The
GOLF MAJORS

Records and Yearbook 2002

ALUN EVANS

A & C Black • London

Published by A&C Black (Publishers) Ltd
37 Soho Square, London W1D 3QZ

Copyright © Alun Evans 1998, 1999, 2002

ISBN 07136 62832

First published in 1998 by Brassey's Sports and 1999 by Aureus Publishing.

A CIP catalogue record for this book is available from the British Library.

ACKNOWLEDGEMENTS
Rand Jerris and Nancy Stulack, USGA Museum, Far Hills
Peter Lewis and Elinor Clark, British Golf Museum, St Andrews
Terry McSweeney and Bob Denney, PGA of America, Palm Beach Gardens
Glenn Greenspan, Augusta National GC
Alan F. Jackson
Sal Johnson

Cover photographs courtesy of Empics, excluding US Masters Trophy, courtesy of Allsport.

Typeset in ITC Cheltenham Light Condensed by Fakenham Photosetting Ltd

Printed & bound in Great Britain by Biddles Ltd, Guildford and Kings Lynn

Contents

List of Abbreviations

a	Amateur
ARG	Argentina
AUS	Australia
BEL	Belgium
BOP	British Open
BRA	Brazil
CAN	Canada
d/q	disqualified
EGY	Egypt
ENG	England
ESP	Spain
FIJ	Fiji
FIN	Finland
FRA	France
GER	Germany (including former West Germany)
NED	Holland
IRL	Ireland (including Northern Ireland and the former Irish Free State)
ITA	Italy
JAP	Japan
KOR	South Korea
MAS	US Masters
MEX	Mexico
NZL	New Zealand
PAR	Paraguay
PGA	US PGA Championship, or Professional Golfers' Association
PUR	Puerto Rico
R&A	Royal and Ancient Club of St Andrews
RSA	South Africa
SCO	Scotland
s/d	Sudden Death
SWE	Sweden
THA	Thailand
TPE	Chinese Taipei/Taiwan (including former Formosa)
TRI	Trinidad and Tobago
URU	Uruguay
USA	United States
USGA	US Golf Association
USO	US Open
WAL	Wales
w/d	withdrawn
ZIM	Zimbabwe (including former Southern Rhodesia and Rhodesia)

Preface

Excepting perhaps Ryder Cup glory, what is it about the Open Championship, the US Open, the US PGA and Masters – the 'Majors' – that has held golfers and golf followers so enthralled throughout history, and, seemingly, increasingly more so over recent decades? Through a variety of historical twists and turns these events have been put on a lofty pedestal, more elevated than the competitions on the respective Tours. This, the third edition of the only book to concentrate solely on the continuing story of *all* the Major Championships, considers the reasons why: their coming to be; their idiosyncrasies; and the landmarks and characters associated with them. Some excellent records and anecdotal histories are to be found across a range of publications (see the bibliography) – but they usually only pertain to one Major Championship or another. Such volumes, quite naturally, promote the credentials of the Championship/Tournament of subject – in short, each Major claims to be the best in one way or another. Because of this, historically there has never been the perceived necessity from within the game's structure to cross-fertilize records for the benefit of the tradition of golf, or its many followers, as other sports do. This is an attempt to set that right.

Since the last edition in 1999, we have witnessed what is undoubtedly the greatest individual feat in the history of the ancient game. Straddling the 2000 and 2001 seasons, Tiger Woods became the first golfer, Hogan and Nicklaus notwithstanding, to achieve one version of golf's Holy Grail. He won, respectively, the US Open, The (British) Open, the US PGA Championship, and finally the Masters at Augusta – all the Majors at one time. Purists will argue that as all the victories didn't occur in one year, this cannot be called the first-ever modern Grand Slam. Whether it is that, a mini-slam or a Tiger Slam, or whatever name anyone cares to give it, it has added the most remarkable chapter yet to the already colourful history of this most prestigious of stories in one of the most venerable of sports.

Readers of the previous editions will note several small differences of inclusion and exclusion, as well as in the textual revisions. In short I have included more records and less narrative. I have also adopted the Olympic abbreviation system (come 2008 who knows?), except, of course where the constituent countries of the British Isles are concerned. Most of the book's layout is self-explanatory, but for those unfamiliar with earlier editions, I should explain the rationale for players' inclusions in Part 3. In this section you will find the only known listing of the top players' records in Major Championships. Adopting the Part 2 premise based on Top 30 finishes (Round of the Last 32 in the Matchplay PGA era), over 2000 records are listed alphabetically. No record is given for years when a Top 30 finish has not been achieved. The symbol [a] after a player's name denotes he was amateur throughout his featured Majors career; 'a' following a finishing position shows the player was an amateur at the time of that event.

As usual, putting this book together has required the support, patience and understanding of several other people and organizations. Thanks, then (in addition to the formal acknowledgements), to my wife Caryl (as usual), Sonia Wilson at A&C Black, Meuryn Hughes for all his efforts over the last three years, and Matt Brown and Jon Marriott at TNT for indulging me.

ALUN EVANS
Milton Keynes, England
October 2001

Part

1 Development of the Major Championships

2 The Championships Year-by-Year

3 The Players

4 The Records

THE BRITISH OPEN CHAMPIONSHIP

Allan Robertson was the subject of many legends. Some say he was never beaten in a singles match, and the pairing of Robertson with his assistant at St Andrews, Tom Morris (Senior, that is), over many years, was probably also undefeated. Whatever the veracity of the stories, it is uniformly regarded that Robertson was the best player of his day in Scotland, which in the mid-18th century meant the world. When he died in 1859, aged just 44, could it be that a new golf tournament was arranged to discover who was to become the new king of golf? Certainly few other valid reasons have been given for the 'Championship', and the format of it, which just happened to be organized for the following year, 1860. Robertson was known in his later life to play less and less singles golf. His influence on the game right up to his untimely death was great, and maybe through his objections such a Championship – single medal play – did not take place any earlier. The idea, however, had been around for a little while.

During the 1850s a founder member of the Prestwick Club (1851) and local squire, Col James Ogilvy Fairlie, was the prime mover in trying to set up a tournament for professionals, based on the less-familiar concept of medal play. Maybe Robertson's refusal to take part suggested there would be little point in trying to hold a competition for the Champion Golfer without him. It maybe more than coincidence, therefore, despite having no support from other Clubs or Societies, that Prestwick went ahead with the competition just one year after Allan Robertson died.

On 16 October 1860, just eight professional golfers went out to play three rounds of Prestwick's 12 holes. Records of scoring are patchy, to say the least, and would be for many years to come; but there is no argument that Tom Morris was beaten into second place by life-long rival Willie Park. Park's reward was a belt of Moroccan leather, buckled in silver, but no winner's prize money would be awarded for a few years. The following year, encouraged by the inaugural success, James Fairlie himself played, as an amateur, making the competition 'open to all the world'. This is undoubtedly where the term 'Open' originated, although it may have just drifted into sporting parlance for the first time without anyone giving its historical importance any real significance. This time 'Old' Tom Morris won the Championship ahead of Park. Morris had become professional at Prestwick some years before, after falling out with Allan Robert-

son. In 1848, the gutta-percha ball, or 'guttie' was introduced. It flew farther, had a longer life, and it was very much cheaper to produce than the old 'feathery' ball. 'Old' Tom wanted to employ the new technology, but as Robertson was famed for his making of featheries, a rift ensued and Morris moved away. He only returned to St Andrews in 1864 after Robertson's death.

The older Morris and Parks dominated the Championship until 1868 when the brief but brilliant career of Tom Morris, Jr began. Just 17 when he won in 1868, this tragic figure came and went like a comet. He was to shine like a brilliant light which illuminated the golf world for the next eight years, before burning out at 25. He won the Open for three years running (1868-70) and the Belt was awarded to him for posterity. Partly because of this, and much off-course politicking, no Championship was held in 1871. When it was relaunched in 1872 Prestwick shared the organization of the event with the prestigious east coast Societies: the Royal and Ancient Club and the Honourable Company of Edinburgh Golfers. It also shared in the outlay for a new trophy, some £30 for the famous silver Claret Jug still presented today. The first winner was inevitably 'Young' Tom Morris, but instead of dominating the world of golf for the next decade and more, this was to be, tragically, his last Open victory. Commonplace among Scottish professionals of the time, Morris was a heavy whisky drinker, and his health began to suffer. In 1874 he was reputedly heart-broken when his wife died in childbirth, and a combination of grief and the resultant need for succour from the bottle killed him. He was found by his father on Christmas morning.

The Open Championship rather patchily consolidated its development over the following two decades by rotating Prestwick with the other Clubs' courses at St Andrews and Musselburgh. The longevity of Messrs Morris and Parks Sr was matched by very few players. The short, spectacular careers of Jamie Anderson and Bob Ferguson, both of whom won three successive Opens, ended in poverty and obscurity, and by the 1890s a great sea change in the game was about to occur.

Golf had been exported from Scotland throughout the world during the 19th century: it had taken root in England even earlier, following the influence of the Stuart kings who inherited the throne of England in 1603. Indeed, it is claimed that the Blackheath Club

was founded in 1608, encouraged by King James I (James VI of Scotland). The British Empire was the catalyst for the world-wide playing of many sports in the 19th century. A certain contretemps with some colonials across the Atlantic ended badly for the British in 1781, however, and discontinued – or changed, through evolution – many sports in the new United States of America. Golf was played in the Carolinas, according to some records, in the mid 18th century, but was then forgotten for almost a century.

The 1890s saw a huge exodus of Scots, and some English, to work as professionals (which also included green-keeping, ball-making and club-making) in the newly, rapidly-forming golf hierarchies of the Eastern Seaboard and Great Lakes cities. The emigrations and the spreading south of the game in Britain meant that the Open took on a less-parochial feel from 1890. Indeed that year it was won by an Englishman, John Ball, for the first time. Ball became, and still is, the youngest-ever competitor in any Major Championship when he competed in the 1878 Open at the tender age of 14. He was, in addition, after the event had run for 30 years, the first amateur to win. In 1892, when Harold Hilton became the second English amateur winner, the competition was extended to four rounds over two days; and the Honourable Company left their nine-hole course at Musselburgh to host the Championship a few miles further along the Firth of Forth, at Muirfield, for the first time. The rota of courses acknowledged the importance of the English improvement in the game when the Open took in English courses at St George's, Sandwich (1894) and Royal Liverpool, Hoylake (1897). And the first world stars of golf appeared.

When JH Taylor won in 1894 and 1895, he was to unwittingly start the age of the so-called 'Great Triumvirate'. Between then and 1914, he (five times), Harry Vardon (six) and James Braid (five) won all but five of the Opens played. Vardon and Taylor toured the US in 1900, competed in the US Open and finished first and second. At the end of their reign however, America became the totally dominant force in world golf – and in the Open Championship, due to the faster US development of all aspects of the game, from administration, golf courses, ball and club technology and players. Few Britons had won the Open since Vardon's last win, and within 25 years of it, total Scottish dominance of the Championship they spawned had evaporated completely. George Duncan won the first post-WW1 Open in 1920, being one of only three Scotsmen, emigrés Jock Hutchison and Tommy

Armour apart, after Braid's last title in 1910, to win the Open again in the 20th century (Sandy Lyle in 1985, then Paul Lawrie in 1999, being the others).

The Royal and Ancient Club (the R&A) had been at the forefront of British golf developments in the 19th century, and particularly so in the terms of rules, which they had based on the Honourable Company's template. By 1897, all the host clubs for the Open had adopted 'St Andrews' rules, thus giving the Club unique hegemony over the sport as a whole, somewhat like the Marylebone Club (MCC) in cricket. Although other countries had developed national bodies to monitor the game, all looked to the R&A on the question of rules (only the USGA in America making any notable amendments independent of St Andrews). After WW1, the British clubs were still organizing the Open Championship as a cartel, and as such differences and inconsistencies occurred. It was decided that some form of rationalization was required if the British national championship was to remain competitive. In 1920, therefore, instead of setting up a national authority for golf, British Clubs vested further powers in the R&A, who took over the running of the Open Championship totally, and still do so today.

The 1920s saw the first phase of American dominance. The flashy Walter Hagen coincided with the Hollywood boom and became the world's first superstar of golf. He won four Opens in a period when only Arthur Havers was a home winner. When Hagen didn't win, it seemed that Bobby Jones must be playing. Inspired by Francis Ouimet's epoch-ending victory over Vardon and Ted Ray in the 1913 US Open, Jones (after tearing up his card in a fit of pique in 1921) won three Open titles in just three further attempts, in a run which also included four US Open wins, and ended with his amazing year of 1930.

The decades leading up to the next war and immediately after it were the bleakest in the history of the Open Championship. The main reasons for this were the inability of the R&A to match the purses on offer across the Atlantic; the sea crossing would take up the time an American professional could spend lucratively employed in another tournament or two Stateside; the difference in the size of the balls (US 1.68" diameter v. GB 1.62"); and the overall strength in depth of the American tournament player against his counterpart in Britain (by 1955 the US team was leading the Great Britain & Ireland team 9-2 in the Ryder Cup series). Little was remembered of the tradition

which started in 1860, and even less was cared. Used to fast, manicured greens and firm, lush fairways, why should the American pro give up all that to play on links courses completely alien to him – and for comparatively little reward? Sam Snead won the 1946 Open at St Andrews, and with little grace criticized the state of the Old Course, pocketed the obviously unsatisfactory cheque and didn't return until 1962. Ben Hogan competed just once, famously in 1953, slammed Carnoustie's greens, and took the old Claret Jug. Many others didn't come at all.

Unfortunately lessons were either not learned, or if they were, there was nothing the R&A could do to reverse the trend. It was hoped that at least without US opposition there would be home victories to celebrate. This was the case in the 30s when American interest dwindled, and there were wins for Cotton, Perry, Padgham, Reg Whitcombe and Burton – but to the concerned onlooker, the Championship paled in comparison with the 1920s heyday of Hagen and Jones, and even the days of the 'Triumvirate'. As a world event it became second division fare.

Immediately after the war, Snead's visit apart, Fred Daly won a low-key affair at Hoylake, and Henry Cotton won his third Open. Maddeningly, Cotton, the best British player of his generation, didn't persevere with his promising early US visits, and thus was not to be the home Champion to inspire a new spate of British world-beaters. Then in 1949, a rotund South African, Arthur D'Arcy Locke, whom all knew as Bobby, brought some international colour back to the Championship. He went on to win three more times in the 1950s, so that even if the Americans stayed away, the new Commonwealth was well represented. If Locke was eclipsed at all during the '50s, it was by Australia's Peter Thomson, who won four times in five years to Locke's four in eight. However, it was to be another South African, globe-trotting Gary Player, who was finally to herald a new dawn for the Open with a win in 1959. The only home winner during this time was Max Faulkner – ironically the only time the Championship was not held in Great Britain – at Portrush in 1951. The only American winner from a Stars and Stripes-starved decade was Ben Hogan, who in 1953 did the hitherto unique treble of Masters, US and British Opens – but was denied any potential Grand Slam as the US PGA frustratingly clashed with Carnoustie.

Meanwhile across the Atlantic the US Tour professional was, through the efforts of the PGA of America, becoming one of the world's most affluent sportsmen. Prize money, sponsorship and royalties were booming thanks mainly to the shrewd marketing of the game to the burgeoning TV networks. At the end of the '50s, the sport had the ideal hero for the television age: Arnold Daniel Palmer. A cigarette-smoking cavalier, his devil-may-care approach almost single-handedly helped to elevate the sport into a media business. The effect was not just restricted to America. Golf, through Palmer, the dashing black-clad figure of Player and the chubby young Golden Bear, Jack Nicklaus, assumed a major world-wide audience for the first time. Television relays and jet aircraft transported the stars across the globe: one of the greatest beneficiaries of all being the increasingly moribund British Open Championship.

Palmer came to St Andrews in 1960 and finished second behind Kel Nagle. Two years later at Troon he became a back-to-back Champion, posting a record 276 and beating the Australian by six shots. The R&A realized they had to accommodate the huge galleries following Palmer: they had to make provision for a new-style golf fan at future Opens. The '60s saw Arnie finally superseded by Nicklaus, but not before Player had won again, Thomson added his fifth title to match Braid and Taylor, and the Open had its oldest winner in an Argentinian faithful of two decades, Roberto de Vicenzo.

If Palmer had re-ignited the spark, the man who actually set the Open ablaze for home supporters was Tony Jacklin. Young, good-looking, a symbol of British confidence in the 1960s, he captured the hearts of the nation at Lytham in 1969. His memorable half in the singles with an over-generous Jack Nicklaus which tied the Ryder Cup at Birkdale later that year, and the win, at Hazeltine in the US Open – all within 12 months – established him as the standard-bearer for the British golfing fight-back against American rule. Whether Britons would have seen world-class golfers like Faldo, Lyle, Woosnam, Montgomerie, Clarke and Westwood if there had been no Tony Jacklin, we will never know. His success in the all-important eyes of America closely followed. He, along with Peter Oosterhuis in the '70s heralded the first signs of improving standards since the days of Dai Rees; and going further back, Henry Cotton and Abe Mitchell. It may be that the Open had been saved forever by Palmer and the rest of the 'Big Three' a decade earlier. Conversely, if there had been no Jacklin, would there have been any resurgence in British, then European golf, to maintain that re-born US interest in the Open. Would

the R&A still be holding its position today, along with the USGA, as the sport's law-makers? Would there be an Open Championship held today in such high regard? Would there still be a Ryder Cup?

Jacklin's presence, however seminal, was, in real performance-terms, relatively short-lived. The Americans' new love affair with the Open carried on apace in the 1970s. Lee Trevino won twice, both times at Jacklin's expense: his chipping-in at the 15th and 18th at Muirfield in 1972 are said to have unnerved the Englishman so much that his game would never be the same again. Tony was never the same player after 1973, whatever the cause. Stylish newcomers Weiskopf and Miller also won, spelling the end of the Nicklaus-Player era and ushering in the tremendous Open run of Tom Watson. Watson won the first of his five links titles at Carnoustie.

In 1979, the Ryder Cup allowed the British and Irish team to become one representative of all Europe. Not that this first selection was too different in composition. Apart from Antonio Garrido, there was only one non-Great Britain & Ireland player: another Spaniard, and current Open Champion, Severiano Ballesteros. When Ballesteros won at Lytham the reception was like that afforded to Jacklin ten years before. The British golf fans had taken a 19 year-old Seve to heart three years earlier when he led the field for 54 holes and chased the ball, and, finally in vain, Johnny Miller, all over the splendid Birkdale links, for a famous second place tie with Nicklaus. From a perspective of European golf, if Jacklin was the standard-bearer, Seve Ballesteros was his bravest captain. Seve illustrated this with some exciting wins in the Open and the Masters, and for Jacklin in the ensuing Ryder Cups – before memorably taking over the Cup mantle himself at Valderrama in 1997.

The Open Championships since 1980 have been much more evenly-spread, with popular British wins for Nick Faldo (three times), Sandy Lyle and most recently, Paul Lawrie; two more for Seve; two for Australian, Greg Norman and one for fellow-countryman, Ian Baker-Finch. The Zimbabwean Nick Price won at Turnberry (the most recent course added to the roster) in 1994. The other wins have gone to America. Bill Rogers was a surprise winner at Sandwich in 1981; Tom Watson picked titles three, four and five; and Mark Calcavecchia collected his only Major at Troon. Significantly perhaps, with wins in recent years from John Daly, Tom Lehman, Justin Leonard, Mark

O'Meara and David Duval, the balance is swinging back to the US. As if destined to be, the Opens that closed the 20th century and began the 21st were blessed with the most historic of championships. Held in 1999 at a monster of a Carnoustie with teeth-like rough, enough to put any US Open to shame, local lad and qualifier Paul Lawrie overturned a ten-stroke overnight lead held by another qualifier, Frenchman Jean Van de Velde. Van de Velde, still leading by three on the 18th tee, thereafter committed golfing suicide in a sporting tragedy without rival. Then at the Home of Golf, the Millennium Open (as almost everything was prefixed in 2000) was won by the bright new star in the golfing firmament, Tiger Woods, by a margin bigger than anything for almost 90 years.

The British Open is without doubt one of the most important of the Majors, if only for its venerable traditions. All the Majors have their own customs and characteristics, levels of prize money and qualifying rigmaroles. However, the Open has the richest history of all, and it is unique as a Major in that it is the only one only to be played each year over links courses. These semi-natural, semi-man-made amalgams of sand, gorse, marram grass with bumpy fairways and bare lies, often criss-crossed by deeply-cut burns and dykes, are the antipathy of the lush, tree-lined parkland courses associated with the US Open (and in more-recent years the US PGA Championship). They bear no resemblance at all to the relatively rough-free, broad avenues and lightning-fast greens of Augusta National – home of the Masters. The exposed tracts, open to the winds of the Firth of Clyde, the Irish Sea, the Channel or the North Sea in an unpredictable British summer, can result in different conditions, and an apparently different golf course, every day – sometimes twice or three times a day. As much for the tradition then, the playing conditions make the Open Championship one of the greatest, if not the greatest, challenges in golf, and very much a Major.

The lessons of the 1930s, '40s and '50s though should tell the R&A there is no room for complacency. Then, the Open Championship was being by-passed by a more vibrant, more commercially aware society 3000 miles away. If it wasn't for the fortuitously timed kick-start given it by the likes of Palmer and Nicklaus there would not have been famous victories for Jacklin, Seve and Faldo, and Britain and Europe could have remained a golfing backwater.

THE US OPEN CHAMPIONSHIP

When John Reid, a Scottish immigrant to the US, asked his friend Bob Lockhart to bring back some golf equipment from a trip home to Scotland, it (indirectly and spontaneously) led to the formation of the St Andrews Club at Yonkers, NY, in 1888. Golf may have been played in America as much as a century earlier, but most golf historians agree that 1888 and St Andrews were the defining moment and location for US golf's amazing explosion.

Six years later the St Andrews Club broke new ground by devising a tournament for the professionals to partner the events that were being organized for amateurs in some of the other infant East Coast clubs. The professionals were (self-?)regarded as the best from the army of Scots, and more than a sprinkling of English, golfers that had taken to crossing the Atlantic to seek their golfing fortunes over the previous few years. By the turn of the century, the proliferation of golf courses in the US, which took the estimated number beyond 1000, indicates just how many Old World pros had come to the States. The 1894 'Championship' at St Andrews (the one at Yonkers) was contested in a matchplay format by Willie Dunn, Campbell and Davis; and Sam Tucker: Dunn winning the first, and unofficial, national title. Willie Dunn had appeared in the Top 10 at the 1883 British Open, and his father (also Willie!) was one of the eight that walked out on Prestwick Links in the inaugural British Open of 1860. Willie Campbell was runner-up to David Brown in the 1886 Open at Musselburgh, while Davis had been the pro at Carnoustie and Hoylake before coming to the Newport, RI Club in 1892. Tucker was the sole Englishman.

Dunn's win was not ratified among the other clubs. However, it forced a meeting to be called for 22 December 1894, to reach a degree of uniformity over such matters as rules and equipment and to set up an authority recognized by all the clubs to organize a national championship. The prime mover here was leading amateur and alumnus of St Andrews University in Scotland, Charles Blair Macdonald. The clubs at St Andrews, Newport, Chicago, Brookline and Shinnecock Hills met in New York City and the United States Golf Association (USGA) was formed as a result. In October 1895 at Newport, running concurrently with the first US Amateur Championship over the same course, the US Open Championship came into being.

The first winner, Horace Rawlins, is a bit of a mystery man. Born on the Isle of Wight in 1874, he was professional at the Mid Herts Club from 1893 to 1894, moving back to the Isle of Wight Ladies Club briefly before arriving at Newport, RI in January 1895. He hadn't competed in the British Open before emigrating, so was an unknown quantity. His four-round, 36-hole (it didn't become a 72-hole championship until 1898) total of 173, suggested that the field was short of quality as well as quantity. Rawlins would never win again.

In 1896, at Shinnecock Hills, the infant Championship nearly didn't take place at all. The professionals objected strongly when caddies John Shippen and Oscar Bunn filed for entry. Shippen was (according to differing reports) either an African-American, or half African-American and half Shinnecock Indian, and Bunn was reported to be a full native American of the same tribe. A stand-off ensued as Theodore Havermayer, the USGA President, ruled that the Open would go on *even if* Shippen and Bunn were the only two competitors. The professionals grudgingly fell into line.

For the first fifteen years the pattern remained broadly the same, with various Smiths, Rosses and Macs dominating the Championship, although Willie Anderson was individually the star of the period, collecting four wins in five years. The dominance of the hired professional who had learned his golf from generations of British experience was the major feature of the early years. The American golfer was still predominantly the gentleman amateur, but slowly, as the new century wore on, a new breed of player, the home-grown caddie/professional, was starting to appear. Standards of play were naturally lower than in Britain in these early years, as even the best of the emigrés, such as Alex Smith, performed only moderately well when they ventured back across the Atlantic to take part in the British Open. This differential was cruelly exposed in 1900 when Harry Vardon and JH Taylor led home the US Open at Chicago by nine and seven strokes respectively.

Then the period of British success came to an abrupt end. Over the next decade, facilitated partly because of America's coming out of the Great War less damaged than Britain, and partly because of there being no line of succession in Britain when the time of the 'Triumvirate' came to a close, the whole emphasis in the golf world swung – permanently – to the other

side of the Atlantic. The catalysts for this turnabout were to be found in the next five years of the US Open.

In 1911, John J. McDermott, two months short of his 20th birthday, erased the memory of his runner-up disappointment from the previous year and became the first American-born winner of the US Open. The following year, proving this was no flash in the pan, he won again at the Buffalo Club. Home-grown talents Mike Brady and Tom McNamara were second on both occasions, suggesting that the dam was about to burst. Then, in 1913, came another twist, and a huge symbolic breakthrough. Francis Ouimet, hanging on to the coat-tails of Harry Vardon (back for the first time since his 1900 success) and Ted Ray – arguably the two best players in the world at the time – to force a three-way play-off, had the temerity to outplay these icons, and make it three US wins in a row. Now the Americans had proved they could beat the very best of British, and no-one saw this more clearly than the confident young man who tied for fourth, just behind the joint leaders. His name was Walter Hagen.

But Ouimet was also an amateur, the first to win the US Open. The heyday of the British Amateur had flick-ered briefly during the 1890s when John Ball and Harold Hilton won the British Open. When Hilton won his second title in 1897, no-one would ever have thought that he would be the last British amateur to win a Major championship. In America, however, with the sport developing so rapidly across all fronts, the style of amateur was different. Unlike the British type of landowner, army officer or socialite, the socio-economic growth of America in the early decades of the 20th century meant that the successful amateur could equally spring from the ranks of the Ivy League colleges, and be the heir of some industrial magnate, or have learned his golf as a caddie and be holding down a regular job. Francis Ouimet was one of the latter. While Hagen was scheming the end of British dominance and the lot of the American professional, Ouimet's victory was stirring the amateur golfing ambitions of a young Atlanta schoolboy – one Robert Tyre Jones, Jr.

Hagen was fast off the mark, winning the first of his two US Opens in the following year. In 1915 and 1916, while all Championship golf was suspended in Europe, two more amateurs, Jerome Travers and Chick Evans, had their names inscribed on the trophy. This made it five American wins in a row and three amateur cham-pions in four years. With the exception of Ted Ray (1920) and various emigrés during the 20s – and on

the back of 16 straight wins between 1895 and 1910 – the next Briton (and only the one since) to win the US Open would be Tony Jacklin in 1970. Thereafter, along with the PGA Championship, the US Open would be viewed as an American preserve. Overseas players did enter from time to time, but they were few and far between. Gary Player's emergence in the '60s hinted at a small but strong southern hemisphere presence thereafter, but a re-emergence of European players didn't come about until the 1980s.

Walter Hagen, in spite of his huge presence in the game, couldn't win a US Open during his purple patch in the 1920s. He collected five PGAs and four British Opens during the decade, but the colourful first superstar of golf's last US Open was in 1919. It was more than a coincidence that he never won a Major when Bobby Jones competed. This was not because Jones won every time, but the mere appearance of the man seemed to jinx Hagen. During the period 1920-30, Jones' US Open performances read 8, 5, 2, W, 2, 2, W, 11, 2, W, W. He, Gene Sarazen and Ralph Guldahl were to be the only multiple winners of the US Open during the '20s and '30s. The Championship remained true to its name with an even spread of one-time winners.

In 1933, Johnny Goodman became the fifth and last amateur US Open Champion. Of the 19 US Opens beginning with Ouimet's win in 1913, and ending with Goodman's triumph at North Shore, amateurs had claimed eight. The brief explosion on to the scene of Guldahl produced wins in 1937 and 1938 and ushered in the dawn of Hogan, Nelson and Snead – and World War II.

During the '30s and even more so after the War, there had been a gradual defining of the type of course required for the national championship. Partly for historical reasons, and partly due to geography, the typical Open course was built in the early part of the century for clubs who bought up large tracts of (usually well-wooded) land close to the industrial conurbations of the East, Mid-west and California. Early golf-course architects often took Scottish links characteristics, such as varying grades of rough and narrow fairways, and adapted them to the parkland environment. Liberal use of water, dog-legging fea-tures and ubiquitous sand were employed to increase the hazards. As the century developed the 'US Open' style of course made it a demanding trial of any aspiring Champion's skills: in the view of archi-tect A.W. Tillinghast (Baltusrol, Fresh Meadow, Inver-ness, Winged Foot), '...a controlled shot to a

closely-guarded green is the surest test of any man's golf'.

In conjunction with this tightening of course criteria, the overwhelming prowess of the American golfer, and the sad decline of the British game, helped to erode the importance of the British Open – at least in American eyes – and promote the US Open as the world's premier championship of golf. It was certainly true that the inauguration of the Masters in 1934 had polarized the British Championship even further. Fewer and fewer US golfers saw the need to support what must have seemed like an outmoded and under-funded competition thousands of miles away. There was a strong argument for the US Open's lead over the other Majors for the next two decades.

In 1947 Lew Worsham beat Sam Snead (already 1942 PGA and 1946 British Open Champion) in a play-off. Sam was never to come as close to the Open title, the only Major he was destined never to win, again. The next few years belonged to Snead's arch-rival, Ben Hogan, whose courage and incredible talent were to make him probably the biggest hero in the annals of the US Open. If Bobby Jones had dominated the event in the 1920s, even by playing a minimum of golf in between, then Hogan matched Jones now, although his limited appearances on a golf course were for other reasons.

In 1948, at the Riviera Country Club, Hogan set one of the Majors' landmark low scores, when he scorched the course in an eight-under par 276. Then in February of the following year, following a head-on collision with a Greyhound bus, Hogan was badly injured. It was felt he may not be able to walk any more, but throughout 1949 he battled against the odds and played again in January 1950. He competed at the US Open at Merion, his golfing talent seemingly undiminished, but faded badly when exhaustion took over. He somehow hung on to force a play-off, and limped to a famous victory over Lloyd Mangrum and George Fazio. Thereafter, he declined to play too much golf – saving himself for the Majors. He only played in one British Open, for example, which he duly won, in 1953: he eschewed the PGA completely because of the potential six or seven days round-by-round grind of stroke-play and matchplay. He effectively only played in the Masters and the US Open; he was to win them both in 1951 and again in 1953. With the British Open win as well in 1953, he became the only golfer to win three Grand Slam tournaments in one season, until matched by Tiger Woods in 2000.

In 1960, a new order took over and Arnold Palmer won over the still-amateur Jack Nicklaus. Nicklaus went on to equal the record of four wins, between 1962 and 1980, and tie with Willie Anderson, Jones and Hogan. Americans continued to dominate during the '60s and '70s with two wins each by Billy Casper and Lee Trevino, but overseas players got a glimpse of success for the first time for many years with wins from Player, Jacklin and David Graham. In the '80s, there was no dominant force, although Curtis Strange did win back-to-back in 1988 and 1989, and there was a popular third win for 'all-time old Champion', Hale Irwin: he was 45 when he claimed the title in 1990. Lee Janzen and the late Payne Stewart had a penchant for doing well in this competition with two wins each between 1989 and 1999, while Ernie Els, winning for the second time at Congressional in 1997, should continue to be a contender for many championships to come.

Since the '60s, the perceived N° 1 status of the US Open among the Majors may be called into question. The charisma of the Masters and the Americans' re-found love affair with the traditions of the British Open have tended to level out the Majors. Since changing from matchplay to strokeplay, the PGA Championship has also come of age in its adoption of 'US Open' type golf courses and more cosmopolitan fields, particularly since the mid-'80s. There is no doubting the claim, however, that the US Open, year-in, year-out, is the toughest test set for the players of all the Majors. Apart from the golf course set-up, it also comes at the end of the first half of the season – a peak time for many golfers: the Masters in April can be too early for some. The competition when it meets, therefore, is potentially at its strongest, both physically and mentally. That, in theory, is what should happen. In practice it only needs a Tiger Woods, as in 2000, to put courses and players into perspective!

THE PGA CHAMPIONSHIP

The excitement created by the exploits of John McDermott, Francis Ouimet and Walter Hagen led to an enormous growth in the game of golf in America. The spread of the sport affected both recreational players and the professional, competitive ranks. The birth of the Tour professional, a player who could devote as much time to tournaments as his members' lessons, his green-keeping and club-repairing duties, introduced a new stratum of golfer: with it came the need to protect his interests.

The British Professional Golfers Association was founded in 1901 and as part of its role it identified sponsors who would support special golfing events. The *News of the World* Sunday newspaper was asked to sponsor the Association's own Championship and by 1916 it was a well-run, well-established 36-hole matchplay competition. On 16 January of that year, a mixture of professional and amateur golfers, course architects and golf industry representatives met in New York City at the invitation of department store entrepreneur, Rodman Wanamaker. Wanamaker could see the potential the new craze for golf could have commercially, and the upshot of the meeting was the creation of the PGA of America (ratified in April 1916) and the Wanamaker-sponsored PGA Championship.

The basis for the competition was matchplay, like its British counterpart, and was only open to professional golfers. The matchplay aspect also complemented the US Amateur Championship and provided a balance to the medal play of the British and US Opens.

Jim Barnes won the first PGA Championship, held in October 1916 at the Siwanoy Country Club, beating Scot Jock Hutchison, 1 up in the final. Barnes also won the second Championship, but had to wait three years to defend it due to World War 1. During the 1920s, Walter Hagen, who had attended that historic January 1916 meeting, won five titles, including four in a row. Before Leo Diegel beat him to go on to win the 1928 Championship, Hagen had gone 22 straight round matches without defeat. Gene Sarazen and Diegel won two PGAs in the '20s, and Sarazen went on to win a third in 1933. Sarazen's second victory – when defending his title in 1923 – featured one of the famous finals. He played a magical shot close to the pin to beat Hagen at the second extra hole. At this time, the 32 qualifiers each year had to endure 36 holes of strokeplay before the matchplay sessions. In 1935, 64 qualifiers went forward to matchplay.

Denny Shute, in 1936 and 1937, became the last player to win back-to-back Championships, before Tiger Woods in 2000. Paul Runyan also won two titles in the 30s. With wartime approaching Byron Nelson was in devastating form, while Sam Snead won the Championship in 1942, the day before he joined the navy. Nelson won in 1940 and was runner-up to Vic Ghezzi in 1941. He was also runner-up, to Bob Hamilton, when the Championship resumed after a break due to the hostilities in 1944. In 1945 Nelson won the PGA for the second time: it was his ninth in a sequence of 11 straight tournament wins that season (the aforementioned Tiger Woods may even struggle to match that record).

The PGA Championship, perhaps because of its format of week-long qualifying strokeplay and matchplay, was not as popular as the US Open with spectators. It may have been something to do also with course selection – some venues were not particularly good. Moreover by guaranteeing a certain number of non-Tour, work-a-day club pros entry the PGA may have reduced the glamour of the event. In order to keep the top pros sweet the prize money was kept competitive with the Open and a new-fangled Tournament down South for amateurs and fancy dans called the Masters. A major blow, however, was the enforced withdrawal, during the 1950s, of just about its greatest star: Ben Hogan. Having won the Championship in 1946 and 1948, Hogan's terrible road accident then precluded his playing in the stamina-sapping elongated event. He stayed away until he was in semi-retirement and the Championship had switched to strokeplay. He would never win again, but finished as high as ninth in 1964, at the age of 52.

The years leading up to and immediately after the dropping of matchplay were fairly nondescript, in that no golfer or group of golfers dominated the Championship. In fact, between 1950 and 1970, even after strokeplay was introduced, the PGA was won by a different player each year. The end of matchplay finally came about when the PGA of America sensed permanent harm to the Championship because of the previously alluded to time and spectator concerns, and that the needs of the new pervasive and persuasive TV phenomenon would have to be met. A proposal by Horton Smith, who was the then President of the PGA of America, to limit matchplay to just the top seven qualifiers from the strokeplay session plus the defending champion, was superseded by one which did away with matchplay altogether. This was certainly

not a happy period for the Championship. Having to overhaul its format comprehensively in order to make it attractive to those outside golf, it was also being criticized from within, with the type and location of courses usually top of the agenda. That the PGA Championship, up to 2001, should have been played on 68 different courses over 26 states in its 83 years says it all. In fairness, it was previous policy for the PGA of America to expand the frontiers of its flagship event, but commercially it was awry. Moreover, the Masters had become a big hit with American TV audiences. Also, from a player's perspective, the PGA's July timing clashed with the British Open too frequently, as well as proving unpopular when the Championship was played in August in the steamier South.

Arnold Palmer failed to leave his mark on the PGA, surprisingly never winning. Typically, however, he couldn't be kept out of the record books. When Bobby Nichols won in 1964, Arnie became the first player to shoot sub-70 rounds throughout without winning. He tied second with Jack Nicklaus. Nicklaus didn't have it all his own way in the '60s, winning just once, in the Dallas heat – not for the first time in a Major at the expense of Bruce Crampton. In 1968, at the age of 48, Julius Boros won, also in Texas (San Antonio), to become the oldest winner of any Major Championship.

Since the 1970s, however, when Nicklaus started to stitch together regular wins, the PGA Championship has made up lost ground. Firstly, there has been some rationalization of the courses. The use of more courses employed by the US Open – Oakland Hills, Inverness, Pebble Beach and Winged Foot, for instance – reduced the roster and made the test as difficult as the Open. It also, finally, took its spot in August, as the finale to the Major Championship season. Over the last 25 years or so the Championship has had a base to move forward and to develop its own style. Before that, constant change, and the dubious quality of both course and player almost reduced the PGA to a non-Major.

Nicklaus went on to emulate Hagen's five wins, and for a while, between 1972 and 1974, Sam Snead was having something of an Indian Summer. Then in his 60s, he collected fourth, ninth, then third positions respectively. He finally called it a day, aged 69 in 1981. He was not the oldest participant, though. Back in 1972 Gene Sarazen (who else?) had appeared at the age of

70 years and 5 months, and shot two 79s to miss the cut. He thus had the distinction, and still does, of being the PGA's oldest competitor and youngest winner (20 years 5 months in 1922). Lee Trevino won twice, in 1974 and 1984, and Tom Watson came as close as he has got to winning the Championship in 1978 when he tied for first with John Mahaffey and Jerry Pate: Mahaffey it was that emerged victorious from the sudden-death play-off. His win was improbable to say the least. After a first round 75, he should never have been in the hunt. By the start of the last round he was still seven behind Watson, but a series of brilliant putts put together a score of 66, while Tom folded to a 73. Watson's chance to join Sarazen, Hogan, Player and Nicklaus as the only players (before you know who in 2000) to have lifted all four Major titles had gone, never to return.

As the PGA Championship has always been an event for the US Tour and Club professional first and foremost, it was not until the breakthrough of Gary Player in 1962 that a true overseas player won the PGA. He repeated the victory in 1972 and since 1979, when Australia's David Graham was victorious, there has been a veritable surge of foreign winners. Whereas the Masters was a favourite event for Europeans in the 1980s and 90s, the golfers of the Southern Hemisphere took to the PGA. Following Player and Graham there have been wins for Australians Wayne Grady and Steve Elkington, and two for Nick Price of Zimbabwe. In between, Larry Nelson picked up two titles, and when Ray Floyd won for the second time in 1982 he tied the record of the longest span between wins of any one Major Championship (13 years). John Daly's fairytale success in 1991 heralded a new breed of super-hitter and paved the way for Tiger Woods, who after stuttering slightly following his first success, won the last Major of the century at Medinah. David Toms then broke all records in 2001.

The PGA Championship today is rightly a Major. Whereas the purist might pine for the days of match-play, no-one can doubt the progress the Championship has made over the last two decades or so. Once dubbed a second-rate parochial competition, now the PGA Championship attracts more overseas golfers than the other US Majors, and, even more importantly, more players from Official World Ranking Top 100 than all other Major Championships.

THE MASTERS TOURNAMENT

After such an extraordinary year as 1930, Robert Tyre Jones, Jr – Bobby Jones – retired from competitive golf. He had nothing else to prove: he had done it all. Being amateur, he played golf in the spare time he allowed himself from his law firm. Being amateur, he couldn't compete with the professional golfers in their own tournament, the PGA Championship. By 1930 he had achieved all that his status would allow him, but in doing so, left a series of golfing records unsurpassed by any amateur in the history of the game: records that even the hugely-talented Tiger Woods, if he had remained amateur at the end of 1996, I'm sure would admit may even have been beyond him.

The 'Grand Slam' is made up of the four Majors as we know them today: the British and US Opens, the US PGA and the Masters. No golfer has ever achieved all four in one season, and only five, Gene Sarazen, Ben Hogan, Jack Nicklaus, Gary Player and Woods, have won every Championship. Back in 1930, the Amateur Championships of America and Britain were also considered 'Majors', and the Grand Slam consisted of these plus both Opens. As an amateur, Jones won the US Amateur title five times and the British equivalent once. He took on and beat the professionals more often than not, winning the first of his four US Open titles in 1923. He also won three British Opens. His main professional rival, Walter Hagen – undoubtedly one of golf's all-time greats himself – despite winning 11 Major Championships, never won one when Jones was in the same field. These feats were achieved in just eight incredible years.

And so to Bobby Jones' *annus mirabilis*: 1930. He appeared in the American Walker Cup side at Sandwich and stayed on to take the British Amateur. In June he went to Hoylake and beat the best of the British, and no small number of American, professionals to lift the Open Championship. The following month at Interlachen he beat an even stronger field for the US Open, before rounding off his competitive career at the Merion Cricket Club in Pennsylvania, winning his fifth US Amateur title. At the end of the year he returned to the law full-time.

During his brief but intensive career Jones had played golf on most of the famous courses on either side of the Atlantic. No longer playing, in 1931 he switched his golfing mind to course construction, and he knew exactly what he wanted to achieve. A resident of Atlanta, Georgia, he was made aware of a 365-acre piece of land a hundred miles or so away at Augusta. It had once been a plant nursery but had gone to the wall during the Depression. Jones, with the backing of financier Clifford Roberts, and Scottish golf course designer, Dr Alister Mackenzie, bought it and planned out a course that would encompass all that was best (in Jones' view) from the courses he'd known as a player. Jones envisioned his course as a private member's club: open only to his closest associates, playing friends, business colleagues and clients. It was, however, intended to be exclusive on a wide geographic front, hence the name it was given – Augusta National. It was also meant to provide a fitting climax to the professionals' winter tour, by invitation (from Jones) to a special tournament. The winter tour was a small offshoot of the professionals' regular summer tour, allowing them to play the Southern States 'out of season' thus avoiding the heat and humidity of other times. Like many clubs in the region, Augusta National closed down for the summer – and still does.

Augusta National was designed so that it wouldn't be too intimidating for Jones' members, yet it would require meticulous planning from the pros to score well. The fairways were wide and accommodating, anything a touch off-line not being penalized too severely. Bobby Jones knew how excruciating the rough could be at the Opens, but he wanted his members to continue to play the course and not be humbled by it. A hook or a slice here would probably result in nothing more punitive than the ball nestling among pine needles, and a member's sense of well-being would remain intact. Moreover, he wanted to make the playing of golf the greatest possible pleasure. No one who has seen, even through TV pictures, Augusta in spring can fail to be uplifted by the beauty of the course, fringed as it is with all manner of flowering shrubs.

In order to beat the par of 72 at Augusta, however, a hole-by-hole strategy is needed. Assuming that the green is reached in regulation, it depends here (more than almost anywhere else) where the ball has landed as to whether a player gets his par, better – or much, much worse. The greens are often huge, always undulating, and usually on several different levels. The approach shot has to be aimed at the 'right' side of the pin. Reading the contours is difficult, and the putting surfaces are lightning-fast. For example, a four foot putt from the 'wrong' side of the hole, not hit with exactly the right speed and borrow, can easily trundle past and roll on 15 feet or a lot more.

Mackenzie and Jones completed the course for Jones' first invitation event, simply called 'The Augusta National Invitational', in March 1934. Mackenzie unfortunately died that year, so he was unaware of the impact the tournament was to make. By the following year the tournament was being dubbed 'The Championship of Champions', but the easier-off-the-tongue sobriquet 'The Masters Tournament' was not long in driving that out. Horton Smith won in 1934, beating one of golf's perennial bridesmaids Craig Wood into second place. Bob Jones came out of retirement to tie 13th with old arch-enemy Walter Hagen. Just like the PGA, it was not regarded as a Major instantly: its status evolved over time. But it's stock as a significant tournament did receive massive impetus after only its second year.

To become a Major Championship, the competition has to be the best; the course has to be one of the toughest; there should at least be tradition in the organization running it. Augusta National was lacking in all three. There was no qualifying – entry was by invitation only; this was no Carnoustie or Olympia Fields; and the club was only formed in 1934. However, to misquote the Bard: 'Some events are born great; some events achieve greatness; and some events have greatness thrust upon them'. The Opens can be thought of as the first; the PGA achieved its status through a workmanlike progress; and the Masters can thank Gene Sarazen, TV and Arnold Palmer for the third!

'Probably the best-known shot in all golf Tournament history', states Augusta National's own *Records of the Masters Tournament*. It alludes to a shot holed from all of 220 yards with fairway spoon (four wood) by a desperate Sarazen on the 15th hole of the final round of the 1935 Tournament. Sarazen was three behind the perenially-unlucky Craig Wood, and his double-eagle or albatross (three under par) on this par-five hole enabled him to tie, and force a play-off which he was to win. In doing so, Sarazen became the first player to win all four Majors as we now know them. The news story was probably blown up out of all proportion, but 'that shot' did take the infant Masters tournament on to the front page. Its real popularity, however, and therefore credibility as a Major, came in the late '50s with TV coverage and, in centre-screen, the man of the people, the risk-taker, the mould-breaking Arnold Palmer. Arnie's incredible escapades were shown on television, the early-season heady combination backdrop of sunshine and Southern flowers making for compulsive viewing. His first win, in 1958, merely set the scene. In 1960, Palmer, one behind the leader Ken Venturi with two to play, improbably birdied both holes to win. Then, in the 1962 three-way play-off, Palmer, three shots behind Gary Player at the turn, scorched the back nine in 31 to win. Comic-hero stuff, and the Masters had arrived.

Since the 1960s, coming as it does early in the season, and being the smallest of all Major Championship fields, the Masters rapidly became a favourite and much-coveted tournament amongst the world's leading golfers. With his great advantage of extra length without compromising on control, Jack Nicklaus was to win an unprecedented and unsurpassed six times, the last occasion in 1986. By that time the newly emerging European force in golf was starting to take a fancy to Augusta in April. Seve Ballesteros had already won twice in the '80s and Bernhard Langer won the first of his two titles the previous year. Sandy Lyle, Nick Faldo (three times), Ian Woosnam and Jose Maria Olazabal would all go on to win over the next few years. American favourite Ben Crenshaw, who's 1984 win was one of the most popular of all time, delighted his supporters with a belated second Green Jacket in 1995. Greg Norman – a runner-up in 1985 and 1986 – had the field at his mercy starting out on the last round of the 1996 Tournament. His six-shot lead was turned into a five-shot deficit by partner Nick Faldo, who ground out a 67 to Greg's 78 to collect a most unlikely third Masters, after the most incredible last round in Majors history.

Then there was 1997. Child prodigy and reigning US Amateur Champion for three years, Eldrick 'Tiger' Woods, took the course and the competition apart, breaking all sorts of records along the way. A new era seemed to be dawning as Woods power play was seen as much of a quantum leap in the sport as was Nicklaus's nearly 40 years before. The much-vaunted Woods, the World No 1 for much of the remainder of the 20th century following his '97 win, was clear favourite to win again in 1998 and 1999. It was his old pal and mentor 41 year-old Mark O'Meara who won in 1998, though, after almost two decades of trying: whilst a popular second Masters was claimed in 1999, on his return to the game after a career-threatening back injury, by Jose Maria Olazabal. Woods' class was to prevail, however, in 2001, when he collected his second Masters as the ultimate part of the Majors quartet he had been constructing since the 2000 US Open. He duly achieved what no other golfer had been able to do: win all four biggies consecutively.

The Masters may be the fourth Major historically, but such is its charm and attraction that every golfer wants to play in it. It is so different to the others. When the Masters was created, the British Open was different from the other Majors in that it was always played on seaside links and had the longest history; the US Open was arguably the sternest test of golf with narrow fairways, bunkers galore and jungle-like rough; the PGA was matchplay with tough qualifying rounds. At that time it was argued that Augusta National was too easy to be a venue for a Major Championship.

But it is the Masters' differences that mark it a Major. As we have said, the approach to Augusta's greens is so critical, especially when pin placement is sometimes a little eccentric. It is exclusive. It is unique in that it is always held at Augusta National. It has a trophy like the others, but it is not a cup: instead the Masters trophy is a silver replica of the Clubhouse at Augusta, itself a replica of a fine *ante bellum*-style Southern homestead. It is different in that the winner is presented with the traditional Green Jacket as a member of the Augusta club – presented and held for him by the previous-year's champion (the first ceremony being conferred upon Sam Snead in 1949). It is different because it calls itself a tournament, not a championship. It is just *so* different!

The Masters oozes sheer style and class, with holes that have names like Tea Olive, Yellow Jasmine, Magnolia, Azalea and Redbud. It's a Major airight, and a most fitting permanent annual tribute to one of *the* master golfers.

Part

THE MAJOR CHAMPIONS: 1860–2001

YEAR	MASTERS	VENUE	US OPEN	VENUE	BRITISH OPEN	VENUE	US PGA	VENUE
1860					Willie Park, Sr	Prestwick		
1861					Tom Morris, Sr	Prestwick		
1862					Tom Morris, Sr	Prestwick		
1863					Willie Park, Sr	Prestwick		
1864					Tom Morris, Sr	Prestwick		
1865					Andrew Strath	Prestwick		
1866					Willie Park, Sr	Prestwick		
1867					Tom Morris, Sr	Prestwick		
1868					Tom Morris, Jr	Prestwick		
1869					Tom Morris, Jr	Prestwick		
1870					Tom Morris, Jr	Prestwick		
1871					*No Championship*			
1872					Tom Morris, Jr	Prestwick		
1873					Tom Kidd	St Andrews		
1874					Mungo Park	Musselburgh		
1875					Willie Park, Sr	Prestwick		
1876					Bob Martin	St Andrews		
1877					Jamie Anderson	Musselburgh		
1878					Jamie Anderson	Prestwick		
1879					Jamie Anderson	St Andrews		
1880					Bob Ferguson	Musselburgh		
1881					Bob Ferguson	Prestwick		
1882					Bob Ferguson	St Andrews		
1883					Willie Fernie	Musselburgh		
1884					Jack Simpson	Prestwick		
1885					Bob Martin	St Andrews		
1886					David Brown	Musselburgh		
1887					Willie Park, Jr	Prestwick		
1888					Jack Burns	St Andrews		
1889					Willie Park, Jr	Musselburgh		
1890					John Ball, Jr (a)	Prestwick		
1891					Hugh Kirkaldy	St Andrews		
1892					Harold Hilton (a)	Muirfield		
1893					Willie Auchterlonie	Prestwick		
1894					JH Taylor	St George's, Sandwich		
1895			Horace Rawlins	Newport GC	JH Taylor	St Andrews		
1896			James Foulis	Shinnecock Hills	Harry Vardon	Muirfield		
1897			Joe Lloyd	Chicago GC	Harold Hilton (a)	Hoylake		
1898			Fred Herd	Myopia Hunt	Harry Vardon	Prestwick		
1899			Willie Smith	Baltimore CC	Harry Vardon	St George's, Sandwich		
1900			Harry Vardon	Chicago GC	JH Taylor	St Andrews		
1901			Willie Anderson	Myopia Hunt	James Braid	Muirfield		
1902			Laurie Auchterlonie	Garden City GC	Sandy Herd	Hoylake		
1903			Willie Anderson	Baltusrol	Harry Vardon	Prestwick		
1904			Willie Anderson	Glen View GC	Jack White	Royal St George's, Sandwich		
1905			Willie Anderson	Myopia Hunt	James Braid	St Andrews		
1906			Alex Smith	Onwentsia	James Braid	Muirfield		
1907			Alex Ross	Philadelphia Cricket Club	Arnaud Massy	Hoylake		
1908			Fred McLeod	Myopia Hunt	James Braid	Prestwick		
1909			George Sargent	Engelwood	JH Taylor	Royal Cinque Ports GC		
1910			Alex Smith	Philadelphia Cricket Club	James Braid	St Andrews		
1911			John McDermott	Chicago GC	Harry Vardon	Royal St George's, Sandwich		
1912			John McDermott	CC of Buffalo	Ted Ray	Muirfield		
1913			Francis Ouimet	Brookline	JH Taylor	Hoylake		
1914			Walter Hagen	Midlothian	Harry Vardon	Prestwick		
1915			Jerome Travers (a)	Baltusrol	*No Championship*			
1916			Chick Evans (a)	Minikahda	*No Championship*		Jim Barnes	Siwanoy CC
1917			*No Championship*		*No Championship*		*No Championship*	
1918			*No Championship*		*No Championship*		*No Championship*	
1919			Walter Hagen	Brae Burn CC	*No Championship*		Jim Barnes	Engineers CC
1920			Ted Ray	Inverness	George Duncan	Royal Cinque Ports GC	Jock Hutchison	Flossmoor CC
1921			Jim Barnes	Columbia CC	Jock Hutchison	St Andrews	Walter Hagen	Inwood
1922		*	Gene Sarazen	Skokie CC	Walter Hagen	Royal St George's, Sandwich	Gene Sarazen	Oakmont
1923			Bobby Jones (a)	Inwood	Arthur Havers	Troon	Gene Sarazen	Pelham GC
1924			Cyril Walker	Oakland Hills	Walter Hagen	Hoylake	Walter Hagen	French Springs
1925			Willie MacFarlane	Worcester CC	Jim Barnes	Prestwick	Walter Hagen	Olympia Fields
1926			Bobby Jones (a)	Scioto CC	Bobby Jones (a)	Royal Lytham & St Anne's	Walter Hagen	Salisbury GL
1927			Tommy Armour	Oakmont	Bobby Jones (a)	St Andrews	Walter Hagen	Cedar Crest
1928			Johnny Farrell	Olympia Fields	Walter Hagen	Royal St George's, Sandwich	Leo Diegel	Five Farms
1929			Bobby Jones (a)	Winged Foot	Walter Hagen	Muirfield	Leo Diegel	Hillcrest CC
1930			Bobby Jones (a)	Interlachen	Bobby Jones (a)	Hoylake	Tommy Armour	Fresh Meadows

THE MAJOR CHAMPIONS: 1860–2001

YEAR	MASTERS	VENUE	US OPEN	VENUE	BRITISH OPEN	VENUE	US PGA	VENUE
1931			Billy Burke	Inverness	Tommy Armour	Carnoustie	Tom Creavy	Wannamoisett CC
1932			Gene Sarazen	Fresh Meadow	Gene Sarazen	Prince's, Sandwich	Olin Dutra	Keller GC
1933			Johnny Goodman (a)	North Shore CC	Denny Shute	St Andrews	Gene Sarazen	Blue Mound CC
1934	Horton Smith	Augusta National	Olin Dutra	Merion	Henry Cotton	Royal St George's, Sandwich	Paul Runyan	Park Club of Buffalo
1935	Gene Sarazen	Augusta National	Sam Parks, Jr	Oakmont	Alf Perry	Muirfield	Johnny Revolta	Twin Hills CC
1936	Horton Smith	Augusta National	Tony Manero	Baltusrol	Alf Padgham	Hoylake	Denny Shute	Pinehurst
1937	Byron Nelson	Augusta National	Ralph Guldahl	Oakland Hills	Henry Cotton	Carnoustie	Denny Shute	Pittsburgh Field Club
1938	Henry Picard	Augusta National	Ralph Guldahl	Cherry Hills	Reg Whitcombe	Royal St George's, Sandwich	Paul Runyan	Shawnee CC
1939	Ralph Guldahl	Augusta National	Byron Nelson	Philadelphia Country Club	Dick Burton	St Andrews	Henry Picard	Pomonock
1940	Jimmy Demaret	Augusta National	Lawson Little	Canterbury GC	*No Championship*		Byron Nelson	Hershey CC
1941	Craig Wood	Augusta National	Craig Wood	Colonial	*No Championship*		Vic Ghezzi	Cherry Hills
1942	Byron Nelson	Augusta National	*No Championship*		*No Championship*		Sam Snead	Sea View CC
1943	*No Championship*	Augusta National	*No Championship*		*No Championship*		*No Championship*	
1944	*No Championship*	Augusta National	*No Championship*		*No Championship*		Bob Hamilton	Manito G & CC
1945	*No Championship*	Augusta National	*No Championship*		*No Championship*		Byron Nelson	Moraine CC
1946	Herman Keiser	Augusta National	Lloyd Mangrum	Canterbury CC	Sam Snead	St Andrews	Ben Hogan	Portland GC
1947	Jimmy Demaret	Augusta National	Lew Worsham	St Louis CC	Fred Daly	Hoylake	Jim Ferrier	Plum Hollow
1948	Claude Harmon	Augusta National	Ben Hogan	Riviera CC	Henry Cotton	Muirfield	Ben Hogan	Norwood Hills CC
1949	Sam Snead	Augusta National	Cary Middlecoff	Medinah	Bobby Locke	Royal St George's, Sandwich	Sam Snead	Hermitage CC
1950	Jimmy Demaret	Augusta National	Ben Hogan	Merion	Bobby Locke	Troon	Chandler Harper	Scioto CC
1951	Ben Hogan	Augusta National	Ben Hogan	Oakland Hills	Max Faulkner	Royal Portrush	Sam Snead	Oakmont
1952	Sam Snead	Augusta National	Julius Boros	Northwood GC	Bobby Locke	Royal Lytham & St Annes	Jim Turnesa	Big Spring CC
1953	Ben Hogan	Augusta National	Ben Hogan	Oakmont	Ben Hogan	Carnoustie	Walter Burkemo	Birmingham CC
1954	Sam Snead	Augusta National	Ed Furgol	Baltusrol	Peter Thomson	Birkdale	Chick Harbert	Keller GC
1955	Cary Middlecoff	Augusta National	Jack Fleck	Olympic CC	Peter Thomson	St Andrews	Doug Ford	Meadowbrook CC
1956	Jack Burke, Jr	Augusta National	Cary Middlecoff	Oak Hill	Peter Thomson	Hoylake	Jack Burke, Jr	Blue Hill G & CC
1957	Doug Ford	Augusta National	Dick Mayer	Inverness	Bobby Locke	St Andrews	Lionel Hebert	Miami Valley GC
1958	Arnold Palmer	Augusta National	Tommy Bolt	Southern Hills	Peter Thomson	Royal Lytham & St Annes	Dow Finsterwald	Llanerch CC
1959	Art Wall	Augusta National	Billy Casper	Winged Foot	Gary Player	Muirfield	Bob Rosburg	Minneapolis GC
1960	Arnold Palmer	Augusta National	Arnold Palmer	Cherry Hills	Kel Nagle	St Andrews	Jay Hebert	Firestone CC
1961	Gary Player	Augusta National	Gene Littler	Oakland Hills	Arnold Palmer	Birkdale	Jerry Barber	Olympia Fields
1962	Arnold Palmer	Augusta National	Jack Nicklaus	Oakmont	Arnold Palmer	Troon	Gary Player	Aronimink GC
1963	Jack Nicklaus	Augusta National	Julius Boros	Brookline	Bob Charles	Royal Lytham & St Annes	Jack Nicklaus	Dallas Athletic Club
1964	Arnold Palmer	Augusta National	Ken Venturi	Congressional	Tony Lema	St Andrews	Bobby Nichols	Columbus CC
1965	Jack Nicklaus	Augusta National	Gary Player	Bellerive	Peter Thomson	Royal Birkdale	Dave Marr	Laurel Valley
1966	Jack Nicklaus	Augusta National	Billy Casper	Olympic CC	Jack Nicklaus	Muirfield	Al Geiberger	Firestone CC
1967	Gay Brewer	Augusta National	Jack Nicklaus	Baltusrol	Roberto de Vicenzo	Hoylake	Don January	Columbine CC
1968	Bob Goalby	Augusta National	Lee Trevino	Oak Hill	Gary Player	Carnoustie	Julius Boros	Pecan Valley
1969	George Archer	Augusta National	Orville Moody	Champions GC	Tony Jacklin	Royal Lytham & St Annes	Ray Floyd	NCR CC
1970	Billy Casper	Augusta National	Tony Jacklin	Hazeltine National	Jack Nicklaus	St Andrews	Dave Stockton	Southern Hills
1971	Charles Coody	Augusta National	Lee Trevino	Merion	Lee Trevino	Royal Birkdale	Jack Nicklaus	PGA National
1972	Jack Nicklaus	Augusta National	Jack Nicklaus	Pebble Beach	Lee Trevino	Muirfield	Gary Player	Oakland Hills
1973	Tommy Aaron	Augusta National	Johnny Miller	Oakmont	Tom Weiskopf	Troon	Jack Nicklaus	Canterbury GC
1974	Gary Player	Augusta National	Hale Irwin	Winged Foot	Gary Player	Royal Lytham & St Annes	Lee Trevino	Tanglewood GC
1975	Jack Nicklaus	Augusta National	Lou Graham	Medinah	Tom Watson	Carnoustie	Jack Nicklaus	Firestone CC
1976	Ray Floyd	Augusta National	Jerry Pate	Atlanta Athletic Club	Johnny Miller	Royal Birkdale	Dave Stockton	Congressional
1977	Tom Watson	Augusta National	Hubert Green	Southern Hills	Tom Watson	Turnberry	Lanny Wadkins	Pebble Beach
1978	Gary Player	Augusta National	Andy North	Cherry Hills	Jack Nicklaus	St Andrews	John Mahaffey	Oakmont
1979	Fuzzy Zoeller	Augusta National	Hale Irwin	Inverness	Seve Ballesteros	Royal Lytham & St Annes	David Graham	Oakland Hills
1980	Seve Ballesteros	Augusta National	Jack Nicklaus	Baltusrol	Tom Watson	Muirfield	Jack Nicklaus	Oak Hill
1981	Tom Watson	Augusta National	David Graham	Merion	Bill Rogers	Royal St George's, Sandwich	Larry Nelson	Atlanta Athletic Club
1982	Craig Stadler	Augusta National	Tom Watson	Pebble Beach	Tom Watson	Royal Troon	Ray Floyd	Southern Hills
1983	Seve Ballesteros	Augusta National	Larry Nelson	Oakmont	Tom Watson	Royal Birkdale	Hal Sutton	Riviera CC
1984	Ben Crenshaw	Augusta National	Fuzzy Zoeller	Winged Foot	Seve Ballesteros	St Andrews	Lee Trevino	Shoal Creek
1985	Bernhard Langer	Augusta National	Andy North	Oakland Hills	Sandy Lyle	Royal St George's, Sandwich	Hubert Green	Cherry Hills
1986	Jack Nicklaus	Augusta National	Ray Floyd	Shinnecock Hills	Greg Norman	Turnberry	Bob Tway	Inverness
1987	Larry Mize	Augusta National	Scott Simpson	Olympic CC	Nick Faldo	Muirfield	Larry Nelson	PGA National
1988	Sandy Lyle	Augusta National	Curtis Strange	Brookline	Seve Ballesteros	Royal Lytham & St Annes	Jeff Sluman	Oak Tree GC
1989	Nick Faldo	Augusta National	Curtis Strange	Oak Hill	Mark Calcavecchia	Royal Troon	Payne Stewart	Kemper Lakes
1990	Nick Faldo	Augusta National	Hale Irwin	Medinah	Nick Faldo	St Andrews	Wayne Grady	Shoal Creek
1991	Ian Woosnam	Augusta National	Payne Stewart	Hazeltine National	Ian Baker-Finch	Royal Birkdale	John Daly	Crooked Stick
1992	Fred Couples	Augusta National	Tom Kite	Pebble Beach	Nick Faldo	Muirfield	Nick Price	Bellrive
1993	Bernhard Langer	Augusta National	Lee Janzen	Baltusrol	Greg Norman	Royal St George's, Sandwich	Paul Azinger	Inverness
1994	Jose Maria Olazabal	Augusta National	Ernie Els	Oakmont	Nick Price	Turnberry	Nick Price	Southern Hills
1995	Ben Crenshaw	Augusta National	Corey Pavin	Shinnecock Hills	John Daly	St Andrews	Steve Elkington	Riviera CC
1996	Nick Faldo	Augusta National	Steve Jones	Oakland Hills	Tom Lehman	Royal Lytham & St Annes	Mark Brooks	Valhalla
1997	Tiger Woods	Augusta National	Ernie Els	Congressional	Justin Leonard	Royal Troon	Davis Love III	Winged Foot
1998	Mark O'Meara	Augusta National	Lee Janzen	Olympic CC	Mark O'Meara	Royal Birkdale	Vijay Singh	Sahalee
1999	Jose Maria Olazabal	Augusta National	Payne Stewart	Pinehurst	Paul Lawrie	Carnoustie	Tiger Woods	Medinah
2000	Vijay Singh	Augusta National	Tiger Woods	Pebble Beach	Tiger Woods	St Andrews	Tiger Woods	Valhalla
2001	Tiger Woods	Augusta National	Retief Goosen	Southern Hills	David Duval	Royal Lytham & St Annes	David Toms	Atlanta Athletic Club

THE MAJOR CHAMPIONSHIPS: 1860–2000

THE OPEN 1860

Prestwick Golf Club, Ayrshire, Scotland
(17 October)

Prestwick was a 12-hole course which went '...dodging in and out among lofty sandhills' and 'The holes were, for the most part, out of sight...', (Horace Hutchinson). The 3799-yard links had a 'bogey' of 48 . Eight men embarked on this inauspicious first occasion, with Willie Park being the first recipient of the Moroccan-leather Belt, but no money.

1	**WILLIE PARK, Sr**	55	59	60	174
	(£Nil)				
2	Tom Morris, Sr	58	59	59	176
3	Andrew Strath				180
4	Robert Andrew				191
5	George Brown				192
6	Charlie Hunter				195
	Alexander Smith				
	William Steel				232?

THE OPEN 1861

Prestwick Golf Club, Ayrshire, Scotland
(26 September)

Regardless of whether the professionals were or were not getting paid, the Championship organizer, Col JO Fairlie, set the scene for the involvement of amateurs by taking part himself. The term 'Open' Championship may have originated from this date, when Fairlie exhorted the Championship as 'being open to all the world'.

1	**TOM MORRIS, Sr**	54	56	53	163
	(£Nil)				
2	Willie Park, Sr	54	54	59	167
3	William Dow	59	58	54	171
4	David Park	58	57	57	172
5	Robert Andrew	58	61	56	175
6	Peter McEwan	56	60	62	178
7	Willie Dunn, Sr	61	59	60	180
8	James Fairlie (a)				184
9	George Brown	60	65	60	185
10	Robert Chambers, Jr (a)				187
11	Jamie Dunn	63	62	63	188
12	Charlie Hunter	67	64	59	190

THE OPEN 1862

Prestwick Golf Club, Ayrshire, Scotland
(11 September)

No monetary prize was offered again, but for the last time. Apart from the belt medals were also distributed, creating a tradition still upheld today. The winning margin of 13 shots still stands as the all-time record for the Open, and for any Major until it was beaten by Tiger Woods' 15-shot margin in the US Open of 2000 – all of 138 years later.

1	**TOM MORRIS, Sr**	52	55	56	163
	(£Nil)				
2	Willie Park, Sr	59	59	58	176
3	Charlie Hunter	60	60	58	178
4	William Dow	60	58	63	181
5	James Knight (a)	62	61	63	186
6	J F Johnston (a)	64	69	75	208
	William Mitchell (a)				
	R Pollock (a)				

THE OPEN 1863

Prestwick Golf Club, Ayrshire, Scotland
(18 September)

After three years of nothing, a £10 purse was shared out among all the professionals, regardless of their finishing positions. Park 2; Morris 1.

1	**WILLIE PARK, Sr**	56	54	58	168
	(£Nil)				
2	Tom Morris, Sr	56	58	56	170
3	David Park	55	63	54	172
4	Andrew Strath	61	55	58	174
5	George Brown	58	61	57	176
6	Robert Andrew	62	57	59	178
7	Charlie Hunter	61	61	62	184
8	James Knight (a)	66	65	59	190
9	James Miller (a)	63	63	66	192
10	James Paxton	65	65	66	196
11=	Peter Chalmers (a)	65	67	65	197
	J F Johnston (a)	66	66	65	197
13	William Mitchell (a)	70	70	66	206
14	William Moffat (a)	75	78	80	233

THE OPEN 1864

Prestwick Golf Club, Ayrshire, Scotland
(16 September)

'Old' Tom Morris squared his private battle with Willie Park. He returned to St Andrews as pro in this year, having been at Prestwick previously. A winner's prize in cash was supplied for the first time.

1	**TOM MORRIS, Sr**	54	58	55	167
	(£6)				
2	Andrew Strath	56	57	56	169
3	Robert Andrew	57	58	60	175
4	Willie Park, Sr	55	67	55	177
5	William Dow	56	58	67	181
6	William Strath	60	62	60	182

THE OPEN 1865

Prestwick Golf Club, Ayrshire, Scotland
(14 September)

Official printed scorecards were introduced for the first time, although judging from the records that remain, not many knew what to do with them. Finally, a winner other than a Morris or a Park was acclaimed.

1	**ANDREW STRATH**	55	54	3	162
	(£8)				
2	Willie Park, Sr	56	52	56	164
3	William Dow				171
4	Bob Kirk	64	54	55	173
5	Tom Morris, Sr	57	61	56	174
6	William Doleman (a)	62	57	59	178
7	Robert Andrew	61	59	59	179
8	William Strath	60	60	62	182
9	William Miller	63	60	66	189
10	Tom Hood (a)	66	66	66	198

THE OPEN 1866

Prestwick Golf Club, Ayrshire, Scotland
(13 September)

How many competitors made up the field at the start? How many completed the Championship, and what were their scores? As the *Ayrshire Express* conceded, '...cards were not given to the secretary and cannot consequently be recorded'. Golfers of the day obviously had no consideration for historians.

1	**WILLIE PARK, Sr**	54	56	59	169
	(£6)				
2	David Park	58	57	56	171
3	Robert Andrew	58	59	59	176
4	Tom Morris, Sr	61	58	59	178
5	Bob Kirk	60	62	58	180
6=	William Doleman (a)	60	60	62	182
	Andrew Strath	61	61	60	182
8	John Allan	60	63	60	183
9	Tom Morris, Jr	63	60	64	187
10	Willie Dunn, Sr	64	63	62	189
11	Tom Hood (a)	61	69	61	191
12	James Hutchison	63	67	64	194

THE OPEN 1867

Prestwick Golf Club, Ayrshire, Scotland
(Date n/k)

'Old' Tom became, at 46 years 99 days, the oldest-ever winner of the Open and any Major until Julius Boros' US PGA title in 1968. Total prize money had dropped to £5.5s from a peak of £20 in 1865, just illustrating how tough it was to put on the Championship in the early years.

1	**TOM MORRIS, Sr**	58	54	58	170
	(£n/k)				
2	Willie Park, Sr	58	56	58	172
3	Andrew Strath	61	57	56	174
4	Tom Morris, Jr	58	59	58	175
5	Bob Kirk	57	60	60	177
6	William Doleman (a)	55	66	57	178
7	Robert Andrew	56	58	65	179
8=	William Dow	62	57	65	184
	T Hunter (a)	62	60	62	184
10	Willie Dunn, Sr	64	63	62	189

THE OPEN 1868

Prestwick Golf Club, Ayrshire, Scotland
(23 September)

The Son of the Father. Enter 'Young' Tom Morris to dominate the Championship for several years and create new scoring records year after year. He recorded the Open's first hole-in-one on the 166(?)-yard 8th hole. At 17 years 5 months 8 days, he became the youngest winner of the Championship – and of any of the Majors.

1	**TOM MORRIS, Jr**	50	55	52	157
	(£6)				
2	Robert Andrew	53	54	52	159
3	Willie Park, Sr	58	50	54	162
4	Bob Kirk	56	59	56	171
5	John Allan	54	55	63	172
6	Tom Morris, Sr	56	62	58	176
7	William Dow	61	58	60	179
8	William Doleman (a)	57	63	61	181
9	Charlie Hunter	60	64	58	182
10	Willie Dunn, Sr	60	63	60	183

THE OPEN 1869

Prestwick Golf Club, Ayrshire, Scotland
(16 September)

Morris, Jr shot the Open's first sub-50 round at Prestwick to steal the title from his Dad. Once again, information on the extent of the field is very patchy.

1	**TOM MORRIS, Jr**	51	54	49	154
	(£6)				
2	Tom Morris, Sr	54	50	53	157
3	S Mure Fergusson (a)	57	54	54	165
4	Bob Kirk	53	58	57	168
5	Davie Strath	53	56	60	169
6	Jamie Anderson	60	56	57	173
7	William Doleman (a)	60	56	59	175
8	G Mitchell-Innes (a)	64	58	58	180

THE OPEN 1870

**Prestwick Golf Club, Ayrshire, Scotland
(15 September)**

Young Tom's third win gave him the Belt outright. He became the first player in an Open to beat the Prestwick 'bogey' of 48, and his winning margin, after his Dad's win in 1862, was the biggest for any Major (apart from being equalled in 1921 by Jim Barnes in the US Open) until Tiger Woods' 12-shot win at Augusta 127 years later. Woods, of course, was to go on to shatter both the Morrisses' records in 2000 at Pebble Beach.

1	**TOM MORRIS, Jr**	47	51	51	149
	(£6)				
2=	Bob Kirk	52	52	57	161
	Davie Strath	54	49	58	161
4	Tom Morris, Sr	56	52	54	162
5	William Doleman (a)	57	56	58	171
6	Willie Park, Sr	60	55	58	173
7	Jamie Anderson	59	57	58	174
8	John Allan	61	58	57	176
9=	A Doleman (a)	61	59	58	178
	Charlie Hunter	58	56	64	178
11	J Brown	66	55	59	180
12	J Millar	66	62	54	182
13	T Hunter (a)	62	63	60	185
14	F Doleman	65	64	60	189
15=	W Boyd	65	59	67	191
	J Hunter	62	65	64	191
17	William Dow	68	64	66	198

THE OPEN – No Championship 1871

Prestwick, undoubtedly, was finding the organization of the Championship tough going, and with the rich East Coast Clubs clamouring for some of the action, the Championship was on rocky ground. It would breathe new life, though, after all the politicking was through, with a new trophy – the famous silver Claret Jug, still presented to the Champion golfer today, was purchased for the not inconsiderable sum of £30 – and the creation of a rotation system between Prestwick, the Hon Co of Edinburgh Golfers at Musselburgh, and the Royal and Ancient Golf Club of St Andrews. It resolved that the competition should be open to all-comers, thus making official Col Fairlie's sentiments of 1861.

THE OPEN 1872

**Prestwick Golf Club, Ayrshire, Scotland
(13 September)**

Tom Morris Jr won his fourth Open at 21: his is the first name on the new trophy – the famous Claret Jug. This was to be the last year of Prestwick's exclusivity in hosting the Open.

1	**TOM MORRIS, Jr**	57	56	53	166
	(£8)				
2	Davie Strath	56	52	61	169
3	William Doleman (a)	63	60	54	177
4=	Tom Morris, Sr	62	60	57	179
	David Park	61	57	61	179
6	Charlie Hunter	60	60	69	189
7	Hugh Brown	65	73	61	199
8	William Hunter (a)	65	63	74	202

THE OPEN 1873

**Royal & Ancient Golf Club, St Andrews, Fife, Scotland
(4 October)**

The first Open Championship to be held at the Old Course was dominated by local St Andrews golfers, of which, Kidd, the winner, was one. Another, David Ayton, was the forerunner of various Aytons' appearances in different Majors spread over the next 80 years or so.

1	**TOM KIDD**	91	88		179
	(£11)				
2	Jamie Anderson	91	89		180
3=	Bob Kirk	91	92		183
	Tom Morris, Jr	94	89		183
5	Davie Strath	97	90		187
6	Walter Gourlay	92	96		188
7	Tom Morris, Sr	93	96		189
9	Henry Lamb (a)	96	96		192
10=	Willie Fernie	101	93		194
	Bob Martin	97	97		194
12=	R Armitage (a)	96	99		195
	Jas Fenton	94	101		195
	JOF Morris	96	99		195
15	S Mure Fergusson (a)	98	101		199
16	R Manzie	96	104		200
17	Jack Morris	106	100		206
18=	David Ayton	111	96		207
	R Thomson	98	109		207
20	John Chisholm	103	105		208
21	Bob Pringle	109	102		211
22	D Brand	110	103		213

THE OPEN 1874

Hon Co of Edinburgh Golfers, Musselburgh, Midlothian, Scotland
(10 April)

Mungo Park (related to the famous late-18th Century explorer of the same name?) beat 'Young' Tom, whose health was now starting to decline. Mungo was the brother of Willie, and his son, also Mungo (!), became a pioneer of golf and course architecture in the United States. His first round 75 was the record low score for any 18 holes; and was only lowered by Harold Hilton, who shot 72 on the much-criticized Muirfield Links in 1892; and by Willie Smith (71), George Duncan (71), James Braid (73&74), and others, on the Old Course as late as 1910. The Hon Co were to be somewhat unusual in the dates they offered for the Championship.

1	**MUNGO PARK**	75	84	159
	(£8)			
2	Tom Morris, Jr	83	78	161
3	George Paxton	80	82	162
4	Bob Martin	85	79	164
5	Jamie Anderson	82	83	165
6=	David Park	83	83	166
	William Thomson	84	82	166
8=	Bob Ferguson	83	84	167
	Tom Kidd	84	83	167
10=	J Fergusson	87	82	169
	G M'Cachnie	79	90	169
	JOF Morris	88	81	169
13	Willie Park, Sr	83	87	170
14=	Tom Hood	83	88	171
	Bob Pringle	85	86	171
16	T Hunter (a)	88	86	174
17	T Brown	87	88	175
18=	Tom Morris, Sr	90	86	176
	Davie Strath	86	90	176
20=	William Cosgrove	88	89	177
	William Doleman (a)	89	88	177
22=	R Cosgrove	92	86	178
	Willie Dunn, SR	87	91	178
24=	J Dow	88	94	182
	Jas Fenton	90	92	182
25	William Brown	91	93	184
26	W Hutchison	90	95	185
27	Charlie Hunter	93	94	187
28	N Patrick	98	98	196
29	D Clayton	99	101	200
30	A Brown	96	106	202

THE OPEN 1875

Prestwick Golf Club, Ayrshire, Scotland
(10 September)

Willie Park picked up his fourth and last title after a few years of indifferent form. It is thought that the Morrises did not compete due the death of 'Young' Tom's wife in childbirth. The even more tragic corollary to this was that Tommy hit the bottle which, I conjunction with his ill-health eventually led to the discovery by 'Old' Tom of his son's body on Christmas morning, 1874. The greatest golfer of his generation was dead at 24.

1	**WILLIE PARK, Sr**	59	59	51	166
	(£8)				
2	Bob Martin	56	58	54	168
3	Mungo Park	59	57	55	171
4	Bob Ferguson	58	56	58	172
5	James Rennie	61	59	57	177
6	Davie Strath	59	61	58	178
7	Bob Pringle	62	58	61	181
8=	William Doleman (a)	65	59	59	183
	Hugh Morrison	62	59	62	183
10	John Campbell	57	66	63	186
11	Neil Boon	67	60	62	189
12	James Guthrie	63	64	66	193
13	Matthew Allan	67	65	62	194
14	James Boyd	67	65	63	195

THE OPEN 1876

Royal & Ancient Golf Club, St Andrews, Fife, Scotland
(30 September)

The first-ever play-off in the Open never took place. Davie Strath protested about a claim against him for disqualification. The decision was that he and Martin should play off, but Strath refused on the basis that his protest had not been properly decided upon. Martin was awarded the Championship.

1	**BOB MARTIN***	86	90	176
	(£10)			
2	Davie Strath	86	90	176
3	Willie Park, Sr	94	89	183
4=	Tom Morris, Sr	90	95	185
	Mungo Park	95	90	185
	William Thomson	90	95	185
7	Henry Lamb (a)	94	92	186
8=	Walter Gourlay	98	89	187
	Bob Kirk	95	92	187
	George Paxton	95	92	187
11	Robert Kinsman	88	100	188
12=	Jamie Anderson	96	93	189
	David Lamb (a)	95	94	189
14=	David Anderson, Sr	93	97	190
	John Thompson	89	101	190

* Play-off: see narrative above

THE OPEN 1877

**Hon Co of Edinburgh Golfers, Musselburgh, Midlothian, Scotland
(6 April)**

The Hon Co continued experimenting with an early-season Championship. Anderson's first of three wins, 'back-to-back', was over four rounds of Musselburgh's nine holes.

1	**JAMIE ANDERSON**	40	42	37	41	160
	(£8)					
2	Bob Pringle	44	38	40	40	162
3=	William Cosgrove	41	39	44	40	164
	Bob Ferguson	40	40	40	44	164
5=	William Brown	39	41	45	41	166
	Davie Strath	45	40	38	43	166
7	Mungo Park					167

THE OPEN 1878

**Prestwick Golf Club, Ayrshire, Scotland
(4 October)**

Jamie Anderson recorded the second 'hole-in-one' in the Championship, following Morris Jr's effort in 1868. Amateur John Ball finished fourth in his first Open: he was also the highest-placed non-Scot to date. He was aged just 14! Ten years later Ball won the embryonic British Amateur Championship on the first of eight occasions (he won it as late as 1912), and in 1890 broke the stranglehold of the Scottish professional in the Open. Until then a Scot had won every Open since the first in 1860.

1	**JAMIE ANDERSON**	53	53	51	157
	(£8)				
2	Bob Kirk	53	55	51	159
3	JOF Morris	50	56	55	161
4=	John Ball, Jr (a)	53	57	55	165
	Bob Martin	57	53	55	165
6=	William Cosgrove	55	56	55	166
	Willie Park, Sr	53	56	57	166
8	Jamie Allan	62	53	52	167
9=	John Allan	55	55	58	168
	Tom Dunn	54	60	54	168
11	Tom Morris, Sr	55	53	63	171
12	Ben Sayers	56	59	58	173
13	Edwin Paxton	58	59	58	175
14	George Strath	63	62	51	176
15	Alex Patrick	62	56	60	178
16	Jack Morris	58	57	64	179
17	Mungo Park	60	58	62	180
18	George Low	57	61	63	181
19	Neil Boon	63	54	66	183
20	William Hunter (a)	67	65	55	187
21	James Moore	62	62	65	189
22	Bob Pringle	62	65	65	192

THE OPEN 1879

**Royal & Ancient Golf Club, St Andrews, Fife, Scotland
(27 September)**

Anderson's 'Hat trick' had the the lowest total of all 36-hole Opens on this, his home course, until Hugh Kirkaldy's 166 in the very last one, in 1891. Joint runner-up, Andrew Kirkaldy, would never win the Open (with four second places, including losing a play-off, surely one of the most unlucky) but went on to become one of the most influential people in the game. Despite a wonderful record at a time when the 'Great Triumvirate' seemed to be winning everything, it was as professional at the R&A, following Tom Morris in 1910, until his death in 1934, that he will always be remembered.

1	**JAMIE ANDERSON**	84	85	169
	(£10)			
2=	Jamie Allan	88	84	172
	Andrew Kirkaldy	86	86	172
4	George Paxton			174
5	Tom Kidd			175
6	Bob Ferguson			176
7	David Anderson, Sr			178
8=	Tom Dunn			179
	Walter Gourlay			179
	JOF Morris	92	87	179
11	AW Smith (a)			180
12=	Willie Fernie			181
	John Kirkaldy			181
	James Rennie			181
15=	Thomas Arundel			184
	David Ayton			184
	Henry Lamb (a)			184
18=	William Doleman (a)			185
	Robert Kinsman			185
	Tom Morris, Sr			185
21	Bob Martin			186
22	Ben Sayers			187
23=	D Corstorphine			189
	Robert Dow			189
	David Grant			189
	Edwin Paxton			189
	Smith (Cambridge)			189
28	Argyll Robertson (a)			190
29=	R Armitage			191
	George Strath			191

THE OPEN 1880

Hon Co of Edinburgh Golfers, Musselburgh, Midlothian, Scotland
(9 April)

The early date of the Championship was inconvenient for Jamie Anderson, and he was unable to compete. This left Bob Ferguson the chance to secure the first of his three wins in a row. Anderson, although featuring strongly over the next few years, never won again, and died in a Poor House in Perth in 1905. So much for the rich pickings of the 19th Century professional golfer.

1	BOB FERGUSON	81	81		162
	(£8)				
2	Peter Paxton	81	86		167
3	Ned Cosgrove	82	86		168
4=	David Brown	86	83		169
	George Paxton	85	84		169
	Bob Pringle	90	79		169
7	Andrew Kirkaldy	85	85		170
8=	William Brown	87	84		171
	David Grant	87	84		171
10=	Thomas Arundel	86	93		179
	T Brown	90	89		179
	Willie Campbell	88	91		179
	J Foreman	92	87		179
14	Willie Park, Sr	89	92		181
15	Willie Park, Jr	92	90		182
16=	A Brown	91	92		183
	D Corstorphine	93	90		183
	George Strath	87	96		183
19	Ben Sayers	91	93		184
20	Mungo Park	95	92		187
21=	R Drummond	96	94		190
	William Thomson	96	94		190
23	James Beveridge	94	97		191

THE OPEN 1881

Prestwick Golf Club, Ayrshire, Scotland
(14 October)

Violent storms reduced the field to 22 starters, of whom only eight finished. The conditions were so bad that Ferguson's winning total was the highest for Prestwick's 36 holes since 'Old' Tom's last win in 1867; and only exceeded by Willie Park's 174 in the inaugural year. About 180 fishermen were drowned in Scottish waters due to the storms.

1	BOB FERGUSON	53	60	57	170
	(£8)				
2	Jamie Anderson	57	60	56	173
3	Ned Cosgrove	61	59	57	177
4	Bob Martin	57	62	59	178
5=	Willie Campbell	60	56	65	181
	Tom Morris, Sr	58	65	58	181
	Willie Park, Jr	66	57	58	181
8	Willie Fernie	65	62	56	183

THE OPEN 1882

Royal & Ancient Golf Club, St Andrews, Fife, Scotland
(30 September)

Ferguson held his three-stroke first round lead to pick up his third consecutive Open. Like Anderson before him, obscurity was to follow in a few years, and he resorted to green-keeping and caddieing thereafter at his home club of Musselburgh.

1	BOB FERGUSON	83	88	171
	(£12)			
2	Willie Fernie	88	86	174
3=	Jamie Anderson	87	88	175
	Fitz Boothby (a)	86	89	175
	John Kirkcaldy	86	89	175
	Bob Martin	89	86	175
7=	David Ayton	90	88	178
	James Mansfield (a)	91	87	178
	Willie Park, Sr	89	89	178
	James Rennie	90	88	178
11=	Tom Kidd	87	93	180
	Henry Lamb (a)	88	92	180
13=	Andrew Alexander	93	88	181
	George Low	95	86	181
	Douglas Rolland	88	93	181
16=	W Honeyman	93	89	182
	William Thomson	95	87	182
18=	Tom Dunn	93	90	183
	Willie Park, Jr	90	93	183
	Ben Sayers	92	91	183
21=	David Anderson, Sr	91	93	184
	Peter Fernie	94	90	184
23=	Jack Burns	97	92	189
	George Forrester	94	95	189
	Bob Pringle	92	97	189
	David Simpson	98	91	189
27	Thomas Arundel	97	93	190
28	James Kirk	101	90	191
29=	James Hunter (a)	92	100	192
	Robert Kinsman	99	93	192

THE OPEN 1883

Hon Co of Edinburgh Golfers, Musselburgh, Midlothian, Scotland
(16 November)

Willie Fernie, despite shooting the only ten to appear on any Major winner's card in history, tied with Ferguson and denied him from making four wins in as many years – by one shot in the first contested play-off. Fernie, although St Andrews born, was then of Dumfries. He thus became the first winner from outside the host clubs, summing up the parochial nature of the Championship to date. Musselburgh played host to the Open in November for the first time, seemingly not happy with its previous, equally-eccentric, habit of April Championships.

1	**WILLIE FERNIE***	75	84	159
	(£n/k)			
2	Ferguson	78	81	159
3	William Brown	83	77	160
4	Bob Pringle	79	82	161
5=	Willie Campbell	80	83	163
	George Paxton	80	83	163
7	Ben Sayers	81	83	164
8	Willie Park, Jr	77	88	165
9	Willie Dunn, Jr	85	81	166
10=	Ben Campbell	81	86	167
	Tom Morris, Sr	86	81	167
	Peter Paxton	85	82	167
	Douglas Rolland (a)	82	85	167
14	T Grossart	82	86	168
15	F Park	84	85	169
16	William Cosgrove	79	91	170
17=	Tom Dunn	87	84	171
	Jack Simpson (a)	90	81	171
19	G Miller (a)	80	92	172
20	D Leitch (a)	88	86	174
21	Thomas Arundel	87	88	175
22	Willie Park, Sr	94	82	176
23	William Thomson	90	87	177
24=	David Brown	88	91	179
	David Grant	89	90	179
26	D Corstorphine	88	93	181
27	Mungo Park	93	89	182
28	Bob Tait	89	94	183
29	George Strath	91	93	184
30	D Baldie (a)	92	93	185

*Willie Fernie (158) beat Bob Ferguson (159) in the 36-Hole Play-off

THE OPEN 1884

Prestwick Golf Club, Ayrshire, Scotland
(Date n/k)

Just about the only thing that was known about the 1884 Prestwick Championship is that Jack Simpson was the only one of several golfing brothers to win the Open. Brother Archie acme closest of the other Simpsons, being runner-up in 1885 and 1890. This misfortune to befall this year's joint-second, Willie Fernie, on more than one occasion in future Championships.

1	**JACK SIMPSON**	78	82	160
	(£n/k)			
2=	Willie Fernie	80	84	164
	Douglas Rolland	81	83	164
4=	Willie Campbell	84	85	169
	Willie Park, Jr	86	83	169
6	Ben Sayers	83	87	170
7=	Tom Dunn			171
	George Fernie			171
9=	Peter Fernie			172
	John Kirkaldy			172
11=	Matthew Allan			173
	Willie Dunn, Jr			173
13=	JOF Morris			174
	Tom Morris, Sr			174
15	Jamie Anderson			175
16=	William Cosgrove			178
	William Doleman (a)			178
18	James Hunter (a)			179
19	David Grant			180
20	G Smith			183

THE OPEN 1885

Royal & Ancient Golf Club, St Andrews, Fife, Scotland
(3 October)

During the 1880s a minor exodus of Scottish pros moved to clubs south of the border, but only a handful of English golfers, all amateur, had ventured north for the Championship. One of the most influential of these, Horace Hutchinson, made his debut this year. Through his playing and writing about golf over the ensuing few years he had much to do with encouraging the burgeoning English talent of the 1890s to participate in the Open.

1	**BOB MARTIN**	84	87	171
	(£10)			
2	Archie Simpson	83	89	172
3	David Ayton	89	84	173
4=	Willie Fernie	89	85	174
	Willie Park, Jr	86	88	174
	Bob Simpson	85	89	174
7	Jack Burns	88	87	175
8	Peter Paxton	85	91	176
9=	Willie Campbell	86	91	177
	JOF Morris	91	86	177
11=	Horace Hutchinson (a)	87	91	178
	John Kirkaldy	94	84	178
13=	Johnny Laidlay (a)	87	92	179
	Jack Simpson	87	92	179
15	Ben Sayers	94	86	180
16=	Leslie Balfour (a)	90	91	181
	William Greig (a)	89	92	181
18=	HSC Everard (a)	90	92	182
	George Fernie	87	95	182
	James Rennie	90	92	182
21	David Anderson, Sr	96	87	183
22	Ben Campbell	88	96	184
23	Willie Brown	91	95	186
24=	Willie Anderson, Sr	90	97	187
	S Mure Fergusson (a)	96	91	187
26	WH Goff (a)	97	91	188
27=	TS Hendry (a)	94	95	189
	Robert Kinsman	96	93	189
29=	Jamie Allan	93	97	190
	William Cosgrove	88	102	190
	Bruce Goff (a)	96	94	190
	Tom Morris, Sr	96	94	190

THE OPEN 1886

Hon Co of Edinburgh Golfers, Musselburgh, Midlothian, Scotland
(5 November)

An unsung champion, David Brown emigrated to America where he tied with Willie Anderson for the US Open as late as 1903 – losing the play-off by two strokes. The Championship could have drifted away in the 1880s; it hadn't really developed beyond a regional event. Despite the Scots traditional antipathy to the Sassenach, it would take a particularly introspective one not to acknowledge the shot in the arm the English were to give the Championship in the next decade.

1	**DAVID BROWN**	79	78	157
	(£8)			
2	Willie Campbell	78	81	159
3	Ben Campbell	79	81	160
4=	Bob Ferguson	82	79	161
	Thomas Gossett	80	81	161
	Willie Park, Jr	84	77	161
	Archie Simpson	82	79	161
8=	Willie Fernie	79	83	162
	David Grant	86	76	162
	Johnny Laidlay (a)	80	82	162
11	JOF Morris	81	82	163
12=	John Lambert	78	86	164
	Thomas McWatt	81	83	164
	Jack Simpson	83	81	164
15	Bob Simpson	84	81	165
16=	Tom Dunn	83	83	166
	Horace Hutchinson (a)	81	85	166
	Bob Pringle	80	86	166
	Ben Sayers	84	82	166
20=	William Cosgrove	84	83	167
	Bob Tait	84	83	167
22	Peter Fernie	85	83	168
23	Peter Paxton	87	82	169
24=	Jacky Ferguson	83	87	170
	George Strath	86	84	170
26	David Simpson	84	88	172
27=	Willie Dunn, Jr	85	88	173
	Tom Morris, Sr	88	85	173
29=	Charlie Crawford	85	89	174
	James Keddie	84	90	174

THE OPEN 1887

Prestwick Golf Club, Ayrshire, Scotland
(16 September)

Willie Jr's win completed the second set of father-son victories. Fittingly it should be the Parks and the Morrises, the fathers having carved up the first five Championships between them. After winning again in 1889, Willie Park Jr increasingly turned his mind to club and ball development; and has been called the father of modern golf course architecture – the classic at Sunningdale being his greatest achievement. He was also the first professional to write on the game: *The Game of Golf* was published in 1896.

1	**WILLIE PARK, Jr**	82	79	161
	(£8)			
2	Bob Martin	81	81	162
3	Willie Campbell	77	87	164
4	Johnny Laidlay (a)	86	80	166
5=	Ben Sayers	83	85	168
	Archie Simpson	81	87	168
7=	Willie Fernie	86	87	173
	David Grant	89	84	173
9	David Brown	82	92	174
10=	Ben Campbell	88	87	175
	Horace Hutchinson (a)	87	88	175
12=	David Ayton	89	87	176
	James Kay	89	87	176
	John Kirkaldy	89	87	176
	Jack Simpson	85	91	176
16	Bob Simpson	90	89	179
17=	George Fernie	92	88	180
	A Monaghan	90	90	180
19	Hugh Kirkaldy	89	92	181
20=	James Boyd	95	87	182
	P Wilson (a)	90	92	182
22=	Allan Macfie (a)	94	90	184
	A Stuart (a)	96	88	184
24	Peter Fernie	95	90	185
25=	JS Carrick (a)	96	90	186
	Jack Morris	93	93	186
27	David McEwan	94	93	187

THE OPEN 1888

Royal & Ancient Golf Club, St Andrews, Fife, Scotland
(6 October)

Jack Burns's win was one of great surprise. He only contested the Championship with any great seriousness during the 1880s, and had just one Top Ten finish before he collected the Claret Jug. Immediately afterwards he moved as pro to the English Midlands. He eventually returned to St Andrews, the place of his birth, to retire from all golf in 1897 – not yet 40. The other side of the coiun was Alex 'Sandy' Herd, who made the Top Ten for the first time in his fourth year of a 54-year span in the Open Championship. His remarkable run included a win in 1902, and seconds in 1892, 1895, 1910 and 1920. He competed in his last Open in 1939, aged 71. His brother Fred won the 1898 US Open.

1	**JACK BURNS**	86	85	171
	(£8)			
2=	David Anderson, Jr	86	86	172
	Ben Sayers	85	87	172
4	Willie Campbell	84	90	174
5	Leslie Balfour (a)	86	89	175
6=	David Grant	88	88	176
	Andrew Kirkaldy	87	89	176
8	Sandy Herd	93	84	177
9	David Ayton	87	91	178
10	Johnny Laidlay (a)	93	87	180
11=	HSC Everard (a)	93	89	182
	Hugh Kirkaldy	98	84	182
	Willie Park, Jr	90	92	182
14=	Laurie Auchterlonie	91	92	183
	Willie Fernie	91	92	183
16=	Bob Martin	86	98	184
	Archie Simpson	91	93	184
18=	Jamie Allan	95	90	185
	Willie Auchterlonie	92	93	185
	John Kirkaldy	92	93	185
	Allan Macfie (a)	94	91	185
	Bob Tait	95	90	185
23=	William Greig (a)	94	92	186
	JOF Morris	96	90	186
25	N Playfair (a)	94	93	187
26	D Leitch (a)	93	96	189
27=	Willie Anderson, Sr	98	92	190
	Tom Morris, Sr	94	96	190
	DG Rose (a)	101	89	190
30	Bob Simpson	90	101	191

THE OPEN 1889

Hon Co of Edinburgh Golfers, Musselburgh, Midlothian, Scotland
(8 November)

The last Championship held at Musselburgh produced a course record winning total in the tie between Willie Jr and Andrew Kirkaldy – the lowest at any venue since the heyday of 'Young' Tom in 1869 and 1870. The Honourable Company, in order to stay involved with the Open, forsook their nine-hole home for Muirfield, further along the southern shores of the Firth of Forth, some 15 miles east of Edinburgh. The end of the second round was played in a November gloom so deep that final pairs had to be guided by street lights, and it triggered, permanently, the move to earlier calendar dates.

1	**WILLIE PARK, Jr** *	39	39	39	38	155
	(£8)					
2	Andrew Kirkaldy	39	38	39	39	155
3	Ben Sayers	39	40	41	39	159
4=	David Brown	43	39	41	39	162
	Johnny Laidlay (a)	42	39	40	41	162
6	Willie Fernie	45	39	40	40	164
7=	Willie Brown	44	43	41	37	165
	Willie Campbell	44	40	42	39	165
	David Grant	41	41	41	42	165
10=	High Kirkaldy	44	39	43	40	166
	William Thomson	43	42	40	41	166
12	Archie Simpson	44	45	37	41	167
13	AM Ross (a)	42	45	42	40	169
14	Jack Burns	47	39	42	42	170

*Willie Park Jr (158) beat Andrew Kirkaldy (163) in the 36-Hole Play-off

THE OPEN 1890

Prestwick Golf Club, Ayrshire, Scotland
(11 September)

With the change of decade, a new wind was starting to blow around a Championship which, both literally and figuratively, had gone really nowhere in its first 30 years. John Ball, returning to the event that he graced as a 14 year-old in 1878, became the first Englishman – and the first amateur – to win the Open Championship. He also pre-empted the great Bobby Jones in doing the 'double' of both the Open and The Amateur Championships in the same year. The invasion had not quite started yet though, as Ball was the only Englishman out of 31 to finish.

1	**JOHN BALL, Jr (a)**	82	82	164
	(£Nil – amateur)			
2=	Willie Fernie	85	82	167
	Archie Simpson	85	82	167
4=	Andrew Kirkaldy	81	89	170
	Willie Park, Jr	90	80	170
6	Horace Hutchinson (a)	87	85	172
7=	David Grant	86	87	173
	Hugh Kirkaldy	82	91	173
9	W McEwan	87	87	174
10	David Brown	85	90	175
11=	James Kay	86	91	177
	Johnny Laidlay (a)	89	88	177
13	D Leitch (a)	86	93	179
14	David Anderson, Jr	90	90	180
15=	John Allan	93	88	181
	Ben Campbell	93	88	181
17=	D Anderson (a)	91	91	182
	David Ayton	97	85	182
19	Ben Sayers	90	93	183
20	A Wright	92	92	184
21	G Fernie	92	94	186
22	RB Wilson	91	96	187
23=	DD Robertson (a)	94	95	189
	Bob Mearns	96	93	189
25	Robert Adam (a)	91	99	190
26	James Mair (a)	98	96	194
27=	James Cunningham	104	95	199
	Charles Whigham (a)	93	106	199
29	James McKay	104	96	200
30	DH Gillan (a)	100	104	204

THE OPEN 1891

Royal & Ancient Golf Club, St Andrews, Fife, Scotland
(6 October)

Hugh was the only Kirkaldy brother to pick up the title although John, and particularly Andrew, as we have already seen, featured prominently. When Andrew became pro at the R&A in 1910 he was in direct succession, not just to Tom Morris, Sr, but before him, to the legendary Allan Robertson. The three held sway at St Andrews in a dynasty unbroken for over 80 years.

1	**HUGH KIRKALDY**	83	83	166
	(£10)			
2=	Willie Fernie	84	84	168
	Andrew Kirkaldy	84	84	168
4	R Mure Fergusson (a)	86	84	170
5	WD More	84	87	171
6	Willie Park, Jr	88	85	173
7	David Brown	88	86	174
8	Willie Auchterlonie	85	90	175
9=	Ben Sayers	91	85	176
	Tom Vardon	89	87	176
11=	John Ball, Jr (a)	94	83	177
	Archie Simpson	86	91	177
13	Sandy Herd	87	91	178
14=	David Grant	84	95	179
	James Kay	93	86	179
	John Kirkaldy	90	89	179
	Bob Mearns	88	91	179
18=	Laurie Auchterlonie	87	93	180
	Charles Hutchings (a)	89	91	180
	Johnny Laidlay (a)	90	90	180
	David Simpson	91	89	180
22=	David Anderson, Jr	90	91	181
	David Ayton	94	87	181
	Ernley RH Blackwell (a)	90	91	181
	Willie Campbell	94	87	181
	Horace Hutchinson (a)	89	92	181
	George Mason	94	87	181
28=	HSC Everard (a)	89	93	182
	William Greig (a)	95	87	182
	RH Johnston (a)	95	87	182
	Freddie Tait (a)	94	88	182

THE OPEN 1892

Hon Co of Edinburgh Golfers, Muirfield, East Lothian, Scotland
(22–23 September)

The first championship to be spread over two days and 72 holes resulted in the second win for an amateur (and again an Englishman) in three years. For the only time in the history of Major Championships, amateurs finished first and second. The Honourable Company of Edinburgh Golfers were hosts at Muirfield, where the championship was held for the first time. Many critics thought that the course was not a sufficient challenge for the Championship and alterations were made for future Opens there. Entry fees, to deter the mere hopefuls, were introduced.

1	**HAROLD HILTON** (a)	78	81	72	74	305
	(£Nil – amateur)					
2=	John Ball, Jr (a)	75	80	74	79	308
	Sandy Herd	77	78	77	76	308
	Hugh Kirkaldy	77	83	73	75	308
5=	James Kay	82	78	74	78	312
	Ben Sayers	80	76	81	75	312
7	Willie Park, Jr	78	77	80	80	315
8	Willie Fernie	79	83	76	78	316
9	Archie Simpson	81	81	76	79	317
10	Horace Hutchinson (a)	74	78	86	80	318
11	Jack White	82	78	78	81	319
12	Tom Vardon	83	75	80	82	320
13=	Edward BH Blackwell (a)	81	82	82	76	321
	Andrew Kirkaldy	84	82	80	75	321
15	S Mure Fergusson (a)	78	82	80	82	322
16=	David Anderson, Jr	76	82	79	87	324
	RT Boothby (a)	81	81	80	82	324
	Ben Campbell	86	83	79	76	324
19=	FA Fairlie (a)	83	87	79	76	325
	William McEwan	79	83	84	79	325
21=	WD More	87	75	80	84	326
	GG Smith (a)	84	82	79	81	326
	Freddie Tait (a)	81	83	84	78	326
24	David Brown	77	82	84	85	328
25=	George Douglas	81	83	86	79	329
	Douglas McEwan	84	84	82	79	329
27	Ernley RH Blackwell (a)	79	81	84	86	330
28=	Leslie Balfour (a)	83	87	80	81	331
	Jack Simpson	84	78	82	87	331
30	Charlie Crawford	79	85	85	84	333

Round Leader(s)
R1   Hutchinson; 74
R2   Hutchinson; 152
R3   Ball; 229

Lowest Scores
R2   More, T Vardon; 75
R3   Hilton 72
R4   Hilton 74

THE OPEN 1893

Prestwick Golf Club, Ayrshire, Scotland
(31 August–1 September)

'Old' Tom Morris – winner of four of the first eight Opens, and playing in the Championship for the 33rd consecutive time, told *The Field* magazine that conditions on the first day were the worst he had ever experienced. The magazine's correspondent was more flowery: '...it rained in the most pitiless fashion from morn to eve....'. Willie Auchterlonie's brother, Laurie, made it a family double when he picked up the US Open in 1902. Willie's winning purse was £1.10.0 more than the *total* prize money two years earlier. With JH Taylor leading after the first round, and Harry Vardon also finishing in the Top 30, things were starting to happen to the Open.

1	**WILLIE AUCHTERLONIE**	78	81	81	82	322
	(£30)				
2	Johnny Laidlay (a)	80	83	80	81	324
3	Sandy Herd	82	81	78	84	325
4=	Andrew Kirkaldy	85	82	82	77	326
	Hugh Kirkaldy	83	79	82	82	326
6=	James Kay	81	81	80	85	327
	Bob Simpson	81	81	80	85	327
8=	John Ball, Jr (a)	83	79	84	86	332
	Harold Hilton (a)	88	81	82	81	332
10=	JH Taylor	75	89	86	83	333
	Jack White	81	86	80	86	333
12	Ben Sayers	87	88	84	76	335
13	Charles Hutchings (a)	81	92	80	84	337
14	Archie Simpson	84	86	84	85	339
15=	S Mure Fergusson (a)	83	85	85	87	340
	John Hunter	87	85	83	85	340
17=	David Grant	86	86	85	84	341
	Joe Lloyd	85	91	84	81	341
19=	LS Anderson (a)	89	83	86	84	342
	PC Anderson (a)	93	84	83	82	342
	Willie Park, Jr	82	89	86	85	342
22	David Anderson, Jr	86	93	83	81	343
23=	John Allan	81	88	83	92	344
	T Carmichael (a)	90	87	82	85	344
	Willie Fernie	86	92	85	81	344
	Bob Mearns	86	84	86	88	344
	Harry Vardon	84	90	81	89	344
28=	FA Fairlie (a)	82	90	88	85	345
	William McEwan	88	84	90	83	345
	Tom Vardon	85	86	82	92	345

Round Leader(s)
R1 JH Taylor; 75
R2 Auchterlonie; 159
R3 Auchterlonie; 240

Lowest Scores
R2 Ball, H Kirkaldy; 79
R3 Herd, 78
R4 Sayers; 76

THE OPEN 1894

St George's Golf Club, Sandwich, Kent, England
(11–12 June)

The English influence in the Open Championship really started to kick in in 1894. The event left Scotland for the first time in an expanded rotation which would also take in Royal Liverpool at Hoylake in 1897. This was the first win for one of the 'Great Triumvirate' of JH Taylor, Harry Vardon and James Braid, who between 1894 and 1914 collected 16 Open Championships – with Vardon also raiding the US Open successfully in 1900. Joe Lloyd, in 17th place, was to achieve greater glory after becoming a part-time emigré, by winning the 1897 US Open.

1	**JH TAYLOR**	84	80	81	81	326
	(£30)				
2	Douglas Rolland	86	79	84	82	331
3	Andrew Kirkaldy	86	79	83	84	332
4	AH Toogood	84	85	82	82	333
5=	Willie Fernie	84	84	86	80	334
	Ben Sayers	85	81	84	84	334
	Harry Vardon	86	86	82	80	334
8	Sandy Herd	83	85	82	88	338
9	Freddie Tait (a)	90	83	83	84	340
10=	AD Blyth (a)	91	84	84	82	341
	James Braid	91	84	82	84	341
12	Willie Park, Jr	88	86	82	87	343
13=	John Ball, Jr (a)	84	89	87	84	344
	David Brown	93	83	81	87	344
	Hugh Kirkaldy	90	85	80	89	344
	Archie Simpson	90	86	86	82	344
17	Joe Lloyd	95	81	86	83	345
18	S Mure Fergusson (a)	87	88	84	87	346
19	Tom Vardon	87	88	82	91	348
20=	CE Dick (a)	85	89	89	90	353
	David Grant	91	84	87	91	353
	David Herd	92	93	84	84	353
23=	Willie Auchterlonie	96	81	93	85	355
	John Rowe	90	90	84	91	355
25=	Stuart Anderson (a)	90	87	91	88	356
	CE Hambro (a)	96	90	82	88	356
	Charles Hutchings (a)	93	85	88	90	356
28	Charles Gibson	92	94	87	84	357
29	Rowland Jones	89	88	93	88	358
30	A Lumsden	90	93	87	89	359

Round Leader(s)
R1 Herd; 83
R2 Taylor; 164
R3 Taylor; 245

Lowest Scores
R2 A Kirkaldy, Rolland; 79
R3 H Kirkaldy; 80
R4 Fernie, H Vardon; 80

THE (BRITISH) OPEN 1895

Royal & Ancient Golf Club, St Andrews, Fife, Scotland
(12–13 June)

Taylor, three behind Herd going into the last round, shot a 78 – four strokes better than anyone in the field – to overhaul the Scotsman over the last 18 holes. Many Brits had left the country by now to seek their fortunes in America, and professional golfers were soon to find out that, at least to begin with, there were some rich pickings for them among the thriving new clubs...

1	**JH TAYLOR**	86	78	80	78	322
	(£30)					
2	Sandy Herd	82	77	82	85	326
3	Andrew Kirkaldy	81	83	84	84	332
4	George Pulford	84	81	83	86	334
5	Archie Simpson	88	85	78	85	336
6=	David Anderson, Jr	86	83	84	84	337
	David Brown	81	89	83	84	337
	Willie Fernie	86	79	86	86	337
9=	Ben Sayers	84	87	85	82	338
	AH Toogood	85	84	83	86	338
	Harry Vardon	80	85	85	88	338
	Tom Vardon	82	83	84	89	338
13=	Laurie Auchterlonie	84	84	85	87	340
	J Robb	89	88	81	82	340
15=	Hugh Kirkaldy	87	87	83	84	341
	Freddie Tait (a)	87	86	82	86	341
17	Johnny Laidlay (a)	91	83	82	86	342
18=	John Ball, Jr (a)	85	85	88	86	344
	L Waters	86	83	85	90	344
20	David Herd	85	85	84	91	345
21	Albert Tingey, Sr	83	88	87	88	346
	Jack White	88	86	85	87	346
23	James Kinnell	84	83	88	92	347
24	Jack Ross	87	84	89	88	348
25=	James Kay	88	85	92	86	351
	David McEwan	85	90	90	86	351
27=	Willie Aveston	89	86	89	89	353
	Douglas McEwan	95	85	92	81	353
	AM Ross (a)	92	85	88	88	353
	Walter Toogood	87	91	88	87	353

Round Leader(s)
R1   H Vardon; 80
R2   S Herd; 159
R3   S Herd 241

Lowest Scores
R2   S Herd; 77
R3   Simpson; 78
R4   Taylor; 78

US OPEN 1895

Newport Golf Club, Newport, Rhode Island
(4 October)

From one island to another – Rawlins left Isle of Wight, England for Rhode Island; where he became pro at the Newport club. The field was made up of British professionals plus Scottish amateur, AW Smith. Runner-up Dunn, whose father had finished seventh in the second-ever British Open, had won the unofficial US national championship in the previous year, but like his father was never destined to win either Major. For the first three years the Championship was held over 36 holes, then followed the 72-hole example of its British counterpart. Just like with its elder brother, the US Open calendar was all over the place in the early years; but , at least, the prize money was realistic from the start.

1	**HORACE RAWLINS**	45	46	41	41	173
	($150)					
2	Willie Dunn, Jr	43	46	44	42	175
3=	James Foulis	46	43	44	43	176
	AW Smith (a)	47	43	44	42	176
5	Willie Davis	45	49	42	42	178
6	Willie Campbell	41	48	42	48	179
7=	John Harland	45	48	43	47	183
	John Patrick	46	48	46	43	183
9	Samuel Tucker	49	48	45	43	185
10	John Reid	49	51	55	51	206

BRITISH OPEN 1896

Hon Co of Edinburgh Golfers, Muirfield, East Lothian, Scotland
(10–11 June)

Harry Vardon was to eclipse his famous Triumvirate cohorts by winning six Opens (and a US Open) to Taylor's and Braid's five. This, his first, followed a marathon play-off after a tie with Taylor at the toughened-up Muirfield course – now reputedly four strokes more difficult than in 1892. Vardon's and Taylor's total was 11 shots poorer than Hilton's four years earlier. 'Old' Tom Morris competed in his last Open, aged 75.

1	**HARRY VARDON***	83	78	78	77	316
	($30)					
2	JH Taylor	77	78	81	80	316
3=	Willie Fernie	78	79	82	80	319
	Freddie Tait (a)	83	75	84	77	319
5	Sandy Herd	72	84	79	85	320
6	James Braid	83	81	79	80	323
7=	David Brown	80	77	81	86	324
	Ben Sayers	83	76	79	86	324
	Andrew Scott	83	84	77	80	324
10	Tom Vardon	83	82	77	83	325
11	Peter McEwan	83	81	80	84	328
12=	Willie Auchterlonie	80	86	81	82	329
	Archie Simpson	85	79	78	87	329
14=	James Kay	77	88	83	82	330
	Andrew Kirkaldy	84	85	79	82	330
	Willie Park, Jr	79	80	83	88	330
17	AH Toogood	81	85	84	84	334
18=	John Hunter	85	79	83	88	335
	Johnny Laidlay (a)	85	82	82	86	335
	David McEwan	83	89	81	82	335
	Jack Ross	83	87	84	81	335
22	Walter Toogood	87	84	80	85	336
23	Harold Hilton (a)	82	85	85	85	337
24=	David Anderson, Jr	86	89	83	81	339
	D Jackson (a)	85	84	82	88	339
	Walter Kirk	85	87	84	83	339
27	David Herd	85	87	86	82	340
28	Albert Tingey, Sr	84	84	88	86	342
29	JW Taylor	87	83	84	90	344
30	Peter Paxton	84	89	86	86	345

* Harry Vardon (157) beat JH Taylor (161) in the 36-Hole Play-off

Round Leader(s)
R1   S Herd; 72
R2   JH Taylor; 155
R3   S Herd; 235

Lowest Scores
R2   Tait; 75
R3   Scott, T Vardon; 77
R4   Tait, H Vardon; 77

US OPEN 1896

Shinnecock Hills Golf Club, Southampton, New York
(18 July)
4423 yards

The Foulis family emigrated from Scotland to America *en bloc* and featured strongly in early Opens. Jim Foulis, part of the next generation, reached the quarter final of the PGA Championship in 1938 and was 11th in the 1946 Masters. John Shippen and Oscar Bunn (who finished 21st) were the first golfers to suffer racial discrimination in a Major. Indeed, they almost were refused entry to the Championship.

1	**JAMES FOULIS**	78	74	152
	($150)			
2	Horace Rawlins	79	76	155
3	Joe Lloyd	76	81	157
4=	George Douglas	79	79	158
	AW Smith (a)	78	80	158
6=	John Shippen	78	81	159
	HJ Wigham (a)	82	77	159
8	Willie Tucker	78	82	160
9	Robert Wilson	82	80	162
10	Alfred Ricketts	80	83	163
11	WH Way	83	81	164
12	Willie Dunn, Jr	78	87	165
13	Willie Davis	83	84	167
14	Willie Campbell	85	85	170
15	WT Hoare	90	81	171
16=	JN Mackrell	89	83	172
	Alex Patrick	86	86	172
	John Reid	88	84	172
19=	Tom Gourlay	82	91	173
	John Patrick	88	85	173
21	Oscar Bunn	89	85	174
22=	John l'Anson	88	92	180
	George Strath	91	89	180
24	John Harrison	92	91	183
25	WW Campbell	91	93	184
26	Willie Norton	87	98	185
27	R Anderson	92	95	187
28	T Warrender	97	93	190

BRITISH OPEN 1897

Royal Liverpool Golf Club, Hoylake, Cheshire, England
(19–20 May)
6150 yards

Hoylake's debut. Hilton's second victory made him the only amateur multiple winner of the Open until the advent of Bobby Jones in the 1920s. Joe Lloyd became the first golfer to play both British and US Opens in the same year.

1	**HAROLD HILTON** (a)	80	75	84	75	314
	(£Nil – amateur)					
2	James Braid	80	74	82	79	315
3=	George Pulford	80	79	79	79	317
	Freddie Tait (a)	79	79	80	79	317
5	Sandy Herd	78	81	79	80	318
6	Harry Vardon	84	80	80	76	320
7=	David Brown	79	82	80	83	324
	Archie Simpson	83	81	81	79	324
	Tom Vardon	81	81	79	83	324
10=	Andrew Kirkaldy	83	83	82	82	330
	JH Taylor	82	80	82	86	330
12=	Ben Sayers	84	78	85	84	331
	S Mure Fergusson (a)	87	83	79	82	331
14=	Peter McEwan	86	79	85	82	332
	TG Renouf	86	79	83	84	332
16	Andrew Scott	83	83	84	83	333
17	John Ball, Jr (a)	78	81	88	87	334
18=	Willie Auchterlonie	84	85	85	81	335
	Jack Graham, (a)	85	80	87	83	335
20=	James Kinnell	82	83	78	93	336
	Joe Lloyd	86	84	82	84	336
22=	Willie Fernie	81	82	93	81	337
	Willie Park, Jr	91	81	83	82	337
	AH Toogood	88	82	84	83	337
25	James Kay	86	81	86	85	338
26	Walter Toogood	87	89	80	83	339
27	James Sherlock	85	86	84	85	340
28	John Rowe	84	86	86	86	342
29	Johnny Laidlay (a)	82	86	86	89	343
30=	John Cuthbert	89	83	87	85	344
	Charles Gibson	88	90	80	86	344
	C Ralph Smith	88	82	94	80	344
	JW Taylor	87	84	85	88	344
	Albert Tingey, Sr	86	86	87	85	344

Round Leader(s)
R1   Ball, Herd; 78
R2   Braid; 154
R3   Braid; 236

Lowest Scores
R2   Braid; 74
R3   Kinnell; 78
R4   Hilton; 75

US OPEN 1897

Chicago Golf Club, Wheaton, Illinois
(17 September)
6682 yards

Lloyd's decision to move to the US in 1897 paid immediate dividends for this much-travelled golfer for his time: he was a summer pro in the US, and spent his winters at the Pau club in South-West France. He collected the US title five months after finishing 20th in the British Open.

1	**JOE LLOYD**	83	79	162
	($150)			
2	Willie Anderson	79	84	163
3=	Willie Dunn, Jr	87	81	168
	James Foulis	80	88	168
5	WT Hoare	82	87	169
6=	Bernard Nicholls	87	85	172
	Alfred Ricketts	91	81	172
8=	David Foulis	86	87	173
	Horace Rawlins	91	82	173
	HJ Wigham (a)	87	86	173
11=	Charles Macdonald (a)	85	89	174
	William Marshall	87	87	174
	Robert Wilson	83	91	174
14	Harry Turpie	85	90	175
15=	Willie Davis	88	89	177
	Robert Foulis	88	89	177
	Willie Tucker	90	87	177
	JA Tyng (a)	86	91	177
19	Findlay Douglas (a)	89	91	180
20	WG Stewart (a)	91	90	181
21=	R Leslie	90	92	182
	RG McAndrews	90	92	182
	George Pearson	93	89	182
24	John Harrison	97	87	184
25=	Samuel Tucker	87	98	185
	WH Way	89	96	185
27	R White	89	97	186
28	Devereux Emmet (a)	98	90	188
29	WB Smith (a)	98	91	189
30	AC Tolifson	91	100	191

BRITISH OPEN 1898

Prestwick Golf Club, Ayrshire, Scotland
(8–9 June)
5732 yds

New restrictions on players' performances were introduced. Competitors who were 20 or more strokes behind the leader at the halfway stage were excluded from the final two rounds. The 'cut' was born. One victim was the last winner at Prestwick, Willie Auchterlonie.

1	**HARRY VARDON**	79	75	77	76	307
	(£30)					
2	Willie Park, Jr	76	75	78	79	308
3	Harold Hilton (a)	76	81	77	75	309
4	JH Taylor	78	78	77	79	312
5	Freddie Tait (a)	81	77	75	82	315
6	David Kinnell	80	77	79	80	316
7	Willie Fernie	79	85	77	77	318
8	John Hunter	82	79	81	77	319
9	TG Renouf	77	79	81	83	320
10=	James Braid	80	82	84	75	321
	Philip Wynn	83	79	81	78	321
12	James Kay	81	81	77	83	322
13=	George Pulford	83	81	78	81	323
	Jack White	82	81	77	83	323
15=	James Kinnell	77	81	78	88	324
	Archie Simpson	83	80	82	79	324
17=	Sandy Herd	80	79	84	82	325
	Peter McEwan	83	83	77	82	325
19=	Ben Sayers	85	78	79	85	327
	Walter Toogood	82	84	83	78	327
21=	JR Gairdner (a)	84	77	82	85	328
	David Herd	79	81	83	85	328
	James Hutchinson	83	79	84	82	328
	Andrew Kirkaldy	82	84	85	77	328
	Peter Paxton	81	82	86	79	328
	Tom Williamson	86	84	77	81	328
27=	C Ralph Smith	84	78	85	82	329
	JW Taylor	83	84	80	82	329
29=	Fred Butel	81	84	86	81	332
	Andrew Scott	83	84	78	87	332
	Bob Simpson	84	81	82	85	332

Round Leader(s)
R1   Hilton, Park; 76
R2   Park; 151
R3   Park; 229

Lowest Scores
R2   Park, Vardon; 75
R3   Tait; 75
R4   Braid, Hilton; 75

US OPEN 1898

Myopia Hunt Club, South Hamilton, Massachusetts
(17–18 July)
6236 yards

The first 72-hole US Open, which meant circumnavigating Myopia's nine holes eight times. While elder brother Sandy was to stay in Scotland and be successful in the British Open over many years, Fred Herd arrived in the US in 1898, and promptly picked the Open Championship. However, he never came close again.

1	**FRED HERD**	84	85	75	84	328
	($150)					
2	Alex Smith	78	86	86	85	335
3	Willie Anderson	81	82	87	86	336
4	Joe Lloyd	87	80	86	86	339
5	Willie Smith	82	91	85	82	340
6	WV Hoare	84	84	87	87	342
7	Willie Dunn, Jr	85	87	87	84	343
8=	John Jones	83	84	90	90	347
	HC Leeds (a)	81	84	93	89	347
	RG McAndrews	85	90	86	86	347
	Bernard Nicholls	86	87	88	86	347
12	Harry Turpie	85	87	86	91	349
13	Alex Findlay	89	88	84	89	350
14=	John Lister	92	88	90	85	355
	Willie Tucker	90	89	87	89	355
16	JF Curtis (a)	87	88	88	93	356
17	John Harland	84	93	93	87	357
18	Willie Davis	91	88	95	85	359
19=	Horace Rawlins	91	90	92	88	361
	JA Tyng (a)	92	91	88	90	361
21=	QA Shaw (a)	88	85	93	98	364
	Jack Youds	92	90	92	90	364
23=	JH Mercer	85	95	93	93	366
	Gilbert Nicholls	91	92	91	92	366
25	John Dunn	91	88	91	97	367
26	Willie Campbell	93	91	97	101	382
27	HR Sweeny (a)	92	97	96	99	384
28	W Rutherford (a)	100	99	98	91	388
29	WE Stoddart	103	95	97	96	391

Round Leader(s)
R1   A Smith; 78
R2   Anderson; 163
R3   Herd; 244

Lowest Scores
R2   Lloyd; 80
R3   Herd; 75
R4   W Smith; 82

BRITISH OPEN 1899

St George's Golf Club, Sandwich, Kent, England
(7–8 June)

6012 yards

Although 101 entered, so many withdrew after the first round, only 28 finished. Vardon's third win in four years was based on his early rounds (152 – easily the best opening 18 holes since the Open went to a 72-hole format). This was the first occasion where the winner led from start to finish over four rounds. It was also Freddie Tait's last Open. He was killed the following year leading a unit of the Black Watch into battle during the Boer War.

1	**HARRY VARDON** (£30)	76	76	81	77	310
2	Jack White	79	79	82	75	315
3	Andrew Kirkaldy	81	79	82	77	319
4	JH Taylor	77	76	83	84	320
5=	James Braid	78	78	85	81	322
	Willie Fernie	79	83	82	78	322
7=	James Kinnell	76	84	80	84	324
	Freddie Tait (a)	81	82	79	82	324
9=	Albert Tingey, Sr	81	81	79	85	326
	Tom Williamson	76	84	80	86	326
11	Ben Sayers	81	79	82	86	328
12=	Harold Hilton (a)	86	80	80	83	329
	TG Renouf	79	82	84	84	329
14	Willie Park, Jr	77	79	85	89	330
15	Willie Aveston	77	86	82	86	331
16=	Sandy Herd	82	81	80	89	332
	Peter Rainford	79	83	83	87	332
	Ted Ray	84	80	84	84	332
	Archie Simpson	84	84	81	83	332
20	Walter Toogood	82	86	81	84	333
21	CE Hambro (a)	78	86	88	82	334
22	T Hutchinson	82	87	82	85	336
23	AH Toogood	83	85	85	84	337
24	William McEwan	84	86	83	85	338
25=	John Ball, Jr (a)	81	82	90	86	339
	Andrew Scott	86	85	87	81	339
	JW Taylor	82	85	86	86	339
28	David Herd	80	88	83	89	340

Round Leader(s)
R1   Vardon, Williamson; 76
R2   Vardon; 152
R3   Vardon; 233

Lowest Scores
R2   Taylor, Vardon; 76
R3   Tait, Tingey; 79
R4   White; 75

US OPEN 1899

Baltimore Country Club, Baltimore, Maryland
(14–15 September)

Willie Smith was one of five brothers from Carnoustie – two of whom won the US Open. Alex was to win in 1906 and 1910. A third brother, Macdonald, had a few close misses in both US and British Opens and was one of the outstanding players in an era to be dominated by Walter Hagen and Bobby Jones. The winning margin is still the biggest in the US Open and only falls behind Morris Sr (13 in 1862 British Open), Morris Jr (12 in 1870) and Tiger Woods (12 in 1997 Masters) in any Major. Willie went on to become pro at Mexico City where he was killed during the Revolution in 1915.

1	**WILLIE SMITH** ($150)	77	82	79	77	315
2=	Val Fitzjohn	85	80	79	82	326
	George Low	82	79	89	76	326
	WH Way	80	85	80	81	326
5	Willie Anderson	77	81	85	84	327
6	Jack Park	88	80	75	85	328
7	Alex Smith	82	81	82	85	330
8	Henry Gullane	81	86	80	84	331
9=	Laurie Auchterlonie	86	87	82	78	333
	Peter Walker	84	86	77	86	333
11	AH Findlay	88	86	79	81	334
12	Alex Campbell	83	80	79	94	336
13=	HM Harriman (a)	87	88	85	79	339
	Alex Patrick	82	83	84	90	339
	Horace Rawlins	81	85	86	87	339
16	Alfred Ricketts	87	85	88	80	340
17	Bernard Nicholls	86	88	85	84	343
18=	David Foulis	83	86	91	85	345
	Harry Turpie	91	88	83	83	345
20=	James Foulis	94	84	88	80	346
	Gilbert Nicholls	90	83	86	87	346
22	Dan Leitch	87	85	85	90	347
23	Ernest Way	85	87	87	89	348
24	W Thompson	82	90	87	90	349
25=	Fred Herd	85	86	93	86	350
	John Shippen	86	88	88	88	350
27=	Robert Braid	85	90	86	90	351
	RS Patrick	85	92	88	86	351
	Willie Tucker	89	91	87	84	351
30=	William Donovan	88	89	91	96	354
	David Hunter	89	86	89	90	354

Round Leader(s)
R1   Anderson, W Smith; 77
R2   Anderson; 158
R3   W Smith; 238

Lowest Scores
R2   Low; 79
R3   Park; 75
R4   Low; 76

BRITISH OPEN 1900

Royal & Ancient Golf Club, St Andrews, Fife, Scotland
(6–7 June)
6323 yds

Taylor's third win was comprehensive and stopped Vardon's amazing run – at least temporarily. 'JH' led 'wire-to-wire' as did Vardon in the previous year, but Taylor also produced the lowest score in every round – a feat never repeated in any Major Championship.

1	**JH TAYLOR**	79	77	78	75	309
	(£50)					
2	Harry Vardon	79	81	80	77	317
3	James Braid	82	81	80	79	322
4	Jack White	80	81	82	80	323
5	Willie Auchterlonie	81	85	80	80	326
6	Willie Park, Jr	80	83	81	84	328
7=	Robert Maxwell (a)	81	81	86	81	329
	Archie Simpson	82	85	83	79	329
9	Ben Sayers	81	83	85	81	330
10=	Sandy Herd	81	85	81	84	331
	Andrew Kirkaldy	87	83	82	79	331
	Tom Vardon	81	85	84	81	331
13	Ted Ray	88	80	85	81	334
14=	David Anderson, Jr	81	87	85	84	337
	Tom Simpson	84	86	83	84	337
16=	William Greig (a)	93	84	80	81	338
	Harold Hilton (a)	83	87	87	81	338
18	JW Taylor	91	81	84	83	339
19=	John Kirkaldy	86	85	87	82	340
	Peter Paxton	87	87	79	87	340
21	Peter McEwan	85	80	89	87	341
22=	PJ Gaudin	85	88	81	88	342
	James Kay	84	81	87	90	342
	FM Mackenzie (a)	88	82	89	83	342
	Andrew Scott	84	84	84	90	342
26=	George Coburn	83	88	83	89	343
	WH Fowler (a)	86	85	88	84	343
	Johnny Laidlay (a)	85	87	85	86	343
29	JM Williamson	87	82	88	89	346
30=	Ted Blackwell (a)	88	86	86	89	349
	C Ralph Smith	83	87	88	91	349

Round Leader(s)
R1 Taylor, H Vardon; 79
R2 Taylor; 156
R3 Taylor; 234

Lowest Scores
R2 Taylor; 77
R3 Taylor; 78
R4 Taylor; 75

US OPEN 1900

Chicago Golf Club, Wheaton, Illinois
(4–5 October)
6032 yards

The roles were reversed a few months later when Vardon, on an exhibition tour of the States, won in Chicago with Taylor second. Vardon became the first player to win two different Majors. A look at the respective Top 20s this year shows the Herd and Auchterlonie brothers represented on both sides of the Atlantic.

1	**HARRY VARDON**	79	78	76	80	313
	($200)					
2	JH Taylor	76	82	79	78	315
3	David Bell	78	83	83	78	322
4=	Laurie Auchterlonie	84	82	80	81	327
	Willie Smith	82	83	79	83	327
6	George Low	84	80	85	82	331
7	Tom Hutchinson	81	87	81	84	333
8	Harry Turpie	84	87	79	84	334
9	Stewart Gardner	85	78	84	89	336
10	Val Fitzjohn	84	83	89	82	338
11=	Willie Anderson	83	88	79	89	339
	Alex Campbell	86	77	93	83	339
13	Alex Smith	90	84	82	84	340
14=	James Foulis	86	88	87	82	343
	Robert Simpson	84	84	88	87	343
16=	Fred Herd	85	89	84	86	344
	Arthur Smith	89	85	85	85	344
	WH Way	88	85	84	87	344
19=	Willie Norton	87	87	84	87	345
	Harry Rawlins	86	84	90	85	345
21	Ernest Way	89	92	81	84	346
22	JB Schlotman	85	94	83	88	350
23=	RG McAndrews	87	93	87	84	351
	Joe Mitchell	88	96	82	85	351
25=	Henry Gullane	89	89	92	82	352
	AC Tolifson	93	87	88	84	352
27=	WV Hoare	90	87	91	85	353
	John Shippen	94	87	89	83	353
29	Robert Foulis	85	89	90	90	354
30	Charles Macdonald (a)	86	90	90	89	355

Round Leader(s)
R1 Taylor; 76
R2 Vardon; 157
R3 Vardon; 233

Lowest Scores
R2 Campbell; 77
R3 Vardon; 76
R4 Bell, Taylor; 78

BRITISH OPEN 1901

Hon Co of Edinburgh Golfers, Muirfield, East Lothian, Scotland
(5–6 June)
5810 yds

Braid established enough of a lead to withstand attacks from Vardon and Taylor over the last round. Just how good this threesome were can be understood from the scoring, all being at least seven shots clear of the rest of field. Braid was due the title after several good finishes in previous years, including second on the same course in 1897. His great years were to come towards the end of the decade though, when he truly (in terms of Open victories) became part of the Triumvirate.

1	**JAMES BRAID** (£50)	79	76	74	80	309
2	Harry Vardon	77	78	79	78	312
3	JH Taylor	79	83	74	77	313
4	Harold Hilton (a)	89	80	75	76	320
5	Sandy Herd	87	81	81	76	325
6	Jack White	82	82	80	82	326
7=	James Kinnell	79	85	86	78	328
	Johnny Laidlay (a)	84	82	82	80	328
9=	PJ Gaudin	86	81	86	76	329
	Jack Graham (a)	82	83	81	83	329
11	Rowland Jones	85	82	81	83	331
12=	Ted Ray	87	84	74	87	332
	TG Renouf	83	86	81	82	332
	Tom Yeoman	85	83	82	82	332
15=	Fred Collins	89	80	81	84	334
	S Mure Fergusson (a)	84	86	82	82	334
	JH Oke	91	83	80	80	334
18=	Andrew Kirkaldy	82	87	86	81	336
	Alf Lewis	85	82	83	86	336
	Willie Park, Jr	78	87	81	90	336
	Andrew Scott	85	80	81	90	336
22=	Charles Neaves	84	87	81	85	337
	L Waters	86	87	86	78	337
24	C Dalziel (a)	82	84	89	83	338
25=	David Herd	90	80	82	87	339
	James Hutchison	84	83	91	81	339
	Jack Ross	84	85	86	84	339
28	Walter Toogood	87	86	85	82	340
29=	Willie Auchterlonie	86	82	88	86	342
	David McEwan	86	84	86	86	342

Round Leader(s)
R1   Vardon; 77
R2   Braid, Vardon; 155
R3   Braid; 229

Lowest Scores
R2   Braid; 76
R3   Braid, Ray, Taylor; 74
R4   Herd, Hilton, Gaudin; 76

US OPEN 1901

Myopia Hunt Club, South Hamilton, Massachusetts
(14–16 June)
6130 yards

No such pond-hopping this year as the Opens virtually clashed, leaving anyone with the ambition to participate in both thwarted by the week-long sea passage. Willie Anderson from North Berwick, Scotland, won the first of his four wins in five years, after beating Alex Smith in the Open's first play-off, and his brother Willie by two. After emigrating in 1897, David Brown, the 1886 British Open winner, participated in his first US Open.

1	**WILLIE ANDERSON*** ($200)	84	83	83	81	331
2	Alex Smith	82	82	87	80	331
3	Willie Smith	84	86	82	81	333
4	Stewart Gardner	86	82	81	85	334
5=	Laurie Auchterlonie	81	85	86	83	335
	Bernard Nicholls	84	85	83	83	335
7	David Brown	86	83	83	84	336
8	Alex Campbell	84	91	82	82	339
9=	George Low	82	89	85	85	341
	Jack Park	87	84	85	85	341
11	James Foulis	88	85	85	89	347
12=	Val Fitzjohn	86	86	89	87	348
	John Jones	87	84	87	80	348
14=	Gilbert Nicholls	87	87	88	87	349
	Robert Simpson	88	87	87	87	349
16	Isaac Mackie	87	88	85	90	350
17=	AH Fenn	87	90	87	87	351
	AG Lockwood (a)	82	89	89	91	351
	Horace Rawlins	90	84	88	89	351
20	Joe Lloyd	90	87	86	89	352
21	Donald Ross	94	86	91	84	355
22=	Walter Clark	88	90	92	87	357
	Alex Taylor	94	84	92	87	357
	Harry Turpie	92	87	88	90	357
25=	David Hunter	91	92	89	87	359
	RS Patrick	90	91	87	91	359
27	Willie Davis	88	91	92	89	360
28=	John Dingwall	89	96	89	87	361
	Ed Fitzjohn	90	86	92	93	361
	John Harland	92	92	93	84	361
	Willie Hunter	88	96	91	86	361
	LC Servas	94	83	91	93	361

* Willie Anderson (85) beat Alex Smith (86) in the 18-Hole Play-off.

Round Leader(s)
R1   Auchterlonie; 81
R2   A Smith; 164
R3   Gardner; 249

Lowest Scores
R2   Gardner, A Smith; 82
R3   Gardner; 81
R4   Jones, A Smith; 80

BRITISH OPEN 1902

Royal Liverpool Golf Club, Hoylake, Cheshire, England
(4–5 June)
6335 yards

Herd won his only Open in a long and distinguished career. He was the first winner to use a rubber-cored Haskell ball and beat Vardon and Braid, who were still using the 'gutty', by one stroke. Braid pulled back seven shots over the last round – not quite enough. Vardon's first round 72 equalled Herd's own record of 1896 and his halfway score of 149 was the first below 150.

1	**SANDY HERD**	77	76	73	81	307
	(£50)					
2=	James Braid	78	76	80	74	308
	Harry Vardon	72	77	80	79	308
4	Robert Maxwell (a)	79	77	79	74	309
5	Tom Vardon	80	76	78	79	313
6=	Harold Hilton (a)	79	76	81	78	314
	James Kinnell	78	80	79	77	314
	JH Taylor	81	76	77	80	314
9	Ted Ray	79	74	85	80	318
10=	Andrew Kirkaldy	77	78	83	82	320
	Arnaud Massy	77	81	78	84	320
12=	Willie Fernie	76	82	84	79	321
	Rowland Jones	79	78	85	79	321
14	SH Fry (a)	78	79	80	85	322
15=	John Ball, Jr (a)	79	79	84	81	323
	John Rowe	79	78	85	81	323
17	James Sherlock	79	84	80	81	324
18	Jack White	82	75	82	86	325
19	Ben Sayers	84	80	80	82	326
20=	TG Renouf	84	82	77	84	327
	Walter Toogood	83	83	80	81	327
22	George Pulford	81	81	85	81	328
23=	F Jackson	80	81	83	85	329
	Willie Park, Jr	79	82	82	86	329
25=	William McEwan	83	84	81	82	330
	Tom Yeoman	85	83	79	83	330
27	C Ralph Smith	85	79	85	82	331
28=	David Herd	82	81	84	85	332
	Peter Rainford	78	79	88	87	332
30=	Archie Simpson	88	79	85	81	333
	Tom Williamson	78	80	90	85	333

Round Leader(s)
R1   H Vardon; 72
R2   H Vardon; 149
R3   Herd; 226

Lowest Scores
R2   Ray; 74
R3   Herd; 73
R4   Braid, Maxwell; 74

US OPEN 1902

Garden City Golf Club, Garden City, New York
(10–11 October)
6170 yards

In another brotherly double, Laurie emulated Willie Auchterlonie's British Open win at Prestwick in 1893, scoring sub-80 in every round for the first time in these Championships. (As visitors to St Andrews will vouch, the family club-making and repair shop started by Willie, who succeeded Andrew Kirkaldy as R&A pro in 1935, still snuggles in the corner of the old grey building which runs parallel to 'Tom Morris', the 18th on the Old Course.) Following the British Open, the Haskell ball was used even more widely. The result was a greater improvement in all-round scoring over previous Championships.

1	**LAURIE AUCHTERLONIE**	78	78	74	77	307
	($200)					
2=	Stewart Gardner	82	76	77	78	313
	Walter Travis (a)	82	82	75	74	313
4	Willie Smith	82	79	80	75	316
5=	Willie Anderson	79	82	76	81	318
	John Shippen	83	81	75	79	318
7	Charles Thom	80	82	80	77	319
8	Harry Turpie	79	85	78	78	320
9	Donald Ross	80	83	78	81	322
10	Alex Ross	83	77	84	79	323
11	Willie Norton	83	82	79	81	325
12=	David Brown	80	88	82	76	326
	George Low	83	84	78	81	326
14=	Jack Campbell	77	87	79	85	328
	Jack Hobens	85	82	80	81	328
16=	AS Griffiths	79	86	82	83	330
	Horace Rawlins	89	83	79	79	330
18=	Gilbert Nicholls	88	86	73	84	331
	Alex Smith	79	86	80	86	331
20=	Alex Campbell	88	82	83	79	332
	James Foulis	81	88	82	81	332
	John Harland	82	82	83	85	332
	Willie Hunter	82	82	81	87	332
24	Fred Herd	82	79	83	89	333
25	Jack Park	79	89	85	81	334
26=	George Braid	85	81	84	85	335
	James Campbell	88	84	82	81	335
28	Bernard Nicholls	89	84	84	79	336
29	John Mackie	88	82	84	84	338
30=	Alex Findlay	85	81	87	86	339
	David Hunter	83	81	91	84	339
	RS Patrick	85	87	84	83	339

Round Leader(s)
R1   Jack Campbell; 77
R2   Auchterlonie; 156
R3   Auchterlonie; 230

Lowest Scores
R2   Gardner; 76
R3   G Nicholls; 73
R4   Travis; 74

BRITISH OPEN 1903

Prestwick Golf Club, Ayrshire, Scotland
(9–10 June)

5948 yards

Vardon joined the Morrises and Willie Park Sr on four Open wins as he coasted home – courtesy of a seven-stroke lead after three rounds. His third round 72 was a record, as were his 54- and 72-hole totals. Brother Tom finished runner-up, his highest-ever position.

1	**HARRY VARDON**	73	77	72	78	300
	(£50)					
2	Tom Vardon	76	81	75	74	306
3	Jack White	77	78	74	79	308
4	Sandy Herd	73	83	76	77	309
5	James Braid	77	79	79	75	310
6=	Andrew Scott	77	77	83	77	314
	Robert Thomson	83	78	77	76	314
8	William Leaver	79	79	77	80	315
9=	George Cawsey	80	78	76	82	316
	JH Taylor	80	82	78	76	316
11=	Andrew Kirkaldy	82	79	78	78	317
	Tom Williamson	76	80	79	82	317
13=	Willie Hunter, Sr	81	74	79	84	318
	Robert Maxwell (a)	82	84	76	76	318
15=	Ernest Gray	77	83	79	80	319
	James Kinnell	78	86	76	79	319
	Willie Park, Jr	78	86	80	75	319
18=	David Kinnell	82	78	80	80	320
	George Pulford	79	86	79	76	320
	AH Toogood	86	77	80	77	320
21=	John Hunter	77	79	84	81	321
	Ben Sayers	79	84	80	78	321
23	Ted Ray	90	78	80	75	323
24=	Willie Fernie	78	81	76	89	324
	James Hepburn	78	82	87	77	324
	Harold Hilton (a)	81	79	83	81	324
	Rowland Jones	82	82	81	79	324
	John Milne	81	86	79	78	324
29=	George Coburn	81	82	75	87	325
	JH Oke	80	81	81	83	325
	Archie Simpson	79	85	80	81	325

Round Leader(s)
R1 Herd, H Vardon; 73
R2 H Vardon; 150
R3 H Vardon; 222

Lowest Scores
R2 W Hunter; 74
R3 H Vardon; 72
R4 T Vardon; 74

US OPEN 1903

Baltusrol Golf Club, Springfield, New Jersey
(8–9 July)

6003 yards

The Open's first visit to (pre-Tillinghast) Baltusrol, Anderson's second win in three years, and the first of three back-to-back wins, may have had something to do with his settling at the Apawamis Club. Prior to 1903 he had been changing clubs annually. He was caught by 1886 British Open Champion, David Brown, in the final round, conceding a six-stroke lead (not helped by an 8 at the 9th), before steeling himself to win the play-off by two.

1	**WILLIE ANDERSON***	73	76	76	82	307
	($200)					
2	David Brown	79	77	75	76	307
3	Stewart Gardner	77	77	82	79	315
4	Alex Smith	77	77	81	81	316
5	Donald Ross	79	79	78	82	318
6	Jack Campbell	76	83	83	77	319
7	Laurie Auchterlonie	75	79	84	83	321
8	Findlay Douglas (a)	77	79	82	84	322
9=	Jack Hobens	76	81	82	84	323
	Alex Ross	83	82	78	80	323
	Willie Smith	80	81	83	79	323
12	Horace Rawlins	82	77	78	87	324
13=	Isaac Mackie	83	80	78	84	325
	FO Reinhart (a)	81	75	89	80	325
15=	Alex Campbell	79	84	80	83	326
	Gilbert Nicholls	86	82	78	80	326
	Walter Travis (a)	83	80	81	82	326
	WH Way	84	79	82	81	326
19	Bernard Nicholls	85	78	82	83	328
20=	Willie Norton	78	81	83	87	329
	David Ogilvie	81	86	81	81	329
22	George Cummings	83	86	77	84	330
23	Harry Turpie	86	82	81	82	331
24=	Joe Lloyd	84	85	80	83	332
	John Reid	82	82	84	84	332
26=	George T Brokaw (a)	78	82	86	87	333
	James Campbell	81	84	82	86	333
	Fred McLeod	83	80	79	91	333
	Arthur Smith	80	87	83	83	333
30	AH Fenn	82	83	83	86	334

* Willie Anderson (82) beat David Brown (84) in the 18-Hole Play-off

Round Leader(s)
R1 Anderson; 73
R2 Anderson; 149
R3 Anderson; 225

Lowest Scores
R2 Reinhart, William Braid (34); 75
R3 Brown; 75
R4 Brown; 76

BRITISH OPEN 1904

Royal St George's Golf Club, Sandwich, Kent, England
(8–10 June)
6223 yards

A nephew of Ben Sayers from North Berwick, Jack White held off the Triumvirate by significantly lowering his numbers each round. He became the first man to break the 300 barrier, and, along with Taylor and Braid, was the first to record a score in the 60s at any Major. St George's had recently received its royal charter and staged the most popularly-contested Open to date. To alleviate congestion with a field of 144, play was taken into a third day for the first time.

1	**JACK WHITE**	80	75	72	69	296
	(£50)					
2=	James Braid	77	80	69	71	297
	JH Taylor	77	78	74	68	297
4	Tom Vardon	77	77	75	72	301
5	Harry Vardon	76	73	79	74	302
6	James Sherlock	83	71	78	77	309
7=	Jack Graham (a)	76	76	78	80	310
	Andrew Kirkaldy	78	79	74	79	310
9	Sandy Herd	84	76	76	75	311
10=	Robert Maxwell (a)	80	80	76	77	313
	Ben Sayers	80	80	76	77	313
12=	Willie Park, Jr	84	72	81	78	315
	Ted Ray	81	81	77	76	315
	Robert Thomson	75	76	80	84	315
	AH Toogood	88	76	74	77	315
16=	George Coburn	79	82	75	80	316
	John Rowe	86	82	75	73	316
17	John Ball, Jr (a)	83	78	79	78	318
18=	George Cawsey	82	80	78	79	319
	Frederick Collins	88	77	75	79	319
	Ernest Gray	84	77	74	84	319
21	JS Worthington (a)	85	79	78	78	320
22	TG Renouf	82	79	79	81	321
23=	PJ Gaudin	79	83	80	80	322
	Alf Matthews	85	81	78	78	322
25	Alec Thompson	86	81	75	81	323
26=	Ted Blackwell (a)	88	77	81	79	325
	George Cawkwell	83	83	79	80	325
	Rowland Jones	89	77	77	82	325
29=	AE Bellworthy	82	84	83	77	326
	James Hepburn	87	80	79	80	326
	Percy Hills	85	83	80	78	326

Round Leader(s)
R1 Thomson; 75
R2 H Vardon; 149
R3 Braid; 226

Lowest Scores
R2 Sherlock; 71
R3 Braid; 69
R4 Taylor; 68

US OPEN 1904

Glen View Club, Golf, Illinois
(8–9 July)

Following the British example, the half-way cut was introduced – excluding those players not within 15 strokes of the lead from further participation. Anderson's scoring, as in the previous year, set new records; with lows of 72 for any round, and 303 for 72 holes. Fred MacKenzie led by two going into the last round, but his 80, coupled with Anderson's record, saw him finish third – six strokes off the winner.

1	**WILLIE ANDERSON**	75	78	78	72	303
	($200)					
2	Gilbert Nicholls	80	76	79	73	308
3	Fred MacKenzie	76	79	74	80	309
4=	Laurie Auchterlonie	80	81	75	78	314
	Bernard Nicholls	80	77	79	78	314
6=	Percy Barrett	78	79	79	80	316
	Stewart Gardner	75	76	80	85	316
	Robert Simpson	82	82	76	76	316
9	James Foulis	83	84	78	82	317
10	Donald Ross	80	82	78	78	318
11=	Jack Hobens	77	82	80	80	319
	Charles Murray	84	81	76	78	319
13	Alex Campbell	81	87	80	82	320
14	Horace Rawlins	79	76	86	81	322
15=	George Braid	82	76	85	81	324
	Alex Ross	87	78	80	79	324
	George Thomson	78	87	81	78	324
18	Alex Smith	78	81	82	85	326
19	David Robertson	82	78	80	88	328
20=	Jack Campbell	80	88	79	82	329
	H Chandler Egan (a)	84	79	83	83	329
	Harry Turpie	81	82	86	80	329
23=	Robert Hunter (a)	83	85	79	84	331
	George Low	89	81	82	79	331
	Alex Taylor	85	83	83	80	331
26=	Kenneth Edwards (a)	84	83	80	85	332
	WH Way	88	83	79	82	332
28	George Cummings	83	83	82	85	333
29=	Tom McDeever	81	82	88	83	334
	Fred McLeod	86	88	81	79	334
	Peter Robertson	82	87	85	80	334
	James Watson	83	83	82	86	334

Round Leader(s)
R1 Anderson, Gardner; 75
R2 Gardner; 151
R3 MacKenzie; 229

Lowest Scores
R2 Foulis; 74
R3 MacKenzie; 74
R4 Anderson; 72

BRITISH OPEN 1905

Royal & Ancient Golf Club, St Andrews, Fife, Scotland
(7–9 June)

6333 yards

Braid's four wins over the next six years were, temporarily, to put him above Vardon *et al* on five Open victories. His record for the decade 1901–10 was something special: W, 2, 5, 2, W, W, 5, W, 2, W. The cut was drawn, as in the previous year's US Open, at 15 behind the leader. The Old Course took its toll on scoring, with only 10 rounds under 80 being recorded in the whole Championship.

1	**JAMES BRAID**	81	78	78	81	318
	(£50)					
2=	Rowland Jones	81	77	87	78	323
	JH Taylor	80	85	78	80	323
4	James Kinnell	82	79	82	81	324
5=	Ernest Gray	82	81	84	78	325
	Arnaud Massy	81	80	82	82	325
7	Robert Thomson	81	81	82	83	327
8	James Sherlock	81	84	80	83	328
9=	Tom Simpson	82	88	78	81	329
	Harry Vardon	80	82	84	83	329
11=	Ted Ray	85	82	81	82	330
	John Rowe	87	81	80	82	330
13=	Willie Park, Jr	84	81	85	81	331
	Tom Williamson	84	81	79	87	331
15	Sandy Herd	80	82	83	87	332
16=	TG Renouf	81	85	84	83	333
	Alex Smith	81	88	86	78	333
18=	JC Johnstone	85	86	84	80	335
	Archie Simpson	87	84	81	83	335
	Tom Watt	86	85	79	85	335
	Jack White	86	83	83	83	335
22=	Fred Collins	86	86	83	81	336
	Percy Hills	87	84	84	81	336
24=	Ernest Foord	85	86	84	83	338
	James Hepburn	84	84	87	83	338
	William Hunter	84	85	88	81	338
	Andrew Kirkaldy	83	83	83	89	338
28=	David Stephenson	84	86	83	86	339
	Walter Toogood	82	83	87	87	339
30	James Kay	85	83	85	87	340

Round Leader(s)
R1   Herd, Taylor, Vardon; 80
R2   Jones; 158
R3   Braid; 237

Lowest Scores
R2   Jones; 77
R3   Braid, T Simpson, Taylor; 78
R4   Gray, Jones, Smith; 78

US OPEN 1905

Myopia Hunt Club, South Hamilton, Massachusetts
(21–22 September)

6300 yards

Willie Anderson secured a place in US Open history when he won his fourth title at Myopia. His feat has never been beaten, and only been matched by Bobby Jones, Ben Hogan and Jack Nicklaus – exalted company indeed. Alex Smith became the second golfer to try his luck at both Opens in one year – finishing 16th at St Andrews and second for the third time in the US Championship.

1	**WILLIE ANDERSON**	81	80	76	77	314
	($200)					
2	Alex Smith	76	80	80	80	316
3=	Percy Barrett	81	80	77	79	317
	Peter Robertson	79	80	81	77	317
5	Stewart Gardner	78	78	85	77	318
6	Alex Campbell	82	76	80	81	319
7=	Jack Hobens	82	80	81	78	321
	Gilbert Nicholls	82	76	84	79	321
9	George Cummings	85	82	75	81	323
10	Arthur Smith	81	77	80	86	324
11=	AG Lockwood (a)	84	85	76	80	325
	Walter Travis (a)	81	80	80	84	325
13=	Alex Ross	79	86	78	83	326
	Willie Smith	86	81	76	83	326
15	George Low	83	82	81	81	327
16=	Joe Lloyd	75	86	83	84	328
	Fred McKenzie	81	85	80	82	328
18	Walter Clark	86	81	82	80	329
19	Fred McLeod	80	84	80	86	330
20=	Tom McNamara	81	79	82	89	331
	Bernard Nicholls	80	82	85	84	331
	George Turnbull	81	88	81	81	331
	WH Way	81	89	84	77	331
24	Laurie Auchterlonie	85	82	79	86	332
25	Donald Ross	83	83	86	81	333
26	Jack Jolly	82	83	85	85	335
	James Maiden	80	86	83	86	335
28	Robert Peebles	81	81	86	88	336
29=	Isaac Mackie	82	82	83	90	337
	Charles Murray	84	85	83	85	337

Round Leader(s)
R1   Lloyd; 75
R2   Gardner, A Smith; 156
R3   A Smith; 236

Lowest Scores
R2   Campbell, G Nicholls; 76
R3   Cummings; 75
R4   Anderson, Gardner, Robertson, Way; 77

BRITISH OPEN 1906

Hon Co of Edinburgh Golfers, Muirfield, East Lothian, Scotland
(13-15 June)
5934 yards

Progressively better scoring gave Braid his second win in a row. Both Taylor and Vardon were in the hunt at the end of R3, but fell away over the last 18. This was the third occasion in seven years when Braid, Taylor and Vardon had finished 1–2–3 in the Open, although not always in that order. Triumvirate indeed. Muirfield, despite being 'toughened'-up was still the shortest course on the roster, and comparatively the easiest.

1	**JAMES BRAID**	77	76	74	73	300
	(£50)					
2	JH Taylor	77	72	75	80	304
3	Harry Vardon	77	73	77	78	305
4	Jack Graham (a)	71	79	78	78	306
5	Rowland Jones	74	78	73	83	308
6	Arnaud Massy	76	80	76	78	310
7	Robert Maxwell (a)	73	78	77	83	311
8=	George Duncan	73	78	83	78	312
	Ted Ray	80	75	79	78	312
	TG Renouf	76	77	76	83	312
11	David Kinnell	78	76	80	79	313
12=	William Hunter	79	76	80	80	315
	William Leaver	80	76	78	81	315
	Tom Vardon	76	81	81	77	315
15=	George Cawsey	79	80	79	78	316
	Thomas Simpson	78	78	81	79	316
	Walter Toogood	83	79	83	71	316
	RW Whitecross (a)	74	83	80	79	316
19=	PJ Gaudin	77	77	80	83	317
	Harry Hamill	83	78	79	77	317
	Sandy Herd	81	79	77	80	317
	David McEwan	79	79	81	78	317
	Tom Williamson	77	77	78	85	317
24=	Tom Ball	78	79	79	82	318
	Ernest Gray	77	77	78	86	318
	Donald Kenny	82	85	83	78	318
	Ernest Riseborough	81	77	80	80	318
28=	James Kinnell	81	75	82	81	319
	Alf Matthews	84	77	80	78	319
30=	Ernest Foord	78	84	78	80	320
	James Hepburn	81	78	84	77	320
	James Kay	80	79	81	80	320
	George Pulford	80	81	81	78	320
	Robert Thomson	76	78	83	83	320

Round Leader(s)
R1 Graham; 71
R2 Taylor; 149
R3 Taylor; 224

Lowest Scores
R2 Taylor; 72
R3 Jones; 73
R4 Toogood; 71

US OPEN 1906

Onwentsia Club, Lake Forest, Illinois
(22-25 March)
6107 yards

Alex Smith led all the way to pick up the first of two US Open titles. In doing do he set a new low total score of 295, bettering the 1903 total by eight shots, and a stroke better than Jack White's British Open record. Three of the Smith brothers finished in the Top 18.

1	**ALEX SMITH**	73	74	73	75	295
	($300)					
2	Willie Smith	73	81	74	74	302
3=	Laurie Auchterlonie	76	78	75	76	305
	James Maiden	80	73	77	75	305
5	Willie Anderson	73	76	74	84	307
6	Alex Ross	76	79	75	80	310
7	Stewart Gardner	80	76	77	78	311
8=	H Chandler Egan (a)	79	78	76	80	313
	Gilbert Nicholls	76	81	77	79	313
10	Jack Hobens	75	84	76	79	314
11=	George Low	79	82	76	79	316
	Bernard Nicholls	79	77	79	81	316
13	Harry Turpie	80	80	76	83	319
14=	Walter Fovargue	77	84	78	81	320
	Jack Jolly	78	82	79	81	320
	Peter Robertson	79	78	80	83	320
17	Alex Baxter	83	81	81	86	321
18=	Fred Brand	78	78	85	81	322
	Alex Campbell	76	84	76	86	322
	George Cummings	79	76	84	83	322
	George Smith	79	76	82	85	322
22=	James Foulis	83	86	79	76	324
	Otto Hackbarth	82	82	82	78	324
	WR Lovekin	77	85	78	84	324
	D McIntosh	79	79	81	85	324
	William Marshall	85	77	81	81	324
27=	James Watson	76	80	81	88	325
	Ernest Way	83	81	80	81	325
29=	George O'Neill	84	82	82	78	326
	David Robertson	82	79	81	84	326

Round Leader(s)
R1 Anderson, A Smith, W Smith; 73
R2 A Smith; 147
R3 A Smith; 220

Lowest Scores
R2 Maiden; 73
R3 A Smith; 73
R4 W Smith; 74

BRITISH OPEN 1907

Royal Liverpool Golf Club, Hoylake, Cheshire, England
(20–21 June)
6355 yards

Arnaud Massy, from La Boulie, France, became the first overseas winner when he outplayed JH Taylor over the final holes. He is the only winner from France and continental Europe had to wait until 1979, and Severiano Ballesteros, for its next winner. France should have collected their second Open in 1999, but the story of the unfortunate Jean van de Velde is too recent – and still too painful – to recall here!

1	**ARNAUD MASSY**	76	81	78	77	312
	(£50)					
2	JH Taylor	79	79	76	80	314
3=	George Pulford	81	78	80	78	317
	Tom Vardon	81	81	80	75	317
5=	James Braid	82	85	75	76	318
	Ted Ray	83	80	79	76	318
7=	George Duncan	83	78	81	77	319
	Harry Vardon	84	81	74	80	319
	Tom Williamson	82	77	82	78	319
10	Tom Ball	80	78	81	81	320
11	PJ Gaudin	83	84	80	76	323
12	Sandy Herd	83	81	83	77	324
13=	Jack Graham (a)	83	81	80	82	326
	Walter Toogood	76	86	82	82	326
15=	John Ball, Jr (a)	88	83	79	77	327
	Frederick Collins	83	83	79	82	327
17=	Alf Matthews	82	80	84	82	328
	Charles Mayo	86	78	82	82	328
	TG Renouf	83	80	82	83	328
20	Reg Gray	83	85	81	80	329
21=	James Bradbeer	83	85	82	80	330
	G Carter	89	80	81	80	330
23	John Rowe	83	83	85	80	331
24	AH Toogood	87	83	85	77	332
25=	William Horne	91	80	81	81	333
	Harry Kidd	84	90	82	77	333
	David McEwan	89	83	80	81	333
	Charles Roberts	86	83	84	80	333
	Alex Smith	85	84	84	80	333
30=	James Kinnell	89	79	80	86	334
	JH Oke	86	85	82	81	334

Round Leader(s)
R1   Massy, W Toogood; 76
R2   Massy; 157
R3   Taylor; 234

Lowest Scores
R2   Williamson; 77
R3   H Vardon; 74
R4   T Vardon; 75

US OPEN 1907

Philadelphia Cricket Club, Chestnut Hill, Pennsylvania
(20–21 June)
5952 yards

Yet another Scot, Alex Ross, added the US Open title to his portfolio. Alex was the brother of the famous golf course designer, Donald, who also finished in 10th place in the Championship this year.

1	**ALEX ROSS**	76	74	76	76	302
	($300)					
2	Gilbert Nicholls	80	73	72	79	304
3	Alex Campbell	78	74	78	75	305
4	Jack Hobens	76	75	73	85	309
5=	George Low	78	76	79	77	310
	Fred McLeod	79	77	79	75	310
	Peter Robertson	81	77	78	74	310
8=	David Brown	75	80	78	78	311
	Bernard Nicholls	76	76	81	78	311
10	Donald Ross	78	80	76	78	312
11=	Laurie Auchterlonie	77	77	83	76	313
	Fred Brand	78	80	73	82	313
13	David Robertson	80	78	75	81	314
14	Tom McNamara	82	79	78	76	315
15	Willie Anderson	81	77	81	77	316
16=	Mike Brady	76	77	84	80	317
	David Hunter	77	75	85	80	317
	Martin O'Loughlin	81	81	77	78	317
19	Jack Campbell	78	79	82	80	319
20	GJ Bouse	78	78	86	78	320
21	Stewart Gardner	81	79	78	83	321
22=	James Campbell	76	85	81	80	322
	Walter Clark	78	81	79	84	322
	Isaac Mackie	82	83	79	78	322
25	Jack Jolly	78	86	81	78	323
26=	David Ogilvie	82	81	81	80	324
	Horace Rawlins	82	76	83	83	324
	WD Robinson	82	84	80	78	324
	Jerome Travers (a)	81	84	80	79	324
30=	WC Gaudin	80	86	82	77	325
	W Ogilvie	80	83	82	80	325

Round Leader(s)
R1   Brown; 75
R2   A Ross; 150
R3   Hobens; 224

Lowest Scores
R2   G Nicholls; 73
R3   G Nicholls; 72
R4   Robertson; 74

BRITISH OPEN 1908

Prestwick Golf Club, Ayrshire, Scotland
(18–19 June)
5948 yards

Leading all the way, Braid lowered the Open (and Majors) record total even further, adding a lowest-to-date 18-hole score of 70; 36-hole total of 144; and 54-holes at 221. He took a six-shot lead into the last round and stretched it to eight.

1	**JAMES BRAID** (£50)	70	72	77	72	291
2	Tom Ball	76	73	76	74	299
3	Ted Ray	79	71	75	76	301
4	Sandy Herd	74	74	79	75	302
5=	David Kinnell	75	73	80	78	306
	Harry Vardon	79	78	74	75	306
7=	Thomas Simpson	75	77	76	79	307
	JH Taylor	79	77	76	75	307
9=	PJ Gaudin	77	76	75	80	308
	Arnaud Massy	76	75	76	81	308
11=	James Edmundson	80	72	76	82	310
	Tom Watt	81	73	78	78	310
13=	John Ball, Jr (a)	74	78	78	81	311
	Fred Collins	78	77	77	79	311
	Ernest Gray	68	79	83	81	311
	William Leaver	79	79	75	78	311
	Tom Vardon	77	79	76	79	311
18=	George Duncan	79	77	80	76	312
	Jack Graham (a)	76	82	76	78	312
	George Pulford	81	77	74	80	312
	Fred Robson	72	79	83	78	312
	AH Toogood	82	76	77	77	312
	Walter Toogood	80	75	78	79	312
24=	George Coburn	77	79	77	81	314
	James Hepburn	80	79	79	76	314
	Rowland Jones	75	77	83	79	314
27	R Andrew (a)	83	78	77	77	315
28=	Willie Aveston	77	77	79	83	316
	TG Renouf	78	78	83	77	316
30=	Charles Mayo	83	79	80	75	317
	Ben Sayers	74	76	84	83	317
	Albert Tingey, Sr	76	82	79	80	317

Round Leaders
R1   Braid; 70
R2   Braid; 142
R3   Braid; 219

Lowest Scores
R2   Ray; 71
R3   Pulford, H Vardon; 74
R4   Braid; 72

US OPEN 1908

Myopia Hunt Club, South Hamilton, Massachusetts
(27–29 August)
6335 yards

The players must have been glad see the back of the Myopia Hunt Club; host to the US Open for the fourth and last time. The course has the dubious distiction of holding the three highest winning totals in USOpen history – 331 (1901), 328 (1898) and now 322. Wind created the havoc in 1908, as much as the golf course itself, though – only Gilbert Nicholls broke 80 twice; and he was disqualified! How 5'4", 108 lbs Fred McLeod withstood it we'll never know. He did, though, to tie with Willie Smith; then went on to win the play-off.

1	**FRED McLEOD*** (£300)	82	82	81	77	322
2	Willie Smith	77	82	85	78	322
3	Alex Smith	80	83	83	81	327
4	Willie Anderson	85	86	80	79	330
5	John Jones	81	81	87	82	331
6=	Jack Hobens	86	81	85	81	333
	Peter Robertson	89	84	77	83	333
8=	Percy Barrett	94	80	86	78	338
	Jock Hutchison	82	84	87	85	338
10=	Richard Kimball	84	86	83	86	339
	Tom McNamara	85	82	86	86	339
12=	Donald Ball	90	81	86	83	340
	Alex Campbell	85	83	89	83	340
	George Low	92	80	84	84	340
	Robert Peebles	85	85	85	85	340
16	David Hunter	87	87	84	83	341
17=	HH Barker	84	85	88	86	343
	Mike Brady	86	87	87	83	343
	Orrin Terry	86	87	83	87	343
20	David Robertson	89	83	86	86	344
21=	Laurie Auchterlonie	85	83	83	95	346
	Harry Rawlins	85	89	88	84	346
23=	Isaac Mackie	94	88	84	81	347
	Alex Ross	89	85	91	82	347
	Walter Travis (a)	90	83	87	87	347
26	Jack Campbell	91	89	87	82	349
27=	David Brown	87	86	91	86	350
	David Ogilvie	91	89	87	83	350
29=	Arthur Smith	97	85	85	85	352
	Herbert Strong	91	89	88	84	352
	WH Way	92	88	87	85	352

* Fred McLeod (77) beat Willie Smith (83) in the 18-Hole Play-off

Round Leader(s)
R1   W Smith; 77
R2   W Smith; 159
R3   W Smith; 244

Lowest Scores
R2   G Nicholls (d/q); 77
R3   P Robertson; 77
R4   McLeod; 77

BRITISH OPEN 1909

Royal Cinque Ports Golf Club, Deal, Kent, England
(10–11 June)
6495 yards

In one of only two visits to Deal, The Open fell into the hands of JH Taylor for the first time since 1900. It was his fourth victory overall, and a triumph for consistently solid scoring. After a few years in America, when he featured in the US Open, Bernard Nicholls returned home to gain a Top Ten place.

1	**JH TAYLOR**	74	73	74	74	295
	(£50)					
2=	Tom Ball	74	75	76	76	301
	James Braid	79	75	73	74	301
4	Charles Johns	72	76	79	75	302
5	TG Renouf	76	78	76	73	303
6	Ted Ray	77	76	76	75	304
7	William Horne	77	78	77	74	306
8=	James Hepburn	78	77	76	76	307
	Sandy Herd	76	75	80	76	307
10=	Bertie Lassen (a)	82	74	74	78	308
	Bernard Nicholls	78	76	77	77	308
	George Pulford	81	76	76	75	308
13	Robert Maxwell (a)	75	80	80	74	309
14=	EP Gaudin	76	77	77	80	310
	Peter Rainford	78	76	76	80	310
16	George Cawsey	79	76	78	78	311
17=	Ben Sayers	79	77	79	77	312
	Robert Thomson	81	79	75	77	312
19=	CK Hutchison (a)	75	81	78	79	313
	Tom Vardon	80	75	80	78	313
21=	Fred Collins	81	78	75	80	314
	George Duncan	77	82	80	75	314
	Ernest Foord	77	80	81	76	314
	Michael Moran	82	81	74	77	314
	Wilfred Reid	77	83	78	76	314
26=	AE Bellworthy	76	84	78	78	316
	Arthur Butchart	80	79	80	77	316
	Douglas Edgar	81	81	76	78	316
	Rowland Jones	80	79	79	78	316
	Harry Vardon	82	77	79	78	316

Round Leader(s)
R1 Johns; 72
R2 Taylor; 147
R3 Taylor; 221

Lowest Scores
R2 Taylor; 73
R3 Braid; 73
R4 Renouf; 73

US OPEN 1909

Englewood Golf Club, Englewood, New Jersey
(24–25 June)
6205 yards: Par 72 (288)

Sargent, after Rawlins and Lloyd, became the third Englishman to win the US Open in its 15 year existence. In something like 50 years, only four Englishmen had won the British Open – accepting that Hilton, Taylor and Vardon were multi-winners – which indicates how great a stranglehold the Scots had, and were, to a lesser degree, still having on the Majors, and golf in general. Sargent shot a new low total for either Open, and McNamara, the first home-grown American talent to lead the US Open, set a record for both Championships at 36 and 54 holes. David Hunter led after the first round with an exceptional 68, only to shoot 84, 84 and 77, to finish tied for 30th.

1	**GEORGE SARGENT**	75	72	72	71	290
	($300)					
2	Tom McNamara	73	69	75	77	294
3	Alex Smith	76	73	74	72	295
4=	Willie Anderson	79	74	76	70	299
	Jack Hobens	75	78	72	74	299
	Isaac Mackie	77	75	74	73	299
7=	Tom Anderson, Jr	78	74	75	73	300
	HH Barker	75	79	73	73	300
	Andrew Campbell	71	75	77	77	300
	Tom Peebles	76	73	73	78	300
	Walter Travis (a)	72	78	77	73	300
12	Mike Brady	76	77	74	75	302
13=	Alex Campbell	75	73	81	74	303
	Fred McLeod	78	76	74	75	303
15=	Orrin Terry	78	80	73	73	304
	FR Upton, Jr (a)	72	79	78	75	304
17	Gilbert Nicholls	73	75	79	79	306
18=	Walter Fovargue	80	76	77	74	307
	David Ogilvie	76	78	79	74	307
20=	Peter Robertson	79	72	78	79	308
	Charles Rowe	74	77	76	81	308
22	Jack Campbell	74	79	75	81	309
23=	Laurie Auchterlonie	78	75	77	71	311
	Findlay Douglas a)	82	76	78	75	311
	Jock Hutchison	79	76	77	79	311
	Tom Vardon	80	75	82	74	311
27=	John Dingwall	79	74	77	72	312
	George Low	78	75	74	85	312
	James Maiden	76	78	80	78	312
30=	Jack Burke, Sr	75	78	81	79	313
	David Hunter	68	84	84	77	313
	Charles Murray	77	75	77	84	313

Round Leader(s)
R1 Hunter; 68
R2 McNamara; 142
R3 McNamara; 217

Lowest Scores
R2 McNamara; 69
R3 Hobens, Sargent; 72
R4 Anderson; 70

US OPEN 1910

Philadelphia Cricket Club, Chestnut Hill, Pennsylvania
(17-18, 20 June)
5956 yards

The US Open preceded the British Open for the first time this year – the last day at Philadelphia Cricket Club was the day before the first at the R&A Club. Alex Smith collected his second Open, in a Monday play-off, after brother MacDonald and Champion-to-be, McDermott, finished in the first-ever three-way tie. Brother Willie was to lead the British Open after 36 holes later that week. Four-time champion, Willie Anderson – aged just 30 – died several months later. Such events in those days were usually alcohol-driven.

1	**ALEX SMITH*** ($300)	73	73	79	73	298
2	John McDermott	74	74	75	75	298
3	Macdonald Smith	74	78	75	71	298
4	Fred McLeod	78	70	78	73	299
5=	Tom McNamara	73	78	73	76	300
	Gilbert Nicholls	73	75	77	75	300
7	Jack Hobens	74	77	74	76	301
8=	Tom Anderson, Jr	72	76	81	73	302
	HH Barker	75	78	77	72	302
	Jock Hutchison	77	76	75	74	302
11	Willie Anderson	74	78	76	75	303
12=	George Low	75	77	79	74	305
	Charles Thom	80	72	78	75	305
14=	Tom Bonnar	78	78	71	80	307
	George Cummings	78	73	79	77	307
16=	Alex Campbell	79	76	80	74	309
	George Sargent	77	81	74	77	309
18=	Jack Campbell	77	77	81	75	310
	James Thomson	74	80	80	76	310
20	Fred Herreshoff (a)	76	77	79	79	311
21	George Smith	76	78	79	80	313
22	Alex Ross	78	84	73	79	314
23=	Otto Hackbarth	79	82	78	76	315
	Martin O'Loughlin	77	82	80	76	315
25	AW Tillinghast (a)	80	81	79	76	316
26	WD Robinson	83	81	78	75	317
27	Jack Burke, Sr	81	77	77	84	319
28=	James Donaldson	80	78	87	75	320
	David Honeyman	83	79	79	79	320
	Irving Stringer	83	77	82	78	320

* Alex Smith (71) beat John McDermott (75) and Macdonald Smith (77) in the 18-Hole Play-off

Round Leader(s)
R1   T Anderson; 72
R2   A Smith; 146
R3   McDermott; 223

Lowest Scores
R2   McLeod; 70
R3   Bonnar; 71
R4   M Smith; 71

BRITISH OPEN 1910

Royal & Ancient Golf Club, St Andrews, Fife, Scotland
(21[rain-affected], 22-24 June)
6487 yds

Braid's magical decade was capped with his fifth Open win – then a record – beating the previous St Andrews low score by ten, and Sandy Herd by four. Only the 60 lowest scorers (and ties) were allowed to proceed to Round Three. Fred MacKenzie, third in the 1904 US Open, had returned (permanently) to his home course to finish 16th; while Willie Smith and Donald Ross were just visiting.

1	**JAMES BRAID** (£50)	76	73	74	76	299
2	Sandy Herd	78	74	75	76	303
3	George Duncan	73	77	71	83	304
4	Laurie Ayton, Sr	78	76	75	77	306
5=	Ted Ray	76	77	74	81	308
	Fred Robson	75	80	77	76	308
	Willie Smith	77	71	80	80	308
8=	EP Gaudin	78	74	76	81	309
	James Kinnell	79	74	77	79	309
	TG Renouf	77	76	75	81	309
	Donald Ross	78	79	75	77	309
12=	Tom Ball	81	77	75	78	311
	PJ Gaudin	80	79	74	78	311
14=	Michael Moran	77	75	79	81	312
	JH Taylor	76	80	78	78	312
16=	Fred MacKenzie	78	80	75	80	313
	William Ritchie	78	74	82	79	313
	Harry Vardon	77	81	75	80	313
19=	John Ball, Jr (a)	79	75	78	82	314
	James Hepburn	78	82	76	78	314
	Tom Williamson	78	80	78	78	314
22=	Arnaud Massy	78	77	81	79	315
	John Rowe	81	74	80	80	315
24=	William Binnie	80	76	77	83	316
	CK Hutchison (a)	82	74	78	82	316
	Wilfred Reid	78	83	77	78	316
	Charles Roberts	81	73	79	83	316
28=	Willie Auchterlonie	79	76	79	83	317
	Ernest Foord	80	77	79	81	317
	Herbert Riseborough	75	81	80	81	317
	James Sherlock	77	81	80	79	317

Round Leader(s)
R1   Duncan; 73
R2   Smith; 148
R3   Duncan; 221

Lowest Scores
R2   Smith; 71
R3   Duncan; 71
R4   Braid, Herd, Robson; 76

US OPEN 1911

Chicago Golf Club, Wheaton, Illinois
(23–24 June)
6605 yards

This was the much-awaited first US Open (and Major championship) win by a native-born American. The unlucky Mike Brady could have entered US golfing folklore, but he was always to be the nearly-man. Born in Philadelphia and not yet 20, McDermott tied with Brady and Scot George Simpson, before easing out Brady in the play-off after Simpson's game was plagued by an attack of rheumatism.

1	**JOHN McDERMOTT***	81	72	75	79	307
	($300)					
2	Mike Brady	76	77	79	75	307
3	George Simpson	76	77	79	75	307
4	Fred McLeod	77	72	76	83	308
5=	Jock Hutchison	80	77	73	79	309
	Gilbert Nicholls	76	78	74	81	309
7=	HH Barker	75	81	77	78	311
	George Sargent	76	77	84	74	311
9=	Peter Robertson	79	76	78	79	312
	Alex Ross	74	75	81	82	312
11	Albert Seckel (a)	78	80	80	75	313
12=	Alex Campbell	81	77	72	84	314
	Harry Turpie	77	76	82	79	314
14	CP Nelson	79	85	74	77	315
15=	James Donaldson	78	81	83	74	316
	George Low	80	78	82	76	316
17	RL Simpson	81	82	75	79	317
18=	John Burke	79	77	78	85	319
	DE Sawyer (a)	84	79	77	79	319
20=	Grange Alves	82	80	73	85	320
	George Cummings	82	80	79	79	320
	Mason Phelps (a)	78	78	78	86	320
23=	H Chandler Egan (a)	81	80	77	83	321
	Robert Gardner (a)	81	78	79	83	321
	JB Simpson	81	82	78	80	321
	Alex Smith	76	78	82	85	321
	RC Watson (a)	82	79	78	82	321
28	Walter Fovargue	83	81	80	78	322
29=	TJ Foulis	79	80	82	83	324
	Otto Hackbarth	78	74	83	89	324
	Robert McDonald	80	82	75	87	324
	Tom McNamara	77	87	79	81	324

* John McDermott (80) beat Mike Brady (82) and George Simpson (86) in the 18-Hole Play-off

Round Leader(s)
R1   Ross; 74
R2   McLeod, Ross; 149
R3   McLeod; 225

Lowest Scores
R2   McDermott, McLeod; 72
R3   Campbell; 72
R4   Donaldson, Sargent; 74

BRITISH OPEN 1911

Royal St George's Golf Club, Sandwich, Kent, England
(26–29 June)
6594 yards

James Braid's record of five victories was short-lived when arch rival Vardon equalled his mark at Sandwich. Arnaud Massy, the 1907 champion, took him to the 35th extra hole, however, for the privilege.

1	**HARRY VARDON***	74	74	75	80	303
	(£50)					
2	Arnaud Massy	75	78	74	76	303
3=	Sandy Herd	77	73	76	78	304
	Horace Hilton (a)	76	74	78	76	304
5=	James Braid	78	75	74	78	305
	Ted Ray	76	72	79	78	305
	JH Taylor	72	76	78	79	305
8	George Duncan	73	71	83	79	306
9	Laurie Ayton, Sr	75	77	77	78	307
10=	James Hepburn	74	77	83	75	309
	Fred Robson	78	74	79	78	309
12	Fred Collins	77	76	83	74	310
13=	J Piper	78	79	80	74	311
	TG Renouf	75	76	79	81	311
15	Tom Ball	76	77	79	80	312
16=	Rowland Jones	80	76	85	72	313
	Charles Mayo	78	78	79	78	313
	Wilfred Reid	78	79	80	76	313
	James Sherlock	73	80	76	84	313
	HE Taylor (a)	83	73	76	81	313
21=	Ernest BH Blackwell (a)	71	81	72	80	314
	Michael Moran	72	78	83	81	314
	William Watt	76	80	79	79	314
24=	Ernest Jones	77	82	81	75	315
	LB Stevens (a)	79	83	77	76	315
	Josh Taylor	79	81	80	75	315
27=	Robert Harris (a)	77	80	76	83	316
	Fred Leach	75	79	87	75	316
29=	Tom R Fernie	80	78	76	83	317
	JC Johnstone	82	79	78	78	317
	AF Kettley	79	77	81	80	317
	James Ockenden	75	78	81	83	317
	Robert Thomson	77	76	85	79	317

* Harry Vardon (143 after 35 holes) beat Arnaud Massy (148 after 34 holes) when Massy conceded at the 35th hole

Round Leader(s)
R1   Blackwell; 71
R2   Duncan; 144
R3   Vardon; 223

Lowest Scores
R2   Duncan; 71
R3   Braid, Massy; 74
R4   R Jones; 72

BRITISH OPEN 1912

Hon Co of Edinburgh Golfers, Muirfield, East Lothian, Scotland
(24–25 June)

6194 yds

Ted Ray was the heir apparent to the Great Triumvirate – except that they were at the top so long, he was himself usurped before he could properly wear the crown. Ray would surely have won more Opens (British, or US – which he collected in 1920) if Braid, Vardon and Taylor had been mere mortals. There was also an enforced sabbatical in the middle of his career, courtesy of Kaiser Wilhelm II. Leading all the way, Ray set a new 54-hole low for the Open of 220.

1	**TED RAY**	71	73	76	75	295
	(£50)					
2	Harry Vardon	75	72	81	71	299
3	James Braid	77	71	77	78	303
4	George Duncan	72	77	78	78	305
5=	Laurie Ayton, Sr	74	80	75	80	309
	Sandy Herd	76	81	76	76	309
7=	Fred Collins	76	79	81	74	310
	Jean Gassiat	76	80	78	76	310
	Reg Wilson	82	75	75	78	310
10	Arnaud Massy	74	77	82	78	311
11=	Charles Mayo	76	77	78	81	312
	JH Taylor	75	76	77	84	312
13=	George Fotheringham	75	78	79	81	313
	Robert Thomson	73	77	80	83	313
15=	Hughie McNeill	76	78	82	78	314
	Michael Moran	76	79	80	79	314
17=	Fred Leach	75	82	81	77	315
	Tom Williamson	80	77	79	79	315
19	TG Renouf	77	80	80	79	316
20=	Douglas Edgar	77	81	80	79	317
	William Horne	73	85	82	77	317
	Wilfred Reid	80	79	79	79	317
23	PJ Gaudin	80	76	82	80	318
24=	FH Frostick	77	80	81	81	319
	Philip Taylor	76	82	81	80	319
26	Tom Ball	75	81	86	78	320
27=	Jas Batley	79	86	80	76	321
	Rowland Jones	78	82	84	77	321
	Charles Pope	83	80	77	81	321
	Charles Roberts	82	81	83	75	321

Round Leaders
R1 Ray; 71
R2 Ray; 144
R3 Ray; 220

Lowest Scores
R2 Braid; 71
R3 Ayton, Wilson; 75
R4 Vardon; 71

US OPEN 1912

Country Club of Buffalo, Buffalo, New York
(1–2 August)

6236 yards: Par 74 (296)

Proving that his 2nd in 1910 and win of the previous year were not flukes, McDermott made it back-to-back victories. He shot an impressive 294 total to lead home fellow 'home-breds', Tom McNamara and Mike Brady. Only Alex Smith of the British imports scored within eight strokes of the winner. In 1911, the USGA officially defined the term 'par'; which meant that McDermott was two 'under' for the Championship.

1	**JOHN McDERMOTT**	74	75	74	71	294
	($300)					
2	Tom McNamara	74	80	73	69	296
3=	Mike Brady	72	75	73	79	299
	Alex Smith	77	70	77	75	299
5	Alex Campbell	74	77	80	71	302
6	George Sargent	72	78	76	77	303
7=	Jack Dowling	76	79	76	74	305
	Otto Hackbarth	77	77	75	76	305
9	Charles Murray	75	78	77	76	306
10=	Tom Anderson, Jr	75	76	81	75	307
	Frank Peebles	73	76	83	75	307
	Walter Travis (a)	73	79	78	77	307
13=	Fred McLeod	79	77	75	77	308
	George Simpson	79	73	77	79	308
15	Percy Barrett	74	73	83	79	309
16=	John G Anderson (a)	80	79	78	73	310
	David Ogilvie	74	83	73	80	310
18=	Jim Barnes	77	73	79	82	311
	John Dingwall	77	77	78	79	311
	Willie MacFarlane	77	81	73	80	311
21=	Jack Croke	74	81	78	79	312
	Tom Vardon	74	83	79	76	312
23=	Jack Campbell	74	75	83	81	313
	George Cummings	78	79	77	79	313
	Jock Hutchison	78	77	82	76	313
26	AH Murray	78	79	79	78	314
27	Charles Rowe	77	78	79	81	315
28=	Dave Robertson	80	82	77	77	316
	Peter Robertson	77	82	81	76	316
30=	David Black	78	77	78	84	317
	David Honeynay	80	82	79	76	317
	David Livie	82	80	76	79	317

Round Leaders
R1 Brady, Sargent; 72
R2 Barrett, Brady, Smith; 147
R3 Brady; 220

Lowest Scores
R2 Smith; 70
R3 Brady, MacFarlane, McNamara, Ogilvie; 73
R4 McNamara; 69

BRITISH OPEN 1913

Royal Liverpool Golf Club, Hoylake, Cheshire, England
(23–24 June)

6455 yards

Taylor joined Vardon and Braid on five Open wins, 19 years after his first success. His margin of eight strokes matched his win of 1900 and Braid's of 1908 – the widest margins of victory in the Open this century. Double US Open Champion, John McDermott, became the first US-born professional to compete in the Championship, finishing tied-5th.

1	**JH TAYLOR** (£50)	73	75	77	79	304
2	Ted Ray	73	74	81	84	312
3=	Michael Moran	76	74	89	74	313
	Harry Vardon	79	75	79	80	313
5=	John McDermott	75	80	77	83	315
	TG Renouf	75	78	84	78	315
7=	James Bradbeer	78	79	81	79	317
	Arnaud Massy	77	80	81	79	317
	James Sherlock	77	86	79	75	317
	Tom Williamson	77	80	80	80	317
11=	Fred Collins	77	85	79	77	318
	Jack Graham (a)	77	79	81	81	318
	Sandy Herd	73	81	84	80	318
14=	Bertie Lassen (a)	79	78	80	82	319
	Charles Roberts	78	79	84	78	319
	Josh Taylor	80	75	85	79	319
17	Philip Taylor	78	81	83	78	320
18=	James Braid	80	79	82	80	321
	Claude Gray	80	81	79	81	321
	Ernest Jones	75	85	81	80	321
	Hughie McNeill	80	81	81	79	321
22=	Jean Gassiat	80	78	86	78	322
	Cyril Hughes	76	78	83	85	322
	Louis Tellier	77	80	85	80	322
25	TL Macnamara	80	78	85	80	323
26	Wilfred Reid	78	82	85	79	324
27=	Arthur Catlin	77	81	81	86	325
	Charles Mayo	83	82	78	82	325
	Thomas Simpson	79	83	85	78	325
30=	Laurie Ayton, Sr	78	83	86	80	327
	Tom Ball	82	83	86	76	327
	GR Buckle	81	80	87	79	327
	Jack B Ross	75	89	84	79	327

Round Leader(s)
R1   Herd, Ray, JH Taylor; 73
R2   Ray; 147
R3   JH Taylor; 225

Lowest Scores
R2   Moran, Ray; 74
R3   McDermott, JH Taylor; 77
R4   Moran; 74

US OPEN 1913

The Country Club, Brookline, Boston, Massachusetts
(22–25 March)

6245 yards: Par 71 (284)

If the Opens of 1911 and 1912 were seminal in that they witnessed the birth of the hitherto embryonic American professional, the Open Championship of 1913 showed how the golf and golfers of the New World would soon outgrow their Old World teachers. Not only did it point to the crumbling hegemony of Britain with Vardon's and Ray's defeat in a playoff – it took US golf on to the front pages; and it heralded a golden era for the successful amateur. Francis Ouimet's destruction of arguably the world's two best players of the time, is one of golf's biggest upsets – and turning points. Already the USGA had improved on the British Championship administration: qualifying rounds were held for the first time, reducing the first round starters to 64, for instance. Now America had the players to lead with as well.

1	**FRANCIS OUIMET* (a)** (Nil – amateur)	77	74	74	79	304
2	Harry Vardon	75	72	78	79	304
3	Ted Ray	79	70	76	79	304
4=	Jim Barnes	74	76	78	79	307
	Walter Hagen	73	78	76	80	307
	Macdonald Smith	71	79	80	77	307
	Louis Tellier	76	76	79	76	307
8	John McDermott	74	74	77	78	308
9	Herbert Strong	75	74	82	79	310
10	Pat Doyle	78	80	73	80	311
11=	WC Fownes, Jr (a)	79	75	78	80	312
	Elmer Loving	76	80	75	81	312
13	Alex Campbell	77	80	76	80	313
14	Mike Brady	83	74	78	80	315
15	Matt Campbell	83	80	77	76	316
16=	Fred Herreshoff (a)	75	78	83	82	318
	Jock Hutchison	77	76	80	85	318
	Tom McNamara	73	86	75	84	318
	Wilfred Reid	75	72	85	86	318
	Alex Smith	82	75	82	79	318
21=	Robert Andrews (a)	83	73	83	80	319
	Jack Croke	72	83	83	81	319
	Charles Murray	80	80	80	79	319
	Peter Robertson	79	80	78	82	319
	George Sargent	75	76	79	89	319
26=	Jack Dowling	77	77	82	85	321
	Charles Thom	76	76	84	85	321
28=	Bob MacDonald	80	79	84	79	322
	Jerome Travers (a)	78	78	81	85	322
30=	Frank Bellwood	79	83	80	81	323
	James Donaldson	79	76	85	83	323
	JH Taylor	81	80	78	84	323

* Francis Ouimet (72) beat Harry Vardon (77) and Ted Ray (78) in the 18-Hole Play-off

Round Leader(s)
R1   Alex Ross (36), M Smith; 71
R2   Reid, Vardon; 147
R3   Ouimet, Ray, Vardon; 225

Lowest Scores
R2   Ray; 70
R3   Doyle; 73
R4   M Campbell, Tellier; 76

BRITISH OPEN 1914

Prestwick Golf Club, Ayrshire, Scotland
(18–19 June)
6122 yds

Vardon's last Open win, his sixth, was a record, and is still unsurpassed. It was the end of an era: the Great War caused a five-year vacuum in the Open Championship, at the end of which the Triumvirate had reached the age of 50. Vardon was to challenge for both Opens in 1920, but that was his parting shot. American hero, Francis Ouimet, who was to add the 1914 US Amateur title to his 1913 US Open, came to Prestwick, but finished well down the field on 332.

1	**HARRY VARDON** (£50)	73	77	78	78	306
2	JH Taylor	74	78	74	83	309
3	Harry Simpson	77	80	78	75	310
4=	Abe Mitchell	76	78	79	79	312
	Tom Williamson	75	79	79	79	312
6	Reg Wilson	76	77	80	80	313
7	James Ockenden	75	76	83	80	314
8=	PJ Gaudin	78	83	80	74	315
	JLC Jenkins (a)	79	80	73	83	315
10=	James Braid	74	82	78	82	316
	George Duncan	77	79	80	80	316
	Arnaud Massy	77	82	75	82	316
	Ted Ray	77	82	76	81	316
14=	James Bradbeer	77	80	80	80	317
	Douglas Edgar	79	75	84	79	317
	Jean Gassiat	76	81	80	80	317
17=	William Hunter	82	77	77	83	319
	Bertie Lassen (a)	85	78	79	77	319
19=	Ernest Foord	82	81	82	76	321
	Cyril Hughes	80	81	80	80	321
21=	Jas Batley	78	83	81	80	322
	Ernest Jones	87	81	80	74	322
	Fred Leach	76	86	78	82	322
	C Ralph Smith	81	79	80	82	322
25=	Walter Hambleton	79	75	86	83	323
	Michael Moran	82	83	82	76	323
	Josh Taylor	82	79	84	78	323
	David Watt	84	80	78	81	323
29=	Sandy Herd	79	87	79	79	324
	CK Hutchison (a)	81	75	82	86	324
	JC Lonie	77	84	82	81	324
	Ernest Whitcombe	74	83	84	83	324

Round Leader(s)
R1   Vardon; 73
R2   Vardon; 150
R3   JH Taylor; 226

Lowest Scores
R2   Edgar, Hambleton, Hutchison; 75
R3   Jenkins; 73
R4   Gaudin, Jones; 74

US OPEN 1914

Midlothian Country Club, Blue Island, Illinois
(20–21 August)
6355 yards: Par 72 (288)

It didn't take long for the infant US golfer to grow up. As if the outbreak of war in Europe signalled the end of the old and the start of the new, 1914 heralded a different order of all things golf. Leading this movement was one Walter Hagen. Finishing fourth behind all the excitement the previous year, Hagen burst on to the scene with a record Round One score of 68; stayed ahead of the field, and won by one stroke from fast-finishing Chick Evans, another emerging amateur. The winning score tied George Sargent's record low total of 1909. Hagen was to go to become the first worldwide superstar of golf – in fact, he probably invented the role, with his brash but charming manner and lavish lifestyle.

1	**WALTER HAGEN** ($300)	68	74	75	73	290
2	Charles Evans, Jr (a)	76	74	71	70	291
3=	Fred McLeod	78	73	75	71	297
	George Sargent	74	77	74	72	297
5=	Mike Brady	78	72	74	74	298
	James Donaldson	72	79	74	73	298
	Francis Ouimet (a)	69	76	75	78	298
8	Louis Tellier	72	75	74	78	299
9=	John McDermott	77	74	74	75	300
	Arthur Smith	79	73	76	72	300
11=	WM Rautenbusch (a)	76	75	75	75	301
	James Simpson	76	71	77	77	301
13=	Jim Barnes	73	76	80	73	302
	Charles Hoffner	77	76	77	72	302
	Tom McNamara	72	71	76	83	302
	Joe Mitchell	77	69	77	79	302
	JJ O'Brien	74	72	77	79	302
	Robert Peebles	78	75	74	75	302
	George Simpson	73	76	76	77	302
20=	Dan Kenny	76	75	76	76	303
	Tom Kerrigan	76	73	77	77	303
22=	Alex Ross	72	75	82	76	305
	Warren Wood (a)	77	73	77	78	305
24	Walter Fovargue	81	71	77	77	306
25=	Jack Munro	83	74	75	75	307
	RM Thompson	79	75	78	75	307
27	Otto Hackbarth	82	75	77	75	309
28=	Fred Brand	78	74	76	82	310
	Jack Burke, Sr	75	77	77	81	310
	CP Nelson	77	81	77	75	310

Round Leader(s)
R1   Hagen; 68
R2   Hagen; 142
R3   Hagen; 217

Lowest Scores
R2   Mitchell; 69
R3   Evans; 71
R4   Evans; 70

BRITISH OPEN 1915

No Championship

US OPEN 1915

Baltusrol Golf Club, Springfield, New Jersey
(22–25 March)

6212 yards: Par 72 (288)

Returning to the original Baltusrol course, The US Open produced its second amateur winner. Jerome Travers had won the matchplay US Amateur title four times. He gave up competitive golf shortly afterwards to concentrate on his Wall Street career.

1	**JEROME TRAVERS (a)**	76	72	73	76	297
	($Nil – amateur)					
2	Tom McNamara	78	71	74	75	298
3	Bob MacDonald	72	77	73	78	300
4=	Jim Barnes	71	75	76	79	301
	Louis Tellier	75	71	76	79	301
6	Mike Brady	76	71	75	80	302
7	George Low	78	74	76	75	303
8=	Jock Hutchison	74	79	76	76	305
	Fred McLeod	74	76	76	79	305
10=	Alex Campbell	76	75	74	81	306
	Emmett French	77	79	75	75	306
	Walter Hagen	78	73	76	79	306
	Tom Kerrigan	78	75	76	77	306
	Gilbert Nicholls	78	81	73	74	306
	Jack Park	77	77	75	77	306
	Wilfred Reid	77	78	75	76	306
	George Sargent	75	77	79	75	306
18	Charles Evans, Jr (a)	71	81	80	75	307
19=	James Donaldson	83	79	76	70	308
	Max Marston (a)	77	77	80	74	308
21	AJ Sanderson	77	76	77	79	309
22=	Jack Dowling	75	79	80	77	311
	Alex Smith	78	76	78	79	311
24=	HH Barker	77	78	80	77	312
	Charles Hoffner	79	79	79	75	312
26=	Joe Mitchell	76	80	74	83	313
	Herbert Strong	83	76	78	76	313
28	George Sayers	76	80	81	77	314
29=	Otto Hackbarth	80	75	79	81	315
	David Ogilvie	75	78	83	79	315
	Ben Sayers	80	79	79	77	315

Round Leader(s)
R1 Barnes, Evans; 71
R2 Barnes, Tellier; 146
R3 Travers; 221

Lowest Scores
R2 Brady, McNamara, Tellier; 71
R3 MacDonald, Nicholls, Travers; 73
R4 Donaldson; 70

BRITISH OPEN 1916

No Championship

US OPEN 1916

Minikahda Club, Minneapolis, Minnesota
(29–30 June)

6130 yards: Par 72 (288)

Chick Evans became the third amateur in four years to win. In doing so he shattered the record for 36 and 54 holes. There is no truth in the rumour that the then recently-formed PGA of America was inaugurated as a protectionist society, and that it wanted the upcoming PGA Championship closed to the pros in order to keep the amateurs out! Tom Vardon, brother of the illustrious Harry, attained his highest US Open position this year after several less-successful visits. Wilfred Reid finished fourth in his first US Open – much higher than in any British Open.

1	**CHARLES EVANS, Jr (a)**	70	69	74	73	286
	($Nil – amateur)					
2	Jock Hutchison	73	75	72	68	288
3	Jim Barnes	71	74	71	74	290
4=	Gilbert Nicholls	73	76	71	73	293
	Wilfred Reid	70	72	79	72	293
	George Sargent	75	71	72	75	293
7	Walter Hagen	73	76	75	71	295
8	Bob MacDonald	74	72	77	73	296
9=	Mike Brady	75	73	75	74	297
	JJ O'Brien	76	72	73	76	297
	Tom Vardon	76	72	75	74	297
12	Jack Dowling	71	76	75	76	298
13=	Walter Fovargue	76	74	74	75	299
	Louis Tellier	74	75	72	78	299
15=	Herbert Lagerblade	77	78	72	73	300
	Tom McNamara	75	79	73	73	300
	Robert Peebles	73	72	76	79	300
	JB Simpson	75	76	76	73	300
19=	Otto Hackbarth	77	80	69	75	301
	George McLean	77	76	74	74	301
21=	James Donaldson	79	75	75	73	302
	Joe Mitchell	75	75	76	76	302
	George Turnbull	83	73	72	74	302
24=	Bert Battell	76	75	75	77	303
	Arthur Fotheringham	78	78	74	73	303
	Fred McLeod	74	75	77	77	303
	George Simpson	76	76	77	74	303
28	Alex Campbell	75	75	75	79	304
29=	Alex Cunningham	79	75	75	77	306
	James Ferguson	74	75	80	77	306
	Tom Kerrigan	79	72	78	77	306

Round Leaders
R1 Evans, Reid; 70
R2 Evans; 139
R3 Evans; 213

Lowest Scores
R2 Evans; 69
R3 Hackbarth; 69
R4 Hutchison; 68

US PGA 1916

**Siwanoy Country Club, Bronxville, New York
(9–14 October)**

MATCHPLAY
32 qualifiers after 36 holes strokeplay
All Rounds 36 holes

Jim Barnes, an Englishman from Cornwall, became the first winner of the Rodman Wanamaker Trophy. The competition was based on the British PGA Championship sponsored by the *News of the World* newspaper – 36-hole matchplay – providing an alternative format for the pros which was already successfully operating in the British and US Amateur Championships. Jock Hutchison had the dubious honour of finishing second in both the year's Majors.

FINAL
JIM BARNES ($500) beat Jock Hutchison, 1up

Round by Round Details

ROUND 1 (Last 32)
Tom Kerrigan bt Charles Adams 6&4; George McLean bt Tom NacNamara 6&5; Alex Smith bt James Ferguson 4&2; JIM BARNES bt George Fotheringham 8&7; Willie MacFarlane bt Robert McNulty 10&9; Mike Brady bt James West 7&6; Emmett French bt Eddie Towns 3&1; Jack Dowling (bye); JJ O'Brien bt Wilfred Reid 1up; George Simpson bt Walter Fovargue 6&5; Bob MacDonald bt Jimmie Donaldson 3&2; Walter Hagen bt JR Thomson 7&6; JOCK HUTCHISON bt Joe Mitchell 11&9; W Brown bt F Clarkson (default); Cyril Walker bt Louis Tellier 4&2; Jack Hobens bt Mike Sherman (default)

ROUND 2 (Last 16)
Kerrigan bt McLean 2&1
BARNES bt Smith 8&7
MacFarlane bt Brady 3&2
Dowling bt French 1up (after 37)
O'Brien bt Simpson 3&2
Hagen bt MacDonald 3&2
HUTCHISON bt Brown 11&9
Walker bt Hobens 5&4

QUARTER FINAL (QF)
BARNES bt Kerrigan 3&1
MacFarlane bt Dowling 2&1
Hagen bt O'Brien 10&9
HUTCHISON bt Walker 5&4

SEMI FINAL (SF)
BARNES bt MacFarlane 6&5
HUTCHISON bt Hagen 2up

BRITISH OPEN 1917

No Championship

US OPEN 1917

No Championship

US PGA 1917

No Championship

BRITISH OPEN 1918

No Championship

US OPEN 1918

No Championship

US PGA 1918

No Championship

BRITISH OPEN 1919

No Championship

US OPEN 1919

Brae Burn Country Club, West Newton, Massachusetts
(9–12 June)

6925 yards: Par 72 (288)

The resurrection of the Majors after World War I saw many familiar faces returning to the golfing fray. Mike Brady, who lost in a play-off against John McDermott in 1911, suffered a similar fate at the hands of Walter Hagen this year. The 'Haig' closed a five-shot gap over the last round to tie.

1	**WALTER HAGEN***	78	73	75	75	301
	($500)					
2	Mike Brady	74	74	73	80	301
3=	Jock Hutchison	78	76	76	76	306
	Tom McNamara	80	73	79	74	306
5=	George McLean	81	75	76	76	308
	Louis Tellier	73	78	82	75	308
7	John Cowan	79	74	75	81	309
8	George Bowden	73	78	75	86	312
	Fred McLeod	78	77	79	78	312
10	Charles Evans, Jr (a)	77	76	82	78	313
11=	Jim Barnes	77	78	79	81	315
	Harry Hampton	79	81	77	78	315
13=	Clarence Hackney	83	78	81	74	316
	Charles Hoffner	72	78	77	89	316
	Isaac Mackie	82	75	78	81	316
16=	Gilbert Nicholls	81	78	82	77	318
	Alex Ross	77	78	77	86	318
18=	Pat Doyle	78	82	76	83	319
	Francis Ouimet (a)	76	79	79	85	319
	James West	79	82	80	78	319
21=	Alex Cunningham	79	81	79	81	320
	Douglas Edgar	80	78	82	80	320
	Wilfred Reid	82	78	80	80	320
24=	Jesse Guilford (a)	79	78	84	80	321
	J Sanderson	85	79	83	74	321
26=	Otto Hackbarth	77	79	82	84	322
	Tom Kerrigan	80	79	82	81	322
	Herbert Lagerblade	79	80	82	81	322
29=	George Fotheringham	81	82	79	81	323
	Bob MacDonald	81	78	80	84	323
	George Sargent	84	79	82	78	323

* Walter Hagen (77) beat Mike Brady (78) in the 18-Hole Play-off

Round Leaders
R1 Hoffner; 72
R2 Brady; 148
R3 Brady, 221

Lowest Scores
R2 Hoffner; 72
R3 Brady; 73
R4 Hackney, McNamara, Sanderson; 74

US PGA 1919

Engineers Country Club, Long Island, New York
(15–20 September)

MATCHPLAY
32 qualifiers after 36 holes strokeplay
All Rounds 36 holes

The hiatus caused by the War didn't stop Barnes from winning his second PGA title. He demolished 1908 US Open Champion Fred McLeod in the final. Apart from Tom Morris, Jr (1870 & 1872) he is the only champion in any Major to have won 'back-to-back' titles but not in successive years. 'Young' Tom did manage three in a row, though, before the British Open break in 1871.

FINAL
JIM BARNES ($500) beat Fred McLeod, 6&5

Round by Round Details

ROUND 1 (Last 32)
JIM BARNES bt Carl Anderson 8&6; Otto Hackbarth bt Joe Sylvester 5&4; Tom Kerrigan bt Bill Mehlhorn 3&2; Emmett French bt Clarence Hackney 7&6; Bob MacDonald bt Tom Boyd 1up; George Fotheringham bt Eddie Loos 8&6; Tom MacNamara bt Louis Martucci 7&6; Jock Hutchison bt John Bredemus 6&5; Harry Hampton bt Jack Hobens 7&6; Douglas Edgar bt Joe Rosman (default); FRED McLEOD bt James Rose 9&7; George Gordon bt Dave Wilson 3&2; Wilfred Reid bt Pat Doyle 1up; Jimmy West bt Willie Kidd (default); Mike Brady bt Louis Tellier 7&6; George McLean bt Johnny Farrell 7&6

ROUND 2 (Last 16)
BARNES bt Hackbarth 3&2
French bt Kerrigan 2up
MacDonald bt Fotheringham 2&1
Hutchison bt MacNamara 8&6
Edgar bt Hampton 5&4
McLEOD bt Gordon 2up
West bt Reid 2&1
McLean bt Brady 6&5

QUARTER FINAL (QF)
BARNES bt French 3&2
MacDonald bt Hutchison 3&2
McLeod bt Edgar 8&6
McLean bt West 9&7

SEMI FINAL (SF)
BARNES bt MacDonald 5&4
McLEOD bt McLean 3&2

BRITISH OPEN 1920

Royal Cinque Ports Golf Club, Deal, Kent, England
(30 June–1 July)
6653 yards

George Duncan's only Open win was extraordinary in its scoring. After shooting two successive 80s, he was 13 behind half-way leader Abe Mitchell, but then his final 36-holes took only 143, which had only previously been bettered by Jack White and James Braid at Sandwich in 1904. This was the second, but also the last, visit to Deal. Many of the pros found it geographically remote (SE England, when the centre of the British golfing universe was still north of the Border) and too close to Sandwich. The R&A took over the running of the Open from the host clubs and some rationalization ensued.

1	**GEORGE DUNCAN** (£75)	80	80	71	72	303
2	Sandy Herd	72	81	77	75	305
3	Ted Ray	72	83	78	73	306
4	Abe Mitchell	74	73	84	76	307
5	Len Holland	80	78	71	79	308
6	Jim Barnes	79	74	77	79	309
7=	Arthur Havers	80	78	81	74	313
	Sydney Wingate	81	74	76	82	313
9=	GR Buckle	80	80	77	78	315
	Archie Compston	79	83	75	78	315
	William Horne	80	81	73	81	315
12	JH Taylor	78	79	80	79	316
13	L Lafitte	75	85	84	73	317
14=	Eric Bannister	78	84	80	76	318
	Harry Vardon	78	81	81	78	318
16=	A Gaudin	81	82	77	79	319
	Charles Johns	82	78	81	78	319
	James Sherlock	82	81	80	76	319
	Philip Taylor	78	84	77	80	319
	Angel de la Torre	84	78	78	79	319
21=	James Braid	79	80	79	82	320
	William B Smith	81	81	77	81	320
	Dick Wheildon	82	78	83	77	320
	Reg Wilson	76	82	78	84	320
25	Cyril Hughes	83	81	80	77	321
26=	WI Hunter (a)	81	80	81	80	322
	Tom Williamson	77	86	79	80	322
28	C Ralph Smith	84	80	79	80	323
29=	Arthur Day	77	83	84	80	324
	Jean Gassiat	79	82	78	85	324
	D Grant (a)	83	76	82	83	324
	Fred Leach	83	82	78	81	324
	Arnaud Massy	81	82	80	81	324
	William Ritchie	79	86	81	78	324

Round Leader(s)
R1 Herd, Ray; 72
R2 Mitchell; 147
R3 Holland; 229

Lowest Scores
R2 Mitchell; 73
R3 Duncan, Holland; 71
R4 Duncan; 72

US OPEN 1920

Inverness Club, Toledo, Ohio
(12–13 August)
6569 yards: Par 72 (288)

Despite a chastening experience in 1913 Ted Ray was not deterred from trying his luck in the US Open one more time. He was 43 in 1920 and was to be the oldest winner of this championship until Ray Floyd, in 1986, then Hale Irwin, four years later, lifted the trophy. In his two visits he tied the lead and was outright winner. His travelling companion, Harry Vardon, was aged 50, and his three visits, spanning 21 years, saw this sequence of results: W, 2, 2. Reigning double PGA Champion, Jim Barnes matched his sixth place in the British Open. In one of those classic era-spanning fields, the likes of Vardon and Alex Ross (tied-27) upheld the honour of the older generation against Jones, Hagen and Sarazen (tied-30).

1	**TED RAY** ($500)	74	73	73	75	295
2=	Jack Burke, Sr	75	77	72	72	296
	Leo Diegel	72	74	73	77	296
	Jock Hutchison	69	76	74	77	296
	Harry Vardon	74	73	71	78	296
6=	Jim Barnes	76	70	76	76	298
	Charles Evans, Jr (a)	74	76	73	75	298
8=	Bobby Jones (a)	78	74	70	77	299
	Willie MacFarlane	76	75	74	74	299
10	Bob McDonald	73	78	71	78	300
11	Walter Hagen	74	73	77	77	301
12	Clarence Hackney	78	74	74	76	302
13	Fred McLeod	75	77	73	79	304
14=	Mike Brady	77	76	74	78	305
	Frank McNamara	78	77	76	74	305
	Charles Rowe	76	78	77	74	305
17=	Laurie Ayton, Sr	75	78	76	77	306
	John Golden	77	80	74	75	306
	Eddie Loos	75	74	73	84	306
20=	Douglas Edgar	73	82	74	78	307
	James West	80	77	75	75	307
22	Harry Hampton	79	76	74	79	308
23=	Tom Kerrigan	77	81	74	77	309
	Gilbert Nicholls	77	82	75	75	309
	JJ O'Brien	82	77	73	77	309
	DK White	78	75	79	77	309
27=	Bill Mehlhorn	78	74	79	79	310
	Peter O'Hara	84	74	74	78	310
	Alex Ross	80	76	77	77	310
30=	George Bowden	74	80	76	81	311
	Charles Hall	77	80	76	78	311
	Willie Kidd	77	81	76	77	311
	George McLean	83	76	73	79	311
	Gene Sarazen	79	79	76	77	311

Round Leaders
R1 Hutchison; 69
R2 Hutchison; 145
R3 Vardon; 218

Lowest Scores
R2 Barnes; 70
R3 Jones; 70
R4 Burke; 72

US PGA 1920

Flossmoor Country Club, Chicago, Illinois
(17–21 August)

MATCHPLAY
32 qualifiers after 36 holes strokeplay
All Rounds 36 holes

Jim Barnes, despite challenging for the other Majors this year, crashed out in Round Two, ending a streak of 11 wins. The final was fought between St Andrews-born Jock Hutchison and JD (Douglas) Edgar of Northumberland, England. Hutchison won to make up for his defeat in the 1916 final. Although never in contention for the British Open, Edgar had taken America by storm when he emigrated in 1918. He beat a high-class field by 16 strokes to win the Canadian Open; was ahead of his time in preaching golfing techniques; and induced such luminaries as Harry Vardon and Tommy Armour to rate him among the very best. He died, in mysterious circumstances, the following year in Atlanta, aged 37.

FINAL
JOCK HUTCHISON ($500) beat Douglas Edgar, 1up

Round by Round Details

ROUND 1 (Last 32)
Alex Cunningham bt Willie MacFarlane 2&1; Peter O'Hara bt Pat Doyle 1up; George McLean bt George Sayers 6&5; Tom Kennett bt Otto Hackbarth 3&1; DOUGLAS EDGAR bt Pat O'Hara 1up; Joe Sylvester bt Tom Boyd 4&3; Bob MacDonald bt Leo Diegel 4&3; Bill Mehlhorn bt Wallie Nelson 3&2; Harry Hampton bt Jack Gordon 6&5; George Thompson bt Isaac Mackie 3&2; Clarence Hackney bt Phil Hesler 3&2; Jim Barnes bt George Bowden 4&3; Charles Mayo bt Lloyd Gullickson 2&1; Louis Tellier bt Joe Rosman 10&9; Laurie Ayton, Sr bt Charles Hoffner 1up (after 39); JOCK HUTCHISON bt Eddie Loos 5&3

ROUND 2 (Last 16)
Peter O'Hara bt Cunningham 5&4
Mclean bt Kennett 2&1
EDGAR bt Sylvester 11&9
MacDonald bt Mehlhorn 1up
Hampton bt Thompson 5&4
Hackney bt Barnes 5&4
Tellier bt Mayo 4&2
HUTCHISON bt Ayton 5&3

QUARTER FINAL (QF)
McLean bt O'Hara 1up (after 38)
EDGAR bt MacDonald 5&4
Hampton bt Hackney 4&3
HUTCHISON bt Tellier 6&5

SEMI FINAL (SF)
EDGAR bt McLean 8&7
HUTCHISON bt Hampton 4&3

BRITISH OPEN 1921

Royal & Ancient Golf Club, St Andrews, Fife, Scotland
(23–25 June)
6487 yds

Jock Hutchison won the Open on the back of the 1920 US PGA Championship. His homecoming resulted in the first win for an American golfer – albeit one who was Scottish born. Hutchison, the amateur, Wethered, and Kerrigan, were all inside James Braid's 1910 St Andrews record, with Hutchison's last round 70 also a record course low in the Championship. Four Americans in the Top 10 signified that the invasion was about to begin.

1	**JOCK HUTCHISON*** (£75)	72	75	79	70	296
2	Roger Wethered (a)	78	75	72	71	296
3	Tom Kerrigan	74	80	72	72	298
4	Arthur Havers	76	74	77	72	299
5	George Duncan	74	75	78	74	301
6=	Jim Barnes	74	74	74	80	302
	Walter Hagen	74	79	72	77	302
	Sandy Herd	75	74	73	80	302
	Joe Kirkwood, Sr	76	74	73	79	302
	Fred Leach	78	75	76	73	302
	Arnaud Massy	74	75	74	79	302
	Tom Williamson	79	71	74	78	302
13=	Abe Mitchell	78	79	76	71	304
	W Pursey	74	82	74	74	304
15	JW Gaudin	78	76	75	76	305
16=	James Braid	77	75	78	76	306
	Len Holland	78	78	76	74	306
	Bill Mehlhorn	75	77	76	78	306
19=	Frank Ball	79	78	74	76	307
	P Hunter (a)	75	78	76	78	307
	Ted Ray	76	72	81	78	307
	William Watt	81	77	75	74	307
23=	Clarence Hackney	77	75	80	76	308
	Henry Kinch	73	77	81	77	308
	Harry Vardon	77	77	80	74	308
26=	Aubrey Boomer	78	80	72	79	309
	Walter Bourne	78	78	75	78	309
	Arthur Butchart	78	80	77	74	309
	Douglas Edgar	82	76	78	73	309
	Emmett French	79	76	75	79	309
	DH Kyle (a)	77	77	81	74	309
	George McLean	76	73	82	78	309
	Hugh Roberts	79	82	74	74	309
	JH Taylor	80	80	75	74	309

* Jock Hutchison (150) beat Roger Wethered (159) in the 36-Hole Play-off

Round Leader(s)
R1 Hutchison; 72
R2 Hutchison; 147
R3 Barnes, Herd; 222

Lowest Scores
R2 Williamson; 71
R3 Boomer, Hagen, Kerrigan, Wethered; 72
R4 Hutchison; 70

US OPEN 1921

Columbia Country Club, Chevy Chase, Maryland
(21–22 July)
6380 yards: Par 70 (280)

Jim Barnes won his third Major in collecting the US Open Championship for the only time. He increased his lead with every round and stretched away to win by nine shots – but still two short of Willie Smith's 1899 record. It was still the greatest margin of victory in the Open in the 20th century. In any Major it has only been bettered by Tiger Woods (15 strokes in the US Open at Pebble Beach in 2000) and Old Tom Morris in 1862, and equalled twice (Young Tommy in 1870 and Woods in his first Masters win in 1997).

1	**JIM BARNES** ($500)	69	75	73	72	289
2=	Walter Hagen	79	73	72	74	298
	Fred McLeod	74	74	76	74	298
4	Charles Evans, Jr (a)	73	78	76	75	302
5=	Emmett French	75	77	74	77	303
	Bobby Jones (a)	78	71	77	77	303
	Alex Smith	75	75	79	74	303
8=	George Duncan	72	78	78	77	305
	Clarence Hackney	74	76	78	77	305
10	Emil Loeffler	74	77	74	81	306
11	Alfred Hackbarth	80	76	82	69	307
12	Eddie Loos	76	79	75	78	308
13	Cyril Walker	78	76	76	79	309
14=	Mike Brady	77	80	78	75	310
	Jess Sweetser (a)	78	78	77	77	310
	Louis Tellier	76	74	78	82	310
17	Gene Sarazen	83	74	77	77	311
18=	Laurie Ayton, Sr	81	74	74	83	312
	Jock Hutchison	75	83	77	77	312
	Peter O'Hara	81	82	76	73	312
21	Charles Murray	75	73	82	83	313
22=	John Golden	77	77	82	78	314
	Otto Hackbarth	79	76	80	79	314
	Harry Hampton	80	78	79	77	314
	Charles Mothersole	81	78	79	76	314
26=	Tom Boyd	81	79	79	76	315
	Bobby Cruickshank	75	77	80	83	315
	Leo Diegel	75	82	83	75	315
	Jesse Guilford (a)	79	75	78	83	315
30=	PO Hart	83	80	76	77	316
	Pat O'Hara	77	78	79	82	316

Round Leader(s)
R1   Barnes; 69
R2   Barnes; 144
R3   Barnes; 217

Lowest Scores
R2   Jones; 71
R3   Hagen; 72
R4   A Hackbarth; 69

US PGA 1921

Inwood Country Club, New Rockaway, New York
(26 September–1 October)

MATCHPLAY
Top 31 PGA available finishers in the 1921 US Open & defending champion (Jock Hutchison)
All Rounds 36 holes

Inwood CC was to become the first host to two different Majors when it would welcome the US Open in 1923. Hagen's first matchplay Major win prefaced a phenomenal run in the middle of the decade. British Open Champion and defending PGA Champion, Jock Hutchison, was beaten in the second round by a 19 year-old New York Italian – a certain Eugene Saraceni, who had just changed his name (although he was probably not yet known as the 'Squire').

FINAL
WALTER HAGEN ($500) beat Jim Barnes, 3&2
Round by Round Details

ROUND 1 (Last 32)
Fred McLeod bt Fred Canausa 1up (after 37); Jack Gordon bt Bill Leach 8&7; Bobby Cruickshank bt Charlie Thom 4&3; JIM BARNES bt Clarence Hackney 3&2; George McLean bt Tom Kerrigan 2&1; Jimmy West bt Jack Pirie 1up (after 37); Charles Clarke bt Peter O'Hara 1up; Emmett French bt Joe Sylvester 8&7; Cyril Walker bt Emil Loeffler 1up (after 37); Charles Mothersole bt Johnny Farrell 1up (after 40); Gene Sarazen bt Harry Hampton 4&3; Jock Hutchison bt Pat O'Hara 1up (after 39); Tom Boyd bt Eddie Towns (default); WALTER HAGEN bt Jack Forrester 6&4; Laurie Ayton, Sr bt TJ Rajoppi 7&6; John Golden bt Robert Barnett 5&3

ROUND 2 (Last 16)
McLeod bt Gordon 4&2
BARNES bt Cruickshank 8&7
McLean bt West 8&7
French bt Clarke 8&7
Walker bt Mothersole 4&2
Sarazen bt Hutchison 8&7
HAGEN bt Boyd 6&5
Golden bt Ayton 1up

QUARTER FINAL (QF)
BARNES bt McLeod 11&9
French bt McLean 5&3
Walker bt Sarazen 5&4
HAGEN bt Golden 8&7

SEMI FINAL (SF)
BARNES bt French 5&4
HAGEN bt Walker 5&4

BRITISH OPEN 1922

Royal St George's Golf Club, Sandwich, Kent, England
(22–23 June)
6616 yards

Hagen's win meant he became the first person to take all three Majors. The Open at Sandwich was his fourth Major in a career haul of 11 – second only in the all-time lists after Jack Nicklaus – and all were achieved in the pre-Masters era.

1	**WALTER HAGEN** (£75)	76	73	79	72	300
2=	Jim Barnes	75	76	77	73	301
	George Duncan	76	75	81	69	301
4	Jock Hutchison	79	74	73	76	302
5	Charles Whitcombe	77	79	72	75	303
6	JH Taylor	73	78	76	77	304
7	Jean Gassiat	75	78	74	79	306
8=	Harry Vardon	79	79	74	75	307
	Thomas Walton	75	78	77	77	307
10	Percy Alliss	75	78	78	77	308
11	Charles Johns	78	76	80	75	309
12=	George Gadd	76	81	76	77	310
	Arthur Havers	78	80	78	74	310
	Len Holland	79	81	74	76	310
	FC Jewell	75	80	78	77	310
	Ernest R Whitcombe	77	78	77	78	310
17=	Aubrey Boomer	75	80	76	80	311
	Dick Wheildon	80	80	76	75	311
18	Abe Mitchell	79	79	78	76	312
19=	Joe Kirkwood, Sr	79	76	80	78	313
	Herbert Osborne	80	81	76	76	313
	Michael Scott (a)	77	83	79	74	313
22=	Willie Hunter, Jr (a)	77	81	75	81	314
	Tom King, Sr	83	78	78	75	314
	W Pursey	77	81	80	76	314
	William B Smith	81	78	74	81	314
26	Archie Compston	81	79	75	80	315
27=	Gus Faulkner	74	81	80	81	316
	Arthur Monk	80	78	78	80	316
	William Watt	82	78	79	77	316
	Tom Williamson	83	77	75	81	316

Round Leaders
R1 Ted Ray (46), Taylor; 73
R2 Hagen; 149
R3 Hutchison; 226

Lowest Scores
R2 Hagen; 73
R3 Whitcombe; 72
R4 Duncan; 69

US OPEN 1922

Skokie Country Club, Glencoe, Illinois
(14–15 July)
6563 yards: Par 70 (280)

Gene Sarazen's long and glittering Majors career really began here at Skokie CC. His final round 68 took him from fifth place and four shots adrift after Round Three, to his first Open title. Little-known Scottish emigrant, John Black, needed two pars to tie and didn't get them. British Open Champion, Walter Hagen, threatened with a record-equalling 68 in Round One and was in the hunt until the last few holes. Admission was charged for the first time.

1	**GENE SARAZEN** ($500)	72	73	75	68	288
2=	John Black	71	71	75	72	289
	Bobby Jones (a)	74	72	70	73	289
4	Bill Mehlhorn	73	71	72	74	290
5	Walter Hagen	68	77	74	72	291
6	George Duncan	76	73	75	72	296
7	Leo Diegel	77	76	73	71	297
8=	Mike Brady	73	75	74	76	298
	John Golden	73	77	77	71	298
	Jock Hutchison	78	74	71	75	298
11=	Laurie Ayton, Sr	72	76	78	73	299
	Johnny Farrell	73	76	75	75	299
13=	Joe Kirkwood, Sr	77	74	75	74	300
	Bob MacDonald	73	76	75	76	300
15	Eddie Loos	75	76	73	77	301
16	Charles Evans, Jr (a)	72	76	74	80	302
17=	George Hackney	74	78	74	77	303
	Abe Mitchell	79	75	76	73	303
19=	Emmett French	76	74	77	78	305
	Jesse Guilford (a)	74	77	76	78	305
	Harry Hampton	76	75	77	77	305
	Charles Hoffner	79	76	77	73	305
	Willie Ogg	79	72	78	76	305
24=	Jim Barnes	74	75	77	80	306
	Cyril Hughes	81	74	77	74	306
	Willie Hunter Jr (a)	75	75	76	80	306
	Fred Wright Jr (a)	76	77	73	80	306
28=	Jack Burke, Sr	76	77	81	73	307
	Bobby Cruickshank	82	74	74	77	307
	Lloyd Gullickson	77	70	83	77	307

Round Leader(s)
R1 Hagen; 68
R2 Black; 142
R3 Jones, Mehlhorn; 216

Lowest Scores
R2 Gullickson; 70
R3 Jones; 70
R4 Sarazen; 68

US PGA 1922

Oakmont Country Club, Oakmont, Pennsylvania
(12–18 August)

MATCHPLAY
64 qualifiers from strokeplay
Rs 1&2, 18 holes; QF, SF, F, 36 holes

Although both Jock Hutchison and Walter Hagen had been reigning PGA Champions when they respectively won the 1921 and 1922 British Opens, Gene Sarazen was the first to win two Majors in the same season. He was made US Open Champion only a month earlier. Hagen missed his opportunity due to other engagements.

FINAL
GENE SARAZEN ($500) beat Emmett French, 1up

Round by Round Details

ROUND 2 (Last 32)
Francis Gallett bt Fred Brand 5&4; Bobby Cruickshank bt Al Watrous 3&2; Jack Burgess bt Peter Walsh 3&2; Charles Rowe bt Tom Boyd 3&1; Frank Sprogell bt Dan Kenny 4&3; GENE SARAZEN bt Willie Ogg 2&1; Jock Hutchison bt Dan Goss 6&4; Harry Hampton bt Charles Hoffner 3&2; Tom Kerrigan bt Charles Hilgendorf 5&4; Johnny Farrell bt Jim Barnes 1up; John Golden bt PJ Gaudin 8&7; Al Ciuci bt George Stark 4&2; Emil Loeffler bt Dave Robertson 4&3; Eddie Towns bt Matt Duffy 1up; RS Miner bt Fred Baroni 1up (after 19); EMMETT FRENCH bt Mike Brady 3&1

ROUND 3 (Last 16)
Cruickshank bt Gallett 7&6
Rowe bt Burgess 6&5
SARAZEN bt Sprogell 9&7
Hutchison bt Hampton 4&3
Kerrigan bt Farrell 4&3
Golden bt Ciuci 3&2
Loeffler bt Towns 3&1
FRENCH by Miner 8&7

QUARTER FINAL (QF)
Cruickshank bt Rowe 3&2
SARAZEN bt Hutchison 3&1
Golden bt Kerrigan 4&3
FRENCH bt Loeffler 4&2

SEMI FINAL (SF)
SARAZEN bt Cruickshank 3&2
FRENCH bt Golden 8&7

BRITISH OPEN 1923

Troon Golf Club, Ayrshire, Scotland
(14–15 June)
6415 yards

For Royal Cinque Ports, read the-not-yet 'Royal' Troon. Troon, along with Royal Lytham in 1925 and Carnoustie in 1931 pulled the Open's centre of gravity further north again, with Sandwich henceforward being the only Open host site in southern England. 20 year-old Arthur Havers held off a clutch of mighty Americans to be the last English winner until Henry Cotton's first win in 1934.

1	**ARTHUR HAVERS**	73	73	73	76	295
	(£75)					
2	Walter Hagen	76	71	74	75	296
3	Macdonald Smith	80	73	69	75	297
4	Joe Kirkwood, Sr	72	79	69	78	298
5	Tom Fernie	73	78	74	75	300
6=	George Duncan	79	75	74	74	302
	Charles Whitcombe	70	76	74	82	302
8=	Herbert Jolly	79	75	75	74	303
	JH Mackenzie	76	78	74	75	303
	Abe Mitchell	77	77	72	77	303
	William Watt	76	77	72	78	303
12=	Gordon Lockhart	78	71	76	79	304
	Ted Ray	79	75	73	77	304
	Tom Williamson	79	78	73	74	304
	Sydney Wingate	80	75	74	75	304
16=	Frank Ball	76	77	77	75	305
	Tom Barber	78	80	76	71	305
	Fred Collins	76	78	72	79	305
19=	Johnny Farrell	79	73	75	79	306
	Angel de la Torre	78	80	74	74	306
	Thomas Walton	77	74	78	77	306
22=	Sid Brews	77	76	72	82	307
	Sandy Herd	82	75	74	76	307
	R Scott, Jr (a)	74	76	79	78	307
25=	Leo Diegel	80	80	73	75	308
	Len Holland	81	75	73	79	308
	FC Jewell	80	78	70	80	308
	James Ockenden	78	79	75	76	308
29=	George Gadd	78	76	79	76	309
	JW Gaudin	80	79	76	74	309
	Fred Robson	82	78	74	75	309
	Reg Wilson	78	77	75	79	309

Round Leader(s)
R1 Whitcombe; 70
R2 Havers, Whitcombe; 146
R3 Havers; 219

Lowest Scores
R2 Hagen, Lockhart; 71
R3 Kirkwood, Smith; 69
R4 Barber; 71

US OPEN 1923

Inwood Country Club, Inwood, New York,
(13–15 July)

6532 yards: Par 72 (288)

Robert Tyre Jones, Jr – Bobby Jones – one of the very few immortals of golf, won the first of his seven open Majors at Inwood. He was virtually retired before the Masters era he was instrumental in creating, and was, as an amateur, excluded from the PGA; so all his Majors were Opens (four US and three British). At that time, the Amateur Championships were considered 'Majors' too, and Jones collected five US and one British. Some archivists therefore have Jones with 13 Majors: and all this between 1923 and 1930. Wee Bobby Cruickshank was one of the greatest players never to win a Major – so there is some irony in his losing to Jones in a play-off for the latter's first of many titles.

1	**BOBBY JONES* (a)**	71	73	76	76	296
	($Nil – amateur)					
2	Bobby Cruickshank	73	72	78	73	296
3	Jock Hutchison	70	72	82	78	302
4	Jack Forrester	75	73	77	78	303
5=	Johnny Farrell	76	77	75	76	304
	Francis Gallett	76	72	77	79	304
	WM Reekie (a)	80	74	75	75	304
8=	Leo Diegel	77	77	76	76	306
	Bill Mehlhorn	73	79	75	79	306
	Al Watrous	74	75	76	81	306
11	Cyril Hughes	74	76	80	77	307
12=	Jim Barnes	78	81	74	75	308
	Joe Kirkwood, Sr	77	77	79	75	308
14=	Charles Evans, Jr (a)	79	80	76	74	309
	Joe Turnesa	76	81	74	78	309
16=	Charles Mothersole	77	80	71	82	310
	Gene Sarazen	79	78	73	80	310
18=	Walter Hagen	77	75	73	86	311
	Willie Ogg	74	76	80	81	311
20=	Mike Brady	74	81	76	81	312
	Macdonald Smith	77	76	81	78	312
22	Emmett French	79	78	77	79	313
23	Cyril Walker	76	78	80	80	314
24=	PO Hart	79	80	78	78	315
	Joe Sylvester	77	80	79	79	315
26=	John Black	82	76	78	80	316
	William Creavy	73	81	77	85	316
	Eddie Held (a)	80	75	79	82	316
29=	Hutt Martin	78	78	76	85	317
	Francis Ouimet (a)	82	75	78	82	317
	George Sargent	77	77	81	82	317

* Bobby Jones (76) beat Bobby Cruickshank (78) in the 18-Hole Play-off

Round Leader(s)
R1   Hutchison; 70
R2   Hutchison; 142
R3   Jones; 220

Lowest Scores
R2   Cruickshank, Gallett, Hutchison; 72
R3   Mothersole; 71
R4   Cruickshank; 73

US PGA 1923

Pelham Golf Club, Pelham Manor, New York
(23–29 September)

MATCHPLAY
64 qualifiers from strokeplay
All Rounds 36 holes

Sarazen made it two PGA wins in a row, but this time Hagen was there to compete. The two met in the final, and their gargantuan battle only ended at the second extra hole. Hagen had clawed back three strokes on the final back nine to take it to sudden-death and must have thought he'd won when Sarazen's tee-shot at the 38th ended up in thick rough. Sarazen, however, hacked out to within two feet of the pin, while an amazed Hagen bunkered his approach.

FINAL
GENE SARAZEN ($ not available) beat Walter Hagen, 1up (after 38)

Round by Round Details

ROUND 2 (Last 32)
Bobby Cruickshank bt Herbert Obendorf 7&5; Ray Derr bt Frank Coltart 5&4; Willie MacFarlane bt Wilfred Reid 3&2; Jack Stait bt Jack Forrester 1up; Jim Barnes bt John Cowan 12&11; Cyril Walker bt Harry Cooper 2&1; Alex Campbell bt Willie Klein 4&3; GENE SARAZEN bt DK White 11&10; Clarence Hackney bt RS Miner 7&6; Fred McLeod bt James Meehan 4&3; WALTER HAGEN bt Jack Elpick 10&9; John Golden bt Robert Barnett 1up; Joe Kirkwood, Sr bt Jimmy West 2up; Johnny Farrell bt Willie Hunter, Jr 4&3; George McLean bt Jimmie Donaldson 6&4; Willie Ogg bt Carl Anderson 12&11

ROUND 3 (Last 16)
Cruickshank bt Derr 1up
MacFarlane bt Stait 5&4
Barnes bt Walker 8&7
SARAZEN bt Campbell 3&2
McLeod bt Hackney 1up
HAGEN bt Golden 4&3
Kirkwood bt Farrell 1up
McLean bt Ogg 1up (after 38)

QUARTER FINAL (QF)
Cruickshank bt MacFarlane 1up (after 39)
SARAZEN bt Barnes 1up
HAGEN bt Mcleod 5&4
McLean bt Kirkwood 5&4

SEMI FINAL (SF)
SARAZEN bt Cruickshank 6&5
HAGEN bt McLean 12&11

US OPEN 1924

Oakland Hill Country Club, Birmingham, Michigan
(5–6 June)
6880 yards: Par 72 (288)

Regional qualifying (East and West) took place for the first time with the lowest 40 and ties making it to Round One. Another 'first' was that steel-shafted putters were allowed. Oakland Hills, at nearly 6900 yards, was the longest course yet used for a Major, and not far short of some of the modern-day monsters. Cyril Walker was the rather surprising winner, his past form in the British Open before he emigrated not suggesting he could best a field which included the likes of Hagen, Jones, Sarazen and Mac Smith.

1	**CYRIL WALKER** ($500)	74	74	74	75	297
2	Bobby Jones (a)	74	73	75	78	300
3	Bill Mehlhorn	72	75	76	78	301
4=	Bobby Cruickshank	77	72	76	78	303
	Walter Hagen	75	75	76	77	303
	Macdonald Smith	78	72	77	76	303
7=	Abe Espinosa	80	71	77	77	305
	Peter O'Hara	76	79	74	76	305
9	Mike Brady	75	77	77	77	306
10=	Charles Evans, Jr (a)	77	77	76	77	307
	Eddie Loos	73	81	75	78	307
	Dave Robertson	73	76	77	81	307
13=	Tommy Armour	78	76	75	80	309
	Clarence Hackney	81	72	78	78	309
15=	Willie Ogg	75	80	76	79	310
	Joe Turnesa	76	78	78	78	310
17=	Walter Bourne	78	76	79	80	313
	Gene Sarazen	74	80	80	79	313
19=	Johnny Farrell	79	76	77	82	314
	Tom Kerrigan	77	74	89	74	314
	Jock Rogers	82	77	77	78	314
22=	Emmett French	79	79	78	79	315
	Joe Kirkwood, Sr	77	80	80	78	315
	James West	81	72	78	84	315
25=	Laurie Ayton, Sr	77	79	84	86	316
	Leo Diegel	78	78	82	78	316
	John Golden	75	83	78	80	316
25=	Jack Stait	79	77	81	79	316
29=	Wiffy Cox	82	76	81	78	317
	Jesse Guilford (a)	80	78	79	80	317

Round Leader(s)
R1 Mehlhorn; 72
R2 Jones, Mehlhorn; 147
R3 Jones, Walker; 222

Lowest Scores
R2 Espinosa; 71
R3 Jock Hutchison (31), O'Hara, Walker; 74
R4 Kerrigan; 74

BRITISH OPEN 1924

Royal Liverpool Golf Club, Hoylake, Cheshire, England
(26–27 June)
6750 yards

Hagen's second Open out of four he was to claim during the '20s was a tight affair. In a high-scoring last round he edged out Ernest Whitcombe – one of the three famous golfing brothers. Bobby Jones didn't compete – and it is worth considering that for all Hagen's successes in the Opens, he never once won when Jones was in the field.

1	**WALTER HAGEN** (£75)	77	73	74	77	301
2	Ernest R Whitcombe	77	70	77	78	302
3=	Frank Ball	78	75	74	77	304
	Macdonald Smith	76	74	77	77	304
5	JH Taylor	75	74	79	79	307
6=	Aubrey Boomer	75	78	76	79	308
	George Duncan	74	79	74	81	308
	Len Holland	74	78	78	78	308
9=	JM Barber	78	77	79	75	309
	George Gadd	79	75	78	77	309
	James Sherlock	76	75	78	80	309
	Percy Weston	76	77	77	79	309
13=	Sandy Herd	76	79	76	79	310
	Gilbert Nicholls	75	78	79	78	310
	Tom Williamson	79	76	80	75	310
16=	JW Gaudin	79	78	80	76	313
	Charles Johns	77	77	78	81	313
18=	James Braid	80	80	78	76	314
	Albert Tingey, Jr	82	81	76	75	314
	Cyril Tolley (a)	73	82	80	79	314
21=	Archie Compston	79	81	76	79	315
	BS Weastell	76	82	78	79	315
23=	Arthur Butchart	82	75	77	82	316
	Rowland Jones	80	73	82	81	316
	Fred Leach	78	74	86	78	316
	William Robertson	84	75	77	80	316
	Fred Robson	83	80	77	76	316
	Sydney Wingate	79	79	82	76	316
29=	Arthur Havers	79	77	86	75	317
	Mark Seymour	74	81	80	82	317

Round Leader(s)
R1 Tolley; 73
R2 Whitcombe; 147
R3 Hagen, Whitcombe; 224

Lowest Scores
R2 Whitcombe; 70
R3 Ball, Duncan, Hagen; 74
R4 Barber, Havers, HJ Osborne (31), Tingey, Williamson; 75

US PGA 1924

French Lick Springs, French Lick, Indiana
(15–20 September)

MATCHPLAY
32 qualifiers after 36 holes strokeplay
(Low – Johnny Farrell, 140)
All Rounds 36 holes

It was Hagen's turn again, in a repeat of the 1921 final. He became the first golfer to hold the British Open and one other Major in the same season, and his win record in Majors between 1919 and 1929 is formidable: 1919, US Open; 1921, PGA; 1922, B Open; 1924, B Open & PGA; 1925, PGA; 1926, PGA; 1927, PGA; 1928, B Open; 1929, B Open.

FINAL
WALTER HAGEN ($ not available)
beat Jim Barnes, 2up

Round by Round Details

ROUND 1 (Last 32)
Willie MacFarlane bt George Dow 5&4; Johnny Farrell bt Neil Christian 2&1; Al Watrous bt George Aulbach 3&1; WALTER HAGEN bt Tom Harmon, Jr 6&5; Al Espinosa bt Arthur Ham 4&2; Francis Gallett bt Bill Mehlhorn 4&3; Bobby Cruickshank bt Willie Ogg 7&5; Ray Derr bt Harry Hampton 2up; Henry Ciuci bt Charles Hoffner 4&2; Dan Williams bt Fred Baroni 4&2; Gene Sarazen bt Fred McLeod 5&4; Larry Nabholtz bt Jack Forrester 1up; Mortie Dutra bt Leo Diegel 3&1; Emmett French bt Jock Robertson 6&4; Jim Barnes bt Mike Brady 1up (after 39); Eddie Towns bt Jock Hutchison 4&3

ROUND 2 (Last 16)
Farrell bt MacFarlane 2&1
HAGEN bt Watrous 4&3
Espinosa bt Gallett 4&3
Derr br Cruickshank 2&1
Ciuci bt Williams 4&3
Nabholtz bt Sarazen 2&1
French bt Dutra 3&1
BARNES bt Towns 10&9

QUARTER FINAL (QF)
HAGEN bt Farrell 3&2
Derr bt Espinosa 2&1
Nabholtz bt Ciuci 5&4
BARNES bt French 6&4

SEMI FINAL (SF)
HAGEN bt Derr 8&7
BARNES bt Nabholtz 1up

US OPEN 1925

Worcester Country Club, Worcester, Massachusetts
(3–5 June)
6430 yards: Par 71 (284)

The era of Scottish-born US Open Champions, and indeed Major winners in general, was just coming to an end. Willie MacFarlane, from Aberdeen, tied with Bob Jones – and tied again on 75 in the first 18-hole play-off. Jones uncharacteristically threw away a four-stroke lead in the second play-off, to allow MacFarlane come home in 72, and beat him by one. Earlier, in Round Two, MacFarlane set a new low score of 67.

1	**WILLIE MacFARLANE***($500)	74	67	72	78	291
2	Bobby Jones (a)	77	70	70	74	291
3=	Johnny Farrell	71	74	69	78	292
	Francis Ouimet (a)	70	73	73	76	292
5=	Walter Hagen	72	76	71	74	293
	Gene Sarazen	72	72	75	74	293
7	Mike Brady	74	72	74	74	294
8	Leo Diegel	73	68	77	78	296
9=	Laurie Ayton, Sr	75	71	73	78	297
	Al Espinosa	72	71	74	80	297
11=	Macdonald Smith	73	79	72	75	299
	Joe Turnesa	76	74	71	78	299
13=	Willie Hunter, Jr	75	77	75	73	300
	Al Watrous	78	73	74	75	300
15=	Bob MacDonald	75	77	77	72	301
	Bill Mehlhorn	78	72	75	76	301
17	Clarence Hackney	78	72	73	79	302
18=	John Golden	76	75	82	70	303
	Tom Kerrigan	75	79	74	75	303
20=	Tom Boyd	73	79	75	77	304
	Jack Forrester	71	76	76	81	304
	Emmett French	77	74	77	76	304
	Francis Gallett	73	70	84	77	304
	Harry Hampton	79	75	76	74	304
	Bob Shave	81	72	77	74	304
26	Charles Mayo	75	74	78	78	305
27=	Jock Hutchison	78	78	79	71	306
	Wilfred Reid	79	75	73	79	306
29=	Jim Barnes	75	76	71	85	307
	George Heron	75	77	77	78	307

* Willie MacFarlane (75,72) beat Bobby Jones (75, 73) after the Second 18-Hole Play-off

Round Leader(s)
R1   Ouimet; 70
R2   MacFarlane; 141
R3   MacFarlane; 213

Lowest Scores
R2   MacFarlane; 67
R3   Farrell; 69
R4   Golden; 70

BRITISH OPEN 1925

Prestwick Golf Club, Ayrshire, Scotland
(25–26 June)
6444 yds

Jim Barnes took his fourth Major title – he had already won the first two PGAs (1916 & 1919) and collected the US Open in 1921. He thus followed Walter Hagen's feat of winning all the contemporary Major Championships. Barnes' win, ahead of 48 year-old Ted Ray and rising British hope, Compston, was in the 23rd and last Open to be played at historic Prestwick. Of the 13 Championships held there between 1860 and 1875, the Morrisses and Willie Park had won a dozen. By 1925, the Ayrshire links, having far too many blind shots for the modern sophisticated golfer, had become a Majors dinosaur.

1	**JIM BARNES**	70	77	79	74	300
	(75)					
2=	Archie Compston	76	75	75	75	301
	Ted Ray	77	76	75	73	301
4	Macdonald Smith	76	69	76	82	303
5	Abe Mitchell	77	76	75	77	305
6=	Percy Alliss	77	80	77	76	310
	Bill Davies	76	76	80	78	310
	JW Gaudin	78	81	77	74	310
	JH Taylor	74	79	80	77	310
	Sydney Wingate	74	78	80	78	310
11=	Robert Harris (a)	75	81	78	77	311
	Fred Robson	80	77	78	76	311
13	HA Gaudin	76	79	77	80	312
14=	Tom Fernie	78	74	77	85	314
	Sandy Herd	76	79	82	77	314
	Joe Kirkwood, Sr	83	79	76	76	314
17=	JI Cruickshank (a)	80	78	82	75	315
	Jack Smith	75	78	82	80	315
	Harry Vardon	79	80	77	79	315
20=	Arthur Havers	77	80	80	79	316
	Duncan McCulloch	76	77	84	79	316
	James Ockenden	80	78	80	78	316
	Reg Whitcombe	81	80	79	76	316
24=	Frank Ball	76	78	81	82	317
	Dick May	82	77	78	80	317
26=	Aubrey Boomer	79	82	76	81	318
	Ernest R Whitcombe	81	83	77	77	318
28=	James Adwick	81	77	82	80	320
	George Duncan	79	77	83	81	320
	Cedric Sayner	83	80	78	79	320
	Cyril Tolley (a)	82	81	78	79	320

Round Leader(s)
R1 Barnes; 70
R2 M Smith; 145
R3 M Smith; 221

Lowest Scores
R2 M Smith; 69
R3 Compston, Mitchell, Ray; 75
R4 Ray; 73

US PGA 1925

Olympia Fields CC, Matteson, Illinois
(21–26 September)

MATCHPLAY
32 qualifiers after 36 holes strokeplay
(Low – Al Watrous, 140)
All Rounds 36 holes

Although convincingly beating Wild Bill Mehlhorn in the final, Walter Hagen's third PGA win in 1925 was not without a fright or two along the way: he was taken into extra holes by Al Watrous and Leo Diegel. Having seen Jim Barnes match a record of his when Barnes won the British Open in June, Hagen now equalled Barnes' (and Sarazen's) feat of back-to-back PGA titles.

FINAL
WALTER HAGEN ($ not available) beat Bill Mehlhorn, 6&5

Round by Round Details

ROUND 1 (Last 32)
WALTER HAGEN bt Al Watrous 1up (after 39); Mike Brady bt JS Collins 10&9; Leo Diegel bt Laurie Ayton, Sr 2&1; Bobby Cruickshank bt Bill Leach 4&3; Harry Cooper bt Jack Blakeslee 7&6; Jack Burke, Sr bt Gene Sarazen 8&7; Johnny Farrell bt William Creavy 6&4; Ray Derr bt Abe Espinosa 4&3; BILL MEHLHORN bt Emmett French 5&4; Al Espinosa bt George Howard 5&3; Tom Kerrigan bt George Smith 5&3; Dan Williams bt Charles Hoffner 4&3; Motrie Dutra bt Willie Ogg 2&1; Ed Dudley bt Mike Patton 3&2; Tommy Armour bt George Griffin 3&1; John Golden bt Dave Robertson 9&8

ROUND 2 (Last 16)
HAGEN bt Brady 7&6
Diegel bt Cruickshank 2&1
Cooper bt Burke 2&1
Farrell bt Derr 1up (after 37)
MEHLHORN bt Al Espinosa 1up
Kerrigan bt Williams 2up
Dutra bt Dudley 6&5
Armour bt Golden 6&5

QUARTER FINAL (QF)
HAGEN bt Diegel 1up (after 40)
Cooper bt Farrell 2&1
MEHLHORN bt Kerrigan 7&6
Dutra bt Armour 2up

SEMI FINAL (SF)
HAGEN bt Cooper 3&1
MEHLHORN bt Dutra 8&6

BRITISH OPEN 1926

Royal Lytham & St Anne's Golf Club, Lancashire, England
(22–24 June)
6456 yards

With sectional qualifying and the expanding of the competition over three days, the Opens were beginning to think in unison – except on the question of the calendar. This year, the British Open preceded its US counterpart once more. The Lancashire links of Royal Lytham were hosting the Championship for the first time: and Bobby Jones won for the first time. He was the first amateur to win since Harold Hilton in 1897.

1	**BOBBY JONES (a)**	72	72	73	74	291
	(£Nil – amateur)					
2	Al Watrous	71	75	69	78	293
3=	Walter Hagen	68	77	74	76	295
	George Von Elm (a)	75	72	76	72	295
5=	Tom Barber	77	73	78	71	299
	Abe Mitchell	78	78	72	71	299
7	Fred McLeod	71	75	76	79	301
8=	Emmett French	76	75	74	78	303
	Jose Jurado	77	76	74	76	303
	Bill Mehlhorn	70	74	79	80	303
10=	HA Gaudin	78	78	71	77	304
	JH Taylor	75	78	71	80	304
12	Tommy Armour	74	76	75	80	305
13=	WL Hartley (a)	74	77	79	76	306
	H Walker	74	77	78	77	306
	Reg Whitcombe	73	82	76	75	306
	Tom Williamson	78	76	76	76	306
17=	Jim Barnes	77	80	72	78	307
	Fred Robson	79	76	77	75	307
	Cyril Walker	79	71	80	77	307
20=	George Duncan	75	79	80	74	308
	Sandy Herd	81	76	75	76	308
21	Herbert Jolly	79	76	79	75	309
22=	Edward Douglas	79	78	75	78	310
	George Gadd	80	71	78	81	310
	Joe Kirkwood, Sr	81	76	78	75	310
	Charles Whitcombe	79	78	75	78	310
26=	James Braid	82	75	75	79	311
	Arthur Havers	75	76	82	78	311
28=	Fred Boobyer	79	79	80	74	312
	Charles Corlett	77	80	76	79	312
	Jean Gassiat	78	78	79	77	312
	J MacDowell	75	82	75	80	312
	Ted Ray	78	80	74	80	312

Round Leader(s)
R1   Hagen; 68
R2   Jones, Mehlhorn; 144
R3   Watrous; 215

Lowest Scores
R2   Gadd, Walker; 71
R3   Watrous; 69
R4   Barber, Mitchell; 71

US OPEN 1926

Scioto Country Club, Columbus, Ohio
(8–10 July)
6675 yards: Par 72 (288)

Returning to the States, Jones picked up his second Major in succession, and became the first player to win both Opens in the same year. Joe Turnesa's second place was to be the start of a runner's-up jinx – on him and his brothers, Mike and Jim – which stretched over many years. Jim eventually broke it by picking up the 1952 PGA title.

1	**BOBBY JONES (a)**	70	79	71	73	293
	($Nil – amateur)					
2	Joe Turnesa	71	74	72	77	294
3=	Leo Diegel	72	76	75	74	297
	Johnny Farrell	76	79	69	73	297
	Bill Mehlhorn	68	75	76	78	297
	Gene Sarazen	78	77	72	70	297
7	Walter Hagen	73	77	74	74	298
8	Willie Hunter, Jr	75	77	69	79	300
9=	Tommy Armour	76	76	74	75	301
	Willie Klein	76	74	75	76	301
	Macdonald Smith	82	76	68	75	301
	Dan Williams	72	74	80	75	301
13=	Al Espinosa	71	79	78	74	302
	Charles Evans, Jr (a)	75	75	73	79	302
	Jack Forrester	76	73	77	76	302
16=	Laurie Ayton, Sr	76	78	76	76	306
	Mike Brady	77	82	76	71	306
	George McLean	74	74	79	79	306
	Jimmy Thomson	77	82	73	74	306
20=	Willie MacFarlane	72	79	75	81	307
	Jock Rogers	80	79	75	73	307
22	Clarence Hackney	77	77	74	80	308
23=	Arthur De Mane	76	80	78	75	309
	PO Hart	76	81	76	76	309
	Harrison Johnston (a)	79	76	77	77	309
	Tom Stevens	79	78	76	76	309
27=	Emmett French	74	79	76	81	310
	Harry Hampton	81	75	78	76	310
	Tom Harmon, Jr	73	81	76	80	310
	Bob MacDonald	77	79	77	77	310
	Eddie Murphy	74	77	80	79	310

Round Leader(s)
R1   Mehlhorn; 68
R2   Mehlhorn; 143
R3   Turnesa; 217

Lowest Scores
R2   Forrester; 73
R3   Smith; 68
R4   Sarazen; 70

US PGA 1926

Salisbury Golf Links, Westbury, Long Island, New York
(20–25 September)

MATCHPLAY
32 qualifiers after 36 holes strokeplay
(Low – Walter Hagen, 140)
All Rounds 36 holes

Bobby Jones may have been having all his own way in the Opens, but in matchplay Walter Hagen was peerless during the mid-'20s. If Jones had been eligible to compete in the PGA, it would have been a mouth-watering prospect to contemplate the two head-to-head. As it was, in 1926, the 'Haig' demolished the opposition round-by-round to take his fourth PGA – and the third in succession.

WALTER HAGEN ($ not available) beat Leo Diegel, 5&3

Round by Round Details

ROUND 1 (Last 32)
Marshall Crichton bt Francis Gallett 1up; Pat Doyle bt Willie Maguire 2&1; Dick Grout bt Jock Hendry 4&3; WALTER HAGEN bt Joe Turnesa 3&2; Dick Linnars bt Fred McLeod 5&4; Johnny Farrell bt Al Watrous 6&5; Harry Hampton bt Larry Nabholtz 6&5; Tom Harmon, Jr bt Al Espinosa 6&4; Abe Espinosa bt Gunnar Nelson 7&6; Mike Brady bt George Aulbach 1up (after 37); LEO DIEGEL bt Mike Patton 8&7; Neal McIntyre bt Bobby Cruickshank 4&2; John Golden bt Harry Cooper 5&3; Gene Sarazen bt Jim Barnes 5&4; Bill Leach bt Laurie Ayton, Sr 3&2; George Christ bt Leo Shea 3&2

ROUND 2 (Last 16)
Doyle by Crichton 3&2
HAGEN bt Grout 7&6
Farrell bt Linnars 6&5
Hampton bt Harmon 6&5
Abe Espinosa bt Brady 1up
DIEGEL bt McIntyre 6&5
Golden bt Sarazen 4&3
Christ bt Leach 1up (after 38)

QUARTER FINAL (QF)
HAGEN bt Doyle 6&5
Farrell bt Hampton 3&1
DIEGEL bt Abe Espinosa 3&2
Golden bt Christ 7&6

SEMI FINAL (SF)
HAGEN bt Farrell 6&5
DIEGEL bt Golden 1up

US OPEN 1927

Oakmont Country Club, Oakmont, Pennsylvania
(14–17 June)
6965 yards: Par 72 (288)

Tommy Armour won the first of his three Majors over the classic Oakmont parkland course. He tied 'Light Horse' Harry Cooper – another for whom a Major Championship was just beyond his grasp – and comfortably won the play-off. Armour was the last Scots-born player to win the US Open. Ted Ray, the Champion of 1920, finished tied-27th, and said farewell to America at the age of 50.

1	**TOMMY ARMOUR***	78	71	76	76	301
	($500)					
2	Harry Cooper	74	76	74	77	301
3	Gene Sarazen	74	74	80	74	302
4	Emmett French	75	79	77	73	304
5	Bill Mehlhorn	75	77	80	73	305
6	Walter Hagen	77	73	76	81	307
7=	Archie Compston	79	74	76	79	308
	Johnny Farrell	81	73	78	76	308
	John Golden	83	77	75	73	308
	Harry Hampton	73	78	80	77	308
11=	Bobby Cruickshank	77	78	76	78	309
	Leo Diegel	78	74	80	77	309
	Bobby Jones (a)	76	77	79	77	309
	Eddie Loos	78	75	79	77	309
15=	Fred Baroni	80	72	79	79	310
	Perry Del Vecchio	79	79	76	76	310
	Arthur Havers	79	77	74	80	310
18=	Al Espinosa	83	80	79	69	311
	Harrison Johnston (a)	73	74	87	77	311
	Willie MacFarlane	82	76	80	73	311
	Macdonald Smith	78	76	81	76	311
	Al Watrous	82	74	78	77	311
23	Jock Hutchison	80	77	77	78	312
24=	Jim Barnes	78	75	81	79	313
	PO Hart	77	77	86	73	313
	Larry Nabholtz	75	81	78	79	313
27=	Ted Ray	76	83	77	78	314
	Joe Turnesa	81	79	78	76	314
29=	Tom Harmon, Jr	79	77	80	79	315
	Bob MacDonald	77	83	78	77	315

* Tommy Armour (76) beat Harry Cooper (79) in the 18-Hole Play-off

Round Leader(s)
R1 Hampton, Johnston; 73
R2 Johnston; 147
R3 Cooper; 224

Lowest Scores
R2 Armour; 71
R3 Cooper, Havers; 74
R4 Espinosa; 69

BRITISH OPEN 1927

Royal & Ancient Golf Club, St Andrews, Fife, Scotland
(13–15 July)
6572 yards

Bobby Jones continued to re-write the record books: record low score for either Open; first back-to-back British Open win for an amateur; third win in a row in eligible Championships (he won both Opens in 1926); and so on. St Andrews introduced a larger scoreboard for spectators – the precursor of the modern leaderboard.

1	**BOBBY JONES (a)**	68	72	73	72	285
	(£Nil –amateur)					
2=	Aubrey Boomer	76	70	73	72	291
	Fred Robson	76	72	69	74	291
4=	Joe Kirkwood, Sr	72	72	75	74	293
	Ernest R Whitcombe	74	73	73	73	293
6	Charles Whitcombe	74	76	71	75	296
7=	Arthur Havers	80	74	73	70	297
	Bert Hodson	72	70	81	74	297
8	Henry Cotton	73	72	77	76	298
9=	Percy Alliss	73	74	73	80	300
	Sandy Herd	76	75	78	71	300
	Phil Perkins (a)	76	78	70	76	300
	Phillip H Rodgers	76	73	74	77	300
	WB Torrance	72	80	74	74	300
	RD Vickers	75	75	77	73	300
	Tom Williamson	75	76	78	71	300
16=	Jim Barnes	76	76	72	77	301
	GR Buckle	77	69	77	78	301
	O Johns	74	78	73	76	301
19=	Donald Curtis	73	76	79	74	302
	Jean Gassiat	76	77	73	76	302
	Tom Stevens	76	73	74	79	302
22=	Archie Compston	74	78	79	72	303
	Len Holland	75	75	71	82	303
	Henry Kinch	80	73	73	77	303
	Jack Smith	81	73	73	76	303
26	Duncan McCulloch	74	77	78	75	304
27=	Chas Gadd	74	74	78	79	305
	Tom King, Jr	73	74	74	84	305
29=	James Braid	75	77	76	78	306
	William Kennett	78	75	75	78	306
	D Murray	72	78	77	79	306
	Ted Ray	78	73	77	78	306
	W Tweddell (a)	78	74	78	76	306
	William Twine	75	78	78	75	306

Round Leader(s)
R1   Jones; 68
R2   Jones; 140
R3   Jones; 213

Lowest Scores
R2   Buckle; 69
R3   Robson; 69
R4   Havers; 70

US PGA 1927

Cedar Crest Country Club, Dallas, Texas
(31 October–6 November)

MATCHPLAY
32 qualifiers after 36 holes strokeplay
(Low – Walter Hagen, 141)
All Rounds 36 holes

Hagen set his remarkable record of four consecutive wins in the PGA. He joined Tom Morris, Jr as the only player in history to win the same Major Championship four times in succession – and the only one to do it four years in a row ('Young' Tom won four British Opens between 1868 and 1872, there being no Championship in 1871).

FINAL
WALTER HAGEN ($ not available) beat Joe Turnesa, 1up

Round by Round Details

ROUND 1 (Last 32)
Tommy Armour bt Johnny Farrell 4&3; Tom Harmon, Jr bt Johnny Perelli 4&3; Tony Manero bt Bobby Cruickshank 4&3; WALTER HAGEN bt Jack Farrell 3&2; Mortie Dutra bt Albert Alcroft 12&11; Charles Guest bt Roland Hancock 3&2; Al Espinosa bt Mel Smith 5&4; Harry Cooper bt Eddie Murphy 7&6; Ed Dudley bt James Gullane 8&7; Gene Sarazen by Jack Curley 1up (after 37); Willie Klein bt Bill Mehlhorn 1up; JOE TURNESA bt Charles McKenna 5&3; John Golden bt Charles Koontz 2&1; Harold Long bt Willie Kidd 4&3; Francis Gallett bt Bob Shave 4&3; Ralph Beach bt Fred Baroni 1up

ROUND 2 (Last 16)
Armour bt Harmon, Jr 7&6
HAGEN bt Manero 11&10
Dutra bt Guest 2up
Espinosa bt Cooper 5&4
Sarazen bt Dudley 4&3
TURNESA bt Klein 1up
Golden bt Long 1up (after 37)
Gallett bt Beach 2up

QUARTER FINAL (QF)
HAGEN bt Armour 4&3
Espinosa bt Dutra 1up
TURNESA bt Sarazen 3&2
Golden bt Gallett 4&2

SEMI FINAL (SF)
HAGEN bt Espinosa 1up (after 37)
TURNESA bt Golden 7&6

BRITISH OPEN 1928

Royal St George's Golf Club, Sandwich, Kent, England
(9-11 June)
6751 yards

Walter Hagen edged away from his 'professional' arch rival, Gene Sarazen (as opposed to Jones, the 'amateur' one, who didn't appear here), over the second 36 holes to win his second Open, both at Sandwich. He lowered his own 1922 record there by eight strokes. In the last appearance of members of the Triumvirate among the finishers, James Braid shot a 316 to finish tied-41st and Harry Vardon tied-47th (317).

1	**WALTER HAGEN**	75	73	72	72	292
	(£75)					
2	Gene Sarazen	72	76	73	73	294
3	Archie Compston	75	74	73	73	295
4=	Percy Alliss	75	76	75	72	298
	Fred Robson	79	73	73	73	298
6=	Jim Barnes	81	73	76	71	301
	Aubrey Boomer	79	73	77	72	301
	Jose Jurado	74	71	76	80	301
9	Bill Mehlhorn	71	78	76	77	302
10	Bill Davies	78	74	79	73	304
11=	Fred Taggart	76	74	77	78	305
	Albert Whiting	78	76	76	75	305
13	Jack Smith	79	77	76	74	306
14=	Phil Perkins (a)	80	79	76	72	307
	William Twine	75	79	77	76	307
16	Stewart Burns	76	74	75	83	308
17	Charles Hezlet (a)	79	76	78	76	309
18=	Henry Cotton	77	75	83	75	310
	Duncan McCulloch	78	78	78	76	310
	George Duncan	75	77	78	80	310
21=	Abe Mitchell	78	75	82	76	311
	Tom Williamson	77	73	77	84	311
23=	Bob Bradbeer	83	76	78	75	312
	George Gadd	83	73	78	78	312
	Jean Gassiat	76	77	81	78	312
	WL Hope (a)	84	75	75	78	312
	James Ockenden	80	78	79	75	312
	Reg Whitcombe	79	77	81	75	312
	Reg Wilson	82	73	77	80	312
	Sydney Wingate	75	82	79	76	312

Round Leader(s)
R1 Mehlhorn; 71
R2 Jurado; 145
R3 Hagen; 220

Lowest Scores
R2 Jurado; 71
R3 Hagen; 72
R4 Barnes; 71

US OPEN 1928

Olympia Fields Country Club, Matteson, Illinois
(21-23 June)
6725 yards: Par 71 (284)

The number of entries had been steadily rising in all Majors, but in 1928, the 1000 mark was passed, here, at Olympia Fields near Chicago, for the first time. Roland Hancock, barely known after qualifying for the matchplay stage of the previous year's PGA Championship, needed to complete 17 and 18 in one over par to become champion. He duly blew it and was forever consigned to golfing oblivion. The Championship went to a tie once more, and although he was to win the fourth of his five US Amateur titles in the coming September, did Jones, as in 1925, give a glimpse of a slight weakness in matchplay golf? Willie MacFarlane beat him in a play-off then: this year it was Johnny Farrell's turn.

1	**JOHNNY FARRELL***	77	74	71	72	294
	($500)					
2	Bobby Jones (a)	73	71	73	77	294
3	Roland Hancock	74	77	72	72	295
4=	Walter Hagen	75	72	73	76	296
	George Von Elm (a)	74	72	76	74	296
6=	Henry Ciuci	70	77	72	80	299
	Waldo Crowder	74	74	76	75	299
	Ed Dudley	77	79	68	75	299
	Bill Leach	72	74	73	80	299
	Gene Sarazen	78	76	73	72	299
	Denny Shute	75	73	79	72	299
	Macdonald Smith	75	77	75	72	299
	Joe Turnesa	74	77	74	74	299
14=	Al Espinosa	74	74	77	75	300
	Willie MacFarlane	73	74	73	80	300
16	Tommy Armour	76	75	77	73	301
17	Jack Forrester	77	76	75	74	302
18=	Billy Burke	74	79	73	77	303
	Neil Christian	80	78	74	71	303
	Leo Diegel	72	79	75	77	303
	Charles Hilgendorf	76	77	79	71	303
22=	Frank Ball	70	81	78	75	304
	Archie Compston	76	81	75	72	304
	Harrison Johnston (a)	77	75	79	73	304
25=	Harry Hampton	77	76	72	80	305
	Leonard Schmutte	71	81	75	78	305
27	Frank Walsh	74	74	80	78	306
28=	Willie Hunter, Jr	73	83	73	78	307
	Felix Serafin	75	76	77	79	307
	Horton Smith	72	79	76	80	307

* Johnny Farrell (143) beat Bobby Jones (144) in the 36-Hole Play-off

Round Leader(s)
R1 Ball, Ciuci; 70
R2 Jones; 144
R3 Jones; 217

Lowest Scores
R2 Craig Wood (46); 70
R3 Dudley; 68
R4 Bill Mehlhorn (49); 70

US PGA 1928

Five Farms Country Club, Baltimore, Maryland
(5-6 June)

MATCHPLAY

32 qualifiers after 36 holes strokeplay
(Low – Al Espinosa, 142)
All Rounds 36 holes

Leo Diegel broke Walter Hagen's four-year run and 22 consecutive match wins in the PGA when he won at the 35th hole in the quarter final. Before that only Gene Sarazen had beaten Hagen in PGA Championship matches – going back to 1921. Diegel then demolished Sarazen before beating top-qualifier, Al Espinosa, in the one-sided final.

FINAL

LEO DIEGEL ($ not available) beat Al Espinosa, 6&5

Round by Round Details

ROUND 1 (Last 32)
Willie McFarlane beat Jim Foulis 9&7; Horton Smith bt Billy Burke 2&1; Glen Spencer bt Fred McDermott 8&6; Perry Del Vecchio bt Jack Burke, Sr 1up (after 37); AL ESPINOSA bt John Golden 8&7; Bob Mac-Donald bt Willie Kidd 2up; Jock Hutchison bt Willie Klein 3&2; Pat Doyle bt Mortie Dutra 6&4; Jim Barnes bt Tommy Armour 3&2; Gene Sarazen bt Bill Mehlhorn 3&2; Al Watrous bt Olin Dutra 2&1; Ed Dudley bt Wiffy Cox 3&2; George Christ bt Albert Alcroft 1up (after 38); LEO DIEGEL bt Tony Manero 10&8; Walter Hagen bt Willie Ogg 4&3; Julian Blanton bt Ed McElligott 9&8

ROUND 2 (Last 16)
Smith bt MacFarlane 1up
Del Vecchio bt Spencer 1up (after 37)
ESPINOSA by MacDonald 1up (after 37)
Hutchison bt Doyle 1up
Sarazen bt Barnes 3&2
Dudley bt Watrous 3&2
DIEGEL bt Christ 6&4
Hagen bt Blanton 2up

QUARTER FINAL (QF)
Smith bt Del Vecchio 2up
ESPINOSA bt Hutchison 5&4
Sarazen bt Dudley 7&6
DIEGEL bt Hagen 2&1

SEMI FINAL (SF)
ESPINOSA bt Smith 6&5
DIEGEL bt Sarazen 9&8

BRITISH OPEN 1929

Hon Co of Edinburgh Golfers, Muirfield, East Lothian, Scotland
(8-10 May)
6738 yards

Hagen repeated his 1928 victory when the first three on the leaderboard were the three Major Champions of 1928. A startling record-equalling 67 in Round 2, and a bad third round from Diegel made the difference; Hagen only having to play solid golf over the last 18 holes to win his fourth – and last – Open. He stands, with a group of players, one behind Taylor, Braid, Peter Thomson and Tom Watson; and two behind Vardon – in the list of most wins.

1	**WALTER HAGEN**	75	67	75	75	292
	(£75)					
2	Johnny Farrell	72	75	76	75	298
3	Leo Diegel	71	69	82	77	299
4=	Percy Alliss	69	76	76	79	300
	Abe Mitchell	72	72	78	78	300
6	Bobby Cruickshank	73	74	78	76	301
7	Jim Barnes	71	80	78	74	303
8=	Gene Sarazen	73	74	81	76	304
	Al Watrous	73	79	75	77	304
10	Tommy Armour	75	73	79	78	305
11	Arthur Havers	80	74	76	76	306
12	Archie Compston	76	73	77	81	307
13=	Johnny Golden	74	73	86	75	308
	Jimmy Thomson	78	78	75	77	308
15=	Aubrey Boomer	74	74	80	81	309
	Herbert Jolly	72	80	78	79	309
	Macdonald Smith	73	78	78	80	309
18=	Sid Brews	76	77	78	79	310
	Bill Davies	79	76	81	74	310
	Ed Dudley	72	80	80	78	310
	Mark Seymour	75	74	78	83	310
22	George Duncan	78	76	81	76	311
23=	William Nolan	80	76	79	77	312
	Phil Perkins (a)	79	73	80	80	312
25=	Jose Jurado	77	73	81	82	313
	W Willis Mackenzie (a)	80	71	80	82	313
	Cedric Sayner	80	75	78	80	313
	Horton Smith	76	76	84	77	313
	Cyril Tolley (a)	74	76	87	76	313
	Joe Turnesa	78	74	81	80	313
	Tom Williamson	73	78	80	82	313

Round Leader(s)
R1 Alliss; 69
R2 Diegel; 140
R3 Hagen; 217

Lowest Scores
R2 Hagen; 67
R3 Hagen, Thomson, Watrous; 75
R4 Barnes, Davies; 74

US OPEN 1929

Winged Foot Golf Club, Mamaroneck, New York
(27-30 June)

6786 yards: Par 72 (288)

Al Espinosa may have wished he hadn't bothered to tie with Bobby Jones. Jones had two 7s in his last round 79 and only made the play-off courtesy of a 12-foot putt on the last green. In his fourth Open play-off though, Jones played golf as majestic as Espinosa's was abject – winning by 23 shots! – and landed his third US Open.

1	**BOBBY JONES* (a)**	69	75	71	79	294
	($Nil – amateur)					
2	Al Espinosa	70	72	77	75	294
3=	Gene Sarazen	71	71	76	78	296
	Denny Shute	73	71	76	76	296
5=	Tommy Armour	74	71	76	76	297
	George Von Elm (a)	79	70	74	74	297
7	Henry Ciuci	78	74	72	75	299
8=	Leo Diegel	74	74	76	77	301
	Peter O'Hara	74	76	73	78	301
10	Horton Smith	76	77	74	75	302
11=	Wiffy Cox	74	76	80	75	305
	JE Rogers	78	76	77	74	305
13=	PO Hart	76	78	75	77	306
	Charles Hilgendorf	72	79	75	80	306
15	Billy Burke	75	80	78	74	307
16=	Louis Chiapetta	78	79	72	79	308
	George Smith	77	77	77	77	308
	Craig Wood	79	71	80	78	308
19=	Walter Hagen	76	81	74	78	309
	Joe Kirkwood, Sr	75	82	76	76	309
21=	Jim Barnes	78	78	81	73	310
	Massie Miller	75	82	75	78	310
23=	Jack Forrester	77	76	75	83	311
	Ted Longworth	74	82	73	82	311
	Macdonald Smith	77	78	80	76	311
26=	Jack Burke, Sr	77	80	74	81	312
	Willie Hunter, Jr	76	77	76	83	312
	Willie MacFarlane	79	78	76	79	312
	Leonard Schmutte	73	75	89	75	312
30=	Tom Boyd	79	80	74	80	313
	Emerick Kocsis	79	76	77	81	313

* Bobby Jones (141) beat Al Espinosa (164) in the
36-Hole Play-off

Round Leader(s)
R1 Jones; 69
R2 Espinosa, Sarazen; 142
R3 Jones; 215

Lowest Scores
R2 Von Elm; 70
R3 Jones; 71
R4 Barnes; 73

US PGA 1929

Hillcrest Country Club, Los Angeles, California
(2-7 December)

MATCHPLAY
32 qualifiers after 36 holes strokeplay
(Low – Fred Morrison, 136)
All Rounds 36 holes

Leo Diegel not only repeated his 1928 win, he had to negotiate previous multiple Champions – Sarazen in the quarter final, Hagen in the semis – in doing it. In his fourth meeting with Hagen in five years, Diegel squared the series. He went on to beat 1928 US Open winner, Johnny Farrell. The Majors hit the West Coast for the first time – hence the date of the Championship. Michigan may not have been so inviting.

FINAL
LEO DIEGEL ($ not available) beat Johnny Farrell, 6&4

Round by Round Details

ROUND 1 (Last 32)
Larry Nabholtz bt Albert Alcroft 1up; Al Watrous bt Neal McIntyre 4&3; Al Espinosa bt Dave Hackney 5&4; Bill Mehlhorn bt Guy Paulsen 7&6; Neil Christian bt Frank Walsh 7&6; Craig Wood bt Horton Smith 1up (after 37); Henry Ciuci bt Clarence Clark 3&2; JOHNNY FARRELL bt John Golden 1up; Tony Manero by Denny Shute 6&5; Eddie Schultz bt Wiffy Cox 5&4; Walter Hagen bt Bob Shave 9&8; Charles Guest bt Mortie Dutra 1up; LEO DIEGEL bt PO Hart 10&9; Herman Barron bt Clarence Doser 5&4; Gene Sarazen bt Jock Hendry 3&2; Fred Morrison bt Joe Kirkwood, Sr 5&4

ROUND 2 (Last 16)
Watrous bt Nabholtz 9&7
Espinosa bt Mehlhorn 1up (after 40)
Wood bt Christian 3&2
FARRELL by Ciuci 3&1
Manero bt Schultz 6&5
Hagen bt Guest 5&4
DIEGEL bt Barron 10&9
Sarazen bt Morrison 3&2

QUARTER FINAL (QF)
Watrous bt Espinosa 2up
FARRELL bt Wood 1up (after 37)
Hagen bt Manero 6&5
DIEGEL bt Sarazen 3&2

SEMI FINAL (SF)
FARRELL bt Watrous 6&5
DIEGEL bt Hagen 3&2

BRITISH OPEN 1930

Royal Liverpool Golf Club, Hoylake, Cheshire, England
(18–20 June)
6750 yards

This was Bobby Jones' year. As if his performances as an amateur over the previous eight years – against amateurs and pros – were not enough, his feats of 1930 will never be repeated. Jones played steady golf to win by two from a clutch of outstanding Americans, and the best of British – who, Compston and Cotton apart, were not of the best vintage.

1	**BOBBY JONES** (a)	70	72	74	75	291
	(£Nil – amateur)					
2=	Leo Diegel	74	73	71	75	293
	Macdonald Smith	70	77	75	71	293
4=	Fred Robson	71	72	78	75	296
	Horton Smith	72	73	78	73	296
6=	Jim Barnes	71	77	72	77	297
	Archie Compston	74	73	68	82	297
8	Henry Cotton	70	79	77	73	299
9=	Tom Barber	75	76	72	77	300
	Auguste Boyer	73	77	70	80	300
	Charles Whitcombe	74	75	72	79	300
12	Bert Hodson	74	77	76	74	301
13=	Abe Mitchell	75	78	77	72	302
	Reg Whitcombe	78	72	73	79	302
15=	Donald Moe (a)	74	73	76	80	303
	Phillip H Rodgers	74	73	76	80	303
17=	Percy Alliss	75	74	77	79	305
	William Large	78	74	77	76	305
	Ernest R Whitcombe	80	72	76	77	305
	Arthur Young	75	78	78	74	305
21=	H Crapper	78	73	80	75	306
	Pierre Hirigoyen	75	79	76	76	306
	Harry Large	79	74	78	75	306
24=	Stewart Burns	77	75	80	75	307
	Bill Davies	78	77	73	79	307
	Arthur Lacey	78	79	74	76	307
	Ted Ray	78	75	76	78	307
	Norman Sutton	72	80	76	79	307
29	Tom Green	73	79	78	78	308
30=	Duncan McCulloch	78	78	79	74	309
	Alf Perry	78	74	75	82	309

Round Leader(s)
R1 Cotton, Jones, M Smith; 70
R2 Jones; 142
R3 Compston; 215

Lowest Scores
R2 Cyril Tolley (52); 71
R3 Compston; 68
R4 M Smith; 71

US OPEN 1930

Interlachen Country Club, Minneapolis, Minnesota
(10–12 July)
6609 yards: Par 72 (288)

The Jones Bandwagon rolled on. Already possessing the British Amateur and Open titles, he won the US Open at Interlachen by 2 from British Open runner-up Mac Smith. In doing so he was the only player under par for the four rounds; he notched up his fourth US Open; and the third leg of the never-to-be-repeated Grand Slam. When he picked up the US Amateur title the following September his challenge was complete, and he retired to practise law full-time at the age of 28.

1	**BOBBY JONES** (a)	71	73	68	75	287
	($Nil – amateur)					
2	Macdonald Smith	70	75	74	70	289
3	Horton Smith	72	70	76	74	292
4	Harry Cooper	72	72	73	76	293
5	Johnny Golden	74	73	71	76	294
6	Tommy Armour	70	76	75	76	297
7	Charles Lacey	74	70	77	77	298
8	Johnny Farrell	74	72	73	80	299
9=	Bill Mehlhorn	76	74	75	75	300
	Craig Wood	73	75	72	80	300
11=	Leo Diegel	75	75	76	75	301
	Johnny Goodman (a)	74	80	72	75	301
	Al Heron (a)	76	78	74	73	301
	Peter O'Hara	75	77	73	76	301
	George Smith	72	81	74	74	301
	George Von Elm (a)	80	74	73	74	301
17=	Ed Dudley	74	75	78	76	303
	Mortie Dutra	76	80	69	78	303
	Charles Guest	76	73	77	77	303
	Walter Hagen	72	75	76	80	303
	Willie Hunter, Jr	76	76	78	73	303
	Bob Shave	76	72	78	77	303
	Joe Turnesa	73	78	78	74	303
	Al Watrous	79	73	73	78	303
25=	Olin Dutra	73	79	78	75	305
	Francis Gallett	76	75	74	80	305
	Denny Shute	76	78	77	74	305
28=	Herman Barron	77	78	74	77	306
	Billy Burke	76	72	82	76	306
	Jack Forrester	73	75	80	78	306
	Charles Hilgendorf	74	81	76	75	306
	Walter Kozak	74	76	78	78	306
	Gene Sarazen	76	78	77	75	306
	Frank Walsh	75	78	77	76	306

Round Leader(s)
R1 M Smith; 70
R2 H Smith; 142
R3 Jones; 212

Lowest Scores
R2 Lacey, H Smith; 70
R3 Jones; 68
R4 M Smith; 70

US PGA 1930

Fresh Meadows Country Club, Flushing, New York
(8–13 September)

MATCHPLAY
32 qualifiers after 36 holes strokeplay (Low – Johnny Farrell, Horton Smith, 145).
All Rounds 36 holes

The 'Silver Scot', Tommy Armour, became the last British-born golfer to win the PGA and it was not until Gary Player in 1962 that the American stranglehold on the Championship was next broken. Ex-champions Hagen and Barnes didn't make it to the matchplay stage, but, another, finalist Gene Sarazen had his best PGA since winning in 1923.

FINAL
TOMMY ARMOUR ($ not available) beat Gene Sarazen, 1up

Round by Round Details

ROUND 1 (Last 32)
Al Watrous bt Eric Seavall 3&1; Charles Lacey bt Charles Guest 3&2; Harold Sampson bt Clarence Ehresman 4&3; Leo Diegel bt Henry Ciuci 8&7; TOMMY ARMOUR bt Clarence Hackney 11&10; Bob Shave bt Joseph Kenny 1up; Denny Shute bt Joe Frank 8&6; Johnny Farrell bt Norman Smith 7&5; GENE SARAZEN bt Charles Schneider 1up; Bob Crowley bt Wiffy Cox 4&3; Harry Cooper bt Bill Mehlhorn 2&1; Al Espinosa bt Mark Fry 2&1; Joe Kirkwood, Sr bt Gunnar Johnson 8&7; JS Collins bt John Golden 5&4; Horton Smith bt Billy Burke 2&1; Laurie Ayton, Sr bt Earl Fry 4&3)

ROUND 2 (Last 16)
Lacey bt Watrous 5&4
Sampson bt Diegel 1up (after 38)
ARMOUR bt Shave 7&5
Farrell bt Shute 1up
SARAZEN bt Crowley 7&6
Espinosa bt Cooper 4&3
Kirkwood bt Collins 1up (after 37)
Horton Smith bt Ayton 5&4

QUARTER FINAL (QF)
Lacey bt Sampson 4&3
ARMOUR bt Farrell 2&1
SARAZEN bt Espinosa 2&1
Kirkwood bt Horton Smith 1up

SEMI FINAL (SF)
ARMOUR bt Lacey 1up
SARAZEN bt Kirkwood 5&4

BRITISH OPEN 1931

Carnoustie Golf Club, Angus, Scotland
(3–5 June)
6900 yards

Reigning US PGA Champion, Tommy Armour, won his third different Major on the Open's first visit to mighty Carnoustie – the longest golf course to that date for any of the Majors. This is also the most-northerly site of any Major Championship course, and, curiously, Argentina– the southernmost stronghold of world golf (with apologies to Chile!) – was well represented, with three players in the first 11 places. In fact Jurado was leading, five better than the winner, going into the last round. Although a naturalized American, Armour was the last Scot to win the Open before Sandy Lyle 54 years later and the last born in Scotland, and to win in Scotland, before the 1999 Champion, Paul Lawrie.

1	**TOMMY ARMOUR**	73	75	77	71	296
	(£100)					
2	Jose Jurado	76	71	73	77	297
3 =	Percy Alliss	74	78	73	73	298
	Gene Sarazen	74	76	75	73	298
5 =	Johnny Farrell	72	77	75	75	299
	Macdonald Smith	75	77	71	76	299
7 =	Marcos Churio	76	75	78	71	300
	Bill Davies	76	78	71	75	300
8	Arthur Lacey	74	80	74	73	301
9 =	Henry Cotton	72	75	79	76	302
	Arthur Havers	75	76	72	79	302
11 =	Gus Faulkner	77	76	76	74	303
	Tomas Genta	75	78	75	75	303
	Abe Mitchell	77	74	77	75	303
	Horton Smith	77	79	75	72	303
	Tom Williamson	77	76	73	77	303
16 =	Marcel Dallemagne	74	77	78	75	304
	William I Hunter	76	75	74	79	304
	William Oke	74	80	75	75	304
	Reg Whitcombe	75	78	71	80	304
20 =	Aubrey Boomer	76	77	80	73	306
	Fred Robson	80	76	76	74	306
22 =	Len Holland	80	74	78	75	307
	Mark Seymour	80	79	75	73	307
	Ernest R Whitcombe	79	76	76	76	307
25 =	Bert Hodson	77	76	78	77	308
	Joe Kirkwood, Sr	75	75	77	81	308
	William Twine	72	78	79	79	308
28 =	Archie Compston	77	76	75	81	309
	Ernest WH Kenyon	75	78	78	78	309
	Duncan McCulloch	76	78	77	78	309
	William McMinn	78	78	79	74	309
	Phillip H Rodgers	77	74	78	80	309
	Charles Whitcombe	80	76	75	78	309

Round Leader(s)
R1 Cotton, Farrell, Twine; 72
R2 Cotton, Jurado; 147
R3 Jurado; 220

Lowest Scores
R2 Jurado; 71
R3 Davies, M Smith, R Whitcombe; 71
R4 Armour, Churio; 71

US OPEN 1931

Inverness Golf Club, Toledo, Ohio
(2–6 July)

6529 yards: Par 71 (284)

It took the sixth play-off in nine years to decide who was to fill the vacuum left by Bobby Jones. (Interestingly, the winner's prize money had doubled during the amateur's reign of domination, so by 1931, the first four-figure winning purse was collected.) The play-off had the effect of doubling the amount of golf the protagonists had to endure, as the result only became known at the 72nd extra hole. Perhaps surprisingly, Billy Burke, and recently-turned pro, Von Elm, tied for the lead ahead of a more-fancied Top Ten, with Burke winning by one shot.

1	**BILLY BURKE***	73	72	74	73	292
	($1000)					
2	George Von Elm	75	69	73	75	292
3	Leo Diegel	75	73	74	72	294
4=	Wiffy Cox	75	74	74	72	295
	Bill Mehlhorn	77	73	75	71	296
	Gene Sarazen	74	78	74	80	296
7=	Mortie Dutra	71	77	73	76	297
	Walter Hagen	74	74	73	76	297
	Phil Perkins (a)	78	76	73	70	297
10=	Al Espinosa	72	78	75	74	299
	Johnny Farrell	78	70	79	72	299
	Macdonald Smith	73	73	75	78	299
13=	Guy Paulsen	74	72	74	80	300
	Frank Walsh	73	77	75	75	300
15=	Herman Barron	71	75	78	77	301
	Harry Cooper	76	75	75	75	301
	Ed Dudley	75	76	76	74	301
	Al Watrous	74	78	76	73	301
19=	Charles Guest	71	75	76	80	302
	Tony Manero	74	75	80	73	302
21=	Olin Dutra	76	76	76	75	303
	John Kinder	79	72	75	77	303
23=	Laurie Ayton, Sr	76	79	74	75	304
	Willie Klein	75	80	70	79	304
25=	Denny Shute	79	73	77	76	305
	Eddie Williams	71	74	81	79	305
27=	Johnny Golden	79	75	78	74	306
	Horton Smith	77	78	75	76	306
29=	Auguste Boyer	75	80	72	80	307
	Henry Ciuci	73	79	81	74	307
	Bill Davies	73	83	74	77	307

* Billy Burke beat George Von Elm after two 36-Hole Play-offs:
  5 July – Burke (149) tied with Von Elm (149)
  6 July – Burke (148) beat Von Elm (149)

Round Leader(s)
R1   Barron, M Dutra, Guest, Williams; 71
R2   Von Elm; 144
R3   Von Elm; 217

Lowest Scores
R2   Von Elm; 69
R3   Klein; 70
R4   Perkins, Sarazen; 70

US PGA 1931

Wannamoisett Country Club, Rumford, Rhode Island
(7–14 September)

MATCHPLAY
31 qualifiers, plus the defending champion (Tommy Armour), after 36 holes strokeplay
(Low – Gene Sarazen; 145)
All Rounds 36 holes

Tom Creavy beat former US Open Champions, Cyril Walker and Gene Sarazen, on his way to a Major at the age of 20. After featuring quite well for the next year or two in the PGA and appearing in the US Open Top 10 of 1934, he was struck down by a debilitating illness and faded into obscurity.

FINAL
TOM CREAVY ($1000) beat Denny Shute, 2&1

Round by Round Details

ROUND 1 (Last 32)
  Paul Runyan bt Arthur Gusa 3&2; Gene Sarazen bt Al Espinosa 9&8; Willie MacFarlane bt Henry Ciuci 3&2; Horton Smith bt Walter Bemish 7&6; Cyril Walker bt Ed Dudley 3&2; John Golden bt Alfred Sargent 3&2; Peter O'Hara bt Walter Hagen 4&3; TOM CREAVY bt Jack Collins 5&4; Bob Crowley bt Pat Circelli 1up; Billy Burke bt Dave Hackney 5&3; Abe Espinosa by Vincent Eldred 4&3; Bill Mehlhorn bt Leo Diegel 3&2; DENNY SHUTE bt Tony Butler 1up (after 38); Jim Foulis bt Johnny Farrell 2up; Tommy Armour bt Joe Kirkwood, Sr 2&1; Walter Murray bt Eddie Schultz 6&5

ROUND 2 (Last 16)
  Sarazen bt Runyan 7&6
  Smith bt McaFarlane 6&5
  Walker bt Golden 5&4
  CREAVY bt O'Hara 2up
  Burke bt Crowley 5&4
  Abe Espinosa bt Mehlhorn 2&1
  SHUTE bt Foulis 2&1
  Armour bt Murray 5&3

QUARTER FINAL (QF)
  Sarazen bt Smith 5&4
  CREAVY bt Walker 3&1
  Burke bt Abe Espinosa 5&3
  SHUTE bt Armour 3&1

SEMI FINAL (SF)
  CREAVY bt Sarazen 5&3
  SHUTE bt Burke 1up

BRITISH OPEN 1932

Prince's Golf Club, Sandwich, Kent, England
(8–10 June)
6983 yards: Par 71 (284)

Sarazen joined Hagen, Barnes and Armour in the select band which had won all three Majors. A record 36- and 54-hole total for any Major to that time set the scene for a comfortable victory. The Prince's Club, adjacent to Royal St George's at Sandwich, was host to the Open for the one and only time.

1	**GENE SARAZEN**	70	69	70	74	283
	(£100)					
2	Macdonald Smith	71	76	71	70	288
3	Arthur Havers	74	71	68	76	289
4=	Percy Alliss	71	71	78	72	292
	Alf Padgham	76	72	74	70	292
	Charles Whitcombe	71	73	73	75	292
7=	Bill Davies	71	73	74	75	293
	Arthur Lacey	73	73	71	76	293
9	Fred Robson	74	71	78	71	294
10=	Archie Compston	74	70	75	76	295
	Henry Cotton	74	72	77	72	295
	Abe Mitchell	77	71	75	72	295
13=	Syd Easterbrook	74	75	72	77	298
	H Prowse	75	75	75	73	298
15=	CS Denny	73	81	72	73	299
	WL Hope (a)	74	79	75	71	299
17=	Tommy Armour	75	70	74	81	300
	Bert Hodson	77	73	77	73	300
	Alf Perry	73	76	77	74	300
	Charlie Ward	73	77	77	73	300
	Reg Whitcombe	75	74	75	76	300
22=	Ernest WH Kenyon	74	73	76	78	301
	Mark Seymour	74	75	81	71	301
	Thomas Torrance (a)	75	73	76	77	301
25=	Alf Beck	78	71	74	79	302
	Lister Hartley (a)	76	73	80	73	302
	Phillip H Rodgers	74	79	75	74	302
	William Twine	80	74	71	77	302
29=	Pierre Hirigoyen	79	73	75	76	303
	LO Munn (a)	74	75	78	76	303
	W Purse	76	75	73	79	303
	Cedric Sayner	74	74	79	76	303
	Percy Weston	75	79	76	73	303

Round Leader (s)
R1   Sarazen; 70
R2   Sarazen; 139
R3   Sarazen; 209

Lowest Scores
R2   Sarazen; 69
R3   Havers; 68
R4   Padgham, Smith; 70

US OPEN 1932

Fresh Meadow Country Club, Flushing, New York
(23–25 June)
68i5 yards: Par 70 (280)

After setting records at the British Open the previous month, Gene Sarazen became the second man after Bobby Jones to lift both Opens in the same season. If the earlier rounds were his strength at Sandwich, it was his final 36-hole low of 136 (including a record for both Opens with his last round of 66) which provided the victory at Fresh Meadow. Englishman, Phil Perkins (runner-up to Bob Jones in the 1928 US Amateur), had just turned professional and led after 54 holes, eventually tying second. His game was somewhat hampered in future after picking up a gun-shot wound to the thigh later that year.

1	**GENE SARAZEN**	74	76	70	66	286
	($1000)					
2=	Bobby Cruickshank	78	74	69	68	289
	Phil Perkins	76	69	74	70	289
4	Leo Diegel	73	74	73	74	294
5	Wiffy Cox	80	73	70	72	295
6	Jose Jurado	74	71	75	76	296
7=	Billy Burke	75	77	74	71	297
	Harry Cooper	77	73	73	74	297
	Olin Dutra	69	77	75	76	297
10	Walter Hagen	75	73	79	71	298
11	Clarence Clark	79	72	74	75	300
12=	Vincent Eldred	78	73	77	73	301
	Paul Runyan	79	77	69	76	301
14=	Henry Ciuci	77	74	77	74	302
	Ed Dudley	80	74	71	77	302
	Johnny Goodman (a)	79	78	77	68	302
	Fred Morrison	˙77	80	69	76	302
	Denny Shute	78	76	76	72	302
	Macdonald Smith	80	76	74	72	302
	Craig Wood	79	71	79	73	302
21=	Tommy Armour	82	73	77	71	303
	George Smith	81	76	72	74	303
23=	Mortie Dutra	77	77	75	75	304
	Joe Kirkwood, Sr	76	77	75	76	304
	Charles Lacey	77	76	78	73	304
	Jack Patroni	79	77	77	71	304
27=	John Fischer (a)	81	78	74	73	306
	Bob MacDonald	82	77	74	73	306
	George Von Elm	79	73	77	77	306
	Al Zimmerman	79	77	73	77	306

Round Score(s)
R1   O Dutra; 69
R2   Jurado, Perkins; 145
R3   Perkins; 219

Lowest Scores
R2   Perkins; 69
R3   Cruickshank, Morrison, Runyan; 69
R4   Sarazen; 66

US PGA 1932

Keller Golf Club, St Paul, Minnesota
(31 August-4 September)

MATCHPLAY

31 qualifiers, plus the defending champion (Tom Creavy),
after 36 holes strokeplay
(Low – Olin Dutra, 140)
All Rounds 36 holes

Olin Dutra proved that his qualifying score was no fluke.
However, he was helped when notables such as Armour,
Cooper and Billy Burke did not making the matchplay 32;
and the early round exits of Horton Smith and Walter
Hagen. In Round One, a generous act by Al Watrous
backfired. Nine up with just 12 to play, he conceded a
testing two-footer to Cruickshank. The match result tells
the story.

FINAL

OLIN DUTRA ($1000) beat Frank Walsh, 4&3

Round by Round Details

ROUND 1 (Last 32)
  OLIN DUTRA bt George Smith 9&8; Reggie Myles bt
  Horton Smith 1up (after 37); Herman Barron bt Neal
  McIntyre 8&7; Abe Espinosa bt Eddie Schultz 4&3;
  Henry Picard bt Charles Lacey 6&4; Ed Dudley bt Joe
  Turnesa 8&7; Al Collins bt Gunnar Nelson 5&4; John
  Golden bt Walter Hagen 1up (after 43); Vincent
  Eldred bt Paul Runyan 1up (after 38); Bobby Cruick-
  shank bt Al Watrous 1up (after 41 holes); Gene Kunes
  bt Craig Wood 3&2; FRANK WALSH bt Ted Long-
  worth 7&6; Ralph Stonehouse bt Vic Ghezzi 6&5; John
  Kinder bt Joe Kirkwood, Sr 1up; Johnny Perelli bt
  Denny Shute 3&2; Tom Creavy bt Jimmy Hines 7&6

ROUND 2 (Last 16)
  DUTRA by Myles 5&3
  Barron bt Espinosa 1up (after 38)
  Dudley bt Picard 10&9
  Collins bt Golden 1up
  Cruickshank bt Eldred 3&1
  WALSH bt Kunes 9&8
  Stonehouse bt Kinder 3&2
  Creavy bt Perelli 1up

QUARTER FINAL (QF)
  DUTRA bt Barron 5&4
  Dudley bt Collins 1up (after 38)
  WALSH bt Cruickshank 8&7
  Creavy bt Stonehouse 3&2

SEMI FINAL (SF)
  DUTRA bt Dudley 3&2
  WALSH bt Creavy 1up (after 38)

US OPEN 1933

North Shore Country Club, Glenview, Illinois
(8–10 June)

6880 yards: Par 72 (288)

Johnny Goodman became the last amateur to win any
Major. He equalled Sarazen's Open low of 66 in Round 2
and was never headed after that. Like Ouimet, Evans and
Jones previously, he won the Open before taking the
Amateur Championship (in 1937). Hagen, aged 41, also
shot a 66 – in Round 4 – his best strokeplay score in the
Majors. From this year on (apart from peculiar changes
around and just after the War with the PGA Championship) the present order of Majors in the golfing calendar was to prevail.

1	**JOHNNY GOODMAN** (a)	75	66	70	76	287
	($Nil –amateur)					
2	Ralph Guldahl	76	71	70	71	288
3	Craig Wood	73	74	71	72	290
4=	Tommy Armour	68	75	76	73	292
	Walter Hagen	73	76	77	66	292
6	Mortie Dutra	75	73	72	74	294
7=	Olin Dutra	75	71	75	74	295
	Gus Moreland (a)	76	76	71	72	295
9=	Clarence Clark	80	72	72	72	296
	Johnny Farrell	75	77	72	72	296
	Willie Goggin	79	73	73	71	296
	Joe Kirkwood, Sr	74	70	79	73	296
13=	Herman Barron	77	77	74	69	297
	Al Watrous	74	76	77	70	297
15=	Henry Ciuci	73	79	74	72	298
	Johnny Revolta	73	76	75	74	298
17=	George Dawson (a)	78	74	71	76	299
	Leo Diegel	78	71	75	75	299
19=	Lester Bolstad (a)	76	74	73	77	300
	Macdonald Smith	77	72	77	74	300
21=	Johnny Golden	79	76	74	72	301
	Archie Hambrick	81	71	75	74	301
	Denny Shute	76	77	72	76	301
24=	Abe Espinosa	76	73	78	75	302
	Horton Smith	75	76	76	75	302
26=	Bob Crowley	75	75	81	72	303
	Ky Laffoon	74	78	79	72	303
	Gene Sarazen	74	77	77	75	303
29=	Harry Cooper	78	76	75	75	304
	Tony Manero	79	73	77	75	304
	Bill Schwartz	75	81	72	76	304
	Frank Walsh	79	73	72	80	304

Round Leader(s)
R1   Armour; 68
R2   Goodman; 141
R3   Goodman; 211

Lowest scores
R2   Goodman; 66
R3   Goodman, Guldahl; 70
R4   Hagen; 66

BRITISH OPEN 1933

Royal & Ancient Golf Club, St Andrews, Fife, Scotland
(5–7 July)
6572 yards

Listed in British records and newspapers under his full name of 'Densmore', Denny Shute won his first Major, and only British Open, at the Home of Golf. In one of the tightest-ever finishes, only three shots covered the first 11 home. Craig Wood tied Shute on 292, but, as was to be his fashion for some years to come it seems, he lost the play-off. Shute's regulation four rounds all took 73 strokes: a consistency not equalled by a winner of a Major Championship, before or since.

1	**DENNY SHUTE***	73	73	73	73	292
	(£100)					
2	Craig Wood	77	72	68	75	292
3=	Leo Diegel	75	70	71	77	293
	Syd Easterbrook	73	72	71	77	293
	Gene Sarazen	72	73	73	75	293
6	Olin Dutra	76	76	70	72	294
7=	Henry Cotton	73	71	72	79	295
	Ed Dudley	70	71	76	78	295
	Abe Mitchell	74	68	74	79	295
	Alf Padgham	74	73	74	74	295
	Reg Whitcombe	76	75	72	72	295
12=	Archie Compston	72	74	77	73	296
	Ernest R Whitcombe	73	73	75	75	296
14=	Auguste Boyer	76	72	70	79	297
	Arthur Havers	80	72	71	74	297
	Joe Kirkwood, Sr	72	73	71	81	297
	Horton Smith	73	73	75	76	297
18=	Aubrey Boomer	74	70	76	78	298
	Jack M'Lean (a)	75	74	75	74	298
	Cyril Tolley (a)	70	73	76	79	298
21	Laurie Ayton, Sr	78	72	76	74	300
22=	Bert Gadd	75	73	73	80	301
	Walter Hagen	68	72	79	82	302
	DC Jones	75	72	78	76	301
	Fred Robertson	71	71	77	82	301
26	Alf Perry	79	73	74	76	302
27	Allan Dailey	74	74	77	78	303
28=	Ross Somerville (a)	72	78	75	79	304
	W Spark	73	72	79	80	304
	Charlie Ward	76	73	76	79	304

* Denny Shute (149) beat Craig Wood (154) in the 36-Hole Play-off

Round Leader(s)
R1 Dudley; 70
R2 Dudley; 141
R3 Easterbrook, Diegel; 146

Lowest Scores
R2 Mitchell; 68
R3 Wood; 68
R4 Dutra, R Whitcombe; 72

US PGA 1933

North Shore Country Club, Glenview, Illinois
(8–13 August)

MATCHPLAY
31 qualifiers, plus the defending champion (Olin Dutra), after 36 holes strokeplay
(Low – Mortie Dutra, Jimmy Hines, 138)
All Rounds 36 holes

'Pretty good for a washed up golfer', commented Gene Sarazen, when he collected his third PGA title – countering a jibe from Tommy Armour that the little man was past his best. Hagen, along with the pair who tied for the British Open a month earlier, Shute and Wood, declined to enter the Championship. I don't think Sarazen minded too much as Major No 6 went into the record books.

GENE SARAZEN ($1000) beat Willie Goggin, 5&4

Round by Round Details

ROUND 1 (Last 32)
Jimmy Hines bt Mortie Dutra 3&2; Henry Picard bt Willie Klein 2&1; Frank Walsh bt Jack Curley 3&2; Tom Creavy bt Dick Metz 3&2; Al Espinosa bt Charles Schneider 3&2; WILLIE GOGGIN bt Leo Diegel 4&3; Paul Runyan bt Al Houghton 6&5; Johnny Revolta bt Alex Gerlak 12&11; Clarence Clark bt Horton Smith 6&5; Ed Dudley bt Ben Pautke 2&1; GENE SARAZEN bt Vincent Eldred 8&7; Harry Cooper bt Dave Hackney 6&5; John Golden bt Gunnar Johnson 4&3; Bobby Cruickshank bt Bunny Torpey 3&2; Johnny Farrell bt Vic Ghezzi 1up; Olin Dutra bt Reggie Myles 4&3

ROUND 2 (Last 16)
Hines bt Picard 5&3
Creavy bt Walsh 2&1
GOGGIN bt Espinosa 9&7
Runyan bt Revolta 2&1
Dudley bt Clark 3&1
SARAZEN bt Cooper 4&3
Golden bt Cruickshank 2&1
Farrell bt Olin Dutra 1up

QUARTER FINAL (QF)
Hines bt Creavy 4&3
GOGGIN bt Runyan 6&5
SARAZEN bt Dudley 6&5
Farrell bt Golden 5&4

SEMI FINAL (SF)
GOGGIN bt Hines 1up
SARAZEN bt Farrell 5&4

THE MASTERS 1934

Augusta National Golf Club, Augusta, Georgia
(22–25 March)

6925 yards: Par 72 (288)

At the inaugural 'Masters' – more properly named at the time the Augusta National Invitational – Horton Smith's 20-foot putt for a birdie at 17 sealed the fate of Craig Wood once again. Bobby Jones came out of retirement to play in this, the tournament he devised, on a course he helped design; and finished in a tie for 13th with his erstwhile adversary, Walter Hagen.

1	**HORTON SMITH**	70	72	70	72	284
	($1500)					
2	Craig Wood	71	74	69	71	285
3=	Billy Burke	72	71	70	73	286
	Paul Runyan	74	71	70	71	286
5	Ed Dudley	74	69	71	74	288
6	Willie MacFarlane	74	73	70	74	291
7=	Al Espinosa	75	70	75	72	292
	Jimmy Hines	70	74	74	74	292
	Harold McSpaden	77	74	72	69	292
	MacDonald Smith	74	70	74	74	292
11=	Mortie Dutra	74	75	71	73	293
	Al Watrous	74	74	71	74	293
13=	Walter Hagen	71	76	70	77	294
	Bobby Jones (a)	76	74	72	72	294
	Denny Shute	73	73	76	72	294
16=	Leo Diegel	73	72	74	76	295
	Ralph Stonehouse	74	70	75	76	295
18=	Ky Laffoon	72	79	72	73	296
	Johnny Revolta	75	72	75	74	296
	Bill Schwartz	75	72	71	78	296
21=	Johnny Golden	71	75	74	77	297
	Charlie Yates (a)	76	72	77	72	297
23=	John Dawson (a)	74	73	76	75	298
	Henry Picard	71	76	75	76	298
25=	Henry Ciuci	74	73	74	78	299
	Tom Creavy	74	73	80	72	299
	Vic Ghezzi	77	74	74	74	299
28=	Bobby Cruickshank	74	74	80	72	300
	Jim Foulis	78	74	76	72	300
	Mike Turnesa	75	74	77	74	300

Round Leader(s)
R1   Emmett French (w/d), Hines, H Smith; 70
R2   H Smith; 142
R3   ¹H Smith; 212

Lowest Scores
R2   Dudley; 69
R3   Wood; 69
R4   McSpaden; 69

US OPEN 1934

Merion Cricket Club, Ardmore, Pennsylvania
(7–9 June)

6694 yards: Par 70 (284)

Olin Dutra made up eight strokes on the 36-hole leader, Bobby Cruickshank, to add a second Major to his 1932 PGA triumph. Despite not having played golf for ten days due to a crippling dysentery, he picked up two birdies on the last nine holes to overhaul Cruickshank, Cox and Sarazen – the last shooting a three-over par seven at the 11th hole.

1	**OLIN DUTRA**	76	74	71	72	293
	($1000)					
2	Gene Sarazen	73	72	73	76	294
3=	Harry Cooper	76	74	74	71	295
	Wiffy Cox	71	75	74	75	295
	Bobby Cruickshank	71	71	77	76	295
6=	Billy Burke	76	71	77	72	296
	Macdonald Smith	75	73	78	70	296
8=	Tom Creavy	79	76	78	76	299
	Ralph Guldahl	78	73	70	78	299
	Jimmy Hines	80	70	77	72	299
	Johnny Revolta	76	73	77	73	299
12=	Joe Kirkwood, Sr	75	73	78	74	300
	Ted Luther	78	71	78	73	300
14=	Willie Hunter, Jr	75	74	80	72	301
	Alvin Krueger	76	75	75	75	301
16	Mark Fry	79	75	74	74	302
17=	Henry Ciuci	74	74	79	76	303
	Leo Diegel	76	71	78	78	303
	Johnny Golden	75	76	74	78	303
	Horton Smith	74	73	79	77	303
21=	Al Espinosa	76	74	76	78	304
	Phil Perkins	78	74	79	73	304
23=	Herman Barron	79	72	76	78	305
	Ky Laffoon	76	73	80	76	305
25=	Lawson Little (a)	83	72	76	75	306
	Eddie Loos	76	75	78	77	306
	Orville White	76	79	76	75	306
28=	Rodney Bliss, Jr (a)	74	73	82	78	307
	Mortie Dutra	74	77	79	77	307
	Zell Eaton (a)	76	73	78	80	307
	Paul Runyan	74	78	79	76	307
	George Schneiter	76	76	79	76	307
	Bill Schwartz	81	74	73	79	307
	George Von Elm	74	76	80	77	307

Round Leader(s)
R1   Cox, Cruickshank; 71
R2   Cruickshank; 142
R3   Sarazen; 218

Lowest Scores
R2   Hines; 70
R3   Guldahl; 70
R4   Creavy; 66

BRITISH OPEN 1934

Royal St George's Golf Club, Sandwich, Kent, England
(27-29 June)
6776 yards

After ten years of American dominance, there was a British winner at Sandwich. Henry Cotton's second round score of 65 was not beaten in the Open until 1977. His 36- and 54-hole totals smashed all existing Majors records. Macdonald Smith was the leading American – 9 behind Cotton – but it is fair to say that the trans-Atlantic presence was not as widespread as in previous years.

1	**HENRY COTTON**	67	65	72	79	283
	(£100)					
2	Sid Brews	76	71	70	71	288
3	Alf Padgham	71	70	75	74	290
4=	Marcel Dallemagne	71	73	71	77	292
	Joe Kirkwood, Sr	74	69	71	78	292
	Macdonald Smith	77	71	72	72	292
7=	Bert Hodson	71	74	74	76	295
	Charles Whitcombe	71	72	74	78	295
9=	Percy Alliss	73	75	71	77	296
	Ernest R Whitcombe	72	77	73	74	296
11	William Twine	72	76	75	74	297
12	John Burton	80	72	72	74	298
13=	Bill Davies	76	68	73	82	299
	Edward Jarman	74	76	74	75	299
	Charlie Ward	76	71	72	70	299
16=	Allan Dailey	74	73	78	75	300
	James McDowall	73	74	76	77	300
	Jack M'Lean (a)	77	76	69	78	300
	Reg Whitcombe	75	76	74	75	300
20	Denny Shute	71	72	80	78	301
21=	Alf Beck	78	72	78	74	302
	Bert Gadd	76	74	74	78	302
	William Nolan	73	71	75	83	302
	Gene Sarazen	75	73	74	80	302
	Percy Weston	72	76	77	77	302
26=	Jimmy Adams	73	78	73	79	303
	Tom Green	75	73	74	81	303
	Alf Perry	76	76	74	77	303
29=	Auguste Boyer	78	75	77	74	304
	LT Cotton	76	73	79	76	304

Round Leader(s)
R1 H Cotton; 67
R2 H Cotton; 132
R3 H Cotton; 204

Lowest Scores
R2 H Cotton; 65
R3 M'Lean; 69
R4 Brews; 71

US PGA 1934

Park Club of Buffalo, Williamsville, New York
(24-29 July)

MATCHPLAY
31 qualifiers, plus the defending champion (Gene Sarazen), after 36 holes strokeplay
(Low Bob Crowley, 138)
All Rounds 36 holes

In a semi final match of incredibly low scoring, Craig Wood wreaked revenge on Denny Shute for his 1933 British Open play-off defeat. Victory was still not to be for Wood, though, as he missed out once more: again after extra holes, to leading Tour money-winner (the first PGA Tour Money List was published this year), Paul Runyan.

FINAL
PAUL RUNYAN ($1000) beat Craig Wood, 1up (after 38)

Round by Round Details

ROUND 1 (Last 32)
Gene Sarazen bt Herman Barron 3&2; Al Watrous bt Errie Ball 8&7; Harry Cooper bt Bill Mehlhorn 4&2; CRAIG WOOD bt Leo Fraser 6&5; Ky Laffoon bt George Smith 12&10; Denny Shute bt Walter Hagen 4&3; Al Houghton bt George Christ 7&6; Fay Coleman bt Leo Diegel 4&2; Dick Metz bt Joe Paletti 6&5; Tommy Armour bt Byron Nelson 4&3; Vic Ghezzi bt Eddie Burke 2&1; PAUL RUNYAN bt Johnny Farrell 8&6; Johnny Revolta bt Jim Foulis 7&6; Gene Kunes bt Orville White 3&2; Ted Turner bt Willie Goggin 1up (after 37); Bob Crowley bt Eddie Loos 3&2

ROUND 2 (Last 16)
Watrous bt Sarazen 4&3
WOOD bt Cooper 4&3
Shute bt Laffoon 3&2
Houghton bt Coleman 4&3
Metz bt Armour 3&2
RUNYAN bt Ghezzi 2&1
Kunes bt Revolta 2&1
Crowley bt Turner 1up

QUARTER FINAL (QF)
WOOD bt Watrous 2&1
Shute bt Houghton 6&5
RUNYAN bt Metz 1up
Kunes bt Crowley 4&3

SEMI FINAL (SF)
WOOD bt Shute 2&1
RUNYAN bt Kunes 4&2

THE MASTERS 1935

Augusta National Golf Club, Augusta, Georgia
(4–8 April)

6925 yards: Par 72 (288)

The chrisma of the Masters was forever set back in 1935, thanks mainly to just one golf shot. Gene Sarazen's albatross on the par-5 15th, achieved by holing a miraculous fairway wood approach from 220 yards, did for poor Craig Wood, yet again. The ensuing newspaper hype brought national attention to this Southern off-season tournament – and the rest is history. Sarazen also made history of another kind. He became the first of only five players (Hogan, Nicklaus, Player and Woods the others) to win all four Majors – the first modern Grand Slam. This was his last Majors win.

1	**GENE SARAZEN***	68	71	73	70	282
	($1500)					
2	Craig Wood	69	72	68	73	282
3	Olin Dutra	70	70	70	74	284
4	Henry Picard	67	68	76	75	286
5	Denny Shute	73	71	70	73	287
6	Lawson Little (a)	74	72	70	72	288
7	Paul Runyan	70	72	75	72	289
8	Vic Ghezzi	73	71	73	73	290
9=	Bobby Cruickshank	76	70	73	72	291
	Jimmy Hines	70	70	77	74	291
	Byron Nelson	71	74	72	74	291
	Joe Turnesa	73	71	74	73	291
13=	Ray Mangrum	68	71	76	77	292
	Johnny Revolta	70	74	73	75	292
15=	Walter Hagen	73	69	72	79	293
	Sam Parks Jr	74	70	74	75	293
17=	John Dawson (a)	75	72	72	75	294
	Al Espinosa	76	72	73	73	294
19=	Clarence Clark	77	75	73	71	296
	Leo Diegel	72	73	74	77	296
	Ed Dudley	73	73	74	76	296
	Harold McSpaden	75	72	75	74	296
	Horton Smith	74	75	74	73	296
	Charlie Yates (a)	75	70	76	75	296
25=	Harry Cooper	73	76	74	74	297
	Bobby Jones (a)	74	72	73	78	297
	Mike Turnesa	72	74	75	76	297
28=	Gene Kunes	76	72	77	73	298
	Ky Laffoon	76	73	72	77	298
	Phil Perkins	77	71	75	75	298

* Gene Sarazen (144) beat Craig Wood (149) in the 36-Hole Play-off

Round Leader(s)
R1   Picard; 67
R2   Picard; 135
R3   Wood; 209

Lowest Scores
R2   Picard; 68
R3   Wood; 68
R4   Sarazen; 70

US OPEN 1935

Oakmont Country Club, Oakmont, Pennsylvania
(6–8 June)

6981 yards: Par 72 (288)

The 11-over par winning total was testimony to the trial that was Oakmont. A look at the final round scores says more than any words can. Sam Parks Jr, fresh out of college, was a surprise winner. He was pro at the nearby South Hills CC, though, and was certainly helped by his local knowledge of the Oakmont beast.

1	**SAM PARKS, Jr**	77	73	73	76	299
	($1000)					
2	Jimmy Thomson	73	73	77	78	301
3	Walter Hagen	77	76	73	76	302
4=	Ray Mangrum	76	76	72	79	303
	Denny Shute	78	73	76	76	303
6=	Alvin Krueger	71	77	78	80	306
	Henry Picard	79	78	70	79	306
	Gene Sarazen	75	74	78	79	306
	Horton Smith	73	79	79	75	306
10=	Dick Metz	77	76	76	78	307
	Paul Runyan	76	77	79	75	307
12=	Olin Dutra	77	76	78	77	308
	Vincent Eldred	75	77	77	79	308
14=	Herman Barron	73	79	78	79	309
	Bobby Cruickshank	78	76	77	78	309
	Mortie Dutra	75	77	80	77	309
	Macdonald Smith	74	82	76	77	309
	Ted Turner	80	71	81	77	309
	Al Watrous	75	80	79	75	309
20	Vic Ghezzi	75	78	81	77	311
21=	Sid Brews	76	81	78	77	312
	Ed Dudley	74	83	75	80	312
	Bill Kaiser	78	82	78	74	312
	Gene Kunes	76	79	77	80	312
	Craig Wood	76	80	79	77	312
26=	Ted Luther	80	76	84	73	313
	Frank Walsh	76	82	82	73	313
28=	Harry Cooper	77	81	79	77	314
	Al Espinosa	75	76	78	85	314
	Willie Hunter, Jr	78	80	80	76	314
	Ky Laffoon	75	83	81	75	314

Round Leader(s)
R1   Krueger; 71
R2   Thomson; 146
R3   Parks, Thomson; 223

Lowest Scores
R2   Turner; 71
R3   Picard; 70
R4   Luther, Walsh; 73

BRITISH OPEN 1935

Hon Co of Edinburgh Golfers, Muirfield, East Lothian, Scotland
(26–28 June)
6806 yds

Once again a light assault from the Americans facilitated another home victory. Alf Perry's only win owed much to an excellent start and a record-equalling third round. With Fred (no relation) also winning at Wimbledon, it was a good year for the Perrys! Double-double Amateur Champion in the making (US & British, 1934–35), Lawson Little, was the best-placed overseas player.

1	**ALF PERRY**	69	75	67	72	283
	(£100)					
2	Alf Padgham	70	72	74	71	287
3	Charles Whitcombe	71	68	73	76	288
4=	Bert Gadd	72	75	71	71	289
	Lawson Little (a)	75	71	74	69	289
6	Henry Picard	72	73	72	75	292
7=	Henry Cotton	68	74	76	75	293
	Syd Easterbrook	75	73	74	71	293
8	William Branch	71	73	76	74	294
9	Laurie Ayton, Sr	74	73	77	71	295
10	Auguste Boyer	74	75	76	71	296
11=	Aubrey Boomer	76	69	75	77	297
	Jack Busson	75	76	70	76	297
	Bill Cox	76	69	77	75	297
	Ernest WH Kenyon	70	74	74	79	297
15=	Percy Alliss	72	76	75	75	298
	JA Jacobs	78	74	75	71	298
17=	W Laidlaw	74	71	75	79	299
	Philip H Rodgers	74	76	74	75	299
	Mark Seymour	75	76	75	73	299
	Macdonald Smith	69	77	75	78	299
	Ernest R Whitcombe	75	72	74	78	299
22=	Reg Cox	75	73	76	76	300
	Sam King	76	74	75	75	300
	Arthur Lacey	71	75	74	80	300
	Laddie Lucas (a)	74	73	72	81	300
26=	Frank Ball	76	75	73	77	301
	Alf Beck	74	76	77	74	301
	Len Holland	72	74	78	77	301
	PWL Risdon (a)	78	74	75	74	301
30=	Sid Brews	79	74	75	74	302
	Dai Rees	75	73	77	77	302
	Cyril Thomson	74	76	75	77	302

Round Leader(s)
R1 Cotton; 68
R2 C Whitcombe; 139
R3 Perry; 211

Lowest Scores
R2 C Whitcombe; 68
R3 Perry; 67
R4 Little; 69

US PGA 1935

Twin Hills Country Club, Oklahoma City, Oklahoma
(18–23 October)

MATCHPLAY
63 qualifiers, plus the defending champion (Paul Runyan), after 36 holes strokeplay
(Low – Walter Hagen, 139)
Rs1&2, 18 holes: R3,QF,SF&F, 36 holes

The Championship format was changed from this year to allow more players into the matchplay stage. It was to remain in this format for most of the remaining years until it gave way to medal play totally in 1958. Johnny Revolta stopped Tommy Armour claiming his second PGA title with a comfortable win in a final which was played in quite wintry conditions.

FINAL
JOHNNY REVOLTA ($1000)
beat Tommy Armour, 5&4

Round by Round Details

ROUND 2 (Last 32)
Paul Runyan bt Mortie Dutra 3&2; Tony Manero bt Clarence Doser 1up; Levi Lynch bt Art Bell 4&2; Al Zimmerman bt Vic Ghezzi 2&1; Pat Cicelli bt Orville White 3&2; JOHNNY REVOLTA bt Jimmy Hines 1up; Alvin Krueger bt Gene Sarazen 2&1; Eddie Schultz bt G Slingerland 2&1; Al Watrous bt Harold Sampson 2&1; Sam Parks, Jr bt Francis Scheider 1up; Horton Smith bt Ray Mangrum 1up; Denny Shute bt Henry Bontempo 4&3; Jimmy Thomson bt JG Collins 6&4; Ed Dudley bt Dick Metz 3&1; Ky Laffoon bt Eddie Loos 1up (after 21); TOMMY ARMOUR bt Charles Schneider 3&2

ROUND 3 (Last 16)
Runyan bt Manero 9&8
Zimmerman bt Lynch 7&6
REVOLTA bt Circelli 4&2
Schultz bt Krueger 1up (after 37)
Watrous bt Parks, Jr 4&3
Smith bt Shute 2&1
Dudley bt Thomson 6&4
ARMOUR bt Laffoon 3&2

QUARTER FINAL (QF)
Zimmerman bt Runyan 3&2
REVOLTA bt Schultz 4&2
Watrous bt Smith 1up
ARMOUR bt Dudley 1up (after 39)

SEMI FINAL (SF)
REVOLTA bt Zimmerman 4&3
ARMOUR bt Watrous 2&1

THE MASTERS 1936

Augusta National Golf Club, Augusta, Georgia
(2–5 April)

6925 yards: Par 72 (288)

Within the course of three years, Horton Smith won his second, and last, Masters, and second and last Major. He overcame Harry Cooper – another with the regular propensity to lose Majors when in contention – to turn a three-shot deficit into a one-stroke victory. Smith chipped in from 50 feet at the 14th and came home under par from there.

1	**HORTON SMITH**	74	71	68	72	285
	($1500)					
2	Harry Cooper	70	69	71	76	286
3	Gene Sarazen	78	67	72	70	287
4=	Bobby Cruickshank	75	69	74	72	290
	Paul Runyan	76	69	70	75	290
6=	Ed Dudley	75	75	70	73	293
	Ky Laffoon	75	70	75	73	293
	Ray Mangrum	76	73	68	76	293
9=	John Dawson (a)	77	70	70	77	294
	Henry Picard	75	72	74	73	294
11=	Walter Hagen	77	74	73	72	296
	Denny Shute	76	68	75	77	296
13=	Wiffy Cox	82	69	75	72	298
	Byron Nelson	76	71	77	74	298
15=	Al Espinosa	72	73	75	79	299
	Vic Ghezzi	77	70	77	75	299
	Harold McSpaden	77	75	71	76	299
	Jimmy Thomson	76	78	71	74	299
	Orville White	78	73	77	71	299
20=	Tommy Armour	79	74	72	75	300
	Chick Chin	76	74	71	79	300
	Lawson Little	75	75	73	77	300
	Sam Parks, Jr	76	75	72	77	300
	Craig Wood	88	67	69	76	300
25	Johnny Revolta	77	72	76	76	301
26	Albert Campbell (a)	82	73	68	79	302
27	Dick Metz	79	78	76	70	303
28	Billy Burke	74	77	74	79	304
29=	Johnny Farrell	78	75	74	78	305
	Joe Kirkwood, Sr	81	76	73	75	305
	Torchy Toda	81	84	75	75	305
	Al Watrous	78	76	73	78	305

Round Leader(s)
R1 Cooper; 70
R2 Cooper; 139
R3 Cooper; 210

Lowest Scores
R2 Sarazen, Wood; 67
R3 Campbell, Mangrum, Smith; 68
R4 Metz, Sarazen; 70

US OPEN 1936

Baltusrol Golf Club, Springfield, New Jersey
(4–6 June)

6866 yards: Par 72 (288)

Just to prove he could do it again, just two months after the Masters, Cooper, five strokes clear over the field, saw Tony Manero charge past with a brilliant 67 to win by two. Chick Evans' 20-year low score of 286 for the US Open had been finally beaten, as had the 283 set (successively) by Sarazen, Cotton and Perry in the British Open. Manero was relatively unknown, and although would be around for a few years, he never won another Major.

1	**TONY MANERO**	73	69	73	67	282
	($1000)					
2	Harry Cooper	71	70	70	73	284
3	Clarence Clark	69	75	71	72	287
4	Macdonald Smith	73	73	72	70	288
5=	Wiffy Cox	74	74	69	72	289
	Ky Laffoon	71	74	70	74	289
	Henry Picard	70	71	74	74	289
8=	Ralph Guldahl	73	70	73	74	290
	Paul Runyan	69	75	73	73	290
10	Denny Shute	72	69	73	77	291
11=	Herman Barron	73	74	69	76	292
	Tom Kerrigan	70	75	72	75	292
	Ray Mangrum	69	71	76	76	292
14=	Charles Kocsis (a)	72	71	73	77	293
	Frank Moore	70	74	75	74	293
	Johnny Revolta	70	71	77	75	293
	Jimmy Thomson	74	73	71	75	293
18=	Billy Burke	72	76	72	74	294
	Vic Ghezzi	70	70	73	81	294
	Willie Goggin	73	73	72	76	294
	Harold McSpaden	75	71	78	70	294
22=	Tommy Armour	74	76	74	71	295
	Johnny Farrell	75	75	70	75	295
	Jerry Gianferante	74	73	71	77	295
	Johnny Goodman (a)	75	73	73	74	295
	Felix Serafin	72	73	74	76	295
	Horton Smith	75	75	72	73	295
28=	Al Brosch	73	75	72	76	296
	Zell Eaton	72	75	72	77	296
	Dick Metz	74	73	73	76	296
	Jack Munger (a)	74	70	76	76	296
	Gene Sarazen	75	72	75	74	296

Round Leader(s)
R1 Clark, Mangrum, Runyon; 69
R2 Ghezzi, Mangrum; 140
R3 Cooper; 211

Lowest Scores
R2 Manero, Shute; 69
R3 Barron, Cox; 69
R4 Manero; 67

BRITISH OPEN 1936

Royal Liverpool Golf Club, Hoylake, Cheshire, England
(24–26 June)

7078 yards

Consistently solid golf gave Alf Padgham his only Open win. Gene Sarazen was there, but precious few other US stars. Although no official par figures are available for the Open Championship courses, where figures do appear they are courtesy of the clubs or contemporary newspaper reports. Over the first 7000+yard course prepared for any Major, Hoylake's scratch score was 76 in 1936.

1	**ALF PADGHAM**	73	72	71	71	287
	(£100)					
2	Jimmy Adams	71	73	71	73	288
3=	Henry Cotton	73	72	70	74	289
	Marcel Dallemagne	73	72	75	69	289
5=	Percy Alliss	74	72	74	71	291
	Tom Green	74	72	70	75	291
	Gene Sarazen	73	75	70	73	291
8=	Arthur Lacey	76	74	72	72	294
	Bobby Locke (a)	75	73	72	74	294
	Reg Whitcombe	72	77	71	74	294
11	Dai Rees	77	71	72	75	295
12=	Dick Burton	74	71	75	76	296
	Bill Cox	70	74	79	73	296
14	Bill Davies	72	76	73	77	298
15=	Aubrey Boomer	74	75	75	75	299
	Wally Smithers	75	73	77	74	299
	Hector Thomson (a)	76	76	73	74	299
	Ted Turner	75	74	76	74	299
19=	Gordon Good	75	73	79	73	300
	Charles Whitcombe	73	76	79	72	300
21=	Max Faulkner	74	74	77	75	301
	Bert Gadd	74	72	77	78	301
23=	Errie Ball	74	77	72	79	302
	Johnny Fallon	78	73	78	73	302
	Francis Francis (a)	73	72	79	78	302
	Willie Goggin	74	78	73	77	302
	Norman Sutton	75	72	78	77	302
28=	Sam King	79	74	75	76	304
	HR Manton	76	78	77	73	304
	Jean Saubaber	74	78	75	77	304

Round Leader(s)
R1 Cox; 70
R2 Adams, Cox; 144
R3 Adams, Cotton; 215

Lowest Scores
R2 Burton, Rees; 71
R3 Cotton, Green, Sarazen; 70
R4 Dallemagne; 69

US PGA 1936

Pinehurst Country Club, Pinehurst, North Carolina
(17–22 November)

MATCHPLAY
63 qualifiers, plus the defending champion (Johnny Revolta), after 36 holes strokeplay
(Low – Fay Coleman, 143)
Rs 1&2, 18 holes: R3,QF,SF&F 36 holes

Shute beat Jimmy Thomson to add a PGA title to his 1933 British Open. It was a bad event for former Champions. Hagen and Diegel didn't qualify, and Sarazen, Armour and Runyan were eliminated in Round One. Defending Champion Revolta also went out early. This was Pinehurst's belated first Major, and even more surprisingly, its only one until it finally gained USGA recognition for the 1999 US Open.

FINAL
DENNY SHUTE beat Jimmy Thompson, 3&2

Round by Round Details

ROUND 2 (Last 32)
Harold McSpaden bt Johnny Revolta 1up (after 19); Leo Walper bt Clarence Hackney 2&1; JIMMY THOMSON bt Willie Klein 3&2; Henry Picard bt Alvin Krueger 5&4; Harry Cooper bt Clarence Doser 3&2; Craig Wood bt Frank Walsh 1up; Bobby Cruickshank bt Errie Ball 2&1; Tony Manero bt Mortie Dutra 6&5; Horton Smith bt Jack Patroni 6&5; Willie Goggin bt Les Madison 5&4; DENNY SHUTE bt Al Zimmerman 3&2; Billy Burke bt Ky Laffoon 4&3; Bill Mehlhorn bt Dick Metz 1up (after 23); Ed Dudley bt Tom LoPresti 2&1; Jimmy Hines bt Ray Mangrum 2&1; Vic Ghezzi bt Fay Coleman 1up

ROUND 3 (Last 16)
McSpaden bt Walper 4&3
THOMSON bt Picard 4&2
Wood bt Cooper 2&1
Manero bt Cruickshank 4&2
Smith bt Goggin 2&1;
SHUTE bt Burke 2&1
Mehlhorn bt Dudley 6&4;
Hines bt Ghezzi 4&3

QUARTER FINAL (QF)
THOMSON bt McSpaden 1up
Wood bt Manero 5&4
SHUTE bt Smith 3&2
Mehlhorn bt Hines 4&2

SEMI FINAL (SF)
THOMSON bt Wood 5&4
SHUTE bt Mehlhorn 1up

THE MASTERS 1937

Augusta National Golf Club, Augusta, Georgia
(1–4 April)

6925 yards: Par 72 (288)

'Lord' Byron Nelson announced his arrival. After a faltering start to his career, the 1937 Masters was his big breakthrough. He set a new low of 66 for the Tournament and led at half-way. Then a bad third round let in Ralph Guldahl for a four-stroke lead going into the last round. A combination of the latter's bad figures thereafter, and Nelson's two-under par last round, turned it all round.

1	**BYRON NELSON**	66	72	75	70	283
	($1500)					
2	Ralph Guldahl	69	72	68	76	285
3	Ed Dudley	70	71	71	74	286
4	Harry Cooper	73	69	71	74	287
5	Ky Laffoon	73	70	74	73	290
6	Jimmy Thomson	71	73	74	73	291
7	Al Watrous	74	72	71	75	292
8=	Tommy Armour	73	75	73	72	293
	Vic Ghezzi	72	72	72	77	293
10=	Leonard Dodson	71	75	71	77	294
	Jimmy Hines	77	72	68	77	294
12	Wiffy Cox	70	72	77	76	295
13=	Clarence Clark	77	75	70	74	296
	Tony Manero	71	72	78	75	296
	Johnny Revolta	71	72	72	81	296
	Denny Shute	74	75	71	76	296
17	Bobby Cruickshank	79	69	71	78	297
18	Sam Snead	76	72	71	79	298
19=	Lawson Little	70	79	74	76	299
	Willie MacFarlane	73	76	73	77	299
	Paul Runyan	74	77	72	76	299
	Felix Serafin	75	76	71	77	299
	Horton Smith	75	72	77	75	299
24=	Ray Mangrum	71	80	72	77	300
	Gene Sarazen	74	80	73	73	300
26=	Craig Wood	79	77	74	71	301
	Charlie Yates (a)	76	73	74	78	301
28	Francis Francis (a)	77	74	75	76	302
29=	Billy Burke	77	71	75	80	303
	Al Espinosa	72	76	79	76	303
	Bobby Jones (a)	79	74	73	77	303

Round Leader(s)
R1 Nelson; 66
R2 Nelson; 138
R3 Guldahl; 209

Lowest Scores
R2 Cooper, Cruickshank; 69
R3 Guldahl, Hines; 68
R4 Nelson; 70

US PGA 1937

Pittsburgh Field Club, Aspinwall, Pennsylvania
(26–30 May)

MATCHPLAY
63 qualifiers, plus the defending champion (Denny Shute),
after 36 holes strokeplay
(Low – Byron Nelson, 139)
Rs1&2, 18 holes: R3,QF,SF&F, 36 holes

Denny Shute's back-to-back PGA titles took his Majors wins to three, and no one has regained a title in such rapid time. The PGA's spring re-scheduling resulted in the 1936 and 1937 Championships being just six months apart. Shute also became the fifth multiple winner of the Championship. He beat Harold 'Jug' McSpaden over extra holes – something that McSpaden had experienced positively against Bunny Torpey and Henry Picard in earlier rounds.

FINAL
DENNY SHUTE ($1000) beat Harold McSpaden, 1up
(after 37)

Round by Round Details

ROUND 2 (Last 32)
DENNY SHUTE bt Olin Dutra 3&2; Ed Dudley bt Pat Wilcox 4&3; Paul Runyan bt Willie Goggin 2&1; Jimmy Hines bt Al Espinosa 1up; Harry Cooper bt Johnny Revolta 1up; Jim Foulis bt Gene Sarazen 1up; Vic Ghezzi bt Sam Parks, Jr 1up; Tony Manero bt Willie MacFarlane 4&3; Byron Nelson bt Craig Wood 4&2; Johnny Farrell bt Charles Schneider 1up; Ky Laffoon bt Billy Burke 2&1; HAROLD McSPADEN bt Bunny Torpey 1up (after 20); Sam Snead bt Alvin Krueger 2up; Henry Picard bt Sam Bernardi 1up; Horton Smith bt Al Watrous 1up (after 19)

ROUND 3 (Last 16)
SHUTE bt Dudley 3&2
Hines bt Runyan 2&1
Cooper bt Foulis 5&4
Manero by Ghezzi 3&1
Nelson bt Farrell 5&4
Laffoon bt Thomson 4&3
McSPADEN bt Snead 3&2
Picard bt Smith 4&3

QUARTER FINAL (QF)
SHUTE bt Hines 4&3
Manero bt Cooper 1up
Laffoon bt Nelson 2up
McSPADEN bt Picard 1up (after 39)

SEMI FINAL (SF)
SHUTE bt Manero 1up
McSPADEN bt Laffoon 2&1

US OPEN 1937

Oakland Hills Country Club, Birmingham, Michigan
(10–12 June)
6880 yards: Par 72 (288)

Guldahl made up for his Masters disappointment with a stunning win, lowering Manero's US Open record of the previous year. The win was the dawn of Guldahl's great but brief reign at the top of world golf. A new era was coming in, with Nelson's Masters win, and the entry of Sam Snead into the record books as runner-up in the 1937 US Open. This started a 38-year span of Majors Top 10s for Snead – he finished tied for 3rd in the PGA as late as 1974 – but this was as close as he would ever get in the US Open: he would never lift his own national title, despite being runner-up on three further occasions.

1	**RALPH GULDAHL** ($1000)	71	69	72	69	281
2	Sam Snead	69	73	70	71	283
3	Bobby Cruickshank	73	73	67	72	285
4	Harry Cooper	72	70	73	71	286
5	Ed Dudley	70	70	71	76	287
6	Al Brosch	74	73	68	73	288
7	Clarence Clark	72	75	73	69	289
8	Johnny Goodman (a)	70	73	72	75	290
9	Frank Strafaci (a)	70	72	77	72	291
10=	Charles Kocsis (a)	72	73	76	71	292
	Henry Picard	71	75	72	74	292
	Gene Sarazen	78	69	71	74	292
	Denny Shute	69	76	75	72	292
14=	Ray Mangrum	75	75	71	72	293
	Paul Runyan	76	72	73	72	293
16=	Billy Burke	75	73	71	75	294
	Jimmy Demaret	72	74	76	72	294
	Sam Parks, Jr	74	74	72	74	294
	Pat Sawyer	72	70	75	77	294
20=	Vic Ghezzi	72	71	78	74	295
	Jimmy Hines	75	72	76	72	295
	Ky Laffoon	74	74	74	73	295
	Harold McSpaden	74	75	73	73	295
	Fred Morrison	71	76	74	74	295
	Byron Nelson	73	78	71	73	295
	Bob Stupple	73	73	73	76	295
	Frank Walsh	70	70	78	77	295
28=	Leo Mallory	73	74	76	73	296
	Toney Penna	76	74	75	71	296
	Johnny Revolta	75	73	75	73	296
	Jimmy Thomson	74	66	78	78	296

Round Leader(s)
R1 Shute, Snead; 69
R2 Dudley, Guldahl, Thomson, Walsh; 140
R3 Dudley; 211

Lowest Scores
R2 Thomson; 66
R3 Cruickshank; 67
R4 Clark, Guldahl; 69

BRITISH OPEN 1937

Carnoustie Golf Club, Angus, Scotland
(7–9 July)
7135 yards

Nelson's good form continued on his only visit to the Open Championship – but he still finished six behind Henry Cotton. Many Americans now saw the British Open as less relevant than their domestic Majors. There were several reasons for this in the '30s. Post-Depression USA was commercially more lucrative for a professional golfer; and the time taken by sea would mean two extra tournaments sacrificed. Also, the US golfers saw themselves post-Vardon, *et al*, as in the ascendancy (the Ryder Cup wins, started in 1927, were going their way). Perhaps Cotton might have been the British champion to throw down the gauntlet in the USA – but he was never encouraged to take them on.

1	**HENRY COTTON** (£100)	74	73	72	71	290
2	Reg Whitcombe	72	70	74	76	292
3	Charles Lacey	76	75	70	72	293
4	Charles Whitcombe	73	71	74	76	294
5	Byron Nelson	75	76	71	74	296
6	Ed Dudley	70	74	78	75	297
7=	Arthur Lacey	75	73	75	75	298
	W Laidlaw	77	72	73	76	298
	Alf Padgham	72	74	76	76	298
10	Horton Smith	77	71	79	72	299
11=	Ralph Guldahl	77	72	74	77	300
	Sam Snead	75	74	75	76	300
13	Bill Branch	72	75	73	81	301
14	Denny Shute	73	73	76	80	302
15=	Percy Alliss	75	76	75	77	303
	Henry Picard	76	77	70	80	303
17=	Jimmy Adams	74	78	76	76	304
	Arthur Havers	77	75	76	76	304
	Bobby Locke (a)	74	74	77	79	304
	Fred Robertson	73	75	78	78	304
21=	Bill Cox	74	77	81	73	305
	Dai Rees	75	73	78	79	305
23	Jack Busson	74	77	79	76	306
24	Tom Collinge	75	75	83	74	307
25	Douglas Cairncross	73	76	77	82	308
26=	Marcel Dallemagne	78	75	79	77	309
	Walter Hagen	76	72	80	81	309
	Jack M'Lean	78	74	81	76	309
29=	John Burton	76	75	82	77	310
	Sam King	79	74	75	82	310
	Ernest E Whitcombe	76	76	81	77	310

Round Leader(s)
R1 Dudley; 70
R2 R Whitcombe; 142
R3 R Whitcombe; 216

Lowest Scores
R2 R Whitcombe; 70
R3 C Lacey; 70
R4 Cotton; 71

THE MASTERS 1938

Augusta National Golf Club, Augusta, Georgia
(1–4 April)
6925 yards: Par 72 (288)

Harry Cooper again came in second (tied this time), once more failing to capitalize on a good start. Henry Picard's first Major was compensation for his 1935 disappointment in the Masters. Leading by four after 36 holes, he fell away badly then, but this time a solid final 36 holes saw him home.

1	**HENRY PICARD**	71	72	72	70	285
	($1500)					
2=	Harry Cooper	68	77	71	71	287
	Ralph Guldahl	73	70	73	71	287
4	Paul Runyan	71	73	74	70	288
5	Byron Nelson	73	74	70	73	290
6=	Ed Dudley	70	69	77	75	291
	Felix Serafin	72	71	78	70	291
8=	Dick Metz	70	77	74	71	292
	Jimmy Thomson	74	70	76	72	292
10=	Vic Ghezzi	75	74	70	74	293
	Jimmy Hines	75	71	75	72	293
	Lawson Little	72	75	74	72	293
13=	Billy Burke	73	73	76	73	295
	Gene Sarazen	78	70	68	79	295
15	Stanley Horne	74	74	77	71	296
16=	Bobby Jones (a)	76	74	72	75	297
	Harold McSpaden	72	75	77	73	297
18=	Bobby Cruickshank	72	75	77	74	298
	Johnny Revolta	73	72	76	77	298
	Tommy Taller	74	69	75	80	298
22=	Chuck Kocsis (a)	76	73	77	73	299
	Horton Smith	75	75	78	71	299
24	Sam Parks, Jr	75	75	76	74	300
25=	Wiffy Cox	74	78	74	75	301
	Ben Hogan	75	76	78	72	301
27=	Ky Laffoon	78	76	74	74	302
	Tony Manero	72	78	82	70	302
	Frank Walsh	74	75	77	76	302
	Al Watrous	73	77	76	76	302

Round Leader(s)
R1   Cooper; 68
R2   Dudley; 139
R3   Picard; 215

Lowest Scores
R2   Dudley, Tailer; 69
R3   Sarazen; 68
R4   Manero, Picard, Runyan, Serafin; 70

US OPEN 1938

Cherry Hills Country Club, Denver, Colorado
(9–11 June)
6888 yards: Par 71 (284)

Guldahl's easy last round ride to a back-to-back win was only the fourth time it had happened in the US Open: Willie Anderson, John McDermott and Bobby Jones were the other successful defending champions. Ray Ainsley set a record I'm pretty sure he would never tell his grandchildren about. He took 19 at the par-four 16th in Round Two and, unsurprisingly, missed the cut.

1	**RALPH GULDAHL**	74	70	71	69	284
	($1000)					
2	Dick Metz	73	68	70	79	290
3=	Harry Cooper	76	69	76	71	292
	Toney Penna	78	72	74	68	292
5=	Byron Nelson	77	71	74	72	294
	Emery Zimmerman	72	71	73	78	294
7=	Frank Moore	79	73	72	71	295
	Henry Picard	70	70	77	78	295
	Paul Runyan	78	72	71	74	295
10	Gene Sarazen	74	74	75	73	296
11=	Vic Ghezzi	79	71	75	72	297
	Jimmy Hines	70	75	69	83	297
	Denny Shute	77	71	72	77	297
	George Von Elm	78	72	71	76	297
15	Willie Hunter, Jr	73	72	78	75	298
16=	Olin Dutra	74	71	77	77	299
	Harold McSpaden	76	67	74	82	299
	Johnny Revolta	74	72	77	76	299
19=	Jim Foulis	74	74	75	77	300
	Horton Smith	80	73	73	74	300
	Al Zimmerman	76	77	75	72	300
22	Charles Lacey	77	75	75	75	302
23	Tommy Armour	78	70	75	80	303
24=	Al Huske	76	79	76	73	304
	Johnny Rogers	71	76	73	84	304
26	Charles Sheppard	79	73	74	79	305
27=	Joe Belfore	75	73	80	78	306
	Stanley Kertes	77	72	82	75	306
	Alvin Krueger	79	69	79	79	306
	Ray Mangrum	77	77	73	79	306

Round Leader(s)
R1   Hines, Picard; 70
R2   Picard; 140
R3   Metz; 211

Lowest Scores
R2   McSpaden; 67
R3   Hines; 69
R4   Penna; 68

BRITISH OPEN 1938

Royal St George's Golf Club, Sandwich, Kent, England
(6–8 July)
6728 yards

Reg Whitcombe, the youngest of the family after Ernest (R) and Charles, improved on his previous-year's runner-up position to take the Open at Sandwich. The winds on the last day were the strongest since Muirfield in 1929, and the Exhibition Tent collapsed. Padgham, downwind, drove the green on the 384-yard 11th for an eagle-two: almost the opposite happened to Cyril Tolley who, into the teeth of the gale on the 14th, saw his one iron clear water only for it to blow back in.

1	**REG WHITCOMBE**	71	71	75	78	295
	(£100)					
2	Jimmy Adams	70	71	78	78	297
3	Henry Cotton	74	73	77	74	298
4=	Dick Burton	71	69	78	85	303
	Jack Busson	71	69	83	80	303
	Allan Dailey	73	72	80	78	303
	Alf Padgham	74	72	75	82	303
8=	Fred Bullock	73	74	77	80	304
	Bill Cox	70	70	84	80	304
10=	Bert Gadd	71	70	84	80	305
	Bobby Locke	73	72	81	79	305
	Charles Whitcombe	71	75	79	80	305
13=	Sid Brews	76	70	84	77	307
	Dai Rees	73	72	79	83	307
15=	JH Ballingall	76	72	83	77	308
	Alf Perry	71	74	77	86	308
17	Arthur Lacey	74	72	82	81	309
18	Bill Shankland	74	72	84	81	311
19	Ernest R Whitcombe	70	77	83	82	312
20=	JL Black	72	72	83	86	313
	PJ Mahon	73	74	83	83	313
22	Jack M'Lean	72	74	83	85	314
23=	Marcel Dallemagne	70	74	86	85	315
	Willie Hastings	74	74	83	84	315
	Sam King	74	73	83	85	315
26=	Johnny Fallon	70	75	82	89	316
	Eustace Storey (a)	77	71	84	84	316
28=	Ernest WH Kenyon	77	71	86	83	317
	Bob Pemberton	74	72	91	80	317
	Cyril Tolley (a)	77	68	86	86	317

Round Leader(s)
R1 Adams, Cox, E Whitcombe, Dallemagne, Fallon; 70
R2 Burton, Busson, Cox; 140
R3 R Whitcombe; 217

Lowest Scores
R2 Tolley; 68
R3 Padgham, R Whitcombe; 75
R4 Cotton; 74

US PGA 1938

Shawnee Country Club, Shawnee-on-Delaware, Pennsylvania
(6–8 July)

MATCHPLAY
63 qualifiers, plus the defending champion (Denny Shute), after 36 holes strokeplay
(Low – Frank Moore, 136)
Rs1&2, 18 holes: R3,QF,SF&F, 36 holes

Paul Runyan immediately followed Denny Shute into the record books as a two-time winner of the PGA. He joined Shute, Jim Barnes, Walter Hagen, Gene Sarazen and Leo Diegel as the only golfers to have won the Championship more than once. Despite being taken to an extra hole by Horton Smith, Runyan had a reasonably trouble-free ride to the final where he demoralized the young Sam Snead.

FINAL
PAUL RUNYAN ($1100) beat Sam Snead, 8&7

Round by Round Details

ROUND 2 (Last 32)
Denny Shute bt John Thoren 7&6; Jimmy Hines bt Frank Walsh 2&1; Byron Nelson bt Alvin Krueger 1up (after 20); Harry Bassler bt Ed Dudley 4&3; Marvin Stahl bt George Whitehead 6&5; Jim Foulis bt Jimmy Thomson 1up; SAM SNEAD bt Terl Johnson 4&3; Felix Serafin bt Ky Laffoon 3&2; Billy Burke bt Frank Moore 1up (after 19); Horton Smith bt Leo Diegel 2&1; Ray Mangrum bt Harold McSpaden 1up (after 20); PAUL RUNYAN bt Tony Manero 3&2; Gene Sarazen bt Harry Nettlebladt 6&5; Jimmy Demaret bt Johnny Revolta 2up; Henry Picard bt Bob Shave 3&2; Dick Metz bt Ralph Guldahl 1up

ROUND 3 (Last 16)
Hines bt Shute 2&1
Nelson bt Bassler 11&10
Foulis bt Stahl 6&5
SNEAD bt Serafin 4&3
Smith bt Burke 3&2
RUNYAN bt Mangrum 1up (after 37)
Sarazen bt Demaret 1up (after 38)
Picard bt Metz 4&3

QUARTER FINAL (QF)
Hines by Nelson 2&1
SNEAD bt Foulis 8&7
RUNYAN bt Smith 4&3
Picard bt Sarazen 3&2

SEMI FINAL (SF)
SNEAD bt Hines 1up
RUNYAN bt Picard 4&3

THE MASTERS 1939

Augusta National Golf Club, Augusta, Georgia
(30–31March, 2 April)

6925 yards: Par 72 (288)

After the trauma of his 8&7 drubbing at the hands of Paul Runyan in the last Major of 1938, Sam Snead may have been forgiven for turning his back on golf after the first Major of 1939. He had already set a new low for all Majors and looked a certainty to win the Masters. Then Ralph Guldahl came home in 33 to set the first-ever sub-280 total. This also established a record of eight-under par for Major Championships.

1	**RALPH GULDAHL**	72	68	70	69	279
	($1500)					
2	Sam Snead	70	70	72	68	280
3=	Billy Burke	69	72	71	70	282
	Lawson Little	72	72	68	70	282
5	Gene Sarazen	73	66	72	72	283
6	Craig Wood	72	73	71	68	284
7	Byron Nelson	71	69	72	75	287
8	Henry Picard	71	71	76	71	289
9	Ben Hogan	75	71	72	72	290
10=	Ed Dudley	75	75	69	72	291
	Toney Penna	72	75	72	72	291
12=	Tommy Armour	71	74	76	72	293
	Vic Ghezzi	73	76	72	72	293
	Harold McSpaden	75	72	74	72	293
15	Denny Shute	78	71	73	72	294
16=	Paul Runyan	73	71	75	76	295
	Felix Serafin	74	76	73	72	295
18=	Chick Harbert	74	73	75	74	296
	Jimmy Thomson	75	71	73	77	296
	Charlie Yates (a)	74	73	74	75	296
21	Tommy Taller	78	75	73	71	297
22	Jimmy Hines	76	73	74	75	298
	Ky Laffoon	72	75	73	78	298
	Frank Moore	75	74	75	74	298
25	Al Watrous	75	75	74	75	299
26=	Tony Manero	76	73	77	74	300
	Horton Smith	75	79	74	72	300
	Willie Turnesa (a)	78	70	79	73	300
29=	Jess Sweetser (a)	75	75	75	77	302
	Frank Walsh	76	76	72	78	302

Round Leader(s)
R1 Burke; 69
R2 Sarazen; 139
R3 Guldahl; 210

Lowest Scores
R2 Sarazen; 66
R3 Little; 68
R4 Snead, Wood; 68

US OPEN 1939

Philadelphia Country Club, West Conshohocken, Pennsylvania
(8–12 June)

6786 yards: Par 69 (276)

Byron Nelson's second Major, after a triple-tie, should also have belonged to the seemingly luckless Sam Snead. Building on a good start, Snead led, or had a share of the lead, throughout. Arriving at the 18th tee he needed a par five to win; shot eight, and didn't even make the play-off. Old hand at being bridesmaid, Craig Wood, had the dubious honour of being the first man to finish second in every Major. He still holds the equally undesirable record of having been beaten in a Majors play-off (extra holes in the PGA) more times than anyone else (now shared with Greg Norman) and, also, in every Major.

1	**BYRON NELSON***	72	73	71	68	284
	($1000)					
2	Craig Wood	70	71	71	72	284
3	Denny Shute	70	72	70	72	284
4	Bud Ward (a)	69	73	71	72	285
5	Sam Snead	68	71	73	74	286
6	Johnny Bulla	72	71	68	76	287
7=	Ralph Guldahl	71	73	72	72	288
	Dick Metz	76	72	71	69	288
9=	Ky Laffoon	76	70	73	70	289
	Harold McSpaden	70	73	71	75	289
	Paul Runyan	76	70	71	72	289
12=	Harry Cooper	71	72	75	72	290
	Ed Dudley	76	72	73	69	290
	Henry Picard	72	72	72	74	290
15	Horton Smith	72	68	75	76	291
16=	Sam Byrd	75	71	72	74	292
	Olin Dutra	70	74	70	78	292
	Clayton Heafner	73	73	66	80	292
	Wilford Wehrle (a)	71	77	69	75	292
20=	Jimmy Hines	73	74	77	69	293
	Johnny Rogers	75	70	69	79	293
22=	Tommy Armour	70	75	69	80	294
	Jimmy Demaret	72	76	72	74	294
	Johnny Revolta	73	76	71	74	294
25=	Bobby Cruickshank	73	74	73	75	295
	Jim Foulis	73	75	77	70	295
	Dutch Harrison	75	72	74	74	295
	Matt Kowal	69	76	75	75	295
29=	Vic Ghezzi	73	71	76	76	296
	Ed Oliver	75	77	72	72	296
	Felix Serafin	80	72	71	73	296

* Byron Nelson beat Craig Wood and Denny Shute after two 18-Hole Play-offs:
11 July – Nelson (68) tied with Wood (68) – Shute (76) eliminated;
12 July – Nelson (70) beat Wood (73)

Round Leader(s)
R1 Snead; 68
R2 Snead; 139
R3 Bulla; 211

Lowest Scores
R2 Smith; 68
R3 Heafner; 66
R4 Nelson; 68

BRITISH OPEN 1939

Royal & Ancient Golf Club, St Andrews, Fife, Scotland
(5–7July)
6842 yds

The last Open Championship before the second great war in Europe was to intervene, was won for the only time by Dick Burton. He does hold the record though for holding the Claret Jug for the longest time! It was the end of an era in more ways than one. The 1902 Champion, Sandy Herd, concluded his 54-year relationship with The Open at the age of 71. In his first Open, in 1885, he was in a field that included one of the originals, 'Old' Tom Morris; and his younger brother Fred had won the US Open as far back as 1898. He is undoubtedly the 'bridge' linking the origins of Major Championships in 1860 to modern times. And, as if to underline the continuity of past and present, both Laurie Aytons, Sr and Jr, members of a particularly elastic St Andrews family, fittingly finished in the 1939 Top 30; whilst Dai Rees would grace the Championship for many years yet, coming second as late as 1961, a century after it all began.

1	**DICK BURTON**	70	72	77	71	290
	(£100)					
2	Johnny Bulla	77	71	71	73	292
3=	Johnny Fallon	71	73	71	79	294
	Sam King	74	72	75	73	294
	Alf Perry	71	74	73	76	294
	Bill Shankland	72	73	72	77	294
	Reg Whitcombe	71	75	74	74	294
8	Martin Pose	71	72	76	76	295
9=	Percy Alliss	75	73	74	74	296
	Ernest WH Kenyon	73	75	74	74	296
	Bobby Locke	70	75	76	75	296
12	Dai Rees	71	74	75	77	297
13=	Jimmy Adams	73	74	75	76	298
	Enrique Bertolino	73	75	75	75	298
	Jimmy Bruen (a)	72	75	75	76	298
	Henry Cotton	74	72	76	76	298
17=	Bill Anderson	73	74	77	75	299
	Enrique Serra	77	72	73	77	299
19	WH Green	75	75	72	78	300
20=	Bill Davies	71	79	74	77	301
	Syd Easterbrook	74	71	80	76	301
	Alex Kyle (a)	74	76	75	76	301
23=	Leonard Crawley (a)	72	76	80	74	302
	Max Faulkner	70	76	76	80	302
25	Harry Busson	70	75	81	77	303
26=	Laurie Ayton, Jr	72	77	78	77	304
	WS Collins	75	74	79	76	304
	Fred Taggart	73	77	76	78	304
29	Aurelio Castanon	77	73	80	75	305
30=	Laurie Ayton, Sr	76	72	82	76	306
	Charlie Ward	71	74	78	83	306

Round Leader(s)
R1 Burton, Busson, Faulkner, Locke; 70
R2 Burton; 142
R3 Fallon; 215

Lowest Scores
R2 Bulla, Easterbrook; 71
R3 Bulla, Fallon; 71
R4 Burton; 71

US PGA 1939

Pomonock Country Club, Flushing, New York
(9–15 July)

MATCHPLAY
64 qualifiers after 36 holes strokeplay
(Low – Dutch Harrison, Ben Hogan, Ky Laffoon, Emerick Kocsis, 138)
Rs1&2, 18 holes: R3,QF,SF&F, 36 holes

Byron Nelson was denied consecutive Majors victories in events in which he had participated (he missed the British Open) in 1939, when Henry Picard birdied the 36th to take the final into overtime – and repeated the dose on the 37th. This was Picard's second Major after collecting the Masters in the previous year, but he was not destined to add to them. Poor health was shortly to curtail his career; but his driver lived for many years and did great things. He gave it to Sam Snead. He also gave some financial assistance to another young hopeful. His name was Ben Hogan!

FINAL
HENRY PICARD ($1100) beat Byron Nelson, 1up (after 37)

Round by Round Details

ROUND 2 (Last 32)
Paul Runyan bt Frank Champ 3&2; Ben Hogan bt Abe Espinosa 5&4; Billy Burke bt Herman Barron 2&1; Dick Metz bt Al Brosch 1up; Tom O'Connor bt Ky Laffoon 2up; Rod Munday bt Jack Ryan 2up; HENRY PICARD v Joe Zarhardt 2up; Al Watrous bt Ken Tucker 5&3; Dutch Harrison bt Johnny Farrell 3&2; Bruce Coltart bt Mike Turnesa 1up (after 21); Clarence Doser bt Ralph Guldahl 2up; Horton Smith bt Ray Mangrum 3&2; Emerick Kocsis bt Vic Ghezzi 3&1; Denny Shute bt Leo Diegel 3&1; Johnny Revolta bt Tony Manero 3&2; BYRON NELSON bt William Francis 3&1

ROUND 3 (Last 16)
Runyan bt Hogan 3&2
Metz bt Burke 6&4
Munday bt O'Connor 2up
PICARD bt Watrous 8&7
Harrison bt Coltart 10&9
Smith bt Doser 4&2
Kocsis bt Shute 3&1
NELSON bt Revolta 6&4

QUARTER FINAL (QF)
Metz bt Runyan 2&1
PICARD bt Munday 2&1
Harrison bt Smith 4&3
NELSON bt Kocsis 10&9

SEMI FINAL (SF)
PICARD bt Metz 1up
NELSON bt Harrison 9&8

THE MASTERS 1940

Augusta National Golf Club, Augusta, Georgia
(4–7 April)
6925 yards: Par 72 (288)

Records fell to Jimmy Demaret, who posted 30 on the back nine; and Lloyd Mangrum, whose low of 64 beat the previous record for any Major. Demaret gradually clawed his way back into the Tournament and eventually won by a then Masters record margin of four. He was to become a feature in a few Masters to come and went on to regain the title in 1947 and 1950. Demaret also has an enviable record unmatched by anyone who has played in the Ryder Cup – played six matches, won six. He was less lucky in the other Majors, though.

1	**JIMMY DEMARET**	67	72	70	71	280
	($1500)					
2	Lloyd Mangrum	64	75	71	74	284
3	Byron Nelson	69	72	74	70	285
4=	Harry Cooper	69	75	73	70	287
	Ed Dudley	73	72	71	71	287
	Willie Goggin	71	72	73	71	287
7=	Henry Picard	71	71	71	75	288
	Sam Snead	71	72	69	76	288
	Craig Wood	70	75	67	76	288
10=	Ben Hogan	73	74	69	74	290
	Toney Penna	73	73	72	72	290
12=	Paul Runyan	72	73	72	74	291
	Frank Walsh	73	75	69	74	291
14=	Sam Byrd	73	74	72	73	292
	Johnny Farrell	76	72	70	74	292
	Ralph Guldahl	74	73	71	74	292
17=	Harold McSpaden	73	71	74	75	293
	Charlie Yates (a)	72	75	71	75	293
19=	Lawson Little	70	77	75	72	294
	Ed Oliver	73	75	74	72	294
21=	Johnny Bulla	73	73	74	75	295
	Dick Metz	71	74	75	75	295
	Gene Sarazen	74	71	77	73	295
	Bud Ward (a)	74	68	75	78	295
	Al Watrous	75	70	73	77	295
26	Jim Ferrier	73	74	75	74	296
27=	Jimmy Hines	75	76	74	72	297
	Johnny Revolta	74	74	74	75	297
29=	Jim Foulis	74	75	73	76	298
	Tony Manero	75	75	73	75	298

Round Leader(s)
R1   Mangrum; 64
R2   Demaret, Mangrum; 139
R3   Demaret; 209

Lowest Scores
R2   Ward; 68
R3   Wood; 67
R4   Cooper, Nelson; 70

US OPEN 1940

Canterbury Golf Club, Cleveland, Ohio
(6–9 June)
6894 yards: Par 72 (288)

Former multiple Amateur Champion, Lawson Little, beat Gene Sarazen after a play-off. Sarazen had pulled back three shots over the final holes to tie. Ed Oliver shot 287, but was disqualified for starting his last round earlier than scheduled due to the threat of a storm. Lawson became the sixth player to have won both US Amateur and Open Championships, but surprisingly he was the first of them to win the US Open as a professional.

1	**LAWSON LITTLE***	72	69	73	73	287
	($1000)					
2	Gene Sarazen	71	74	70	72	287
3	Horton Smith	69	72	78	69	288
4	Craig Wood	72	73	72	72	289
5=	Ralph Guldahl	73	71	76	70	290
	Ben Hogan	70	73	74	73	290
	Lloyd Mangrum	75	70	71	74	290
	Byron Nelson	72	74	70	74	290
9	Dick Metz	75	72	72	72	291
10=	Ed Dudley	73	75	71	73	292
	Frank Walsh	73	69	71	79	292
12=	Tommy Armour	73	74	75	71	293
	Harold McSpaden	74	72	70	77	293
	Henry Picard	73	73	71	76	293
15	Vic Ghezzi	70	74	75	75	294
16=	Jim Foulis	73	73	77	72	295
	Gene Kunes	76	72	73	74	295
	Johnny Revolta	73	74	72	76	295
	Sam Snead	67	74	73	81	295
20=	Andrew Gibson	71	75	77	73	296
	Jimmy Hines	73	74	77	72	296
	Felix Serafin	77	74	71	74	296
23=	Jock Hutchison, Jr	73	72	75	77	297
	Eddie Kirk	73	77	74	73	297
	Wilford Wehrle (a)	78	73	72	74	297
	Leland Wilcox	75	73	74	75	297
27	Ray Mangrum	73	78	75	72	298
28	Johnny Farrell	75	77	76	71	299
29=	Bruce Coltart	80	72	74	74	300
	Jim Ferrier (a)	73	74	78	75	300
	Al Huske	70	80	76	74	300
	Sam Parks, Jr	69	74	79	78	300
	Henry Ransom	75	77	74	74	300
	Jack Ryan	75	75	77	73	300
	Andrew Szwedko	76	77	76	71	300

* Lawson Little (70) beat Gene Sarazen (73) in the 18-Hole Play-off

Round Leader(s)
R1   Snead; 67
R2   Little, Smith, Snead; 141
R3   Walsh; 213

Lowest Scores
R2   Little, Walsh; 69
R3   McSpaden, Nelson, Sarazen; 70
R4   Smith; 69

BRITISH OPEN 1940

No Championship

US PGA 1940

Hershey Country Club, Hershey, Pennsylvania
(26 August–2 September)

MATCHPLAY
64 qualifiers after 36 holes strokeplay
(Low – Dick Metz, 140)
Rs1,2&3, 18 holes: QF,SF&F, 36 holes

Byron Nelson matched Hagen, Sarazen, Barnes and Armour by winning his third different Major. Poor old Sam Snead was still searching for his first title when he went down to Nelson at the 36th hole. He must have thought a win would never come. Hagen's victory was his 40th and last match win in the PGA, while rival Sarazen, in beating Ray Mangrum, notched up win No 43 – and still had some years to go.

FINAL
BYRON NELSON ($1100) beat Sam Snead, 1up

Round by Round Details

ROUND 2 (Last 32)
Henry Picard bt Alex Gerlak 4&3; Gene Sarazen bt Ray Mangrum 2&1; Jimmy Hines bt Ray Hill 2&1; SAM SNEAD bt Charles Sheppard 3&2; Ed Dudley bt John Gibson 2&1; Paul Runyan bt Al Watrous 3&2; Walter Hagen bt Vic Ghezzi 2&1; Harold McSpaden bt Herman Keiser 2&1; Dick Metz bt Ky Laffoon 3&2; BYRON NELSON bt Frank Walsh 1up (after 20); Arthur Clark bt Billy Burke 1up; Eddie Kirk bt Jimmy Demaret 2&1; Al Brosch bt Red Francis 5&4; Ben Hogan bt Harry Nettlebladt 5&4; Ralph Guldahl bt John Kinder 6&5; Jim Foulis bt Craig Wood 1up (after 19)

ROUND 3 (Last 16)
Sarazen bt Picard 1up
SNEAD bt Hines 2&1
Runyan bt Dudley 4&3
McSpaden bt Hagen 1up
NELSON bt Metz 2&1
Kirk bt Clark 5&4
Hogan bt Brosch 5&4
Guldahl bt Foulis 5&3

QUARTER FINAL (QF)
SNEAD by Sarazen 1up
McSpaden bt Runyan 8&6
NELSON bt Kirk 6&5
Guldahl bt Hogan 3&2

SEMI FINAL (SF)
SNEAD bt McSpaden 5&4
NELSON bt Guldahl 3&2

THE MASTERS 1941

Augusta National Golf Club, Augusta, Georgia
(3–6 April)
6925 yards: Par 72 (288)

Craig Wood's luck had changed. After a decade and more of disappointment he won his first Major. The US entered the War before the end of the year, so Wood's success seemed to arrive just in time. His win equalled the record under-par score – eight – and set a new first 36-hole low for the Masters.

1	**CRAIG WOOD**	66	71	71	72	280
	($1500)					
2	Byron Nelson	71	69	73	70	283
3	Sam Byrd	73	70	68	74	285
4	Ben Hogan	71	72	75	68	286
5	Ed Dudley	73	72	75	68	288
6=	Vic Ghezzi	77	71	71	70	289
	Sam Snead	73	75	72	69	289
8	Lawson Little	71	70	74	75	290
9=	Willie Goggin	71	72	72	76	291
	Harold McSpaden	75	74	72	70	291
	Lloyd Mangrum	71	72	72	76	291
12=	Jimmy Demaret	77	69	71	75	292
	Clayton Heafner	73	70	76	73	292
14=	Harry Cooper	72	73	75	73	293
	Ralph Guldahl	76	71	75	71	293
17	Jack Ryan	73	74	74	74	295
18	Denny Shute	77	75	74	70	296
19=	Dick Chapman (a)	76	73	70	78	297
	Jimmy Hines	76	74	75	72	297
	Gene Kunes	76	74	76	71	297
	Dick Metz	74	72	75	76	297
	Sam Parks, Jr	75	76	75	71	297
	Toney Penna	73	74	80	70	297
	Gene Sarazen	76	72	74	75	297
	Felix Serafin	72	79	74	72	297
	Horton Smith	74	72	77	74	297
28	Ray Mangrum	76	70	78	74	298
29=	Jim Ferrier	75	76	73	75	299
	Jim Foulis	76	75	71	77	299
	Martin Pose	77	74	76	72	299

Round Leader(s)
R1 Wood; 66
R2 Wood; 137
R3 Wood; 208

Lowest Scores
R2 Demaret, Nelson; 69
R3 Byrd; 68
R4 Dudley, Hogan; 68

US OPEN 1941

**Colonial Country Club, Fort Worth, Texas
(5–7 June)**

7005 yards: Par 70 (280)

As if to make up for all his previous failures, Craig Wood made it two in a row when he won the US Open's visit to the beast of Colonial for the first time. Just as sweet as the win was being able to turn the tables on Denny Shute – something of a *bête noir* to Wood over the years. Par golf over the second 36 holes kept him ahead of the field.

1	**CRAIG WOOD**	73	71	70	70	284
	($1000)					
2	Denny Shute	69	75	72	71	287
3=	Johnny Bulla	75	71	72	71	289
	Ben Hogan	74	77	68	70	289
5=	Herman Barron	75	71	74	71	291
	Paul Runyan	73	72	71	75	291
7=	Dutch Harrison	70	82	71	71	294
	Harold McSpaden	71	75	74	74	294
	Gene Sarazen	74	73	72	75	294
10=	Ed Dudley	74	74	74	73	295
	Lloyd Mangrum	73	74	72	76	295
	Dick Metz	71	74	76	74	295
13=	Henry Ransom	72	74	75	75	296
	Horton Smith	73	75	73	75	296
	Sam Snead	76	70	77	73	296
	Harry Todd (a)	72	77	76	71	296
17=	Lawson Little	71	73	79	74	297
	Byron Nelson	73	73	74	77	297
19	Vic Ghezzi	70	79	77	72	298
20	Gene Kunes	71	79	74	75	299
21=	Ralph Guldahl	79	76	72	73	300
	Clayton Heafner	72	72	78	78	300
	Johnny Palmer	74	76	76	74	300
24	Jimmy Hines	74	75	76	76	301
25	Joe Zarhardt	74	76	77	75	302
26=	Sam Byrd	76	78	75	74	303
	Herman Keiser	74	77	76	76	303
	Johnny Morris	72	73	81	77	303
	Henry Picard	77	79	72	75	303
30=	Jim Ferrier	77	71	81	75	304
	Jerry Gianferante	76	77	74	77	304
	Bud Ward (a)	76	77	75	76	304

Round Leader(s)
R1 Shute; 69
R2 Heafner, Little, Shute, Wood; 144
R3 Wood; 214

Lowest Scores
R2 Snead; 70
R3 Hogan; 68
R4 Hogan, Wood; 70

BRITISH OPEN 1941

No Championship

US PGA 1941

**Cherry Hills Country Club, Denver, Colorado
(7–13 July)**

MATCHPLAY
63 qualifiers, plus the defending champion (Byron Nelson), after 36 holes strokeplay
(Low – Sam Snead, 138)
Rs1&2, 18 holes: R3,QF,SF&F, 36 holes

Wood's bid to win all three US Majors in one season failed at the second fence in the PGA, when he was hammered 6&5 by little-known Mark Fry. Vic Ghezzi had been competing in the PGA for some years without proceeding to the later stages. Now wins over Lloyd Mangrum in the semi final and an overtime win in the final over Byron Nelson made him a worthy Champion.

FINAL
VIC GHEZZI ($1100) beat Byron Nelson, 1up
(after 38)

Round by Round Details

ROUND 2 (Last 32)
BYRON NELSON bt William Heinlein 1up; Ralph Guldahl bt Gene Kunes 2&1; Ben Hogan bt Bud Oakley 2up; Horton Smith bt Ralph Stonehouse 3&2; Denny Shute bt Jim Foulis 1up; Leonard Ott bt Jack Ryan (default); Bruce Coltart bt George Fazio 1up (after 19); Gene Sarazen bt Toney Penna 1up (after 19); Sam Snead bt Phil Greenwaldt 7&6; Mike Turnesa bt Harry Bassler 4&2; Mark Fry bt Craig Wood 6&5; Lloyd Mangrum bt Charles Sheppard 3&1; Jack Grout bt Fay Coleman 1up; VIC GHEZZI bt Augie Nordone 1up; Harold McSpaden bt George Schneiter 3&2; Jimmy Hines bt Ed Dudley 3&2

ROUND 3 (Last 16)
NELSON bt Guldahl 4&3
Hogan bt Smith 2&1
Shute bt Ott 5&3
Sarazen bt Coltart 9&7
Snead bt Turnesa 1up
Mangrum bt Fry 1up
GHEZZI bt Grout 1up
Hines bt McSpaden 6&4

QUARTER FINAL (QF)
NELSON bt Hogan 2&1
Sarazen bt Shute 7&6
Mangrum bt Snead 6&4
GHEZZI bt Hines 6&4

SEMI FINAL (SF)
NELSON bt Sarazen 2up
GHEZZI bt Mangrum 1up

BRITISH OPEN 1942

No Championship

US OPEN 1942

No Championship

THE MASTERS 1942

Augusta National Golf Club, Augusta, Georgia
(9–13 April)

6925 yards: Par 72 (288)

In a clash of the Titans, two of the biggest names in the game at that time went to an historic play-off. Hogan had reduced Nelson's 36-hole lead of eight to tie on a record-equalling 280 after the latter's 135 – another Masters low. In the play-off, Hogan raced away to lead by three, but starting at the sixth, Nelson started to reel him in and pass him to win by one. Three greats from the previous generation, Tommy Armour, Bobby Jones and Gene Sarazen, were in a bunch tied 28th.

1	**BYRON NELSON***	68	67	72	73	280
	($1500)					
2	Ben Hogan	73	70	67	70	280
3	Paul Runyan	67	73	72	71	283
4	Sam Byrd	68	68	75	74	285
5	Horton Smith	67	73	74	73	287
6	Jimmy Demaret	70	70	75	75	290
7=	Dutch Harrison	74	70	71	77	292
	Lawson Little	71	74	72	75	292
	Sam Snead	78	69	72	73	292
10=	Chick Harbert	73	73	72	75	293
	Gene Kunes	74	74	74	71	293
12	Jimmy Thomson	73	70	74	77	294
13	Chandler Harper	75	75	76	69	295
14	Willie Goggin	74	70	78	74	296
15=	Bobby Cruickshank	72	79	71	75	297
	Jim Ferrier	71	76	80	70	297
	Henry Picard	75	72	75	75	297
18=	Harry Cooper	74	77	76	72	299
	Harold McSpaden	74	72	79	74	299
	Felix Serafin	75	74	77	73	299
21	Ralph Guldahl	74	74	76	76	300
22	Toney Penna	74	79	73	75	301
23=	Billy Burke	71	79	80	72	302
	Herman Keiser	74	74	78	76	302
	Craig Wood	72	75	72	73	302
26=	Jim Foulis	75	71	79	78	303
	Johnny Palmer	78	75	75	75	303
28=	Tommy Armour	74	79	76	75	304
	Bobby Jones (a)	72	75	79	78	304
	Gene Sarazen	80	74	75	75	304
	Bud Ward (a)	76	73	80	75	304
	Charlie Yates (a)	78	76	74	76	304

* Byron Nelson (69) beat Ben Hogan (70) in the 18-Hole Play-off

Round Leader(s)

R1 Runyan, Smith; 67
R2 Nelson; 135
R3 Nelson; 207

Lowest Scores

R2 Nelson; 67
R3 Hogan; 67
R4 Harper; 69

US PGA 1942

Sea View Country Club, Atlantic City, New Jersey
(23–31 May)

MATCHPLAY
31 qualifiers, plus the defending champion (Vic Ghezzi), after 36 holes strokeplay
(Low – Harry Cooper, 138)
All Rounds 36 holes

Unlike the other Majors, World War II did not disrupt the PGA Championship in the same way. There was no Championship in 1943, but otherwise it was business as usual. Some pros had volunteered, others had been conscripted, but in 1942 the PGA could still attract a strong field. There was a military feel to the final, all the same, when Army Corporal (shortly to become Sergeant) Jim Turnesa lost out to Sam Snead, due to join the US Navy the following day, in a closer match than most people predicted. Snead made his Majors breakthrough at last, and went to war.

FINAL
SAM SNEAD ($1000) beat Jim Turnesa, 2&1

Round by Round Details

ROUND 1 (Last 32)
Jimmy Demaret bt Vic Ghezzi 4&3; Tom Harmon, Jr bt Bruce Coltart 3&2; Craig Wood bt Rod Munday 5&4; Leland Gibson bt Jimmy Gauntt 10&9; SAM SNEAD bt Sam Byrd 7&6; Willie Goggin bt Eddie Burke 2&1; Ed Dudley bt Denny Shute 3&2; Toney Penna bt Jimmy Hines 3&2; Harry Cooper bt Mike Turnesa 3&1; Lloyd Mangrum bt Dick Metz 6&5; Byron Nelson bt Harry Nettlebladt 5&3; Joe Kirkwood, Sr bt Jimmy Thomson 4&2; JIM TURNESA bt Dutch Harrison 6&5; Harold McSpaden bt Sam Parks, Jr 7&5; Ben Hogan bt Ben Loving 7&6; Ky Laffoon bt Vic Bass 12&11

ROUND 2 (Last 16)
Demaret bt Harmon 3&2
Wood bt Gibson 7&6
SNEAD bt Goggin 9&8
Dudley bt Penna 4&2
Cooper bt Mangrum 1up
Nelson bt Kirkwood 2&1
JIM TURNESA bt McSpaden 1up
Hogan bt Laffoon 9&8

QUARTER FINAL (QF)
Demaret bt Wood 7&6
SNEAD bt Dudley 1up
Nelson bt Cooper 1up (after 39)
JIM TURNESA bt Hogan 2&1

SEMI FINAL (SF)
SNEAD bt Demaret 3&2
JIM TURNESA bt Nelson 1up (after 37)

THE MASTERS 1943

No Championship

BRITISH OPEN 1943

No Championship

US OPEN 1943

No Championship

US PGA 1943

No Championship

THE MASTERS 1944

No Championship

BRITISH OPEN 1944

No Championship

US OPEN 1944

No Championship

US PGA 1944

Manito Golf & Country Club, Spokane, Washington (14–20 August

MATCHPLAY
32 qualifiers after 36 holes strokeplay
(Low – Byron Nelson)
All Rounds 36 holes

There was a less-familiar look to the competitors when the Championship resumed in 1944. It looked to be a foregone conclusion for Byron Nelson as he coasted through an under-strength field to meet little-known Bob Hamilton. Hamilton was 10–1 to beat Nelson, but in one of golf's biggest upsets, he did just that. Hamilton did less well in future – hampered as he was with burns from an aircraft accident, although he reappeared to contest the 1946 Masters. Winner's prize money rocketed, although it was paid in War Bonds.

FINAL
BOB HAMILTON ($3500) beat Byron Nelson, 1up

Round by Round Details

ROUND 1 (Last 32)
 BYRON NELSON bt Mike DeMassey 5&4; Mark Fry bt Neil Christian 2&1; Willie Goggin bt Purvis Ferree 8&7; Tony Manero bt Clayton Aleridge 1up (after 38); Sam Byrd bt WA Stackhouse 4&3; Chuck Congdon bt Henry Williams, Jr 7&6; Ed Dudley bt Steve Savel 7&6; Jimmy Hines bt Thurman Edwards 7&6; Harold McSpaden bt Bruce Coltart 7&5; Fred Annon bt Harry Nettlebladt 5&4; BOB HAMILTON bt Gene Kunes 6&5; Harry Bassler bt Joe Mozel 6&5; Art Bell bt Joe Zarhardt 1up (after 37); Craig Wood bt Jimmy D'Angelo 5&4; Toney Penna bt Morrie Gravatt 3&2; George Schneiter bt Ted Longworth 7&6

ROUND 2 (Last 16)
 NELSON bt Fry 7&6
 Goggin bt Manero 4&3
 Congdon bt Byrd 2&1
 Dudley bt Hines 1up (after 37)
 McSpaden bt Annon 8&7
 HAMILTON bt Bassler 6&5
 Bell bt Wood 3&2
 Schneiter bt Penna 4&3

QUARTER FINAL (QF)
 NELSON bt Goggin 4&3
 Congdon bt Dudley 6&5
 HAMILTON bt McSpaden 2&1
 Schneiter bt Bell 2&1

SEMI FINAL (SF)
 NELSON bt Congdon 8&7
 HAMILTON bt Schneiter 1up

THE MASTERS 1945

No Championship

BRITISH OPEN 1945

No Championship

US OPEN 1945

No Championship

US PGA 1945

MATCHPLAY
31 qualifiers, plus the defending champion (Bob Hamilton), after 36 holes strokeplay
(Low – Byron Nelson, Johnny Revolta, 138)
All Rounds 36 holes

If 1930 was the year of Bobby Jones, then surely 1945 was to be Byron Nelson's year. Although no other Major was played, the PGA Championship was part of the Players' Tour, which had restarted the previous year. From March to August 1945, he won every tournament he entered, to put together a sequence of wins, which just like Jones' achievement in 1930' will surely never be beaten (eh, Tiger?). He won 11 altogether, including the PGA in July – which, with the winner's purse at $3750, was the richest of the Majors for several years to come.

FINAL
BYRON NELSON ($3750) beat Sam Byrd, 4&3

Round by Round Details

ROUND 1 (Last 32)
  Jack Grout bt Bob Hamilton 5&4; Ky Laffoon bt Felix Serafin 4&3; Clarence Doser bt Harold McSpaden 5&4; Toney Penna bt Wayne Timberman 2up; Johnny Revolta bt Frank Kringle 10&9; SAM BYRD bt Augie Nordone 4&3; Herman Barron bt Harry Nettlebladt 5&3; Vic Ghezzi bt Ed Dudley 7&6; BYRON NELSON bt Gene Sarazen 4&3; Mike Turnesa bt John Gibson 5&4; Denny Shute bt Barney Clark 4&3; Bob Kepler bt George Schneiter 2&1; Terl Johnson bt Dutch Harrison 1up; Ralph Hutchison bt Ted Huge 6&5; Jim Turnesa bt Byron Harcke 6&5; Claude Harmon bt Verl Stinchcomb 2&1

ROUND 2 (Last 16)
  Laffoon bt Grout 5&4
  Doser bt Penna 1up
  BYRD bt Revolta 2&1
  Ghezzi bt Barron 2up
  NELSON bt Mike Turnesa 1up
  Shute bt Kepler 5&4
  Hutchison bt Johnson 6&5
  Harmon bt Jim Turnesa 8&7

QUARTER FINAL (QF)
  Doser bt Laffoon 2&1
  BYRD bt Ghezzi 7&6
  NELSON bt Shute 3&2
  Harmon bt Hutchison 4&3

SEMI FINAL (SF)
  BYRD bt Doser 7&6
  NELSON bt Harmon 5&4

THE MASTERS 1946

Augusta National Golf Club, Augusta, Georgia
(4–7 April)
6925 yards: Par 72 (288)

Normal service was resumed in 1946 with all Majors taking place. Herman Keiser surprisingly won the first post-war Masters, leaving Ben Hogan then with the longest reign of any golfer as runner-up in a Major – at least for a few months. Keiser's excellent start meant that Hogan had to charge the last round. This he duly did and had the chance to tie on the 18th when Keiser three-putted. That Hogan followed suit in an identical fashion was somewhat of an anticlimax.

1	**HERMAN KEISER**	69	68	71	74	282
	($2500)					
2	Ben Hogan	74	70	69	70	283
3	Bob Hamilton	75	69	71	72	287
4=	Jimmy Demaret	75	70	71	73	289
	Jim Ferrier	74	72	68	75	289
	Ky Laffoon	74	73	70	72	289
7=	Chick Harbert	69	75	76	70	290
	Clayton Heafner	74	69	71	76	290
	Byron Nelson	72	73	71	74	290
	Sam Snead	74	75	70	71	290
11	Jim Foulis	75	70	72	74	291
12	Cary Middlecoff (a)	72	76	70	74	292
13=	Vic Ghezzi	71	79	67	76	293
	George Schneiter	73	73	72	75	293
15	Fred Haas	71	75	68	80	294
16=	Johnny Bulla	72	76	73	74	295
	Lloyd Mangrum	76	75	72	72	295
18	Claude Harmon	76	75	74	71	296
19	Chandler Harper	74	76	73	74	297
20	Frank Stranahan (a)	76	74	73	75	298
21=	Lawson Little	74	74	78	73	299
	Toney Penna	71	73	80	75	299
	Felix Serafin	76	75	79	69	299
	Horton Smith	78	77	75	69	299
25=	Herman Barron	74	73	74	79	300
	Henry Picard	79	73	72	77	300
	Denny Shute	79	77	71	73	300
	Jimmy Thomson	72	70	79	79	300
29=	Gene Kunes	76	72	77	76	301
	Harold McSpaden	75	74	75	77	301
	Al Zimmerman	76	76	74	75	301

Round Leader(s)
R1   Harbert, Keiser; 69
R2   Keiser; 137
R3   Keiser; 208

Lowest Scores
R2   Keiser; 68
R3   Ghezzi; 67
R4   Serafin, Smith; 69

US OPEN 1946

Canterbury Golf Club, Cleveland, Ohio
(13–16 June)
6880 yards: Par 72 (288)

Vic Ghezzi was denied his second Major and Nelson his sixth, when Lloyd Mangrum won the three-way play-off at Cleveland. The first play-off was indecisive, and in the repeat, with Mangrum three down to Ghezzi and two to Hogan with six to play, all looked lost. Three successive birdies changed all that, and Mangrum's second 72 was too good for the others.

1	**LLOYD MANGRUM***	74	70	68	72	284
	($1500)					
2=	Vic Ghezzi	71	69	72	72	284
	Byron Nelson	71	71	69	73	284
4=	Herman Barron	72	72	72	69	285
	Ben Hogan	72	68	73	72	285
6=	Jimmy Demaret	71	74	73	68	286
	Ed Oliver	71	71	74	70	286
8=	Chick Harbert	72	78	67	70	287
	Dick Metz	76	70	72	69	287
10=	Dutch Harrison	75	71	72	70	288
	Lawson Little	72	69	76	71	288
12=	Ed Furgol	77	69	74	69	289
	Clayton Heafner	75	72	71	71	289
	Henry Picard	71	73	71	74	289
15=	Claude Harmon	72	77	70	72	291
	Chandler Harper	76	74	67	74	291
	Steve Kovach	71	72	73	75	291
	Toney Penna	69	97	74	71	291
19=	Gene Kunes	74	73	73	72	292
	Sam Snead	69	75	74	74	292
21	Paul Runyan	75	72	76	70	293
22=	Johnny Bulla	72	74	73	75	294
	Henry Ransom	71	73	73	77	294
	Harry Todd	75	73	70	76	294
	Lew Worsham	73	74	76	71	294
26=	Leland Gibson	74	71	78	72	295
	Smiley Quick (a)	75	76	72	72	295
	Mike Turnesa	70	76	74	75	295
	Ellsworth Vines	73	72	75	75	295
	Bud Ward (a)	74	77	72	72	295

* Lloyd Mangrum beat Vic Ghezzi and Byron Nelson after two 18-Hole Play-offs:
   am) Mangrum (72) tied with Ghezzi (72) and Nelson (72)
   (pm) Mangrum (72) beat Ghezzi (73) and Nelson (73)

Round Leader(s)
R1   Penna, Snead; 69
R2   Ghezzi, Hogan; 140
R3   Nelson; 211

Lowest Scores
R2   Hogan; 68
R3   Harbert, Harper; 67
R4   Demaret; 68

BRITISH OPEN 1946

Royal & Ancient Golf Club, St Andrews, Fife, Scotland
(3–5 July)
6923 yds

It was fitting for the the first post-war Open Championship, just like the last before the War, should be held over the Old Course at St Andrews. Unfortunately, Sam Snead did not consider his second Major all that important (compare the respective prize money, for one thing), and the Americans stayed away in their droves for another decade and more. All but one, that is: Johnny Bulla remained faithful to the British Open for several years to come – and it was he that relieved Ben Hogan of his longevity crown for a Majors runner-up, set the previous April at Augusta.

1	**SAM SNEAD**	71	70	74	75	290
	(£150)					
2=	Johnny Bulla	71	72	72	79	294
	Bobby Locke	69	74	75	76	294
4=	Henry Cotton	70	70	76	79	295
	Norman von Nida	70	76	74	75	295
	Dai Rees	75	67	73	80	295
	Charlie Ward	73	73	73	76	295
8=	Fred Daly	77	71	76	74	298
	Joe Kirkwood, Sr	71	75	78	74	298
10	Lawson Little	78	75	72	74	299
11	Harry Bradshaw	76	75	76	73	300
12	Dick Burton	74	76	76	76	302
13	Bill Shankland	76	76	77	75	304
14=	Bill Anderson	76	76	78	75	305
	Reg Whitcombe	71	76	82	76	305
16	Laurie Ayton, Jr	77	74	80	75	306
17	Percy Alliss	74	72	82	79	307
18=	Archie Compston	77	74	77	80	308
	Frank Jowle	78	74	76	80	308
	Arthur Lees	77	71	78	82	308
21=	G Knight	77	75	82	76	310
	Ernest E Whitcombe	75	79	77	79	310
23=	RK Bell (a)	81	73	81	77	312
	JA Jacobs	76	77	80	79	312
25=	Alf Perry	78	77	78	80	313
	James Wilson (a)	78	76	81	78	313
27=	Flory van Donck	76	78	83	78	315
	A Dowie (a)	81	71	80	83	315
	AM Robertson	79	75	80	81	315
30=	Tom Haliburton	78	76	81	81	316
	Alf Padgham	79	74	76	87	316
	Ronnie White (a)	76	79	84	77	316

Round Leader(s)
R1   Locke; 69
R2   Cotton; 140
R3   Bulla, Rees, Snead; 215

Lowest Scores
R2   Rees; 67
R3   Bulla, Little; 72
R4   Bradshaw; 73

US PGA 1946

Portland Golf Club, Portland, Oregon
(19–25 August)

MATCHPLAY
63 qualifiers, plus the defending champion (Byron Nelson), after 36 holes strokeplay
(Low – Jim Ferrier, 134)
Rs1&2, 18 holes: R3,QF,SF&F, 36 holes

After a compacted matchplay format during the War years, the PGA reverted to the 1941 set-up once more. Australian Jim Ferrier shot a round of 63 in his record qualifying score, and although the field was back to strength, no one could stop Ben Hogan ripping it apart. Big defeats of Art Bell and Frank Moore preceded the semi final demolition of Jimmy Demaret. Hogan then blasted away Ed Oliver in the final. Byron Nelson, after his amazing year previously, and with a haul of five Majors, dramatically and prematurely retired from tournament golf. He did, however, play in a dwindling number of Major Championships for another 20 years.

FINAL
BEN HOGAN ($3500) beat Ed Oliver, 6&4

Round by Round Details

ROUND 2 (Last 32)
Byron Nelson bt Larry Lamberger 3&2; Herman Barron bt Fay Coleman 3&2; ED OLIVER bt Dick Metz 3&1; Chandler Harper bt Jimmy Thomson 2&1; Dutch Harrison bt Toney Penna 1up; Harold McSpaden bt Bob Hamilton 4&3; Chuck Congdon bt Newton Bassler 1up (after 19); George Schneiter bt Sam Snead 6&5; Jim Ferrier bt Lawson Little 3&2; Jimmy Demaret bt Dave Tinsley 3&2; Jim Turnesa bt Henry Ransom 1up; Dick Shoemaker bt Vic Ghezzi 1up; BEN HOGAN bt William Heinlein 4&3; Art Bell bt Al Nelson 4&3; Frank Moore bt George Fazio 2&1; Harry Bassler bt Lew Worsham 1up

ROUND 3 (Last 16)
Nelson bt Barron 3&2
OLIVER bt Harper 5&4
McSpaden bt Harrison 4&3
Congdon bt Schneiter 2&1
Demaret bt Ferrier 3&2
Turnesa bt Shoemaker 5&4
HOGAN bt Bell 5&4
Moore bt Harry Bassler 4&3

QUARTER FINAL (QF)
OLIVER bt Nelson 1up
McSpaden bt Congdon 5&3
Demaret bt Turnesa 6&5
HOGAN bt Moore 5&4

SEMI FINAL (SF)
OLIVER bt McSpaden 6&5
HOGAN bt Demaret 10&9

THE MASTERS 1947

Augusta National Golf Club, Augusta, Georgia
(3–6 April)
6925 yards: Par 72 (288)

Jimmy Demaret, badly beaten finalist in the PGA of 1946, was on much more familiar territory in the first Major of 1947 at Augusta National. Charged with a Round One 69, he led from start to finish to win his second Masters. The outstanding amateur of the next decade, Frank Stranahan, finished tied-second. Recent retiree Nelson obviously hadn't read the script for appearances by former pros!

1	**JIMMY DEMARET** ($2500)	69	71	70	71	281
2=	Byron Nelson	69	72	72	70	283
	Frank Stranahan (a)	73	72	70	68	283
4=	Ben Hogan	75	68	71	70	284
	Harold McSpaden	74	69	70	71	284
6=	Jim Ferrier	70	71	73	72	286
	Henry Picard	73	70	72	71	286
8=	Chandler Harper	77	72	68	70	287
	Lloyd Mangrum	76	73	68	70	287
	Dick Metz	72	72	72	71	287
	Ed Oliver	70	72	74	71	287
	Toney Penna	71	70	75	71	287
13	Johnny Bulla	70	75	74	69	288
14=	Dick Chapman (a)	72	71	74	72	289
	Lawson Little	71	71	76	71	289
	Bobby Locke	74	74	71	70	289
17=	Herman Barron	71	71	74	74	290
	Fred Haas	70	74	73	73	290
	Johnny Palmer	70	73	74	73	290
20	Denny Shute	73	75	72	71	291
21	Vic Ghezzi	73	77	71	71	292
22=	Horton Smith	72	70	76	75	293
	Sam Snead	72	71	75	75	293
24=	Herman Keiser	74	75	73	72	294
	Ellsworth Vines	75	71	75	73	294
26=	Claude Harmon	73	69	76	77	295
	Gene Sarazen	75	76	74	70	295
	George Schneiter	70	75	78	72	295
29=	Dutch Harrison	74	71	74	77	296
	Clayton Heafner	75	73	75	73	296
	Cary Middlecoff	71	69	76	80	296
	Harry Todd	74	74	71	77	296

Round Leader(s)
R1   Demaret, Nelson; 69
R2   Demaret, Middlecoff; 140
R3   Demaret; 210

Lowest Scores
R2   Hogan; 68
R3   Harper, Mangrum; 68
R4   Stranahan; 68

US OPEN 1947

St Louis Country Club, St Louis, Missouri
(12–15 June)
6532 yards: Par 71 (284)

Sam Snead never won the US Open – the only jewel missing from his otherwise glittering crown. In the previous September the original trophy was destroyed by fire. Old trophy or new, Snead was never to get as close as 1947, when he and Lew Worsham tied. Worsham won the play-off on the last green in controversial circumstances. Worsham asked for a measure after Snead had already addressed his 2½ foot putt. The measure still meant that Snead was first to putt. He missed, but Worsham made his to win.

1	**LEW WORSHAM*** ($2000)	70	70	71	71	282
2	Sam Snead	72	70	70	70	282
3=	Bobby Locke	68	74	70	73	285
	Ed Oliver	73	70	71	71	285
5	Bud Ward (a)	69	72	73	73	287
6=	Jim Ferrier	71	70	74	74	289
	Vic Ghezzi	74	73	73	69	289
	Leland Gibson	69	76	73	71	289
	Ben Hogan	70	75	70	74	289
	Johnny Palmer	72	70	75	72	289
	Paul Runyan	71	74	72	72	289
12	Chick Harbert	67	72	81	70	290
13=	Ed Furgol	70	75	72	74	291
	Dutch Harrison	76	72	70	73	291
	Dick Metz	69	70	78	74	291
	Bill Nary	77	71	70	73	291
	Frank Stranahan (a)	73	74	72	72	291
	Harry Todd	67	75	77	72	291
19=	Claude Harmon	74	72	74	72	292
	Gene Kunes	71	77	72	72	292
	George Payton	71	75	75	71	292
	Alfred Smith	70	73	76	73	292
23=	Sam Byrd	72	74	70	77	293
	Joe Kirkwood, Sr	72	73	70	78	293
	Lloyd Mangrum	72	72	69	75	293
	James McHale, Jr (a)	79	72	65	77	293
27=	Herman Barron	74	71	75	74	294
	Billy Burke	74	75	71	74	294
29=	Bob Hamilton	75	71	75	74	295
	Henry Ransom	67	74	79	75	295

* Lew Worsham (69) beat Sam Snead (70) in the
   18-Hole Play-off

Round Leader(s)
R1   Harbert, Ransom, Todd; 67
R2   Harbert, Metz; 139
R3   Worsham; 211

Lowest Scores
R2   Demaret (39); 69
R3   McHale Jr; 65
R4   Ghezzi; 69

US PGA 1947

Plum Hollow Country Club, Detroit, Michigan
(18–24 June)

MATCHPLAY
63 qualifiers, plus the defending champion (Ben Hogan), after 36 holes strokeplay
(Low – Jimmy Demaret, 137)
Rs1&2, 18 holes: R3,QF,SF&F, 36 holes

Jim Ferrier became the first non-American born winner of the PGA since Tommy Armour in 1930. It was also the first final since 1937 without Hogan, Nelson or Snead. Good putting (just 52 over the 35 holes played) was Ferrier's secret. It was just as well, as his driving off the tee and approach play were erratic. It is reported that he struck spectators on seven occasions during the course of the final!

FINAL
JIM FERRIER ($3500) beat Chick Harbert, 5&4

Round by Round Details

ROUND 2 (Last 32)
Ky Laffoon bt Toney Penna 1up; Gene Sarazen bt Sam Snead 2&1; Dick Metz bt Henry Ransom 1up; Art Bell bt Johnny Bulla 4&3; Claude Harmon bt Jim Milward 5&3; JIM FERRIER bt Herman Barron 3&2; Mike Turnesa bt Chandler Harper 1up (after 22); Lloyd Mangrum bt Ed Dudley 4&3; Vic Ghezzi bt Earl Martin 6&5; Jim Turnesa bt Walter Ambo 4&3; Lew Worsham bt Clarence Doser 5&4; Reggie Myles bt George Schneiter 1up; CHICK HARBERT bt Clayton Heafner 1up (after 20); Ed Oliver bt Harry Bassler 4&3; Eddie Joseph bt Lloyd Wadkins 1up; Leland Gibson bt Jack Smith 3&2

ROUND 3 (Last 16)
Laffoon bt Sarazen 4&3
Bell bt Metz 1up (after 37)
FERRIER bt Harmon 1up (after 37)
Mangrum bt Mike Turnesa 1up
Ghezzi bt Jim Turnesa 4&3
Worsham bt Myles 7&6
HARBERT bt Oliver 3&2
Gibson bt Joseph 1up (after 37)

QUARTER FINAL (QF)
Bell bt Laffoon 2up
FERRIER bt Mangrum 4&3
Ghezzi bt Worsham 3&2
HARBERT bt Gibson 2up

SEMI FINAL (SF)
FERRIER bt Bell 10&9
HARBERT bt Ghezzi 6&5

BRITISH OPEN 1947

Royal Liverpool Golf Club, Hoylake, Cheshire, England
(2–4 July)
6960 yards

Ulsterman Fred Daly became the only player, to date, from the island of Ireland to win a Major. As Liverpool is often considered a cultural extension of the Emerald Isle, I suppose the win at Hoylake was apposite. Laurie Ayton is the third generation of that family to feature in Major Championships, although sadly, none has ever threatened to win.

1	**FRED DALY**	73	70	78	72	293
	(£150)					
2=	Reg Horne	77	74	72	71	294
	Frank Stranahan (a)	71	79	72	72	294
4	Bill Shankland	76	74	75	70	295
5	Dick Burton	77	71	77	71	296
6=	Johnny Bulla	80	72	74	71	297
	Henry Cotton	69	78	74	76	297
	Sam King	75	72	77	73	297
	Arthur Lees	75	74	72	76	297
	Norman von Nida	74	76	71	76	297
	Charlie Ward	76	73	76	72	297
12	Jimmy Adams	73	80	71	75	299
13=	Alf Padgham	75	75	74	76	300
	Reg Whitcombe	75	77	71	77	300
15=	Laurie Ayton, Jr	69	80	74	79	302
	Fred Bullock	74	78	78	72	302
17	Norman Sutton	77	76	73	77	303
18=	Vic Ghezzi	75	78	72	79	304
	Alf Perry	76	77	70	81	304
	Ernest E Whitcombe	77	76	74	77	304
21=	Dai Rees	77	74	73	81	305
	Flory van Donck	73	76	81	75	305
23	Alan Waters	75	78	76	77	306
24	John Burton	73	79	76	71	309
25=	Harry Busson	80	76	71	83	310
	JA Jacobs	75	80	76	79	310
27=	Ken Bousfield	78	76	79	78	311
	Arthur Havers	80	76	79	76	311
	N Quigley	79	77	76	79	311
	B Shepard	78	78	77	78	311

Round Leader(s)
R1 Ayton, Cotton; 69
R2 Daly, 143
R3 Daly, Lees, Von Nida; 221

Lowest Scores
R2 Daly; 70
R3 Perry; 70
R4 Shankland; 70

THE MASTERS 1948

Augusta National Golf Club, Augusta, Georgia
(8–11 April)

6925 yards: Par 72 (288)

Claude Harmon, father of Butch, the coach of Tiger Woods and others half a century later, was the first non-tournament playing professional to win the Masters. No one would have noticed – he equalled Ralph Guldahl's low score set in 1939 and won by the biggest margin to date!

1	**CLAUDE HARMON** ($2500)	70	70	69	70	279
2	Cary Middlecoff	74	71	69	70	284
3	Chick Harbert	71	70	70	76	287
4=	Jim Ferrier	71	71	75	71	288
	Lloyd Mangrum	69	73	75	71	288
6=	Ed Furgol	70	72	73	74	289
	Ben Hogan	70	71	77	71	289
8=	Byron Nelson	71	73	72	74	290
	Harry Todd	72	67	80	71	290
10=	Herman Keiser	70	72	76	73	291
	Bobby Locke	71	71	74	75	291
	Dick Metz	71	72	75	73	291
13=	Johnny Bulla	74	72	76	71	293
	Dutch Harrison	73	77	73	70	293
	Skee Riegel (a)	71	74	73	75	293
16=	Al Smith	73	73	74	74	294
	Sam Snead	74	75	72	73	294
18=	Jimmy Demaret	73	72	78	72	295
	Ed Dudley	73	76	75	71	295
	Vic Ghezzi	75	73	73	74	295
	Fred Haas	75	75	76	69	295
	Bob Hamilton	72	72	76	75	295
23=	Art Bell	71	74	74	77	296
	Gene Sarazen	77	74	73	72	296
25=	Herman Barron	73	77	71	76	297
	Henry Cotton	72	73	75	77	297
	Henry Picard	73	73	74	77	297
28=	Johnny Palmer	75	73	76	74	298
	Elsworth Vines	76	71	77	74	298
30=	Bud Ward (a)	74	74	77	74	299
	Lew Worsham	74	78	71	76	299

Round Leader(s)
R1 Mangrum; 69
R2 Todd; 139
R3 Harmon; 209

Lowest Scores
R2 Todd; 67
R3 Harman, Middlecoff; 69
R4 Haas; 69

US PGA 1948

Norwood Hills Country Club, St Louis, Missouri
(8–10 June)

MATCHPLAY
63 qualifiers, plus the defending champion (Jim Ferrier), after 36 holes strokeplay
(Low – Skip Alexander, 134)
Rs1&2, 18 holes: R3,QF,SF&F, 36 holes

The PGA was still playing musical chairs with the Majors' calendar. While the Masters and both Open Championship dates remained quite static, the PGA in 1947 was the third Major of the season; 1948 and 1949 it was second on the roster; 1950 through to 1953, back to third; and fourth from then on. Even then it didn't settle into its August slot until 1969 and, rather eccentrically, it took place in 1971 in February! The Hogan era was well and truly here as he added a second PGA to his 1946 title, with a third Turnesa brother experiencing the anguish of runner-up in a Major. An accident involving a Greyhound bus on 2 February 1949 was to cut short Hogan's PGA career. He was to return to it again only in 1960, when the event had become matchplay.

FINAL
BEN HOGAN ($3500) beat Mike Turnesa, 7&6

Round by Round Details

ROUND 2 (Last 32)
Claude Harmon bt Jim Ferrier 1up; Henry Ransom bt Lloyd Mangrum 3&2; Sam Snead bt Frank Moore 4&3; Leland Gibson bt Pete Cooper 1up; Johnny Bulla bt Armand Farina 4&3; Ky Laffoon bt Chandler Harper 3&2; MIKE TURNESA bt Zell Eaton 1up (after 21); Al Smith bt Jimmy Hines 4&3; Skip Alexander bt Al Brosch 2up; Chick Harbert bt Eddie Burke 1up (after 26); BEN HOGAN bt Johnny Palmer 1up; Gene Sarazen bt Jackson Bradley 2&1; Jimmy Demaret bt George Getchell 3&1; Lew Worsham bt Errie Ball 7&6; Ed Oliver bt Sherman Elworthy 3&2; George Fazio bt Henry Williams Jr 7&6

ROUND 3 (Last 16)
Harmon bt Ransom 2&1
Snead bt Gibson 5&3
Bulla bt Laffoon 6&5
TURNESA bt Smith 3&2
Harbert bt Alexander 11&10
HOGAN bt Sarazen 1up
Demaret bt Worsham 3&2
Fazio bt Oliver 1up

QUARTER FINAL (QF)
Harmon bt Snead 1up (after 42)
TURNESA bt Bulla 6&5
HOGAN bt Harbert 2&1
Demaret bt Fazio 5&4

SEMI FINAL (SF)
TURNESA bt Harmon 1up (after 37)
HOGAN bt Demaret 2&1

US OPEN 1948

Riviera Country Club, Pacific Palisades, California
(10–12 June)
7020 yards: Par 71 (284)

Ben Hogan's first US Open win was his second Major in successive events, and third in total. His 276 was a landmark record in the US Open. It was not lowered until Jack Nicklaus' 275 at Baltusrol in 1967. In fact, up until 1964 only one total bettered this in any Major – 274 in the 1954 Masters by Hogan himself.

1	**BEN HOGAN**	67	72	68	69	276
	($2000)					
2	Jimmy Demaret	71	70	68	69	278
3	Jim Turnesa	71	69	70	70	280
4	Bobby Locke	70	69	73	70	282
5	Sam Snead	69	69	73	72	283
6	Lew Worsham	67	74	71	73	285
7	Herman Barron	73	70	71	72	286
8=	Johnny Bulla	73	72	75	67	287
	Toney Penna	70	72	73	72	287
	Smiley Quick	73	71	69	74	287
11	Skip Alexander	71	73	71	73	288
12=	Charles Congdon	71	70	71	77	289
	Harold McSpaden	74	69	69	77	289
14=	Vic Ghezzi	72	74	74	70	290
	Leland Gibson	71	76	69	74	290
	Otto Greiner	74	73	71	72	290
	Herman Keiser	71	71	73	75	290
	George Schneiter	73	68	75	74	290
	Herschel Spears	72	71	76	71	290
	Ellsworth Vines	75	72	69	74	290
21=	Joe Kirkwood, Jr	72	70	72	77	291
	Lloyd Mangrum	71	72	74	74	291
	Cary Middlecoff	74	71	73	73	291
	Alfred Smith	73	72	77	69	291
25=	Art Bell	72	75	71	74	292
	Pete Cooper	76	72	72	72	292
	George Fazio	72	72	76	72	292
28=	Marty Furgol	72	74	73	74	293
	Chick Harbert	72	72	77	72	293
	Joe Kirkwood, Sr	73	75	73	72	293
	Frank Moore	73	75	73	72	293

Round Leader(s)
R1 Hogan, Worsham; 67
R2 Snead; 138
R3 Hogan; 207

Lowest Scores
R2 Schnieter; 68
R3 Demaret, Hogan; 68
R4 Bulla; 67

BRITISH OPEN 1948

Hon Co of Edinburgh Golfers, Muirfield, East Lothian, Scotland
(30 June–2 July)
6806 yards

Cotton won his third Open at the age of 41, courtesy of a second round of 66 – a score only previously beaten by his own 65 at Sandwich, 14 years before. This gave him enough of a cushion to hold off defending champion Fred Daly. US veteran, 54 year-old Bobby Cruickshank, finished down the field on 302.

1	**HENRY COTTON**	71	66	75	72	284
	(£150)					
2	Fred Daly	72	71	73	73	289
3=	Roberto de Vicenzo	70	73	72	75	290
	Jack Hargreaves	76	68	73	73	290
	Norman von Nida	71	72	76	71	290
	Charlie Ward	69	72	75	74	290
7=	Johnny Bulla	74	72	73	72	291
	Sam King	69	72	74	76	291
	Alf Padgham	73	70	71	77	291
	Flory van Donck	69	73	73	76	291
11=	Mario Gonzales	76	72	70	75	293
	EC Kingsley (a)	77	69	77	70	293
	Arthur Lees	73	79	73	78	293
	Alan Waters	75	71	70	77	293
15=	Max Faulkner	75	71	74	74	294
	Dai Rees	73	71	76	74	294
	Ernest E Whitcombe	74	73	73	74	294
18=	Dick Burton	74	70	74	77	295
	Frank Jowle	70	78	74	73	295
	Reg Whitcombe	77	67	77	74	295
21=	Ken Bousfield	76	71	73	76	296
	Johnny Fallon	73	74	74	75	296
23=	Tom Haliburton	73	74	76	74	297
	Alf Perry	77	71	76	73	297
	Frank Stranahan (a)	77	71	75	74	297
	Norman Sutton	72	73	77	75	297
27	Claude Harmon	75	73	78	72	298
28=	Otway Hayes	74	73	75	78	300
	Reg Horne	71	77	73	79	300
30=	Arthur Clark	74	71	75	81	301
	Harold Gould	75	73	78	75	301

Round Leader(s)
R1 King, Van Donck, Ward; 69
R2 Cotton; 137
R3 Cotton; 212

Lowest Scores
R2 Cotton; 66
R3 Gonzales, Waters; 70
R4 Kingsley; 70

THE MASTERS 1949

Augusta National Golf Club, Augusta, Georgia
(7–10 April)

6925 yards: Par 72 (288)

Snead's first Masters win was all down to a superb last 36 holes. The final round 67 included eight birdies. This was his second Major success, but another was just around the corner. Bulla, after two experiences in the British Open, became a Majors runner-up for the third time. He was also third in the 1941 US Open, and must be considered unlucky not to have become a Majors winner. This was the first occasion upon which the famous Green Jacket was awarded to the winner by the Augusta National Club.

1	**SAM SNEAD**	73	75	67	67	282
	($2750)					
2=	Johnny Bulla	74	73	69	69	285
	Lloyd Mangrum	69	74	72	70	285
4=	Johnny Palmer	73	71	70	72	286
	Jim Turnesa	73	72	71	70	286
6	Lew Worsham	76	75	70	68	289
7	Joe Kirkwood, Jr	73	72	70	75	290
8=	Jimmy Demaret	76	72	73	71	292
	Clayton Heafner	71	74	72	75	292
	Byron Nelson	75	70	74	73	292
11=	Claude Harmon	73	75	73	72	293
	Herman Keiser	75	68	78	72	293
13=	Herman Barron	73	75	71	75	294
	Leland Gibson	71	74	77	72	294
	Bobby Locke	74	74	74	72	294
16=	Charles R Coe (a)	77	72	72	74	295
	John Dawson (a)	78	72	72	73	295
	Jim Ferrier	77	72	67	79	295
19=	Tony Holguin	81	70	71	74	296
	Frank Stranahan (a)	70	77	75	74	296
21=	Pete Cooper	76	75	72	74	297
	Henry Picard	74	77	73	73	297
23=	Bob Hamilton	77	79	69	73	298
	Dutch Harrison	73	78	75	72	298
	Lawson Little	72	77	73	76	298
	Cary Middlecoff	76	77	72	73	298
	Toney Penna	74	76	76	72	298
	Horton Smith	75	72	78	73	298
29	Fred Haas	75	70	75	79	299
30–	Skip Alexander	74	77	75	74	300
	George Fazio	78	76	71	75	300
	Dick Metz	71	76	76	77	300
	Skee Riegel (a)	75	74	74	77	300

Round Leader(s)
R1   Mangrum; 69
R2   Keiser, Mangrum; 143
R3   Palmer; 214

Lowest Scores
R2   Keiser; 68
R3   Ferrier, Snead; 67
R4   Snead; 67

US PGA 1949

Hermitage Country Club, Richmond, Virginia
(25–31 May)

MATCHPLAY
64 qualifiers (the defending champion Ben Hogan was unable to compete) after 36 holes strokeplay
(Low – Ray Hill, 136)
Rs1&2, 18 holes: R3, QF, SF&F, 36 holes

It is often very difficult to win the Masters Tournament and the PGA Championship in the same season. They are usually at the opposite ends of the calendar, which requires the sustaining of form in a notoriously fickle sport over several months, or the ability to 'peak' twice in the same year. Sam Snead's feat was no doubt facilitated by another springtime PGA – and the absence of Ben Hogan due to his horrendous road accident.

FINAL
SAM SNEAD ($3500) beat Johnny Palmer, 3&2

Round by Round Details

ROUND 2 (Last 32)
Ray Hill bt Jack Isaacs 3&2; Walter Romans bt Frank Moore 4&2; Herman Barron bt Jimmy Thomson 2&1; LLoyd Mangrum bt Bob Hamilton 3&2; JOHNNY PALMER bt Clay Gaddie 8&6; Lew Worsham by George Schneiter 5&4; Henry Williams Jr bt Jack Harden 1up; Al Brosch bt Horton Smith 5&4; SAM SNEAD bt Henry Ransom 3&1; Dave Douglas bt Mike DeMassey 3&2; Jimmy Demaret by George Fazio 3&1; Jim Turnesa bt Johnny Bulla 1up; Clyton Heafner bt Claude Harmon 2&1; Jack Patroni bt Jimmy Johnson 1up; Jim Ferrier bt Skip Alexander 1up; Marty Furgol bt Eddie Burke 2&1

ROUND 3 (Last 16)
Hill bt Romans 5&4
Mangrum bt Barron 4&3
PALMER bt Worsham 2&1
Williams Jr bt Brosch 7&6
SNEAD bt Douglas 1up
Demaret bt Turnesa 5&3
Heafner bt Patroni 5&4
Ferrier bt Furgol 8&6

QUARTER FINAL (QF)
Mangrum bt Hill 7&6
PALMER bt Williams Jr 7&6
SNEAD bt Demaret 4&3
Ferrier bt Heafner 3&2

SEMI FINAL (SF)
PALMER bt Mangrum 6&5
SNEAD bt Ferrier 3&2

US OPEN 1949

Medinah Country Club, Medinah, Illinois
(9–11 June)
6936 yards: Par 71 (284)

Hogan was crippled for 12 months and played no part in any of the 1949 Majors. Cary Middlecoff won the first of his two Opens, winning at Medinah by just holding off late challenges by Heafner, and especially Snead.

1	**CARY MIDDLECOFF** ($2000)	75	67	69	75	286
2=	Clayton Heafner	72	71	71	73	287
	Sam Snead	73	73	71	70	287
4=	Bobby Locke	74	71	73	71	289
	Jim Turnesa	78	69	70	72	289
6=	Dave Douglas	74	73	70	73	290
	Buck White	74	68	70	78	290
8=	Pete Cooper	71	73	74	73	291
	Claude Harmon	71	72	74	74	291
	Johnny Palmer	71	75	72	73	291
11=	Eric Monti	75	72	70	75	292
	Herschel Spears	76	71	71	74	292
13	Al Brosch	70	71	73	79	293
14=	Johnny Bulla	73	75	72	74	294
	Lloyd Mangrum	74	74	70	76	294
	Skee Riegel (a)	72	75	73	74	294
	Harry Todd	76	72	73	73	294
	Ellsworth Vines	73	72	71	78	294
19=	Fred Haas	74	73	73	75	295
	Les Kennedy	69	74	79	73	295
	Gene Webb	73	77	70	75	295
22	Ralph Guldahl	71	75	73	77	296
23=	Jim Ferrier	74	75	74	74	297
	Chick Harbert	70	78	75	74	297
	Jack Isaacs	73	73	74	77	297
	Horton Smith	72	75	74	76	297
27=	Skip Alexander	76	72	77	73	298
	Herman Barron	70	78	76	74	298
	Sam Bernardi	80	69	76	73	298
	Jack Burke, Jr	74	74	75	75	298
	Charles Farlow	70	77	76	75	298
	James McHale, Jr (a)	72	76	74	76	298
	Craig Wood	76	73	76	73	298
	Lew Worsham	71	76	71	80	298

Round Leader(s)
R1 Kennedy; 69
R2 Brosch; 141
R3 Middlecoff; 211

Lowest Scores
R2 Middlecoff; 67
R3 Middlecoff; 69
R4 Snead; 70

BRITISH OPEN 1949

Royal St George's Golf Club, Sandwich, Kent, England
(6–8 July)
6728 yards

In 1949, Bobby Locke of South Africa was undoubtedly the best non-American golfer in the world. He had already won several times on the US tour and featured well in the US Open; and was about to embark on an orgy of British Open Championships. He had to endure an epic second 36-hole dogfight with Harry Bradshaw – then a somewhat easier head-to-head in the play-off. Bradshaw's Round Two 77 was not helped by his having to play one shot out of a broken beer bottle. It meant having to address the bottle and hope that the follow-through would pick up the ball as well. It did! In an attempt to attract a more international field, the R&A doubled the winner's prize money. The Americans were not impressed.

1	**BOBBY LOCKE*** (£300)	69	76	68	70	283
2	Harry Bradshaw	68	77	68	70	283
3	Roberto de Vicenzo	68	75	73	69	285
4=	Sam King	71	69	74	72	286
	Charlie Ward	73	71	70	72	286
6=	Max Faulkner	71	71	71	74	287
	Arthur Lees	74	70	72	71	287
8=	Jimmy Adams	67	77	72	72	288
	Johnny Fallon	69	75	72	72	288
	Wally Smithers	72	75	70	71	288
11=	Ken Bousfield	69	77	76	67	289
	Bill Shankland	69	73	74	73	289
13	Frank Stranahan (a)	71	73	74	72	290
14=	Bill Branch	71	75	74	71	291
	Dick Burton	73	70	74	74	291
	J Knipe	76	71	72	72	291
17	Walter Lees	74	72	69	78	293
18	Alan Waters	70	76	75	73	294
19	Norman Sutton	69	78	75	73	295
20=	Reg Horne	73	74	75	74	296
	Arthur Lacey	72	73	73	78	296
	Gregor McIntosh	70	77	76	73	296
	William McMinn	70	75	78	73	296
	EA Southerden	69	76	74	77	296
26	Herbert Osborne	73	74	75	76	298
27	Johnny Bulla	71	73	76	79	299
28	Ugo Grappasoni	70	76	77	77	300
29	Ernest WH Kenyon	72	75	77	77	301
30	Bill White	74	71	80	78	303

* Bobby Locke (135) beat Harry Bradshaw (147) in the 36-Hole Play-off

Round Leader(s)
R1 Adams; 67
R2 King; 140
R3 Bradshaw, Faulkner, Locke; 68

Lowest Scores
R2 King, 69
R3 Bradshaw, Locke; 68
R4 Bousfield; 67

THE MASTERS 1950

Augusta National Golf Club, Augusta, Georgia
(6–9 April)

6925 yards: Par 72 (288)

Jim Ferrier conceded seven strokes over the final six holes to lose to Jimmy Demaret. Although Demaret kept up the pressure by playing these holes in two under par, Ferrier's game collapsed, dropping five shots. Demaret's win was his third – the first to achieve this number in the Masters. After 12 months, when to walk again was considered optimistic, Ben Hogan finished in par to tie for 4th place, with part-timer Nelson in fifth.

1	**JIMMY DEMARET**	70	72	72	69	283
	($2400)					
2	Jim Ferrier	70	67	73	75	285
3	Sam Snead	71	74	70	72	287
4=	Ben Hogan	73	68	71	67	288
	Byron Nelson	75	70	69	74	288
6	Lloyd Mangrum	76	74	73	68	291
7=	Clayton Heafner	74	77	69	72	292
	Cary Middlecoff	75	76	68	73	292
9	Lawson Little	70	73	75	75	293
10=	Fred Haas	74	76	73	71	294
	Gene Sarazen	80	70	72	72	294
12=	Roberto de Vicenzo	76	76	73	71	296
	Horton Smith	70	79	75	72	296
14=	Skip Alexander	78	74	73	72	297
	Vic Ghezzi	78	75	70	74	297
	Leland Gibson	78	73	72	74	297
	Herman Keiser	75	72	75	75	297
	Joe Kirkwood, Jr	75	74	77	71	297
	Henry Picard	74	71	77	75	297
	Frank Stranahan (a)	74	79	73	71	297
21=	George Fazio	73	74	78	73	298
	Toney Penna	71	75	77	75	298
	Skee Riegel	69	75	78	76	298
24=	Chick Harbert	76	75	73	75	299
	Johnny Palmer	72	76	76	75	299
26	Eric Monti	74	79	74	73	300
27=	Herschel Spears	70	74	79	78	301
	Norman Von Nida	77	74	74	76	301
29=	Billy Burke	80	75	76	71	302
	Pete Cooper	74	77	77	74	302

Round Leader(s)
R1   Riegel; 69
R2   Ferrier; 137
R3   Ferrier; 210

Lowest Scores
R2   Ferrier; 67
R3   Middlecoff; 68
R4   Mangrum; 68

US OPEN 1950

Merion Golf Club, Ardmore, Pennsylvania
(8–11 June)

6694 yards: Par 70 (280)

Lee Mackey's Round One record score of 64 was the lowest for any round in any Major to that date. Ben Hogan's comeback was complete when he repeated his 1948 Open win at the Riviera CC here at Merion (now less one Cricket Club). He was to achieve it the hard way, however, when strictly speaking still recuperating from his accident, he was involved in a three-way tie. The 36-holes on the final day proved almost too much for him, but, refreshed for the Sunday play-off, he shot a 69 to win comfortably. This lesson was to dissuade Hogan from playing too much golf; and thereafter the demanding matchplay schedule of the PGA Championship was eschewed in favour of the Opens and the Masters.

1	**BEN HOGAN***	72	69	72	74	287
	($4000)					
2	Lloyd Mangrum	72	70	69	76	287
3	George Fazio	73	72	72	70	287
4	Dutch Harrison	72	67	73	76	288
5=	Jim Ferrier	71	69	74	75	289
	Joe Kirkwood, Jr	71	74	74	70	289
	Henry Ransom	72	71	73	73	289
8	Bill Nary	73	70	74	73	290
9	Julius Boros	68	72	77	74	291
10=	Cary Middlecoff	71	71	71	79	292
	Johnny Palmer	73	70	70	79	292
12=	Al Besselink	71	72	76	75	294
	Johnny Bulla	74	66	78	76	294
	Dick Mayer	73	76	73	72	294
	Henry Picard	71	71	79	73	294
	Skee Riegel	73	69	79	73	294
	Sam Snead	73	75	72	74	294
18=	Skip Alexander	68	74	77	76	295
	Fred Haas	73	74	76	72	295
20=	Jimmy Demaret	72	77	71	76	296
	Marty Furgol	75	71	72	78	296
	Dick Metz	76	71	71	78	296
	Bob Toski	73	69	80	74	296
	Harold Williams	69	75	75	77	296
25=	Bobby Cruickshank	72	77	76	72	297
	Ted Kroll	75	72	78	72	297
	Lee Mackey, Jr	64	81	75	77	297
	Paul Runyan	76	73	73	75	297
29=	Pete Cooper	75	72	76	75	298
	Henry Williams, Jr	69	76	76	77	298

* Ben Hogan (69) beat Lloyd Mangrum (73) and George Fazio (75) in the 18-Hole Play-off

Round Leader(s)
R1   Mackey Jr; 64
R2   Harrison; 139
R3   Mangrum; 211

Lowest Scores
R2   Bulla; 66
R3   Mangrum; 69
R4   Fazio, Kirkwood Jr; 70

US PGA 1950

Scioto Country Club, Columbus, Ohio
(21–27 June)

MATCHPLAY
63 qualifiers, plus the defending champion (Sam Snead),
after 36 holes strokeplay
(Low – Sam Snead, 140)
Rs1&2, 18 holes: R3,QF,SF&F, 36 holes

Hogan's absence, and the defeat of Sam Snead in Round
Two, made for a very open PGA Championship at Scioto.
Experienced campaigners like Jimmy Demaret and Lloyd
Mangrum were then favourites; but it was 36-year old
Chandler Harper who defeated Demaret in the semi final
to go on and gain his only Major. The final was played
between two men who's best PGA record between them
previously was when Harper made the third round in
1946.

FINAL
CHANDLER HARPER ($3500) beat Henry Williams
Jr, 4&3

Round by Round Details

ROUND 2 (Last 32)
Eddie Burke bt Sam Snead 1up; Ray Gafford by
Leonard Schmutte 1up; Denny Shute bt Elsworth
Vines 4&3; Jimmy Demaret bt Rod Munday 5&3; Lloyd
Mangrum bt Skip Alexander 1up; Chick Harbert bt
Harold Williams 5&3; Bob Toski bt George Fazio 1up;
CHANDLER HARPER bt Dick Metz 1up; Claude
Harmon bt Al Brosch 2&1; HENRY WILLIAMS Jr by
Emery Thomas 6&5; Elmer Reed bt Jim Ferrier 5&4;
Dave Douglas bt Jimmy Hines 5&4; Jackson Bradley by
George Shafer 4&3; Henry Picard bt Clarence Doser
4&2; Johnny Palmer bt Lew Worsham 4&2; Ted Kroll
bt Al Watrous 2&1

ROUND 3 (Last 16)
Gafford bt Burke 4&3
Demaret bt Shute 4&3
Mangrum bt Harbert 6&5
HARPER bt Toski 2&1
WILLIAMS Jr bt Harmon 1up (after 38)
Douglas bt Reed 3&2
Picard bt Bradley 1up
Palmer bt Kroll 1up

QUARTER FINAL (QF)
Demaret bt Gafford 5&4
HARPER bt Mangrum 1up
WILLIAMS Jr bt Douglas 1up
Picard bt Palmer 10&8

SEMI FINAL (SF)
HARPER bt Demaret 2&1
WILLIAMS Jr bt Picard 1up (after 38)

BRITISH OPEN 1950

Troon Golf Club, Ayrshire, Scotland
(5–7 July)
6583 yards

From this year onward, apart for the odd US Open,
Locke, after 15 wins on the US Tour, concentrated his
time more in Europe and his native South Africa. He collected the first back-to-back Open Championship win
since Walter Hagen's in 1929. In doing so he set a new
low of 279. Johnny Bulla apart, the American professional
interest waned even further, as the PGA Championship
only finished eight days before the Open started; and
there was still quite a disparity in the respective purses.

1	**BOBBY LOCKE** (£300)	69	72	70	68	279
2	Roberto de Vicenzo	72	71	68	70	281
3=	Fred Daly	75	72	69	66	282
	Dai Rees	71	68	72	71	282
5=	Max Faulkner	72	70	70	71	283
	Eric Moore	74	68	73	68	283
7=	Fred Bullock	71	71	71	71	284
	Arthur Lees	68	76	68	72	284
9=	Sam King	70	75	68	73	286
	Frank Stranahan (a)	77	70	73	66	286
	Flory van Donck	73	71	72	70	286
12=	Jimmy Adams	73	75	69	70	287
	Wally Smithers	74	70	73	70	287
14=	Johnny Bulla	73	70	71	74	288
	Hector Thomson	71	72	73	72	288
16	Harry Bradshaw	73	71	75	70	289
17=	Reg Horne	73	75	71	71	290
	James McHale (a)	73	73	74	70	290
	Ernest E Whitcombe	69	76	72	73	290
20=	Alf Padgham	77	71	74	69	291
	John Panton	76	69	70	76	291
	Norman von Nida	74	72	76	69	291
23	Eric Brown	73	73	73	73	292
24=	Trevor Allen	77	70	75	71	293
	Bill Branch	71	69	78	75	293
	Stewart Field	73	71	73	76	293
	Norman Sutton	71	75	74	73	293
	Bill White	74	74	73	72	293
29	Fred Allott	72	71	77	74	294
30=	David Blair (a)	72	72	77	74	295
	H Hassanein	73	72	77	73	295

Round Leader(s)
R1 Lees; 68
R2 Rees; 139
R3 De Vicenzo, Locke, Rees; 211

Lowest Scores
R2 Moore, Rees; 68
R3 De Vicenzo, King, Lees; 68
R4 Daly, Stranahan; 66

THE MASTERS 1951

Augusta National Golf Club, Augusta, Georgia
(22–25 March)

6925 yards: Par 72 (288)

Ben Hogan won his first Masters Tournament, thereby keeping his incredible comeback going. It was his seventh Major title, and second since his accident. Recently turned professional, 1947 US Amateur Champion Skee Riegel finished at six under par for the Tournament, but he had to succumb to the power and experience of Hogan in Round Four.

1	**BEN HOGAN**	70	72	70	68	280
	($3000)					
2	Skee Riegel	73	68	70	71	282
3=	Lloyd Mangrum	69	74	70	73	286
	Lew Worsham	71	71	72	72	286
5	Dave Douglas	74	69	72	73	288
6	Lawson Little	72	73	72	72	289
7	Jim Ferrier	74	70	74	72	290
8=	Johnny Bulla	71	72	73	75	291
	Byron Nelson	71	73	73	74	291
	Sam Snead	69	74	68	80	291
11	Jack Burke, Jr	73	72	74	73	292
12=	Charles R Coe (a)	76	71	73	73	293
	Cary Middlecoff	73	73	69	78	293
	Gene Sarazen	75	74	73	71	293
15=	Ed Furgol	80	71	72	71	294
	Dutch Harrison	76	71	76	71	294
17	Julius Boros	76	72	74	73	295
18=	George Fazio	68	74	74	80	296
	Bob Toski	75	73	73	75	296
20=	Al Besselink	76	73	71	77	297
	Dick Chapman (a)	72	76	72	77	297
	Clayton Heafner	74	72	73	78	297
	Joe Kirkwood, Jr	73	71	78	75	297
	Roberto de Vicenzo	75	74	74	74	297
25=	Ted Kroll	76	75	71	76	298
	Dick Mayer	71	75	79	73	298
	Bill Nary	76	73	73	76	298
	Henry Ransom	74	74	74	76	298
	Sam Urzetta	73	72	78	75	298
30=	Jimmy Demaret	76	74	78	71	299
	Johnny Palmer	73	74	77	75	299

Round Leader(s)
R1 Fazio; 68
R2 Riegel; 141
R3 Riegel, Snead; 211

Lowest Scores
R2 Riegel; 68
R3 Snead; 68
R4 Hogan; 68

US OPEN 1951

Oakland Hills Country Club, Birmingham, Michigan
(14–15 June)

6927 yards: Par 70 (280)

Hogan made it two US Opens in a row – and wins in the last three consecutive Major Championships he had entered. Still playing only a modicum of golf to conserve his strength, but enough to stay sharp, Hogan made it a last round special performance once again, burning up Oakland Hills in 67 – 32 for the back nine. He considered this his best ever round of golf.

1	**BEN HOGAN**	76	73	71	67	287
	($4000)					
2	Clayton Heafner	72	75	73	69	289
3	Bobby Locke	73	71	74	73	291
4=	Julius Boros	74	74	71	74	293
	Lloyd Mangrum	75	74	74	70	293
6=	Al Besselink	72	77	72	73	294
	Dave Douglas	75	70	75	74	294
	Fred Hawkins	76	72	75	71	294
	Paul Runyan	73	74	72	75	294
10=	Al Brosch	73	74	76	72	295
	Smiley Quick	73	76	74	72	295
	Skee Riegel	75	76	71	73	295
	Sam Snead	71	78	72	74	295
14=	Jimmy Demaret	74	74	70	78	296
	Lew Worsham	76	71	76	73	296
16=	Charles Kocsis (a)	75	74	76	72	297
	Henry Ransom	74	74	76	73	297
	Buck White	76	75	74	72	297
19=	Raymond Gafford	76	74	74	74	298
	Johnny Revolta	78	72	72	76	298
21=	Charles Bassler	79	71	74	75	299
	Joe Kirkwood, Jr	74	78	73	74	299
23	Marty Furgol	78	72	74	76	300
24=	Cary Middlecoff	76	73	79	73	301
	Ed Oliver	81	71	77	72	301
	Johnny Palmer	73	78	76	74	301
	Henry Picard	78	73	78	72	301
	Earl Stewart	74	74	78	75	301
29=	Tommy Bolt	77	72	75	78	302
	Roberto de Vicenzo	75	76	74	77	302
	Fred Haas	77	75	77	73	302
	George Kinsman	75	73	75	79	302
	Sam Urzetta (a)	78	71	78	75	302
	Bo Wininger (a)	75	71	77	79	302

Round Leader(s)
R1 Snead; 71
R2 Locke; 144
R3 Demaret, Locke; 218

Lowest Scores
R2 Johnny Bulla (52), Douglas; 70
R3 Demaret; 70
R4 Hogan; 67

US PGA 1951

Oakmont Country Club, Oakmont, Pennsylvania
(27June–3 July)

MATCHPLAY
63 qualifiers, plus the defending champion (Chandler Harper), after 36 holes strokeplay
(Low – Pete Cooper, Claude Harmon, Lloyd Mangrum, 142)
Rs1&2, 18 holes: R3,QF,SF&F, 36 holes

After squeaking past Fred Haas in Round One, and needing three extra holes before disposing of Marty Furgol, Sam Snead really came to life in the semi final. From there he annihilated Charles Bassler and Walter Burkemo to become the last multiple PGA Champion until Nicklaus repeated his own first win in 1971. In between there was a sequence of 19 different winners in succession.

FINAL
SAM SNEAD ($3500) beat Walter Burkemo, 7&6

Round by Round Details

ROUND 2 (Last 32)
  Charles Bassler bt Jim Turnesa 5&4; George Bolesta bt Ed Oliver 2&1; Al Brosch bt Lew Worsham 5&4; Jack Harden bt Toney Penna 5&3; Lloyd Mangrum bt Buck White 2&1; SAM SNEAD bt Marty Furgol 1up (after 21); Jack Burke, Jr bt Gene Sarazen 5&3; Gene Kunes bt Ray Gafford 2&1; Dick Shoemaker bt Lawson Little 2&1; WALTER BURKEMO bt Chick Harbert 1up (after 19); Vic Ghezzi bt Rod Munday 4&3; Reggie Myles by Mike Pavella 1up (after 20); Jackson Bradley bt Denny Shute 2&1; Elsworth Vines bt Henry Picard 1up; Jim Ferrier bt Milon Marusic 3&2; Johnny Bulla bt Bob Hamilton 5&3

ROUND 3 (Last 16)
  Bassler bt Bolesta 1up (after 37)
  Brosch bt Harden 6&5
  SNEAD bt Mangrum 3&2
  Burke Jr bt Kunes 4&3
  BURKEMO by Shoemaker 2&1
  Myles bt Ghezzi 1up
  Vines bt Bradley 2&1
  Bulla bt Ferrier 9&8

QUARTER FINAL (QF)
  Bassler bt Brosch 1up
  SNEAD bt Burke Jr 2&1
  BURKEMO bt Myles 1up
  Vines bt Bulla 1up

SEMI FINAL (SF)
  SNEAD bt Bassler 9&8
  BURKEMO bt Vines 1up (after 37)

BRITISH OPEN 1951

Royal Portrush Golf Club, Co Antrim, Northern Ireland
(4–6 July)
6802 yards

The Open left the shores of Great Britain for the one and only time and visited picturesque Royal Portrush. Max Faulkner interrupted Bobby Locke's recent stranglehold, building up enough of any early lead to hold off fast-finishing Argentinian, Antonio Cerda. This year, the US PGA and the British Open effectively overlapped, with the finals of the former held on the day before the first round in Ulster. The Open Championship and the US Majors were never further apart.

1	**MAX FAULKNER**	71	70	70	74	285
	(£300)				
2	Antonio Cerda	74	72	71	70	287
3	Charlie Ward	75	73	74	68	290
4=	Jimmy Adams	68	77	75	72	292
	Fred Daly	74	70	75	73	292
6=	Bobby Locke	71	74	74	74	293
	Bill Shankland	73	76	72	72	293
	Norman Sutton	73	70	74	76	293
	Peter Thomson	70	75	73	75	293
	Harry Weetman	73	71	75	74	293
11	John Panton	73	72	74	75	294
12=	Dick Burton	74	77	71	73	295
	Dai Rees	70	77	76	72	295
	Frank Stranahan (a)	75	75	72	73	295
15	Harry Bradshaw	80	71	74	71	296
16	Eric Cremin	73	75	75	74	297
17=	Kep Enderby (a)	76	74	75	73	298
	Alan Waters	74	75	78	71	298
19=	Ugo Grappasoni	73	73	77	76	299
	Jack Hargreaves	73	78	79	69	299
	WJ Henderson	77	73	76	73	299
	Kel Nagle	76	76	72	75	299
	Christy O'Connor, Sr	79	74	72	74	299
24=	Joe Carr (a)	75	76	73	76	300
	P Traviani	74	79	73	74	300
	Flory van Donck	72	76	76	76	300
	Ernest E Whitcombe	74	74	76	76	300
28=	J McKenna	74	76	76	76	302
	Alan Poulton	77	77	73	75	302
	Wally Smithers	75	73	76	78	302

Round Leader(s)
R1 Adams; 68
R2 Faulkner; 141
R3 Faulkner; 211

Lowest Scores
R2 Daly, Faulkner, Sutton; 70
R3 Faulkner; 70
R4 Ward; 68

THE MASTERS 1952

Augusta National Golf Club, Augusta, Georgia
(3–6 July)
6925 yards: Par 72 (288)

Sam Snead overcame high winds, which affected scoring generally over the last two rounds, to post 286 – the only score better than par in the Tournament. It was his second Masters win and sixth Major. Ray Gafford tied for the lead after Round One with a 69 – then followed it with an 80, and an eventual 49th place.

1	**SAM SNEAD**	70	67	77	72	286
	($4000)					
2	Jack Burke, Jr	76	67	78	69	290
3=	Al Besselink	70	76	71	74	291
	Tommy Bolt	71	71	75	74	291
	Jim Ferrier	72	70	77	72	291
6	Lloyd Mangrum	71	74	75	72	292
7=	Julius Boros	73	73	76	71	293
	Fred Hawkins	71	73	78	71	293
	Ben Hogan	70	70	74	79	293
	Lew Worsham	71	75	73	74	293
11	Cary Middlecoff	72	72	72	78	294
12	Johnny Palmer	69	74	75	77	295
13	Johnny Revolta	71	71	77	77	296
14=	George Fazio	72	71	78	76	297
	Claude Harmon	73	74	77	73	297
	Chuck Kocsis (a)	75	78	71	73	297
	Ted Kroll	74	74	76	73	297
	Skee Riegel	75	71	78	73	297
19=	Joe Kirkwood, Jr	71	77	74	76	298
	Frank Stranahan (a)	72	74	76	76	298
21=	Doug Ford	71	74	79	75	299
	Bobby Locke	74	71	79	75	299
	E Harvie Ward, Jr (a)	72	71	78	78	299
24=	Arnold Blum (a)	74	77	77	74	302
	Clayton Heafner	76	74	74	78	302
	Byron Nelson	72	75	78	77	302
27=	Skip Alexander	71	73	77	82	303
	Smiley Quick	73	76	79	75	303
	Norman Von Nida	77	77	73	76	303
30=	Dave Douglas	76	69	81	78	304
	Vic Ghezzi	77	77	76	74	304
	Ed Oliver	72	72	77	83	304
	Horton Smith	74	73	77	80	304

Round Leader(s)
R1 Ray Gafford (49), Palmer; 69
R2 Snead; 137
R3 Hogan, Snead; 214

Lowest Scores
R2 Burke, Snead; 67
R3 Besselink, Kocsis ; 71
R4 Burke; 69

US OPEN 1952

Northwood Golf Club, Dallas, Texas
(12–14 June)
6782 yards: Par 70 (280)

Julius Boros didn't turn professional until 1950, when he was already 30 years old. This was his first of three Major victories – the other two were to occur in the next decade, when he was to set records for his age. The odds were in favour of Hogan winning again when he equalled the Open 36-hole low score. The heat and 36 holes on the last day were too much for him this time though.

1	**JULIUS BOROS**	71	71	68	71	281
	($4000)					
2	Ed Oliver	71	72	70	72	285
3	Ben Hogan	69	69	74	74	286
4	Johnny Bulla	73	68	73	73	287
5	George Fazio	71	69	75	75	290
6	Dick Metz	70	74	76	71	291
7=	Tommy Bolt	72	76	71	73	292
	Ted Kroll	71	75	76	70	292
	Lew Worsham	72	71	74	75	292
10=	Lloyd Mangrum	75	74	72	72	293
	Sam Snead	70	75	76	72	293
	Earl Stewart	76	75	70	72	293
13=	Clarence Doser	71	73	73	77	294
	Harry Todd	71	76	74	73	294
15=	Al Brosch	68	79	77	71	295
	Jimmy Demaret	74	77	73	71	295
	Milon Marusic	73	76	74	72	295
	Horton Smith	70	73	76	76	295
19=	Doug Ford	74	74	74	74	296
	James Jackson (a)	74	76	75	71	296
	Bill Trombley	72	73	81	70	296
22=	Leland Gibson	73	76	72	76	297
	Paul Runyan	73	78	73	73	297
24=	Chick Harbert	75	75	73	75	298
	Cary Middlecoff	75	74	75	74	298
	Felice Torza	74	76	70	78	298
	Bo Wininger	78	72	69	79	298
28=	Zell Eaton	71	79	73	76	299
	Raymond Gafford	77	74	75	73	299
	Dick Mayer	74	77	69	79	299
	Stan Mosel (a)	71	77	75	76	299
	P Patrick	74	76	73	76	299

Round Leader(s)
R1 Brosch; 68
R2 Hogan; 138
R3 Boros; 210

Lowest Scores
R2 Bulla; 68
R3 Boros; 68
R4 Kroll, Trombley; 70

US PGA 1952

Big Spring Country Club, Louisville, Kentucky
(18–25 June)

MATCHPLAY
63 qualifiers plus the defending champion (Sam Snead)
after 36 holes strokeplay
(Low – Dutch Harrison, 136)
Rs1&2, 18 holes: R3,QF,SF&F, 36 holes

At the age of 40, and after 26 years and four Major
Championship second places for him and his brothers
(Joe and Mike), Jim Turnesa finally buried the family jinx
at Big Spring. The youngest of the seven Turnesa brothers to make a mark was Willie – he won the US Amateur
title in 1938 and 1948, but he never turned pro. Sam
Snead, the defending champion, went out in Round One
to Lew Worsham.

FINAL
JIM TURNESA ($3500) beat Chick Harbert, 1up

Round by Round Details

ROUND 2 (Last 32)
Ray Honsberger bt Jim Ferrier 1up; Ted Kroll bt Lloyd
Mangrum 2up; Cary Middlecoff bt Charles Harter 3&2;
Al Smith bt Labron Harris 1up (after 19); JIM TUR-
NESA bt Chandler Harper 3&1; Roberto de Vicenzo bt
Jack Burke Jr 1up; Clarence Doser bt Bob Gajda 3&2;
Jack Isaacs bt Marty Furgol 3&2; Fred Haas bt Lew
Worsham 1up; Milon Marusic bt Zell Eaton (default);
Henry Williams Jr bt Jack Jones 1up; CHICK HAR-
BERT bt Leonard Schmutte 3&2; Frank Champ bt John
Trish 2&1; Walter Burkemo bt Dave Douglas 1up; Vic
Ghezzi bt Mel Carpenter 5&3; Bob Hamilton bt Sam
Bernardi 3&1

ROUND 3 (Last 16)
Kroll bt Honsberger 1up (after 38)
Middlecoff bt Smith 4&2
TURNESA bt de Vicenzo 5&4
Doser bt Isaacs 1up
Haas bt Marusic 1up (after 38)
HARBERT bt Williams Jr 6&5
Champ bt Burkemo 3&1
Hamilton bt Ghezzi 9&8

QUARTER FINAL (QF)
Kroll bt Middlecoff 1up (after 38)
TURNESA bt Doser 2&1
HARBERT bt Haas 2&1
Hamilton bt Champ 2&1

SEMI FINAL (SF)
TURNESA bt Kroll 4&2;
HARBERT bt Hamilton 2&1

BRITISH OPEN 1952

Royal Lytham & St Anne's Golf Club, Lancashire, England
(9–11 July)
6657 yards

Emulating Harry Vardon and James Braid, Locke won his
third Open in four years. He held firm in the last round
under the challenge of young Australian, Peter Thomson.
Gene Sarazen, at the age of 50, made a creditable 17th
place, 18 years after his success at Prince's, Sandwich.
Otherwise the field was almost totally bereft of an American challenge.

1	**BOBBY LOCKE** (£300)	69	71	74	73	287
2	Peter Thomson	68	73	77	70	288
3	Fred Daly	67	69	77	76	289
4	Henry Cotton	75	74	74	71	294
5=	Antonio Cerda	73	73	76	73	295
	Sam King	71	74	74	76	295
7	Flory van Donck	74	75	71	76	296
8	Fred Bullock	76	72	72	77	297
9=	Harry Bradshaw	70	74	75	79	298
	Eric Brown	71	72	78	77	298
	Willie Goggin	71	74	75	78	298
	Arthur Lees	76	72	76	74	298
	Syd Scott	75	69	76	78	298
	Norman von Nida	77	70	74	77	298
15=	John Panton	72	72	78	77	299
	Harry Weetman	74	77	71	77	299
17=	Max Faulkner	72	76	79	73	300
	Gene Sarazen	74	73	77	76	300
	Wally Smithers	73	74	76	77	300
20	Norman Sutton	72	74	79	76	301
21=	Fred Allott	77	71	76	78	302
	Ken Bousfield	72	73	79	78	302
	Jimmy Hines	73	78	74	77	302
	Eddie Noke	72	78	76	76	302
25=	JA Jacobs	74	72	81	76	303
	Alan Poulton	71	74	76	82	303
27=	Jack Hargreaves	75	75	79	75	304
	John Jacobs	72	76	79	77	304
	JW Jones (a)	73	70	78	83	304
	Dai Rees	76	74	77	77	304

Round Leader(s)
R1 Daly; 67
R2 Daly; 136
R3 Daly; 213

Lowest Scores
R2 Daly, Scott; 69
R3 Van Donck, Weetman; 71
R4 Thomson; 70

THE MASTERS 1953

Augusta National Golf Club, Augusta, Georgia
(9–12 April)

6925 yards: Par 72 (288)

Ben Hogan, in winning his second Masters title, lowered the Masters' and all Majors' low score to 274. In doing so he trimmed the Augusta National Tournament's record, and beat the field, by five shots. Conditions were benign, but Hogan played what was reported as 'the best 72-hole stretch of golf played by anyone anywhere'. The Masters' record low was to stand until taken by Nicklaus in 1965, and equalled by Ray Floyd 11 years later. Tiger Woods further lowered it in 1997. Porky Oliver collected another runner-up spot to add his 1946 PGA and previous year's US Open.

1	**BEN HOGAN** ($5000)	70	69	66	69	274
2	Ed Oliver	69	73	67	70	279
3	Lloyd Mangrum	74	68	71	69	282
4	Bob Hamilton	71	69	70	73	283
5=	Tommy Bolt	71	75	68	71	285
	Chick Harbert	68	73	70	74	285
7	Ted Kroll	71	70	73	72	286
8	Jack Burke, Jr	78	69	69	71	287
9	Al Besselink	69	75	70	74	288
10=	Julius Boros	73	71	75	70	289
	Chandler Harper	74	72	69	74	289
	Fred Hawkins	75	70	74	70	289
13	Johnny Palmer	74	73	72	71	290
14=	Frank Stranahan (a)	72	75	69	75	291
	E Harvie Ward, Jr (a)	73	74	69	75	291
16=	Charles R Coe (a)	75	74	72	71	292
	Jim Ferrier	74	71	76	71	292
	Dick Mayer	73	72	71	76	292
	Sam Snead	71	75	71	75	292
	Earl Stewart, Jr	75	72	70	75	292
21=	Jerry Barber	73	76	72	72	293
	Doug Ford	73	73	72	75	293
23=	Leland Gibson	73	71	72	78	294
	Al Mengert	77	70	75	72	294
	Dick Metz	73	72	71	78	294
26	Fred Haas	74	73	71	77	295
27=	Cary Middlecoff	75	76	68	77	296
	Jim Turnesa	73	74	73	76	296
29=	Skip Alexander	72	78	74	73	297
	Byron Nelson	73	73	78	73	297
	Skee Riegel	74	72	76	75	297
	Felice Torza	78	73	72	74	297
	Bo Wininger	80	70	72	75	297

Round Leader(s)
R1 Harbert; 68
R2 Hogan; 139
R3 Hogan; 205

Lowest Scores
R2 Mangrum; 68
R3 Hogan; 66
R4 Hogan, Mangrum; 69

US OPEN 1953

Oakmont Country Club, Oakmont, Pennsylvania
(11–13 June)

6916 yards: Par 72 (288)

Returning to Oakmont for the first time since 1935 (although the course was host site to the PGA Championship just two years before), the US Open saw Hogan rewriting the record books once again. In beating top rival Snead by six strokes, Hogan drew level with Willie Anderson's and Bobby Jones' four US Opens; and it was the first wire-to-wire win since Jim Barnes in 1921. He also repeated his 1951 feat of lifting the Masters and US Open in the same year.

1	**BEN HOGAN** ($5000)	67	72	73	71	283
2	Sam Snead	72	69	72	76	289
3	Lloyd Mangrum	73	70	74	75	292
4=	Pete Cooper	78	75	71	70	294
	Jimmy Demaret	71	76	71	76	294
	George Fazio	70	71	77	76	294
7=	Ted Kroll	76	71	74	74	295
	Dick Metz	75	70	74	76	295
9=	Marty Furgol	73	74	76	73	296
	Jay Hebert	72	72	74	78	296
	Frank Souchak (a)	70	76	76	74	296
12=	Fred Haas	74	73	72	78	297
	Bill Ogden	71	78	75	73	297
14=	Jack Burke, Jr	76	73	72	77	298
	Dutch Harrison	77	75	70	76	298
	Bobby Locke	78	70	74	76	298
17=	Julius Boros	75	72	76	76	299
	Clarence Doser	74	76	78	71	299
	Bill Nary	76	74	73	76	299
	Jim Turnesa	75	78	72	74	299
21=	Gardner Dickinson	77	73	76	74	300
	Doug Ford	74	77	74	75	300
	Al Mengert	75	71	78	76	300
	Bob Rosburg	76	72	78	74	300
	Frank Stranahan (a)	75	75	75	75	300
26=	Clayton Heafner	75	75	76	75	301
	James McHale, Jr (a)	79	74	75	73	301
	Peter Thomson	80	73	73	75	301
	Art Wall	80	72	77	72	301
30=	Louis Barbaro	72	79	74	77	302
	Jerry Barber	72	75	76	79	302
	Toby Lyons	73	78	74	77	302

Round Leader(s)
R1 Hogan; 67
R2 Hogan; 139
R3 Hogan; 212

Lowest Scores
R2 Snead; 69
R3 Harrison; 70
R4 Cooper; 70

US PGA 1953

Birmingham Club, Birmingham, Michigan
(1–7 July)

63 qualifiers plus the defending champion (Jim Turnesa) after 36 holes strokeplay
(Low – Johnny Palmer, 136)
Rs1&2, 18 holes: R3,QF,SF&F, 36 holes

Once more the PGA clashed with the British Open, so even if Ben Hogan did contemplate a Grand Slam in 1953, he would have been denied it. His antipathy to the six-day ardour of the PGA Championship remained, and he was persuaded to try the British Open. Walter Burkemo was a local boy and his wins leading up to, and in, the final were cheered on by a partisan crowd. His one and only Major win, and his second place in the PGA in 1951, picked him out as a match-player and he was selected for the 1953 Ryder Cup. He lost his only match.

FINAL
WALTER BURKEMO ($5000) beat Felice Torza, 2&1

Round by Round Details

ROUND 2 (Last 32)
FELICE TORZA bt Jim Turnesa 4&3; Wally Ulrich bt Buck White 2&1; Jimmy Clark bt Cary Middlecoff 5&4; Henry Williams Jr bt Charles Bassler 3&1; Jack Isaacs bt Fred Haas 1up; Labron Harris bt Marty Furgol 1up; Al Smith bt Iverson Martin 3&2; Henry Ransom bt Bob Toski 3&2; Jackson Bradley bt Tommy Bolt 1up; Dave Douglas bt Sam Snead 1up (after 19); WALTER BURKEMO bt Mike Turnesa 3&1; Pete Cooper bt Leonard Dodson 6&5; Bill Nary bt Dutch Harrison 1up; Jim Browning bt Broyles Plemmons 3&1; Ed Furgol bt Jim Ferrier 3&1; Claude Harmon bt Jack Grout 4&2

ROUND 3 (Last 16)
TORZA bt Ulrich 1up (after 38)
Clark bt Williams Jr 4&3
Isaacs bt Harris 5&4
Ransom bt Smith 1up
Douglas bt Bradley 1up (after 37)
BURKEMO bt Cooper 3&2
Nary bt Browning 6&5
Harmon bt Furgol 5&3

QUARTER FINAL (QF)
TORZA bt Clark 1up
Isaacs bt Ransom 1up
BURKEMO bt Douglas 2up
Harmon bt Nary 6&5

SEMI FINAL (SF)
TORZA bt Isaacs 1up (after 39)
BURKEMO bt Harmon 1up

BRITISH OPEN 1953

Carnoustie Golf Club, Angus, Scotland
(8–10 July)
7103 yards

Ben Hogan paid his one and only visit to the Open Championship, adapted very quickly to conditions and the size of the ball – the British still used the 1.62" small ball, whereas the American big ball (1.68") had been in operation since 1932 – and won the title. His round-by-round improvement brought a score of 282, and meant he was the first, and only, golfer to win three modern Majors in one season, until the feat was matched by Tiger Woods in 2000. In doing so he joined Sarazen as the second man to achieve the Slam of all four titles. This was, however, to be his last Major title (his ninth, two behind Walter Hagen). He had played in few other tournaments apart from the Majors since the accident in 1949, but his sequence in Majors played between 1950 and 1953, inclusive, was remarkably: 4, W, W, W, 7, 3, W, W, W.

1	**BEN HOGAN**	73	71	70	68	282
	(£500)					
2=	Antonio Cerda	75	71	69	71	286
	Dai Rees	72	70	73	71	286
	Frank Stranahan (a)	70	74	73	69	286
	Peter Thomson	72	72	71	71	286
6	Roberto de Vicenzo	72	71	71	73	287
7	Sam King	74	73	72	71	290
8	Bobby Locke	72	73	74	72	291
9=	Peter Alliss	75	72	74	71	292
	Eric Brown	71	71	75	75	292
11	Fred Daly	73	75	71	75	294
12	Max Faulkner	74	71	73	77	295
13	Arthur Lees	76	76	72	72	296
14=	THT Fairbairn	74	71	73	79	297
	John Jacobs	79	74	71	73	297
	Harry Weetman	80	73	72	72	297
17=	H Hassanein	78	71	73	76	298
	Eric Lester	83	70	72	73	298
	Charlie Ward	78	71	76	73	298
20=	Reg Horne	76	74	75	74	299
	Flory van Donck	77	71	78	73	299
22=	Syd Scott	74	74	78	74	300
	Hector Thomson	76	74	74	76	300
24=	Reg Knight	74	79	74	74	301
	Lloyd Mangrum	75	76	74	76	301
	Christy O'Connor, Sr	77	77	72	75	301
27=	Ugo Grappasoni	77	75	72	78	302
	John Panton	79	74	76	73	302
29=	R Ferguson	77	75	74	77	303
	Tom Haliburton	75	76	76	76	303
	Alan Poulton	75	77	75	76	303
	Norman Sutton	76	72	76	79	303

Round Leader(s)
R1   Stranahan; 70
R2   Brown, Rees; 142
R3   de Vicenzo, Hogan; 214

Lowest Scores
R2   Lester, Rees; 70
R3   Cerda; 69
R4   Hogan; 68

THE MASTERS 1954

Augusta National Golf Club, Augusta, Georgia
(8–12 April)

6925 yards: Par 72 (288)

Hogan could have made that famous sequence four in a row had not Sam Snead chipped away at the great man's lead in Round Four. Hogan slipped to three over for the round, allowing Snead to force a tie through his solid par play. Snead then won the head-to-head between the world's two greatest players of the time, and two of the very best of all-time, to become a three-time Masters Champion.

1	**SAM SNEAD***	74	73	70	72	289
	($5000)					
2	Ben Hogan	72	73	69	75	289
3	Billy Joe Patton (a)	70	74	75	71	290
4=	Dutch Harrison	70	79	74	68	291
	Lloyd Mangrum	71	75	76	69	291
6=	Jerry Barber	74	76	71	71	292
	Jack Burke, Jr	71	77	73	71	292
	Bob Rosburg	73	73	76	70	292
9=	Al Besselink	74	74	74	72	294
	Cary Middlecoff	73	76	70	75	294
11	Dick Chapman (a)	75	75	75	70	294
12=	Tommy Bolt	73	74	72	77	296
	Chick Harbert	73	75	75	73	296
	Byron Nelson	73	76	74	73	296
	Lew Worsham	74	74	74	74	296
16=	Julius Boros	76	79	68	74	297
	Jay Hebert	79	74	74	70	297
	Peter Thomson	76	72	76	73	297
	Ken Venturi (a)	76	74	73	74	297
20=	Charles R Coe (a)	76	75	73	74	298
	E Harvie Ward, Jr (a)	78	75	74	71	298
22=	Walter Burkemo	74	77	75	73	299
	Pete Cooper	73	76	75	75	299
	Marty Furgol	76	79	75	69	299
	Gene Littler	79	75	73	72	299
	Ed Oliver	75	75	75	74	299
	Earl Stewart, Jr	78	75	75	71	299
	Bob Toski	80	74	71	74	299
29=	Jimmy Demaret	80	75	72	73	300
	Vic Ghezzi	73	79	73	75	300
	Dick Mayer	76	75	72	77	300

* Sam Snead (70) beat Ben Hogan (71) in the 18-hole Play-off

Round Leader(s)
R1   Harrison, Patton; 70
R2   Patton; 144
R3   Hogan; 214

Lowest Scores
R2   Thomson; 72
R3   Boros; 68
R4   Harrison; 68

US OPEN 1954

Baltusrol Golf Club, Springfield, New Jersey
(17–19 June)

7027 yards: Par 70 (280)

National TV covered the 1954 US Open to witness Ed Furgol claim his only Major championship. Furgol, who played with a withered left arm after a childhood accident, just did enough to hold off 1953 US Amateur Champion, just turned professional, Gene Littler over the final holes. Amateur, Billy Joe Patton, after leading and almost tying the Masters, took the lead again here, at Baltusrol, after 18 holes.

1	**ED FURGOL**	71	70	71	72	284
	($6000)					
2	Gene Littler	70	69	76	70	285
3=	Lloyd Mangrum	72	71	72	71	286
	Dick Mayer	72	71	70	73	286
5	Bobby Locke	74	70	74	70	288
6=	Tommy Bolt	72	72	73	72	289
	Fred Haas	73	73	71	72	289
	Ben Hogan	71	70	76	72	289
	Shelley Mayfield	73	75	72	69	289
	Billy Joe Patton (a)	69	76	71	73	289
11=	Cary Middlecoff	72	71	72	75	290
	Sam Snead	72	73	72	73	290
13=	Rudy Horvath	75	72	71	73	291
	Al Mengert	71	72	73	75	291
15=	Jack Burke, Jr	73	73	72	75	293
	Claude Harmon	75	72	72	74	293
17	Jay Hebert	77	70	70	77	294
18=	Marty Furgol	73	74	73	75	295
	Leland Gibson	72	77	69	77	295
	Bob Toski	70	74	78	73	295
21=	Dick Chapman (a)	77	67	77	75	296
	Johnny Weitzel	74	76	69	77	296
23=	Julius Boros	78	71	78	70	297
	William Campbell (a)	75	73	73	76	297
	Max Evans	76	74	73	74	297
	Lew Worsham	72	77	77	71	297
27=	George Fazio	74	77	74	73	298
	Ted Kroll	70	79	73	76	298
29=	Jimmy Demaret	79	71	76	73	299
	Dick Metz	75	75	72	77	299
	Johnny Revolta	72	75	73	79	299
	Bob Rosburg	74	77	74	74	299

Round Leader(s)
R1   Patton; 69
R2   Littler; 139
R3   Furgol; 212

Lowest Scores
R2   Chapman; 67
R3   Gibson, Weitzel; 69
R4   Mayfield; 69

BRITISH OPEN 1954

Birkdale Golf Club, Southport, Lancashire, England
(7–9 July)
6867 yards

Following Ben Hogan's famous interruption the previous year, Bobby Locke must have wondered what had happened to his Open supremacy when Peter Thomson improved on two previous runner-up spots to gain his first Open success, putting the South African into joint-second place. Sarazen again belied his age, and there were Top 10 performances from other US veterans, Jim Turnesa and Jimmy Demaret. To put British golf of this era in perspective, the US won six of the seven Ryder Cups in the period 1949–61. Over the same period, apart from Faulkner in 1951, the Opens were carved up by two Americans, two South Africans and two Australians. The British had to wait until Tony Jacklin in 1969 for their next home success. Classic Birkdale, scheduled for use when World War Two arrived, finally got on the roster for the Open.

1	**PETER THOMSON**	72	71	69	71	283
	(£750)					
2=	Bobby Locke	74	71	69	70	284
	Dai Rees	72	71	69	72	284
	Syd Scott	76	67	69	72	284
5=	Jimmy Adams	73	75	69	69	286
	Antonio Cerda	71	71	73	71	286
	Jim Turnesa	72	72	71	71	286
8=	Peter Alliss	72	74	71	70	287
	Sam King	69	74	74	70	287
10=	Jimmy Demaret	73	71	74	71	289
	Flory van Donck	77	71	70	71	289
12=	Alfonso Angelini	76	70	73	71	290
	Harry Bradshaw	72	72	73	73	290
	JW Spence	69	72	74	75	290
15=	Bobby Halsall	72	73	73	73	291
	Peter Toogood (a)	72	75	73	71	291
17=	Ugo Grappasoni	72	75	74	71	292
	C Kane	74	72	74	72	292
	Gene Sarazen	75	74	73	70	292
20=	Norman Drew	76	71	74	72	293
	Max Faulkner	73	78	69	73	293
	Jack Hargreaves	77	72	77	67	293
	John Jacobs	71	73	80	69	293
	Eric Lester	72	75	73	73	293
	Christy O'Connor, Sr	74	72	72	75	293
	Lambert Topping	75	76	69	73	293
27=	Norman Sutton	70	80	72	72	294
	EB Williamson	76	73	75	70	294
29=	Jimmy Hitchcock	73	72	76	74	295
	Ben Shelton	74	77	71	73	295
	Frank Stranahan (a)	73	75	71	76	295

Round Leader(s)
R1 Alliss, Spence; 69
R2 Spence, 141
R3 Rees, Scott, Thomson; 212

Lowest Scores
R2 Scott; 67
R3 Adams, Faulkner, Locke, Rees, Scott, Thomson, Topping; 69
R4 Hargreaves; 67

US PGA 1954

Merion Golf Club, Ardmore, Pennsylvania
(8–11 June)

MATCHPLAY
63 qualifiers plus the defending champion (Walter Burkemo) after 36 holes strokeplay
(Low – Ed Oliver, 136)
Rs1&2, 18 holes: R3,QF,SF&F, 36 holes

Settling finally (give or take a year) for its position in the Majors calendar, the 1954 PGA Championship was won by 1952 runner-up Chick Harbert. Walter Burkemo again confirmed his reputation in matchplay, but was no match in this instance for Harbert, who took control of the final early into the second 18 holes.

FINAL
CHICK HARBERT ($5000) beat Walter Burkemo, 4&3

Round by Round Details

ROUND 2 (Last 32)
Tommy Bolt bt Arthur Doering 2&1; Jim Browning bt Ed Furgol 1up; Sam Snead bt Jin Milward 4&3; Dutch Harrison bt Johnny Palmer 4&3; Charles Bassler bt Bill Trombley 5&4; Jerry Barber bt Fred Haas 1up (after 19); CHICK HARBERT bt John O'Donnell 3&1; Ed Oliver bt Bill Nary (1up); WALTER BURKEMO bt Claude Harmon 2&1; Johnny Revolta bt Toby Lyons 5&4; Roberto de Vicenzo bt Henry Ransom; 4&3; Elroy Marti bt Henry Williams Jr 2up; Cary Middlecoff bt Bob Toski 2&1; Ted Kroll bt Max Evans 1up (after 24); Shelley Mayfield bt Wally Ulrich 5&4; Horton Smith bt Jack Isaacs 3&2

ROUND 3 (Last 16)
Bolt bt Browning 2&1
Snead bt Harrison 4&3
Barber bt Bassler 1up (after 38)
HARBERT bt Oliver 3&1
BURKEMO bt Revolta 4&3
de Vicenzo bt Marti 8&6
Middlecoff bt Kroll 5&4
Mayfield bt Smith 3&2

QUARTER FINAL (QF)
Bolt bt Snead 1up (after 39)
HARBERT bt Barber 1up
BURKEMO bt de Vicenzo 5&4
Middlecoff bt Mayfield 3&1

SEMI FINAL (SF)
HARBERT bt Bolt 1up
BURKEMO bt Middlecoff 1up (after 37)

THE MASTERS 1955

Augusta National Golf Club, Augusta, Georgia
(7–10 April)

6925 yards: Par 72 (288)

Thanks to a blistering 65 in Round Two, Cary Middlecoff finished a remarkable seven shots clear of Hogan, and eight of Snead. This was the second Major victory for trained dentist, 'Doc' Middlecoff, having beaten Snead into second place earlier, in the 1949 US Open at Medinah. 1954 US Amateur Champion, 26 year-old Arnold Daniel Palmer, finished tenth.

1	**CARY MIDDLECOFF** ($5000)	72	65	72	70	279
2	Ben Hogan	73	68	72	73	286
3	Sam Snead	72	71	74	70	287
4=	Julius Boros	71	75	72	71	289
	Bob Rosburg	72	72	72	73	289
	Mike Souchak	71	74	72	72	289
7	Lloyd Mangrum	74	73	72	72	291
8=	E Harvie Ward, Jr (a)	77	69	75	71	292
	Stan Leonard	77	73	68	74	292
10=	Dick Mayer	78	72	72	71	293
	Byron Nelson	72	75	74	72	293
	Arnold Palmer	76	76	72	69	293
13=	Jack Burke, Jr	67	76	71	80	294
	Skee Riegel	73	73	73	75	294
15=	Walter Burkemo	73	73	72	77	295
	Jay Hebert	75	74	74	72	295
	Frank Stranahan	77	76	71	71	295
18=	Joe Conrad (a)	77	71	74	75	297
	Billy Maxwell (a)	77	72	77	71	297
	Johnny Palmer	77	73	72	75	297
	Peter Thomson	74	73	74	76	297
22=	Tommy Bolt	76	70	77	75	298
	Gene Littler	75	72	76	75	298
24=	Pete Cooper	73	73	78	75	299
	Ed Furgol	74	72	78	75	299
	Hillman Robbins, Jr (a)	77	76	74	72	299
27	Max Evans	76	75	75	76	302
28=	William L Goodloe, Jr (a)	74	73	81	75	303
	Claude Harmon	77	75	78	73	303
30=	Don Cherry	79	75	78	82	304
	Bud Ward	77	73	77	77	304

Round Leader(s)
R1   Burke; 67
R2   Middlecoff; 137
R3   Middlecoff; 209

Lowest Scores
R2   Middlecoff; 65
R3   Leonard; 68
R4   Palmer; 69

US OPEN 1955

Olympic Country Club, San Francisco, California
(16–19 June)

6700 yards: Par 70 (280)

Jack Fleck, in his first full year on the Tour, sensationally held his nerve to beat 43 year-old Ben Hogan in a play-off. He had arrived there after birdying two of the last four holes to tie. With a par of 70, the difficult Olympic CC course took its toll, and only seven rounds were played under par throughout the Championship – including the play-off. Fittingly, Fleck achieved three of them. After his momentous year in 1953, Hogan's Majors sequence read: 2, 6, 2, 2. He was never to get any higher again.

1	**JACK FLECK*** ($6000)	76	69	75	67	287
2	Ben Hogan	72	73	72	70	287
3=	Tommy Bolt	67	77	75	73	292
	Sam Snead	79	69	70	74	292
5=	Julius Boros	76	69	73	77	295
	Bob Rosburg	78	74	67	76	295
7=	Doug Ford	74	77	74	71	296
	Bud Holscher	77	75	71	73	296
	E Harvie Ward, Jr (a)	74	70	76	76	296
10=	Jack Burke, Jr	71	77	72	77	297
	Mike Souchak	73	79	72	73	297
12=	Shelley Mayfield	75	76	75	72	298
	Frank Stranahan	80	71	76	71	298
14	Walker Inman, Jr	70	75	76	78	299
15	Gene Littler	76	73	73	78	300
16=	Al Mengert	76	76	72	77	301
	Smiley Quick	76	74	74	77	301
	Art Wall	77	78	72	74	301
19=	Fred Hawkins	73	78	75	76	302
	George Schneiter	78	74	77	73	302
21=	Bob Harris	77	71	78	77	303
	Cary Middlecoff	76	78	74	75	303
	Arnold Palmer	77	76	74	76	303
	Ernie Vossler	77	76	76	74	303
25=	Marty Furgol	76	77	78	73	304
	Leland Gibson	76	78	76	74	304
27	Billy Maxwell	77	74	75	79	305
28=	Art Bell	74	76	81	75	306
	Max Evans	77	73	76	80	306
	Dow Finsterwald	84	71	74	77	306
	Eric Monti	76	76	78	76	306
	Byron Nelson	77	74	80	75	306
	Charles Rotar	76	75	80	75	306

* Jack Fleck (69) beat Ben Hogan (72) in the 18-Hole Play-off

Round Leader(s)
R1   Bolt; 67
R2   Bolt, Ward; 144
R3   Hogan; 217

Lowest Scores
R2   Boros, Fleck, Snead; 69
R3   Rosburg; 67
R4   Fleck; 67

BRITISH OPEN 1955

Royal & Ancient Golf Club, St Andrews, Fife, Scotland
(6–8 July)
6526 yards

Despite never winning a tournament, Johnny Fallon came close to the Open Championship twice – both times at St Andrews. In 1939 he finished third, and went one better in 1955. Peter Thomson won his second Open in a row, but the aficionados gathered around the Old Course more to see the legend that was Byron Nelson. Effectively retired for almost a decade, he decided to take a golfing 'holiday' in Europe. Aged 43, he won the French Open, but his last British Open placing was 33rd, after shooting 296.

1	**PETER THOMSON**	71	68	70	72	281
	(£1000)					
2	Johnny Fallon	73	67	73	70	283
3	Frank Jowle	70	71	69	74	284
4	Bobby Locke	74	69	70	72	285
5=	Ken Bousfield	71	75	70	70	286
	Antonio Cerda	73	71	71	71	286
	Bernard Hunt	70	71	74	71	286
	Flory van Donck	71	72	71	72	286
	Harry Weetman	71	71	70	74	286
10=	Romualdo Barbieri	71	71	73	72	287
	Christy O'Connor, Sr	71	75	70	71	287
12=	Eric Brown	69	70	73	76	288
	Fred Daly	75	72	70	71	288
	John Jacobs	71	70	71	76	288
15=	Iain Anderson	71	72	77	69	289
	Willie John Henderson	74	71	72	72	289
17=	DF Smalldon	70	69	78	73	290
	Arturo Soto	72	73	72	73	290
20=	Ed Furgol	71	76	72	73	292
	Kel Nagle	72	72	74	74	292
	Syd Scott	69	77	73	73	292
23=	Harry Bradshaw	72	70	73	78	293
	Bill Branch	75	72	73	73	293
	Joe Conrad (a)	72	76	74	71	293
	Bobby Halsall	71	74	76	72	293
	Reg Horne	72	75	75	71	293
28=	H Hassanein	73	72	76	73	294
	Dai Rees	69	79	73	73	294
	Norman Sutton	71	74	75	74	294

Round Leader(s)
R1 Brown, Rees, Scott; 69
R2 Brown, Smalldon, Thomson; 139
R3 Thomson; 209

Lowest Scores
R2 Fallon; 67
R3 Jowle; 69
R4 Anderson; 69

US PGA 1955

Meadowbrook Country Club, Northville, Michigan
(20–26 July)

MATCHPLAY
64 qualifiers after 36 holes strokeplay
(Low – Doug Ford, 136)
Rs1&2, 18 holes: R3,QF,SF&F, 36 holes

Doug Ford became only the fourth player, after Walter Hagen, in 1926 and 1927;Olin Dutra in 1932; and, not surprisingly in 1945, Byron Nelson, to shoot the lowest qualifying score and then go on to win the matchplay series. He overcame reigning Masters Champion, Cary Middlecoff, in a final that could have gone either way until he picked up birdies at 29, 30 and 32, for a three shot lead he was not going to give away.

FINAL
DOUG FORD beat Cary Middlecoff, 4&3

Round by Round Details

ROUND 2 (Last 32)
  Brien Charter bt Lionel Hebert 1up; Don Fairfield bt Vic Ghezzi 1up (after 23); Shelley Mayfield by Gene Sarazen 4&3; Claude Harmon bt Eldon Briggs 2&1; Ed Furgol bt Gus Salerno 1up (after 20); Fred Hawkins bt Fred Haas 2up; Wally Ulrich bt Leonard Wagner 2up; DOUG FORD bt Ted Kroll 2&1; Johnny Palmer bt Chick Harbert 1up; Lew Worsham bt Ray Hill 2&1; Tommy Bolt bt Sam Snead 3&2; Jack Fleck bt Jay Hebert 2&1; CARY MIDDLECOFF bt Bill Nary 3&2; Mike Pavella bt Jim Browning 4&3; Marty Furgol bt Tony Holguin 1up; Jack Burke Jr bt Dave Douglas 8&6

ROUND 3 (Last 16)
  Fairfield bt Charter 2&1
  Mayfield bt Harmon 1up
  Hawkins bt E Furgol 6&5
  FORD bt Ulrich 12&10
  Worsham bt Palmer 6&5
  Bolt bt Fleck 3&1
  MIDDLECOFF bt Pavella 8&6
  Burke Jr bt M Furgol 2&1

QUARTER FINAL (QF)
  Mayfield bt Fairfield 3&2
  FORD bt Hawkins 5&4
  Bolt bt Worsham 8&7
  MIDDLECOFF bt Burke Jr 1up (after 40)

SEMI FINAL (SF)
  FORD bt Mayfield 4&3
  MIDDLECOFF bt Bolt 4&3

THE MASTERS 1956

Augusta National Golf Club, Augusta, Georgia
(5–8 April)

6925 yards: Par 72 (288)

Jack Burke achieved what his father never could when he won a Major Championship, and in the most dramatic fashion at Augusta. Amateur Ken Venturi led Cary Middlecoff by four going into the last round, with Burke back in the pack, eight off the lead. The young Venturi crumbled in a generally high-scoring round, allowing Burke to come through on the rails to win by one.

1	**JACK BURKE, Jr**	72	71	75	71	289
	($6000)					
2	Ken Venturi (a)	66	69	75	80	290
3	Cary Middlecoff	67	72	75	77	291
4=	Lloyd Mangrum	72	74	72	74	292
	Sam Snead	73	76	72	71	292
6=	Jerry Barber	71	72	76	75	294
	Doug Ford	70	72	75	77	294
8=	Tommy Bolt	68	74	78	76	296
	Ben Hogan	69	78	74	75	296
	Shelley Mayfield	68	74	80	74	296
11	Johnny Palmer	76	74	74	73	297
12=	Pete Cooper	72	70	77	79	298
	Gene Littler	73	77	74	74	298
	Billy Joe Patton (a)	70	76	79	73	298
	Sam Urzetta	73	75	76	74	298
16	Bob Rosberg	70	74	81	74	299
17=	Walter Burkemo	72	74	78	76	300
	Roberto de Vicenzo	75	72	78	75	300
	Hillman Robbins, Jr (a)	73	73	78	76	300
	Mike Souchak	73	73	74	80	300
21	Arnold Palmer	73	75	74	79	301
22=	Frank Stranahan	72	75	79	76	302
	Jim Turnesa	74	74	74	80	302
24=	Julius Boros	73	78	72	80	303
	Dow Finsterwald	74	73	79	77	303
	Ed Furgol	74	75	78	76	303
	Stan Leonard	75	75	79	74	303
	Al Mengert	74	72	79	78	303
29=	Al Balding	75	78	77	74	304
	Vic Ghezzi	74	77	77	76	304
	Fred Haas	78	72	75	79	304
	Fred Hawkins	71	73	76	84	304
	Walker Inman, Jr	73	75	74	82	304

Round Leader(s)

R1   Venturi; 66
R2   Venturi; 135
R3   Venturi; 210

Lowest Scores

R2   Venturi; 69
R3   Boros, Mangrum, Snead; 72
R4   Burke, Snead; 71

US OPEN 1956

Oak Hill Country Club, Rochester, New York
(14–16 June)

6902 yards: Par 70 (280)

Cary Middlecoff never topped the US Money list, but he had a most successful career in the decade and a half immediately after WW2, winning 40 Tour events in total, tying him No 7 of all time, with Walter Hagen. Middlecoff's second US Open and third Major, however, came after a nail-biting few minutes watching his pursuers. Putting to tie, first Hogan (for a par) missed a 2_ footer on the 17th; then Boros (for birdie) rattled the cup on the final hole. Peter Thomson, in the middle of his unassailable period in the British Open, finished in his highest position in a US Major.

1	**CARY MIDDLECOFF**	71	70	70	70	281
	($6000)					
2=	Julius Boros	71	71	71	69	282
	Ben Hogan	72	68	72	70	282
4=	Ed Furgol	71	70	73	71	285
	Ted Kroll	72	70	70	73	285
	Peter Thomson	70	69	75	71	285
7	Arnold Palmer	72	70	72	73	287
8	Ken Venturi (a)	77	71	68	73	289
9=	Jerry Barber	72	69	74	75	290
	Wes Ellis, Jr	71	70	71	78	290
	Doug Ford	71	75	70	74	290
12	Billy Maxwell	72	71	76	72	291
13	Billy Joe Patton (a)	75	73	70	74	292
14=	Billy Casper	75	71	71	76	293
	Pete Cooper	73	74	76	70	293
	Fred Haas	72	71	72	78	293
17=	Henry Cotton	74	72	73	75	294
	Dutch Harrison	72	76	72	74	294
	Jay Hebert	71	76	73	74	294
	Bill Ogden	76	73	76	69	294
	Bob Toski	76	71	74	73	294
22=	Errie Ball	71	75	73	76	295
	Tommy Bolt	74	71	73	77	295
24=	Johnny Bulla	77	72	73	74	296
	Robert Kay	75	74	76	71	296
	Sam Snead	75	71	77	73	296
27=	Roberto de Vicenzo	76	69	77	75	297
	Doug Higgins	74	75	72	76	297
29=	Walter Burkemo	73	74	76	75	298
	Mike Dietz	73	74	70	81	298
	Shelley Mayfield	75	71	75	77	298
	Mike Souchak	78	71	72	77	298
	Frank Taylor, Jr (a)	72	71	80	75	298

Round Leader(s)

R1   Bob Rosburg (45); 68
R2   Thomson; 139
R3   Middlecoff; 211

Lowest Scores

R2   Hogan; 68
R3   Venturi; 68
R4   Boros, Ogden; 69

BRITISH OPEN 1956

Royal Liverpool Golf Club, Hoylake, Cheshire, England
(4–6 July)
6960 yards

Peter Thomson achieved something that had not happened since Bob Ferguson did it in 1882: namely, win the Open Championship three times in succession. Only Jamie Anderson and Tom Morris Jr, moving progressively backwards from Ferguson, had managed the same: and only Willie Anderson (US Open) and Walter Hagen (PGA) – in the history of the other Major Championships – had achieved it. No one has done it since.

1	**PETER THOMSON**	70	70	72	74	286
	(£1000)					
2	Flory van Donck	71	74	70	74	289
3	Roberto de Vicenzo	71	70	79	70	290
4	Gary Player	71	76	73	71	291
5	John Panton	74	76	72	70	292
6=	Enrique Bertolino	69	72	76	76	293
	Henry Cotton	72	76	71	74	293
8=	Antonio Cerda	72	81	68	73	294
	Mike Souchak	74	74	74	72	294
10=	Christy O'Connor, Sr	73	78	74	70	295
	Harry Weetman	72	76	75	72	295
12	Frank Stranahan	72	76	72	76	296
13=	Bruce Crampton	76	77	72	72	297
	Angel Miguel	71	74	75	77	297
	Dai Rees	75	74	75	73	297
16	John Jacobs	73	77	76	72	298
17=	Al Balding	70	81	76	73	300
	Jack Hargreaves	72	80	75	73	300
	Ricardo Rossi	75	77	72	76	300
	Dave Thomas	70	78	77	75	300
	Charlie Ward	73	75	78	74	300
22=	Ken Bousfield	73	77	76	75	301
	Gerard de Wit	76	73	74	78	301
	Eric Lester	70	76	77	78	301
25=	Jimmy Adams	75	76	76	75	302
	Laurie Ayton, Jr	74	78	78	72	302
	Eric Moore	75	75	78	74	302
28=	KWC Adwick	77	76	74	76	303
	Syd Scott	78	74	74	77	303
	DF Smalldon	68	79	78	78	303

Round Leader(s)
R1   Smalldon; 68
R2   Thomson; 140
R3   Thomson; 212

Lowest Scores
R2   de Vicenzo, Thomson; 70
R3   Cerda; 68
R4   de Vicenzo, O'Connor, Panton; 70

US PGA 1956

Blue Hill Golf & Country Club, Canton, Massachusetts
(20–24 July)

MATCHPLAY
128 players
Rs1,2,3&4, 18 holes: QF,SF&F, 36 holes

In the penultimate year of matchplay, the format was changed again to allow 128 competitors to qualify for that stage and cut down on two days of qualifying. Jack Burke became the 11th player to win two or more Majors in the same season – by doing the difficult Masters-PGA double. He beat Ted Kroll, who had finished well up in the US Open, in the final. Kroll strolled to the final after a semi final which saw Bill Johnston commit golfing suicide with a morning 81.

FINAL
JACK BURKE, Jr ($5000) beat Ted Kroll, 3&2

Round by Round Details

ROUND 3 (Last 32)
Walter Burkemo bt Doug Ford 5&3; Bill Johnston bt Tony Fortino 4&3; Henry Ransom bt Claude Harmon 1up (after 23); Lew Worsham bt Shelley Mayfield 5&4; Sam Snead bt Bob Toski 4&3; Gene Sarazen bt Mike Krak 3&2; TED KROLL bt Michael Rooney 3&2; Jim Turnesa bt Jack Fleck 1up; Charles Harper Jr bt Babe Lichardus 1up; JACK BURKE Jr bt Fred Haas 1up (after 20); Fred Hawkins bt Art Wall 1up (after 19); Lionel Hebert bt Skee Riegel 3&1; Toby Lyons bt Charles Lepre 3&2; Terl Johnson bt Charles DuPree 4&2; Robert Kay bt Mike Fetchick 1up; Ed Furgol bt Jerry Barber 2&1

ROUND 4 (Last 16)
Johnston bt Burkemo 1up
Ransom bt Worsham 2up
Snead bt Sarazen 5&4
KROLL bt Turnesa 1up
BURKE Jr bt Harper Jr 3&2
Hawkins bt Hebert 4&3
Johnson bt Lyons 1up (after 19)
Furgol bt Kay 4&3

QUARTER FINAL (QF)
Johnston bt Ransom 3&2
KROLL bt Snead 2&1
BURKE Jr bt Hawkins 4&2
Furgol bt Johnson 1up

SEMI FINAL (SF)
KROLL bt Johnston 10&8
BURKE Jr bt Furgol 1up (after 37)

THE MASTERS 1957

Augusta National Golf Club, Augusta, Georgia
(4–7 April)

6925 yards: Par 72 (288)

A 36-hole cut was applied for the first time in the 1957 Masters. Doug Ford added to his 1955 PGA title thanks to a six-shot swing over the last 18 holes, and has become one of a very few veteran golfers to use the lifetime winner's exemption to play in the Masters quite literally – even into the following century, aged almost 80! Round Three leader Sam Snead shot par, but Ford's record last round 66 took him from three behind to three in front. Still on an ageist theme, Snead, aged 45 was second, and Masters expert Jimmy Demaret, who finished third, was 47. Henry Cotton, making a rare visit to the US was 13th at the age of 50; Byron Nelson 16th at 45.

1	**DOUG FORD**	72	73	72	66	283
	($8750)					
2	Sam Snead	72	68	74	72	286
3	Jimmy Demaret	72	70	75	70	287
4	E Harvie Ward, Jr (a)	73	71	71	73	288
5	Peter Thomson	72	73	73	71	289
6	Ed Furgol	73	71	72	74	290
7=	Jack Burke, Jr	71	72	74	74	291
	Dow Finsterwald	74	74	73	70	291
	Arnold Palmer	73	73	69	76	291
10	Jay Hebert	74	72	76	70	292
11=	Marty Furgol	73	74	73	73	293
	Stan Leonard	75	72	68	78	293
13=	Henry Cotton	73	73	72	76	294
	Frank M Taylor, Jr (a)	74	74	77	69	294
	Ken Venturi	74	76	74	70	294
16=	Al Balding	73	73	73	76	295
	Billy Casper	75	75	75	70	295
	Mike Fetchick	74	73	72	76	295
	Fred Hawkins	75	74	72	74	295
	Byron Nelson	74	72	73	76	295
21=	Bruce Crampton	72	75	78	71	296
	Al Mengert	75	75	71	75	296
	Henry Ransom	75	73	72	76	296
24=	Johnny Palmer	77	73	73	74	297
	Gary Player	77	72	75	73	297
26=	Jerry Barber	73	77	78	70	298
	Jack Fleck	76	74	75	73	298
28=	Bill Johnston	77	70	78	74	299
	Lawson Little	76	72	77	74	299
	Lloyd Mangrum	77	71	74	77	299

Round Leader(s)
R1   Burke; 71
R2   Snead; 140
R3   Snead; 214

Lowest Scores
R2   Snead; 68
R3   Leonard; 68
R4   Ford; 66

US OPEN 1957

Inverness Golf Club, Toledo, Ohio
(13–15 June)

6919 yards: Par 70 (280)

Dick Mayer won his only Major and stopped a Middlecoff double when he outplayed him in the play-off. A tie had resulted after 72 holes when Mayer's 138 over the first 36 holes (shared with Billy Joe Patton) was compensated by Middlecoff's 136 over the last 36 (this equalled a 25 year-old record set by Gene Sarazen at Fresh Meadow). Demaret was again in the hunt and was leading going into Round Four.

1	**DICK MAYER***	70	68	74	70	282
	($7200)					
2	Cary Middlecoff	71	75	68	68	282
3	Jimmy Demaret	68	73	70	72	283
4=	Julius Boros	69	75	70	70	284
	Walter Burkemo	74	73	72	65	284
6=	Fred Hawkins	72	72	71	71	286
	Ken Venturi	69	71	75	71	286
8=	Roberto de Vicenzo	72	70	72	76	290
	Chick Harbert	68	79	71	72	290
	Billy Maxwell	70	76	72	72	290
	Billy Joe Patton (a)	70	68	76	76	290
	Sam Snead	74	74	69	73	290
13=	Mike Fetchick	74	71	71	75	291
	Dow Finsterwald	74	72	72	73	291
	William Hyndman III (a)	77	73	72	69	291
	Frank Stranahan	72	76	69	74	291
17=	Don Fairfield	78	72	73	69	292
	Jim Ferree	74	74	73	71	292
	Doug Ford	69	71	80	72	292
	Bud Ward	70	74	70	78	292
21	Bo Wininger	70	71	76	76	293
22=	George Bayer	73	77	69	75	294
	Joe Campbell (a)	74	72	73	75	294
	Ed Oliver	74	73	73	74	294
	Peter Thomson	71	72	74	77	294
26=	Jack Fleck	72	76	73	74	295
	Gerald Kesselring	74	71	75	75	295
	Sam Penecale	71	73	73	78	295
	E Harvie Ward, Jr (a)	72	75	74	74	295
30=	Leo Biagetti	73	75	72	76	296
	Johnny Revolta	76	74	74	72	296

* Dick Mayer (72) beat Cary Middlecoff (79) in the 18-Hole Play-off

Round Leader(s)
R1   Demaret, Harbert; 68
R2   Mayer, Patton; 138
R3   Demaret; 211

Lowest Scores
R2   Mayer, Patton; 68
R3   Middlecoff; 68
R4   Burkemo; 65

BRITISH OPEN 1957

Royal & Ancient golf Club, St Andrews, Fife, Scotland
(3-5 July)
6936 yards

TV cameras caught the finish 'live' for the first time as Bobby Locke regained the crown after four years from Peter Thomson. This was Locke's fourth and last Open (and Major) win, to put him level with Willie Park Sr and Tom Morris (Sr and Jr); but one behind Taylor and Braid, two behind Vardon (who also, of course, was US Open Champion in 1900). Token American interest came in the form of current US Open runner-up, Cary Middlecoff, and the now professional Frank Stranahan.

1	**BOBBY LOCKE**	69	72	68	70	279
	(£1000)					
2	Peter Thomson	73	69	70	70	282
3	Eric Brown	67	72	73	71	283
4	Angel Miguel	72	72	69	72	285
5=	Tom Haliburton	72	73	68	73	286
	Dick Smith (a)	71	72	72	71	286
	Dave Thomas	72	74	70	70	286
	Flory van Donck	72	68	74	72	286
9=	Antonio Cerda	71	71	72	73	287
	Henry Cotton	74	72	69	72	287
	Max Faulkner	74	70	71	72	287
12=	Peter Alliss	72	74	74	68	288
	Harry Weetman	75	71	71	71	288
14	Cary Middlecoff	72	71	74	72	289
15=	Norman Drew	70	75	71	74	290
	Eric Lester	71	76	70	73	290
	Sebastian Miguel	71	75	76	68	290
	John Panton	71	72	74	73	290
19=	Harry Bradshaw	73	74	69	75	291
	Johnny Fallon	75	67	73	76	291
	Christy O'Connor, Sr	77	69	72	73	291
	Frank Stranahan	74	71	74	72	291
23	Jimmy Hitchcock	69	74	73	76	292
24=	Reg Horne	76	72	72	73	293
	Bernard Hunt	72	72	74	75	293
	Sam King	76	72	70	75	293
	Gary Player	71	74	75	73	293
	Trevor Wilkes	75	73	71	74	293
29	Harold Henning	75	73	71	75	294
30=	Laurie Ayton, Jr	67	76	75	77	295
	Peter Butler	77	71	74	73	295
	Reg Knight	71	73	75	76	295
	Dai Rees	73	72	79	71	295
	Norman Sutton	69	76	73	77	295

Round Leader(s)
R1 Ayton, Brown; 67
R2 Brown; 139
R3 Locke; 209

Lowest Scores
R2 Fallon; 67
R3 Haliburton, Locke; 68
R4 Alliss, Miguel; 68

US PGA 1957

Miami Valley Golf Club, Dayton, Ohio
(17-21 July4-7 April)

MATCHPLAY
128 players
Rs1,2,3&4, 18 holes: QF,SF&F, 36 holes

Due to commercial demands brought on by the burgeoning TV era, and not altogether approved of by the purists and the professionals, matchplay in the PGA was brought to a close in 1957. To be fair, the Championship still took five days as against three for the other Majors – so it was a little unwieldy, and not particularly spectator-friendly when fewer and fewer matches were on offer as the matchplay rounds ground on in their eliminatory fashion. Medal play ensued thereafter. Lionel Hebert beat Dow Finsterwald in the last final.

FINAL
LIONEL HEBERT ($8000) beat Dow Finsterwald, 3&1

Round by Round Details

ROUND 3 (Last 32)
Milon Marusic bt Mike Krak 2&1; Donald Whitt bt Ellsworth Vines 4&3; Ted Kroll bt Ewing Pomeroy 4&3; Dick Mayer bt Al Smith 5&3; Warren Smith bt Skee Riegel 3&2; Charles Sheppard bt Buck White 1up; Sam Snead bt John Thoren 3&2; DOW FINSTERWALD bt Joe Kirkwood Jr 2&1; Mike Souchak bt Brien Charter 4&3; LIONEL HEBERT bt Charles Farlow 3&1; Claude Harmon bt Charles Bassler 4&3; Tommy Bolt bt Eldon Briggs 7&6; Henry Ransom bt Herman Keiser 5&3; Walter Burkemo bt Tony Holguin 1up; Jay Hebert bt Charles Harper Jr 1up; Doug Ford bt Bob Gajda 3&2

ROUND 4 (Last 16)
Whitt bt Marusic 2&1
Mayer bt Kroll 1up
Sheppard bt Smith 4&3
FINSTERWALD bt Snead 2&1
L HEBERT bt Souchak 2&1
Harmon bt Bolt 1up
Burkemo bt Ransom 5&4
J Hebert bt Ford 3&2

QUARTER FINAL (QF)
Whitt bt Mayer 2&1
FINSTERWALD bt Sheppard 2up
L HEBERT bt Harmon 2&1
Burkemo bt J Hebert 3&2

SEMI FINAL (SF)
FINSTERWALD bt Whitt 2up
L HEBERT bt Burkemo 3&1

THE MASTERS 1958

Augusta National Golf Club, Augusta, Georgia
(3–6 April)
6925 yards: Par 72 (288)

It was somehow appropriate that the first five-figure winner's purse in a Major Championship should go to Arnold Palmer. Over the next two decades he, more than anyone else, is associated with the commercial revolution that took place in golf. Arnie's first win made him, at 28, the youngest winner of the Masters since Byron Nelson in 1938. He was almost caught by Ford and Hawkins over the last holes, but they both missed holeable birdie putts on the 18th. The aforementioned Nelson, along with fellow veterans Snead, Demaret and Hogan, gave a nostalgic glow to the Top Twenty.

1	**ARNOLD PALMER**	70	73	68	73	284
	($11250)					
2=	Doug Ford	74	71	70	70	285
	Fred Hawkins	71	75	68	71	285
4=	Stan Leonard	72	70	73	71	286
	Ken Venturi	68	72	74	72	286
6=	Cary Middlecoff	70	73	69	75	287
	Art Wall	71	72	70	74	287
8	Billy Joe Patton (a)	72	69	73	74	288
9=	Claude Harmon	71	76	72	70	289
	Jay Hebert	72	73	73	71	289
	Billy Maxwell (a)	71	70	72	76	289
	Al Mengert	73	71	69	76	289
13	Sam Snead	72	71	68	79	290
14=	Jimmy Demaret	69	79	70	73	291
	Ben Hogan	72	77	69	73	291
	Mike Souchak	72	75	73	71	291
17=	Dow Finsterwald	72	71	74	75	292
	Chick Harbert	69	74	73	76	292
	Bo Winninger	69	73	71	79	292
20=	Billy Casper	76	71	72	74	293
	Byron Nelson	71	77	74	71	293
22	Phil Rodgers	77	72	73	72	294
23=	Charles R Coe (a)	73	76	69	77	295
	Ted Kroll	73	75	75	72	295
	Peter Thomson	72	74	73	76	295
26=	Al Balding	75	72	71	78	296
	Bruce Crampton	73	76	72	75	296
	William Hyndman III (a)	71	76	70	79	296
29=	George Bayer	74	75	72	76	297
	Arnold Blum (a)	72	74	75	76	297
	Joe E Campbell (a)	73	75	74	75	297

Round Leader(s)
R1   Venturi; 68
R2   Venturi; 140
R3   Palmer, Snead; 211

Lowest Scores
R2   Patton; 69
R3   Hawkins, Palmer, Snead; 68
R4   Ford, Harmon; 70

US OPEN 1958

Southern Hills Country Club, Tulsa, Oklahoma
(12–14 June)
6907 yards: Par 70 (280)

The number of entries topped 2000 for the first time; and Sam Snead, after 18 consecutive years of making the final day, missed the cut. Irascible Tommy Bolt's famous temper was generally kept in check as he led all the way to collect his solitary Major Championship victory. A second Top Five placing in two years for Walter Burkemo belied the myth he was just a matchplay golfer, and despite a wrist injury, Ben Hogan still finished in the Top 10. The younger generation was represented by a young South African, who almost emulated Palmer's feat in the Masters: one Gary Jim Player.

1	**TOMMY BOLT**	71	71	69	72	283
	($8000)					
2	Gary Player	75	68	73	71	287
3	Julius Boros	71	75	72	71	289
4	Gene Littler	74	73	67	76	290
5=	Walter Burkemo	75	74	70	72	291
	Bob Rosburg	75	74	72	70	291
7=	Jay Hebert	77	76	71	69	293
	Don January	79	73	68	73	293
	Dick Metz	71	78	73	71	293
10=	Ben Hogan	75	73	75	71	294
	Tommy Jacobs	76	75	71	72	294
	Frank Stranahan	72	72	75	75	294
13=	Billy Casper	79	70	75	71	295
	Charles R Coe (a)	75	71	75	74	295
	Marty Furgol	75	74	74	72	295
16	Bob Goetz	75	75	77	69	296
17=	Tom Nieporte	75	73	74	75	297
	Jerry Pittman	75	77	71	74	297
19=	Jerry Barber	79	73	73	73	298
	Bruce Crampton	73	75	74	76	298
	Jim Ferree	76	74	73	75	298
	Jerry Magee	76	77	75	70	298
23=	Dutch Harrison	76	76	73	74	299
	Dick Mayer	76	74	71	78	299
	Arnold Palmer	75	75	77	72	299
	Earl Stewart	75	74	77	73	299
27=	Stan Dudas	76	73	76	75	300
	Don Fairfield	78	75	72	75	300
	Mike Fetchick	78	76	73	73	300
	Labron Harris	74	72	77	77	300
	Billy Maxwell	78	76	76	70	300
	Cary Middlecoff	75	79	75	71	300
	Bo Winninger	78	74	74	74	300

Round Leader(s)
R1   Bolt, Boros, Metz; 71
R2   Bolt; 142
R3   Bolt; 211

Lowest Scores
R2   Player; 68
R3   Littler; 67
R4   Hebert, Goetz; 69

BRITISH OPEN 1958

Royal Lytham & St Anne's Golf Club, Lancashire, England
(2–4 July)
6635 yards

The game of musical chairs between Locke and Thomson continued at Lytham. Between them they had claimed the Open eight times since 1949. Only Max Faulkner (1951) and Ben Hogan (1953) disturbed their party game. Thomson's fourth win placed him alongside Locke in the all-time lists, and only James Braid had more wins in the century to date. Thomson's incredible sequence in the event since 1952 read: 2, 2, W, W, W, 2, W! In 1958, he was taken to the wire – and beyond – by Welshman Dave Thomas. Good finishes from a couple of much-loved ancients, Cotton and Sarazen.

I	**PETER THOMSON*** (£1000)	66	72	67	73	278
2	Dave Thomas	70	68	69	71	278
3=	Eric Brown	73	70	65	71	279
	Christy O'Connor, Sr	67	68	73	71	279
5=	Leopoldo Ruiz	71	65	72	73	281
	Flory van Donck	70	70	67	74	281
7	Gary Player	68	74	70	71	283
8=	Henry Cotton	68	75	69	72	284
	Eric Lester	73	66	71	74	284
	Harry Weetman	73	67	73	71	284
11=	Peter Alliss	72	70	70	73	285
	Don Swaelens	74	67	74	70	285
13	Harold Henning	70	71	72	73	286
14=	Jean Garaialde	69	74	72	72	287
	Dai Rees	77	69	71	70	287
16=	Max Faulkner	68	71	71	78	288
	Bobby Locke	76	70	72	70	288
	Eric Moore	72	72	70	74	288
	Gene Sarazen	73	73	70	72	288
20=	AB Coop	69	71	75	75	290
	Fred Daly	71	74	72	73	290
	Norman Drew	69	72	75	74	290
	Christy Greene	75	71	72	72	290
24=	Harry Bradshaw	70	73	72	76	291
	Gerard de Wit	71	75	72	73	291
26=	Antonio Cerda	72	71	74	75	292
	Sebastian Miguel	74	71	73	74	292
	Trevor Wilkes	76	70	69	77	292
29	Angel Miguel	71	70	75	77	293
30=	Bernard Hunt	70	70	76	79	295
	Sam King	71	73	76	75	295
	David Snell	72	72	72	79	295

* Peter Thomson (139) beat Dave Thomas (143) in the 36-Hole Play-off

Round Leader(s)
R1 Thomson; 66
R2 O'Connor; 135
R3 Thomson; 205

Lowest Scores
R2 Ruiz; 65
R3 Thomson, Van Donck; 67
R4 Locke, Rees, Swaelens; 70

US PGA 1958

Llanerch Country Club, Havertown, Pennsylvania
(17–20 July)
6710 yards: Par 70 (280)

Dow Finsterwald became the first strokeplay winner of the PGA – atoning for his defeat by Lionel Hebert in the last matchplay final the previous year. It was Lionel's brother, Jay, who was the early threat this time. For Sam Snead, the scenario was not too dissimilar from the Masters of the previous year. Again he led into the final round, but was once more overhauled by a superb round. This time, for Doug Ford's 66, read Finsterwald's 67.

I	**DOW FINSTERWALD** ($5500)	67	72	70	67	276
2	Billy Casper	73	67	68	70	278
3	Sam Snead	73	67	67	73	280
4	Jack Burke, Jr	70	72	69	70	281
5=	Tommy Bolt	72	70	73	70	285
	Julius Boros	72	68	73	72	285
	Jay Hebert	68	71	73	73	285
8=	Buster Cupit	71	74	69	73	287
	Ed Oliver	74	73	71	69	287
	Mike Souchak	75	69	69	74	287
11=	Doug Ford	72	70	70	76	288
	Bob Rosburg	71	73	76	68	288
	Art Wall	71	78	67	72	288
14=	Fred Hawkins	72	75	70	73	290
	Dick Mayer	69	76	69	76	290
16=	John Barnum	75	69	74	73	291
	Walter Burkemo	76	73	66	76	291
	Lionel Hebert	69	73	74	75	291
	Bo Wininger	76	73	69	73	291
20=	Ted Kroll	69	74	75	74	292
	Cary Middlecoff	71	73	76	72	292
	Eric Monti	73	71	73	75	292
	Bob Toski	79	70	71	72	292
	Ken Venturi	72	73	74	73	292
25=	Pete Cooper	74	77	73	69	293
	George Fazio	72	74	73	74	293
	Bob Gajda	75	70	75	73	293
	Billy Maxwell	75	69	74	75	293
29=	Dick Shoemaker	79	72	73	70	294
	Don Whitt	71	72	73	78	294

Round Leader(s)
R1 Finsterwald; 67
R2 Finsterwald, Hebert; 139
R3 Snead; 207

Lowest Scores
R2 Casper, Snead; 67
R3 Burkemo; 66
R4 Finsterwald; 67

THE MASTERS 1959

Augusta National Golf Club, Augusta, Georgia
(2–5 April)

6925 yards: Par 72 (288)

Art Wall was to be the leading money winner on the Tour in 1959 – set up by the biggest-ever first prize in a Major to date. His 66 in Round Four to squeeze out Middlecoff was remarkable in its five-under-par sequence over the last four holes. Wall was a remarkable golfer in many ways. He won a Tour tournament aged 51 as late as 1975; he also claims the world record for holes-in-one – an astonishing 42! This was to be his only Major win, though.

1	**ART WALL**	73	74	71	66	284
	($15000)					
2	Cary Middlecoff	74	71	68	72	285
3	Arnold Palmer	71	70	71	74	286
4=	Stan Leonard	69	74	69	75	287
	Dick Mayer	73	75	71	68	287
6	Charles R Coe (a)	74	74	67	73	288
7	Fred Hawkins	77	71	68	73	289
8=	Julius Boros	75	69	74	72	290
	Jay Hebert	72	73	72	73	290
	Gene Littler	72	75	72	71	290
	Billy Maxwell (a)	73	71	72	74	290
	Billy Joe Patton (a)	75	70	71	74	290
	Gary Player	73	75	71	71	290
14=	Chick Harbert	74	72	74	71	291
	Chandler Harper	71	74	74	72	291
	Ted Kroll	76	71	73	71	291
	Ed Oliver	75	69	73	74	291
18=	Dow Finsterwald	79	68	73	72	292
	Jack Fleck	74	71	71	76	292
	William Hyndman III (a)	73	72	76	71	292
	Bo Wininger	75	70	72	75	292
22=	Walter Burkemo	75	70	71	77	293
	Chuck Kocsis (a)	73	75	70	75	293
	Sam Snead	74	73	72	74	293
25=	Don Cherry	77	71	75	71	294
	Doug Ford	76	73	73	72	294
	Paul Harney	75	69	77	73	294
	Angel Miguel	72	72	76	74	294
	Mike Souchak	73	71	74	76	294
30=	Tommy Bolt	72	75	72	76	295
	Ben Hogan	73	74	76	72	295
	Bob Rosburg	75	74	73	73	295
	Dave Thomas	73	71	77	74	295

Round Leader(s)
R1   Leonard; 69
R2   Palmer; 141
R3   Leonard, Palmer; 212

Lowest Scores
R2   Finsterwald; 68
R3   Coe; 67
R4   Wall; 66

US OPEN 1959

Winged Foot Golf Club, Mamaroneck, New York
(11–13 June)

6873 yards: Par 70 (280)

The increasing number of entrants forced the introduction of local and final qualifying sessions. Billy Casper hung on to his halfway lead to head up an unfancied Top Four. Disappointing last rounds for Palmer, Hogan and Snead reduced the pressure on him in a Championship where his putting (which was to become his career trademark) had kept his scores together. He putted just 122 times throughout.

1	**BILLY CASPER**	71	68	69	74	282
	($12000)					
2	Bob Rosburg	75	70	67	71	283
3=	Claude Harmon	72	71	70	71	284
	Mike Souchak	71	70	72	71	284
5=	Doug Ford	72	69	72	73	286
	Arnold Palmer	71	69	72	74	286
	Ernie Vossler	72	70	72	72	286
8=	Ben Hogan	69	71	71	76	287
	Sam Snead	73	72	67	75	287
10	Dick Knight	69	75	73	73	290
11=	Dow Finsterwald	69	73	75	74	291
	Fred Hawkins	76	72	69	74	291
	Ted Kroll	71	73	73	74	291
	Gene Littler	69	74	75	73	291
15=	Dave Marr	75	73	69	75	292
	Gary Player	71	69	76	76	292
17=	Gardner Dickinson	77	70	71	75	293
	Jay Hebert	73	70	78	72	293
19=	Jack Fleck	74	74	69	77	294
	Mac Hunter	75	74	73	72	294
	Don January	71	73	73	77	294
	Cary Middlecoff	71	73	73	77	294
	Johnny Pott	77	72	70	75	294
	Bo Wininger	71	73	72	78	294
25	Joe Campbell	73	71	75	76	295
26=	Chick Harbert	78	68	76	74	296
	Billy Maxwell	75	75	70	76	296
28=	Julius Boros	76	74	72	75	297
	Lionel Hebert	71	74	70	82	297
	Henry Ransom	72	77	71	77	297
	Fred Wampler	74	73	75	75	297

Round Leader(s)
R1   Finsterwald, Hogan, Knight, Littler; 69
R2   Casper; 139
R3   Casper; 208

Lowest Scores
R2   Cooper, Harbert; 68
R3   Rosburg, Snead; 67
R4   Harman, Rosburg, Souchak; 71

BRITISH OPEN 1959

Hon Co of Edinburgh Golfers, Muirfield, East Lothian, Scotland
(1–3 July)
6806 yds

Gary Player had announced his arrival on the world golfing scene when he finished fourth in the British Open in 1956 and second in the US Open in 1958. The South African's first Major Championship win of an illustrious career coincided with the nadir of the Open's gradual decline in comparative importance with the US Open. A glance at the comparative prize money is enough on its own to suggest why. The influx of top-class American challengers had dwindled to a trickle since the mid '30s until, by 1959, there were none. Amazingly, it was to change very quickly indeed...

1	**GARY PLAYER**	75	71	70	68	284
	(£1000)					
2=	Fred Bullock	68	70	74	74	286
	Flory van Donck	70	70	73	73	286
4	Syd Scott	73	70	73	71	287
5=	Reid Jack (a)	71	75	68	74	288
	Sam King	70	74	68	76	288
	Christy O'Connor, Sr	73	74	72	69	288
	John Panton	72	72	71	73	288
9=	Dai Rees	73	73	69	74	289
	Leopoldo Ruiz	72	74	69	74	289
11=	Michael Bonallack (a)	70	72	72	76	290
	Ken Bousfield	73	73	71	73	290
	Jimmy Hitchcock	75	68	70	77	290
	Bernard Hunt	73	75	71	71	290
	Arnold Stickley	68	74	77	71	290
16=	Peter Alliss	76	72	76	67	291
	Harry Bradshaw	71	76	72	72	291
	Antonio Cerda	69	74	73	75	291
	Harry Weetman	72	73	76	70	291
	Guy Wolstenholme (a)	78	70	73	70	291
21=	Neil Coles	72	74	71	75	292
	Jean Garaialde	75	70	74	73	292
23=	Harold Henning	73	73	72	76	294
	Geoff Hunt	72	73	74	75	294
	Reg Knight	71	71	74	78	294
	Peter Mills	75	71	72	76	294
	JR Moses	72	73	73	76	294
	Peter Thomson	74	74	72	74	294
29=	Jimmy Adams	71	74	75	75	295
	Tom Haliburton	74	69	74	78	295
	Bobby Locke	73	73	76	73	295
	PJ Shanks	76	70	75	74	295
	Ernest E Whitcombe	71	77	74	73	295

Round Leader(s)
R1   Bullock, Stickley; 68
R2   Bullock; 138
R3   Bullock, King; 212

Lowest Scores
R2   Haliburton; 69
R3   Jack, King; 68
R4   Alliss; 67

US PGA 1959

Minneapolis Golf Club, Louis park, Minnesota
(30 July–2 August)
6850 yards: Par 70 (280)

Bob Rosburg made up for his second place disappointment in the US Open by taking his one and only Major title at Minneapolis. Nine people tied at the end of Round One, on 69 (three of whom, Dick Hart, Chuck Klein and Mike Krak, would miss the cut: Jackson Bradley finished in 31st place) – the largest leadership grouping at the end of any round in any Major. Rosburg, nine behind Barber at halfway, and six shots adrift after 54 holes, blasted a final round 66 to win by one.

1	**BOB ROSBURG**	71	72	68	66	277
	($8250)					
2=	Jerry Barber	69	65	71	73	278
	Doug Sanders	72	66	68	72	278
4	Dow Finsterwald	71	68	71	70	280
5=	Bob Goalby	72	69	72	68	281
	Mike Souchak	69	67	71	74	281
	Ken Venturi	70	72	70	69	281
8=	Cary Middlecoff	72	68	70	72	282
	Sam Snead	71	73	68	70	282
10	Gene Littler	69	70	72	73	284
11=	Doug Ford	71	73	71	70	285
	Billy Maxwell	70	76	70	69	285
	Ed Oliver	75	70	69	71	285
14=	Paul Harney	74	71	71	70	286
	Tommy Jacobs	73	71	68	74	286
	Arnold Palmer	72	72	71	71	286
17=	Tommy Bolt	76	69	68	74	287
	Jack Burke, Jr	70	73	72	72	287
	Walter Burkemo	69	72	73	73	287
	Billy Casper	69	71	73	74	287
	Pete Cooper	78	70	68	71	287
	Buster Cupit	70	72	72	73	287
	Babe Lichardus	71	73	72	71	287
	Ernie Vossler	75	71	72	69	287
25=	Jay Hebert	72	70	69	77	288
	Ted Kroll	72	74	71	71	288
	Art Wall	70	72	73	73	288
28=	Clare Emery	74	74	72	69	289
	Chick Harbert	73	71	71	74	289
	Fred Hawkins	72	69	72	76	289

Round Leader(s)
R1   Barber, Jackson Bradley (31), Burkemo, Casper,
      Dick Hart (Cut), Chuck Klein (Cut), Mike Krak
      (Cut), Littler, Souchak; 69
R2   Barber; 134
R3   Barber; 205

Lowest Scores
R2   Barber; 65
R3   Bolt, Cooper, Jacobs, Rosburg, Sanders, Snead; 68
R4   Rosburg; 66

THE MASTERS 1960

Augusta National Golf Club, Augusta, Georgia
(7–10 April)
6925 yards: Par 72 (288)

Palmer's second Masters triumph swept in the new decade like the breath of fresh air the '60s' was to become on many fronts. Post-War colourless austerity, and cloying formalities and conventions gave way to new freedoms of expression; none freer than in golf, personified by the phenomenon of Arnold Palmer. The people's man, he took the playing of golf into a new dimension through his vision and daring. He almost single-handedly, through the media of press and, particularly, TV, popularized the sport for spectators; and created a surge in new players like at no time before. At Augusta in 1960, in front of a TV audience sitting on the edge of their seats, he dramatically birdied 17 and 18 to beat the disbelieving Ken Venturi by one.

1	**ARNOLD PALMER**	67	73	72	70	282
	($17500)					
2	Ken Venturi	73	69	71	70	283
3	Dow Finsterwald	71	70	72	71	284
4	Billy Casper	71	71	71	74	287
5	Julius Boros	72	71	70	75	288
6=	Walter Burkemo	72	69	75	73	289
	Ben Hogan	73	68	72	76	289
	Gary Player	72	71	72	74	289
9=	Lionel Hebert	74	70	73	73	290
	Stan Leonard	72	72	72	74	290
11=	Jack Burke, Jr	72	72	74	74	292
	Sam Snead	73	74	72	73	292
13=	Ted Kroll	72	76	71	74	293
	Jack Nicklaus (a)	75	71	72	75	293
	Billy Joe Patton	75	72	74	72	293
16=	Bruce Crampton	74	73	75	72	294
	Claude Harmon	69	72	75	78	294
	Fred Hawkins	69	78	72	75	294
	Mike Souchak	72	75	72	75	294
20=	Tommy Bolt	73	74	75	73	295
	Don January	70	72	74	79	295
	Ed Oliver	74	75	73	73	295
	Bob Rosburg	74	74	71	76	295
	Frank M Taylor, Jr (a)	70	74	73	78	295
25=	Tommy Aaron	74	75	75	73	297
	Doug Ford	74	72	80	81	297
	Billy Maxwell (a)	72	71	79	75	297
	Dave Ragan	74	73	75	75	297
29=	George Bayer	73	73	80	72	298
	Deane Beman (a)	71	72	77	78	298
	Richard Crawford	74	72	75	77	298
	Doug Sanders	73	71	81	73	298

Round Leader(s)
R1   Palmer; 67
R2   Palmer; 140
R3   Palmer; 212

Lowest Scores
R2   Hogan; 68
R3   Boros; 70
R4   Palmer, Venturi; 70

US OPEN 1960

Cherry Hills Country Club, Denver, Colorado
(16–18 June)
7004 yards: Par 71 (284)

Two months later Palmer was still rolling on. Once more, he saved his heroics until Round Four. Trailing leader Mike Souchak by seven strokes, he went out in a record-equalling 30, to make 65 and leapfrog the leading pack. With a proper sense of the occasion, Jack William Nicklaus also entered the scene, when he took the highest place claimed by an amateur since Goodman's win in 1933. Along with Palmer and British Open Champion, Player, the emergence of the 'Golden Bear' heralded the modern version of the Great Triumvirate, more prosaically titled 'The Big Three'. From Arnie's 1958 Masters win to Jack's in 1986, they were to scoop 34 Major titles between them.

1	**ARNOLD PALMER**	72	71	72	65	280
	($14400)					
2	Jack Nicklaus (a)	71	71	69	71	282
3=	Julius Boros	73	69	68	73	283
	Dow Finsterwald	71	69	70	73	283
	Jack Fleck	70	70	72	71	283
	Dutch Harrison	74	70	70	69	283
	Ted Kroll	72	69	75	67	283
	Mike Souchak	68	67	73	75	283
9=	Jerry Barber	69	71	70	74	284
	Don Cherry (a)	70	71	71	72	284
	Ben Hogan	75	67	69	73	284
12=	George Bayer	72	72	73	69	286
	Billy Casper	71	70	73	72	286
	Paul Harney	73	70	72	71	286
15=	Bob Harris	73	71	71	72	287
	Johnny Pott	75	68	69	75	287
17=	Dave Marr	72	73	70	73	288
	Donald Whitt	75	69	72	72	288
19=	Jackson Bradley	73	73	69	74	289
	Bob Goalby	73	70	72	74	289
	Gary Player	70	72	71	76	289
	Sam Snead	72	69	73	75	289
23=	Al Feminelli	75	71	71	73	290
	Lloyd Mangrum	72	73	71	74	290
	Bob Rosburg	72	75	71	72	290
	Ken Venturi	71	73	74	72	290
27=	Claude Harmon	73	73	75	70	291
	Lionel Hebert	73	72	71	75	291
	Bob Shave, Jr	72	71	71	77	291
	Richard Stranahan	70	73	73	75	291

Round Leader(s)
R1   Souchak; 68
R2   Souchak; 135
R3   Souchak; 208

Lowest Scores
R2   Rex Baxter (33), Hogan, Souchak; 67
R3   Boros; 68
R4   Palmer; 65

BRITISH OPEN 1960

Royal & Ancient Golf Club, St Andrews, Fife, Scotland
(6–8 July)
6936 yards

Perhaps sensing a Grand Slam on the cards, Palmer remembered from somewhere deep inside there was that other Championship across the water. It may have become marginalized in the eyes of America, but it still had to be won if the clean sweep of the traditional Majors was to be claimed. Be that his reason or not, Palmer heralded the return of the Americans to the Open, and the world of golf owes him a huge debt of gratitude for that. Another final round charge just failed to net him the Centenary Open Championship, denying him Ben Hogan's treble of 1953 and what was to become his best chance of immortality, golfing or otherwise. The Commonwealth succession continued in the person of Australian Kel Nagle: Palmer's presence, however, had introduced a new style of play – and player – to the Open, and he would be back.

1	**KEL NAGLE**	69	67	71	71	278
	(£1250)					
2	Arnold Palmer	70	71	70	68	279
3=	Roberto de Vicenzo	67	67	75	73	282
	Harold Henning	72	72	69	69	282
	Bernard Hunt	72	73	71	66	282
6	Guy Wolstenholme (a)	74	70	71	68	283
7	Gary Player	72	71	72	69	284
8	Joe Carr (a)	72	73	67	73	285
9=	David Blair (a)	70	73	71	72	286
	Eric Brown	75	68	72	71	286
	Dai Rees	73	71	73	69	286
	Syd Scott	73	71	67	75	286
	Peter Thomson	72	69	75	70	286
	Harry Weetman	74	70	71	71	286
15	Ramon Sota	74	72	71	70	287
16=	Fidel de Luca	69	73	75	71	288
	Reid Jack (a)	74	71	70	73	288
	Angel Miguel	72	73	72	71	288
	Ian Smith	74	70	73	71	288
20	Peter Mills	71	74	70	74	289
21=	Ken Bousfield	70	75	71	74	290
	Alec Deboys (a)	76	70	73	71	290
	George Low	72	74	71	73	290
	John MacDonald	76	71	69	74	290
	Ralph Moffitt	72	71	76	71	290
26=	Bill Johnson	75	74	71	71	291
	Sebastian Miguel	73	68	74	76	291
28=	Laurie Ayton, Jr	73	69	75	75	292
	Fred Boobyer	74	74	73	71	292
	Geoff Hunt	76	69	72	75	292
	Jimmy Martin	72	72	72	76	292

Round Leader(s)
R1 de Vicenzo; 67
R2 de Vicenzo; 134
R3 Nagle; 207

Lowest Scores
R2 de Vicenzo, Nagle; 67
R3 Carr, Scott; 67
R4 Hunt; 66

US PGA 1960

Firestone Country Club, Akron, Ohio
(21–24 July)
7165 yards: Par 70 (280)

Jay Hebert followed younger brother Lionel as PGA Champion; the only brothers to achieve this (albeit one matchplay, one medal play). He pipped 1947 winner, Jim Ferrier, for the 1960 title. The only other sets of brothers to win Majors are: the Parks, Sr – Willie & Mungo (British Open); the Auchterlonies – Willie (British Open) and Laurie (US Open); the Herds – Fred (US Open) and Sandy (British Open); and the Smiths – Willie and Alex (both US Open). Palmer's outstanding year looked set to continue when he led after Round One, but two poor middle rounds dropped him to seventh.

1	**JAY HEBERT**	72	67	72	70	281
	($11000)					
2	Jim Ferrier	71	74	66	71	282
3=	Doug Sanders	70	71	69	73	283
	Sam Snead	68	73	70	72	283
5	Don January	70	70	72	72	284
6	Wes Ellis, Jr	72	72	72	69	285
7=	Doug Ford	75	70	69	72	286
	Arnold Palmer	67	74	75	70	286
9	Ken Venturi	70	72	73	72	287
10=	Fred Hawkins	73	69	72	74	288
	Dave Marr	75	71	69	73	288
12=	Bill Collins	71	75	71	73	290
	Ted Kroll	73	71	72	74	290
	Mike Souchak	73	73	70	74	290
15=	Pete Cooper	73	74	70	74	291
	Dow Finsterwald	73	73	69	76	291
	Johnny Pott	75	72	72	72	291
18=	Paul Harney	69	78	73	72	292
	Lionel Hebert	75	72	70	75	292
	Gene Littler	74	70	75	73	292
	Tom Nieporte	72	74	74	72	292
22=	Dave Ragan	75	75	68	75	293
	Mason Rudolph	72	71	76	74	293
24=	Julius Boros	76	73	72	73	294
	Walter Burkemo	72	77	73	72	294
	Billy Casper	73	75	75	71	294
	Billy Maxwell	74	77	72	71	294
	Ernie Vossler	71	77	74	72	294
29=	Jack Burke, Jr	73	72	78	72	295
	Cary Middlecoff	73	74	73	75	295
	Bo Wininger	73	77	71	74	295

Round Leader(s)
R1 Palmer; 67
R2 Hebert; 139
R3 Sanders; 210

Lowest Scores
R2 Hebert; 67
R3 Ferrier; 66
R4 Ellis, Jr; 69

THE MASTERS 1961

Augusta National Golf Club, Augusta, Georgia
(6–10 April: Sunday play washed out)
6925 yards: Par 72 (288)

In a Masters of 'firsts', Gary Player's first Masters and second Major victory came after an extra day was required due to the weather. He collected golf's first $20000 winning purse and was the first non-American to win the Masters (and the first since Jim Ferrier in the 1947 PGA to win any US Major). His victory was built on a 54 hole-total of 206, allowing him a cushion of four strokes over Palmer and six over Coe (emulating Nicklaus' feat as an amateur at the previous year's US Open) going into Round Four. He was to need every one.

1	**GARY PLAYER**	69	68	69	74	280
	($20000)					
2=	Charles R Coe, Jr (a)	72	71	69	69	281
	Arnold Palmer	68	69	73	71	281
4=	Tommy Bolt	72	71	74	68	285
	Don January	74	68	72	71	285
6	Paul Harney	71	73	68	74	286
7=	Jack Burke, Jr	76	70	68	73	287
	Billy Casper	72	77	69	69	287
	Bill Collins	74	72	67	74	287
	Jack Nicklaus (a)	70	75	70	72	287
11=	Walter Burkemo	74	69	73	72	288
	Robert Gardner (a)	74	71	72	71	288
	Doug Sanders	76	71	68	73	288
	Ken Venturi	72	71	72	73	288
15=	Stan Leonard	72	74	72	74	289
	Gene Littler	72	73	72	72	289
	Bob Rosburg	68	73	73	75	289
	Sam Snead	74	73	69	73	289
19=	Dick Mayer	76	72	70	73	291
	Johnny Pott	71	75	72	73	291
	Peter Thomson	73	76	68	74	291
22=	Roberto de Vicenzo	73	74	71	74	292
	Lew Worsham	74	71	73	74	292
24=	Antonio Cerda	73	73	72	75	293
	Fred Hawkins	74	75	72	72	293
	Ted Kroll	73	70	72	78	293
27	Al Balding	74	74	70	76	294
28=	Mason Rudolph	77	69	72	77	295
	Mike Souchak	75	72	75	73	295
30=	Jay Hebert	72	75	69	80	296
	Lionel Hebert	74	69	74	79	296

Round Leader(s)
R1 Palmer, Rosburg; 68
R2 Palmer, Player; 137
R3 Player; 206

Lowest Scores
R2 January, Player; 68
R3 Collins; 67
R4 Bolt; 68

US OPEN 1961

Oakland Hills Club, Augusta, Georgia
(4–7 April)
6907 yards: Par 7 (280)

Gene Littler's US Open win, after a fine closing round had taken him past Sanders, Goalby and Souchak, came relatively early in a long career. After winning the US Amateur in 1953 (thereby becoming the eighth player to pick up the US Amateur-US Open double), much was expected; but perhaps he just missed that dedicated edge which is required to get to the very top, and remain there, in any field. Ben Hogan missed a Top 10 finish for the first time in any Open in which he competed since 1940.

1	**GENE LITTLER**	73	68	72	68	281
	($14000)					
2=	Bob Goalby	70	72	69	71	282
	Doug Sanders	72	67	71	72	282
4=	Jack Nicklaus (a)	75	69	70	70	284
	Mike Souchak	73	70	68	73	284
6=	Dow Finsterwald	72	71	71	72	286
	Doug Ford	72	69	71	74	286
	Eric Monti	74	67	72	73	286
9=	Jacky Cupit	72	72	67	76	287
	Gardner Dickinson	72	69	71	75	287
	Gary Player	75	72	69	71	287
12=	Deane Beman (a)	74	72	72	70	288
	Al Geiberger	71	70	73	74	288
14=	Dave Douglas	72	72	75	70	289
	Ben Hogan	71	72	73	73	289
	Arnold Palmer	74	75	70	70	289
17=	Billy Casper	74	71	73	72	290
	Dutch Harrison	74	71	76	69	290
	Kel Nagle	71	71	74	74	290
	Sam Snead	73	70	74	73	290
21	Bob Rosburg	72	67	74	78	291
22=	Tommy Bolt	70	73	73	76	292
	Bob Brue	69	72	73	78	292
	Bruce Crampton	71	71	74	76	292
	Jim Ferrier	74	72	71	75	292
	Billy Maxwell	73	74	72	73	292
27=	Jack Fleck	73	71	79	70	293
	Ted Kroll	78	69	73	73	293
29=	Edward Brantly	75	70	72	77	294
	Chick Harbert	75	71	69	79	294
	Robert Harrison	79	70	71	74	294
	Milon Marusic	75	74	71	74	294
	Jerry Steelsmith	74	74	72	74	294

Round Leader(s)
R1 Brue; 69
R2 Rosburg, Sanders; 139
R3 Sanders; 210

Lowest Scores
R2 Bob Harris (34), Monti, Rosburg, Sanders; 67
R3 Cupit; 67
R4 Littler; 68

BRITISH OPEN 1961

Birkdale Golf Club, Southport, Lancashire, England
(12–14 July)
6844 yards

Dai Rees, according to Peter Alliss and others, was probably the best British player never to win his native Championship. He was undoubtedly the best golfer to come out of Wales until Ian Woosnam appeared on the scene; and was captain of the victorious British Ryder Cup team of 1957, when he beat Ed Furgol in the Singles, 7&6. His third runner-up place in the Open, aged 48, after a tooth-and-nail struggle with the best player in the world, was to be his last serious challenge. Palmer's first win in the Open seemed inevitable after his runner's-up place the previous year, and the spectacle did even more to encourage his compatriots to return, despite the prize money.

1	**ARNOLD PALMER**	70	73	69	72	284
2	Dai Rees	68	74	71	72	285
3=	Neil Coles	70	77	69	72	288
	Christy O'Connor, Sr	71	77	67	73	288
5=	Eric Brown	73	76	70	70	289
	Kel Nagle	68	75	75	71	289
7	Peter Thomson	75	72	70	73	290
8=	Peter Alliss	73	75	72	71	291
	Ken Bousfield	71	77	75	68	291
10=	Harold Henning	68	74	75	76	293
	Syd Scott	76	75	71	71	293
12	Ramon Sota	71	76	72	76	295
13	AB Coop	71	79	73	74	297
14=	Norman Johnson	69	80	70	79	298
	Reg Knight	71	80	73	74	298
	Angel Miguel	73	79	74	72	298
	Sebastian Miguel	71	80	70	77	298
18=	Dennis Hutchinson	72	80	74	73	299
	Paul Runyan	75	77	75	72	299
20=	Harry Bradshaw	73	75	78	74	300
	Peter Butler	72	76	78	74	300
	John Jacobs	71	79	76	74	300
	Lionel Platts	70	80	71	79	300
26=	Jean Garaialde	69	81	76	75	301
	Brian Huggett	72	77	75	77	301
	Eric Lester	71	77	75	78	301
	Ralph Moffitt	73	80	73	75	301
30=	David Miller	69	79	80	74	302
	George Will	74	75	75	78	302

Round Leader(s)
R1 Henning, Nagle, Rees; 68
R2 Henning, Rees; 142
R3 Palmer; 212

Lowest Scores
R2 Thomson; 72
R3 O'Connor, Sr; 67
R4 Bousfield; 68

US PGA 1961

Olympia Fields Country Club, Matteson, Illinois
(27–31 July)
6722 yards: Par 70 (280)

With three holes to play, Don January led Jerry Barber by four strokes. Thanks to two dropped shots and three big putts by Barber (two for birdie), the latter drew level; and after a few traumas, went on to win the play-off. At 45, Barber was the oldest man to win the PGA, and he overtook Ted Ray's 1920 record to become the oldest player of the century to win a Major – at least for a few years, until Julius Boros took both records away from him.

1	**JERRY BARBER***	69	67	71	70	277
	($11000)					
2	Don January	72	66	67	72	277
3	Doug Sanders	70	68	74	68	280
4	Ted Kroll	72	68	70	71	281
5=	Wes Ellis, Jr	71	71	68	72	282
	Doug Ford	69	73	74	66	282
	Gene Littler	71	70	72	69	282
	Arnold Palmer	73	72	69	68	282
	Johnny Pott	71	73	67	71	282
	Art Wall	67	72	73	70	282
11=	Paul Harney	70	73	69	71	283
	Cary Middlecoff	74	69	71	69	283
13	Jay Hebert	68	72	72	72	284
14	Walter Burkemo	71	71	73	70	285
15=	Billy Casper	74	72	69	71	286
	Bob Goalby	73	72	68	73	286
	Ernie Vossler	68	72	71	75	286
	Don Whitt	76	72	70	68	286
19=	Gardner Jackson	71	71	71	74	287
	Jack Fleck	70	74	73	70	287
	Bob Rosburg	70	71	73	73	287
22=	George Bayer	73	71	72	72	288
	Don Fairfield	70	71	74	73	288
	Fred Hawkins	75	73	71	69	288
	Dave Marr	72	74	73	69	288
	Shelley Mayfield	70	74	72	72	288
27=	Billy Maxwell	71	72	73	73	289
	Sam Snead	72	71	71	75	289
29=	Charles Bassler	73	73	72	72	290
	Bob Keller	72	73	72	73	290
	Al Mengert	72	74	72	72	290
	Gary Player	72	74	71	73	290

* Jerry Barber (67) beat Don January (68) in the
18-Hole Play-off

Round Leader(s)
R1 Wall; 67
R2 Barber; 136
R3 January; 205

Lowest Scores
R2 January; 66
R3 January, Pott; 67
R4 Ford; 66

THE MASTERS 1962

Augusta National Golf Club, Augusta, Georgia
(5–9 April)

6925 yards: Par 72 (288)

There could be no quibbling about quality at Augusta in 1962. All the 1961 Major Champions featured in the Top Five in the spring Major; two of them, along with Dow Finsterwald, in the three-way play-off. Palmer's supremacy was maintained, however, when he reeled in Gary Player – the pretender to his crown (?) – pulling back three shots to win with a blistering home nine of 31.

1	**ARNOLD PALMER***	70	66	69	75	280
	($20000)					
2	Gary Player	67	71	71	71	280
3	Dow Finsterwald	74	68	65	73	280
4	Gene Littler	71	68	71	72	282
5=	Jerry Barber	72	72	69	74	287
	Jimmy Demaret	73	73	71	70	287
	Billy Maxwell (a)	71	73	72	71	287
	Mike Souchak	70	72	74	71	287
9=	Charles R Coe (a)	72	74	71	71	288
	Ken Venturi	75	70	71	72	288
11=	Julius Boros	69	73	72	76	290
	Gay Brewer	74	71	70	75	290
	Jack Fleck	72	75	74	69	290
	Harold Henning	75	73	72	70	290
15=	Billy Casper	73	73	73	72	291
	Gardner Dickinson	70	71	72	78	291
	Paul Harney	74	71	74	72	291
	Jack Nicklaus	74	75	70	72	291
	Sam Snead	72	75	70	74	291
20=	Jacky Cupit	73	73	72	74	292
	Lionel Hebert	72	73	71	76	292
	Don January	71	73	74	74	292
	Johnny Pott	77	71	75	69	292
24	Al Balding	75	68	78	72	293
25=	Bob Charles	75	72	73	74	294
	Bob Goalby	74	74	73	73	294
	Ted Kroll	72	74	72	76	294
	Dave Ragan	70	73	76	75	294
29=	Bill Collins	75	70	75	75	295
	Bruce Crampton	72	75	74	74	295
	Cary Middlecoff	75	74	73	73	295
	Lew Worsham	75	70	78	72	295

* Arnold Palmer (68) beat Gary Player (71) and Dow Finsterwald (77) in the 18-hole Play-off

Round Leader(s)
R1   Player; 67
R2   Palmer; 136
R3   Palmer; 205

Lowest Scores
R2   Palmer; 66
R3   Finsterwald; 65
R4   Fleck, Pott; 69

US OPEN 1962

Oakmont Country Club, Oakmont, Pennsylvania
(14–17 June)

6894 yards: Par 72 (288)

Two months later Palmer was not so lucky in the play-off. He succumbed to 22 year-old Jack Nicklaus, who was in his first year as a professional. Nicklaus became the first player since Bobby Jones to hold the US Amateur and US Open titles at the same time. The balance of power was changing again. Although Palmer would remain at the very top for some years yet, this was, without doubt, the start of Jack Nicklaus' first golden era. Between 1962 and 1986 – a record span – a blend of power and precision never before witnessed on a golf course was to reap him a harvest of 18 Majors, seven more than the next man, Walter Hagen.

1	**JACK NICKLAUS***	72	70	72	69	283
	($17500)					
2	Arnold Palmer	71	68	73	71	283
3=	Bobby Nichols	70	72	70	73	285
	Phil Rodgers	74	70	69	72	285
5	Gay Brewer	73	72	73	69	287
6=	Tommy Jacobs	74	71	73	70	288
	Gary Player	71	71	72	74	288
8=	Doug Ford	74	75	71	70	290
	Gene Littler	69	74	72	75	290
	Billy Maxwell	71	70	75	74	290
11=	Doug Sanders	74	74	74	69	291
	Art Wall	73	72	72	74	291
13	Bob Rosburg	70	69	74	79	292
14=	Deane Beman (a)	74	72	80	67	293
	Bob Goalby	73	74	73	73	293
	Mike Souchak	75	73	72	73	293
17=	Jacky Cupit	73	72	72	77	294
	Jay Hebert	75	72	73	74	294
	Earl Stewart	75	73	75	71	294
	Donald Whitt	73	71	75	75	294
	Bo Wininger	73	74	69	78	294
22	Miller Barber	73	70	77	75	295
23=	Gardner Dickinson	76	74	75	71	296
	Lionel Hebert	75	72	75	74	296
25=	Stan Leonard	72	73	78	74	297
	Edward Meister, Jr (a)	78	72	76	71	297
27	Frank Boynton	71	75	74	78	298
28=	Joe Campbell	78	71	72	78	299
	Dave Douglas	74	70	72	83	299
	Paul Harney	73	73	71	72	299
	Dean Refram	75	73	77	74	299
	Mason Rudolph	74	74	73	78	299

* Jack Nicklaus (71) beat Arnold Palmer (74) in the 18-Hole Play-off

Round Leader(s)
R1   Littler; 69
R2   Palmer, Rosburg; 139
R3   Palmer, Nichols; 212

Lowest Scores
R2   Palmer; 68
R3   Rodgers, Wininger; 69
R4   Beman; 67

BRITISH OPEN 1962

Troon Golf Club, Ayrshire, Scotland
(11-13 July)
6583 yards

Nicklaus was not to get quite all his own way yet. He won't forget his first visit to Troon, where rounds of 80 and 79 contributed to a humbling score of 305, and a tie for 34th place. Palmer, on the other hand, found the links much to his liking: he set a new record low for the Championship and tied Hogan's famous score in the 1948 US Open. His lead from the end of the second round increased from two, to four, to six, over Kel Nagle. Impressive.

1	**ARNOLD PALMER**	71	69	67	69	276
	(£1400)					
2	Kel Nagle	71	71	70	70	282
3=	Brian Huggett	75	71	74	69	289
	Phil Rodgers	75	70	72	72	289
5	Bob Charles	75	70	70	75	290
6=	Sam Snead	76	73	72	71	292
	Peter Thomson	70	77	75	70	292
8=	Peter Alliss	77	69	74	73	293
	Dave Thomas	77	70	71	75	293
10	Syd Scott	77	74	75	68	294
11	Ralph Moffitt	75	70	74	76	295
12=	Jean Garaialde	76	73	76	71	296
	Sebastian Miguel	72	79	73	72	296
	Harry Weetman	75	73	73	75	296
	Ross Whitehead	74	75	72	75	296
16=	Roger Foreman	77	73	72	75	297
	Bernard Hunt	74	75	75	73	297
	Dennis Hutchinson	78	73	76	70	297
	Jimmy Martin	73	72	76	76	297
	Christy O'Connor, Sr	74	78	73	72	297
	John Panton	74	73	79	71	297
22	AB Coop	76	75	75	72	298
23	Don Swaelens	72	79	74	74	299
24=	Brian Bamford	77	73	74	76	300
	Lionel Platts	78	74	76	72	300
	Guy Wolstenholme	78	74	76	72	300
27=	Hugh Boyle	73	78	74	76	301
	Keith MacDonald	69	77	76	79	301
29	George Low	77	75	77	73	302
30=	Harry Bradshaw	72	75	81	75	303
	Harold Henning	74	73	79	77	303
	Jimmy Hitchcock	78	74	72	79	303

Round Leader(s)
R1   MacDonald; 69
R2   Palmer; 140
R3   Palmer; 207

Lowest Scores
R2   Alliss, Palmer; 69
R3   Palmer; 67
R4   Scott; 68

US PGA 1962

Aronimink Golf Club, Newtown Square, Pennsylvania
(19-22 July)
7045 yards: Par 70 (280)

Gary Player – in just four years – won his third different Major. He was the 10th player to achieve it, and the first non-American born player since Tommy Armour in 1931. Two of the other nine, Snead and Palmer, were also in the Top 20. Scoring was tough on this 7000+-yard, Par 70 course.

1	**GARY PLAYER**	72	67	69	70	278
	($13000)					
2	Bob Goalby	69	72	71	67	279
3=	George Bayer	69	70	71	71	281
	Jack Nicklaus	71	75	69	67	281
5	Doug Ford	69	69	73	71	282
6	Bobby Nichols	72	70	71	70	283
7=	Jack Fleck	74	69	70	71	284
	Paul Harney	70	73	72	69	284
	Dave Ragan	72	74	70	68	284
10	Jay Hebert	73	72	70	70	285
11=	Julius Boros	73	69	74	70	286
	Dow Finsterwald	73	70	70	73	286
	Chick Harbert	68	76	69	73	286
	Bob McCallister	74	66	70	76	286
15=	Cary Middlecoff	73	66	74	74	287
	Doug Sanders	76	69	73	69	287
17=	Jack Burke, Jr	73	69	71	75	288
	Bruce Crampton	76	73	67	72	288
	Billy Farrell	73	71	73	71	288
	Arnold Palmer	71	72	73	72	288
	Sam Snead	75	70	71	72	288
	Frank Stranahan	69	73	72	74	288
23=	Fred Haas	75	71	74	69	289
	Tommy Jacobs	73	73	73	70	289
	Gene Littler	73	75	72	69	289
	Art Wall	72	75	71	71	289
27=	Joe Campbell	70	74	74	73	291
	Don January	70	74	72	75	291
	Johnny Pott	71	77	71	72	291
30=	Tommy Bolt	72	74	72	74	292
	Pete Cooper	73	71	74	74	292
	Buster Cupit	76	70	76	70	292
	Wes Ellis, Jr	75	72	73	72	292
	Dick Hart	70	73	76	73	292
	Ted Kroll	73	70	76	73	292
	Shelley Mayfield	74	70	74	74	292
	Tom Nieporte	75	75	69	73	292
	Don Whitt	74	73	70	75	292

Round Leader(s)
R1   John Barnum (57); 66
R2   Ford; 138
R3   Player; 208

Lowest Scores
R2   McCallister, Middlecoff; 66
R3   Crampton; 67
R4   Nicklaus, Goalby; 67

THE MASTERS 1963

Augusta National Golf Club, Augusta, Georgia
(4–7 April)

6925 yards: Par 72 (288)

Nicklaus' second Major was gained when confronting Augusta National at its most difficult. Weather conditions accounted for the relatively high scoring, but Jack made the best of it when it relented during Round Two. At 23, he was the youngest winner of the Masters to that date.

1	**JACK NICKLAUS**	74	66	74	72	286
	($20000)					
2	Tony Lema	74	69	74	70	287
3=	Julius Boros	76	69	71	72	288
	Sam Snead	70	73	74	71	288
5=	Dow Finsterwald	74	73	73	69	289
	Ed Furgol	70	71	74	74	289
	Gary Player	71	74	74	70	289
8	Bo Wininger	69	72	77	72	290
9=	Don January	73	75	72	71	291
	Arnold Palmer	74	73	73	71	291
11=	Billy Casper	79	72	71	70	292
	Bruce Crampton	74	74	72	72	292
	Doug Ford	75	73	75	69	292
	Mike Souchak	69	70	79	74	292
15=	Bob Charles	74	72	76	71	293
	Chen Ching-po	76	71	71	75	293
	Billy Maxwell (a)	72	75	76	70	293
	Dick Mayer	73	70	80	70	293
	Mason Rudolph	75	72	72	74	293
	Dan Sikes	74	76	72	71	293
21=	Stan Leonard	74	72	73	75	294
	Johnny Pott	75	76	74	69	294
	Art Wall	75	74	73	72	294
24=	Wes Ellis, Jr	74	72	79	70	295
	Gene Littler	77	72	78	68	295
	Bobby Nichols	76	74	73	72	295
27	Jay Hebert	70	70	81	75	296
28=	George Bayer	71	75	84	67	297
	Tommy Jacobs	78	74	73	72	297
	Doug Sanders	73	74	77	73	297
	Alvie Thompson	79	72	75	71	297

Round Leader(s)
R1 Souchak, Wininger; 69
R2 Souchak; 139
R3 Nicklaus; 214

Lowest Scores
R2 Nicklaus; 66
R3 Boros, Casper, Ching-po; 71
R4 Bayer; 67

US OPEN 1963

The Country Club Club, Brookline, Boston, Massachusetts
(20–23 June)

6925 yards: Par 72 (288)

The US Open returned to Brookline to celebrate 50 years of Francis Ouimet's mould-breaking win over Vardon and Ray. Mentioning Ted Ray, we move from the youngest winner of the Masters to the oldest American winner of the US Open: Julius Boros, in adding to his 1952 Open title, was just 26 day's younger than Ray when the Englishman won at Inverness in 1920. A three-way play-off resulted when Boros caught Palmer, who missed a two-footer at the 17th; and Jackie Cupit, who dropped three shots over 17 and 18. Paul Harney also bogeyed the last to miss the play-off.

1	**JULIUS BOROS***	71	74	76	72	293
	($17500)					
2	Jacky Cupit	70	72	76	75	293
3	Arnold Palmer	73	69	77	74	293
4	Paul Harney	78	70	73	73	294
5=	Bruce Crampton	74	72	75	74	295
	Tony Lema	71	74	74	76	295
	Billy Maxwell	73	73	75	74	295
8=	Walter Burkemo	72	71	76	77	296
	Gary Player	74	75	75	72	296
10	Dan Sikes	77	73	73	74	297
11	Don January	72	74	78	75	299
12=	Dow Finsterwald	73	69	79	79	300
	Dave Ragan	78	74	74	74	300
14=	Mike Fetchick	74	76	75	77	302
	Lionel Hebert	71	79	76	76	302
	Davis Love, Jr	71	74	78	79	302
	Bobby Nichols	74	75	75	78	302
	Dean Refram	72	71	80	79	302
19=	Bob Charles	74	76	76	77	303
	Ken Still	76	75	78	74	303
21=	Jack Burke, Jr	75	76	78	75	304
	Gardner Dickinson	76	71	78	79	304
	Gene Littler	75	77	80	72	304
	Dave Marr	75	74	77	78	304
	Bob McCallister	75	77	76	76	304
	Doug Sanders	77	74	75	78	304
27=	Otto Greiner	74	75	76	80	305
	Ted Makalena	75	77	76	77	305
	Mason Rudolph	76	75	78	76	305
30=	Bob Goetz	79	72	00	75	306
	Bill Ogden	73	76	78	79	306

* Julius Boros (70) beat Jacky Cupit (73) and Arnold Palmer (76) in the 18-Hole Play-off

Round Leader(s)
R1 Bob Gadja (46); 69
R2 Cupit, Finsterwald, Palmer; 142
R3 Cupit; 218

Lowest Scores
R2 Finsterwald, Palmer; 69
R3 Harney, Sikes; 73
R4 Boros, Littler, Player; 72

BRITISH OPEN 1963

Royal Lytham & St Anne's Golf Club, Lancashire, England
(10–12 July)
6836 yards

So far the only left-handed player to win a Major, and the first from New Zealand, Bob Charles tied with Phil Rodgers before comfortably winning the play-off. They both, along with third-placed Nicklaus, beat the Lytham links scratch score of 70 (280), playing off Championship tees, which accumulatively added 79 yards to the members' course

1	**BOB CHARLES***	68	72	66	71	277
	(£1500)					
2	Phil Rodgers	67	68	73	69	277
3	Jack Nicklaus	71	67	70	70	278
4	Kel Nagle	69	70	73	71	283
5	Peter Thomson	67	69	71	78	285
6	Christy O'Connor, Sr	74	68	76	68	286
7=	Gary Player	75	70	72	70	287
	Ramon Sota	69	73	73	72	287
9=	Jean Garaialde	72	69	72	75	288
	Sebastian Miguel	73	69	73	73	288
11=	Bernard Hunt	72	71	73	73	289
	Alex King	71	73	73	72	289
13	Sewsunker Sewgolum	71	74	73	72	290
14=	Brian Allen	75	71	71	74	291
	Brian Huggett	73	74	70	74	291
	Hugh Lewis	71	77	69	74	291
	Ian MacDonald	71	71	74	75	291
18=	Peter Alliss	74	71	77	80	292
	Frank Phillips	70	73	75	74	292
20=	Neil Coles	73	75	72	73	293
	Max Faulkner	77	71	71	74	293
	Harold Henning	76	68	71	78	293
	Malcolm Leeder	76	73	74	70	293
	John MacDonald	73	75	75	70	293
	Brian Wilkes	70	77	74	72	293
26=	Jimmy Hitchcock	75	73	70	76	294
	Arnold Palmer	76	71	71	76	294
	Doug Sewell	75	72	73	74	294
	Dave Thomas	74	74	75	71	294
30=	Ken Bousfield	73	75	71	76	295
	Tom Haliburton	68	73	77	77	295
	Tony Jacklin	73	72	76	74	295

* Bob Charles (140) beat Phil Rodgers (148) in the 36-Hole Play-off

Round Leader(s)
R1   Rodgers, Thomson; 67
R2   Rodgers; 135
R3   Charles; 206

Lowest Scores
R2   Nicklaus; 67
R3   Charles; 66
R4   O'Connor, Sr; 68

US PGA 1963

Dallas Athletic Club, Dallas, Texas
(18–21 July)
7046 yards: Par 71 (284)

Nicklaus emulated Gary Player's feat of the previous year – except Jack's third different Major was achieved in just a two-year span. He also became only the fourth player, after Sarazen, Nelson and Hogan to lift all the US Majors; the fourth player after Snead, Hogan and Jack Burke, Jr to do the Masters-PGA double in the same year; and the eighth to have won two Majors in one season. And this was only his second full year as a pro!

1	**JACK NICKLAUS**	69	73	69	68	279
	($13000)					
2	Dave Ragan	75	70	67	69	281
3=	Bruce Crampton	70	73	65	74	282
	Dow Finsterwald	72	72	66	72	282
5=	Al Geiberger	72	73	69	70	284
	Billy Maxwell	73	71	69	71	284
7	Jim Ferrier	73	73	70	69	285
8=	Gardner Dickinson	72	74	74	66	286
	Tommy Jacobs	74	72	70	70	286
	Bill Johnson	71	72	72	71	286
	Gary Player	74	75	67	70	286
	Art Wall	73	76	66	71	286
13=	Julius Boros	69	72	73	73	287
	Bob Charles	69	76	72	70	287
	Tony Lema	70	71	77	69	287
	Jack Sellman	75	70	74	68	287
17=	Manuel de la Torre	71	71	74	72	288
	Wes Ellis, Jr	71	74	71	72	288
	Bob Goalby	74	70	74	70	288
	Dick Hart	66	72	76	74	288
	Dave Hill	73	72	69	74	288
	Doug Sanders	74	69	70	75	288
23=	Paul Harney	72	74	71	72	289
	Bobby Nichols	74	73	71	71	289
	Mason Rudolph	69	75	71	74	289
	Mike Souchak	72	72	73	72	289
27=	Doug Ford	70	72	71	77	290
	JC Goosie	74	74	74	68	290
	Fred Haas	80	70	70	70	290
	Sam Snead	71	73	70	76	290
	Earl Stewart	70	77	70	73	290
	Bert Weaver	76	73	71	70	290
	Bo Wininger	75	71	71	73	290

Round Leader(s)
R1   Hart; 66
R2   Hart; 138
R3   Crampton; 208

Lowest Scores
R2   Sanders; 69
R3   Crampton; 65
R4   Dickinson; 66

THE MASTERS 1964

Augusta National Golf Club, Augusta, Georgia
(9–12 April)

6925 yards: Par 72 (288)

Arnold Palmer led all the way to win an unprecedented fourth Masters; putting him above Sam Snead and Jimmy Demaret. His victory by six from Dave Marr was his seventh and last Major, and he joined a stellar band of golfers on this mark: Vardon, Jones, Sarazen and Snead. 49 year-old former PGA Champion, Jim Ferrier, was a surprising Top Ten finisher.

1	**ARNOLD PALMER**	69	68	69	70	276
	($20000)					
2=	Dave Marr	70	73	69	70	282
	Jack Nicklaus	71	73	71	67	282
4	Bruce Devlin	72	72	67	73	284
5=	Billy Casper	76	72	69	69	286
	Jim Ferrier	71	73	69	73	286
	Paul Harney	73	72	71	70	286
	Gary Player	69	72	72	73	286
9=	Dow Finsterwald	71	72	75	69	287
	Ben Hogan	73	75	67	72	287
	Tony Lema	75	68	74	70	287
	Mike Souchak	73	74	70	70	287
13=	Peter Butler	72	72	69	75	288
	Al Geiberger	75	73	70	70	288
	Gene Littler	70	72	78	68	288
	Johnny Pott	74	70	71	73	288
	Dan Sikes	76	68	71	73	288
18=	Don January	70	72	75	72	289
	Billy Maxwell (a)	73	73	69	74	289
	Mason Rudolph	75	72	69	73	289
21=	Bruce Crampton	74	72	73	71	290
	Kel Nagle	69	77	71	73	290
	Chi Chi Rodriguez	71	73	73	73	290
	Bo Wininger	74	71	69	76	290
25=	Deane Beman (a)	74	71	70	76	291
	Gay Brewer	75	72	73	71	291
	Gary Cowan (a)	71	77	72	71	291
	Bobby Nichols	75	71	75	70	291
	Phil Rodgers	75	72	72	72	291
30=	Jay Hebert	74	74	69	75	292
	Dean Refram	74	72	73	73	292

Round Leader(s)
R1   Bob Goalby (37), Davis Love, Jr (34); Nagle, Palmer, Player; 69
R2   Palmer, 137
R3   Palmer; 206

Lowest Scores
R2   Lema, Palmer, Sikes; 68
R3   Devlin, Hogan; 67
R4   Nicklaus; 67

US OPEN 1964

Congressional Country Club, Bethesda, Maryland
(18–20 June)

7053 yards: Par 70 (280)

After two momentous failures in the Masters, Ken Venturi at last put his past behind him to take a Major Championship. In 1956, as an amateur, he blew up and shot a last-round 80 to concede nine strokes to Jack Burke, and the Tournament. Then in 1960, the nightmare returned' this time in the guise of Arnold Palmer's birdie-birdie finish, to pip him at the last. On this occasion Venturi, however, came from behind in Round Four to overtake the collapsing Tommy Jacobs, who in the second round had equalled Lee Mackey's 14 year-old low.

1	**KEN VENTURI**	72	70	66	70	278
	($17500)					
2	Tommy Jacobs	72	64	70	76	282
3	Bob Charles	72	72	71	68	283
4	Billy Casper	71	74	69	71	285
5=	Gay Brewer	76	69	73	68	286
	Arnold Palmer	68	69	75	74	286
7	Bill Collins	70	71	74	72	287
8	Dow Finsterwald	73	72	71	72	288
9=	Johnny Pott	71	73	73	72	289
	Bob Rosburg	73	73	70	73	289
11=	George Bayer	75	73	72	71	291
	Don January	75	73	74	69	291
	Gene Littler	73	71	74	73	291
14=	Bruce Crampton	72	71	75	74	292
	Terry Dill	73	73	75	71	292
	Ray Floyd	73	70	72	77	292
	Ed Furgol	72	74	72	74	292
	Al Geiberger	74	70	75	73	292
	Bobby Nichols	72	72	76	72	292
20	Tony Lema	71	72	75	75	293
21=	Lionel Hebert	73	74	72	75	294
	Bill Ogden	73	73	73	75	294
23=	Ted Makalena	73	74	75	73	295
	Jack Nicklaus	72	73	77	73	295
	Gary Player	75	74	74	74	295
	Dudley Wysong	74	73	75	73	295
27	Charles Sifford	72	70	77	77	296
28=	Jacky Cupit	75	71	75	76	297
	Don Fairfield	75	72	74	76	297
	John Farquhar (a)	74	73	77	73	297
	Labron Harris, Jr	72	76	74	75	297

Round Leader(s)
R1   Palmer; 68
R2   Jacobs; 136
R3   Jacobs; 206

Lowest Scores
R2   Jacobs; 64
R3   Venturi; 66
R4   Brewer, Charles; 68

BRITISH OPEN 1964

Royal & Ancient Golf Club, St Andrews, Fife, Scotland
(8–10 July)
6936 yards: Par 72 (288)

'Champagne' Tony Lema won the Open Championship at his first attempt. His nine-under-par performance over the Old Course was stunning, finishing five clear of Nicklaus, who had hauled himself into contention early in Round Four. Lema's star seemed to be in the ascendant. He was to finish prominently in a few more Majors, but before his true worth could be assessed, he was tragically killed in a private plane crash in 1966.

1	**TONY LEMA**	73	68	68	70	279
	(£1500)				
2	Jack Nicklaus	76	74	66	68	284
3	Roberto de Vicenzo	76	72	70	67	285
4	Bernard Hunt	73	74	70	70	287
5	Bruce Devlin	72	72	73	73	290
6=	Christy O'Connor, Sr	71	73	74	73	291
	Harry Weetman	72	71	75	73	291
8=	Harold Henning	78	73	71	70	292
	Angel Miguel	73	76	72	71	292
	Gary Player	78	71	73	70	292
11	Doug Sanders	78	73	74	68	293
12	Frank Phillips	77	75	72	70	294
13=	Jean Garaialde	71	74	79	72	296
	Christy Greene	74	76	73	73	296
	Ralph Moffitt	76	72	74	74	296
	Dave Thomas	75	74	75	72	296
17=	Alex Caygill	77	74	71	75	297
	Bob Charles	79	71	69	78	297
19=	Malcolm Gregson	78	70	74	76	298
	John MacDonald	78	74	74	72	298
	A Murray	77	73	76	72	298
	Phil Rodgers	74	79	74	71	298
	Syd Scott	75	74	73	76	298
24=	AB Coop	75	72	76	76	299
	Doug Ford	75	76	76	72	299
	Liang-Huan Lu	76	71	78	74	299
	Jimmy Martin	74	72	79	74	299
	Peter Thomson	79	73	72	75	299
29	George Will	74	79	71	76	300
30=	Peter Butler	78	75	74	74	301
	Geoff Hunt	77	75	74	75	301
	Ramon Sota	77	74	74	76	301

Round Leader(s)
R1 Garaialde, O'Connor, Sr; 71
R2 Lema; 141
R3 Lema; 209

Lowest Scores
R2 Lema; 68
R3 Nicklaus; 66
R4 de Vicenzo; 67

US PGA 1964

Columbus Country Club, Columbus, Ohio
(16–19 July)
6851 yards: Par 70 (280)

In a Championship of records, 28-year-old Bobby Nicholls, partially paralysed only a few years earlier, won over Nicklaus and Palmer by three strokes. Record-equalling 64s came from Nicholls and Nicklaus: the new low total of 271 for the PGA, was, by three strokes, the record for any Major Championship. A consistent player for the next decade or so, Nicholls never won another Major, and his form left him after he was struck, along with Lee Trevino and Jerry Heard, by lightning during the Western Open in 1975.

1	**BOBBY NICHOLS**	64	71	69	67	271
	($18000)				
2=	Jack Nicklaus	67	73	70	64	274
	Arnold Palmer	68	68	69	69	274
4	Mason Rudolph	73	66	68	69	276
5=	Tom Nieporte	68	71	68	72	279
	Ken Venturi	72	65	73	69	279
7	Bo Wininger	69	68	73	70	280
8	Gay Brewer	72	71	71	67	281
9=	Billy Casper	68	72	70	72	282
	Jon Gustin	69	76	71	66	282
	Ben Hogan	70	72	68	72	282
	Tony Lema	71	68	72	71	282
13=	Ed Furgol	71	69	72	71	283
	Billy Maxwell	72	71	70	70	283
	Gary Player	70	71	71	71	283
	Mike Souchak	67	73	71	72	283
17=	Walter Burkemo	70	71	72	71	284
	Jacky Cupit	72	71	72	69	284
19=	Bob Charles	68	71	73	73	285
	Al Geiberger	73	72	72	68	285
21=	Tommy Aaron	72	74	70	70	286
	Julius Boros	70	73	71	72	286
23=	Gardner Dickinson	74	74	68	71	287
	Mike Fetchick	74	73	74	66	287
	Ed Kroll	75	72	72	68	287
	Ted Kroll	72	73	72	70	287
	Dick Rhyan	71	72	71	73	287
28=	Bill Bisdorf	73	72	73	70	288
	Jim Ferree	70	72	75	71	288
	Dick Hart	73	73	72	70	288
	George Knudson	76	69	72	71	288
	Doug Sanders	71	73	76	68	288

Round Leader(s)
R1 Nichols; 64
R2 Nichols; 135
R3 Nichols; 204

Lowest Scores
R2 Venturi; 65
R3 Dickinson, Chick Harbert (44), Hogan, Nieporte, Rudolph; 68
R4 Nicklaus; 64

THE MASTERS 1965

Augusta National Golf Club, Augusta, Georgia
(8–11 April)

6925 yards: Par 72 (288)

The following year in the Masters, the records kept on coming. Jack Nicklaus dismantled Ben Hogan's Masters low score, and equalled Lloyd Mangrum's 1940 course record 64, when he shot 271, 17 under par, to win. The under-par figures and the margin of victory – nine strokes – were also records, and the low total matched Bobby Nichols' outstanding effort in the previous year's PGA, to become the best-equal for any Major to that date.

1	**JACK NICKLAUS**	67	71	64	69	271
	($20000)				
2=	Arnold Palmer	70	68	72	70	280
	Gary Player	69	72	72	73	280
4	Mason Rudolph	70	75	66	72	283
5	Dan Sikes	67	72	71	75	285
6=	Gene Littler	71	74	67	74	286
	Ramon Sota	71	73	70	72	286
8=	Frank Beard	68	77	72	70	287
	Tommy Bolt	69	78	69	71	287
10	George Knudson	72	73	69	74	288
11=	Tommy Aaron	67	74	71	77	289
	Bruce Crampton	72	72	74	71	289
	Paul Harney	74	74	71	70	289
	Doug Sanders	69	72	74	74	289
15=	George Bayer	69	74	75	72	290
	Bruce Devlin	71	76	73	70	290
	Wes Ellis, Jr	69	76	72	73	290
	Tommy Jacobs	71	74	72	73	290
	Kel Nagle	75	70	74	71	290
	Byron Nelson	70	74	72	74	290
21=	Dow Finsterwald	72	75	72	72	291
	Ben Hogan	71	75	71	74	291
	Tony Lema	67	73	77	74	291
24=	Terry Dill	72	73	75	72	292
	Al Geiberger	75	72	74	71	292
26=	Bernard Hunt	71	74	74	74	293
	Tomoo Ishii	74	74	70	75	293
	Billy Maxwell (a)	74	72	76	71	293
	Tom Nieporte	71	73	75	74	293
	Bo Wininger	70	72	75	76	293

Round Leader(s)
R1 Player; 65
R2 Nicklaus, Palmer, Player; 138
R3 Nicklaus; 202

Lowest Scores
R2 Palmer; 68
R3 Nicklaus; 64
R4 Nicklaus; 69

US OPEN 1965

Bellerive Country Club, St Louis, Missouri
(17–21 June)

7191 yards: Par 70 (280)

South Africa's Gary Player became the first overseas winner of the US Open since Ted Ray in 1920: he beat 1960 British Open Champion Kel Nagle after a play-off. In doing so he joined Gene Sarazen and Ben Hogan as only one of three golfers to win all four Majors at that time – the Grand Slam? It was certainly called this in the long years between the Bobby Jones version (two Opens, two Amateur titles) and the astounding feat of Tiger Woods in 2000–01, when it was thought that such a level of superiority could never occur again. Time to rethink the terminology! Player achieved his four different Majors feat in just six years, compared with seven for Hogan (who, of course only entered the British Open once) and 13 for Sarazen (who had to wait 13 years from his first win for the Masters to offer itself).

1	**GARY PLAYER***	70	70	71	71	282
	($26000)				
2	Kel Nagle	68	73	72	69	282
3	Frank Beard	74	69	70	71	284
4=	Julius Boros	72	75	70	70	287
	Al Geiberger	70	76	70	71	287
6=	Bruce Devlin	72	73	72	71	288
	Ray Floyd	72	72	76	68	288
8=	Tony Lema	72	74	73	70	289
	Gene Littler	73	71	73	72	289
	Dudley Wysong	72	75	70	72	289
11=	Deane Beman (a)	69	73	76	72	290
	Mason Rudolph	69	72	73	76	290
	Doug Sanders	77	73	69	71	290
14	Billy Maxwell	76	73	71	71	291
15	Steve Oppermann	72	77	73	70	292
16	Gay Brewer	72	74	71	76	293
17=	Billy Casper	73	73	76	72	294
	Charles Huckaby	73	74	73	74	294
	George Knudson	80	69	73	72	294
	Bob Verwey	73	74	75	72	294
21=	Gardner Dickinson	77	73	71	74	295
	Eric Monti	76	71	75	73	295
23	Lou Graham	70	77	76	73	296
24=	Wes Ellis, Jr	73	76	77	71	297
	Labron Harris, Jr	74	76	74	73	297
	Ted Kroll	76	74	72	75	297
	Sam Snead	75	71	77	74	297
28=	Dutch Harrison	78	72	72	76	298
	Tommy Jacobs	76	71	74	77	298
	Dean Refram	71	79	72	76	298
	Terry Wilcox	74	73	73	78	298

* Gary Player (71) beat Kel Nagle (74) in the 18-Hole Play-off

Round Leader(s)
R1 Nagle; 68
R2 Player; 140
R3 Player; 211

Lowest Scores
R2 Beard, Knudson; 69
R3 Sanders; 69
R4 Floyd; 68

BRITISH OPEN 1965

Royal Birkdale Golf Club, Southport, Lancashire, England
(7-9 July)
7037 yards: Par 73 (292)

Returning to the scene of his very first Open victory in 1954, Peter Thomson picked up his fifth win, and thereby joined Braid and Taylor on this mark, just one behind Harry Vardon's all-time record. It will always be argued that Thomson's four wins during the '50s were somewhat devalued because the competition was not of the very best; an argument strengthened by Thomson's modest success in US Majors. However, no one can doubt his fifth, and final, win, with a strong American contingent trailing in his wake. Birkdale had, at last, like its inclusion on the Open roster, received its long-overdue Royal Charter.

1	**PETER THOMSON**	74	68	72	71	285
	(£1750)					
2=	Brian Huggett	73	68	76	70	287
	Christy O'Connor, Sr	69	73	74	71	287
4	Roberto de Vicenzo	74	69	73	72	288
5=	Bernard Hunt	74	74	70	71	289
	Tony Lema	68	72	75	74	289
	Kel Nagle	74	70	73	72	289
8=	Bruce Devlin	71	69	75	75	290
	Sebastian Miguel	72	73	72	73	290
10=	Max Faulkner	74	72	74	73	293
	John Panton	74	74	75	70	293
12=	Hugh Boyle	73	69	76	76	294
	Neil Coles	73	74	77	70	294
	Jack Nicklaus	73	71	77	73	294
	Lionel Platts	72	72	73	77	294
16	Arnold Palmer	70	71	75	79	295
17=	Eric Brown	72	70	77	77	296
	Tommy Horton	75	73	76	72	296
	Cobie Legrange	76	73	75	72	296
	Guy Wolstenholme	72	75	77	72	296
21=	Brian Bamford	72	76	74	75	297
	Christy Greene	72	77	74	74	297
	Dennis Hutchinson	74	72	76	75	297
	George Will	75	69	74	79	297
25=	Fred Boobyer	74	73	73	78	298
	Tony Jacklin	75	73	73	77	298
	Doug Sewell	72	75	74	77	298
	Ramon Sota	75	70	78	75	298
29=	Michael Burgess (a)	74	73	78	74	299
	Harry Weetman	76	69	80	74	299

Round Leader(s)
R1 Lema; 68
R2 Devlin, Lema; 140
R3 Thomson; 214

Lowest Scores
R2 Huggett, Thomson; 68
R3 Hunt; 70
R4 Coles, Huggett, Panton; 70

US PGA 1965

Laurel Valley Golf Club, Ligonier, Pennsylvania
(12-15 August)
7090 yards: Par 71 (284)

Dave Marr won his only Major when he firstly cast off Tommy Aaron's challenge (whose 40 going out in Round Four put him out of contention); then held firm to weather assaults from Nicklaus and Casper. 53 year-old ex-Champions, Sam Snead and Ben Hogan, came home sixth and 15th, respectively, while contemporary giants of the game, Palmer and Player, could only tie 33rd.

1	**DAVE MARR**	70	69	70	71	280
	($25000)					
2=	Billy Casper	70	70	71	71	282
	Jack Nicklaus	69	70	72	71	282
4	Bo Wininger	73	72	72	66	283
5	Gardner Dickinson	67	74	69	74	284
6=	Bruce Devlin	68	75	72	70	285
	Sam Snead	68	75	70	72	285
8=	Tommy Aaron	66	71	72	78	287
	Jack Burke, Jr	75	71	72	69	287
	Jacky Cupit	72	76	70	69	287
	Rod Funseth	75	72	69	71	287
	Bob McCallister	76	68	70	73	287
13=	Wes Ellis, Jr	73	76	70	69	288
	RH Sykes	71	71	71	75	288
15=	Ben Hogan	72	75	72	70	289
	Mike Souchak	70	72	77	70	289
17=	Julius Boros	75	72	73	70	290
	Ray Floyd	68	73	72	77	290
19	Al Geiberger	74	71	71	75	291
20=	Bruce Crampton	77	74	70	71	292
	Jack Fleck	76	71	72	73	292
	Doug Ford	73	70	77	72	292
	Gordon Jones	72	76	71	73	292
	George Knudson	75	69	73	75	292
	Kel Nagle	74	75	71	72	292
	Mason Rudolph	67	76	75	74	292
	Doug Sanders	71	73	74	74	292
28=	Gay Brewer	75	70	73	75	293
	Paul Kelly	76	71	75	71	293
	Gene Littler	78	70	70	75	293
	Johnny Pott	76	70	74	73	293

Round Leader(s)
R1 Aaron; 66
R2 Aaron; 137
R3 Aaron, Marr; 209

Lowest Scores
R2 McCallister; 68
R3 Funseth, Dickinson; 69
R4 Wininger; 66

THE MASTERS 1966

Augusta National Golf Club, Augusta, Georgia
(7–11 April)

6925 yards: Par 72 (288)

Nicklaus' third Masters win was the first ever back-to-back. His fifth Major title took him equal with Braid and Taylor, Byron Nelson and Peter Thomson; but it was not his easiest. In a Tournament where the lead changed hands 17 times, a play-off seemed inevitable. Finally, Nicklaus had more trouble seeing off Tommy Jacobs than Gay Brewer, who struggled to a 78.

1	**JACK NICKLAUS*** ($20000)	68	76	72	72	288
2=	Gay Brewer	74	72	72	70	288
	Tommy Jacobs	75	71	70	72	288
4=	Arnold Palmer	74	70	74	72	290
	Doug Sanders	74	70	75	71	290
6=	Don January	71	73	73	75	292
	George Knudson	73	76	72	71	292
8=	Ray Floyd	72	73	74	74	293
	Paul Harney	75	68	76	74	293
10=	Billy Casper	71	75	76	72	294
	Jay Hebert	72	74	73	75	294
	Bob Rosburg	73	71	76	74	294
13=	Tommy Aaron	74	73	77	71	295
	Peter Butler	72	71	79	73	295
	Ben Hogan	74	71	73	77	295
16	Ken Venturi	75	74	73	74	296
17=	Tommy Bolt	75	72	78	72	297
	Bruce Crampton	74	75	71	77	297
	Terry Dill	75	72	74	76	297
	Doug Ford	75	73	73	76	297
	Phil Rodgers	76	73	75	73	297
22=	Frank Beard	77	71	77	73	298
	Chen Ching-po	75	77	76	70	298
	Roberto de Vicenzo	74	76	74	74	298
	Harold Henning	77	74	70	77	298
	Tony Lema	74	74	74	76	298
	Bobby Nichols	77	73	74	74	298
28=	Julius Boros	77	73	73	76	299
	Bruce Devlin	75	77	72	77	299
	Gardner Dickinson	76	75	76	72	299
	James A Grant (a)	74	74	78	73	299
	Gary Player	74	77	76	72	299

* Jack Nicklaus (70) beat Tommy Jacobs (72) and Gay Brewer (78) in the 18-hole Play-off

Round Leader(s)
R1   Nicklaus; 68
R2   Butler, Harney; 143
R3   Jacobs, Nicklaus; 216

Lowest Scores
R2   Harney; 68
R3   Henning, Jacobs; 70
R4   Brewer, Ching-po; 70

US OPEN 1966

Olympic Country Club, San Francisco, California
(16–20 June)

6719 yards: Par 70 (280)

Arnold Palmer's attempt to collect his second US Open, and eighth Major, folded on the back nine of the final round. Although he eventually succumbed to Billy Casper in a play-off, in the fourth round of regulation play Palmer dropped seven shots to the eventual winner, after blitzing the outward holes in 32. This was Casper's second title, following his win at Winged Foot in 1959. Unknown Rives McBee equalled the low score of 64 in Round Two.

1	**BILLY CASPER*** ($26500)	69	68	73	68	278
2	Arnold Palmer	71	66	70	71	278
3	Jack Nicklaus	71	71	69	74	285
4=	Tony Lema	71	74	70	71	286
	Dave Marr	71	74	68	73	286
6	Phil Rodgers	70	70	73	74	287
7	Bobby Nichols	74	72	71	72	289
8=	Wes Ellis, Jr	71	75	74	70	290
	Johnny Miller (a)	70	72	74	74	290
	Mason Rudolph	74	72	71	73	290
	Doug Sanders	70	75	74	71	290
12	Ben Hogan	72	73	76	70	291
13=	Rod Funseth	75	75	69	73	292
	Rives McBee	76	64	74	78	292
15=	Bob Murphy (a)	73	72	75	73	293
	Gary Player	78	72	74	69	293
17=	George Archer	74	72	76	72	294
	Frank Beard	76	74	69	75	294
	Julius Boros	74	69	77	74	294
	Don January	73	73	75	73	294
	Ken Venturi	73	77	71	73	294
22=	Walter Burkemo	76	72	70	77	295
	Bob Goalby	71	73	71	80	295
	Dave Hill	72	71	79	73	295
	Bob Verwey	72	73	75	75	295
26=	Miller Barber	74	76	77	69	296
	Bruce Devlin	74	75	71	76	296
	Al Mengert	67	77	71	81	296
	Bob Shave	76	71	74	75	296
30=	Tommy Aaron	73	75	71	78	297
	Deane Beman (a)	75	76	70	76	297
	Al Geiberger	75	75	74	73	297
	Vince Sullivan	77	73	73	74	297

* Billy Casper (69) beat Arnold Palmer (73) in the 18-Hole Play-off

Round Leader(s)
R1   Mengert; 67
R2   Casper, Palmer; 137
R3   Palmer; 207

Lowest Scores
R2   McBee; 64
R3   Marr; 68
R4   Casper; 68

BRITISH OPEN 1966

Hon Co of Edinburgh Golfers, Muirfield, East Lothian, Scotland
(6-9 July)
6887 yards

Jack Nicklaus became the fourth golfer to win a clean sweep of all the Major Championships. Nicklaus' record is the greatest of them all, and could claim as such even at the time. The Bobby Jones Grand Slams included six Amateur titles, but no Masters or PGA (through no fault of his own); Nicklaus had two Amateur Championships (although not the British Amateur) as well as matching the professional deeds of Sarazen, Hogan and Player. It is, indeed an unique achievement. Moreover, his professional Grand Slam was accumulated in easily the fastest time – just four years. The R&A decided to follow the example of the US Open and spread the Championship over four days. The Masters had been a four-day event since inception, and the PGA since opting for medal play.

1	**JACK NICKLAUS**	70	67	75	70	282
	(£2100)					
2=	Doug Sanders	71	70	72	70	283
	Dave Thomas	72	73	69	69	283
4=	Bruce Devlin	73	69	74	70	286
	Kel Nagle	72	68	76	70	286
	Gary Player	72	74	71	69	286
	Phil Rodgers	74	66	70	76	286
8=	Dave Marr	73	76	69	70	288
	Sebastian Miguel	74	72	70	72	288
	Arnold Palmer	73	72	69	74	288
	Peter Thomson	73	75	69	71	288
12	RH Sikes	73	72	73	72	290
13=	Harold Henning	71	69	75	76	291
	Christy O'Connor, Sr	73	72	74	72	291
15	Julius Boros	73	71	76	72	292
16=	Peter Butler	73	65	80	75	293
	Alex Caygill	72	71	73	77	293
	Jimmy Hitchcock	70	77	74	72	293
	Ronnie Shade (a)	71	70	75	77	293
20=	Peter Alliss	74	72	75	73	294
	Roberto de Vicenzo	74	72	71	77	294
	Doug Sewell	76	69	74	75	294
23=	Eric Brown	78	72	71	74	295
	Peter Townsend (a)	73	75	72	75	295
	George Will	74	75	73	73	295
26	Keith MacDonald	75	74	70	77	296
27=	Michael Bonallack (a)	73	76	75	73	297
	Dennis Hutchinson	74	73	73	77	297
	Bob Stanton	73	72	73	79	297
30=	Fred Boobyer	72	76	77	73	298
	Bobby Cole (a)	73	75	73	77	298
	Christy Greene	72	76	76	74	298
	Alan Henning	73	73	74	78	298
	Tony Jacklin	74	76	72	76	298
	Tony Lema	71	76	76	75	298

Round Leader(s)
R1 Hitchcock, Nicklaus; 70
R2 Nicklaus; 137
R3 Rodgers; 210

Lowest Scores
R2 Rodgers; 66
R3 Marr, Palmer, Thomas, Thomson; 69
R4 Player, Thomas; 69

US PGA 1966

Firestone Country Club, Akron, Ohio
(21-24 July)
7180 yards: Par 70 (280)

Al Geiberger was the only player to achieve par as the course defeated the likes of Casper and Player (two over); Boros, Palmer and Snead (three over); and Nicklaus (eight over). It was the only Major Championship success for Geiberger, who is one of the few golfers who will be remembered for something other than a win in a Major Championship. His 59 in the 1977 Memphis Classic was the first sub-60 score in a US Tour event. He went out in 30, back in 29, and shot 11 birdies, one eagle and no bogeys.

1	**AL GEIBERGER**	68	72	68	72	280
	($25000)					
2	Dudley Wysong	74	72	66	72	284
3=	Billy Casper	73	73	70	70	286
	Gene Littler	75	71	71	69	286
	Gary Player	73	70	70	73	286
6=	Julius Boros	69	72	75	71	287
	Jacky Cupit	70	73	73	71	287
	Arnold Palmer	75	73	71	68	287
	Doug Sanders	69	74	73	71	287
	Sam Snead	68	71	75	73	287
11	Frank Beard	73	72	69	74	288
12=	Dow Finsterwald	74	70	73	72	289
	Jay Hebert	75	73	70	71	289
	Don January	69	71	73	76	289
15=	Paul Harney	74	73	71	72	290
	Bill Martindale	73	75	70	72	290
	Ken Venturi	74	75	69	72	290
18=	Gardner Dickinson	74	72	73	72	291
	Ray Floyd	74	75	74	68	291
	Dave Marr	75	75	68	73	291
	Ernie Vossler	77	70	75	69	291
22=	Tommy Aaron	71	72	75	74	292
	Frank Boynton	73	74	73	72	292
	Billy Farrell	73	70	71	78	292
	Jack Nicklaus	75	71	75	71	292
	Mason Rudolph	74	73	76	69	292
27	Gay Brewer	73	73	76	71	293
28=	Butch Baird	73	74	73	74	294
	Bruce Devlin	76	71	71	76	294
	Ron Howell	76	71	75	72	294
	Don Massengale	74	72	75	73	294
	Dan Sikes	72	76	74	72	294
	RH Sikes	75	72	73	74	294

Round Leader(s)
R1 Geiberger, Snead; 68
R2 Snead; 139
R3 Geiberger; 208

Lowest Scores
R2 Farrell, Finsterwald, Player, James Riggins (75), Vossler; 70
R3 Wysong; 66
R4 Floyd, Palmer; 68

THE MASTERS 1967

Augusta National Golf Club, Augusta, Georgia
(6-9 April)
6925 yards: Par 72 (288)

After disappointing in the three-way play-off the previous year, Gay Brewer won his only Major – one stroke clear of 1964 PGA Champion Bobby Nichols, at Augusta National. With Bert Yancey fading, Brewer and Nichols fought tooth and nail over the last round, the winner getting in front for the first time at the 13th.

1	**GAY BREWER**	73	68	72	67	280
	($20000)					
2	Bobby Nichols	72	69	70	70	281
3	Bert Yancey	67	73	71	73	284
4	Arnold Palmer	73	73	70	69	285
5	Julius Boros	71	70	70	75	286
6=	Paul Harney	73	71	74	69	287
	Gary Player	75	69	72	71	287
8=	Tommy Aaron	75	68	74	71	288
	Lionel Hebert	77	71	67	73	288
10=	Roberto de Vicenzo	73	72	74	71	290
	Bruce Devlin	74	70	75	71	290
	Ben Hogan	74	73	66	77	290
	Mason Rudolph	72	76	72	70	290
	Sam Snead	72	76	71	71	290
15	Jacky Cupit	73	76	67	75	291
16=	George Archer	75	67	72	78	292
	Wes Ellis, Jr	79	71	74	68	292
	Tony Jacklin	71	70	74	77	292
	Dave Marr	73	74	70	75	292
	Doug Sanders	74	72	73	73	292
21=	Jay Hebert	72	77	68	76	293
	Bob Rosburg	73	72	76	72	293
	Ken Venturi	76	73	71	73	293
24=	Peter Butler	72	73	77	72	294
	Billy Casper	70	74	75	75	294
26=	Frank Beard	74	75	75	71	295
	Tommy Bolt	72	77	72	74	295
	Don January	74	74	76	71	295
28=	Gene Littler	72	74	74	75	295
	Juan Rodriguez	73	73	73	76	295

Round Leader(s)
R1   Yancey; 67
R2   Yancey; 140
R3   Boros, Nichols, Yancey; 211

Lowest Scores
R2   Archer; 67
R3   Hogan; 66
R4   Brewer; 67

US OPEN 1967

Baltusrol Golf Club, Springfield, New Jersey
(15-18 June)
6925 yards: Par 72 (288)

Arnold Palmer may have been the first person in US Open history to shoot below 280 on more than one occasion, but he could not stop Nicklaus' second Open win, nor his lowering of the record total: a record which had stood since 1948 when Ben Hogan took the Riviera Country Club apart. At 27, Nicklaus was now well into one of his purple patches; collecting his seventh Major, to catch Vardon, Jones, Sarazen, Snead and Palmer. The company was now becoming very elevated!

1	**JACK NICKLAUS**	71	67	72	65	275
	($30000)					
2	Arnold Palmer	69	68	73	69	279
3	Don January	69	72	70	70	281
4	Billy Casper	69	70	71	72	282
5	Lee Trevino	72	70	72	70	284
6=	Deane Beman	69	71	71	73	284
	Gardner Dickinson	70	73	68	73	284
	Bob Goalby	72	71	70	71	284
9=	Dave Marr	70	74	70	71	285
	Kel Nagle	70	72	72	71	285
	Art Wall	69	73	72	71	285
12=	Al Balding	75	72	71	68	286
	Wes Ellis, Jr	74	69	70	73	286
	Gary Player	69	73	73	71	286
15	Tom Weiskopf	72	71	74	70	287
16=	Dutch Harrison	70	76	72	70	288
	Jerry Pittman	72	72	75	69	288
18=	Miller Barber	71	71	69	78	289
	Marty Fleckman (a)	67	73	69	80	289
	Paul Harney	71	75	72	71	289
	Dave Hill	76	69	69	75	289
	Bob Verwey	75	71	69	74	289
23=	Bruce Devlin	72	68	77	73	290
	Billy Farrell	76	71	73	70	290
	Howie Johnson	74	73	71	72	290
	Bob Murphy (a)	73	73	75	69	290
	Bobby Nichols	74	71	73	72	290
28=	Charles Coody	77	71	75	68	291
	Mike Fetchick	73	71	76	71	291
	Al Geiberger	71	73	73	74	291
	Lou Graham	71	75	76	69	291
	Labron Harris, Jr	75	71	72	73	291
	Ken Venturi	74	74	72	71	291

Round Leader(s)
R1   Fleckman; 67
R2   Palmer; 137
R3   Fleckman; 209

Lowest Scores
R2   Dick Lotz (60), Nicklaus; 67
R3   Dickinson; 68
R4   Nicklaus; 65

BRITISH OPEN 1967

Royal Liverpool Golf Club, Hoylake, Cheshire, England
(12–15 July)
6995 yards

Already 44, Argentinian Roberto de Vicenzo became Britain's Champion Golfer, after being runner-up as far back as 1950. This, the best player to come out of South America, was to collect 12 different national titles in all, over a professional career spanning 40 years. He then progressed to the Seniors Tour, winning the US title twice, and the World's senior title in 1974. The Royal Liverpool Golf Club at Hoylake sadly played host to the Open for the 10th and last time – or so it seemed…

1	**ROBERTO DE VICENZO** (£2100)	70	71	67	70	278
2	Jack Nicklaus	71	69	71	69	280
3 =	Clive Clark	70	73	69	72	284
	Gary Player	72	71	67	74	284
5	Tony Jacklin	73	69	73	70	285
6 =	Harold Henning	74	70	71	71	286
	Sebastian Miguel	72	74	68	72	286
8 =	Al Balding	74	71	69	73	287
	Hugh Boyle	74	74	71	68	287
	Bruce Devlin	70	70	72	75	287
	Tommy Horton	74	74	69	70	287
	Peter Thomson	71	74	70	72	287
13 =	Deane Beman	72	76	68	73	289
	M Hoyle	74	75	69	71	289
	Stanley Peach	71	75	73	70	289
	Lionel Platts	68	73	72	76	289
	Guy Wolstenholme	74	71	73	71	289
18 =	Barry Coxon	73	76	71	70	290
	Hedley Muscroft	72	73	72	73	290
	Doug Sanders	71	73	73	73	290
21	Christy O'Connor, Sr	70	74	71	76	291
22 =	Dennis Hutchinson	73	72	71	76	292
	Peter Mills	72	75	73	72	292
	Kel Nagle	70	74	69	79	292
25 =	Brian Barnes	71	75	74	73	293
	Robin Davenport	76	69	75	73	293
	Barry Franklin	70	74	73	76	293
	Brian Huggett	73	75	72	73	293
29 =	Fred Boobyer	70	71	74	79	294
	Jimmy Hume	69	72	73	80	294

Round Leader(s)
R1   Platts; 68
R2   Nicklaus; 140
R3   de Vicenzo; 208

Lowest Scores
R2   Jacklin, Nicklaus; 69
R3   de Vicenzo, Player; 67
R4   Boyle; 68

US PGA 1967

Columbine Country Club, Denver, Colorado
(20–24 July)
6925 yards: Par 72 (288)

Columbine hosted a Major for the one and only time and holds the record as being the longest course for any Major to date. For Don January, who had perished in the 1961 play-off, the extra holes this time were not to hold any gremlins. His 69 was too good for Massengale's one-under-par effort. In regulation play, overnight leader-by-three, Sykes had completely blown it, and for once Nicklaus was left behind too, in this two Dons-and-a-Dan shake down.

1	**DON JANUARY*** ($25000)	71	72	70	68	281
2	Don Massingale	70	75	70	66	281
3 =	Jack Nicklaus	67	75	69	71	282
	Dan Sikes	69	70	70	73	282
5 =	Julius Boros	69	76	70	68	283
	Al Geiberger	73	71	69	70	283
7 =	Frank Beard	71	74	70	70	285
	Don Bies	69	70	76	70	285
	Bob Goalby	70	74	68	73	285
	Gene Littler	73	72	71	69	285
11 =	Billy Farrell	75	72	69	70	286
	Dave Hill	66	73	74	73	286
	Ken Venturi	73	74	71	68	286
14 =	Sam Carmichael	75	71	69	72	287
	Lionel Hebert	75	71	70	71	287
	Bobby Nichols	75	75	67	70	287
	Arnold Palmer	70	71	72	74	287
	RH Sikes	72	71	71	73	287
19	Billy Casper	75	70	75	68	288
20 =	Tommy Aaron	70	65	76	78	289
	Bill Bisdorf	72	71	77	69	289
	Dick Crawford	76	73	73	67	289
	Ray Floyd	74	69	74	72	289
	Mike Souchak	70	73	70	76	289
25	Wes Ellis Jr	76	71	72	71	290
26 =	Bruce Crampton	71	77	74	69	291
	Earl Stewart	77	70	72	72	291
28 =	Gay Brewer	75	74	71	72	292
	Gardner Dickinson	75	72	69	76	292
	Phil Rodgers	71	76	72	73	292
	Mason Rudolph	72	73	73	74	292
	Doug Sanders	72	71	76	73	292

* Don January (69) beat Don Massingale (71) in the 18-Hole Play-off

Round Leader(s)
R1   Hill; 66
R2   Aaron; 135
R3   Sikes; 209

Lowest Scores
R2   Aaron; 65
R3   Nichols; 67
R4   Massengale; 66

THE MASTERS 1968

Augusta National Golf Club, Augusta, Georgia
(11-14 April)

6925 yards: Par 72 (288)

Following his late-career win in the British Open in 1967, Roberto de Vicenzo tied with Bob Goalby; after birdieing 17 and dropping a shot at the last. The Argentinian was annoyed about that bogey at 18, but completely distraught when he was penalized one stroke for signing an incorrect card. The three at 17 was entered as a four – a mistake that was to haunt de Vicenzo, and Tommy Aaron, who was marking his playing partner's card, for some time to come. Goalby, in rather unsatisfactory circumstances, became outright winner.

1	**BOB GOALBY**	70	70	71	66	277
	($20000)					
2	Roberto de Vicenzo	69	73	70	66	278
3	Bert Yancey	71	71	72	65	279
4	Bruce Devlin	69	73	69	69	280
5=	Frank Beard	75	65	71	70	281
	Jack Nicklaus	69	71	74	67	281
7=	Tommy Aaron	68	72	72	69	282
	Ray Floyd	71	71	69	71	282
	Lionel Hebert	72	71	71	68	282
	Jerry Pittman	70	73	70	69	282
	Gary Player	72	67	71	72	282
12=	Miller Barber	75	69	68	71	283
	Doug Sanders	76	69	70	68	283
14=	Don January	71	68	72	73	284
	Mason Rudolph	73	73	72	66	284
16=	Julius Boros	73	71	70	71	285
	Billy Casper	68	75	73	69	285
	Tom Weiskopf	74	71	69	71	285
19	Bob Charles	75	71	70	70	286
20=	Dave Marr	74	71	71	71	287
	Kermit Zarley	70	73	74	70	287
22=	George Archer	75	71	72	70	288
	Gardner Dickinson	74	71	72	71	288
	Marvin Giles III (a)	71	72	72	73	288
	Harold Henning	72	71	71	74	288
	Tony Jacklin	69	73	74	72	288
	Art Wall	74	74	73	67	288
28=	Jay Hebert	74	71	71	73	289
	George Knudson	75	71	72	71	289
30=	Charles Coody	76	72	72	70	290
	Al Geiberger	76	70	72	72	290
	Kel Nagle	76	71	72	71	290
	Bobby Nichols	74	73	73	70	290
	Bob Rosburg	74	73	71	72	290

Round Leader(s)
R1   Casper; 68
R2   January, Player; 139
R3   Player; 210

Lowest Scores
R2   Beard; 65
R3   Barber; 68
R4   Yancey; 65

US OPEN 1968

Oak Hill Country Club, Rochester, New York
(13-16 June)

6962 yards: Par 70 (280)

Equalling Jack Nicklaus' previous year low total, Lee Trevino became the first man in history to win any Major with all four rounds under par and sub-70. When he wasn't winning, Nicklaus was notching up a high percentage of second places. Bert Yancey set a new Open 54-hole low of 205; and Sam Snead, then 56, still made the Top 10. Entries for the Open passed 3000 for the first time.

1	**LEE TREVINO**	69	68	69	69	275
	($30000)					
2	Jack Nicklaus	72	70	70	67	279
3	Bert Yancey	67	68	70	76	281
4	Bobby Nichols	74	71	68	69	282
5=	Don Bies	70	70	75	69	284
	Steve Spray	73	75	71	65	284
7=	Bob Charles	73	69	72	71	285
	Jerry Pittman	73	67	74	71	285
9=	Gay Brewer	71	71	75	69	286
	Billy Casper	75	68	71	72	286
	Bruce Devlin	71	69	75	71	286
	Al Geiberger	72	74	68	72	286
	Sam Snead	73	71	74	68	286
	Dave Stockton	72	73	69	72	286
15	Dan Sikes	71	71	73	72	287
16=	George Archer	74	72	73	69	288
	Julius Boros	71	71	71	75	288
	Charles Coody	69	71	72	76	288
	Rod Funseth	74	72	69	73	288
	Dave Hill	74	68	74	72	288
	Gary Player	76	69	70	73	288
22=	Mac McLendon	72	76	70	71	289
	Hugh Royer, Jr	75	72	73	69	289
24=	Miller Barber	74	68	78	70	290
	Roberto de Vicenzo	72	76	72	70	290
	Bob Erickson	75	68	72	75	290
	Don January	71	75	71	73	290
	Bob Lunn	74	73	73	70	290
	Pat Schwab	76	70	75	69	290
	Tom Weiskopf	75	72	70	73	290
	Larry Ziegler	71	71	74	74	290

Round Leader(s)
R1   Yancey; 67
R2   Yancey; 135
R3   Yancey; 205

Lowest Scores
R2   Pittman; 67
R3   Geiberger, Nichols; 68
R4   Spray; 65

BRITISH OPEN 1968

Carnoustie Golf Club, Angus, Scotland
(10–13 July)
7252 yards: Par 72 (288)

Gary Player won his fifth Major when he won the Open at Carnoustie; and over the longest course yet set for the Championship. He beat a strong field which boasted six other Majors winners among the Top Ten and ties. A 54-hole cut was introduced for the first time, reducing the number to 45 who went out on the last day.

1	**GARY PLAYER** (£3000)	74	71	71	73	289
2=	Bob Charles	72	72	71	76	291
	Jack Nicklaus	76	69	73	73	291
4	Billy Casper	72	68	74	78	292
5	Maurice Bembridge	71	75	73	74	293
6=	Brian Barnes	70	74	80	71	295
	Gay Brewer	74	73	72	76	295
	Neil Coles	75	76	71	73	295
9	Al Balding	74	76	74	72	296
10=	Roberto de Vicenzo	77	72	74	74	297
	Bruce Devlin	77	73	72	75	297
	Arnold Palmer	77	71	72	77	297
13=	Peter Alliss	73	78	72	75	298
	Bobby Cole	75	76	72	75	298
	Tommy Horton	77	74	73	74	298
	Brian Huggett	76	71	75	76	298
	Kel Nagle	74	75	75	74	298
18=	Eric Brown	76	76	74	73	299
	Tony Jacklin	72	72	75	80	299
	Paddy Skerritt	72	73	77	77	299
21=	Michael Bonallack (a)	70	77	74	79	300
	Sebastian Miguel	73	75	76	76	300
	DL Webster	77	71	78	74	300
24=	Alex Caygill	79	76	71	75	301
	Keith MacDonald	80	71	73	77	301
	Peter Thomson	77	71	78	75	301
27=	Malcolm Gregson	77	75	76	74	302
	Bob Shaw	75	76	73	78	302
	Dave Thomas	75	71	78	78	302
	Sandy Wilson	73	81	74	74	302

Round Leader(s)
R1   Barnes, Bonallack; 70
R2   Barnes, Charles, Jacklin; 144
R3   Casper; 214

Lowest Scores
R2   Casper; 68
R3   Caygill, Charles, Coles, Player; 71
R4   Barnes; 71

US PGA 1968

Pecan Valley Country Club, San Antonio, Texas
(18–21 July)
7096 yards: Par 70 (280)

If Julius Boros failed by a few days to set the record for the oldest winner of the US Open in 1963, he made up for it when winning the PGA Championship at Pecan Valley, at the age of 48. Before that, the oldest winner of any Major was 46 year-old Tom Morris, Sr; and the oldest within the century, Jerry Barber in 1961, also in the PGA, was positively juvenile at 45!

1	**JULIUS BOROS** ($25000)	71	71	70	69	281
2=	Bob Charles	72	70	70	70	282
	Arnold Palmer	71	69	72	20	282
4=	George Archer	71	69	74	69	283
	Marty Fleckman	66	72	72	73	283
6=	Frank Beard	68	70	72	74	284
	Billy Casper	74	70	70	70	284
8=	Miller Barber	70	70	72	73	285
	Frank Boynton	70	73	72	70	285
	Charles Coody	70	77	70	68	285
	Al Geiberger	70	73	71	71	285
	Bob Goalby	73	72	70	70	285
	Lou Graham	73	70	70	72	285
	Doug Sanders	72	67	73	73	285
	Dan Sikes	70	72	73	70	285
	Kermit Zarley	72	75	68	70	285
17=	Dave Hill	72	74	69	71	286
	Mason Rudolph	69	75	70	72	286
	Dave Stockton	75	71	68	72	286
20=	Gay Brewer	71	72	72	72	287
	Al Mengert	71	73	70	73	287
	Dick Rhyan	72	72	68	75	287
23=	Bruce Crampton	71	75	70	72	288
	Lee Trevino	69	71	72	76	288
	Bert Yancey	75	71	70	72	288
26=	Tommy Aaron	73	73	73	70	289
	Don Bies	69	73	74	73	289
	Dick Crawford	71	75	73	70	289
	Steve Reid	73	73	71	72	289
30=	Gardner Dickinson	74	69	76	71	290
	Lionel Hebert	75	71	70	74	290
	Gene Littler	73	74	74	69	290
	Bob Lunn	72	75	72	71	290

Round Leader(s)
R1   Fleckman; 66
R2   Beard, Fleckman; 138
R3   Beard, Fleckman; 210

Lowest Scores
R2   Sanders; 67
R3   Rhyan, Stockton, Zarley; 68
R4   Coody; 68

THE MASTERS 1969

Augusta National Golf Club, Augusta, Georgia
(10–13 April)
6925 yards: Par 72 (288)

George Archer only came to prominence in Major Championships in the PGA of 1968, when he finished fourth, two behind Julius Boros. Billy Casper, who had made all the running, wilted, leaving Archer the Masters Champion when Tom Weiskopf and Canadian George Knudson couldn't mount a sufficient challenge over the final holes.

1	**GEORGE ARCHER**	67	73	69	72	281
	($20000)					
2=	Billy Casper	66	71	71	74	282
	George Knudson	70	73	69	70	282
	Tom Weiskopf	71	71	69	71	282
5=	Charles Coody	74	68	69	72	283
	Don January	74	73	70	66	283
7	Miller Barber	71	71	68	74	284
8=	Tommy Aaron	71	71	73	70	285
	Lionel Hebert	69	73	70	73	285
	Gene Littler	69	75	70	71	285
11	Mason Rudolph	69	73	74	70	286
12	Dan Sikes	69	71	73	74	287
13=	Bruce Crampton	69	73	74	72	288
	Al Geiberger	71	71	74	72	288
	Harold Henning	73	72	71	72	288
	Takaaki Kono	71	75	68	74	288
	Bert Yancey	69	75	71	73	288
18	Dave Stockton	71	71	75	72	289
19=	Frank Beard	72	74	70	74	290
	Deane Beman	74	73	74	69	290
	Bruce Devlin	67	70	76	77	290
	Dale Douglass	73	72	71	74	290
	Lee Trevino	72	74	75	69	290
19=	Frank Beard	72	74	70	74	290
	Deane Beman	74	73	74	69	290
	Bruce Devlin	67	70	76	77	290
	Dale Douglass	73	72	71	74	290
	Lee Trevino	72	74	75	69	290
24=	Jack Burke, Jr	73	72	70	76	291
	Dave Hill	75	73	72	71	291
	Jack Nicklaus	68	75	72	76	291
27	Arnold Palmer	73	75	70	74	292
28	Johnny Pott	72	72	71	78	293
29=	Roberto Bernardini	76	71	72	75	294
	Bob Charles	70	76	72	76	294
	Gardner Dickinson	73	74	71	76	294
	Bobby Nichols	78	69	74	73	294

Round Leader(s)
R1   Casper; 66
R2   Casper, Devlin; 137
R3   Casper; 208

Lowest Scores
R2   Coody; 68
R3   Barber, Kono; 68
R4   January; 66

US OPEN 1969

Champions Golf Club, Houston, Texas
(12–15 June)
6967 yards: Par 70 (280)

Failing to make the cut in his first attempt the previous year, former career soldier Orville Moody won his only Major in only his second year on the Tour. Miller Barber held a three-stroke lead over Moody after 54 holes, butwent to pieces, allowing Moody to close out Beman, Geiberger and 1959 PGA Champion, Bob Rosburg, over the final 18.

1	**ORVILLE MOODY**	71	70	68	72	281
	($30000)					
2=	Deane Beman	68	69	73	72	282
	Al Geiberger	68	72	72	70	282
	Bob Rosburg	70	69	72	71	282
5	Bob Murphy	66	74	72	71	283
6=	Miller Barber	67	71	68	78	284
	Bruce Crampton	73	72	68	71	284
	Arnold Palmer	70	73	69	72	284
9	Bunky Henry	70	72	68	75	285
10=	George Archer	69	74	73	70	286
	Bruce Devlin	73	74	70	69	286
	Dave Marr	75	69	71	71	286
13=	Julius Boros	71	73	70	73	287
	Charles Coody	72	68	72	75	287
	Dale Douglass	76	69	70	72	287
	Ray Floyd	79	68	68	72	287
	Dave Hill	73	74	70	70	287
	Howie Johnson	72	73	72	70	287
	Dean Refram	69	74	70	74	287
	Phil Rodgers	76	70	69	72	287
	Kermit Zarley	74	72	70	71	287
22=	Bob Stanton	74	70	71	73	288
	Tom Weiskopf	69	75	71	73	288
	Bert Yancey	71	71	74	72	288
25=	Joe Campbell	73	74	73	69	289
	Richard Crawford	70	75	73	71	289
	Tony Jacklin	71	70	73	75	289
	Bobby Mitchell	72	74	66	77	289
	Jack Nicklaus	74	67	75	73	289
	Dave Stockton	75	69	72	73	289

Round Leader(s)
R1   Murphy; 66
R2   Beman; 137
R3   Barber; 206

Lowest Scores
R2   Nicklaus, Bob E Smith (31); 67
R3   Mitchell; 66
R4   Campbell, Devlin; 69

BRITISH OPEN 1969

Royal Lytham & St Anne's Golf Club, Lancashire, England
(9–12 July)
6848 yards: Par 71 (284)

After a wait of 18 years, the old Claret Jug was lifted by a home player again. Englishman Tony Jacklin became a national hero when he finished four under par, and ahead of three former Champions, to win at Lytham. As if to mark the occasion, the R&A's winner's prize was increased in 1969 by over 40% – a realistic increase, perhaps, but still way off the American pace of increases in the recent past. It may be simplistic to say that Jacklin's emergence at the top of world golf, albeit for a short time, was a pivotal point in the game's history, in that the emphasis of total American dominance was to change. But his exploits did act as a catalyst in Britain: the interest in golf surged; within the next 15 years, two multiple Majors winners, Faldo and Lyle, had emerged; others would also challenge and become the basis for parity or better in the Ryder Cup.

1	**TONY JACKLIN**	68	70	70	72	280
	(£4250)					
2	Bob Charles	66	69	75	72	282
3=	Roberto de Vicenzo	72	73	66	72	283
	Peter Thomson	71	70	70	72	283
5	Christy O'Connor, Sr	71	65	74	74	284
6=	Davis Love, Jr	70	73	71	71	285
	Jack Nicklaus	75	70	68	72	285
8	Peter Alliss	73	74	73	66	286
9	Kel Nagle	74	71	72	70	287
10	Miller Barber	69	75	75	69	288
11=	Neil Coles	75	76	70	68	289
	Tommy Horton	71	76	70	72	289
	Cobie Legrange	79	70	71	69	289
	Guy Wolstenholme	70	71	76	72	289
15	Gay Brewer	76	71	68	75	290
16=	Eric Brown	73	76	69	73	291
	Bruce Devlin	71	73	75	72	291
	Harold Henning	72	71	75	73	291
	Brian Huggett	72	72	69	78	291
	Orville Moody	71	70	74	76	291
	Peter Townsend	73	70	76	72	291
	Bert Yancey	72	71	71	77	291
23=	Bernard Hunt	73	71	75	73	292
	Gary Player	74	68	76	74	292
25=	Fred Boobyer	74	70	76	73	293
	Billy Casper	70	70	75	78	293
	Alex Caygill	71	67	79	76	293
28=	Hedley Muscroft	68	77	73	76	294
	Peter Tupling (a)	73	71	78	72	294
30=	Max Faulkner	71	74	76	74	295
	Jean Garaialde	69	77	76	73	295
	Mike Ingham	73	73	74	75	295
	Don Swaelens	72	73	76	74	295

Round Leader(s)
R1   Charles; 66
R2   Charles; 135
R3   Jacklin; 208

Lowest Scores
R2   O'Connor; 65
R3   De Vicenzo; 66
R4   Alliss; 66

US PGA 1969

NCR Country Club, Dayton, Ohio
(14–17 August)
6925 yards: Par 72 (288)

Raymond Floyd led all the way to win the first of his two PGA titles, and four Majors, in holding out Gary Player over the last round. Player was the subject of anti-apartheid demonstrations during the Championship, but displaying his famous iron will he pushed Floyd right to the wire. He pulled back four shots over the last round, and just failed to tie. As in the PGA of 1959, it was claustrophobic at the top of the Round One leaderboard, with nine tying for the lead.

1	**RAY FLOYD**	69	66	67	74	276
	($35000)					
2	Gary Player	71	65	71	70	277
3	Bert Greene	71	68	68	71	278
4	Jimmy Wright	71	68	69	71	279
5=	Miller Barber	73	75	64	68	280
	Larry Ziegler	69	71	70	70	280
7=	Charles Coody	69	71	72	69	281
	Orville Moody	70	68	71	72	281
	Terry Wilcox	72	71	72	66	281
10	Frank Beard	70	75	68	69	282
11=	Don Bies	74	64	71	74	283
	Bunky Henry	69	68	70	76	283
	Larry Mowry	69	71	69	74	283
	Jack Nicklaus	70	68	74	71	283
15=	Bruce Crampton	70	70	72	72	284
	Dave Hill	74	75	67	68	284
	Don January	75	70	70	69	284
	Chi Chi Rodriguez	72	72	71	69	284
19=	Howie Johnson	73	68	72	72	285
	Johnny Pott	69	75	71	70	285
21=	Ron Cerrudo	74	66	70	76	286
	Bobby Cole	72	74	71	69	286
	Bob Lunn	69	74	73	70	286
	Tom Shaw	69	75	73	70	286
25=	Julius Boros	72	74	70	71	287
	Gay Brewer	74	71	76	66	287
	Bob Dickson	74	72	70	71	287
	Tony Jacklin	73	70	73	71	287
	George Knudson	70	75	67	75	287
	Fred Marti	73	70	71	73	287
	Dan Sikes	71	74	69	73	287

Round Leader(s)
R1   Coody, Floyd, Al Geiberger (35), Henry, Lunn, Mowry, Pott, Shaw, Ziegler; 69
R2   Floyd; 135
R3   Floyd; 202

Lowest Scores
R2   Bies; 64
R3   Barber; 64
R4   Brewer, Wilcox; 66

THE MASTERS 1970

Augusta National Golf Club, Augusta, Georgia
(9–13 April)

6925 yards: Par 72 (288)

Billy Casper compensated for his defeat the previous year when he took the Masters in a play-off from 1961 Open Champion Gene Littler. The final round was very tight with five players jockeying for the lead, before Casper and Littler prevailed. This was Casper's third Major victory, following two successes in the US Open.

1	**BILLY CASPER*** ($25000)	72	68	68	71	279
2	Gene Littler	69	70	70	70	279
3	Gary Player	74	68	68	70	280
4	Bert Yancey	69	70	72	70	281
5=	Tommy Aaron	68	74	69	72	283
	Dave Hill	73	70	70	70	283
	Dave Stockton	72	72	69	70	283
8	Jack Nicklaus	71	75	69	69	284
9	Frank Beard	71	76	68	70	285
10=	Bob Lunn	70	70	75	72	287
	Chi Chi Rodriguez	70	76	73	68	287
12=	Charles Coody	70	74	67	77	288
	Bert Greene	75	71	70	72	288
	Tony Jacklin	73	74	70	71	288
	Don January	76	73	69	70	288
	Takaaki Kono	75	68	71	74	288
17	Bob Charles	75	71	71	72	289
18=	Howie Johnson	75	71	73	71	290
	Dick Lotz	74	72	72	72	290
	Orville Moody	73	72	71	74	290
21=	Miller Barber	76	73	77	65	291
	Terry Wilcox	79	70	70	72	291
23=	Deane Beman	74	72	72	74	292
	Julius Boros	75	71	74	72	292
	Charles R Coe (a)	74	71	72	75	292
	Bob Murphy	78	70	73	71	292
	Sam Snead	76	73	71	72	292
	Tom Weiskopf	73	73	72	74	292
29=	Yung-Yo Hsieh	75	75	69	74	293
	Jimmy Wright	75	72	71	75	293

* Billy Casper (69) beat Gene Littler (74) in the 18-hole Play-off

Round Leader(s)
R1 Aaron; 68
R2 Littler, Yancey; 139
R3 Casper; 208

Lowest Scores
R2 Casper, Kono, Player; 68
R3 Coody; 67
R4 Barber; 65

US OPEN 1970

Hazeltine National Golf Club, Minneapolis, Minnesota
(18–21 June)

7151 yards: Par 72 (288)

Reigning British Open Champion Jacklin achieved a rare double with a remarkable win at Hazeltine. His victory by seven shots was the biggest since Jim Barnes in 1921; he led wire-to-wire, increasing his lead round-by-round; he was the only player under par. He also rather put the golf world of 1970 into perspective by being the first Brit to hold the both Opens simultaneously since Vardon's transatlantic conquest in 1900. (In only one other similar instance, Jock Hutchison was the reigning US PGA champion when he won the British Open in 1921, but had effectively emigrated.) Going forward to 1970 at Hazeltine, second-placed Dave Hill was so critical of Robert Trent Jones' alterations to the golf course, that he was fined $150 by the USGA for his remarks.

1	**TONY JACKLIN** ($30000)	71	70	70	70	281
2	Dave Hill	75	69	71	73	288
3=	Bob Charles	76	71	75	67	289
	Bob Lunn	77	72	70	70	289
5	Ken Still	78	71	71	71	291
6	Miller Barber	75	75	72	70	292
7	Gay Brewer	75	71	71	76	293
8=	Billy Casper	75	75	71	73	294
	Bruce Devlin	75	75	71	73	294
	Lee Trevino	77	73	74	70	294
	Larry Ziegler	75	73	73	73	294
12=	Julius Boros	73	75	70	77	295
	Bobby Cole	78	75	71	71	295
	Joel Goldstrand	76	76	71	72	295
	Howie Johnson	75	72	75	73	295
	Gene Littler	77	72	71	75	295
	Bobby Mitchell	74	78	74	69	295
18=	Al Balding	75	74	75	72	296
	Paul Harney	78	73	75	70	296
	Johnny Miller	79	73	73	71	296
	Randy Wolff	78	67	76	75	296
22=	Frank Beard	75	73	79	70	297
	Richard Crawford	74	71	76	76	297
	Ray Floyd	78	73	70	76	297
	Ted Hayes, Jr	79	73	73	72	297
	Bert Yancey	81	72	73	71	297
27=	Chi Chi Rodriguez	73	77	75	73	298
	Mason Rudolph	73	75	73	77	298
	Dan Sikes	81	69	72	76	298
30=	George Archer	76	73	77	73	299
	Bruce Crampton	79	71	74	75	299
	Bunky Henry	80	68	77	74	299
	Dave Marr	82	69	74	74	299
	Kel Nagle	78	75	73	73	299
	Tom Weiskopf	76	73	78	72	299

Round Leader(s)
R1 Jacklin; 71
R2 Jacklin; 141
R3 Jacklin; 211

Lowest Scores
R2 Wolff; 67
R3 Boros, Floyd, Jacklin, Lunn; 70
R4 Charles; 67

BRITISH OPEN 1970

Royal & Ancient Golf Club, St Andrews, Fife, Scotland
(8–11 July)
6951 yards: Par 72 (288)

Doug Sanders never won a Major, but will always be remembered for his glorious failure at the 1970 Open at St Andrews. Once Trevino fell away, Sanders always seemed to have the edge over Nicklaus. However, needing a par four at the relatively easy 18th, he missed a three-foot putt for outright victory. In the play-off, Sanders, one behind going to the last, birdied the same hole – only for Nicklaus to do likewise and pick up his second Open, and first Major in, what was for him, a barren three years.

1	**JACK NICKLAUS***	68	69	73	73	283
	(£5250)					
2	Doug Sanders	68	71	71	73	283
3=	Harold Henning	67	72	73	73	285
	Lee Trevino	68	68	72	77	285
5	Tony Jacklin	67	70	73	76	286
6=	Neil Coles	65	74	72	76	287
	Peter Oosterhuis	73	69	69	76	287
8	Hugh Jackson	69	72	73	74	288
9=	Tommy Horton	66	73	75	75	289
	John Panton	72	73	73	71	289
	Peter Thomson	68	74	73	74	289
12	Arnold Palmer	68	72	76	74	290
13=	Maurice Bembridge	67	74	75	76	292
	Bob Charles	72	73	73	74	292
	JC Richardson	67	72	76	77	292
	Bert Yancey	71	71	73	77	292
17=	Roberto Bernadini	75	69	74	75	293
	Billy Casper	71	74	73	75	293
	Clive Clark	69	70	77	77	293
	Roberto de Vicenzo	71	76	71	75	293
	Christy O'Connor, Sr	72	68	74	79	293
22=	Walter Godfrey	71	75	74	74	294
	Tom Weiskopf	70	74	72	78	294
	Guy Wolstenholme	68	77	72	77	294
25=	Bruce Devlin	72	76	72	75	295
	Graham Marsh	75	72	74	74	295
	Ronnie Shade	72	75	69	79	295
28=	Stuart Brown	73	73	71	79	296
	Bobby Cole	71	76	71	78	296
	Brian Huggett	68	78	73	77	296
	Tom Shaw	73	71	73	79	296

* Jack Nicklaus (72) beat Doug Sanders (73) in the 18-Hole Play-off

Round Leader(s)
R1 Coles; 65
R2 Trevino; 136
R3 Trevino; 208

Lowest Scores
R2 O'Connor, Trevino; 68
R3 Oosterhuis, Shade; 69
R4 Panton; 71

US PGA 1970

Southern Hills Country Club, Tulsa, Oklahoma (4–7 April)
6962 yards: Par 70 (280)

Arnold Palmer's third runner-up spot in the PGA was to be his last serious attempt to be the fifth player to win all four Majors. The PGA title was ever to elude him after Dave Stockton's Round Three 66 took him clear of the field at Southern Hills. Although Arnie gradually clawed his way back he couldn't make enough of an impact on the leader to exert the required pressure to make him crack.

1	**DAVE STOCKTON**	70	70	66	73	279
	(£40000)					
2=	Bob Murphy	71	73	71	66	281
	Arnold Palmer	70	72	69	70	281
4=	Larry Hinson	69	71	74	68	282
	Gene Littler	72	71	69	70	282
6=	Bruce Crampton	73	75	68	67	283
	Jack Nicklaus	68	76	73	66	283
8=	Ray Floyd	71	73	65	75	284
	Dick Lotz	72	70	75	67	284
10=	Billy Maxwell	72	71	73	69	285
	Mason Rudolph	71	70	73	71	285
12=	Don January	73	71	73	69	286
	Johnny Miller	68	77	70	71	286
	Gary Player	74	68	74	70	286
	Sam Snead	70	75	68	73	286
16=	Al Geiberger	72	74	71	71	288
	Mike Hill	70	71	74	73	288
18=	Billy Casper	72	70	74	73	289
	Bruce Devlin	75	70	71	73	289
	Al Mengert	76	72	70	71	289
	Dan Sikes	74	70	75	70	289
22=	Lou Graham	75	68	74	73	290
	Bob Stanton	71	74	72	73	290
	Bert Yancey	74	69	75	72	290
	Kermit Zarley	73	74	73	70	290
26=	Julius Boros	72	71	72	76	291
	Bob Charles	74	73	72	72	291
	Terry Dill	72	71	75	73	291
	Bobby Nichols	72	76	72	72	291
	Lee Trevino	72	77	77	65	291

Round Leader(s)
R1 Miller, Nicklaus; 68
R2 Hinson, Stockton; 140
R3 Stockton; 206

Lowest Scores
R2 Graham, Player; 68
R3 Floyd; 65
R4 Trevino; 65

US PGA 1971

PGA National Golf Club, Palm Beach Gardens, Florida
(25–28 February)
7096 yards: Par 72 (288)

Going completely against the grain of previous years, the 1971 PGA Championship was held in February, at the PGA of America's home course, making it the first, not the last, Major of the season. The time of year made no difference to Jack Nicklaus though. He won, coasting home with shots to spare. In winning, he performed a unique double Grand Slam. Nicklaus became – and still is – the only golfer to win all the Major Championships at least twice.

1	**JACK NICKLAUS**	66	69	70	73	281
	($40000)				
2	Billy Casper	71	73	71	68	283
3	Tommy Bolt	72	74	69	69	284
4=	Miller Barber	72	68	75	70	285
	Gary Player	71	73	68	73	285
6=	Gibby Gilbert	74	67	72	73	286
	Dave Hill	74	71	71	70	286
	Jim Jamieson	72	72	72	70	286
9=	Jerry Heard	73	71	72	71	287
	Bob Lunn	72	70	73	72	287
	Fred Marti	72	71	74	70	287
	Bob Rosburg	74	72	70	71	287
13=	Frank Beard	74	71	73	70	288
	Bob Charles	70	75	70	73	288
	Bruce Devlin	71	71	74	72	288
	Larry Hinson	71	73	73	71	288
	Lee Trevino	71	73	75	69	288
18=	Herb Hooper	74	71	73	71	289
	Arnold Palmer	75	71	70	73	289
20=	Johnny Miller	71	76	72	71	290
	Bob E Smith	73	70	75	72	290
22=	Brad Anderson	71	75	75	70	291
	Chuck Courtney	74	71	74	72	291
	Hale Irwin	73	72	72	74	291
	Jerry McGee	73	74	71	73	291
	John Schroeder	72	74	74	71	291
	Tom Weiskopf	72	70	77	72	291
	Larry Wood	74	71	72	74	291
	Bert Yancey	71	74	70	76	291
30=	Terry Dill	75	68	75	74	292
	Gene Borek	72	70	73	77	292
	Rod Funseth	72	47	75	71	292
	Al Geiberger	74	69	77	72	292

Round Leader(s)
R1   Nicklaus; 69
R2   Nicklaus; 138
R3   Nicklaus; 208

Lowest Scores
R2   Gilbert; 67
R3   Player; 68
R4   Casper; 68

THE MASTERS 1971

Augusta National Golf Club, Augusta, Georgia
(8–11 April)
6925 yards: Par 72 (288)

In 1969, dropped shots over the last three holes cost Charles Coody the Masters Tournament. Two years on, despite Johnny Miller's six-under-par charge to hole 16 in the final round, Coody held his game together to see him off, and Miller eventually ran out of steam. Jack Nicklaus, of all people, couldn't sustain his momentum in the final round after leading for three days.

1	**CHARLES COODY**	66	73	70	70	279
	($25000)				
2=	Johnny Miller	72	73	68	68	281
	Jack Nicklaus	70	71	68	72	281
4=	Don January	69	69	73	72	283
	Gene Littler	72	69	73	69	283
6=	Gary Player	72	72	71	69	284
	Ken Still	72	71	72	69	284
	Tom Weiskopf	71	69	72	72	284
9=	Frank Beard	74	73	69	70	286
	Roberto de Vicenzo	76	69	72	69	286
	Dave Stockton	72	73	69	72	286
12	Bert Greene	73	73	71	70	287
13=	Billy Casper	72	73	71	72	288
	Bruce Devlin	72	70	72	74	288
	Ray Floyd	69	75	73	71	288
	Hale Irwin	69	72	71	76	288
	Bob Murphy	69	70	76	73	288
18=	Bruce Crampton	73	72	74	70	289
	Arnold Palmer	73	72	71	73	289
20=	Dave Eichelberger	76	71	70	73	290
	Orville Moody	79	69	70	72	290
22=	Tommy Aaron	76	72	74	69	291
	Bobby Mitchell	72	70	74	75	291
24=	Al Geiberger	73	75	72	72	292
	Dick Lotz	77	72	73	70	292
	Steve Melnyk	73	70	75	74	292
27=	Dale Douglass	70	71	76	76	293
	Dave Hill	74	73	70	76	293
	Art Wall	71	76	72	74	293
30=	Larry Hinson	75	71	76	72	294
	Yung-Yo Hsieh	75	69	77	73	294
	Juan Rodriguez	73	75	71	75	294
	Larry Ziegler	73	70	77	74	294

Round Leader(s)
R1   Coody; 66
R2   January; 138
R3   Coody, Nicklaus; 209

Lowest Scores
R2   Hsieh, January, Littler, Moody, de Vicenzo, Weiskopf; 69
R3   Miller, Nicklaus; 68
R4   Miller; 68

US OPEN 1971

Merion Golf Club, Ardmore, Pennsylvania
(17–21 June)
6544 yards: Par 70 (280)

Lee Trevino's second US Open win came after a superb 68 saw off Jack Nicklaus in a play-off. Amateur Jim Simons held a two-stroke lead at the end of Round Three, thanks to a sparkling 65. Nicklaus collected his second consecutive Majors runner-up prize of the season, after lifting the Masters title; while 1971 winner, Tony Jacklin, missed the cut, as had five other defending champions from over the previous eight years. Entries passed 4000 for the first time.

1	**LEE TREVINO***	70	72	69	69	280
	($30000)					
2	Jack Nicklaus	69	72	68	71	280
3=	Jim Colbert	69	69	73	71	282
	Bob Rosburg	71	72	70	69	282
5=	George Archer	71	70	70	72	283
	Johnny Miller	70	73	70	70	283
	Jim Simons (a)	71	71	65	76	283
8	Ray Floyd	71	75	67	71	284
9=	Gay Brewer	70	70	73	72	285
	Larry Hinson	71	71	70	73	285
	Bobby Nichols	69	72	69	75	285
	Bert Yancey	75	69	69	72	285
13=	Bob Charles	72	75	69	70	286
	Bobby Cole	72	71	72	71	286
	Jerry Heard	73	71	73	69	286
	Jerry McGee	72	67	77	70	286
	Chi Chi Rodriguez	70	71	73	72	286
	Lanny Wadkins (a)	68	75	75	68	286
19=	Homero Blancas	71	71	75	70	287
	Dave Eichelberger	72	72	70	73	287
	Bob Goalby	68	76	74	69	287
	Hale Irwin	72	73	72	70	287
	Ken Still	71	72	69	75	287
24=	Dick Lotz	72	72	73	71	288
	Arnold Palmer	73	68	73	74	288
	Bob E Smith	71	74	71	72	288
27=	Ben Crenshaw (a)	74	74	68	73	289
	Bruce Devlin	72	69	71	77	289
	Don January	75	73	71	70	289
	Ralph Johnston	70	75	73	71	289
	Bob Lunn	71	73	71	74	289
	Bobby Mitchell	72	74	72	71	289
	Orville Moody	71	71	76	71	289
	Gary Player	76	71	72	70	289
	John Schroeder	72	73	69	75	289
	Kermit Zarley	74	70	72	73	289

* Lee Trevino (68) beat Jack Nicklaus (71) in the 18-Hole Play-off

Round Leader(s)
R1 Labron Harris (46); 67
R2 Colbert, Bob Erickson (37); 138
R3 Simons; 207

Lowest Scores
R2 Erickson, McGee; 67
R3 Simons; 65
R4 Wadkins; 68

BRITISH OPEN 1971

Royal Birkdale Golf Club, Southport, Lancashire, England
(7–9 July)
7080 yards: Par 73 (292)

The year of 'Mr Lu' and his constantly-doffed pork-pie hat: and the first of Lee Trevino's British Opens. Liang-Huan Lu, from Taiwan, charmed the Birkdale crowds – and TV audiences – as he so nearly became the first Asian golfer to win a Major. Trevino's Round One 69 was to make all the difference as the pair matched each other's scores from there in. His second consecutive Major of the year meant he joined Jones (twice), Sarazen and Hogan as the only players to lift both Opens in the same year.

1	**LEE TREVINO**	69	70	69	70	278
	(£5500)					
2	Liang-Huan Lu	70	70	69	70	279
3	Tony Jacklin	69	70	70	71	280
4	Craig DeFoy	72	72	68	69	281
5=	Charles Coody	74	71	70	68	283
	Jack Nicklaus	71	71	72	69	283
7=	Billy Casper	70	72	75	67	284
	Gary Player	71	70	71	72	284
9=	Doug Sanders	73	71	74	67	285
	Peter Thomson	70	73	73	69	285
11=	Harry Bannerman	73	71	72	71	287
	Roberto de Vicenzo	71	70	72	74	287
	Kel Nagle	70	75	73	69	287
	Ramon Sota	72	72	70	73	287
	Dave Stockton	74	74	68	71	287
	Bert Yancey	75	70	71	71	287
17	Dale Hayes	71	72	70	75	288
18=	Bob Charles	77	71	71	70	289
	Peter Oosterhuis	76	71	66	76	289
20=	Bernard Hunt	74	73	73	70	290
	Howie Johnson	69	76	72	73	290
22=	Michael Bonallack (a)	71	72	75	73	291
	Neil Coles	76	72	72	71	291
	Hugh Jackson	71	73	72	75	291
25=	Peter Butler	73	73	73	73	292
	Vicente Fernandez	69	79	73	71	292
	Malcolm Gregson	71	71	73	77	292
	Brian Huggett	73	73	74	72	292
	Bill Large	73	75	73	71	292
	John Lister	74	71	74	73	292
	Doug Sewell	73	74	74	71	292
	Randall Vines	75	71	73	73	292

Round Leader(s)
R1 Fernandez, Jacklin, Johnson, Trevino; 69
R2 Jacklin, Trevino; 139
R3 Trevino; 208

Lowest Scores
R2 de Vicenzo, Jacklin, Lu, Player, Trevino, Yancey; 70
R3 Oosterhuis; 66
R4 Casper, Sanders; 67

THE MASTERS 1972

Augusta National Golf Club, Augusta, Georgia
(6–9 April)

6925 yards: Par 72 (288)

After a period of three seasons when he won nothing, Jack Nicklaus was winning Majors again – and continuing to break records. He won his fourth Masters, tying the record of Arnold Palmer; and tenth Major overall – one ahead of Ben Hogan, one behind Walter Hagen. Australian Bruce Crampton was to follow Jack home in this, and his next two, Major Championship wins. In fact all Crampton's four Majors second places were behind Nicklaus. Is that fair?

1	**JACK NICKLAUS** ($25000)	68	71	73	74	286
2=	Bruce Crampton	72	75	69	73	289
	Bobby Mitchell	73	72	71	73	289
	Tom Weiskopf	74	71	70	74	289
5=	Homero Blancas	76	71	69	74	290
	Bruce Devlin	74	75	70	71	290
	Jerry Heard	73	71	72	74	290
	Jim Jamieson	72	70	71	77	290
	Jerry McGee	73	74	71	72	290
10=	Gary Player	73	75	72	71	291
	Dave Stockton	76	70	74	71	291
12=	George Archer	73	75	72	72	292
	Charles Coody	73	70	74	75	292
	Al Geiberger	76	70	74	72	292
	Steve Melnyk	72	72	74	74	292
	Bert Yancey	72	69	76	75	292
17=	Billy Casper	75	71	74	74	294
	Bob Goalby	73	76	72	73	294
19=	Ben Crenshaw (a)	73	74	74	74	295
	Takaaki Kono	76	72	73	74	295
	Lanny Wadkins	72	72	77	74	295
22=	Bob Charles	72	76	74	74	296
	Roberto de Vicenzo	75	69	76	76	296
	Gardner Dickinson	77	72	73	74	296
	Hubert Green	75	74	74	73	296
	Paul Harney	71	69	75	81	296
27=	Tony Jacklin	72	76	75	74	297
	Tom Kite	74	74	76	73	297
	Sam Snead	69	75	76	77	297
30	JC Snead	74	77	72	75	298

Round Leader(s)
R1 Nicklaus; 68
R2 Nicklaus; 139
R3 Nicklaus; 212

Lowest Scores
R2 Harney, de Vicenzo, Yancey; 69
R3 Blancas, Crampton; 69
R4 Devlin, Player, Stockton; 71

US OPEN 1972

Pebble Beach Golf Links, Pebble Beach, California
(15–18 June)

6812 yards: Par 72 (288)

Spectacular Pebble Beach played host to a Major Championship for the first time – and it proved a tough test. Nicklaus' second Major win in a row was the fifth time the Masters–US Open double in the same year was recorded. Craig Wood, Ben Hogan (twice) and Arnold Palmer had previously accomplished it. It was Jack's third US Open title and it also put him level with Walter Hagen atop the all-time lists with 11 – Masters (4), US Open (3), British Open (2), PGA (2). Mason Rudolph shot the low score for Rounds One and Four, but scored 80 and 86 in between to finish in 40th place.

1	**JACK NICKLAUS** ($30000)	71	73	72	74	290
2	Bruce Crampton	74	70	73	76	293
3	Arnold Palmer	77	68	73	76	294
4=	Homero Blancas	74	70	76	75	295
	Lee Trevino	74	72	71	78	295
6	Kermit Zarley	71	73	73	79	296
7	Johnny Miller	74	73	71	79	297
8	Tom Weiskopf	73	74	73	78	298
9=	Chi Chi Rodriguez	71	75	78	75	299
	Cesar Sanudo	72	72	78	77	299
11=	Billy Casper	74	73	79	74	300
	Don January	76	71	74	79	300
	Bobby Nichols	77	74	72	77	300
	Bert Yancey	75	79	70	76	300
15=	Don Massengale	72	81	70	78	301
	Orville Moody	71	77	79	74	301
	Gary Player	72	76	75	78	301
	Jim Simons (a)	75	75	79	72	301
19=	Lou Graham	75	73	75	79	302
	Tom Kite (a)	75	73	79	75	302
21=	Al Geiberger	80	74	76	73	303
	Paul Harney	79	72	75	77	303
	Bobby Mitchell	74	80	73	76	303
	Charles Sifford	79	74	72	78	303
25=	Gay Brewer	77	77	72	78	304
	Rod Funseth	73	73	84	74	304
	Lanny Wadkins	76	68	79	81	304
	Jim Wiechers	74	79	69	82	304
29=	Miller Barber	76	76	73	80	305
	Julius Boros	77	77	74	77	305
	Dave Eichelberger	76	71	80	78	305
	Lee Elder	75	71	79	80	305
	Jerry Heard	73	74	77	81	305
	Dave Hill	74	78	74	79	305
	Tom Watson	74	79	76	76	305

Round Leader(s)
R1 Moody, Nicklaus, Rodriguez, Mason Rudolph (40), Tom Shaw (40), Zarley; 71
R2 Blancas, Crampton, Nicklaus, Sanudo, Wadkins, Zarley; 144
R3 Nicklaus; 216

Lowest Scores
R2 Palmer, Wadkins; 68
R3 Wiechers; 69
R4 Mason Rudolph (40); 70

BRITISH OPEN 1972

Hon Co of Edinburgh Golfers, Muirfield, East Lothian, Scotland
(12–15 July)
6892 yards: Par 71 (284)

Lee Trevino's back-to-back Open win was destined to be. In the third round, he scrambled five consecutive birdies over the final five holes with an array of chips-in and outlandish putting unlikely to be seen again...or so Tony Jacklin hoped. It was bad enough watching his immaculate 67 being overhauled by Trevino's antics in Round Three; but when, tied going into the 72nd hole, he was 15 feet away in three, and saw Trevino, through the back of the green in four, run it in, it destroyed Jacklin – some say as a golfing force forever. Jacklin three-putted and allowed a Nicklaus charge to deprive him even of second place: Jack, like Arnold Palmer in 1960, just failing to emulate Ben Hogan's 1953 three Majors in-a-row record.

1	**LEE TREVINO**	71	70	66	71	278
	(£5500)					
2	Jack Nicklaus	70	72	71	66	279
3	Tony Jacklin	69	72	67	72	280
4	Doug Sanders	71	71	69	70	281
5	Brian Barnes	71	72	69	71	283
6	Gary Player	71	71	76	67	285
7=	Guy Hunt	75	72	67	72	286
	Arnold Palmer	73	73	69	71	286
	David Vaughan	74	73	70	69	286
	Tom Weiskopf	73	74	70	69	286
11=	Clive Clark	72	71	73	71	287
	Dave Marr	70	74	71	72	287
13=	Roberto Bernadini	73	71	76	68	288
	Peter Townsend	70	72	76	70	288
15=	Peter Butler	72	75	73	69	289
	Bob Charles	75	70	74	70	289
	Jan Dorrestein	74	71	72	72	289
	Johnny Miller	76	66	72	75	289
19=	Harry Bannerman	77	73	73	67	290
	Frank Beard	70	76	74	70	290
	Maurice Bembridge	73	71	75	71	290
	Bert Yancey	73	72	72	73	290
23=	Craig DeFoy	70	75	71	75	291
	Doug McClelland	73	74	72	72	291
	Christy O'Connor, Sr	73	74	73	71	291
26=	Bruce Devlin	75	70	77	70	292
	Brian Huggett	73	72	79	68	292
28=	John Garner	71	71	76	75	293
	Jerry Heard	75	75	71	72	293
	Peter Oosterhuis	75	75	73	70	293

Round Leader(s)
R1   Jacklin; 69
R2   Jacklin, Trevino; 141
R3   Trevino; 207

Lowest Scores
R2   Miller; 66
R3   Trevino; 66
R4   Nicklaus; 66

US PGA 1972

Oakland Hills Country Club, Birmingham, Michigan
(3–6 August)
6815 yards: Par 70 (280)

Just when it was rumoured that Gary Player was losing his form; and like Arnold Palmer – another of the 'Big Three' – it was said he would never win another Major, he picked up his second PGA title, and sixth Major Championship victory. Player's win ranked him above Taylor, Braid, Nelson and Thomson in the all-time lists, but still one behind the next group of Vardon, Jones, Sarazen, Snead and the aforementioned Palmer.

1	**GARY PLAYER**	71	71	67	72	281
	($45000)					
2=	Tommy Aaron	71	71	70	71	283
	Jim Jamieson	69	72	72	70	283
4=	Billy Casper	73	70	67	74	284
	Ray Floyd	69	71	74	70	284
	Sam Snead	70	74	71	69	284
7=	Gay Brewer	71	70	70	74	285
	Jerry Heard	69	70	72	74	285
	Phil Rodgers	71	72	68	74	285
	Doug Sanders	72	72	68	73	285
11=	Hale Irwin	71	69	75	71	286
	Lee Trevino	73	71	71	71	286
13=	Jack Nicklaus	72	75	68	72	287
	Dan Sikes	70	72	73	72	287
15	Charles Coody	71	73	70	74	288
16=	Miller Barber	73	74	72	70	289
	Hubert Green	75	71	73	70	289
	Arnold Palmer	69	75	72	73	289
	Lanny Wadkins	74	68	72	75	289
20=	Johnny Miller	70	76	70	74	290
	Bob Shaw	72	72	74	72	290
	JC Snead	72	72	71	75	290
	Larry Wise	74	71	67	78	290
24=	Bruce Crampton	73	74	68	76	291
	Lee Elder	73	71	71	76	291
	Chi Chi Rodriguez	71	74	73	73	291
	Bob E Smith	72	69	76	74	291
	Art Wall	72	71	75	73	291
29=	Jerry McGee	73	74	72	73	292
	Mike Souchak	73	73	71	75	292
	Jim Wiechers	70	73	69	80	292
	Bert Yancey	72	74	71	75	292

Round Leader(s)
R1   Buddy Allin (53), Stan Thirsk (72); 68
R2   Heard; 139
R3   Player; 209

Lowest Scores
R2   Wadkins; 68
R3   Casper, Player, Wise; 67
R4   Snead; 69

THE MASTERS 1973

Augusta National Golf Club, Augusta, Georgia
(5–9 April: Saturday washed out)
6925 yards: Par 72 (288)

Tommy Aaron, a local boy, won his first and last Major ahead of JC Snead – Sam's nephew. Englishman Peter Oosterhuis held a three-shot lead going into the last day, but couldn't keep it all together, as Aaron, Snead and Jamieson challenged. A string of eight consecutive birdies helped Jack Nicklaus race up the leaderboard to tie with the Briton and Jamieson.

1	**TOMMY AARON**	68	73	74	68	283
	($30000)					
2	JC Snead	70	71	73	70	284
3=	Jim Jamieson	73	71	70	71	285
	Jack Nicklaus	69	77	73	66	285
	Peter Oosterhuis	73	70	68	74	285
6=	Bob Goalby	73	70	71	74	288
	Johnny Miller	75	69	71	73	288
8=	Bruce Devlin	73	72	72	72	289
	Jumbo Ozaki	69	74	73	73	289
10=	Gay Brewer	75	66	74	76	291
	Gardner Dickinson	74	70	72	75	291
	Don January	75	71	75	70	291
	Chi Chi Rodriguez	72	70	73	76	291
14=	Hubert Green	72	74	75	71	292
	Mason Rudolph	72	72	77	71	292
	Dave Stockton	72	74	71	75	292
17=	Billy Casper	75	73	72	73	293
	Bob Dickson	70	71	76	76	293
	Lou Graham	77	73	72	71	293
	Babe Hiskey	74	73	72	74	293
	Gene Littler	77	72	71	73	293
	Kermit Zarley	74	71	77	71	293
24=	Frank Beard	73	75	71	76	295
	Ben Crenshaw (a)	73	72	74	76	295
	Paul Harney	77	71	74	73	295
	Bobby Nichols	79	72	76	68	295
	Arnold Palmer	77	72	76	70	295
29=	Bob Charles	74	70	74	78	296
	Charles Coody	74	73	79	70	296
	David Graham	72	74	77	73	296
	Sam Snead	74	76	73	73	296
	Lanny Wadkins	75	74	71	76	296

Round Leader(s)
R1   Aaron; 68
R2   Aaron, Brewer, Dickson, Snead; 141
R3   Oosterhuis; 211

Lowest Scores
R2   Brewer; 66
R3   Oosterhuis; 68
R4   Nicklaus; 66

US OPEN 1973

Oakmont Country Club, Oakmont, Pennsylvania
(14–17 June)
6921 yards: Par 71 (284)

Johnny Miller followed up his second place at Augusta with a first Majors success in the US Open at Oakmont. In doing so he beat the Championship low round score of 64, jointly held by Lee Mackey, Tommy Jacobs and Rives McBee – his 63 being the lowest score in any Major, which is still to be beaten.

1	**JOHNNY MILLER**	71	69	76	63	279
	($35000)					
2	John Schlee	73	70	67	70	280
3	Tom Weiskopf	73	69	69	70	281
4=	Jack Nicklaus	71	69	74	68	282
	Arnold Palmer	71	71	68	72	282
	Lee Trevino	70	72	70	70	282
7=	Julius Boros	73	69	68	73	283
	Jerry Heard	74	70	66	73	283
	Lanny Wadkins	74	69	75	65	283
10	Jim Colbert	70	68	74	72	284
11	Bob Charles	71	69	72	74	286
12	Gary Player	67	70	77	73	287
13=	Al Geiberger	73	72	71	72	288
	Ralph Johnston	71	73	76	68	288
	Larry Ziegler	73	74	69	72	288
16	Ray Floyd	70	73	75	71	289
17	Marvin Giles (a)	74	69	74	73	290
18=	Gene Littler	71	74	70	76	291
	Rocky Thompson	73	71	71	76	291
20=	Rod Funseth	75	74	70	74	293
	Hale Irwin	73	74	75	71	293
	Denny Lyons	72	74	75	72	293
	Bob Murphy	77	70	75	71	293
	Bobby Nichols	75	71	74	73	293
25=	Miller Barber	74	71	71	78	294
	Frank Beard	74	75	68	77	294
	Tom Shaw	73	71	74	76	294
	Bert Yancey	73	70	75	76	294
29=	Don Bies	77	73	73	72	295
	Charles Coody	74	74	73	74	295
	John Mahaffey	74	72	74	75	295
	Chi Chi Rodriguez	75	71	75	74	295
	Sam Snead	75	74	73	73	295

Round Leader(s)
R1   Player; 67
R2   Player; 137
R3   Boros, Heard, Palmer, Schlee; 210

Lowest Scores
R2   Gene Borek (38); 65
R3   Heard, 66
R4   Miller; 63

BRITISH OPEN 1973

Troon Golf Club, Ayrshire, Scotland
(11–14 July)
7064 yards: Par 72 (288)

Tom Weiskopf's good finish in the US Open was during a run of superb form on the US Tour. He had already tied for second in the Masters, and running up to Pebble Beach, his results sequence read: W, W, 2, W. He played one other Tour event between the Opens, and must have been disappointed to finish fifth. His win at Troon, therefore, was as expected as it was popular – for if the game of golf awarded marks for artistic impression, then Weiskopf would have won more than one Major. US Open Champion, Johnny Miller, added another runner-up prize to his Masters earlier in the year.

1	**TOM WEISKOPF**	68	67	71	70	276
	(£5500)					
2=	Neil Coles	71	72	70	66	279
	Johnny Miller	70	68	69	72	279
4	Jack Nicklaus	69	70	76	65	280
5	Bert Yancey	69	69	73	70	281
6	Peter Butler	71	72	74	69	286
7=	Bob Charles	73	71	73	71	288
	Christy O'Connor, Sr	73	68	74	73	288
	Lanny Wadkins	71	73	70	74	288
10=	Brian Barnes	76	67	70	76	289
	Gay Brewer	76	71	72	70	289
	Harold Henning	73	73	73	70	289
	Lee Trevino	75	73	73	68	289
14=	Tony Jacklin	75	73	72	70	290
	Doug McClelland	76	71	69	74	290
	Arnold Palmer	72	76	70	72	290
	Gary Player	76	69	76	69	290
18=	Hugh Baiocchi	75	74	69	74	292
	Hugh Boyle	75	75	69	73	292
	Bruce Crampton	71	76	73	72	292
	Bruce Devlin	72	78	71	71	292
	Bernard Gallacher	73	69	75	75	292
	DJ Good	75	74	73	70	292
	Dave Hill	75	74	74	69	292
	Peter Oosterhuis	80	71	69	72	292
	Eddie Polland	74	73	73	72	292
	Peter Wilcock	71	76	72	73	292
28=	Roberto de Vicenzo	72	75	74	72	293
	Chi Chi Rodriguez	72	73	73	75	293
	Doug Sanders	79	72	72	70	293

Round Leader(s)
R1 Weiskopf; 68
R2 Weiskopf; 135
R3 Weiskopf; 206

Lowest Scores
R2 Barnes, Weiskopf; 67
R3 Baiocchi, Boyle, McClelland, Miller, Oosterhuis; 69
R4 Nicklaus; 65

US PGA 1973

Canterbury Golf Club, Cleveland, Ohio
(9–12 August)
6852 yards: Par 71 (284)

Jack Nicklaus made history when he won his 12th Major and became the greatest player of Major Championships the game had ever seen. In passing Walter Hagen's total, he also – to the statistician's delight – eclipsed the old version of 'Grand Slam' titles, which include the US and British Amateur Championship, held by Bobby Jones for 43 years. Nicklaus' two US Amateur wins took his grand haul past Jones' tally of 13 Amateur and Open titles.

1	**JACK NICKLAUS**	72	68	68	69	277
	($45000)					
2	Bruce Crampton	71	73	67	70	281
3=	Mason Rudolph	69	70	70	73	282
	JC Snead	71	74	68	69	282
	Lanny Wadkins	73	69	71	69	282
6=	Don Iverson	67	72	70	74	283
	Dan Sikes	72	68	72	71	283
	Tom Weiskopf	70	71	71	71	283
9=	Hale Irwin	76	72	68	68	284
	Sam Snead	71	71	71	71	284
	Kermit Zarley	76	71	68	69	284
12=	Bobby Brue	70	72	73	70	285
	Jim Colbert	72	70	69	74	285
	Larry Hinson	73	70	71	71	285
	Denny Lyons	73	70	67	75	285
	Dave Stockton	72	69	75	69	285
	Tom Watson	75	70	71	69	285
18=	Al Geiberger	67	76	74	69	286
	Gibby Gilbert	70	70	73	73	286
	Bob Goalby	75	70	71	70	286
	Jim Jamieson	71	73	71	71	286
	Johnny Miller	72	71	74	69	286
	Lee Trevino	76	70	73	67	286
24=	Miller Barber	73	73	70	71	287
	Bruce Devlin	73	70	74	70	287
	Lee Elder	71	76	70	70	287
	Mike Hill	69	73	75	70	287
	Chi Chi Rodriguez	72	71	74	70	287
	Bert Yancey	74	72	69	72	287
30=	Don Bies	70	72	71	75	288
	Lou Graham	74	71	73	70	288
	John Mahaffey	75	71	72	70	288
	Orville Moody	73	74	70	71	288

Round Leader(s)
R1 Geiberger, Iverson; 67
R2 Iverson, Rudolph; 139
R3 Nicklaus; 208

Lowest Scores
R2 Charles Coody (35), Nicklaus, Sikes; 68
R3 Buddy Allin (34), Crampton, Lyons; 67
R4 Trevino; 67

THE MASTERS 1974

Augusta National Golf Club, Augusta, Georgia
(11–14 April)

6925 yards: Par 72 (288)

Augusta saw Gary Player's seventh Major win, but only his second Masters, and after a record 13-year span. 1970 PGA Champion Dave Stockton had led for much of the Tournament, but was caught and passed by Player in an exciting back nine. A nine iron to within inches of the pin at 17 set up the birdie that clinched it for the popular South African. Maurice Bembridge, a rare English visitor, equalled the low score with a 64 to finish tied for ninth.

1	**GARY PLAYER**	71	71	66	70	278
	($35000)					
2=	Dave Stockton	71	66	70	73	280
	Tom Weiskopf	71	69	70	70	280
4=	Jim Colbert	67	72	69	73	281
	Hale Irwin	68	70	72	71	281
	Jack Nicklaus	69	71	72	69	281
7=	Bobby Nichols	73	68	68	73	282
	Phil Rodgers	72	69	68	73	282
9=	Maurice Bembridge	73	74	72	64	283
	Hubert Green	68	70	74	71	283
11=	Bruce Crampton	73	72	69	70	284
	Jerry Heard	70	70	73	71	284
	Dave Hill	71	72	70	71	284
	Arnold Palmer	76	71	70	67	284
15=	Buddy Allin	73	73	70	69	285
	Miller Barber	75	67	72	71	285
	Ralph Johnston	72	71	70	72	285
	Johnny Miller	72	74	69	70	285
	Dan Sikes	69	71	74	71	285
20=	Chi Chi Rodriguez	70	74	71	71	286
	Sam Snead	72	72	71	71	286
22=	Frank Beard	69	70	72	76	287
	Ben Crenshaw	75	70	70	72	287
	Ray Floyd	69	72	76	70	287
	Bob Goalby	76	71	72	68	287
26=	Julius Boros	75	70	69	74	288
	John Schlee	75	71	71	71	288
	JC Snead	73	68	74	73	288
29=	Charles Coody	74	72	76	67	289
	Don Iverson	68	74	73	74	289

Round Leader(s)
R1   Colbert; 67
R2   Stockton; 137
R3   Stockton; 207

Lowest Scores
R2   Stockton; 66
R3   Player; 66
R4   Bembridge; 64

US OPEN 1974

Winged Foot Golf Club, Mamaroneck, New York
(13–16 June)

6961 yards: Par 70 (280)

Hale Irwin won his first Major by playing solid golf over the tough West Course at Winged Foot. That he was seven over par is testament to the demands of the golf course. 23 year-old Tom Watson held the lead after 54 holes, but collapsed – coming home in 41, as the pack overwhelmed him.

1	**HALE IRWIN**	73	70	71	73	287
	($35000)					
2	Forrest Fezler	75	70	74	70	289
3=	Lou Graham	71	75	74	70	290
	Bert Yancey	76	69	73	72	290
5=	Jim Colbert	72	77	69	74	292
	Arnold Palmer	73	70	73	76	292
	Tom Watson	73	71	69	79	292
8=	Tom Kite	74	70	77	72	293
	Gary Player	70	73	77	73	293
10=	Buddy Allin	76	71	74	73	294
	Jack Nicklaus	75	74	76	69	294
12=	Frank Beard	77	69	72	77	295
	John Mahaffey	74	73	75	73	295
	Larry Ziegler	78	68	78	71	295
15=	Ray Floyd	72	71	78	75	296
	Mike Reasor	71	76	76	73	296
	Tom Weiskopf	76	73	72	75	296
18=	Dale Douglass	77	72	72	76	297
	Al Geiberger	75	76	78	68	297
	David Graham	73	75	76	73	297
21=	JC Snead	76	71	76	75	298
	Leonard Thompson	75	75	76	72	298
23=	Bruce Crampton	72	77	76	74	299
	Larry Hinson	75	76	75	73	299
	Bobby Mitchell	77	73	73	76	299
26=	Hubert Green	81	67	76	76	300
	Jim Jamieson	77	73	75	75	300
	Chi Chi Rodriguez	75	75	77	73	300
	Lanny Wadkins	75	73	76	76	300
30=	Ron Cerrudo	78	75	75	73	301
	Rod Funseth	73	75	78	75	301
	David Glenz	76	74	75	76	301
	Rik Massengale	79	72	74	76	301
	Jerry McGee	77	72	78	74	301

Round Leader(s)
R1   Player; 70
R2   Floyd, Irwin, Palmer, Player; 143
R3   Watson; 213

Lowest Scores
R2   Green; 67
R3   Colbert, Watson; 69
R4   Geiberger; 68

BRITISH OPEN 1974

Royal Lytham and St Anne's Golf Club, Lancashire, England
(10–13 July)
6822 yards: Par 71 (284)

Gary Player won his third Open and eighth Major in all when he was the only one to beat par at Royal Lytham. He climbed to fourth place outright in the all-time Major winners list, behind Nicklaus, Hagen and Hogan. The British Open, thanks to its support from Player (champion first in 1959) and the Americans led by Palmer and Nicklaus, was unrecognizable from a decade or so before. Only one Englishman finished in the cosmopolitan Top 10, which also featured two South Africans, five Americans, a Taiwanese and a Belgian

1	**GARY PLAYER**	69	68	75	70	282
	(£5500)					
2	Peter Oosterhuis	71	71	73	71	286
3	Jack Nicklaus	74	72	70	71	287
4	Hubert Green	71	74	72	71	288
5=	Danny Edwards	70	73	76	73	292
	Liang-Huan Lu	72	72	75	73	292
7=	Bobby Cole	70	72	76	75	293
	Don Swaelens	77	73	74	69	293
	Tom Weiskopf	72	72	74	75	293
10	Johnny Miller	72	75	73	74	294
11=	John Garner	75	78	73	69	295
	David Graham	76	74	76	69	295
13=	Neil Coles	72	75	75	74	296
	Al Geiberger	76	70	76	74	296
	John Morgan	69	75	76	76	296
	Alan Tapie	73	77	73	73	296
	Peter Townsend	79	76	72	69	296
18=	Peter Dawson	74	74	73	76	297
	Tony Jacklin	74	77	71	75	297
	Gene Littler	77	76	70	74	297
	Dewitt Weaver	73	80	70	74	297
22=	Ronnie Shade	78	75	73	72	298
	Lanny Wadkins	78	71	75	74	298
24=	Bernard Gallacher	76	72	76	75	299
	Angel Gallardo	74	77	75	73	299
	Hale Irwin	76	73	79	71	299
	Christy O'Connor, Jr	78	76	72	73	299
28=	Ben Crenshaw	74	80	76	70	300
	David Jagger	80	71	76	73	300
	Doug McClelland	75	79	73	73	300

Round Leader(s)
R1 Morgan, Player; 69
R2 Player; 137
R3 Player; 212

Lowest Scores
R2 Player; 68
R3 Littler, Nicklaus, Weaver; 70
R4 Garner, Graham, Swaelens, Townsend; 69

US PGA 1974

Tanglewood Golf Club, Clemmons, North Carolina
(8–11 August)
7050 yards: Par 70 (280)

Wet conditions throughout the Championship favoured the maverick shotmaking genius that was Lee Trevino. He won his first PGA, and fifth Major, after shooting an opening 73 which left him tied-43rd, five shots off the lead. Thereafter he played brilliant golf in the conditions to card 203 for the last 54 holes. Jack Nicklaus continued to collect as many runner-up prizes as wins. Sam Snead, at the age of 62, was having a remarkable Indian summer in the PGA, finishing fourth, ninth and third over the last three years. It was 32 years after his first of seven Major titles.

1	**LEE TREVINO**	73	66	68	69	276
	($45000)					
2	Jack Nicklaus	69	69	70	69	277
3=	Bobby Cole	69	68	71	71	279
	Hubert Green	68	68	73	70	279
	Dave Hill	74	69	67	69	279
	Sam Snead	69	71	71	68	279
7	Gary Player	73	64	73	70	280
8	Al Geiberger	70	70	75	66	281
9=	Don Bies	73	71	68	70	282
	John Mahaffey	72	72	71	67	282
11=	Tommy Aycock	73	68	73	70	284
	Frank Beard	73	67	69	75	284
	Lee Elder	74	69	72	69	284
	Ray Floyd	68	73	74	70	284
	Mike Hill	76	72	68	68	284
	Tom Watson	69	72	73	70	284
17=	Gay Brewer	72	72	72	69	285
	Tom Jenkins	70	73	71	71	285
	John Schlee	68	67	75	75	285
	Dan Sikes	71	75	71	68	285
	Leonard Thompson	69	71	70	75	285
22=	Stan Brion	71	71	74	70	286
	Bruce Devlin	70	74	70	72	286
24=	Don Massengale	74	71	70	72	287
	JC Snead	72	72	75	68	287
26=	Larry Hinson	74	73	69	72	288
	Dave Stockton	71	73	70	74	288
28=	Jim Colbert	70	76	70	73	289
	Gene Littler	76	72	70	71	289
	Arnold Palmer	72	75	70	72	289
	Victor Regalado	70	72	77	70	289

Round Leader(s)
R1 Green, Floyd, Schlee; 68
R2 Schlee; 135
R3 Trevino; 207

Lowest Scores
R2 Player; 64
R3 Hill; 67
R4 Geiberger; 66

THE MASTERS 1975

Augusta National Golf Club, Augusta, Georgia
(10–13 April)
6925 yards: Par 72 (288)

Nicklaus' fifth win was a record for the Masters, while Tom Weiskopf equalled Ben Hogan's four second places. The two fought out a real dogfight over the last nine holes, but when Weiskopf missed his birdie putt on 18, Jack was home and dry for Major No 13. Attempting to make up 11 shots on Nicklaus over the last 36 holes, Johnny Miller fired 131, but just failed to tie for the lead when he again missed a putt for birdie at the last.

1	**JACK NICKLAUS**	68	67	73	68	276
	($40000)					
2=	Johnny Miller	75	71	65	66	277
	Tom Weiskopf	69	72	66	70	277
4=	Hale Irwin	73	74	71	64	282
	Bobby Nichols	67	74	72	69	282
6	Billy Casper	70	70	73	70	283
7	Dave Hill	75	71	70	68	284
8=	Hubert Green	74	71	70	70	285
	Tom Watson	70	70	72	73	285
10=	Tom Kite	72	74	71	69	286
	JC Snead	69	72	75	70	286
	Lee Trevino	71	70	74	71	286
13=	Arnold Palmer	69	71	75	72	287
	Larry Ziegler	71	73	74	69	287
15=	Bobby Cole	73	71	73	71	288
	Rod Curl	72	70	76	70	288
	Bruce Devlin	72	70	76	70	288
	Allen Miller	68	75	72	73	288
	Art Wall	72	74	72	70	288
20=	Buddy Allin	73	69	73	74	289
	Ralph Johnston	74	73	69	73	289
22=	Hugh Baiocchi	76	72	72	70	290
	Pat Fitzsimons	73	68	79	70	290
	Gene Littler	72	72	72	74	290
	Graham Marsh	75	70	74	71	290
26=	Miller Barber	74	72	72	73	291
	Maurice Bembridge	75	72	75	69	291
	Jerry Heard	71	75	72	73	291
	Dave Stockton	72	72	73	74	291
30=	George Burns	72	72	76	72	292
	Ben Crenshaw	72	71	75	74	292
	Forrest Fezler	76	71	71	74	292
	Ray Floyd	72	73	79	68	292
	Gary Player	72	74	73	73	292
	Victor Regalado	76	72	72	72	292
	Bert Yancey	74	71	74	73	292

Round Leader(s)
R1　Nichols; 67
R2　Nicklaus; 135
R3　Weiskopf; 207

Lowest Scores
R2　Nicklaus; 67
R3　Miller; 65
R4　Irwin; 64

US OPEN 1975

Medinah Country Club, Medinah, Illinois
(19–23 June)
7032 yards: Par 71 (284)

With three strokes covering the first 11 players home, a play-off was perhaps inevitable. Frank Beard led by three going into the final round from Tom Watson and Pat Fitzsimmons, but all played Round Four poorly allowing John Mahaffey through to tie with Lou Graham, who took a one-over five at the last. Graham steadied himself for the play-off to win his only Major. Unusually, Jack Nicklaus dropped a shot at each of the last three holes, and fell back into the pack.

1	**LOU GRAHAM***	74	72	68	73	287
	($40000)					
2	John Mahaffey	73	71	72	71	287
3=	Frank Beard	74	69	67	78	288
	Ben Crenshaw	70	68	76	74	288
	Hale Irwin	74	71	73	70	288
	Bob Murphy	74	73	72	69	288
7=	Jack Nicklaus	72	70	75	72	289
	Peter Oosterhuis	69	73	72	75	289
9=	Pat Fitzsimons	67	73	73	77	290
	Arnold Palmer	69	75	73	73	290
	Tom Watson	67	68	78	77	290
12=	Ray Floyd	76	71	72	72	291
	Andy North	75	72	72	72	291
14=	Joe Inman, Jr	72	72	71	77	292
	Rik Massengale	71	74	71	76	292
	Eddie Pearce	75	71	70	76	292
	Jim Wiechers	68	73	76	75	292
18=	Terry Dill	72	69	77	75	293
	Hubert Green	74	73	68	78	293
	Gary Groh	73	74	73	73	293
	Jay Haas (a)	74	69	72	78	293
	Grier Jones	69	73	79	72	293
	Jerry Pate (a)	79	70	72	72	293
24=	Buddy Allin	76	70	73	75	294
	Miller Barber	74	71	71	78	294
	Dale Douglass	71	77	72	74	294
	Forrest Fezler	73	75	71	75	294
	Kermit Zarley	73	71	75	75	294
29=	Tommy Aaron	73	71	82	69	295
	David Graham	71	76	74	74	295
	Jerry Heard	77	67	78	73	295
	Don January	75	71	74	75	295
	Steve Melnyk	75	73	74	73	295
	Ed Sneed	75	74	73	73	295
	Nate Starks	75	72	76	72	295
	Lee Trevino	72	75	73	75	295
	Tom Weiskopf	75	71	74	75	295

* Lou Graham (71) beat John Mahaffey (73) in the 18-Hole Play-off

Round Leader(s)
R1　Fitzsimons, Watson; 67
R2　Watson; 135
R3　Beard; 210

Lowest Scores
R2　Heard; 67
R3　Beard; 67
R4　Aaron, Murphy; 69

BRITISH OPEN 1975

Carnoustie Golf Club, Angus, Scotland
(9–12 July)
7065 yards: Par 72 (288)

After succumbing to final round pressures in the US Open the previous month, and blowing up at Winged Foot in 1974, there was something of a question mark over Tom Watson's credentials when it came to converting winning positions into wins in Major Championships. There was always going to be something different about seaside golf for Watson, however – especially in Scotland – as he became only the third American after Ben Hogan and Tony Lema to play the British Open (and its particular links-land game) 'blind', and win at the first attempt. Jack Newton conceded seven shots to Watson over the last 36 holes, to allow the play-off which Watson narrowly won. With attendances increasing every year, it was felt that the facilities offered by Carrnoustie were not up to scratch, and there was a real fear that what Gary Player described as the greatest golf course in the world would be lost to the roster forever. New creature comforts were (rather belatedly) put in place for it to rejoin the Open roadshow in 1999.

1	TOM WATSON*	71	67	69	72	279
	(£7500)					
2	Jack Newton	69	71	75	74	279
3=	Bobby Cole	72	66	66	76	280
	Johnny Miller	71	69	66	74	280
	Jack Nicklaus	69	71	68	72	280
6	Graham Marsh	72	67	71	71	281
7=	Neil Coles	72	69	67	74	282
	Peter Oosterhuis	68	70	71	73	282
9	Hale Irwin	69	70	69	75	283
10=	George Burns	71	73	69	71	284
	John Mahaffey	71	68	69	76	284
12=	Bob Charles	74	73	70	69	286
	Paul Leonard	70	69	73	74	286
	Andries Oosthuizen	69	69	70	78	286
15	Tom Weiskopf	73	72	70	72	287
16=	Maurice Bembridge	75	73	67	73	288
	Arnold Palmer	74	72	69	73	288
	Alan Tapie	70	72	67	79	288
19=	Bernard Gallacher	72	67	72	78	289
	Lon Hinckle	76	72	69	72	289
	Tommy Horton	72	71	71	75	289
	Sam Torrance	72	74	71	72	289
23=	Brian Barnes	71	74	72	73	290
	Hugh Baiocchi	72	72	73	73	290
	Danny Edwards	70	74	71	75	290
	Ray Floyd	71	72	76	71	290
	Martin Foster	72	74	73	71	290
28=	Roberto de Vicenzo	71	74	72	74	291
	David Graham	74	70	72	75	291
	Simon Hobday	70	70	76	75	291
	Guy Hunt	73	68	76	74	291

* Tom Watson (71) beat Jack Newton (72) in the 18-Hole Play-off

Round Leader(s)
R1 Oosterhuis; 68
R2 Cole, Oosterhuis, Oosthuizen, Watson; 138
R3 Cole; 204

Lowest Scores
R2 Cole; 66
R3 Newton; 65
R4 Charles; 69

US PGA 1975

Firestone Country Club, Akron, Ohio
(7–10 August)
7180 yards: Par 70 (280)

Jack Nicklaus, who else, became the first person to do the Masters-PGA double in the same year twice. Sam Snead and Jack Burke Jr were the only other players to achieve the feat once. Playing steady golf based on an overnight four-shot lead, Nicklaus coasted to his 14th Major, ahead of Bruce Crampton – runner up to Jack for the fourth time in a Major Championship. Crampton had the consolation of setting a new low of 63, however – the best in the PGA – and matched Johnny Miller, in the 1973 US Open, to tie for the all-time low round score in a Major to date.

1	JACK NICKLAUS	70	68	67	71	276
	($45000)					
2	Bruce Crampton	71	63	75	69	278
3	Tom Weiskopf	70	71	70	68	279
4	Andy North	72	74	70	65	281
5=	Billy Casper	69	72	72	70	283
	Hale Irwin	72	65	73	73	283
7=	Dave Hill	71	71	74	68	284
	Gene Littler	76	71	66	71	284
9	Tom Watson	70	71	71	73	285
10=	Buddy Allin	73	72	70	71	286
	Ben Crenshaw	73	72	71	70	286
	Ray Floyd	70	73	72	71	286
	David Graham	72	70	70	74	286
	Don January	72	70	71	73	286
	John Schlee	71	68	75	72	286
	Leonard Thompson	74	69	72	71	286
17=	Dale Douglass	74	72	74	67	287
	Gibby Gilbert	73	70	77	67	287
	Mike Hill	72	71	70	74	287
	Steve Melnyk	71	72	74	70	287
	Gil Morgan	73	71	71	72	287
22=	Ed Dougherty	69	70	72	77	288
	Mark Hayes	67	71	75	75	288
	Chi Chi Rodriguez	73	72	74	69	288
25=	Jerry Heard	75	70	70	74	289
	Mac McLendon	73	71	70	75	289
	Bob Murphy	75	68	69	77	289
28=	Larry Hinson	68	73	72	77	290
	John Mahaffey	71	70	75	74	290
	JC Snead	73	67	75	75	290
	Bob Wynn	69	69	80	72	290

Round Leader(s)
R1 Hayes; 67
R2 Crampton; 134
R3 Nicklaus; 205

Lowest Scores
R2 Crampton; 63
R3 Littler; 66
R4 North; 65

THE MASTERS 1976

Augusta National Golf Club, Augusta, Georgia
(8–11 April)

6925 yards: Par 72 (288)

Ray Floyd's second Major came as a result of spectacular scoring at Augusta. In tying Jack Nicklaus' all-time low for the Masters (and any Major Championship) he set new 36-and 54-hole record scores, to win by eight – only one shot less than Jack's 1965 margin. At the end of Round Three Floyd led Nicklaus by eight, but as the latter faded, and Ben Crenshaw charged, he held firm to maintain the same gap.

1	**RAY FLOYD**	65	66	70	70	271
	($40000)					
2	Ben Crenshaw	70	70	72	67	279
3=	Jack Nicklaus	67	69	73	73	282
	Larry Ziegler	67	71	72	72	282
5=	Charles Coody	72	69	70	74	285
	Hale Irwin	71	77	67	70	285
	Tom Kite	73	67	72	73	285
8	Billy Casper	71	76	71	69	287
9=	Roger Maltbie	72	75	70	71	288
	Graham Marsh	73	68	75	72	288
	Tom Weiskopf	73	71	70	74	288
12=	Jim Colbert	71	72	74	72	289
	Lou Graham	68	73	72	76	289
	Gene Littler	71	72	74	72	289
15=	Al Geiberger	75	70	73	73	291
	Dave Hill	69	73	76	73	291
	Jerry McGee	71	73	72	75	291
	Curtis Strange (a)	71	76	73	71	291
19=	Buddy Allin	69	76	72	75	292
	Bruce Devlin	77	69	72	74	292
	Hubert Green	71	66	78	77	292
	Dale Hayes	75	74	73	70	292
23=	Gay Brewer	75	74	71	73	293
	Rik Massengale	70	72	78	73	293
	Johnny Miller	71	73	74	75	293
	Peter Oosterhuis	76	74	75	68	293
27	Bruce Crampton	74	76	71	73	294
28=	Bob Murphy	72	74	76	73	295
	Eddie Pearce	71	71	79	74	295
	Gary Player	73	73	70	79	295
	Lee Trevino	75	75	69	76	295
	Art Wall	74	71	75	75	295

Round Leader(s)
R1 Floyd; 65
R2 Floyd; 131
R3 Floyd; 201

Lowest Scores
R2 Floyd, Green; 66
R3 Irwin; 67
R4 Crenshaw; 67

US OPEN 1976

Atlanta Athletic Club, Altanta, Georgia
(17–20 June)

7015 yards: Par 70 (280)

Spectators, numbering more than 100000 for the four days for the first time, witnessed Jerry Pate play golf of a consistently high standard to win from 1966 PGA Champion, Al Geiberger, and the British Open Champion of 1973, Tom Weiskopf. After Nicklaus in 1962, Pate, at 22, was the youngest US Open winner since Bobby Jones in 1923.

1	**JERRY PATE**	71	69	69	68	277
	($42000)					
2=	Al Geiberger	70	69	71	69	279
	Tom Weiskopf	73	70	68	68	279
4=	Butch Baird	71	71	71	67	280
	John Mahaffey	70	68	69	73	280
6	Hubert Green	72	70	71	69	282
7	Tom Watson	74	72	68	70	284
8=	Ben Crenshaw	72	68	72	73	285
	Lyn Lott	71	71	70	73	285
10	Johnny Miller	74	72	69	71	286
11=	Rod Funseth	70	70	72	75	287
	Jack Nicklaus	74	70	75	68	287
13	Ray Floyd	70	75	71	72	288
14=	Mark Hayes	74	74	70	71	289
	Don January	71	74	69	75	289
	Mike Morley	71	71	70	77	289
	Andy North	74	72	69	74	289
	JC Snead	73	69	71	76	289
19=	Danny Edwards	73	75	70	72	290
	Randy Glover	72	74	76	68	290
21=	Dave Eichelberger	73	70	74	74	291
	Larry Nelson	75	74	70	72	291
21=	Dave Eichelberger	73	70	74	74	291
	Larry Nelson	75	74	70	72	291
23=	Joe Inman	75	73	74	70	292
	Calvin Peete	76	69	74	73	292
	Gary Player	72	77	73	70	292
26=	Hale Irwin	75	72	75	71	293
	Tom Jenkins	72	74	75	72	293
28=	Lou Graham	75	74	72	73	294
	Barry Jaeckel	74	77	69	74	294
	Grier Jones	76	69	71	78	294
	Wayne Levi	74	73	74	73	294
	Bob E Smith	72	75	74	73	294

Round Leader(s)
R1 Mike Reid (a, 50); 67
R2 Mahaffey; 138
R3 Mahaffey; 207

Lowest Scores
R2 Mahaffey, Crenshaw; 68
R3 Weiskopf, Watson; 68
R4 Baird; 67

BRITISH OPEN 1976

Royal Birkdale Golf Club, Southport, Lancashire, England
(7–10 July)
7001 yards: Par 72 (288)

Johnny Miller became the 13th winner of both Opens, first achieved by Harry Vardon when he claimed the US Open in 1900. In doing so he pulled away from the exciting, erratic Spaniard – the 19 year-old Severiano Ballesteros – with a blistering last round 66. Over the final 36 holes Miller played sensible, percentage golf: he used his one iron off the tee no fewer than 21 times. His achievement, however, almost took a back seat to Ballesteros' antics. Flirting with the Birkdale dunes, his scrambling brilliance was shown to the world for the first time. This was no ordinary golfer.

1	**JOHNNY MILLER**	72	68	73	66	279
	(£7500)					
2=	Seve Ballesteros	69	69	73	74	285
	Jack Nicklaus	74	70	72	69	285
4	Ray Floyd	76	67	73	70	286
5=	Hubert Green	72	70	78	68	288
	Tommy Horton	74	69	72	73	288
	Mark James	76	72	74	66	288
	Tom Kite	70	74	73	71	288
	Christy O'Connor, Jr	69	73	75	71	288
10=	George Burns	75	69	75	70	289
	Peter Butler	74	72	73	70	289
	Vicente Fernandez	79	71	69	70	289
	Norio Suzuki	69	75	75	70	289
14	Brian Barnes	70	73	75	72	290
15=	Eamonn Darcy	78	71	71	71	291
	John Fourie	71	74	75	71	291
17=	Graham Marsh	71	73	72	76	292
	Jack Newton	70	74	76	72	292
	Tom Weiskopf	73	72	76	71	292
	Guy Wolstenholme	76	72	71	73	292
21=	Stewart Ginn	78	72	72	71	293
	David Graham	77	70	75	71	293
	Simon Hobday	79	71	75	68	293
	Chi-San Hsu	81	69	71	72	293
	David Huish	73	74	72	74	293
	Bob Shearer	76	73	75	69	293
	Alan Tapie	74	72	75	72	293
28=	Neil Coles	74	77	70	73	294
	Nick Faldo	78	71	76	69	294
	Gary Player	72	72	79	71	294
	Doug Sanders	77	73	73	71	294

Round Leader(s)
R1 Ballesteros, O'Connor, Suzuki; 69
R2 Ballesteros; 138
R3 Ballesteros; 211

Lowest Scores
R2 Floyd; 67
R3 Fernandez; 69
R4 James, Miller; 66

US PGA 1976

Congressional CC, Bethesda, Maryland
(12–16 August – rain affected)
7054 yards: Par 70 (280)

Dave Stockton won the PGA Championship for the second time. He repeated his 1970 success by holing an awkward ten-foot putt for par at the last, to avoid a play-off with the 1967 and 1969 Champions. Congressional was at its meanest – denying par over 72 holes to any competitor.

1	**DAVE STOCKTON**	70	72	69	70	281
	($45000)					
2=	Ray Floyd	72	68	71	71	282
	Don January	70	69	71	72	282
4=	David Graham	70	71	70	72	283
	Jack Nicklaus	71	69	69	74	283
	Jerry Pate	69	73	72	69	283
	John Schlee	72	71	70	70	283
8=	Charles Coody	68	72	67	77	284
	Ben Crenshaw	71	69	74	70	284
	Jerry McGee	68	72	72	72	284
	Gil Morgan	66	68	75	75	284
	Tom Weiskopf	65	74	73	72	284
13=	Tom Kite	66	72	73	75	286
	Gary Player	70	69	72	75	286
15=	Lee Elder	68	74	70	75	287
	Mark Hayes	69	72	73	73	287
	Mike Hill	72	70	73	72	287
	Mike Morley	69	72	72	74	287
	Arnold Palmer	71	76	68	72	287
	JC Snead	74	71	70	72	287
	Tom Watson	70	74	70	73	287
22=	Lou Graham	74	70	70	74	288
	Jerry Heard	72	74	69	73	288
	Dave Hill	76	66	75	71	288
	Joe Inman Jr	72	69	74	73	288
	Gene Littler	71	69	73	75	288
	Don Massengale	71	74	73	70	288
	Leonard Thompson	73	69	72	74	288
29	Joe Porter	72	71	70	76	289
30=	Hubert Green	73	70	73	74	290
	Grier Jones	71	70	75	74	290
	Rik Massengale	71	72	73	74	290
	Bob Zender	69	71	73	77	290

Round Leader(s)
R1 Weiskopf; 65
R2 Morgan; 134
R3 Coody; 207

Lowest Scores
R2 Hill; 66
R3 Coody; 67
R4 Pate; 69

THE MASTERS 1977

Augusta National Golf Club, Augusta, Georgia
(7–10 April)
6925 yards: Par 72 (288)

Reigning British Open Champion, Tom Watson, won his second Major in under a year, when he beat off a challenge from Jack Nicklaus in a spree of spectacular low-scoring on the final day. Nicklaus' sequence of scores in the Majors before this event and following his success in the 1973 PGA, were as follows: 4, 10, 3, 2, W, 7, 3, W, 3, 11, 2, 4 – recording an amazing consistency, and posing a threat at every Championship. Watson's 20-foot birdie putt at 17 sealed his victory.

1	**TOM WATSON**	70	69	70	67	276
	($40000)					
2	Jack Nicklaus	72	70	70	66	278
3=	Tom Kite	70	73	70	67	280
	Rik Massengale	70	73	67	70	280
5	Hale Irwin	70	74	70	68	282
6=	David Graham	75	67	73	69	284
	Lou Graham	75	71	69	69	284
8=	Ben Crenshaw	71	69	69	76	285
	Ray Floyd	71	72	71	71	285
	Hubert Green	67	74	72	72	285
	Don January	69	76	69	71	285
	Gene Littler	71	72	73	69	285
	John Schlee	75	73	69	68	285
14=	Billy Casper	72	72	73	69	286
	Jim Colbert	72	71	69	74	286
	Rod Funseth	72	67	74	73	286
	Jerry Pate	70	72	74	70	286
	Tom Weiskopf	73	71	71	71	286
19=	George Archer	74	74	69	70	287
	Andy Bean	74	70	71	72	287
	Danny Edwards	72	74	68	73	287
	Lee Elder	76	68	72	71	287
	Gary Player	71	70	72	74	287
24=	Billy Kratzert	69	71	78	70	288
	Andy North	74	74	71	69	288
	Arnold Palmer	76	71	71	70	288
	Bob Wynn	75	73	70	70	288
28=	Isao Aoki	73	76	70	70	289
	Bruce Lietzke	73	71	72	73	289
	Jerry McGee	73	73	72	71	289

Round Leader(s)
R1   Green; 67
R2   Funseth, Watson; 139
R3   Crenshaw, Watson; 209

Lowest Scores
R2   Funseth, Graham, Bob Shearer (37); 67
R3   Massengale; 67
R4   Nicklaus; 66

US OPEN 1977

Southern Hills Country Club, Tulsa, Oklahoma
(16–19 June)
6873 yards: Par 70 (280)

Hubert Green hung on to a lead he'd had since the first day to squeeze out 1975 Champion, Lou Graham, whose record-equalling last 36 holes took him to within one of a tie. Shooting birdie-par-bogey over the last 3 holes, Green just about handled the pressure to stay ahead of Graham, already waiting nervously in the Clubhouse.

1	**HUBERT GREEN**	69	67	72	70	278
	($45000)					
2	Lou Graham	72	71	68	68	279
3	Tom Weiskopf	71	71	68	71	281
4	Tom Purtzer	69	69	72	72	282
5=	Jay Haas	72	68	71	72	283
	Gary Jacobsen	73	70	67	73	283
7=	Terry Diehl	69	68	73	74	284
	Lyn Lott	73	72	71	67	284
	Tom Watson	74	72	71	67	284
10=	Rod Funseth	69	70	72	74	285
	Al Geiberger	70	71	75	69	285
	Mike McCullough	73	73	69	70	285
	Jack Nicklaus	74	68	71	72	285
	Peter Oosterhuis	71	70	74	70	285
	Gary Player	72	67	71	75	285
16=	Wally Armstrong	71	70	70	75	286
	Joe Inman, Jr	70	70	72	74	286
	Steve Melnyk	70	73	70	73	286
19=	Bill Kratzert	73	69	75	70	287
	Bruce Lietzke	74	68	71	74	287
	Jerry McGee	76	69	76	66	287
	Arnold Palmer	70	72	73	72	287
23=	Sam Adams	70	69	76	73	288
	Andy Bean	71	70	68	79	288
	Ron Streck	73	73	71	71	288
26	Gay Brewer	73	72	70	74	289
27=	George Archer	73	72	74	71	290
	Tom Kite	71	73	70	76	290
	John Lister	72	73	68	77	290
	Johnny Miller	71	73	70	76	290
	Mike Morley	70	73	74	73	290
	Don Padgett	70	74	66	80	290
	JC Snead	72	75	68	75	290
	Lee Trevino	74	70	73	73	290

Round Leader(s)
R1   Diehl, Funseth, Green, Grier Jones (35), Florentino Molina (39), Larry Nelson (54), Purtzer; 69
R2   Green; 136
R3   Green; 208

Lowest Scores
R2   Green, Player, Jim Simons (35); 67
R3   Padgett; 66
R4   McGee; 66

BRITISH OPEN 1977

Turnberry GC, Ayrshire, Scotland
(6-9 July)
6875 yards: Par 70 (280)

The Open came to Turnberry, a few miles south of Prestwick and Troon, for the first time, and the Ailsa course with its dramatic sea views saw more than its fair share of drama on the links. Some argue that this was the best-ever Open, perhaps the best-ever Major. Tom Watson defended his title and became the fifth player to do the Masters-British Open double in the same year – following no lesser lights than Hogan, Palmer, Nicklaus (twice, of course) and Player. His 268, in a wonderfully stirring two-horse race with Nicklaus, beat the Championship record by eight shots and lowered Jack's, Bobby Nichols' and Ray Floyd's record score for any Major. Watson also set a new low of 130 for 36-holes. Nicklaus, until Augusta earlier in the year, was not used to seeing a rival withstand the kind of pressure he was putting on Watson: in the end was bested by his young compatriot. Even so, much of a private duel was this titanic struggle, Jack's second place was ten shots clear of US Open Champion, Hubert Green. Mark Hayes' 63 was a new Championship low and tied with Johnny Miller's and Bruce Crampton's record for any Major.

1	**TOM WATSON**	68	70	65	65	268
	(£10000)					
2	Jack Nicklaus	68	70	65	66	269
3	Hubert Green	72	66	74	67	279
4	Lee Trevino	68	70	72	70	280
5=	George Burns	70	70	72	69	281
	Ben Crenshaw	71	69	66	75	281
7	Arnold Palmer	73	73	67	69	282
8	Ray Floyd	70	73	68	72	283
9=	Mark Hayes	76	63	72	73	284
	Tommy Horton	70	74	65	75	284
	Johnny Miller	69	74	67	74	284
	John Schroeder	66	74	73	71	284
13=	Howard Clark	72	68	72	74	286
	Peter Thomson	74	72	67	73	286
15=	Seve Ballesteros	69	71	73	74	287
	Peter Butler	71	68	75	73	287
	Bobby Cole	72	71	71	73	287
	Guy Hunt	73	71	71	72	287
	Graham Marsh	73	69	71	74	287
	Jerry Pate	74	70	70	73	287
	Bob Shearer	72	69	72	74	287
22=	Peter Dawson	74	68	73	73	288
	John Fourie	74	69	70	75	288
	Gary Player	71	74	74	69	288
	Tom Weiskopf	74	71	71	72	288
26=	Gaylord Burrows	69	72	68	80	289
	Martin Foster	67	74	75	73	289
	Angel Gallardo	78	65	72	74	289
	David Ingram	73	74	70	72	289
	Roger Maltbie	71	66	72	80	289
	Rik Massengale	73	71	74	71	289
	John O'Leary	74	73	68	74	289
	Norio Suzuki	74	71	69	75	289

Round Leader(s)
R1   Schroeder; 66
R2   Maltbie; 137
R3   Nicklaus, Watson; 203

Lowest Scores
R2   Hayes; 63
R3   Horton; 65
R4   Watson; 65

US PGA 1977

Pebble Beach Golf Links, Pebble Beach, California
(11-14 August)
6804 yards: Par 72 (288)

In the first-ever sudden-death play-off employed in any Major, Lanny Wadkins won his only Major when he beat 1961 US Open Champion, Gene Littler. The tie was somewhat presented to Wadkins, who, five shots adrift at the turn, saw Littler bogey five of the next six holes – and Jack Nicklaus, who was then tying with Littler, dropped a shot at the 17th. Wadkins then drew level with Littler by shooting the only birdie of his round at the last.

1	**LANNY WADKINS***	69	71	72	70	282
	($45000)					
2	Gene Littler	67	69	70	76	282
3	Jack Nicklaus	69	71	70	73	283
4	Charles Coody	70	71	70	73	284
5	Jerry Pate	73	70	69	73	285
6=	Al Geiberger	71	70	73	72	286
	Lou Graham	71	73	71	71	286
	Don January	75	69	70	72	286
	Jerry McGee	68	70	77	71	286
	Tom Watson	68	73	71	74	286
11=	Joe Inman, Jr	72	69	73	73	287
	Johnny Miller	70	74	73	70	287
13=	Tom Kite	73	73	70	72	288
	Lee Trevino	71	73	71	73	288
15=	George Cadle	69	73	70	77	289
	Bruce Lietzke	74	70	74	71	289
	Gil Morgan	74	68	70	77	289
	Leonard Thompson	72	73	69	75	289
19=	George Archer	70	73	76	72	291
	George Burns	71	76	70	74	291
	Mark Hayes	68	75	74	74	291
	Arnold Palmer	72	73	73	73	291
	John Schroeder	73	76	68	74	291
	JC Snead	76	71	72	72	291
25=	Miller Barber	77	68	69	78	292
	Grier Jones	72	74	72	74	292
	Bill Kratzert	71	76	75	70	292
	Lyn Lott	76	75	67	74	292
	Bob Murphy	72	72	72	76	292
	Jim Simons	74	74	69	75	292

* Lanny Wadkins beat Gene Littler at the 3rd extra hole in Sudden Death Play-off

Round Leader(s)
R1   Littler; 67
R2   Littler; 136
R3   Littler; 206

Lowest Scores
R2   Morgan, Barber; 68
R3   Danny Edwards (36), Lott; 67
R4   Kratzert, Miller, Wadkins; 70

THE MASTERS 1978

Augusta National Golf Club, Augusta, Georgia
(6–9 April)

6925 yards: Par 72 (288)

Gary Player, aged 42, won his ninth and last Major Championship at the Masters, thus drawing level with Ben Hogan to tie third on the all-time list. His first Major was back in 1959 when he lifted the British Open title at Muirfield, and his span of wins matched the 20 years of JH Taylor (1894–1913). Seven birdies over the last ten holes turned back the clock and set up his third Masters win – an improbable result when Hubert Green was defending a seven-shot lead after Round Three, and went round the last 18 holes in par. Tommy Nakajima of Japan shot a 13 at the 13th. Unlucky for some, perhaps: certainly for accident-prone Tommy. He missed the cut.

1	**GARY PLAYER**	72	72	69	64	277
	($45000)				
2=	Rod Funseth	73	66	70	69	278
	Hubert Green	72	69	65	72	278
	Tom Watson	73	68	68	69	278
5=	Wally Armstrong	72	70	70	68	280
	Billy Kratzert	70	74	67	69	280
7	Jack Nicklaus	72	73	69	67	281
8	Hale Irwin	73	67	71	71	282
9=	David Graham	75	69	67	72	283
	Joe Inman, Jr	69	73	72	69	283
11=	Don January	72	70	72	70	284
	Jerry McGee	71	73	71	69	284
	Tom Weiskopf	72	71	70	71	284
14=	Peter Oosterhuis	74	70	70	71	285
	Lee Trevino	70	69	72	74	285
16=	Ray Floyd	76	71	71	68	286
	Lindy Miller (a)	74	71	70	71	286
18=	Seve Ballesteros	74	71	68	74	287
	Tom Kite	71	74	71	71	287
	Gil Morgan	73	73	70	71	287
	Jerry Pate	72	71	72	72	287
	Ed Sneed	74	70	70	73	287
	Lanny Wadkins	74	70	73	70	287
24=	Miller Barber	75	67	73	73	288
	Andy Bean	76	68	73	71	288
	Gene Littler	72	68	70	78	288
	Leonard Thompson	72	69	75	72	288
28	Bobby Cole	77	70	70	72	289
29=	Gay Brewer	73	71	69	77	290
	Mac McLendon	72	72	72	74	290
	Bill Rogers	76	70	68	76	290

Round Leader(s)
R1 John Schlee (44); 68
R2 Funseth, Trevino; 139
R3 Green; 206

Lowest Scores
R2 Funseth; 66
R3 Green; 65
R4 Player; 64

US OPEN 1978

Cherry Hills Country Club, Denver, Colorado
(15–18 June)

7083 yards: Par 71 (284)

No one beat par at Cherry Hills. Andy North went to four under par after seven holes on the last day, a lead of five, with the benefit of two birdies. Then the next few holes saw some eccentric scoring from him: bogey, bogey, bogey, birdie, birdie, bogey, double-bogey! Despite that he still maintained a diminishing lead. At the 15th it was cut to just one stroke when Dave Stockton birdied, but Stockton's own bogey at the 18th meant North only needed the same to win. He duly obliged.

1	**ANDY NORTH**	70	70	71	74	285
	($45000)				
2=	JC Snead	70	72	72	72	286
	Dave Stockton	71	73	70	72	286
4=	Hale Irwin	69	74	75	70	288
	Tom Weiskopf	77	73	70	68	288
6=	Andy Bean	72	72	71	74	289
	Bill Kratzert	72	74	70	73	289
	Johnny Miller	78	69	68	74	289
	Jack Nicklaus	73	69	74	73	289
	Gary Player	71	71	70	77	289
	Tom Watson	74	75	70	70	289
12=	Ray Floyd	75	70	76	70	291
	Joe Inman, Jr	72	72	74	73	291
	Mike McCullough	75	75	73	68	291
	Lee Trevino	72	71	75	73	291
16=	Seve Ballesteros	75	69	71	77	292
	Artie McNickle	74	75	70	73	292
	Jerry Pate	73	72	74	73	292
	Bob Shearer	78	72	71	71	292
20=	Wally Armstrong	73	73	74	73	293
	Phil Hancock	71	73	75	74	293
	Tom Kite	73	73	70	77	293
	Bruce Lietzke	72	73	72	76	293
24=	Dale Douglass	74	75	74	72	295
	Tom Purtzer	75	72	72	76	295
	Victor Regalado	74	72	73	76	295
27=	Jerry McGee	74	76	71	75	296
	Pat McGowan	74	73	72	77	296
	Peter Oosterhuis	72	72	78	74	296
30=	Billy Casper	71	76	73	77	297
	Bobby Clampett (a)	70	73	80	84	297
	Charles Coody	74	76	76	71	297
	Rod Curl	78	72	74	73	297
	Lee Elder	76	73	73	75	297

Round Leader(s)
R1 Irwin; 69
R2 North; 140
R3 North; 211

Lowest Scores
R2 Ballesteros, Nicklaus, Miller, Bill Rogers (44); 69
R3 Miller; 68
R4 McCullough, Weiskopf; 68

BRITISH OPEN 1978

Royal & Ancient Golf Club, St Andrews, Fife, Scotland
(12–15 July)
6933 yards: Par 72 (288)

It was totally fitting that Jack Nicklaus should win what was to be his last Open Championship at the Home of Golf. It was his 15th Major and his first for three years; and it presented him with a record that may never be beaten (Mr Woods may disagree!). He became the only player to win each of the Grand Slam titles three times or more; and still no-one else apart from Sarazen, Hogan and Player have achieved the feat even once. New Zealander Simon Owen, building on his Round Three 67, took the lead when he chipped in at the 15th. At this point he was playing the best golf of the round, and an upset seemed likely. Then he dropped two shots over the last three holes to tie second. After his disaster in the Masters, Nakajima effectively put himself out of contention when he took nine at the 17th (Road Hole) in the third round.

1	**JACK NICKLAUS**	71	72	69	69	281
	(£12500)				
2=	Ben Crenshaw	70	69	73	71	283
	Ray Floyd	69	75	71	68	283
	Tom Kite	72	69	72	70	283
	Simon Owen	70	75	67	71	283
6	Peter Oosterhuis	72	70	69	73	284
7=	Isao Aoki	68	71	73	73	285
	Nick Faldo	71	72	70	72	285
	John Schroeder	74	69	70	72	285
	Bob Shearer	71	69	74	71	285
11=	Michael Cahill	71	72	75	68	286
	Dale Hayes	74	70	71	71	286
	Orville Moody	73	69	74	70	286
14=	Mark Hayes	70	75	75	67	287
	Jumbo Ozaki	72	69	75	71	287
	Tom Watson	73	68	70	76	287
17=	Seve Ballesteros	69	70	76	73	288
	Bob Byman	72	69	74	73	288
	Guy Hunt	71	73	71	73	288
	Tommy Nakajima	70	71	76	71	288
	Tom Weiskopf	69	72	72	75	288
22=	Bernard Gallacher	72	71	76	70	289
	Nick Job	73	75	68	73	289
24=	Antonio Garrido	73	71	76	70	290
	Hale Irwin	75	71	76	78	290
	Carl Mason	70	74	72	74	290
	Jack Newton	69	76	71	74	290
	Peter Thomson	72	70	72	76	290
29=	Tienie Britz	73	74	72	72	291
	Hubert Green	78	70	67	76	291
	John Morgan	74	68	77	72	291
	Greg Norman	72	73	74	72	291
	Lee Trevino	75	72	73	71	291

Round Leader(s)
R1   Aoki; 68
R2   Aoki, Crenshaw; 139
R3   Aoki, Crenshaw, Nicklaus, Oosterhuis; 212

Lowest Scores
R2   Morgan, Watson; 68
R3   Owen; 67
R4   Hayes; 67

US PGA 1978

Oakmont CC, Oakmont, Pennsylvania
(3–6 August)
6989 yards: Par 72 (284)

Trailing Tom Watson by seven strokes going into the last round, John Mahaffey shot a 66 to tie with him and Jerry Pate for a play-off. He then birdied the second extra hole to win the first three-way sudden-death play-off, and his only Majors title. This was the first strokeplay PGA Championship hosted by Oakmont CC, but two were held there in matchplay days – and five US Opens to that date. This made Oakmont the most-used venue for Majors in the US after Augusta National.

1	**JOHN MAHAFFEY***	75	67	68	66	276
	($50000)				
2=	Jerry Pate	72	70	66	68	276
	Tom Watson	67	69	67	73	276
4=	Gil Morgan	76	71	66	67	280
	Tom Weiskopf	73	67	69	71	280
6	Craig Stadler	70	74	67	71	282
7=	Andy Bean	72	72	70	70	284
	Graham Marsh	72	74	68	70	284
	Lee Trevino	69	73	70	74	284
10	Fuzzy Zoeller	75	69	73	68	285
11	Joe Inman, Jr	72	68	69	77	286
12=	Hale Irwin	73	71	73	70	287
	Bill Kratzert	70	77	73	67	287
	Larry Nelson	76	71	70	70	287
	John Schroeder	76	69	70	72	287
16=	Ben Crenshaw	69	71	75	73	288
	Phil Hancock	70	73	70	75	288
	Grier Jones	70	73	71	74	288
19=	Wally Armstrong	71	73	75	70	289
	George Burns	79	68	70	72	289
	Bob Gilder	74	71	70	74	289
	Don January	73	72	75	69	289
	Bobby Nichols	75	67	73	74	289
	Dave Stockton	68	75	74	72	289
	Kermit Zarley	75	71	67	76	289
26=	George Cadle	74	74	74	68	290
	Rod Curl	76	72	73	70	290
	Hubert Green	71	71	74	74	290
	Peter Oosterhuis	73	72	72	73	290
	Gary Player	76	72	71	71	290
	Greg Powers	75	70	75	70	290
	Bob Shearer	73	73	71	73	290
	Bob Zender	73	69	74	74	290

* John Mahaffey beat Jerry Pate and Tom Watson at the 2nd extra hole in the Sudden Death Play-off

Round Leader(s)
R1   Watson; 67
R2   Watson; 136
R3   Watson; 203

Lowest Scores
R2   George Archer (61), Mahaffey, Nichols, Weiskopf; 67
R3   Morgan, Pate; 66
R4   Mahaffey; 66

THE MASTERS 1979

Augusta National Golf Club, Augusta, Georgia
(12–15 April)
6925 yards: Par 72 (288)

Frank Urban (Fuzzy) Zoeller wrote himself into the record books with his first Major triumph, by winning the first-ever sudden-death play-off in the Masters. He also collected the first $50000 winner's prize at Augusta, although the 1978 PGA Championship claims that for the first Major. Ed Sneed saw fame and glory dissipate after squandering a five-stroke lead at the start of the day. Even after the 15th he was still three clear, but three bogeys necessitated a play-off. For Tom Watson, following the afore-mentioned 1978 PGA Championship, it was his second successive three-way sudden-death play-off; but he was to be no luckier at the Masters. Zoeller's birdie at the second extra hole saw to that.

1	**FUZZY ZOELLER***	70	71	69	70	280
	($50000)					
2=	Ed Sneed	68	67	69	76	280
	Tom Watson	68	71	70	71	280
4	Jack Nicklaus	69	71	72	69	281
5	Tom Kite	71	72	68	72	283
6	Bruce Lietzke	67	75	68	74	284
7=	Craig Stadler	69	66	74	76	285
	Leonard Thompson	68	70	73	74	285
	Lanny Wadkins	73	69	70	73	285
10=	Hubert Green	74	69	72	71	286
	Gene Littler	74	71	69	72	286
12=	Seve Ballesteros	72	68	73	74	287
	Miller Barber	75	64	72	76	287
	Jack Newton	70	72	69	76	287
	Andy North	72	72	74	69	287
	Lee Trevino	73	71	70	73	287
17=	Lee Elder	73	70	74	71	288
	Ray Floyd	70	68	73	77	288
	Billy Kratzert	73	68	71	76	288
	Artie McNickle	71	72	74	71	288
	Gary Player	71	72	74	71	288
22	JC Snead	73	71	72	73	289
23=	Bobby Clampett	73	71	73	73	290
	Lou Graham	69	71	76	74	290
	Joe Inman, Jr	68	71	76	75	290
	Hale Irwin	72	70	74	74	290
	Jim Simons	72	70	75	73	290
28=	Tommy Aaron	72	73	76	70	291
	Andy Bean	69	74	74	74	291
	Graham Marsh	71	72	73	75	291

* Fuzzy Zoeller beat Ed Sneed and Tom Watson at the second extra hole of the Sudden-death Play-off

Round Leader(s)
R1 Lietzke; 67
R2 Sneed, Stadler; 135
R3 Sneed; 204

Lowest Scores
R2 Barber; 64
R3 Kite, Lietzke; 68
R4 Nicklaus, North; 69

US OPEN 1979

Inverness Golf Club, Toledo, Ohio
(14–17 June)
6982 yards: Par 71 (284)

Hale Irwin was the only player to meet par over the tough 72 holes at Inverness. It was enough to give him another US Open title to add to his victory of 1974. Leading Tom Weiskopf by three overnight, he had extended his advantage to five by the 16th. Then the wheels almost came off. At the 17th, bunkered and two-putting, he carded a double-bogey six, then found sand again at the last, to limp home finally just two ahead.

1	**HALE IRWIN**	74	68	67	75	284
	($50000)					
2=	Jerry Pate	71	74	69	72	286
	Gary Player	73	73	72	68	286
4=	Larry Nelson	71	68	76	73	288
	Bill Rogers	71	72	73	72	288
	Tom Weiskopf	71	74	67	76	288
7	David Graham	73	73	70	73	289
8	Tom Purtzer	70	69	75	76	290
9=	Keith Fergus	70	77	72	72	291
	Jack Nicklaus	74	77	72	68	291
11=	Ben Crenshaw	75	71	72	75	293
	Lee Elder	74	72	69	78	293
	Andy North	77	74	68	74	293
	Calvin Peete	72	75	71	75	293
	Ed Sneed	72	73	75	73	293
16=	Bob Gilder	77	70	69	78	294
	Graham Marsh	77	71	72	74	294
	Jim Simons	74	74	78	68	294
19=	Al Geiberger	74	74	69	78	295
	Lee Trevino	77	73	73	72	295
	Lanny Wadkins	73	74	71	77	295
	Bobby Walzel	74	72	71	78	295
	DA Weibring	74	76	71	74	295
24	Hubert Green	74	77	73	72	296
25=	Andy Bean	70	76	71	80	297
	Lou Graham	70	75	77	75	297
	Wayne Levi	77	73	75	72	297
	Bob Murphy	72	79	69	77	297
	Bobby Nichols	76	75	71	75	297
	Mike Reid	74	75	74	74	297
	Bob E Smith	77	71	69	80	297

Round Leader(s)
R1 Bean, Fergus, Graham, Purtzer; 70
R2 Nelson, Purtzer; 139
R3 Irwin; 209

Lowest Scores
R2 Irwin, Nelson; 68
R3 Irwin, Weiskopf; 67
R4 Nicklaus, Player, Simons; 68

BRITISH OPEN 1979

Royal Lytham and St Anne's Golf Club, Lancashire, England
(18–21 July)
6822 yards: Par 71 (284)

Ballesteros' victory at Lytham will not be remembered for the first Open Championship to be won by a continental European since Arnaud Massy in 1907, but for the manner in which it was won. A new star in the ascendant, the flamboyant Spaniard was aggressive and headstrong, foolish and cavalier in his approach to the game: and he announced himself to the world, displaying all those characteristics in just 18 holes on Saturday 21 July 1979. Bashing his way from rough to sand, to car park to green, with scant regard for the fairway – only replacing brute strength with sublime touch when he neared his destination – Seve broke the hearts of Crenshaw and Nicklaus. As much as past icons like Ouimet, Jones, Hogan, Palmer or Nicklaus, he was changing the face of golf once again: and European golf, and an unprecedented pan-European golfing unity, was stirring.

1	**SEVE BALLESTEROS**	73	65	75	70	283
	(£15000)					
2=	Ben Crenshaw	72	71	72	71	286
	Jack Nicklaus	72	69	73	72	286
4	Mark James	76	69	69	73	287
5	Rodger Davis	75	70	70	73	288
6	Hale Irwin	68	68	75	78	289
7=	Isao Aoki	70	74	72	75	291
	Bob Byman	73	70	72	76	291
	Graham Marsh	74	68	75	74	291
10=	Bob Charles	78	72	70	72	292
	Greg Norman	73	71	72	76	292
	Jumbo Ozaki	75	69	75	73	292
13=	Wally Armstrong	74	74	73	72	293
	Terry Gale	71	74	75	73	293
	John O'Leary	73	73	74	73	293
	Simon Owen	75	76	74	68	293
17=	Peter McEvoy (a)	71	74	72	77	294
	Lee Trevino	71	73	74	76	294
19=	Ken Brown	72	71	75	77	295
	Nick Faldo	74	74	78	69	295
	Sandy Lyle	74	76	75	70	295
	Orville Moody	71	74	76	74	295
	Gary Player	77	74	69	75	295
24=	Tony Jacklin	73	74	76	73	296
	Tohru Nakamura	77	75	67	77	296
26=	Jerry Pate	69	74	76	78	297
	Ed Sneed	76	75	70	76	297
	Peter Thomson	76	75	72	74	297
	Tom Watson	72	68	76	81	297
30=	Mark Hayes	75	75	77	71	298
	Simon Hobday	75	77	71	75	298
	Tom Kite	73	74	77	74	298
	Bill Longmuir	65	74	77	82	298
	Armando Saavedra	76	76	73	73	298
	Bobby Verwey	75	77	74	72	298

Round Leader(s)
R1   Longmuir; 65
R2   Irwin; 136
R3   Irwin; 211

Lowest Scores
R2   Ballesteros; 65
R3   Nakamura; 67
R4   Owen; 68

US PGA 1979

Oakland Hills CC, Birmingham, Michigan
(2–5 August)
7014 yards: Par 70 (280)

David Graham became the second Australian, after Jim Ferrier in 1947, to take the PGA Championship. With play-offs coming thick and fast in recent Majors, this PGA was no exception; but while Ben Crenshaw played beautifully for his Round Four 67, Graham's 65 could have been a 63 (he double-bogeyed the last), and no play-off would have been necessary. Graham then sank two very-missable putts before birdieing the third extra hole for victory. This was Crenshaw's fourth second place in a Major, and second in succession, and was spoken of at the time as the best golfer around never to have won such a coveted title.

1	**DAVID GRAHAM***	69	68	70	65	272
	($60000)					
2	Ben Crenshaw	69	67	69	67	272
3	Rex Caldwell	67	70	66	71	274
4	Ron Streck	68	71	69	68	276
5=	Gibby Gilbert	69	72	68	69	278
	Jerry Pate	69	69	69	71	278
7=	Jay Haas	68	69	73	69	279
	Don January	69	70	71	69	279
	Howard Twitty	70	73	69	67	279
10=	Lou Graham	69	74	68	69	280
	Gary Koch	71	71	71	67	280
12=	Andy Bean	76	69	68	68	281
	Jerry McGee	73	69	71	68	281
	Jack Renner	71	74	66	70	281
	Tom Watson	66	72	69	74	281
16=	Bob Gilder	73	71	68	70	282
	Hubert Green	69	70	72	71	282
	Bruce Lietzke	69	69	71	73	282
	Gene Littler	71	71	67	73	282
	Graham Marsh	69	70	71	72	282
21=	Bob Byman	73	72	69	69	283
	John Schroeder	72	72	70	69	283
23=	Frank Conner	70	73	69	72	284
	Rod Funseth	70	69	76	69	284
	Peter Jacobsen	70	74	67	73	284
	Gary Player	73	70	70	71	284
	Alan Tapie	73	65	76	70	284
28=	Miller Barber	73	72	69	71	285
	George Burns	71	74	67	73	285
	Mark McCumber	75	68	70	72	285
	Artie McNickle	69	70	72	74	285
	Gil Morgan	72	73	70	70	285
	Larry Nelson	70	75	70	70	285
	Ed Sneed	77	67	70	71	285

* David Graham beat Ben Crenshaw at 3rd extra hole in Sudden Death Play-off

Round Leader(s)
R1   Watson; 66
R2   Crenshaw; 136
R3   Caldwell; 203

Lowest Scores
R2   Tapie; 65
R3   Caldwell, Renner; 66
R4   D Graham; 65

THE MASTERS 1980

Augusta National Golf Club, Augusta, Georgia
(10–13 April)

6925 yards: Par 72 (288)

Seve Ballesteros led the Masters by ten strokes going into the back nine on the last day. Typically, the flawed genius made some unspeakable errors coming home, so that in the end his lead was cut to four. If he had just parred in from the turn, the Masters low total was his for the taking. But that was not the Ballesteros way. As it was, Seve's second Major was his first in the US and, after leading wire-to-wire, he became, at 23, the youngest winner of the Masters to that time, taking away just one record from Jack Nicklaus.

1	**SEVE BALLESTEROS** ($55000)	66	69	68	72	275
2=	Gibby Gilbert	70	74	68	67	279
	Jack Newton	68	74	69	68	279
4	Hubert Green	68	74	71	67	280
5	David Graham	66	73	72	70	281
6=	Ben Crenshaw	76	70	68	69	283
	Ed Fiori	71	70	69	73	283
	Tom Kite	69	71	74	69	283
	Larry Nelson	69	72	73	69	283
	Jerry Pate	72	68	76	67	283
	Gary Player	71	71	71	70	283
12=	Andy Bean	74	72	68	70	284
	Tom Watson	73	69	71	71	284
14=	Jim Colbert	72	70	70	73	285
	Jack Renner	72	70	72	71	285
	JC Snead	73	69	69	74	285
17=	Ray Floyd	75	70	74	67	286
	Jay Haas	72	74	70	70	286
19=	Billy Kratzert	73	69	72	73	287
	Gil Morgan	74	71	75	67	287
	Calvin Peete	73	71	76	67	287
	Jim Simons	70	70	72	75	287
	Fuzzy Zoeller	72	70	70	75	287
24=	Andy North	70	72	69	77	288
	Arnold Palmer	73	73	73	69	288
26=	Keith Fergus	72	71	72	74	289
	Lou Graham	71	74	71	73	289
	Jay Sigel (a)	71	71	73	74	289
	Craig Stadler	74	70	72	73	289
	Dave Stockton	74	70	76	69	289
	Lee Trevino	74	71	70	74	289

Round Leader(s)
R1 Ballesteros, Graham, Jeff Mitchell (41); 66
R2 Ballesteros; 135
R3 Ballesteros; 203

Lowest Scores
R2 Rex Caldwell (38); 66
R3 Ballesteros, Bean, Crenshaw, Gilbert; 68
R4 Floyd, Gilbert, Green, Morgan, Pate, Peete; 67

US OPEN 1980

Baltusrol GC, Springfield, New Jersey
(12–15 June)

7076 yards: Par 70 (280)

1980 was to be Jack Nicklaus' last really big year in Major Championships. Tom Watson's year-round play on the US Tour had been superior to Jack's for the last three seasons, but now turning 40, he honed himself pre-season for one last assault on the Majors. After disappointing in the Masters, he won the Open for the fourth time and joined the ranks of Willie Anderson, Bobby Jones and Ben Hogan, setting a new low total in the process. This included a 63, which tied Johnny Miller (1973) and Tom Weiskopf (in Round One) on the US Open record round score.

1	**JACK NICKLAUS** ($55000)	63	71	70	68	272
2	Isao Aoki	68	68	68	70	274
3=	Keith Fergus	66	70	70	70	276
	Lon Hinkle	66	70	69	71	276
	Tom Watson	71	68	67	70	276
6=	Mark Hayes	66	71	69	74	280
	Mike Reid	69	67	75	69	280
8=	Hale Irwin	70	70	73	69	282
	Mike Morley	73	68	69	72	282
	Andy North	68	75	72	67	282
	Ed Sneed	72	70	70	70	282
12=	Bruce Devlin	71	70	70	72	283
	Joe Hager	72	70	71	70	283
	Lee Trevino	68	72	69	74	283
	Bobby Wadkins	72	71	68	72	283
16=	Joe Inman, Jr	74	69	69	72	284
	Pat McGowan	69	69	73	73	284
	Gil Morgan	73	70	70	71	284
	Bill Rogers	69	71	70	73	284
	Craig Stadler	73	67	69	75	284
	Curtis Strange	69	74	71	70	284
22=	Gary Hallberg (a)	74	68	70	73	285
	Peter Jacobsen	70	69	72	74	285
	Jim Simons	70	72	71	72	285
	JC Snead	69	71	73	72	285
26=	Jay Haas	67	74	70	75	286
	Mark Lye	68	72	77	69	286
28=	George Burns	75	69	73	70	287
	David Edwards	73	68	72	74	287
	John Mahaffey	72	73	69	73	287
	Calvin Peete	67	76	74	70	287

Round Leader(s)
R1 Nicklaus; 63
R2 Nicklaus; 134
R3 Aoki, Nicklaus; 204

Lowest Scores
R2 Reid, Stadler; 67
R3 Hubert Green (32); 65
R4 North; 67

BRITISH OPEN 1980

Hon Co of Edinburgh Golfers, Muirfield, East Lothian, Scotland
(17–20 July)
6892 yards: Par 71 (284)

Tom Watson collected his third Open on Scottish links (all different) ahead of a resurgent Lee Trevino, and the nearly-man of the time, Ben Crenshaw. Eight Americans, an Englishman, a Scotsman and an Australian made up the Top 10 and tie. Watson's fourth Major rubber-stamped the contention that he was the best player in the world in 1980. Finally, after lagging so far behind for so much of the century, the Open was accorded almost parity in prize money with its American counterparts. Twenty years previously, that would have been unthinkable.

1	**TOM WATSON** (£25000)	68	70	64	69	271
2	Lee Trevino	68	67	71	69	275
3	Ben Crenshaw	70	70	68	69	277
4=	Carl Mason	72	69	70	69	280
	Jack Nicklaus	73	67	71	69	280
6=	Andy Bean	71	69	70	72	282
	Ken Brown	70	68	68	76	282
	Hubert Green	77	69	64	72	282
	Craig Stadler	72	70	69	71	282
10=	Gil Morgan	70	70	71	72	283
	Jack Newton	69	71	73	70	283
12=	Isao Aoki	74	74	63	73	284
	Nick Faldo	69	74	71	70	284
	Sandy Lyle	70	71	70	73	284
	Larry Nelson	72	70	71	71	284
16=	John Bland	73	70	70	73	285
	Jerry Pate	71	67	74	73	285
	Tom Weiskopf	72	72	71	70	285
19=	Seve Ballesteros	72	68	72	74	286
	Bruce Lietzke	74	69	73	70	286
	Bill Rogers	76	73	68	69	286
	Norio Suzuki	74	68	72	72	286
23=	Gary Cullen	72	72	69	74	287
	Bill McColl	75	73	68	71	287
	Mark McNulty	71	73	72	71	287
	Peter Oosterhuis	72	71	75	69	287
27=	Tom Kite	72	72	74	70	288
	Nick Price	72	71	71	74	288
29=	Hugh Baiocchi	76	67	69	77	289
	Neil Coles	75	69	69	76	289
	David Graham	73	71	68	77	289

Round Leader(s)
R1 Trevino, Watson; 68
R2 Trevino; 135
R3 Watson; 202

Lowest Scores
R2 Horacio Carbonetti (Cut); 64
R3 Aoki; 63
R4 Crenshaw, Mason, Nicklaus, Oosterhuis, Rogers, Trevino, Watson; 69

US PGA 1980

Oak Hill CC, Rochester, New York
(7–10 August)
6964 yards: Par 70 (280)

Gene Sarazen in 1922 was the only man in history to win both American National Championships – the US Open and the US PGA – in the same season. 58 years later, the feat was eventually emulated by Jack Nicklaus. Jack thus added yet another record, or share of a record, to his name. He stretched his lead in the all-time list with this 1980 double to 17 Majors, and tied Walter Hagen's redoubtable PGA record of five wins. As an aesthetically boring piece of PGA of America forward planning, the host site for the Championship was the third in a row to feature the King of the Forest (after Oakmont and Oakland Hills)!

1	**JACK NICKLAUS**	70	69	66	69	274
2	Andy Bean	72	71	68	70	281
3=	Lon Hinckle	70	69	69	75	283
	Gil Morgan	68	70	73	72	283
5=	Curtis Strange	68	72	72	72	284
	Howard Twitty	68	74	71	71	284
7	Lee Trevino	74	71	69	69	285
8=	Bill Rogers	71	71	72	72	286
	Bobby Walzel	68	76	71	71	286
10=	Terry Diehl	72	72	68	76	288
	Peter Jacobsen	71	73	74	70	288
	Jerry Pate	72	73	70	73	288
	Tom Watson	75	74	72	67	288
	Tom Weiskopf	71	73	72	72	288
15=	John Mahaffey	71	77	69	72	289
	Andy North	72	70	73	74	289
17=	George Archer	70	73	75	72	290
	Ray Floyd	70	76	71	73	290
	Joe Inman, Jr	72	71	75	72	290
20=	Rex Caldwell	73	70	73	75	291
	Rod Curl	74	71	75	71	291
	Tom Kite	73	70	76	72	291
	Bob Murphy	68	80	72	71	291
	Jack Newton	72	73	73	73	291
	Alan Tapie	74	75	69	73	291
26=	Lee Elder	70	75	74	73	292
	David Graham	69	75	73	75	292
	Gary Player	72	74	71	75	292
	Leonard Thompson	71	75	73	73	292
30=	Jim Colbert	73	75	77	68	293
	Bruce Devlin	76	73	71	73	293
	Bob Eastwood	72	73	73	75	293
	David Edwards	73	76	73	71	293
	Hale Irwin	69	76	74	74	293
	Bruce Lietzke	71	75	74	73	293
	Artie McNickle	71	71	76	75	293
	Scott Simpson	74	74	74	71	293
	Mike Sullivan	71	74	76	72	293
	Doug Tewell	73	71	75	74	293
	Lanny Wadkins	76	72	72	73	293

Round Leader(s)
R1 Craig Stadler (55); 67
R2 Morgan; 138
R3 Nicklaus; 205

Lowest Scores
R2 Ed Sneed (55); 66
R3 Nicklaus; 66
R4 Watson; 67

THE MASTERS 1981

Augusta National Golf Club, Augusta, Georgia
(9–12 April)
6925 yards: Par 72 (288)

Tom Watson's contemporary superiority over Jack Nicklaus continued into 1981, when he won the first Major of the year at Augusta. A Round Three 75 undid Jack, who held a four-shot lead after 36 holes, and he had to settle for second place with Johnny Miller. This win was Watson's second Green Jacket and fifth Major overall.

1	**TOM WATSON**	71	68	70	71	280
	($60000)					
2=	Johnny Miller	69	72	73	68	282
	Jack Nicklaus	70	65	75	72	282
4	Greg Norman	69	70	72	72	283
5=	Tom Kite	74	72	70	68	284
	Jerry Pate	71	72	71	70	284
7	David Graham	70	70	74	71	285
8=	Ben Crenshaw	71	72	70	73	286
	Ray Floyd	75	71	71	69	286
	John Mahaffey	72	71	69	74	286
11=	George Archer	74	70	72	71	287
	Hubert Green	70	70	74	73	287
	Peter Jacobsen	71	70	72	74	287
	Bruce Lietzke	72	67	73	75	287
15=	Gay Brewer	75	68	71	74	288
	Bob Gilder	72	75	69	72	288
	Gary Player	73	73	71	71	288
	Jim Simons	70	75	71	72	288
19=	Don Pooley	71	75	72	71	289
	Curtis Strange	69	79	70	71	289
21=	John Cook	70	71	72	77	290
	Gil Morgan	74	73	70	73	290
	Calvin Peete	75	70	71	74	290
	Lanny Wadkins	72	71	71	76	290
25=	Jim Colbert	73	68	74	76	291
	Hale Irwin	73	74	70	74	291
	Wayne Levi	72	71	73	75	291
28=	Gibby Gilbert	71	71	76	74	292
	Lon Hinkle	69	70	74	79	292
	Sandy Lyle	73	70	76	73	292

Round Leader(s)
R1 Hinckle, Miller, Norman, Strange; 69
R2 Nicklaus; 135
R3 Watson; 209

Lowest Scores
R2 Nicklaus; 65
R3 Gilder, Mahaffey; 69
R4 Kite, Miller; 68

US OPEN 1981

Merion Golf Club, Ardmore, Pennsylvania
(18–21 June)
6544 yards: Par 70 (280)

David Graham added the US Open to the PGA Championship he picked up in 1979. He became the first Australian to win the US Open and the first overseas player since Tony Jacklin in 1970. Turning a three-stroke deficit going into the last day into a victory by the same margin, thanks to a fine 67, he turned the tables on George Burns who had led from Round Two.

1	**DAVID GRAHAM**	68	68	70	67	273
	($55000)					
2=	George Burns	69	66	68	73	276
	Bill Rogers	70	68	69	69	276
4=	John Cook	68	70	71	70	279
	John Schroeder	71	68	69	71	279
6=	Frank Conner	71	72	69	68	280
	Lon Hinkle	69	71	70	70	280
	Jack Nicklaus	69	68	71	72	280
	Sammy Rachels	70	71	69	70	280
	Chi Chi Rodriguez	68	73	67	72	280
11=	Isao Aoki	72	71	71	67	281
	Ben Crenshaw	70	75	64	72	281
	Jim Thorpe	66	73	70	72	281
14=	Mark Hayes	71	70	72	69	282
	Calvin Peete	73	72	67	70	282
	Lanny Wadkins	71	68	72	71	282
17=	Bruce Lietzke	70	71	71	71	283
	Jack Renner	68	71	72	72	283
	Curtis Strange	71	69	72	71	283
20=	Tom Kite	73	74	67	70	284
	Larry Nelson	70	73	69	72	284
	Mike Reid	71	72	69	72	284
23=	Johnny Miller	69	71	73	72	285
	Scott Simpson	72	67	71	75	285
	Tom Watson	70	69	73	73	285
26=	Jim Colbert	71	69	77	69	286
	Bruce Devlin	73	71	70	72	286
	Rik Massengale	70	75	70	71	286
	Jerry Pate	70	69	72	75	286
	Gary Player	72	72	71	71	286
	Craig Stadler	71	76	68	71	286
	Tom Valentine	69	68	72	77	286

Round Leader(s)
R1 Thorpe; 66
R2 Burns; 135
R3 Burns; 203

Lowest Scores
R2 Burns; 66
R3 Crenshaw; 64
R4 Aoki, Graham; 67

BRITISH OPEN 1981

Royal St George's Golf Club, Sandwich, Kent, England
(16–19 July)
6857 yards: Par 70 (280)

The Open returned to Sandwich after a break of 32 years. Bill Rogers, who had finished strongly to tie for second in the US Open the previous month, played the best golf of his life to win on a links course at his first attempt – as had Hogan, Lema and Watson before him. His strength lay in the middle rounds, enabling him to take a five-shot lead into the last 18, and comfortably hold off two young European hopefuls, Langer and James – and double-Majors winner Floyd, who was never to get closer than this in the Open.

1	**BILL ROGERS**	72	66	67	71	276
	(£25000)					
2	Bernhard Langer	73	67	70	70	280
3=	Ray Floyd	74	70	69	70	283
	Mark James	72	70	68	73	283
5=	Sam Torrance	72	69	73	70	284
	Bruce Lietzke	76	69	71	69	285
	Manuel Pinero	73	74	68	70	285
8=	Howard Clark	72	76	70	68	286
	Ben Crenshaw	72	67	76	71	286
	Brian Jones	73	76	66	71	286
11=	Isao Aoki	71	73	69	74	287
	Nick Faldo	77	68	69	73	287
	Lee Trevino	77	67	70	73	287
14=	Brian Barnes	76	70	70	72	288
	Eamonn Darcy	79	69	70	70	288
	David Graham	71	71	74	72	288
	Nick Job	70	69	75	74	288
	Sandy Lyle	73	73	71	71	288
19=	Gordon J Brand	78	65	74	72	289
	Graham Marsh	75	71	72	71	289
	Jerry Pate	73	73	69	74	289
	Peter Townsend	73	70	73	73	289
23=	Hubert Green	75	72	74	69	290
	Tony Jacklin	71	71	73	75	290
	Mark McNulty	74	74	74	68	290
	Jack Nicklaus	83	66	71	70	290
	Simon Owen	71	74	70	75	290
	Arnold Palmer	72	74	73	71	290
	Nick Price	77	68	76	69	290
	Tom Watson	73	69	75	73	290

Round Leader(s)
R1 Job; 70
R2 Rogers; 138
R3 Rogers; 205

Lowest Scores
R2 Nicklaus, Rogers; 66
R3 Jones; 66
R4 Clark, McNulty; 68

US PGA 1981

Atlanta Athletic Club, Duluth, Atlanta, Georgia
(6–9 August)
7070 yards: PAR 70 (280)

Vietnam veteran Larry Nelson won his first Major at the Atlanta Athletic Club – just a few minutes from his front door. He hung on to Bob Murphy's coat-tails as Murphy blazed away with a 66, 69 start, then pulled away from the field with a 66 of his own to take a lead of four over Fuzzy Zoeller. He maintained the differential over the final round to cruise home.

1	**LARRY NELSON**	70	66	66	71	273
	($60000)					
2	Fuzzy Zoeller	70	68	68	71	277
3	Dan Pohl	69	67	73	69	278
4=	Isao Aoki	75	68	66	70	279
	Keith Fergus	71	71	69	68	279
	Bob Gilder	74	69	70	76	279
	Tom Kite	71	67	69	72	279
	Bruce Lietzke	70	70	71	68	279
	Jack Nicklaus	71	68	71	69	279
	Greg Norman	73	67	68	71	279
11=	Vance Heafner	68	70	70	72	280
	Andy North	68	69	70	73	280
	Jerry Pate	71	68	70	71	280
	Tommy Valentine	73	70	71	66	280
15	JC Snead	70	71	70	70	281
16=	David Edwards	71	69	70	72	282
	Hale Irwin	71	74	68	69	282
18	Bob Murphy	66	69	73	75	283
19=	John Cook	72	69	70	73	284
	Ray Floyd	71	70	71	72	284
	Jay Haas	73	68	74	69	284
	Joe Inman, Jr	73	71	67	73	284
	Don January	70	72	70	72	284
	Gil Morgan	70	69	74	71	284
	Don Pooley	74	70	69	71	284
	Tom Purtzer	70	70	73	71	284
27=	Bobby Clampett	75	71	70	69	285
	Hubert Green	71	74	71	69	285
	Peter Jacobsen	74	71	71	69	285
	Bill Rogers	72	75	66	72	285
	Curtis Strange	73	72	74	66	285
	Tom Weiskopf	71	72	72	70	285

Round Leader(s)
R1 Murphy; 66
R2 Murphy; 135
R3 Nelson; 202

Lowest Scores
R2 Nelson; 66
R3 Aoki, Nelson, Rogers; 66
R4 Gilder, Strange, Valentine; 66

THE MASTERS 1982

Augusta National Golf Club, Augusta, Georgia
(8–11 April)
6925 yards: Par 72 (288)

Craig Stadler answered the $64000 question when he defeated Dan Pohl in the sudden-death play-off. He was being asked it all through the second half of the Tournament as Pohl, who shot an anonymous 150 for the first 36, then tore up the golf course with two 67s. He made up six shots on the 'Walrus', but Stadler clung on for a tie, steadied himself, and prevailed in overtime to claim his only Major victory.

1	**CRAIG STADLER***	75	69	67	73	284
	($64000)					
2	Dan Pohl	75	75	67	67	284
3=	Seve Ballesteros	73	73	68	71	285
	Jerry Pate	74	73	67	71	285
5=	Tom Kite	76	69	73	69	287
	Tom Watson	77	69	70	71	287
7=	Ray Floyd	74	72	69	74	289
	Larry Nelson	79	71	70	69	289
	Curtis Strange	74	70	73	72	289
10=	Andy Bean	75	72	73	70	290
	Mark Hayes	74	73	73	70	290
	Tom Weiskopf	75	72	68	75	290
	Fuzzy Zoeller	72	76	70	72	290
14	Bob Gilder	79	71	66	75	291
15=	Yakata Hagawa	75	74	71	72	292
	Jack Nicklaus	69	77	71	75	292
	Gary Player	74	73	71	74	292
	Jim Simons	77	74	69	72	292
19	David Graham	73	77	70	73	293
20=	Peter Jacobsen	78	75	70	71	294
	Bruce Lietzke	76	75	69	74	294
	Jodie Mudd (a)	77	74	67	76	294
	Jack Renner	72	75	76	71	294
24=	Ben Crenshaw	74	80	70	71	295
	Danny Edwards	75	74	74	72	295
	Morris Hatalsky	73	77	75	70	295
	Wayne Levi	77	76	72	70	295
	Peter Oosterhuis	73	74	75	73	295
	John Schroeder	77	71	70	77	295
30=	George Archer	79	74	72	71	296
	Calvin Peete	77	72	73	74	296

* Craig Stadler beat Dan Pohl in the Sudden-death Play-off

Round Leader(s)
R1   Nicklaus; 69
R2   Stadler, Strange; 144
R3   Stadler; 211

Lowest Scores
R2   Kite, Stadler, Watson; 69
R3   Gilder; 66
R4   Pohl; 67

US OPEN 1982

Pebble Beach Golf Links, Pebble Beach, California
(17–20 June)
6815 yards: Par 72 (288)

Watson's penchant for seaside golf, and delight in keeping Jack Nicklaus at bay, was doubly manifested at Pebble Beach. His first, and only US Open, was won after another momentous struggle between the two great golfers; and was only settled at the 17th, when Tom memorably pitched in for a birdie. He birdied the last for good measure and undid Jack once more, just as he had done at Augusta and Turnberry in 1977. Only the PGA Championship stood in his way from becoming, at the time, only the fifth player to win all the Major titles. Unfortunately, as another has since achieved it in the comparative twinkling of an eye, Tom would seem to be timed out on this final quest. Another record was set, however, for the number of entries filed, taking the figure over 5000 for the first time.

1	**TOM WATSON**	72	72	68	70	282
	($60000)					
2	Jack Nicklaus	74	70	71	69	284
3=	Bobby Clampett	71	73	72	70	286
	Dan Pohl	72	74	70	70	286
	Bill Rogers	70	73	69	74	286
6=	David Graham	73	72	69	73	287
	Jay Haas	75	74	70	68	287
	Gary Koch	78	73	69	67	287
	Lanny Wadkins	73	76	67	71	287
10=	Bruce Devlin	70	69	75	74	288
	Calvin Peete	71	72	72	73	288
12=	Chip Beck	76	75	69	69	289
	Danny Edwards	71	75	73	70	289
	Lyn Lott	72	71	75	71	289
15=	Larry Rinker	74	67	75	74	290
	Scott Simpson	73	69	72	76	290
	JC Snead	73	75	71	71	290
	Fuzzy Zoeller	72	76	71	71	290
19=	Ben Crenshaw	76	74	68	73	291
	Larry Nelson	74	72	74	71	291
	Hal Sutton	73	76	72	70	291
22=	Mike Brannan	75	74	71	72	292
	Joe Hager	78	72	72	70	292
	Gene Littler	74	75	72	71	292
	John Mahaffey	77	72	70	73	292
	Gil Morgan	75	75	68	74	292
	Andy North	72	71	77	72	292
	Craig Stadler	76	70	70	76	292
29	Tom Kite	73	71	75	74	293
30=	Isao Aoki	77	74	72	71	294
	Don Bies	73	74	74	73	294
	George Burns	72	72	70	80	294
	Peter Oosterhuis	73	78	67	76	294
	Greg Powers	77	71	74	72	294
	Jack Renner	74	71	77	72	294
	Jim Thorpe	72	73	72	77	294

Round Leader(s)
R1   Devlin, Rogers; 70
R2   Devlin; 139
R3   Rogers, Watson; 212

Lowest Scores
R2   Rinker; 67
R3   Oosterhuis, Wadkins; 67
R4   Koch; 67

BRITISH OPEN 1982

Royal Troon Golf Club, Ayrshire, Scotland
(15–18 July)
7067 yards: Par 72 (288)

The Open Championship offered the richest first prize in Major Championship golf since 1894, when, of course, there were no others. Troon GC's Royal Charter in the Queen's Silver Jubilee year of 1977, That year Tom Watson won his second British Open 20 miles down the coast at Turnberry, and in 1982 collected his fourth – all at different Scottish courses. Watson, seven behind a self-destructing Bobby Clampett at half-way, and four adrift of Nick Price going out on the last day, maintained a champion's nerve to edge out an international pack, headed by home favourite, Oosterhuis. Tom joined the Morrises, Willie Park Sr, Walter Hagen and Bobby Locke on four wins: he also, with Bobby Jones (twice), Gene Sarazen, Ben Hogan and Lee Trevino became one of the only winners of both Opens in the same year.

1	**TOM WATSON**	69	71	74	70	284
	(£32000)					
2=	Peter Oosterhuis	74	67	74	70	285
	Nick Price	69	69	74	73	285
4=	Nick Faldo	73	73	71	69	286
	Masahiro Kuramoto	71	73	71	71	286
	Tom Purtzer	76	66	75	69	286
	Des Smyth	70	69	74	73	286
8=	Sandy Lyle	74	66	73	74	287
	Fuzzy Zoeller	73	71	73	70	287
10=	Bobby Clampett	67	66	78	77	288
	Jack Nicklaus	77	70	72	69	288
12	Sam Torrance	73	72	73	71	289
13=	Seve Ballesteros	71	75	73	71	290
	Bernhard Langer	70	69	78	73	290
15=	Ben Crenshaw	74	75	72	70	291
	Ray Floyd	74	73	77	67	291
	Curtis Strange	72	73	76	70	291
	Denis Watson	75	69	73	74	291
19	Ken Brown	70	71	79	72	292
20=	Isao Aoki	75	69	75	74	293
	Tohru Nakamura	77	68	77	71	293
22=	Jose Maria Canizares	71	72	79	72	294
	Johnny Miller	71	76	75	72	294
	Bill Rogers	73	70	76	75	294
25=	Bernard Gallacher	75	71	74	75	295
	Graham Marsh	76	76	72	71	295
27=	David Graham	73	70	76	77	296
	Jay Haas	78	72	75	71	296
	Greg Norman	73	75	76	72	296
	Arnold Palmer	71	73	78	74	296
	Lee Trevino	78	72	71	75	296

Round Leader(s)
R1   Clampett; 67
R2   Clampett; 133
R3   Clampett; 211

Lowest Scores
R2   Clampett, Lyle, Purtzer; 66
R3   Faldo, Kuramoto, Trevino; 71
R4   Floyd; 67

US PGA 1982

Southern Hills Country Club, Tulsa, Oklahoma
(5–8 August)
6862 yards: PAR 70 (280)

Raymond Floyd's third Major was also his second PGA, after a gap of 13 years – the longest wait for a second win in any single Major (shared with Gary Player's record in the Masters, 1961–74). Floyd's records were not to stop there: 63 equalled the all-time low in the PGA and any Major; 131 was a new 36-hole record for the PGA; his 200 was the low for any 54 holes in any Major; and Floyd became the only winner of the PGA wire-to-wire on more than one occasion. 52 year-old Gene Littler, the 1961 US Open Champion, shot the low score of Round Three.

1	**RAY FLOYD**	63	69	68	72	272
	($65000)					
2	Lanny Wadkins	71	68	69	67	275
3=	Fred Couples	67	71	72	66	276
	Calvin Peete	69	70	68	69	276
5=	Jay Haas	71	66	68	72	277
	Greg Norman	66	69	70	72	277
	Jim Simons	68	67	73	69	277
8	Bob Gilder	66	68	72	72	278
9=	Lon Hinkle	70	68	71	71	280
	Tom Kite	73	70	70	67	280
	Jerry Pate	72	69	70	69	280
	Tom Watson	72	69	71	68	280
13	Seve Ballesteros	71	68	69	73	281
14=	Nick Faldo	67	70	73	72	282
	Curtis Strange	72	70	71	69	282
16=	Jim Colbert	70	72	72	69	283
	Dan Halldorson	69	71	72	71	283
	Bruce Lietzke	73	71	70	69	283
	Jack Nicklaus	74	70	72	67	283
	Tom Herman	73	69	73	68	283
	Craig Stadler	71	70	70	72	283
22=	Danny Edwards	71	71	68	74	284
	Gil Morgan	76	66	68	74	284
	Peter Oosterhuis	72	72	74	66	284
	Mark Pfeil	68	73	76	67	284
	Ron Streck	71	72	71	70	284
	Doug Tewell	72	70	72	70	284
	Leonard Thompson	72	72	71	69	284
29=	Mike Holland	71	73	70	71	285
	Bill Rogers	73	71	70	71	285
	Hal Sutton	72	68	70	75	285

Round Leader(s)
R1   Floyd; 63
R2   Floyd; 132
R3   Floyd; 200

Lowest Scores
R2   Haas, Morgan; 66
R3   Gene Littler (49); 67
R4   Couples, Oosterhuis; 66

THE MASTERS 1983

Augusta National Golf Club, Augusta, Georgia
(7–11 April: Friday washed out)
6925 yards: Par 72 (288)

Ballesteros' second Masters win, and his third Major triumph, was a typical mixture of brilliance and bravura. He shot a last round 69 to overhaul the crumbling 1982 Champion Craig Stadler, and the reigning PGA Champion, Ray Floyd. Eligible 'bridesmaids', Crenshaw and Kite, were still awaiting the bouquet to be thrown in their direction. Both shot sub-70 in the last round but had too much ground to make up on the irrepressible Spaniard.

1	**SEVE BALLESTEROS**	68	70	73	69	280
	($90000)				
2=	Ben Crenshaw	76	70	70	68	284
	Tom Kite	70	72	73	69	284
4=	Ray Floyd	67	72	71	75	285
	Tom Watson	70	71	71	73	285
6=	Hale Irwin	72	73	72	69	286
	Craig Stadler	69	72	69	76	286
8=	Gil Morgan	67	70	76	74	287
	Dan Pohl	74	72	70	71	287
	Lanny Wadkins	73	70	73	71	287
11	Scott Simpson	70	73	72	73	288
12=	George Archer	71	73	71	74	289
	Wayne Levi	72	70	74	73	289
	Johnny Miller	72	72	71	74	289
	J C Snead	68	74	74	73	289
16=	Keith Fergus	70	69	74	77	290
	Tommy Nakajima	72	70	72	76	290
	Jack Renner	67	75	78	70	290
19	Isao Aoki	70	76	74	71	291
20=	Nick Faldo	70	70	76	76	292
	Mark Hayes	71	73	76	72	292
	Peter Jacobsen	73	71	76	72	292
	Peter Oosterhuis	73	69	78	72	292
	Lee Trevino	71	72	72	77	292
	Tom Weiskopf	75	72	71	74	292
	Fuzzy Zoeller	70	74	76	72	292
27=	Jay Haas	73	69	73	78	293
	Scott Hoch	74	69	74	76	293
	Hal Sutton	73	73	70	77	293
30=	Greg Norman	71	74	70	79	294
	Andy North	72	75	72	75	294

Round Leader(s)
R1   Floyd, Morgan, Renner; 67
R2   Morgan; 137
R3   Floyd, Stadler; 210

Lowest Scores
R2   Fred Couples (32), Jodie Mudd (42); 68
R3   Stadler; 69
R4   Crenshaw; 68

US OPEN 1983

Oakmont Country Club, Oakmont, Pennsylvania
(16–20 June)
6972 yards: Par 71 (284)

Larry Nelson's second Major followed his 1981 PGA triumph – but victory was far from his mind after the first 36 holes, when he was standing on 148, seven shots back, and tying for 25th place. He then broke the US Open record for 36 holes with a ten-under-par 132 – four strokes better than the previous low. Arnold Palmer equalled Gene Sarazen's record of 31 consecutive US Open appearances, and finished tied for 60th.

1	**LARRY NELSON**	75	73	65	67	280
	($72000)				
2	Tom Watson	72	70	70	69	281
3	Gil Morgan	73	72	70	68	283
4=	Seve Ballesteros	69	74	69	74	286
	Calvin Peete	75	68	70	73	286
6	Hal Sutton	73	70	73	71	287
7	Lanny Wadkins	72	73	74	69	288
8=	David Graham	74	75	73	69	291
	Ralph Landrum	75	73	69	74	291
10=	Chip Beck	73	74	74	71	292
	Andy North	73	71	72	76	292
	Craig Stadler	76	74	73	69	292
13=	Lennie Clements	74	71	75	73	293
	Ray Floyd	72	70	72	79	293
	Pat McGowan	75	71	75	72	293
	Mike Nicolette	76	69	73	75	293
	David Ogrin	75	69	75	74	293
	Scott Simpson	73	71	73	76	293
	Jim Thorpe	75	70	75	73	293
20=	Tom Kite	75	76	70	73	294
	Griff Moody	76	72	73	73	294
	Gary Player	73	74	76	71	294
	DA Weibring	71	74	80	79	294
24=	Gary Koch	78	71	72	74	295
	Tom Weiskopf	75	73	74	73	295
26=	Bob Ford	76	73	75	72	296
	Ken Green	77	73	71	75	296
	Mark Hayes	75	72	74	75	296
	Tommy Nakajima	75	74	74	73	296
	Joey Rassett	72	69	78	77	296
	Curtis Strange	74	72	78	72	296

Round Leader(s)
R1   Ballesteros, John Mahaffey (34),
       Bob Murphy (50); 69
R2   Mahaffey, Rassett; 141
R3   Ballesteros, Watson; 212

Lowest Scores
R2   Peete; 68
R3   Nelson; 65
R4   Nelson; 67

BRITISH OPEN 1983

Royal Birkdale Golf Club, Southport, Lancashire, England
(14–17 July)

6968 yards: Par 71 (284)

Playing steady golf as only he could, Tom Watson capitalized on a good start and some mistakes by Craig Stadler to take the lead after 54 holes. He was headed by Nick Faldo briefly in Round Four, but kept his game together better than the 26 year-old Englishman, who was urged on by an excited home crowd. Last round charges from Andy Bean, and twice US Open Champion, Hale Irwin, were not enough to deter Watson – nor was a new final round low for the Championship by Australian, Graham Marsh. Watson, proving he could win south of the border, joined the rarified level of five Open wins – joint-second all-time with Taylor, Braid and Thomson, and one behind Vardon. This was his eighth and last (?) Major title.

I	**TOM WATSON**	67	68	70	70	275
	(£40000)					
2=	Andy Bean	70	69	70	67	276
	Hale Irwin	69	68	72	67	276
4	Graham Marsh	69	70	74	64	277
5	Lee Trevino	69	66	73	70	278
6=	Seve Ballesteros	71	71	69	68	279
	Harold Henning	71	69	70	69	279
8=	Denis Durnian	73	66	74	67	280
	Nick Faldo	68	68	71	73	280
	Christy O'Connor, Jr	72	69	71	68	280
	Bill Rogers	67	71	73	69	280
12=	Peter Jacobsen	72	69	70	70	281
	Craig Stadler	64	70	72	75	281
14=	Ray Floyd	72	66	69	75	282
	David Graham	71	69	67	75	282
	Gary Koch	75	71	66	70	282
	Mike Sullivan	72	68	74	68	282
	Fuzzy Zoeller	71	71	67	73	282
19=	Tienie Britz	71	74	69	69	283
	Bernard Gallacher	72	71	70	70	283
	Hubert Green	69	74	72	68	283
	Jay Haas	73	72	68	70	283
	Simon Hobday	70	73	70	70	283
	Greg Norman	75	71	70	67	283
	Brian Waites	70	70	73	70	283
26=	Howard Clark	71	72	69	72	284
	Eamonn Darcy	69	72	74	69	284
	Rodger Davis	70	71	70	73	284
29=	Terry Gale	72	66	72	75	285
	Mark James	70	70	74	71	285
	Tom Kite	71	72	72	70	285
	CS Lu	71	72	74	68	285
	Mike McCullough	74	69	72	70	285
	Tohru Nakamura	73	69	72	71	285
	Jack Nicklaus	71	72	72	70	285
	Curtis Strange	74	68	70	73	285
	Hal Sutton	68	71	75	71	285
	Lanny Wadkins	72	73	72	68	285

Round Leader(s)
R1   Stadler; 64
R2   Stadler; 134
R3   Watson; 205

Lowest Scores
R2   Durnian, Floyd, Gale, Trevino; 66
R3   Koch; 66
R4   Marsh; 64

US PGA 1983

Riviera Country Club, Pacific Palisades, California
(4–7 August)

6946 yards: Par 71 (284)

The Riviera CC, scene of Hogan's and Demaret's dismantling of the US Open and all-Majors low total in 1948, was host to a Major Championship for the first time since. Although the 1948 figure was lowered, the impact on the golfing world this time around was not so great – unless of course your name was Hal Sutton. Nothing could have seemed better for Sutton, winning his first Major in the season following his 'Rookie of the Year' award; but he had to withstand heavy pressure from Nicklaus and Peter Jacobsen to win through. The winner's prize money broke through the six-figure dollar mark for the first time in any Major.

I	**HAL SUTTON**	65	66	72	71	274
	($100000)					
2	Jack Nicklaus	73	65	71	66	275
3	Peter Jacobsen	73	70	68	65	276
4	Pat McGowan	68	67	73	69	277
5	John Fought	67	69	71	71	278
6=	Bruce Lietzke	67	71	70	71	279
	Fuzzy Zoeller	72	71	67	69	279
8	Dan Pohl	72	70	69	69	280
9=	Ben Crenshaw	68	66	71	77	282
	Jay Haas	68	72	69	73	282
	Mike Reid	69	71	72	70	282
	Scott Simpson	66	73	70	73	282
	Doug Tewell	74	72	69	67	282
14=	Keith Fergus	68	70	72	73	283
	David Graham	79	69	74	70	283
	Hale Irwin	72	70	73	68	283
	Roger Maltbie	71	71	71	70	283
	Jim Thorpe	68	72	74	69	283
	Lee Trevino	70	68	74	71	283
20=	John Cook	74	71	68	71	284
	Danny Edwards	67	76	71	70	284
	Ray Floyd	69	75	71	69	284
23=	Chip Beck	72	71	70	72	285
	Fred Couples	71	70	73	71	285
	Jerry Pate	69	72	70	74	285
	Don Pooley	72	68	74	71	285
27=	Seve Ballesteros	71	76	72	67	286
	Bobby Wadkins	73	72	74	67	286
	Buddy Whitten	66	70	73	77	286
30=	Andy Bean	71	73	71	72	287
	Bob Boyd	70	77	72	68	287
	Johnny Miller	72	75	73	67	287
	Mark Pfeil	73	71	70	73	287
	Jim Simons	69	75	72	71	287
	Tom Weiskopf	76	70	69	72	287

Round Leader(s)
R1   Sutton; 65
R2   Sutton; 131
R3   Sutton; 203

Lowest Scores
R2   Nicklaus; 65
R3   Barry Jaeckel (42), Zoeller; 67
R4   Jacobsen; 65

THE MASTERS 1984

Augusta National Golf Club, Augusta, Georgia
(12–15 April)

6925 yards: Par 72 (288)

After ten Top 10 finishes, including three runners-up places, Ben Crenshaw cast off the mantle of 'best player never to have won a Major' and won the 1984 Masters by two from Tom Watson. In doing so he collected Augusta's first $100000+ prize, and left Tom Kite to wonder when it was going to happen for him. Kite held the third round lead, but disintegrated over the last day to finish five shots behind the crowd's favourite, Ben.

1	**BEN CRENSHAW**	67	72	70	68	277
	($108000)					
2	Tom Watson	74	67	69	69	279
3=	David Edwards	71	70	72	67	280
	Gil Morgan	73	71	69	67	280
5	Larry Nelson	76	69	66	70	281
6=	Ronnie Black	71	74	69	68	282
	David Graham	69	70	70	73	282
	Tom Kite	70	68	69	75	282
	Mark Lye	69	66	73	74	282
10	Fred Couples	71	73	67	72	283
11=	Rex Caldwell	71	71	69	73	284
	Wayne Levi	71	72	69	72	284
	Larry Mize	71	70	71	72	284
	Jack Renner	71	73	71	69	284
15=	Nick Faldo	70	69	70	76	285
	Ray Floyd	70	73	70	72	285
	Calvin Peete	79	66	70	70	285
18=	Andy Bean	71	70	72	73	286
	Danny Edwards	72	71	70	73	286
	Jack Nicklaus	73	73	70	70	286
21=	Jay Haas	74	71	70	72	287
	Hale Irwin	70	71	74	72	287
	Gary Player	71	72	73	71	287
	Payne Stewart	76	69	68	74	287
25=	Isao Aoki	69	72	73	74	288
	George Archer	70	74	71	73	288
	Rick Fehr (a)	72	71	70	75	288
	Peter Jacobsen	72	70	75	71	288
	Greg Norman	75	71	73	69	288
	Tom Purtzer	69	74	76	69	288

Round Leader(s)
R1   Crenshaw; 67
R2   Lye; 135
R3   Kite; 207

Lowest Scores
R2   Lye, Peete; 66
R3   Nelson; 66
R4   Edwards, Morgan; 67

US OPEN 1984

Winged Foot Golf Club, Mamaroneck, New York
(14–18 June)

6930 yards: Par 70 (280)

Fuzzy Zoeller won his second Major Championship, beating Greg Norman after 18 extra holes. The 'Fuz' led by three at the turn in regulation play, but Norman scrambled on to level terms, thanks to a birdie at 17, then a 15-yard putt to save par at the last. After such a good finish Norman should have had the upper hand psychologically for the start of the ensuing play-off, but he was mortified when Zoeller sank a putt of almost 25 yards at the second play-off hole. Norman double-bogeyed, and that was the beginning of the end for the 'Shark'. He would rue this and several other missed opportunities to win Majors in the years to come.

1	**FUZZY ZOELLER***	71	66	69	70	276
	($94000)					
2	Greg Norman	70	68	69	69	276
3	Curtis Strange	69	70	74	68	281
4=	Johnny Miller	74	68	70	70	282
	Jim Thorpe	68	71	70	73	282
6	Hale Irwin	68	68	69	79	284
7=	Peter Jacobsen	72	73	73	67	285
	Mark O'Meara	71	74	71	69	285
9=	Fred Couples	69	71	74	72	286
	Lee Trevino	71	72	69	74	286
11=	Andy Bean	70	71	75	71	287
	Jay Haas	73	73	70	71	287
	Tim Simpson	72	71	68	76	287
	Lanny Wadkins	72	71	72	72	287
	Tom Watson	72	72	74	69	287
16=	Isao Aoki	72	70	72	74	288
	Lennie Clements	69	76	72	71	288
	Mark McCumber	71	73	71	73	288
	Tom Purtzer	73	72	72	71	288
	Hal Sutton	72	72	74	70	288
21=	Chip Beck	72	74	71	72	289
	David Graham	71	72	70	76	289
	Gil Morgan	70	74	72	73	289
	Jack Nicklaus	71	71	70	77	289
25=	Bill Glasson	72	75	71	72	290
	Joe Hager	74	73	71	72	290
	Peter Oosterhuis	73	71	71	75	290
	Scott Simpson	72	75	74	69	290
	Mike Sullivan	70	73	70	77	290
30=	Jim Albus	77	69	74	71	291
	Seve Ballesteros	69	73	74	75	291
	Hubert Green	68	75	72	76	291
	John Mahaffey	72	74	77	68	291

* Fuzzy Zoeller (67) beat Greg Norman (75) in the 18-Hole Play-off

Round Leader(s)
R1   Mike Donald (34), Green, Irwin, Thorpe; 68
R2   Irwin; 136
R3   Irwin; 205

Lowest Scores
R2   Zoeller; 66
R3   Simpson; 68
R4   Jacobsen; 67

BRITISH OPEN 1984

Royal & Ancient Golf Club, St Andrews, Fife, Scotland
(19–22 July)

6933 yards: Par 72

Seve Ballesteros won his second Open to double his haul of Major wins, thereby denying Tom Watson immortality and a share in Harry Vardon's record of six Open wins. The two were neck-and-neck coming to the 17th when Ballesteros (via the rough, of course) found the green in regulation for the first time that week. The usually rock-steady Watson sent his approach over the green to within two feet of the wall abutting the road by which the 17th hole at St Andrews is named. A dropped shot here coincided with Seve's birdie at 18, and there was no way back for Tom.

1	**SEVE BALLESTEROS**	69	68	70	69	276
	(£50000)					
2=	Bernard Langer	71	68	68	71	278
	Tom Watson	71	68	66	73	278
4=	Fred Couples	70	69	74	68	281
	Lanny Wadkins	70	69	73	69	281
6=	Nick Faldo	69	68	76	69	282
	Greg Norman	67	74	74	67	282
8	Mark McCumber	74	67	72	70	283
9=	Hugh Baiocchi	72	70	70	72	284
	Ian Baker-Finch	68	66	71	79	284
	Graham Marsh	70	72	73	67	284
	Ronan Rafferty	74	72	67	71	284
	Sam Torrance	74	74	66	70	284
14=	Andy Bean	72	69	75	69	285
	Bill Bergin	75	73	66	71	285
	Ken Brown	74	71	72	68	285
	Hale Irwin	75	68	70	72	285
	Sandy Lyle	75	71	72	67	285
	Peter Senior	74	70	70	71	285
	Lee Trevino	70	67	75	73	285
	Fuzzy Zoeller	71	72	71	71	285
22=	Ben Crenshaw	72	75	70	69	286
	Peter Jacobsen	67	73	73	73	286
	Tom Kite	69	71	74	72	286
	Gil Morgan	71	71	71	73	286
	Corey Pavin	71	74	72	69	286
	Paul Way	73	72	69	72	286
28=	Terry Gale	71	74	72	70	287
	Jaime Gonzalez	69	71	76	71	287
	Craig Stadler	75	70	70	72	287

Round Leader(s)
R1 Jacobsen, Norman; 67
R2 Baker-Finch; 134
R3 Baker-Finch, Watson; 205

Lowest Scores
R2 Baker-Finch; 66
R3 Bergin, Torrance, Watson; 66
R4 Lyle, Marsh, Norman; 67

US PGA 1985

Shoal Creek Country Club, Birmingham, Alabama
(16–19 August)

7145 yards: Par 72 (288)

Lee Trevino, at 44, won his second PGA, ten years after his win at Tanglewood. In doing so he frustrated Gary Player, then 48, and prevented him from achieving his tenth Major win – even though the South African shot a PGA low of 63 in Round Two. Lanny Wadkins, Champion in 1977, fought hard against the veteran maestros, but first he, then Player, buckled under the power of Trevino's impressive play on the greens. The affable Texan walked away with the record prize for any Major. This was his sixth Major title (two Masters, two British Opens and two PGA Championships – like Sam Snead, Trevino, too, missed out in the US Open), and became 11th overall on the all-time list.

1	**LEE TREVINO**	69	68	67	69	273
	($125000)					
2=	Gary Player	74	63	69	71	277
	Lanny Wadkins	68	69	68	72	277
4	Calvin Peete	71	70	69	68	278
5	Seve Ballesteros	70	69	70	70	279
6=	Gary Hallberg	69	71	68	72	280
	Larry Mize	71	69	67	73	280
	Scott Simpson	69	69	72	70	280
	Hal Sutton	74	73	64	69	280
10=	Russ Cochran	73	68	73	67	281
	Tommy Nakajima	72	68	67	74	281
	Victor Regalado	69	69	73	70	281
13	Ray Floyd	68	71	69	74	282
14=	Hubert Green	70	74	66	73	283
	Mike Reid	68	72	72	71	283
16=	Andy Bean	69	75	70	70	284
	Donnie Hammond	70	69	71	74	284
18=	Peter Jacobsen	70	72	72	71	285
	Craig Stadler	71	73	73	68	285
20=	Fred Couples	72	72	75	67	286
	Nick Faldo	69	73	74	70	286
	Keith Fergus	72	72	72	70	286
	John Mahaffey	72	72	72	70	286
	Corey Pavin	73	72	74	67	286
25=	Chip Beck	69	77	70	71	287
	Rex Caldwell	71	71	74	71	287
	Jim Colbert	71	72	74	70	287
	Hale Irwin	71	70	74	72	287
	Jack Nicklaus	77	70	71	69	287
	Mark O'Meara	75	69	71	72	287
	Tim Simpson	73	70	72	72	287
	Doug Tewell	72	71	71	73	287

Round Leader(s)
R1 Floyd, Reid, Wadkins; 68
R2 Trevino, Wadkins; 137
R3 Trevino; 204

Lowest Scores
R2 Player; 63
R3 Sutton; 64
R4 Cochran, Couples, Pavin; 67

THE MASTERS 1985

Augusta National Golf Club, Augusta, Georgia
(11–14 April)
6925 yards: Par 72 (288)

After tying second with Tom Watson at St Andrews the previous year, Bernhard Langer became the first German, and only the third continental European (after Arnaud Massy and Ballesteros) to win a Major Championship. Seve jointly led the chasing group, but despite catching the overnight leaders Floyd and Strange, he had no answer to the German's final-round 68. In the wake of the Spaniard, the European challenge on the Majors – and the Masters, in particular – albeit piecemeal at this stage, had begun.

1	**BERNHARD LANGER**	72	74	68	68	282
	($126000)					
2=	Seve Ballesteros	72	71	71	70	284
	Ray Floyd	70	73	69	72	284
	Curtis Strange	80	65	68	71	284
5	Jay Haas	73	73	72	67	285
6=	Gary Hallberg	68	73	75	70	286
	Bruce Lietzke	72	71	73	70	286
	Jack Nicklaus	71	74	72	69	286
	Craig Stadler	73	67	76	70	286
10=	Fred Couples	75	73	69	70	287
	David Graham	74	71	71	71	287
	Lee Trevino	70	73	72	72	287
	Tom Watson	69	71	75	72	287
14=	Bill Kratzert	73	77	69	69	288
	John Mahaffey	72	75	70	71	288
16=	Isao Aoki	72	74	71	72	289
	Gary Koch	72	70	73	74	289
18=	Wayne Levi	75	72	70	73	290
	Mark McCumber	73	73	79	65	290
	Sam Randolph (a)	70	75	72	73	290
	Tim Simpson	73	72	75	70	290
	Jim Thorpe	73	71	72	74	290
	Lanny Wadkins	72	73	72	73	290
24	Mark O'Meara	73	76	72	70	291
25=	Andy Bean	72	74	73	73	292
	Nick Faldo	73	73	75	71	292
	Sandy Lyle	78	65	76	73	292
	Johnny Miller	77	68	76	71	292
	Corey Pavin	72	75	75	70	292
	Payne Stewart	69	71	76	76	292

Round Leader(s)
R1   Hallberg; 68
R2   Stadler, Stewart, Watson; 140
R3   Floyd; 212

Lowest Scores
R2   Lyle, Strange; 65
R3   Langer, Strange; 68
R4   McCumber; 65

US OPEN 1985

Oakland Hills Country Club, Birmingham, Michigan
(13–16 June)
6966 yards: Par 70 (280)

Andy North repeated his 1978 win at Cherry Hills by shakily holding off Dave Barr of Canada, and Taiwan's T-C Chen. Chen had led from the start and was four strokes clear coming to the 5th in Round Four. He looked as if he was about to be Asia's breakthrough winner in Major Championships, but then lost all his advantage with a disastrous eight. North went ahead, but bogeyed 9, 10 and 11 and slipped behind Barr. Nerves got to everybody in the run-in and all but North dropped shots up to 17. He then bogeyed the final hole, but having a two-stroke buffer at the tee, he nervously edged home.

1	**ANDY NORTH**	70	65	70	74	279
2=	Dave Barr	70	68	70	72	280
	Tze-Chung Chen	65	69	69	77	280
	Denis Watson	72	65	73	70	280
5=	Seve Ballesteros	71	70	69	71	281
	Payne Stewart	70	70	71	70	281
	Lanny Wadkins	70	72	69	70	281
8	Johnny Miller	74	71	68	69	282
9=	Rick Fehr	69	67	73	74	283
	Corey Pavin	72	68	73	70	283
	Jack Renner	72	69	72	70	283
	Fuzzy Zoeller	71	69	72	71	283
13	Tom Kite	69	70	71	74	284
14	Hale Irwin	73	72	70	70	285
15=	Andy Bean	69	72	73	72	286
	Jay Haas	69	66	77	74	286
	Greg Norman	72	71	71	72	286
	Mark O'Meara	72	67	75	72	286
	Don Pooley	73	69	73	71	286
	Tony Sills	75	70	71	70	286
	Scott Simpson	73	73	68	72	286
	Joey Sindelar	72	72	69	73	286
23=	Ray Floyd	72	67	73	75	287
	David Frost	74	68	74	71	287
	Fred Funk	75	70	72	70	287
	David Graham	73	72	74	68	287
	Gil Morgan	71	72	72	72	287
	Mike Reid	69	75	70	73	287
	Tom Sieckmann	73	73	70	71	287
	Hal Sutton	74	71	74	68	287

Round Leader(s)
R1   Chen; 65
R2   Chen; 134
R3   Chen; 203

Lowest Scores
R2   North; Watson; 65
R3   Miller, Simpson; 68
R4   Graham, Sutton; 68

BRITISH OPEN 1985

Royal St George's Golf Club, Sandwich, Kent, England
(18–21 July)
6857 yards: Par 70 (280)

Jock Hutchison and Tommy Armour excepted (who, in 1921 and 1931, were domiciled in the USA), George Duncan was the last Scotsman to win the Open Championship – in 1920. This was a desperate return for a nation which had given the world the ancient game. Then, as a consequence of the sport's resurgence in Britain and Europe – with Jacklin perhaps the catalyst, and Ballesteros very much its swash-buckling lead role – Sandy Lyle won his first Major amid patriotic scenes at St George's. With this result, Langer's win at the Masters, and the development of Faldo and the emergence of Ian Woosnam and others, the Ryder Cup – the British Isles and Europe against the Americans (since 1979) – was won for the 1st time since 1957.

1	**SANDY LYLE**	68	71	73	70	282
	(£65000)				
2	Payne Stewart	70	75	70	68	283
3=	David Graham	68	71	70	75	284
	Bernhard Langer	72	69	68	75	284
	Christy O'Connor, Jr	64	76	72	72	284
	Mark O'Meara	70	72	70	72	284
	Jose Rivero	74	72	70	68	284
8=	Anders Forsbrand	70	76	69	70	285
	Tom Kite	73	73	67	72	285
	DA Weibring	69	71	74	71	285
11=	Jose Maria Canizares	72	75	70	69	286
	Eamonn Darcy	76	68	74	68	286
	Peter Jacobsen	71	74	68	73	286
	Gary Koch	75	72	70	69	286
	Fuzzy Zoeller	69	76	70	71	286
16=	Simon Bishop	71	75	72	69	287
	Greg Norman	71	72	71	73	287
	Sam Torrance	74	74	69	70	287
	Ian Woosnam	70	71	71	75	287
20=	Ian Baker-Finch	71	73	74	70	288
	Jaime Gonzalez	72	72	73	71	288
	Mark James	71	78	66	73	288
	Graham Marsh	71	75	69	73	288
	Lee Trevino	73	76	68	71	288
25=	Gordon J Brand	73	72	72	72	289
	Michael Cahill	72	74	71	72	289
	David Frost	70	74	73	72	289
	Robert Lee	68	73	74	74	289
	Kristen Moe	70	76	73	70	289
	Jose Maria Olazabal (a)	72	76	71	70	289
	Philip Parkin	68	76	77	68	289
	Manuel Pinero	71	73	72	73	289

Round Leader(s)
R1 O'Connor; 64
R2 Graham, Lyle; 139
R3 Graham, Langer; 209

Lowest Scores
R2 Darcy; 68
R3 James; 66
R4 Darcy, Parkin, Rivero, Stewart; 68

US PGA 1985

Cherry Hills Country Club, Englewood, Denver, Colorado
(8–11 August)
7145 yards: P 72 (288)

Lee Trevino, leading at the halfway point, could not consolidate it to win back-to-back PGAs. His 75 in Round Three let in 1977 US Open Champion Hubert Green for his second Major. After eight years of anonymous performances, Green, despite his early pedigree, was not expected to win another Major title. 'They' obviously failed to tell Hubert that!

1	**HUBERT GREEN**	67	69	70	72	278
	($125000)				
2	Lee Trevino	66	68	75	71	280
3=	Andy Bean	71	70	72	68	281
	Tze-Ming Chen	69	76	71	65	281
5	Nick Price	73	73	65	71	282
6=	Fred Couples	70	65	76	72	283
	Buddy Gardner	73	73	70	67	283
	Corey Pavin	66	75	73	69	283
	Tom Watson	67	70	74	72	283
10=	Peter Jacobsen	66	71	75	72	284
	Lanny Wadkins	70	69	73	72	284
12=	Scott Hoch	70	73	73	69	285
	Tom Kite	69	75	71	70	285
	Dan Pohl	72	74	69	70	285
	Scott Simpson	72	68	72	73	285
	Payne Stewart	72	72	73	68	285
	Doug Tewell	64	72	77	72	285
18=	Bob Gilder	73	70	74	69	286
	Wayne Levi	72	69	74	71	286
	Bruce Lietzke	70	74	72	70	286
	Calvin Peete	69	72	75	70	286
	Craig Stadler	72	73	74	67	286
23=	Tze-Chung Chen	73	74	74	66	287
	John Mahaffey	74	73	71	69	287
	Larry Mize	71	70	73	73	287
	Larry Nelson	70	74	71	72	287
	Willie Wood	71	73	74	69	287
28=	Roger Maltbie	69	73	72	74	288
	Gil Morgan	69	77	72	70	288
	Mark O'Meara	71	76	71	70	288
	Joey Sindelar	71	75	71	71	288

Round Leader(s)
R1 Tewell; 64
R2 Trevino; 134
R3 Green; 206

Lowest Scores
R2 Couples; 65
R3 Price; 65
R4 Chen; 65

THE MASTERS 1986

Augusta National Golf Club, Augusta, Georgia
(10-13 April)

6925 yards: Par 72 (288)

I doubt if there was ever a more popular win in the Majors than the one achieved at Augusta by Jack Nicklaus in 1986. Then aged 46, and not having won a Major for six years, the odds on the Golden Bear picking up another title, to add to the seemingly insurmountable tally of 17, were very long indeed. Nearly-men old and new, Kite and Norman (who agonizingly bogeyed the last), were shattered by a vintage Nicklaus charge which took him to a final round 65 — and title No18. In doing so, he became the oldest winner of the Masters, and the third-oldest Major winner of all time (after Julius Boros and Tom Morris, Sr). Along the way he had collected six Masters — a record; four US Opens — a tied record; three British Opens; and five PGAs — another tied record. Looking at the winner's prize money, did Tom and Greg consider Jack's appetite for Major titles gross?

1	**JACK NICKLAUS**	74	71	69	65	279
	($144000)					
2=	Tom Kite	70	74	68	68	280
	Greg Norman	70	72	68	70	280
4	Seve Ballesteros	71	68	72	70	281
5	Nick Price	79	69	63	71	282
6=	Jay Haas	76	69	71	67	283
	Tom Watson	70	74	68	71	283
8=	Tommy Nakajima	70	71	71	72	284
	Payne Stewart	75	71	69	69	284
	Bob Tway	70	73	71	70	284
11=	Donnie Hammond	73	71	67	74	285
	Sandy Lyle	76	70	68	71	285
	Mark McCumber	76	67	71	71	285
	Corey Pavin	71	72	71	71	285
	Calvin Peete	75	71	69	70	285
16=	Dave Barr	70	77	71	68	286
	Ben Crenshaw	71	71	74	70	286
	Gary Koch	69	74	71	72	286
	Bernhard Langer	74	68	69	75	286
	Larry Mize	75	74	72	65	286
23=	Tze-Chung Chen	69	73	75	71	288
	Roger Maltbie	71	75	69	73	288
25=	Bill Glasson	72	74	72	71	289
	Peter Jacobsen	75	73	68	73	289
	Scott Simpson	76	72	67	74	289
28=	Danny Edwards	71	71	72	76	290
	David Graham	76	72	74	68	290
	Johnny Miller	74	70	77	69	290

Round Leader(s)
R1   Ken Green (44), Bill Kratzert (42); 68
R2   Ballesteros; 139
R3   Norman; 210

Lowest Scores
R2   McCumber; 67
R3   Price; 63
R4   Mize, Nicklaus; 65

US OPEN 1986

Shinnecock Hills Golf Club, Southampton, New York
(12-15 June)

6912 yards: Par 70 (280)

90 years after hosting the second National Championship, the US Open returned to a very different-looking Shinnecock Hills. Ray Floyd, 43, picked up his fourth Major title; but in this, his first US Open win, he beat Ted Ray's 66 year-old record for the being the oldest winner by some five months (and like Nicklaus in the Masters a few weeks before, found himself in the Top 10 for the oldest Majors winners). He also joined a group of only 12 players at that time to have won three different Majors — Tom Watson being the last to do so in 1982. High quality last rounds by Chip Beck and Lanny Wadkins weren't quite enough, and shooting a 66 of his own, Floyd came home two strokes ahead. 54-hole leader, Greg Norman, fell away again.

1	**RAY FLOYD**	75	68	70	66	279
	($115000)					
2=	Chip Beck	75	73	68	65	281
	Lanny Wadkins	74	70	72	65	281
4=	Hal Sutton	75	70	66	71	282
	Lee Trevino	74	68	69	71	282
6=	Ben Crenshaw	76	69	69	69	283
	Payne Stewart	76	68	69	70	283
8=	Bernhard Langer	74	70	70	70	284
	Mark McCumber	74	71	68	71	284
	Jack Nicklaus	77	72	67	68	284
	Bob Tway	70	73	69	72	284
12=	Greg Norman	71	68	71	75	285
	Denis Watson	72	70	71	72	285
14	Mark Calcavecchia	75	75	72	65	287
15=	David Frost	72	72	77	67	288
	David Graham	76	71	69	72	288
	Gary Koch	73	73	71	71	288
	Jodie Mudd	73	75	69	71	288
	Joey Sindelar	81	66	70	71	288
	Craig Stadler	74	71	74	69	288
	Scott Verplank	75	72	67	74	288
	Bobby Wadkins	75	69	72	72	288
	Fuzzy Zoeller	75	74	71	68	288
24=	Seve Ballesteros	75	73	68	73	289
	Andy Bean	76	72	73	68	289
	Lennie Clements	75	72	67	75	289
	Dave Eichelberger	80	70	72	67	289
	Larry Mize	75	71	73	70	289
	Calvin Peete	77	73	70	69	289
	Don Pooley	75	71	74	69	289
	Mike Reid	74	73	76	66	289
	Larry Rinker	77	71	70	71	289
	Tom Watson	72	71	71	75	289

Round Leader(s)
R1   Tway; 70
R2   Norman; 139
R3   Norman; 210

Lowest Scores
R2   Sindelar; 66
R3   Reid, Sutton; 66
R4   Beck, Calcavecchia, Wadkins; 65

BRITISH OPEN 1986

Turnberry Golf Club, Ayrshire, Scotland
(17–20 July)
6957 yards: Par 70 (280)

Greg Norman put away, at least for a while, former miseries – including the recent US Open final round failure – and silenced his critics to boot, when he won wonderfully win over a Turnberry links whipped up by heavy winds. His belated first Major was a performance of power tempered by worldy-wise experience, and anchored by a record second round 63. Now 31, his five years on the European Tour (as much as his previous close calls) helped him tame the conditions and silence the field. He seemed to have broken his jinx and was destined to win more Major honours – he had always seemed to have the game to win a clutch of Major titles – but, as we are about to see, old habits were to return. Only two Americans from a strong contingent made the Top Ten.

1	**GREG NORMAN** (£70000)	74	63	74	69	280
2	Gordon J Brand	71	68	75	71	285
3=	Bernhard Langer	72	70	76	68	286
	Ian Woosnam	70	74	70	72	286
5	Nick Faldo	71	70	76	70	287
6=	Seve Ballesteros	76	75	73	64	288
	Gary Koch	73	72	72	71	288
8=	Brian Marchbank	78	70	72	69	289
	Tommy Nakajima	74	67	71	77	289
	Fuzzy Zoeller	75	73	72	69	289
11=	Jose Maria Canizares	76	68	73	73	290
	David Graham	75	73	70	72	290
	Christy O'Connor, Jr	75	71	75	69	290
14=	Andy Bean	74	73	73	71	291
	Curtis Strange	79	69	74	69	291
16=	Ray Floyd	78	67	73	74	292
	Anders Forsbrand	71	73	77	71	292
	Jose Maria Olazabal	78	69	72	73	292
19=	Bob Charles	76	72	73	72	293
	Manuel Pinero	78	71	70	74	293
21=	Derrick Cooper	72	79	72	71	294
	Ben Crenshaw	77	69	75	73	294
	Danny Edwards	77	73	70	74	294
	Vicente Fernandez	78	70	71	75	294
	Robert Lee	71	75	75	73	294
	Philip Parkin	78	70	72	74	294
	Ronan Rafferty	75	74	75	70	294
	Vaughan Somers	73	77	72	72	294
	Sam Torrance	78	69	71	76	294
30=	Masahiro Kuramoto	77	73	73	72	295
	Sandy Lyle	78	73	70	74	295
	John Mahaffey	75	73	75	72	295
	Ian Stanley	72	74	78	71	295
	DA Weibring	75	70	76	74	295

Round Leader(s)
R1   Woosnam; 70
R2   Norman; 137
R3   Norman; 211

Lowest Scores
R2   Norman; 63
R3   Edwards, Graham, Lyle, Pinero, Woosnam; 70
R4   Ballesteros; 64

US PGA 1986

Inverness Club, Toledo, Ohio
(7–10 August)
6982 yards: Par 71 (284)

In only his second year on the US Tour, Bob Tway was to burst Greg Norman's Turnberry bubble, and allow all the old doubts about his losing Majors from winning positions to return. Norman, leading all the way, and by four going into the last round, was caught by Tway as he squandered shots around the turn. Even so, Norman played the better golf over the last three holes, but Tway, missing every green, managed to get up and down. Then, in the cruellest manner of all, when brittle confidence starts to crumble, Tway unbelievably chipped in from a bunker for a birdie at 18, when again Norman was better placed. Greg's much easier chip from some light fringe rough was then to tie, but suddenly, the crowd knew, and so did Greg, it didn't look favourite to drop. And so it didn't, leaving Tway scampering about in bemused ecstasy. Uniquely, Norman had held the lead at the start of the final round in every Major of 1986.

1	**BOB TWAY** ($140000)	72	70	64	70	276
2	Greg Norman	65	68	69	76	278
3	Peter Jacobsen	68	70	70	71	279
4	DA Weibring	71	72	68	69	280
5=	Bruce Lietzke	69	71	70	71	281
	Payne Stewart	70	67	72	72	281
7=	David Graham	75	69	71	67	282
	Mike Hulbert	69	68	74	71	282
	Jim Thorpe	71	67	73	71	282
10	Doug Tewell	73	71	68	71	283
11=	Ben Crenshaw	72	73	72	67	284
	Donnie Hammond	70	71	68	75	284
	Lonnie Nielsen	73	69	72	70	284
	Lee Trevino	71	74	69	70	284
	Lanny Wadkins	71	75	70	68	284
16=	Chip Beck	71	73	71	70	285
	Jack Nicklaus	70	68	72	75	285
	Don Pooley	71	74	69	71	285
	Tony Sills	71	72	69	73	285
	Tom Watson	72	69	72	72	285
21=	Ronnie Black	68	71	74	73	286
	David Frost	70	73	68	75	286
	Wayne Grady	68	76	71	71	286
	Corey Pavin	71	72	70	73	286
	Hal Sutton	73	71	70	72	286
26=	Ken Green	71	72	71	73	287
	Hale Irwin	76	70	73	68	287
	Tom Kite	72	73	71	71	287
	Dan Pohl	71	71	74	71	287
30=	Wayne Levi	68	73	71	76	288
	Calvin Peete	72	73	69	74	288
	Gene Sauers	69	73	70	76	288
	Jeff Sluman	70	71	76	71	288
	Craig Stadler	67	74	73	74	288
	Ian Woosnam	72	70	75	71	288

Round Leader(s)
R1   Norman; 65
R2   Norman; 133
R3   Norman; 202

Lowest Scores
R2   Stewart, Thorpe, Mark Wiebe (47); 67
R3   Tway; 64
R4   Crenshaw, Graham; 67

THE MASTERS 1987

Augusta National Golf Club, Augusta, Georgia
(9–12 April)

6925 yards: Par 72 (288)

Greg Norman must have hoped that the memory of the previous August's PGA nightmare would have faded during the winter, and have disappeared altogether with the optimistic airs of spring. He certainly came to Augusta full of expectation, and a third-round 66 took him to the wire to tie with twice-Champion Ballesteros, and hitherto modest performer, Larry Mize. Seve blew out on the first extra hole. Norman was on the green, and with Mize to the right of it, over 40 yards from the flag, Greg was in prime position. The unthinkable happened, and the nightmare of Inverness returned when Mize, in an action which in a less-gentlemanly sport would surely have been classed as sadistic, freakily chipped in. Norman was crushed once more.

I	**LARRY MIZE***	70	72	72	71	285
	($162000)				
2=	Seve Ballesteros	73	71	70	71	285
	Greg Norman	73	74	66	72	285
4=	Ben Crenshaw	75	70	67	74	286
	Roger Maltbie	76	66	70	74	286
	Jodie Mudd	74	72	71	69	286
7=	Jay Haas	72	72	72	73	289
	Bernhard Langer	71	72	70	76	289
	Jack Nicklaus	74	72	73	70	289
	Tom Watson	71	72	74	72	289
	DA Weibring	72	75	71	71	289
12=	Chip Beck	75	72	70	73	290
	Tze-Chung Chen	74	69	71	76	290
	Mark McCumber	75	71	69	75	290
	Curtis Strange	71	70	73	76	290
	Lanny Wadkins	73	72	70	75	290
17=	Paul Azinger	77	73	69	72	291
	Mark Calcavecchia	73	72	78	68	291
	Sandy Lyle	77	74	68	72	291
	Craig Stadler	74	74	72	71	291
21	Bobby Wadkins	76	69	73	74	292
22=	Gary Koch	76	75	72	70	293
	Nick Price	73	73	71	76	293
24=	John Cook	69	73	74	78	294
	Tom Kite	73	74	74	73	294
	Mark O'Meara	75	74	71	74	294
27=	David Graham	73	77	72	73	295
	Donnie Hammond	73	75	74	73	295
	Corey Pavin	71	71	81	72	295
	Scott Simpson	72	75	72	76	295
	Denis Watson	76	74	73	72	295
	Fuzzy Zoeller	76	71	76	72	295

* Larry Mize beat Seve Ballesteros and Greg Norman in the Sudden-death Play-off

Round Leader(s)
R1   Cook; 69
R2   Strange; 141
R3   Crenshaw, Maltbie; 212

Lowest Scores
R2   Maltbie; 66
R3   Norman; 66
R4   Calcavecchia; 68

US OPEN 1987

Olympic Golf Club, San Francisco, California
(16–19 June)

6709 yards: Par 70 (280)

Overnight leader Tom Watson was denied a second US Open title when Scott Simpson birdied 14, 15, and 16 on the final stretch to overtake him and win his only Major title. Watson was undergoing a long slump in form, but still managed to raise his game for the events that mattered, and just failed to tie Simpson when his 45-foot putt for birdie at the 18th ended up inches from the hole.

I	**SCOTT SIMPSON**	71	68	70	68	277
	($150000)				
2	Tom Watson	72	65	71	70	278
3	Seve Ballesteros	68	75	68	71	282
4=	Ben Crenshaw	67	72	72	72	283
	Bernhard Langer	69	69	73	72	283
	Larry Mize	71	68	72	72	283
	Curtis Strange	71	72	69	71	283
	Bobby Wadkins	71	71	70	71	283
9=	Lennie Clements	70	70	70	74	284
	Tommy Nakajima	68	70	74	72	284
	Mac O'Grady	71	69	72	72	284
	Dan Pohl	75	71	69	69	284
	Jim Thorpe	70	68	73	73	284
14=	Isao Aoki	71	73	70	71	285
	Bob Eastwood	73	66	75	71	285
	Tim Simpson	76	66	70	73	285
17=	Mark Calcavecchia	73	68	73	72	286
	David Frost	70	72	71	73	286
	Kenny Knox	72	71	69	74	286
	Jodie Mudd	72	75	71	68	286
	Jumbo Ozaki	71	69	72	74	286
	Nick Price	69	74	69	74	286
	Jim Woodward	71	74	72	69	286
24=	Jay Don Blake	70	75	71	71	287
	Danny Edwards	72	70	72	73	287
	Peter Jacobsen	72	71	71	73	287
	John Mahaffey	72	72	67	76	287
	Steve Pate	71	72	72	72	287
	Don Pooley	74	72	72	69	287
	Craig Stadler	72	68	74	73	287

Round Leader(s)
R1   Crenshaw; 67
R2   Watson, Mark Wiebe (58); 137
R3   Watson; 208

Lowest Scores
R2   Watson; 65
R3   Keith Clearwater (31); 64
R4   Ken Green (31), Mudd, Simpson; 68

BRITISH OPEN 1987

Hon Co of Edinburgh Golfers, Muirfield, East Lothian, Scotland
(16–19 July)
6963 yards: Par 71 (280)

Nick Faldo, for many years seen by many Englishmen as the heir-apparent to Tony Jacklin, eventually came out of the shadow of the double Open winner (and nearly three years of technical rehabilitation with guru David Leadbeater) to win his first Major. He had been playing the Open since 1976 when he was a teenager, and although consistently winning on the European Tour, he was not by his own demanding standards making the breakthrough in the Majors. Leadbeater effectively rebuilt Faldo's swing. He won in the Muirfield *haar* (sea mist), grinding down Paul Azinger with 18 straight pars in Round Four, eventually nudging ahead at the last when the American missed his 30-foot par putt.

1	**NICK FALDO** (£75000)	68	69	71	71	279
2=	Paul Azinger	68	68	71	73	280
	Rodger Davis	64	73	74	69	280
4=	Ben Crenshaw	73	68	72	68	281
	Payne Stewart	71	66	72	72	281
6	David Frost	70	68	70	74	282
7	Tom Watson	69	69	71	74	283
8=	Nick Price	68	71	72	73	284
	Craig Stadler	69	69	71	75	284
	Ian Woosnam	71	69	72	72	284
11=	Mark Calcavecchia	69	70	72	74	285
	Graham Marsh	69	70	72	74	285
	Mark McNulty	71	69	75	70	285
	Jose Maria Olazabal	70	73	70	72	285
	Jumbo Ozaki	69	72	71	73	285
	Hal Sutton	71	70	73	71	285
17=	Ken Brown	69	73	70	74	286
	Eamonn Darcy	74	69	72	71	286
	Ray Floyd	72	68	70	76	286
	Wayne Grady	70	71	76	69	286
	Bernhard Langer	69	69	76	72	286
	Sandy Lyle	76	69	71	70	286
	Mark Roe	74	68	72	72	286
	Lee Trevino	67	74	73	72	286
25	Gerard Taylor	69	68	75	75	287
26=	Gordon Brand, Jr	73	70	75	70	288
	David Feherty	74	70	77	67	288
	Larry Mize	68	71	76	73	288
29=	Danny Edwards	71	73	72	73	289
	Anders Forsbrand	73	69	73	74	289
	Ken Green	67	76	74	72	289
	Lanny Wadkins	72	71	75	71	289
	Fuzzy Zoeller	71	70	76	72	289

Round Leader(s)
R1   Davis; 64
R2   Azinger; 136
R3   Azinger; 207

Lowest Scores
R2   Stewart; 66
R3   Brown, Floyd, Frost, Olazabal; 70
R4   Feherty; 67

US PGA 1987

PGA National Golf Club, Palm Beach Gardens, Florida
(6–9 August)
7002 yards: Par 72 (288)

Larry Nelson may not have been the most consistent performer in the Majors, but he is only one of 15 players to have won the PGA Championship more than once. When the Championship returned to the Florida home of the PGA, he tied with 1977 Champion Lanny Wadkins then added to his 1981 success when Wadkins bogeyed the first hole in sudden death.

1	**LARRY NELSON*** ($150000)	70	72	73	72	287
2	Lanny Wadkins	70	70	74	73	287
3=	Scott Hoch	74	74	71	69	288
	DA Weibring	73	72	67	76	288
5=	Mark McCumber	74	69	69	77	289
	Don Pooley	73	71	73	72	289
7=	Ben Crenshaw	72	70	74	74	290
	Bobby Wadkins	68	74	71	77	290
9	Curtis Strange	70	76	71	74	291
10=	Seve Ballesteros	72	70	72	78	292
	David Frost	75	70	71	76	292
	Tom Kite	72	77	71	72	292
	Nick Price	76	71	70	75	292
14=	Curt Byrum	74	75	68	76	293
	David Edwards	69	75	77	72	293
	Ray Floyd	70	70	73	80	293
	Dan Pohl	71	78	75	69	293
	Jeff Sluman	72	69	78	74	293
	Tom Watson	70	79	73	71	293
20	Peter Jacobsen	73	75	73	73	294
21=	Jim Hallett	73	78	73	71	295
	Bernhard Langer	70	78	77	70	295
	Gil Morgan	75	74	70	76	295
24=	Ken Brown	73	74	73	76	296
	Jack Nicklaus	76	73	74	73	296
	Gene Sauers	76	74	68	78	296
	Payne Stewart	72	75	75	74	296
28=	Ronnie Black	76	70	76	75	297
	Bobby Clampett	71	72	77	77	297
	Russ Cochran	73	76	69	79	297
	John Cook	76	70	72	79	297
	Brad Fabel	73	73	77	74	297
	Nick Faldo	73	73	77	74	297
	Jay Haas	74	70	76	77	297
	Bruce Lietzke	75	76	74	72	297
	Roger Maltbie	74	72	75	76	297
	Chris Perry	75	75	74	73	297
	Craig Stadler	75	72	75	75	297
	Hal Sutton	73	74	74	76	297

* Larry Nelson beat Lanny Wadkins at the 1st extra hole in Sudden Death Play-off

Round Leader(s)
R1   Wadkins; 68
R2   Floyd, Wadkins; 140
R3   McCumber, Weibring; 212

Lowest Scores
R2   McCumber, Sluman; 69
R3   Weibring; 67
R4   Hoch, Pohl; 69

THE MASTERS 1988

Augusta National Golf Club, Augusta, Georgia
(7–10 April)

6925 yards: Par 72 (288)

Sandy Lyle became the first Briton to win the Masters, and the third European in the decade to date. His Round Two 67 gave him the platform, and he led again after 54 holes. However, Mark Calcavecchia then caught Lyle and they were level when Lyle teed off at the last. Going for birdie, the Scot caught a fairway trap some 140 yards from the flag. Then, in one of the most dramatic approaches seen at Augusta's 18th, Lyle's seven iron sailed out of the bunker, over the pin and it spun back to within ten feet of the hole. He birdied against Calcavecchia's par to take the Green Jacket.

1	**SANDY LYLE**	71	67	72	71	281
	($183800)					
2	Mark Calcavecchia	71	69	72	70	282
3	Craig Stadler	76	69	70	68	283
4	Ben Crenshaw	72	73	67	72	284
5=	Fred Couples	75	68	71	71	285
	Greg Norman	77	73	71	64	285
	Don Pooley	71	72	72	70	285
8	David Frost	73	74	71	68	286
9=	Bernhard Langer	71	72	71	73	287
	Tom Watson	72	71	73	71	287
11=	Seve Ballesteros	73	72	70	73	288
	Ray Floyd	80	69	68	71	288
	Lanny Wadkins	74	75	69	70	288
14=	Nick Price	75	76	72	66	289
	Doug Tewell	75	73	68	73	289
16=	Mark McNulty	74	71	73	72	290
	Dan Pohl	78	70	69	73	290
	Fuzzy Zoeller	76	66	72	76	290
19=	Tze-Chung Chen	76	73	72	70	291
	Hubert Green	74	70	75	72	291
21=	Chip Beck	73	70	76	73	292
	Jack Nicklaus	75	73	72	72	292
	Curtis Strange	76	70	72	74	292
24	Mark McCumber	79	71	72	71	293
25=	Isao Aoki	74	74	73	73	294
	Gary Koch	72	73	74	75	294
	Payne Stewart	75	76	71	72	294
	Robert Wrenn	69	75	76	74	294
29	Rodger Davis	77	72	71	75	295
30=	Nick Faldo	75	74	75	72	296
	Steve Jones	74	74	75	73	296
	Mac O'Grady	74	73	76	73	296

Round Leader(s)
R1   Larry Nelson (33), Wrenn; 69
R2   Lyle; 138
R3   Lyle; 210

Lowest Scores
R2   Zoeller; 66
R3   Crenshaw; 67
R4   Norman; 64

US OPEN 1988

The Country Club, Brookline, Boston, Massachusetts
(16–20 June)

7010 yards: Par 71 (284)

Sandy Lyle projected his Masters form into the Open to shoot 68 and share the lead, but dropped out of contention after that. Another Briton, Nick Faldo, was trying to emulate Tony Jacklin by winning the US Open while still Britain's Champion Golfer, and tied with Curtis Strange when Strange bogeyed the 17th. The play-off – the third in three visits to Brookline (including the momentous 1913 affair between Ouimet, Vardon and Ray) – saw Curtis play much the better golf, and he held the lead from the 7th, Faldo bogeying three of the last four holes.

1	**CURTIS STRANGE***	70	67	69	72	278
	($180000)					
2	Nick Faldo	72	67	68	71	278
3=	Mark O'Meara	71	72	66	71	280
	Steve Pate	72	69	72	67	280
	DA Weibring	71	69	68	72	280
6=	Paul Azinger	69	70	76	66	281
	Scott Simpson	69	66	72	74	281
8=	Bob Gilder	68	69	70	75	282
	Fuzzy Zoeller	73	72	71	66	282
10=	Fred Couples	72	67	71	73	283
	Payne Stewart	73	73	70	67	283
12=	Andy Bean	71	71	72	70	284
	Ben Crenshaw	71	72	74	67	284
	Larry Mize	69	67	72	76	284
	Dan Pohl	74	72	69	69	284
	Lanny Wadkins	70	71	70	73	284
17=	Ray Floyd	73	72	73	67	285
	Hale Irwin	71	71	72	71	285
	Mark McNulty	73	72	72	68	285
	Joey Sindelar	76	68	70	71	285
21=	Chip Beck	73	72	71	70	286
	Bob Eastwood	74	72	69	71	286
	Scott Hoch	71	72	71	72	286
	Peter Jacobsen	76	70	76	64	286
25=	Dave Barr	73	72	72	20	287
	Jay Haas	73	67	74	73	287
	Sandy Lyle	68	71	75	73	287
	Billy Mayfair (a)	71	72	71	73	287
	Craig Stadler	70	73	71	73	287
	Bob Tway	77	68	73	69	287
	Mark Wiebe	75	70	73	69	287

* Curtis Strange (71) beat Nick Faldo (75) in the 18-Hole Play-off

Round Leader(s)
R1   Gilder, Lyle, Mike Nicolette (40); 68
R2   Simpson; 135
R3   Strange; 206

Lowest Scores
R2   Simpson; 66
R3   O'Meara; 66
R4   Jacobsen; 64

BRITISH OPEN 1988

Royal Lytham and St Anne's Golf Club, Lancashire, England
(14–18 July – Saturday washed out)
6857 yards: Par 71 (284)

Seve Ballesteros' third Open victory and fifth Major title came where it all started for the Spaniard in 1979. At his lucky Lytham links, Ballesteros' stunning 65 broke the heart of defending Champion Faldo and only Zimbabwean Nick Price could mount a challenge. In the end he had to capitulate to Seve's masterful performance. Rain washed away the third day's play, disappointing the 36000 crowd, and, after 117 Opens over 128 years, there was play on a Monday.

1	**SEVE BALLESTEROS**	67	71	70	65	273
	(£80000)					
2	Nick Price	70	67	69	69	275
3	Nick Faldo	71	69	68	71	279
4=	Fred Couples	73	69	71	68	281
	Gary Koch	71	72	70	68	281
6	Peter Senior	70	73	70	69	282
7=	Isao Aoki	72	71	73	67	283
	David Frost	71	75	69	68	283
	Sandy Lyle	73	69	67	74	283
	Payne Stewart	73	75	68	67	283
11=	Brad Faxon	69	74	70	71	284
	David J Russell	71	74	69	70	284
13=	Larry Nelson	73	71	68	73	285
	Eduardo Romero	72	71	69	73	285
	Curtis Strange	79	69	69	68	285
16=	Andy Bean	71	70	71	74	286
	Ben Crenshaw	73	73	68	72	286
	Don Pooley	70	73	69	74	286
	Jose Rivero	75	69	70	72	286
20=	Gordon Brand, Jr	72	76	68	71	287
	Bob Charles	71	74	69	73	287
	Rodger Davis	76	71	72	68	287
	Tom Kite	75	71	73	68	287
	Bob Tway	71	71	72	73	287
25=	Jack Nicklaus	75	70	75	68	288
	Ian Woosnam	76	71	72	69	288
27	Mark O'Meara	75	69	75	70	289
28=	Tommy Armour III	73	72	72	73	290
	Chip Beck	72	71	74	73	290
	Jim Benepe	75	72	70	73	290
	Howard Clark	71	72	75	72	290
	Mark McNulty	73	73	72	72	290
	Tom Watson	74	72	72	72	290

Round Leader(s)
R1 Ballesteros; 67
R2 Price; 137
R3 Faldo, Price; 208

Lowest Scores
R2 Price; 67
R3 Lyle; 67
R4 Ballesteros; 65

US PGA 1988

Oak Tree Golf Club, Edmond, Oklahoma
(11–14 August)
7015 yards: Par 71 (284)

Just as Ballesteros had done at Royal Lytham the previous month, a charging 65 from Jeff Sluman gave him a Major Championship win – except, unlike with Seve, this was Sluman's first. For Paul Azinger it was sense of Muirfield *déjà vu*, but instead of being ground down by Nick Faldo, he was blasted away by Sluman. All-round scoring was lower than expected on a notoriously difficult course.

1	**JEFF SLUMAN**	69	70	68	65	272
	($160000)					
2	Paul Azinger	67	66	71	71	275
3	Tommy Nakajima	69	68	74	67	278
4=	Tom Kite	72	69	71	67	279
	Nick Faldo	67	71	70	71	279
6=	Bob Gilder	66	75	71	68	280
	Dave Rummells	73	64	68	75	280
8	Dan Pohl	69	71	70	71	281
9=	Ray Floyd	68	68	74	72	282
	Steve Jones	69	68	72	73	282
	Kenny Knox	72	69	68	73	282
	Greg Norman	68	71	72	71	282
	Mark O'Meara	70	71	70	71	282
	Payne Stewart	70	69	70	73	282
15=	John Mahaffey	71	71	70	71	283
	Craig Stadler	68	73	75	67	283
17=	Mark Calcavecchia	73	69	70	72	284
	Ben Crenshaw	70	71	69	74	284
	David Graham	70	67	73	74	284
	Mark McNulty	73	70	67	74	284
	Jay Overton	68	66	76	74	284
	Corey Pavin	71	70	75	68	284
	Nick Price	74	70	67	73	284
	Richard Zokol	70	70	74	70	284
25=	Ronnie Black	71	71	70	73	285
	Jay Don Blake	71	73	72	69	285
	David Edwards	71	69	77	68	285
	Scott Hoch	74	69	68	74	285
	Blaine McCallister	73	67	75	70	285
	Lanny Wadkins	74	69	70	72	285

Round Leader(s)
R1 Gilder; 66
R2 Azinger; 133
R3 Azinger; 204

Lowest Scores
R2 Rummells; 64
R3 McNulty, Price; 67
R4 Sluman; 65

THE MASTERS 1989

Augusta National Golf Club, Augusta, Georgia
(6–9 April)

6925 yards: Par 72 (288)

With Nick Faldo winning his second Major in successive years, he also perpetuated the mini-stranglehold that Europeans had on the Masters. After Ballesteros (twice), Langer and Lyle, Faldo's win meant that half the decade's Masters titles went overseas – a somewhat different picture to the previous 46 years of the Tournament. Faldo had to put together something special over the last round after an incongruous 77 in Round Three, and his best-of-the-event 65 tied him with Scott Hoch. This set him up for the play-off win and the first prize of $200000 – a record for any Major.

1	**NICK FALDO***	68	73	77	65	283
	($200000)					
2	Scott Hoch	69	74	71	69	283
3=	Ben Crenshaw	71	72	70	71	284
	Greg Norman	74	75	68	67	284
5	Seve Ballesteros	71	72	73	69	285
6	Mike Reid	72	71	71	72	286
7	Jodie Mudd	73	76	72	76	287
8=	Chip Beck	74	76	70	68	288
	Jose Maria Olazabal	77	73	70	68	288
	Jeff Sluman	74	72	74	68	288
11=	Fred Couples	72	76	74	67	289
	Ken Green	74	69	73	73	289
	Mark O'Meara	74	71	72	72	289
14=	Paul Azinger	75	75	69	71	290
	Don Pooley	70	77	76	67	290
	Tom Watson	72	73	74	71	290
	Ian Woosnam	74	76	71	69	290
18=	David Frost	76	72	73	70	291
	Tom Kite	72	72	72	75	291
	Jack Nicklaus	73	74	73	71	291
	Jumbo Ozaki	71	75	73	72	291
	Curtis Strange	74	71	74	72	291
	Lee Trevino	67	74	81	69	291
24=	Tom Purtzer	71	76	73	72	292
	Payne Stewart	73	75	74	70	292
26=	Bernhard Langer	74	75	71	73	293
	Larry Mize	72	77	69	75	293
	Steve Pate	76	75	74	68	293
	Lanny Wadkins	76	71	73	73	293
	Fuzzy Zoeller	76	74	69	74	293

* Nick Faldo (5,3) beat Scott Hoch (5,4) in the Sudden-death Play-off

Round Leader(s)
R1   Trevino; 67
R2   Faldo, Trevino; 141
R3   Crenshaw; 213

Lowest Scores
R2   Green; 69
R3   Norman; 68
R4   Faldo; 65

US OPEN 1989

Oak Hill Country Club, Rochester, New York
(15–18 June)

6902 yards: Par 70 (280)

Curtis Strange became the first player since Ben Hogan in 1951 to win back-to-back US Opens, and the sixth in all. Along with Hogan, he joined Willie Anderson, John McDermott, Bobby Jones and Ralph Guldahl. His win over Chip Beck, Mark McCumber and Welshman Ian Woosnam was a little more comfortable than his play-off win over Faldo the previous year. He could afford to three-putt the 18th and still win. With odds against it happening of 332000/1, four players – Doug Weaver, Mark Wiebe, Jerry Pate and Nick Price – all achieved a hole-in-one on the 167-yard 6th, and all within a few hours during Round Two.

1	**CURTIS STRANGE**	71	64	73	70	278
	($200000)					
2=	Chip Beck	71	69	71	68	279
	Mark McCumber	70	68	72	69	279
	Ian Woosnam	70	68	73	68	279
5=	Brian Claar	71	72	68	69	280
6=	Jumbo Ozaki	70	71	68	72	281
	Scott Simpson	67	70	69	75	281
8	Peter Jacobsen	71	70	71	70	282
9=	Paul Azinger	71	72	70	70	283
	Hubert Green	69	72	74	68	283
	Tom Kite	67	69	69	78	283
	Jose Maria Olazabal	69	72	70	72	283
13=	Scott Hoch	70	72	70	72	284
	Mark Lye	71	69	72	72	284
	Larry Nelson	68	73	68	75	284
	Tom Pernice	67	75	68	74	284
	Payne Stewart	66	75	72	71	284
18=	Jay Don Blake	66	71	72	76	285
	Nick Faldo	68	72	73	72	285
	David Frost	73	72	70	70	285
21=	Fred Couples	74	71	67	74	286
	Steve Elkington	70	70	78	68	286
	Bill Glasson	73	70	70	73	286
	Nolan Henke	75	69	72	70	286
	DA Weibring	70	74	73	69	286
26=	Ray Floyd	68	74	74	71	287
	Don Pooley	74	69	71	73	287
	Robert Wrenn	74	71	73	69	287
29=	Emlyn Aubrey	69	73	73	73	288
	Dan Pohl	71	71	73	73	288
	Hal Sutton	69	75	72	72	288
	Scott Taylor	69	71	76	72	288

Round Leader(s)
R1   Blake, Bernhard Langer (59), Stewart; 66
R2   Strange; 135
R3   Kite; 205

Lowest Scores
R2   Strange; 64
R3   Couples; 67
R4   Beck, Elkington, Green, Woosnam; 68

BRITISH OPEN 1989

Royal Troon Golf Club, Ayrshire, Scotland
(20–23 July)
7067 yards: Par 71 (284)

Another play-off was needed to settle a Major when the 1988 Masters runner-up, Mark Calcavecchia, tied with Australians Wayne Grady and Greg Norman at Troon. This time, however, it was an experimental four-hole play-off, starting at the 15th; and should there still be a tie after the 18th has been played, a further rotation of the same holes would take place. Norman had fought his way into contention with a record-equalling regulation fourth round score, only to miss out again when it really mattered. Grady lost touch early in the play-off, and after controlling events early on, Norman's game collapsed over holes 3 and 4, to let Calcavecchia back in.

1	**MARK CALCAVECCHIA***	71	68	68	68	275
	(£80000)					
2=	Wayne Grady	68	67	69	71	275
	Greg Norman	69	70	72	64	275
4	Tom Watson	69	68	68	72	277
5	Jodie Mudd	73	67	68	70	278
6=	Fred Couples	68	71	68	72	279
	David Feherty	71	67	69	72	279
8=	Paul Azinger	68	73	67	72	280
	Eduardo Romero	68	70	75	67	280
	Payne Stewart	72	65	69	74	280
11=	Nick Faldo	71	71	70	69	281
	Mark McNulty	75	70	70	66	281
13=	Roger Chapman	76	68	67	71	282
	Howard Clark	72	68	72	70	282
	Mark James	69	70	71	72	282
	Steve Pate	69	70	73	70	282
	Craig Stadler	73	69	69	71	282
	Philip Walton	69	74	69	70	282
19=	Derrick Cooper	69	70	76	68	283
	Tom Kite	70	74	67	72	283
	Larry Mize	71	74	66	72	283
	Don Pooley	73	70	69	71	283
23=	Davis Love III	72	70	73	69	284
	Jose Maria Olazabal	68	72	69	75	284
	Vijay Singh	71	73	69	71	284
26=	Chip Beck	75	69	68	73	285
	Stephen Bennett	75	69	68	73	285
	Scott Simpson	73	66	72	74	285
	Lanny Wadkins	72	70	69	74	285
30=	Ian Baker-Finch	72	69	70	75	286
	Mark Davis	77	68	67	74	286
	Jeff Hawkes	75	67	69	75	286
	Peter Jacobsen	71	74	71	70	286
	Gary Koch	72	71	74	69	286
	Brian Marchbank	69	74	73	70	286
	Miguel Martin	68	73	73	72	286
	Jack Nicklaus	74	71	71	70	286
	Jumbo Ozaki	71	73	70	72	286

* Mark Calcavecchia (4-3-3-3) beat Wayne Grady
(4-4-4-4) and Greg Norman (3-3-4-x) in the 4-Hole
Play-off

Round Leader(s) **Lowest Scores**
R1 Azinger, Couples, R2 Stewart; 65
  Grady, Martin, R3 Mize; 66
  Olazabal, R4 Norman; 64
  Romero; 68
R2 Grady; 135
R3 Grady; 204

US PGA 1989

Kemper Lakes Golf Club, Hawthorn Woods, Illinois
(10–13 August)
7217 yards: Par 72 (288)

For the first time in the same year, the three American Majors paid out the same amount to the winner. Payne Stewart, along with Australia's Rodger Davis, the only two top golfers of the day who regularly wore traditional plus-twos (or -fours) or knicker(bocker)s, collected his first Major title, after some strong performances in the recent past. Putting aside a shaky start, two strong middle rounds put Stewart in contention. However, by the 13th hole in Round Four, a win for him looked most unlikely after allowing a six-shot gap to develop behind Mike Reid. Then a combination of brilliant play from Stewart (four birdies) and Mike Reid's capitulation (bogey at 16, double-bogey at 17), allowed Payne to squeeze by, and also pip Andy Bean – already home with a 66.

1	**PAYNE STEWART**	74	66	69	67	276
	($200000)					
2=	Andy Bean	70	67	74	66	277
	Mike Reid	66	67	70	74	277
	Curtis Strange	70	68	70	69	277
5	Dave Rummells	68	69	69	72	278
6	Ian Woosnam	68	70	70	71	279
7=	Scott Hoch	69	69	69	73	280
	Craig Stadler	71	64	72	73	280
9=	Nick Faldo	70	73	69	69	281
	Ed Fiori	70	67	75	69	281
	Tom Watson	67	69	74	71	281
12=	Seve Ballesteros	72	70	66	74	282
	Jim Gallagher Jr	73	69	68	72	282
	Greg Norman	74	71	67	70	282
	Mike Sullivan	76	66	67	73	282
	Mark Wiebe	71	70	69	72	282
17=	Isao Aoki	72	71	65	75	283
	Ben Crenshaw	68	72	72	71	283
	Buddy Gardner	72	71	70	70	283
	Davis Love III	73	69	72	69	283
	Blaine McCallister	71	72	70	70	283
	Larry Mize	73	71	68	71	283
	Chris Perry	67	70	70	76	283
24=	Tommy Armour	70	69	73	72	284
	Dan Pohl	71	69	74	70	284
	Jeff Sluman	75	70	69	70	284
27=	David Frost	70	74	69	72	285
	Mike Hulbert	70	71	72	72	285
	Peter Jacobsen	70	70	73	72	285
	Jack Nicklaus	68	72	73	72	285
	Tim Simpson	69	70	73	73	285
	Brian Tennyson	71	69	72	73	285
	Howard Twitty	72	71	68	74	285

Round Leader(s)
R1 Reid, Leonard Thompson (34); 66
R2 Reid; 133
R3 Reid; 203

Lowest Scores
R2 Stadler; 64
R3 Aoki; 65
R4 Bean; 66

THE MASTERS 1990

Augusta National Golf Club, Augusta, Georgia
(5–8 April)

6925 yards: Par 72 (288)

Nick Faldo joined Jack Nicklaus (1965–66) as the only players to have won consecutive Masters Tournaments. This time Faldo needed to play-off against 48 year-old Raymond Floyd, and became the only man in Majors history to have to play off to win back-to-back titles. It was his third Major win. Mike Donald's 64 led by two after the first day: he then shot an 82 to make the cut by one. He followed this by playing the final 54 holes in 19-over par – a Masters record since the halfway cut was introduced in 1957 – to finish 47th out of 49.

1	**NICK FALDO***	71	72	66	69	278
	($225000)					
2	Ray Floyd	70	68	68	72	278
3=	John Huston	66	74	68	75	283
	Lanny Wadkins	72	73	70	68	283
5	Fred Couples	74	69	72	69	284
6	Jack Nicklaus	72	70	69	74	285
7=	Seve Ballesteros	74	73	68	71	286
	Bill Britton	68	74	71	73	286
	Bernhard Langer	70	73	69	74	286
	Scott Simpson	74	71	68	73	286
	Curtis Strange	70	73	71	72	286
	Tom Watson	77	71	67	71	286
13	Jose Maria Olazabal	72	73	68	74	287
14=	Ben Crenshaw	72	74	73	69	288
	Scott Hoch	71	68	73	76	288
	Tom Kite	75	73	66	74	288
	Larry Mize	70	76	71	71	288
	Ronan Rafferty	72	74	69	73	288
	Craig Stadler	72	70	74	72	288
20=	Mark Calcavecchia	74	73	73	69	289
	Steve Jones	77	69	72	71	289
	Fuzzy Zoeller	72	74	73	70	289
23	Jumbo Ozaki	70	71	77	72	290
24=	Donnie Hammond	71	74	75	71	291
	Gary Player	73	74	68	76	291
	Lee Trevino	78	69	72	72	291
27=	Wayne Grady	72	75	72	73	292
	Andy North	71	73	77	71	292
	Jeff Sluman	78	68	75	71	292
30=	Peter Jacobsen	67	75	76	75	293
	Jodie Mudd	74	70	73	76	293
	Ian Woosnam	72	75	70	76	293

* Nick Faldo (4,4) beat Ray Floyd (4,5) at the 2nd Sudden-death Play-off hole

Round Leader(s)
R1　Mike Donald (47); 64
R2　Floyd; 138
R3　Floyd; 206

Lowest Scores
R2　Floyd, Hoch, Sluman; 68
R3　Faldo, Kite; 66
R4　Wadkins; 68

US OPEN 1990

Medinah Country Club, Medinah, Illinois
(14–18 June)

7195 yards: Par 72 (288)

No concessions are given for age, as 45 year-old Hale Irwin will tesify. He was taken into a sudden-death extension to the play-off – effectively made to play 91 holes – for the privilege of becoming the oldest winner of the US Open. It was his third win; only Anderson, Jones, Hogan and Nicklaus had achieved more. Irwin beat Mike Donald, who led him by four shots going into the last regulation 18 holes. Donald, whose misadventures in the Masters that year had not fazed him, had won his private duel with Billy Ray Brown, only to find Irwin in the Clubhouse on 280 as well. There was a new record for entries filed – 6198.

1	**HALE IRWIN***	69	70	74	67	280
	($220000)					
2	Mike Donald	67	70	72	71	280
3=	Billy Ray Brown	69	71	69	72	281
	Nick Faldo	72	72	68	69	281
5=	Mark Brooks	68	70	72	73	283
	Greg Norman	72	73	69	69	283
	Tim Simpson	66	69	75	73	283
8=	Scott Hoch	70	73	69	72	284
	Steve Jones	67	76	74	67	284
	Jose Maria Olazabal	73	69	69	73	284
	Tom Sieckmann	70	74	68	72	284
	Craig Stadler	71	70	72	71	284
	Fuzzy Zoeller	73	70	68	73	284
14=	Jim Benepe	72	70	73	70	285
	John Huston	68	72	73	72	285
	John Inman	72	71	70	72	285
	Larry Mize	72	70	69	74	285
	Larry Nelson	74	67	69	75	285
	Scott Simpson	66	73	73	73	285
	Jeff Sluman	66	70	74	75	285
21=	Steve Elkington	73	71	73	69	286
	Curtis Strange	73	70	68	75	286
	Ian Woosnam	70	70	74	72	286
24=	Paul Azinger	72	72	69	74	287
	Webb Heintzelman	70	75	74	68	287
	Jumbo Ozaki	73	72	74	68	287
	Corey Pavin	74	70	73	70	287
	Billy Tuten	74	70	72	71	287
29=	Chip Beck	71	71	73	73	288
	Brian Claar	70	71	71	76	288
	Mike Hulbert	76	66	71	75	288
	Phil Mickelson (a)	74	71	71	72	288

* Hale Irwin (74) beat Mike Donald (74) at the 1st extra hole after the 18-Hole Play-off was tied

Round Leader(s)
R1　S Simpson, T Simpson, Sluman; 66
R2　T Simpson; 135
R3　Brown, Donald; 209

Lowest Scores
R2　Hulbert; 66
R3　Faldo, Jack Nicklaus (33), Craig Parry (46), Mike Reid (33), Sieckmann, Strange, Zoeller; 68
R4　Irwin, Jones; 67

BRITISH OPEN 1990

Royal & Ancient Golf Club, St Andrews, Fife, Scotland
(19–22 July)
6933 yards: Par 72 (288)

Nick Faldo shot the lowest total for any Major since Tom Watson's all-time low of 268 (and Nicklaus' 269) at Turnberry in 1977. In some ways, Faldo's performance could be consideredeven better, in that his total was 18 under par, compared to Watson's 12 under. He finished five ahead of reigning PGA Champion Payne Stewart and Zimbabwean Mark McNulty, themselves leading home a classy-looking Top 10. It was Faldo's second Open Championship, and fourth Major, in less than four years. In that time, influenced, at least psychologically, by the Leadbeater technique, his Majors sequence read: W, 28, 30, 2, 3, 4, W, 18, 11, 9, W, 3, W – a consistent run which over a period of time has only been put together by the very best in golfing history.

1	**NICK FALDO**	67	65	67	71	270
	(£85000)					
2=	Mark McNulty	74	68	68	65	275
	Payne Stewart	68	68	68	71	275
4=	Jodie Mudd	72	66	72	66	276
	Ian Woosnam	68	69	70	69	276
6=	Ian Baker-Finch	68	72	64	73	277
	Greg Norman	66	66	76	69	277
8=	David Graham	72	71	70	66	279
	Donnie Hammond	70	71	68	70	279
	Steve Pate	70	68	72	69	279
	Corey Pavin	71	69	68	71	279
12=	Paul Broadhurst	74	69	63	74	280
	Robert Gamez	70	72	67	71	280
	Tim Simpson	70	69	69	72	280
	Vijay Singh	70	69	72	69	280
16=	Peter Jacobsen	68	70	70	73	281
	Steve Jones	72	67	72	70	281
	Sandy Lyle	72	70	67	72	281
	Frank Nobilo	72	67	68	74	281
	Jose Maria Olazabal	71	67	71	72	281
	Mark Roe	71	70	72	68	281
22=	Eamonn Darcy	71	71	72	68	282
	Craig Parry	68	68	69	77	282
	Jamie Spence	72	65	73	72	282
25=	Fred Couples	71	70	70	72	283
	Christy O'Connor, Jr	68	72	71	72	283
	Nick Price	70	67	71	75	283
	Jose Rivero	70	70	70	73	283
	Jeff Sluman	72	70	70	71	283
	Lee Trevino	69	70	73	71	283

Round Leader(s)
R1   Norman; 66
R2   Faldo, Norman; 132
R3   Faldo; 199

Lowest Scores
R2   Faldo, Spence; 65
R3   Broadhurst; 63
R4   McNulty; 65

US PGA 1990

Shoal Creek Country Club, Birmingham, Alabama
(9–12 August)
7145 yards: Par 72 (288)

Wayne Grady no doubt benefitted from the experience of tying for the British Open in 1989. He played mistake-free par golf along the back nine in the last round while the leader, Fred Couples, feeling the pressure of the Australian's metronomic scoring, lost out through bogeys at 13, 14, 15 and 16. Grady became the third Australian, after Jim Ferrier and David Graham, to hold the PGA title.

1	**WAYNE GRADY**	72	67	72	71	282
	($225000)					
2	Fred Couples	69	71	73	72	285
3	Gil Morgan	77	72	65	72	286
4	Bill Britton	72	74	72	71	289
5=	Chip Beck	70	71	78	71	290
	Billy Mayfair	70	71	75	74	290
	Loren Roberts	73	71	70	76	290
8=	Mark McNulty	74	72	75	71	292
	Don Pooley	75	74	71	72	292
	Tim Simpson	71	73	75	73	292
	Payne Stewart	71	72	70	79	292
12=	Hale Irwin	77	72	70	74	293
	Larry Mize	72	68	76	77	293
14=	Billy Andrade	75	72	73	74	294
	Morris Hatalsky	73	78	71	72	294
	Jose Maria Olazabal	73	77	72	72	294
	Corey Pavin	73	75	72	74	294
	Fuzzy Zoeller	72	71	76	75	294
19=	Bob Boyd	74	74	71	76	295
	Nick Faldo	71	75	80	69	295
	Blaine McCallister	75	73	74	73	295
	Greg Norman	77	69	76	73	295
	Mark O'Meara	69	76	79	71	295
	Tom Watson	74	71	77	73	295
	Mark Wiebe	74	73	75	73	295
26=	Mark Brooks	78	69	76	73	296
	Peter Jacobsen	74	75	71	76	296
	Chris Perry	75	74	72	75	296
	Ray Stewart	73	73	75	75	296
	Brian Tennyson	71	77	71	77	296

Round Leader(s)
R1   Bobby Wadkins (66); 68
R2   Grady; 139
R3   Grady; 211

Lowest Scores
R2   Grady; 67
R3   Morgan; 65
R4   Faldo; 69

THE MASTERS 1991

Augusta National Golf Club, Augusta, Georgia
(11–14 April)
6925 yards: Par 72 (288)

Woosnam's win at Augusta took him to the top of the World Ranking. Over the previous half-dozen years or so the Welshman had not set the Majors world alight, but had made his name as a winner of tournaments worldwide, with a game based on long driving (for his 5'4" frame) and silky iron play. If his putting had been half as good again, maybe he would have been in contention in more Majors, both before and after this: once in contention, he knew how to win. Not that that was so much in evidence that April at Augusta, coming to the 72nd hole. Woosie, tied with the young Spaniard Olazabal and the old maestro Watson, missed the green with his approach. His scramble up to five feet and down for a par, though, while the others dropped shots, was good enough to claim his one-and-only Major.

1	**IAN WOOSNAM**	72	66	67	72	277
	($243000)					
2	Jose Maria Olazabal	68	71	69	70	278
3=	Ben Crenshaw	70	73	68	68	279
	Steve Pate	72	73	69	65	279
	Lanny Wadkins	67	71	70	71	279
	Tom Watson	68	68	70	73	279
7=	Ian Baker-Finch	71	70	69	70	280
	Andrew Magee	70	72	68	70	280
	Jodie Mudd	70	70	71	69	280
10=	Hale Irwin	70	70	75	66	281
	Tommy Nakajima	74	71	67	69	281
12=	Mark Calcavecchia	70	68	77	67	282
	Nick Faldo	72	73	67	70	282
	Billy Mayfair	72	72	72	66	282
	Craig Stadler	70	72	71	69	282
	Fuzzy Zoeller	70	70	75	67	282
17=	Ray Floyd	71	68	71	73	283
	Jim Gallagher, Jr	67	74	71	71	283
	Peter Jacobsen	73	70	68	72	283
	Mark McCumber	67	71	73	72	283
	Larry Mize	72	71	66	74	283
22=	Seve Ballesteros	75	70	69	70	284
	Steve Elkington	72	69	74	69	284
	Rocco Mediate	72	69	71	72	284
	Corey Pavin	73	70	69	72	284
	Scott Simpson	69	73	69	73	284
27=	Jay Don Blake	74	72	68	71	285
	Mark O'Meara	74	68	72	71	285
29=	Morris Hatalsky	71	72	70	73	286
	John Huston	73	72	71	70	286
	Jeff Sluman	71	71	72	72	286

Round Leader(s)
R1 Gallagher, McCumber, Wadkins; 67
R2 Watson; 136
R3 Woosnam; 205

Lowest Scores
R2 Billy Ray Brown (42); 65
R3 Mize; 66
R4 Pate; 65

US OPEN 1991

Hazeltine National Golf Club, Minneapolis, Minnesota
(13–17 June)
7149 yards: Par 72 (288)

Payne Stewart had been injured for much of the early season, and didn't compete in the Masters. However, fit again, he led home an all-American Top Ten to collect his second Major Championship – adding to the PGA title he won in 1989. Leading almost throughout, he eventually surrendered the lead to 1987 Champion Scott Simpson, who stretched away by. Simpson then bogeyed 16 and 18 while Stewart parred in, to make it the third US Open play-off in four years. Both played nondescript golf, but Stewart was just the steadier to win. A freak lightning storm on the first day unfortunately killed a spectator – something which coincidentally, and unhappily, occurred again in the same year at Crooked Stick, during the PGA Championship.

1	**PAYNE STEWART***67	70	73	72	282
	($235000)				
2	Scott Simpson	70	68	72	72	282
3=	Fred Couples	70	70	75	70	285
	Larry Nelson	73	72	72	68	285
5	Fuzzy Zoeller	72	73	74	67	286
6	Scott Hoch	69	71	74	73	287
7	Nolan Henke	67	71	77	73	288
8=	Ray Floyd	73	72	76	68	289
	Jose Maria Olazabal	73	71	75	70	289
	Corey Pavin	71	67	79	72	289
11=	Jim Gallagher, Jr	70	72	75	73	290
	Hale Irwin	71	75	70	74	290
	Davis Love III	70	76	73	71	290
	Craig Parry	70	73	73	74	290
	DA Weibring	76	71	75	68	290
16=	Nick Faldo	72	74	73	72	291
	Sandy Lyle	72	70	74	75	291
	Tom Watson	73	71	77	70	291
19=	Mark Brooks	73	73	73	73	292
	Billy Ray Brown	73	71	77	71	292
	John Cook	76	70	72	74	292
	Peter Persons	70	75	75	72	292
	Nick Price	74	69	71	78	292
	Tom Sieckmann	74	70	74	74	292
	Craig Stadler	71	66	77	75	292
26=	Rick Fehr	74	69	73	77	293
	Jodie Mudd	71	70	77	75	293
	Mike Reid	74	72	74	73	293
	Bob Tway	75	69	75	74	293

* Payne Stewart (75) beat Scott Simpson (77) in the 18-Hole Play-off

Round Leader(s)
R1 Henke, Stewart; 67
R2 Stewart; 137
R3 Simpson, Stewart; 210

Lowest Scores
R2 Pavin; 67
R3 Irwin; 70
R4 Zoeller; 67

BRITISH OPEN 1991

Royal Birkdale Golf Club, Southport, Lancashire, England
(18–21 July)
6940 yards: Par 70 (280)

In 1984, then aged 23, Australian Ian Baker-Finch shot a fourth-round 79 over the Old Course at St Andrews to bow out of Open Championship contention. That, after 54 holes of 68, 66, 71 (205) and a share of the lead, gave birth to one of the most unkind tabloid nicknames ever conjured: Ian Baker-*Flinch*. Baker-Finch was not the first person to blow up in the last round of a Major, and won't be the last, but the combination of surnames made him a headline writer's delight. It was with some satisfaction, then, when the most famous hyphen in golf became the first double-barrelled surname to win any Major (not that there had been many in contention over the years). This time, the Australian saved all his sparkling golf to the end, shooting a record-equalling Round Three score, and birdieing five of the first seven holes on the last day. Although chased hard by compatriot Mike Harwood, this burst of scoring secured him the title. Englishman Richard Boxhall, trailing the lead in Round Three by just three, freakishly broke his leg while driving off the 3rd tee.

1	**IAN BAKER-FINCH**	71	71	64	66	272
	(£90000)					
2	Mike Harwood	68	70	69	67	274
3=	Fred Couples	72	69	70	64	275
	Mark O'Meara	71	68	67	69	275
5=	Eamonn Darcy	73	68	66	70	277
	Jodie Mudd	72	70	72	63	277
	Bob Tway	75	66	70	66	277
8	Craig Parry	71	70	69	68	278
9=	Seve Ballesteros	66	73	69	71	279
	Bernhard Langer	71	71	70	67	279
	Greg Norman	74	68	71	66	279
12=	Roger Chapman	74	66	71	69	280
	Rodger Davis	70	71	73	66	280
	Vijay Singh	71	69	69	71	280
	Magnus Sunesson	72	73	68	67	280
	David Williams	74	71	68	67	280
17=	Chip Beck	67	78	70	66	281
	Paul Broadhurst	71	73	68	69	281
	Nick Faldo	68	75	70	68	281
	Barry Lane	68	72	71	70	281
	Mark Mouland	68	74	68	71	281
	Peter Senior	74	67	71	69	281
	Andrew Sherborne	73	70	68	70	281
	Lee Trevino	71	72	71	67	281
	Ian Woosnam	70	72	69	70	281
26=	Wayne Grady	69	70	73	70	282
	Mark James	72	68	70	72	282
	Colin Montgomerie	71	69	71	71	282
	Mike Reid	68	71	70	73	282
	Eduardo Romero	70	73	68	71	282
	Tom Watson	69	72	72	69	282

Round Leader(s)
R1   Ballesteros; 66
R2   Harwood; 138
R3   Baker-Finch, O'Meara; 206

Lowest Scores
R2   Chapman, Tway; 66
R3   Baker-Finch; 64
R4   Mudd; 63

US PGA 1991

Crooked Stick Golf Club, Carmel, Indiana
(8–11 August)
7295 yards: Par 72 (288)

Every sport has its share of fairy stories – golf more than most. There have not been many more remarkable than when John Daly won the PGA in 1991. Virtually unknown, he didn't qualify high enough to merit an automatic entry for the Championship. In fact, he was only ninth on the reserve list – ninth alternate. His chance only came when Nick Price scratched to be at the birth of his child, and several higher on the list declined the invitation to play. Daly, without any hang-ups it seemed, hit the ball consistently longer, and usually straighter, than any player before in the history of the Majors, and certainly longer and straighter than those at Crooked Stick that week. Without a practice round, he shot a 69 and, from Round Two onwards, his ferocious hitting backed up by some magical pressure putting, he was not headed, finally victorious by three strokes.

1	**JOHN DALY**	69	67	69	71	276
	($230000)					
2	Bruce Lietzke	68	69	72	70	279
3	Jim Gallagher, Jr	70	72	72	67	281
4	Kenny Knox	67	71	70	74	282
5=	Bob Gilder	73	70	67	73	283
	Steven Richardson	70	72	72	69	283
7=	David Feherty	71	74	71	68	284
	Ray Floyd	69	74	72	69	284
	John Huston	70	72	70	72	284
	Steve Pate	70	75	70	69	284
	Craig Stadler	68	71	69	76	284
	Hal Sutton	74	67	72	71	284
13=	Jay Don Blake	75	70	72	68	285
	Andrew Magee	69	73	68	75	285
	Payne Stewart	74	70	71	70	285
16=	Nick Faldo	70	69	71	76	286
	Ken Green	68	73	71	74	286
	Wayne Levi	73	71	72	70	286
	Sandy Lyle	68	75	71	72	286
	Rocco Mediate	71	71	73	71	286
	Gil Morgan	70	71	74	71	286
	Howard Twitty	70	71	75	70	286
23=	Seve Ballesteros	71	72	71	73	287
	Chip Beck	73	73	70	71	287
	Mike Hulbert	72	72	73	70	287
	Jack Nicklaus	71	72	73	71	287
27=	Fred Couples	74	67	76	71	288
	Rick Fehr	70	73	71	74	288
	Jim Hallett	69	74	73	72	288
	Mark McNulty	75	71	69	73	288
	Loren Roberts	72	74	72	70	288

Round Leader(s)
R1   Knox, Ian Woosnam (48); 67
R2   Daly; 136
R3   Daly; 205

Lowest Scores
R2   Daly, Couples, Sutton; 67
R3   Gilder; 67
R4   Gallagher; 67

THE MASTERS 1992

Augusta National Golf Club, Augusta, Georgia
(9–12 April)
6925 yards: Par 72 (288)

Ian Woosnam, tying with Craig Parry at halfway, looked to be on course to a successful defence of his title, but disappointingly fell away to finish eight shots adrift of Freddie Couples at the end. Parry still led after 54 holes, but the Australian of Woosnam-esque stature also crumpled, shooting a final round 78. Couples' first Major was extremely popular, and he played a consistently, and on times brilliantly, set of four rounds to head Ray Floyd – six months short of his 50th birthday – by two.

1	**FRED COUPLES**	69	67	69	70	275
	($270000)					
2	Ray Floyd	69	68	69	71	277
3	Corey Pavin	72	71	68	67	278
4=	Mark O'Meara	74	67	69	70	280
	Jeff Sluman	65	74	70	71	280
6=	Ian Baker-Finch	70	69	68	74	281
	Nolan Henke	70	71	70	70	281
	Larry Mize	73	69	71	68	281
	Greg Norman	70	70	73	68	281
	Steve Pate	73	71	70	67	281
	Nick Price	70	71	67	73	281
	Ted Schultz	68	69	72	72	281
13=	Nick Faldo	71	72	68	71	282
	Wayne Grady	68	75	71	68	282
	Bruce Lietzke	69	72	68	73	282
	Craig Parry	69	66	69	78	282
	Dillard Pruitt	75	68	70	69	282
	Scott Simpson	70	71	71	70	282
19=	Billy Ray Brown	70	74	70	69	283
	John Daly	71	71	73	68	283
	Mike Hulbert	68	74	71	70	283
	Andrew Magee	73	70	70	70	283
	Ian Woosnam	69	66	73	75	283
	Fuzzy Zoeller	71	70	73	69	283
25=	Bruce Fleisher	73	70	72	69	284
	Jim Gallagher, Jr	74	68	71	71	284
	John Huston	69	73	73	69	284
	Davis Love III	68	72	72	72	284
	Craig Stadler	70	71	70	73	284
	DA Weibring	71	68	72	73	284

Round Leader(s)
R1 Sluman, Lanny Wadkins (48); 65
R2 Parry, Woosnam; 135
R3 Parry; 204

Lowest Scores
R2 Parry, Woosnam; 66
R3 Price; 67
R4 Mark Calcavecchia (31); 65

US OPEN 1992

Pebble Beach Golf Links, Pebble Beach, California
(18–21 June)
6809 yards: Par 72 (288)

Tom Kite probably held the tag of 'best player never...', etc longer than most. He had appeared in the US Open as far back as 1970, and had achieved a runner-up slot in three Major Championships. Kite may have thought, at the age of 42, his career (in which he at the time became the biggest money-earner in golf history) was going to end without that elusive claim to immortality – a Major. It took a wild and windy Pebble Beach to elevate his status into Majors folklore. It was a US Open that confirmed Jeff Sluman's credentials as a worthy Majors Champion (he won the 1988 PGA title); the promise of Scotsman, Colin Montgomerie; and 46 year-old Gil Morgan's last serious attempt to win.

1	**TOM KITE**	71	72	70	72	285
	($275000)					
2	Jeff Sluman	73	74	69	71	287
3	Colin Montgomerie	70	71	77	70	288
4=	Nick Faldo	70	76	68	77	291
	Nick Price	71	72	77	71	291
6=	Billy Andrade	72	74	72	74	292
	Jay Don Blake	70	74	75	73	292
	Bob Gilder	73	70	75	74	292
	Mike Hulbert	74	73	70	75	292
	Tom Lehman	69	74	72	77	292
	Joey Sindelar	74	72	68	78	292
	Ian Woosnam	72	72	69	79	292
13=	Ian Baker-Finch	74	71	72	76	293
	John Cook	72	72	74	75	293
	Mark McCumber	70	76	73	74	293
	Gil Morgan	66	69	77	81	293
17=	Fred Couples	72	70	78	74	294
	Andy Dillard	68	70	79	77	294
	Wayne Grady	74	76	81	73	294
	Andrew Magee	77	69	72	76	294
	Tray Tyner	74	72	78	70	294
	Willie Wood	70	75	75	74	294
23=	Seve Ballesteros	71	76	69	79	295
	Brad Bryant	71	76	75	73	295
	Jay Haas	70	77	74	74	295
	Donnie Hammond	73	73	73	76	295
	Dudley Hart	76	71	71	77	295
	Jim Kane	73	71	76	75	295
	Bernhard Langer	73	72	75	75	295
	Billy Mayfair	74	73	75	73	295
	Jumbo Ozaki	77	70	72	76	295
	Curtis Strange	67	78	76	74	295

Round Leader(s)
R1 Morgan; 66
R2 Morgan; 135
R3 Morgan; 212

Lowest Scores
R2 Grady; 66
R3 Faldo, Scott Simpson (64), Sindelar; 68
R4 Montgomerie; Tyner; 70

BRITISH OPEN 1992

Hon Co of Edinburgh Golfers, Muirfield, East Lothian, Scotland
(16–19 July)
6970 yds: Par (284)

Nick Faldo won his third Open (second at Muirfield) to match the feat of Jones, Cotton, Player, Nicklaus and Ballesteros during the 20th Century. He's still tied-11th on the all-time list of Open winners however, only halving Vardon's haul of titles. At the same venue in 1987, Paul Azinger was the American worn down by Faldo's attritional style. This time, after wasting a four-shot lead overnight, he stood on the 15th tee two behind another American, John Cook, with the tide going the way of his rival. Faldo's reserves of grit are famously deep, however, and *the* outstanding winner of Majors over a period of twn years from the mid-80s to the mid-90s proved why, when he birdied 15 and 17, forcing Cook to crack on 18, and win by one. Faldo's first 36 holes in 130 remains the record low for any Major to date.

1	**NICK FALDO**	66	64	69	73	272
	(£95000)					
2	John Cook	66	67	70	70	273
3	Jose Maria Olazabal	70	67	69	68	274
4	Steve Pate	64	70	69	73	276
5=	Gordon Brand, Jr	65	68	72	74	279
	Ernie Els	66	69	70	74	279
	Donnie Hammond	70	65	70	74	279
	Robert Karlsson	70	68	70	71	279
	Malcolm Mackenzie	71	67	70	71	279
	Andrew Magee	67	72	70	70	279
	Ian Woosnam	65	73	70	71	279
12=	Chip Beck	71	68	67	74	280
	Ray Floyd	64	71	73	72	280
	Sandy Lyle	68	70	70	72	280
	Mark O'Meara	71	68	72	69	280
	Larry Rinker	69	68	70	73	280
	Jamie Spence	71	68	70	71	280
18	Greg Norman	71	72	70	68	281
19=	Ian Baker-Finch	71	71	72	68	282
	Hale Irwin	70	73	67	72	282
	Tom Kite	70	69	71	72	282
22=	Paul Lawrie	70	72	68	73	283
	Peter Mitchell	69	71	72	71	283
	Tom Purtzer	68	69	75	71	283
25=	Billy Andrade	69	71	70	74	284
	Peter Senior	70	69	70	75	284
	Duffy Waldorf	69	70	73	72	284
28=	Mark Calcavecchia	69	71	73	72	285
	Russ Cochran	71	68	72	74	285
	Mats Lanner	72	68	71	74	285
	Mark McNulty	71	70	70	74	285
	Jodie Mudd	71	69	74	71	285
	Craig Parry	67	71	76	71	285

Round Leader(s)
R1   Floyd, Pate; 64
R2   Faldo; 130
R3   Faldo; 199

Lowest Scores
R2   Faldo; 64
R3   Beck, Irwin; 67
R4   Baker-Finch, Norman, Olazabal; 68

US PGA 1992

Bellerive Country Club, St Louis, Missouri
(13–16 August)
7024 yards: PAR 71 (284)

John Cook was to be unlucky again at Bellerive, but this time he may have taken some comfort knowing that Nick Price was also a two-time second placer (British Opens in 1982 and 1988) before landing his first Major. Sadly for Cook, it seems this was to be his last great assault on a Major Championship. Zimbabwean Price, who with an English father and Welsh mother, spent much of his early career on the European circuit before settling in the US – where he had established himself as one of the world's best players. Faldo's charge to become the first European to win the Wanamaker Trophy did not fluster the calm African who, after the leader throughout, Gene Sauers, blew up, held on for a comfortable win.

1	**NICK PRICE**	70	70	68	70	278
	($280000)					
2=	John Cook	71	72	67	71	281
	Nick Faldo	68	70	76	67	281
	Jim Gallagher, Jr	72	66	72	71	281
	Gene Sauers	67	69	70	75	281
6	Jeff Maggert	71	72	65	74	282
7=	Russ Cochran	69	69	76	69	283
	Dan Forsman	70	73	70	70	283
9=	Brian Claar	68	73	73	70	284
	Anders Forsbrand	73	71	70	70	284
	Duffy Waldorf	74	73	68	69	284
12=	Billy Andrade	72	71	70	72	285
	Corey Pavin	71	73	70	71	285
	Jeff Sluman	73	71	72	69	285
15=	Mark Brooks	71	72	68	75	286
	Brad Faxon	72	69	75	70	286
	Greg Norman	71	74	71	70	286
18=	Steve Elkington	74	70	71	72	287
	Rick Fehr	74	73	71	69	287
	John Huston	73	75	71	68	287
21=	Bill Britton	70	77	70	71	288
	Fred Couples	69	73	73	73	288
	Lee Janzen	74	71	72	71	288
	Tom Kite	73	73	69	73	288
	Gil Morgan	71	69	73	75	288
	Tommy Nakajima	71	75	69	73	288
	Tom Purtzer	72	72	74	70	288
28=	Mike Hulbert	74	74	70	71	289
	Peter Jacobsen	73	71	72	73	289
	Larry Nelson	72	68	75	74	289
	Joe Ozaki	76	72	74	67	289
	Tom Wargo	72	72	73	72	289

Round Leader(s)
R1   Sauers, Craig Stadler (48); 67
R2   Sauers; 136
R3   Sauers; 206

Lowest Scores
R2   Gallagher, Steven Richardson (48); 66
R3   Maggert; 65
R4   Faldo, Ozaki; 67

THE MASTERS 1993

Augusta National Golf Club, Augusta, Georgia
(8–11 April)
6925 yards: Par 72 (288)

Eight years after winning his first Masters, Bernhard Langer proved he was still a force in world golf with a repeat victory at Augusta. It was also ten years after Seve Ballesteros' second win, which paved the way for Lyle, Faldo (twice) and Woosnam, along with Langer, to dominate the event for Europe. Jose Maria Olazabal apart, the German was the only European to finish in this year's Top 10: a signal, perhaps, along with form from the other Majors later in the year, that the US were to retain the Ryder Cup this year. Winner's prize money topped $300000 for the first time.

I	**BERNHARD LANGER**	68	70	69	70	277
	($306000)					
2	Chip Beck	72	67	72	70	281
3=	John Daly	70	71	73	69	283
	Steve Elkington	71	70	71	71	283
	Tom Lehman	67	75	73	68	283
	Lanny Wadkins	69	72	71	71	283
7=	Dan Forsman	69	69	73	73	284
	Jose Maria Olazabal	70	72	74	68	284
9=	Brad Faxon	74	70	72	69	285
	Payne Stewart	74	70	72	69	285
11=	Seve Ballesteros	74	70	71	71	286
	Ray Floyd	68	71	74	73	286
	Anders Forsbrand	71	74	75	66	286
	Corey Pavin	67	75	73	71	286
	Scott Simpson	72	71	71	72	286
	Fuzzy Zoeller	75	67	71	73	286
17=	Mark Calcavecchia	71	70	74	72	287
	Jeff Sluman	71	72	71	73	287
	Howard Twitty	70	71	73	73	287
	Ian Woosnam	71	74	73	69	287
21=	Russ Cochran	70	69	73	76	288
	Fred Couples	72	70	74	72	288
	Sandy Lyle	73	71	71	73	288
	Jeff Maggert	70	67	75	76	288
	Larry Mize	67	74	74	73	288
	Mark O'Meara	75	69	73	71	288
27=	Nolan Henke	76	69	71	73	289
	Hale Irwin	74	69	74	72	289
	Jack Nicklaus	67	75	76	71	289
	Joey Sindelar	72	69	76	72	289

Round Leader(s)
R1   Lehman, Mize, Nicklaus, Pavin; 67
R2   Maggert; 137
R3   Langer; 207

Lowest Scores
R2   Beck, Maggert, Zoeller; 67
R3   Langer, 69
R4   Forsbrand; 66

US OPEN 1993

Baltusrol Golf Club, Springfield, New Jersey
(17–20 June)
7152 yards: Par 70 (280)

Failing to make the cut in three former attempts, it was deemed a little early in his career for 28 year-old Lee Janzen to win a Major. However, leading from Round Two, he headed a strong field thereafter, and held on to be a worthy winner from 1991 Champion Payne Stewart. Joey Sindelar tied for the first round lead with a 66. He then shot a 79 to miss the cut. John Daly, the 1991 PGA Champion and prodigious hitter extrordinaire, playing the 630-yard 17th – the longest hole in Majors history – drove, then one-ironed the green in two.

I	**LEE JANZEN**	67	67	69	69	272
	($290000)					
2	Payne Stewart	70	66	68	70	274
3=	Paul Azinger	71	68	69	69	277
	Craig Parry	66	74	69	68	277
5=	Scott Hoch	66	72	72	68	278
	Tom Watson	70	66	73	69	278
7=	Ernie Els	71	73	68	67	279
	Ray Floyd	68	73	70	68	279
	Fred Funk	70	72	67	70	279
	Nolan Henke	72	71	67	69	279
11=	John Adams	70	70	69	71	280
	David Edwards	70	72	66	72	280
	Nick Price	71	66	70	73	280
	Loren Roberts	70	70	71	69	280
	Jeff Sluman	71	71	69	69	280
16=	Fred Couples	68	71	71	71	281
	Barry Lane	74	68	70	69	281
	Mike Standly	70	69	70	72	281
19=	Ian Baker-Finch	70	70	70	72	282
	Dan Forsman	73	71	70	68	282
	Tom Lehman	71	70	71	70	282
	Blaine McCallister	68	73	73	68	282
	Steve Pate	70	71	71	70	282
	Corey Pavin	68	69	75	70	282
25=	Chip Beck	72	68	72	71	283
	Mark Calcavecchia	70	70	71	72	283
	John Cook	75	66	70	72	283
	Wayne Levi	71	69	69	74	283
	Rocco Mediate	68	72	73	70	283
	Joe Ozaki	70	70	74	69	283
	Kenny Perry	74	70	68	71	283
	Curtis Strange	73	68	75	67	283

Round Leader(s)
R1   Hoch, Parry, Joey Sindelar (Cut); 66
R2   Janzen; 134
R3   Janzen; 203

Lowest Scores
R2   Cook, Price, Stewart, Watson; 66
R3   Edwards; 66
R4   Steve Lowery (33); 66

BRITISH OPEN 1993

Royal St George's Golf Club, Sandwich, Kent, England
(15–18 July)
6860 yards: Par 72 (280)

Greg Norman set the lowest score in Majors history when his blitzing 64 in the last round gave him a two-shot lead over reigning Champion Nick Faldo. Visiting nonegenarian and golfing 'squire' Gene Sarazen said he had witnessed nothing like it in golf before. Norman's 13-under par 267 was one lower than Tom Watson's at Turnberry in 1977, where Norman won his only other title. In repeating his win he scotched further accusations of his fragility in Major Championships, but he was not to get rid of them completely. Ernie Els shot four sub-70 rounds, but only finished sixth – the lowest position for such an achievement in a Major Championship. Nick Faldo and Payne Stewart each tied with the all-time low of 63. The winning prize money reached six figures in Pounds Sterling for the first time.

1	**GREG NORMAN**	66	68	69	64	267
	(£100000)					
2	Nick Faldo	69	63	70	67	269
3	Bernhard Langer	67	66	70	67	270
4=	Corey Pavin	68	66	68	70	272
	Peter Senior	66	69	70	67	272
6=	Ernie Els	68	69	69	68	274
	Paul Lawrie	72	68	69	65	274
	Nick Price	68	70	67	69	274
9=	Fred Couples	68	66	72	69	275
	Wayne Grady	74	68	64	69	275
	Scott Simpson	68	70	71	66	275
12	Payne Stewart	71	72	70	63	276
13	Barry Lane	70	68	71	68	277
14=	Mark Calcavecchia	66	73	71	68	278
	John Daly	71	66	70	71	278
	Tom Kite	72	70	68	68	278
	Mark McNulty	67	71	71	69	278
	Gil Morgan	70	68	70	70	278
	Jose Rivero	68	73	67	70	278
	Fuzzy Zoeller	66	70	71	71	278
21=	Peter Baker	70	67	74	68	279
	Howard Clark	67	72	70	70	279
	Jesper Parnevik	68	74	68	69	279
24=	Rodger Davis	68	71	71	70	280
	David Frost	69	73	70	68	280
	Mark Roe	70	71	73	66	280
27=	Seve Ballesteros	68	73	69	71	281
	Mark James	70	70	70	71	281
	Malcolm Mackenzie	72	71	71	67	281
	Larry Mize	67	69	74	71	281
	Yoshinori Mizumaki	69	69	73	70	281
	Iain Pyman (a)	68	72	70	71	281
	Des Smyth	67	74	70	70	281

Round Leader(s)
R1 Calcavecchia, Norman, Senior, Zoeller; 66
R2 Faldo; 132
R3 Faldo, Pavin; 202

Lowest Scores
R2 Faldo; 63
R3 Grady; 64
R4 Stewart; 63

US PGA 1993

Inverness Club, Toledo, Ohio
(12–15 August)
7024 yards: Par 71 (284)

Paul Azinger, twice a runner-up in Majors (British Open 1987 and the PGA itself a year later), and close finisher in the US Open earlier in the year, eventually collected an overdue Major Championship. Greg Norman's propensity to fail in Majors showdowns continued, as he succumbed once again to events at Inverness. Here, in 1986, it was Bob Tway's greenside bunker blow: this time it was down to Greg himself. He rimmed the hole from four feet to bogey the second extra hole in the play-off. Vijay Singh, from Fiji, the greatest golfer to come from the South Seas, shot a record-equalling 63 in Round Two.

1	**PAUL AZINGER***	69	66	69	68	272
	($300000)					
2	Greg Norman	68	68	67	69	272
3	Nick Faldo	68	68	69	68	273
4	Vijay Singh	68	63	73	70	274
5	Tom Watson	69	65	70	72	276
6=	John Cook	72	66	68	71	277
	Bob Estes	69	66	69	73	277
	Dudley Hart	66	68	71	72	277
	Nolan Henke	72	70	67	68	277
	Scott Hoch	74	68	68	67	277
	Hale Irwin	68	69	67	73	277
	Phil Mickelson	67	71	69	70	277
	Scott Simpson	64	70	71	72	277
14=	Steve Elkington	67	66	74	71	278
	Brad Faxon	70	70	65	73	278
	Bruce Fleisher	69	74	67	68	278
	Gary Hallberg	70	69	68	71	278
	Lanny Wadkins	65	68	71	74	278
	Richard Zokol	66	71	71	70	278
20=	Jay Haas	69	68	70	72	279
	Eduardo Romero	67	67	74	71	279
22=	Lee Janzen	70	68	71	72	281
	Jim McGovern	71	67	69	74	281
	Frank Nobilo	69	66	74	72	281
	Gene Sauers	68	74	70	69	281
	Greg Twiggs	70	69	70	72	281
	Ian Woosnam	70	71	68	72	281
28=	Peter Jacobsen	71	67	74	70	282
	Billy Mayfair	68	73	70	71	282
	Loren Roberts	67	67	76	72	282

* Paul Azinger beat Greg Norman a the 2nd extra hole in a Sudden Death Play-off

Round Leader(s)
R1 Simpson; 64
R2 Singh; 131
R3 Norman; 203

Lowest Scores
R2 Singh; 63
R3 Faxon; 65
R4 Hoch; 67

THE MASTERS 1994

Augusta National Golf Club, Augusta, Georgia
(7–10 April)

6925 yards: Par 72 (288)

The rich promise of Jose Maria Olazabal matured at Augusta, as Seve's prodigy and countryman won a Major for the first time. Six off the lead after Round One (held by 1987 Masters Champion, Larry Mize, in his best Majors performance since that year), Olazabal powered his way up the leaderboard. Ollie went around the final 54 holes in 11 under par to overtake third-round leader, Tom Lehman. This win made it nine Masters wins for Europeans since Ballesteros himself 1980, and the third for Spain.

1	**JOSE MARIA OLAZABAL**	74	67	69	69	279
	($360000)					
2	Tom Lehman	70	70	69	72	281
3	Larry Mize	68	71	72	71	282
4	Tom Kite	69	72	71	71	283
5=	Jay Haas	72	72	72	69	285
	Jim McGovern	72	70	71	72	285
	Loren Roberts	75	68	72	70	285
8=	Ernie Els	74	67	74	71	286
	Corey Pavin	71	72	73	70	286
10=	Ian Baker-Finch	71	71	71	74	287
	Ray Floyd	71	74	71	72	287
	John Huston	72	72	74	69	287
13	Tom Watson	70	71	73	74	288
14	Dan Forsman	74	66	76	73	289
15=	Chip Beck	71	71	75	74	291
	Brad Faxon	71	73	73	74	291
	Mark O'Meara	75	70	76	70	291
18=	Seve Ballesteros	70	76	75	71	292
	Ben Crenshaw	74	73	73	72	292
	David Edwards	73	72	73	74	292
	Bill Glasson	72	73	75	72	292
	Hale Irwin	73	68	79	72	292
	Greg Norman	70	70	75	77	292
	Lanny Wadkins	73	74	73	72	292
25=	Bernhard Langer	74	74	72	73	293
	Jeff Sluman	74	75	71	73	293
27=	Scott Simpson	74	74	73	73	294
	Vijay Singh	70	75	74	75	294
	Curtis Strange	74	70	75	75	294
30=	Lee Janzen	75	71	76	73	295
	Craig Parry	75	74	73	73	295

Round Leader(s)
R1   Mize; 68
R2   Mize; 139
R3   Lehman; 209

Lowest Scores
R2   Forsman; 66
R3   Lehman, Olazabal; 69
R4   Haas, Huston, Olazabal; 69

US OPEN 1994

Oakmont Country Club, Oakmont, Pennsylvania
(16–20 June)

6946 yards: Par 71 (284)

There was a three-way play-off in the US Open for the first time since Brookline in 1963. Arnold Palmer, along with Jacky Cupit, missed out to Julius Boros that year: now Arnold, aged 64, started the US Open for the last time. Ernie Els, 40 years his junior, became the first South African since Gary Player to win the Championship, and only the thrd after Bobby Locke and Player to win any Major Championship. After 18 holes, Colin Montgomerie was eliminated, leaving Els to fight it out, sudden death, with Loren Roberts. It took two holes before Roberts' bogey let in Ernie. The Round One leaderboard had a nostalgic feel to it: Tom Watson led Jack Nicklaus by one.

1	**ERNIE ELS***	69	71	66	73	279
	($320000)					
2=	Colin Montgomerie	71	65	73	70	279
	Loren Roberts	76	69	74	70	279
4	Curtis Strange	70	70	70	70	280
5	John Cook	73	65	73	71	282
6=	Tom Watson	68	73	68	74	283
	Clark Dennis	71	71	70	71	283
	Greg Norman	71	71	69	72	283
9=	Jeff Maggert	71	68	75	70	284
	Frank Nobilo	69	71	68	76	284
	Jeff Sluman	72	69	72	71	284
	Duffy Waldorf	74	68	73	69	284
13=	David Edwards	73	65	75	72	285
	Scott Hoch	72	72	70	71	285
	Jim McGovern	73	69	74	69	285
16=	Fred Couples	72	71	69	74	286
	Steve Lowery	71	71	68	76	286
18=	Seve Ballesteros	72	72	70	73	287
	Hale Irwin	69	69	71	78	287
	Scott Verplank	70	72	75	70	287
21=	Steve Pate	74	66	71	77	288
	Sam Torrance	72	71	76	69	288
23=	Bernhard Langer	72	72	73	72	289
	Kirk Triplett	70	71	71	77	289
25=	Chip Beck	73	73	70	74	290
	Craig Parry	78	68	71	73	290
	Mike Springer	74	72	73	71	290
28=	Lennie Clements	73	71	73	75	292
	Jim Furyk	74	69	74	75	292
	Davis Love III	74	72	74	72	292
	Jack Nicklaus	69	70	77	76	292
	Jumbo Ozaki	70	73	69	80	292

* Ernie Els (74) beat Colin Montgomerie (78) and tied with Loren Roberts (74) in the 18-Hole Play-off, before winning at the second extra hole

Round Leader(s)
R1   Watson; 68
R2   Montgomerie; 136
R3   Els; 206

Lowest Scores
R2   Cook, Edwards, Montgomerie; 65
R3   Roberts; 64
R4   McGovern, Torrance, Waldorf; 69

BRITISH OPEN 1994

Turnberry Golf Club, Ayrshire, Scotland
(14–17 July)
6957 yards: Par 70 (280)

Nick Price was to end 1994 atop the World Ranking: only Langer (in the first week of the Ranking), Ballesteros, Faldo, Woosnam and Couples, on times, took that spot from the dominant Greg Norman since the computerized tables were first produced in 1986. Greg was to regain the No 1 position for the eighth time again in 1995. Price's second Major occurred in a display of blistering scoring over the Turnberry Links. His battle-royal throughout Round Four with Jesper Parnevik culminated in the Swede – going to the last two ahead – dropping a shot at the last, while Price was holing a 17-yard putt for eagle at the 17th.

1	NICK PRICE	69	66	67	66	268
	(£110000)					
2	Jesper Parnevik	68	66	68	67	269
3	Fuzzy Zoeller	71	66	64	70	271
4=	David Feherty	68	69	66	70	273
	Anders Forsbrand	72	71	66	64	273
	Mark James	72	67	66	68	273
7	Brad Faxon	69	65	67	73	274
8=	Nick Faldo	75	66	70	64	275
	Tom Kite	71	69	66	69	275
	Colin Montgomerie	72	69	65	69	275
11=	Mark Calcavecchia	71	70	67	68	276
	Russell Claydon	72	71	68	65	276
	Jonathan Lomas	66	70	72	68	276
	Mark McNulty	71	70	68	67	276
	Larry Mize	73	69	64	70	276
	Frank Nobilo	69	67	72	68	276
	Greg Norman	71	67	69	69	276
	Ronan Rafferty	71	66	65	74	276
	Tom Watson	68	65	69	74	276
20=	Mark Brooks	74	64	71	68	277
	Peter Senior	68	71	67	71	277
	Vijay Singh	70	68	69	70	277
	Greg Turner	65	71	70	71	277
24=	Andrew Coltart	71	69	66	72	278
	Ernie Els	69	69	69	71	278
	Bob Estes	72	68	72	66	278
	Peter Jacobsen	69	70	67	72	278
	Paul Lawrie	71	69	70	68	278
	Tom Lehman	70	69	70	69	278
	Jeff Maggert	69	74	67	68	278
	Terry Price	74	65	71	68	278
	Loren Roberts	68	69	69	72	278
	Mike Springer	72	67	68	71	278
	Craig Stadler	71	69	66	72	278

Round Leader(s)
R1 Turner; 65
R2 Watson; 133
R3 Faxon, Zoeller; 201

Lowest Scores
R2 Brooks; 64
R3 Mize, Zoeller; 64
R4 Faldo, Forsbrand; 64

US PGA 1994

Southern Hills Country Club, Tulsa, Oklahoma
(11–14 August)
6824 yards: PAR 70 (280)

Nick Price's 11-under par 269 was a new low for the PGA Championship and formed part of a remarkable 23-under par back-to-back Majors double for the Zimbabwean. He became the first golfer since Faldo in 1990 to win more than one Major in the same season; and only the second person to achieve the British Open-PGA double in the same year since Walter Hagen's achievement 70 years before. His win by six strokes over an outstanding field emphasised Price's superiority in 1994.

1	NICK PRICE	67	65	70	67	269
	($310000)					
2	Corey Pavin	70	67	69	69	275
3	Phil Mickelson	68	71	67	70	276
4=	John Cook	71	67	69	70	277
	Nick Faldo	73	67	71	66	277
	Greg Norman	71	69	67	70	277
7=	Steve Elkington	73	70	66	69	278
	Jose Maria Olazabal	72	66	70	70	278
9=	Ben Crenshaw	70	67	70	72	279
	Tom Kite	72	68	69	70	279
	Loren Roberts	69	72	67	71	279
	Tom Watson	69	72	67	71	279
	Ian Woosnam	68	72	73	66	279
14	Jay Haas	71	66	68	75	280
15=	Glen Day	70	69	70	72	281
	Mark McNulty	72	68	70	71	281
	Larry Mize	72	72	67	70	281
	Kirk Triplett	71	69	71	70	281
19=	Bill Glasson	71	73	68	70	282
	Mark McCumber	73	70	71	68	282
	Craig Parry	70	69	70	73	282
	Craig Stadler	70	70	74	68	282
	Curtis Strange	73	71	68	70	282
	Fuzzy Zoeller	69	71	72	70	282
25=	Ernie Els	68	71	69	75	283
	David Frost	70	71	69	73	283
	Barry Lane	70	73	68	72	283
	Bernhard Langer	73	71	67	72	283
	Jeff Sluman	70	72	66	75	283
30=	Bob Boyd	72	71	70	71	284
	Lennie Clements	74	70	69	71	284
	Brad Faxon	72	73	73	66	284
	Wayne Grady	75	68	71	70	284
	Sam Torrance	69	75	69	71	284
	Richard Zokol	77	67	67	73	284

Round Leader(s)
R1 Colin Montgomerie (36), Price; 67
R2 Price; 132
R3 Price; 202

Lowest Scores
R2 Blaine McCallister (36); 64
R3 Elkington, Sluman; 66
R4 Faldo, Faxon, Woosnam; 66

THE MASTERS 1995

Augusta National Golf Club, Augusta, Georgia
(6–9 April)
6925 yards: Par 72 (288)

Ben Crenshaw's second Masters, and second Major, was an emotional occasion. 'Gentle' Ben had been one of the game's most popular players for over two decades; and when he won his second Green Jacket, 11 years after the first, and just a few days after the death of his friend and mentor, Harvey Penick, no one complained. Davis Love III, whose grandfather and father had featured in various Majors over the years, was beginning to assume the mantle that Crenshaw once had – and Kite had discarded in 1992.

1	**BEN CRENSHAW**	70	67	69	68	274
	($396000)					
2	Davis Love III	69	69	71	66	275
3=	Jay Haas	71	64	72	70	277
	Greg Norman	73	68	68	68	277
5=	Steve Elkington	73	67	67	72	279
	David Frost	66	71	71	71	279
7=	Scott Hoch	69	67	71	73	280
	Phil Mickelson	66	71	70	73	280
9	Curtis Strange	72	71	65	73	281
10=	Fred Couples	71	69	67	75	282
	Brian Henninger	70	68	68	76	282
12=	Lee Janzen	69	69	74	71	283
	Kenny Perry	73	70	71	69	283
14=	Hale Irwin	69	72	71	72	284
	Jose Maria Olazabal	66	74	72	72	284
	Tom Watson	73	70	69	72	284
17=	Paul Azinger	70	72	73	70	285
	Brad Faxon	76	69	69	71	285
	Ray Floyd	71	70	70	74	285
	John Huston	70	66	72	77	285
	Colin Montgomerie	71	69	76	69	285
	Corey Pavin	67	71	72	75	285
	Ian Woosnam	69	72	71	73	285
24=	David Edwards	69	73	73	71	286
	Nick Faldo	70	70	71	75	286
	David Gilford	67	73	75	71	286
	Loren Roberts	72	69	72	73	286
	Duffy Waldorf	74	69	67	76	286
29=	Bob Estes	73	70	76	68	287
	Jumbo Ozaki	70	74	70	73	287

Round Leader(s)
R1 Frost, Mickelson, Olazabal; 66
R2 Haas; 135
R3 Crenshaw, Henninger; 206

Lowest Scores
R2 Haas; 64
R3 Strange; 65
R4 Love; 66

US OPEN 1995

Shinnecock Hills Golf Club, Southampton, New York
(15–18 June)
6912 yards: PAR 70 (280)

Davis Love was inheriting the label 'the best player never to have won a Major', championship by championship, and this was reinforced when the US Open celebrated its centennial at Shinnecock. Corey Pavin had also been linked with the tag, but his first win eliminated him from the maiden stakes to leave Love, with another creditable performance, looking over his shoulder for new competition in Mickelson and Montgomerie. Greg Norman finished second for the seventh time in a Major.

1	**COREY PAVIN**	72	69	71	68	280
	($350000)					
2	Greg Norman	68	67	74	73	282
3	Tom Lehman	70	72	67	74	283
4=	Bill Glasson	69	70	76	69	284
	Jay Haas	70	73	72	69	284
	Neal Lancaster	70	72	77	65	284
	Davis Love III	72	68	73	71	284
	Jeff Maggert	69	72	77	66	284
	Phil Mickelson	68	70	72	74	284
10=	Frank Nobilo	72	72	70	71	285
	Vijay Singh	70	71	72	72	285
	Bob Tway	69	69	72	75	285
13=	Brad Bryant	71	75	70	70	286
	Lee Janzen	70	72	72	72	286
	Mark McCumber	70	71	77	68	286
	Nick Price	66	73	73	74	286
	Mark Roe	71	69	74	72	286
	Jeff Sluman	72	69	74	71	286
	Steve Stricker	71	70	71	74	286
	Duffy Waldorf	72	70	75	69	286
21=	Billy Andrade	72	69	74	72	287
	Pete Jordan	74	71	71	71	287
	Brett Ogle	71	75	72	69	287
	Payne Stewart	74	71	73	69	287
	Scott Verplank	72	69	71	75	287
	Ian Woosnam	72	71	69	75	287
	Fuzzy Zoeller	69	74	76	68	287
28=	David Duval	70	73	73	72	288
	Gary Hallberg	70	76	69	73	288
	Mike Hulbert	74	72	72	70	288
	Miguel Jimenez	72	72	75	69	288
	Colin Montgomerie	71	74	75	68	288
	Jose Maria Olazabal	73	70	72	73	288
	Jumbo Ozaki	69	68	80	71	288
	Scott Simpson	67	75	74	72	288

Round Leader(s)
R1 Price; 66
R2 Norman; 135
R3 Lehman, Norman; 209

Lowest Scores
R2 Norman; 67
R3 Lehman; 67
R4 Lancaster; 65

BRITISH OPEN 1995

Royal & Ancient Golf Club, St Andrews, Fife, Scotland
(20–23 July)
6933 yards: Par 72 (288)

John Daly, flirting with alcoholics' rehabilitation centres since his 1991 PGA triumph, held his nerve to outplay an emotionally-drained Constantino Rocca in the four-hole play-off. After completing Round Four, Daly was in the Clubhouse watching the Italian approach Tom Morris' green. Rocca needed to chip and putt for two to tie. With not much green to work with, he fluffed his shot, and saw his ball roll back into the Valley of Sin and stop 20 yards or so from the pin. Daly, with TV cameras watching his every gesture, kept calm, but must have thought the Claret Jug was his. His expression hardly changed when Costantino sensationally holed his second approach attempt with the putter: but the Italian collapsed in a mixture of relief and exhausion. Despite seeing the Jug dashed away from his lips at the last, it was Daly, in overtime, who stayed the calmer to win his second Major.

1	**JOHN DALY*** (£125000)	67	71	73	71	282
2	Costantino Rocca	69	70	70	73	282
3=	Steven Bottomley	70	72	72	69	283
	Mark Brooks	70	69	73	71	283
	Michael Campbell	71	71	65	76	283
6=	Steve Elkington	72	69	69	74	284
	Vijay Singh	68	72	73	71	284
8=	Bob Estes	72	70	71	72	285
	Mark James	72	75	68	70	285
	Corey Pavin	69	70	72	74	285
11=	Ernie Els	71	68	72	75	286
	Brett Ogle	73	69	71	73	286
	Payne Stewart	72	68	75	71	286
	Sam Torrance	71	70	71	74	286
15=	Robert Allenby	71	74	71	71	287
	Ben Crenshaw	67	72	76	72	287
	Brad Faxon	71	67	75	74	287
	Per-Ulrik Johansson	69	78	68	72	287
	Greg Norman	71	74	72	70	287
20=	Andrew Coltart	70	74	71	73	288
	David Duval	71	75	70	72	288
	Barry Lane	72	73	68	75	288
	Peter Mitchell	73	74	71	70	288
24=	Mark Calcavecchia	71	72	72	74	289
	Bill Glasson	68	74	72	75	289
	Lee Janzen	73	73	71	72	289
	Bernhard Langer	72	71	73	73	289
	Jesper Parnevik	75	71	70	73	289
	Katsuyoshi Tomori	70	68	73	78	289
	Steven Webster (a)	70	72	74	73	289

* John Daly beat Costantino Rocca in the 4-Hole Play-off

Round Leader(s)
R1 Crenshaw, Daly; 67
R2 Daly, Faxon; 138
R3 Campbell; 207

Lowest Scores
R2 Faxon; 67
R3 Campbell; 65
R4 Bottomley; 69

US PGA 1995

Riviera Country Club, Pacific Palisades, California
(10–13 August)
6956 yards: PAR 71 (284)

Colin Montgomerie tied the record low score in Major Championships, but without actually winning. A famous quiz question at the time, expunged from the record books after all the goings on at Atlanta AC in 2001. Colin's 267 took him level with Steve Elkington, whose 25-foot birdie putt sealed the play-off. One record that does remain is the 132 Elkington shot for the second 36 holes: it is the lowest such total for any Major (until Atlanta, 2001!) and, along with Davis Love in 1997, still the lowest second half to win any Major. If the Europeans had taken a shine to the Masters, then the PGA was starting to become the preserve of golfers from the Southern Hemisphere. Between 1916 and 1962 only Australia's Jim Ferrier and South Africa's Gary Player had taken the trophy ahead of native or naturalized Americans. Following Player's second win in 1972, David Graham, Wayne Grady, Price (twice), Ernie Els, and now Elkington, had won the Championship – the last five in six years.

1	**STEVE ELKINGTON*** ($360000)	68	67	68	64	267
2	Colin Montgomerie	68	67	67	65	267
3=	Ernie Els	66	65	66	72	269
	Jeff Maggert	66	69	65	69	269
5	Brad Faxon	70	67	71	63	271
6=	Bob Estes	69	68	68	68	273
	Mark O'Meara	64	67	69	73	273
8=	Jay Haas	69	71	64	70	274
	Justin Leonard	68	66	70	70	274
	Steve Lowery	69	68	68	69	274
	Jeff Sluman	69	67	68	70	274
	Craig Stadler	71	66	66	71	274
13=	Jim Furyk	68	70	69	68	275
	Miguel Jimenez	69	69	67	70	275
	Payne Stewart	69	70	69	67	275
	Kirk Triplett	71	69	68	67	275
17=	Michael Campbell	71	65	71	69	276
	Constantino Rocca	70	69	68	69	276
	Curtis Strange	72	68	68	68	276
20=	Greg Norman	66	69	70	72	277
	Jesper Parnevik	69	69	70	69	277
	Duffy Waldorf	69	69	67	72	277
23=	Woody Austin	70	70	70	68	278
	Nolan Henke	68	73	67	70	278
	Peter Jacobsen	69	67	71	71	278
	Lee Janzen	66	70	72	70	278
	Bruce Lietzke	73	68	67	70	278
	Billy Mayfair	68	68	72	70	278
	Steve Stricker	75	64	69	70	278
	Sam Torrance	69	69	69	71	278

* Steve Elkington beat Colin Montgomerie at the 1st extra hole in a Sudden Death Play-off

Round Leader(s)
R1 Michael Bradley (54); 63
R2 Els, O'Meara; 131
R3 Els; 197

Lowest Scores
R2 Stricker; 64
R3 Haas; 64
R4 Faxon; 63

THE MASTERS 1996

Augusta National Golf Club, Augusta, Georgia
(11–14 April)
6925 yards: Par 72 (288)

Perhaps this was the most astonishing final round in Majors history. World No 1 Greg Norman, twice winner of the British Open, became a Majors runner-up for the eigthth, and perhaps most-damaging, time when he sur-rendered a six-shot overnight lead to Nick Faldo. His game then collapsed completely, finally losing by five in an 11-stroke swing of fortune. Norman's Majors weakness within a sport he had otherwise dominated for much of the previous decade cannot be questioned. His eight run-ners-up places put him tied with Sam Snead in third place of all time. But Sam won seven Majors as well, and pro-portionately the best players have had a similar number of winning and second place positions. Above Snead and Norman are Nicklaus with 18 seconds and 18 wins; fol-lowed by Palmer (nine and seven, respectively). Against Faldo, Norman's capitulation included a seven-shot swing in as many holes, and ten over the last 12. Faldo, to his credit, still shot a best-of-the-day 67 for his sixth Major – joint-11th all-time with Lee Trevino – and proved himself to be one of the best head-to-head scrappers in the his-tory of the Majors.

1	**NICK FALDO** ($435000)	69	67	73	67	276
2	Greg Norman	63	69	71	78	281
3	Phil Mickelson	65	73	72	72	282
4	Frank Nobilo	71	71	72	69	283
5=	Scott Hoch	67	73	73	71	284
	Duffy Waldorf	72	71	69	72	284
7=	Davis Love III	72	71	74	68	285
	Jeff Maggert	71	73	72	69	285
	Corey Pavin	75	66	73	71	285
10=	David Frost	70	68	74	74	286
	Scott McCarron	70	70	72	74	286
12=	Ernie Els	71	71	72	73	287
	Lee Janzen	68	71	75	73	287
	Bob Tway	67	72	76	72	287
15=	Mark Calcavecchia	71	73	71	73	288
	Fred Couples	78	68	71	71	288
17	John Huston	71	71	71	76	289
18=	Paul Azinger	70	74	76	70	290
	David Duval	73	72	69	76	290
	Tom Lehman	75	70	72	73	290
	Mark O'Meara	72	71	75	72	290
	Nick Price	71	75	70	74	290
23=	Larry Mize	75	71	77	68	291
	Loren Roberts	71	73	72	75	291
25=	Brad Faxon	69	77	72	74	292
	Ray Floyd	70	74	77	71	292
27=	Bob Estes	71	71	79	72	293
	Justin Leonard	72	74	75	72	293
29=	John Daly	71	74	71	78	294
	Jim Furyk	75	70	78	71	294
	Jim Gallagher, Jr	70	76	77	71	294
	Hale Irwin	74	71	77	72	294
	Scott Simpson	69	76	76	73	294
	Craig Stadler	73	72	71	78	294
	Ian Woosnam	72	69	73	80	294

Round Leader(s)
R1   Norman; 63
R2   Norman; 132
R3   Norman; 203

Lowest Scores
R2   Pavin; 66
R3   Duval, Waldorf; 69
R4   Faldo; 67

US OPEN 1996

Oakland Hills Country Club, Birmingham, Michigan
(13–16 June)
6996 yards: Par 70 (280)

Steve Jones had to pre-qualify for the Open – being the first winner to do so since 1976, when Jerry Pate had to endure the same ordeal. Jones had faded from the golf scene a few years previously due to an awful motorcycle accident, but it was he who had the right stuff as holes were running out. Jones, Davis Love and Tom Lehman were battling for supremacy. Love should have been in the Clubhouse with a 67, but missed a putt on the 18th reminiscent of that required to win the British Open in 1970 by Doug Sanders. After also bogeying 17, he could only sit and wait. Driving off the 18th tee Lehman found a fairway bunker to nullify any hope he had of making the green in regulation. Jones steadied and drove truly down the middle to set up the par that was to win it.

1	**STEVE JONES** ($405000)	74	66	69	69	278
2=	Tom Lehman	71	72	65	71	279
	Davis Love III	71	69	70	69	279
4	John Morse	68	74	68	70	280
5=	Ernie Els	72	67	72	70	281
	Jim Furyk	72	69	70	70	281
7=	Ken Green	73	67	72	70	282
	Scott Hoch	73	71	71	67	282
	Vijay Singh	71	72	70	69	282
10=	Lee Janzen	68	75	71	69	283
	Colin Montgomerie	70	72	69	72	283
	Greg Norman	73	66	74	70	283
13=	Dan Forsman	72	71	70	71	284
	Frank Nobilo	69	71	70	74	284
	Tom Watson	70	71	71	72	284
16=	David Berganio, Jr	69	72	72	72	285
	Mark Brooks	76	68	69	72	285
	Stewart Cink	69	73	70	73	285
	John Cook	70	71	71	73	285
	Nick Faldo	72	71	72	70	285
	Mark O'Meara	72	73	68	72	285
	Sam Torrance	71	69	71	74	285
23=	Billy Andrade	72	69	72	73	286
	Woody Austin	67	72	72	75	286
	Brad Bryant	73	71	74	68	286
	Peter Jacobsen	71	74	70	71	286
27=	John Daly	72	69	73	73	287
	Pete Jordan	71	74	72	70	287
	Jack Nicklaus	72	74	69	72	287
	Payne Stewart	67	71	76	73	287
	Curtis Strange	74	73	71	69	287

Round Leader(s)
R1   Austin, Stewart; 67
R2   Stewart; 138
R3   Lehman; 208

Lowest Scores
R2   Jones, Norman; 66
R3   Lehman; 65
R4   Hoch; 67

BRITISH OPEN 1996

Royal Lytham and St Anne's Golf Club, Lancashire, England
(18–21 July)

6892 yards: PAR 71 (284)

With the first prize doubling within four years, the 125th Open, although mostly dominated by the top Americans, was still not supported by as many as the R&A would have liked. Demands imposed upon them by the ever-more competitive PGA Tour forced many to stay at home – especially those not exempt and who would have to have invested extra time in qualifying. This would change in a few years, with the inclusion of the British Open as an official PGA Tour event, and some events leading up to the Open counting as qualifying tournaments. Nick Faldo kept home hopes alive with three successive 68s, but was too far away from Tom Lehman's 54-hole record score of 198 to make an impression. With the weather calm, Lytham was a bit of a pussy cat for a change, and low scoring was the norm. 1994 US Open Champion, Ernie Els, and 45 year-old Mark McCumber, kept up the pressure, and Mark Brooks was in the hunt as he was the previous year. But Lehman's cushion was to prove too comfortable. His disappointing two-over par 73 still gave him a two-stroke advantage at the end. After several good finishes in the past, his first Major was well deserved. Mentioning pussy cats, three-time US Amateur Champion, one Tiger Woods, introduced himself to the British public. The face of professional golf was soon to change unrecognizably in a very short space of time.

1	**TOM LEHMAN**	67	67	64	73	271
	(£200000)					
2=	Ernie Els	68	67	71	67	273
	Mark McCumber	67	69	71	66	273
4	Nick Faldo	68	68	68	70	274
5=	Mark Brooks	67	70	68	71	276
	Jeff Maggert	69	70	72	65	276
7=	Fred Couples	67	70	69	71	277
	Peter Hedblom	70	65	75	67	277
	Greg Norman	71	68	71	67	277
	Greg Turner	72	69	68	68	277
11=	Alexander Cejka	73	67	71	67	278
	Darren Clarke	70	68	69	71	278
	Vijay Singh	69	67	69	73	278
14=	David Duval	76	67	66	70	279
	Paul McGinley	69	65	74	71	279
	Mark McNulty	69	71	70	69	279
	Shigeki Maruyama	68	70	69	72	279
18=	Padraig Harrington	68	68	73	71	280
	Rocco Mediate	69	70	69	72	280
	Loren Roberts	67	69	72	72	280
	Michael Welch	71	68	73	68	280
22=	Jay Haas	70	72	71	68	281
	Mark James	70	68	75	68	281
	Carl Mason	68	70	70	73	281
	Steve Stricker	71	70	66	74	281
	Tiger Woods (a)	75	66	70	70	281
27=	Paul Broadhurst	65	72	64	71	282
	Ben Crenshaw	73	68	71	70	282
	Tom Kite	77	66	69	70	282
	Peter Mitchell	71	68	71	72	282
	Frank Nobilo	70	72	68	72	282
	Corey Pavin	70	66	74	72	282

Round Leader(s)
R1 Broadhurst; 65
R2 Lehman, McGinley; 134
R3 Lehman; 198

Lowest Scores
R2 Hedblom, McGinley; 65
R3 Lehman; 64
R4 Maggert; 65

US PGA 1996

Valhalla Golf Club, Louisville, Kentucky
(8–11 August)

7144 yards: PAR 72 (288)

Carrying on his good form from Royal Lytham, Mark Brooks from Texas was involved in the finish once again. This time his immediate competition came from Kenny Perry, who was two strokes clear of the field going to the last hole. Round Three leader Russ Cochrane had blown up and challenges from Vijay Singh and Steve Elkington were dissipating. With Perry's lead then reduced to one after a waywide drive, Brooks birdied the last to force extra holes. He repeated the dose at the same hole in the play-off. The two-shot swing at the end of regulation play was a stern lesson to Perry. A popular local player, he was actively playing to the crowd going to the 18th tee, almost in premature celebration. He should have remembered Jesper Parnevik's horror two years before at Turnberry, when he set up for the 18th two ahead of Nick Price – and failed to make the play-off.

1	**MARK BROOKS***	68	70	69	70	277
	($430000)					
2	Kenny Perry	66	72	71	68	277
3=	Steve Elkington	67	74	67	70	278
	Tommy Tolles	69	71	71	67	278
5=	Justin Leonard	71	66	72	70	279
	Jesper Parnevik	73	67	69	70	279
	Vijay Singh	69	69	69	72	279
8=	Lee Janzen	68	71	71	70	280
	Per-Ulrik Johansson	73	72	66	69	280
	Phil Mickelson	67	67	74	72	280
	Larry Mize	71	70	69	70	280
	Frank Nobilo	69	72	71	68	280
	Nick Price	68	71	69	72	280
14=	Mike Brisky	71	69	69	72	281
	Tom Lehman	71	71	69	70	281
	Joey Sindelar	73	72	69	67	281
17=	Russ Cochran	68	72	65	77	282
	David Edwards	69	71	72	70	282
	Brad Faxon	72	68	73	69	282
	Jim Furyk	70	70	73	69	282
	Greg Norman	68	72	69	73	282
	Tom Watson	69	71	73	69	282
	DA Weibring	71	73	71	67	282
24=	Emlyn Aubrey	69	74	72	68	283
	Miguel Angel Jimenez	71	71	71	70	283
26=	Fred Funk	73	69	73	69	284
	Mark O'Meara	71	70	74	69	284
	Corey Pavin	71	74	70	69	284
	Curtis Strange	73	70	68	73	284
	Steve Stricker	73	72	72	67	284

* Mark Brooks beat Kenny Perry at the 1st extra hole in a Sudden-death Play-off

Round Leader(s)
R1 Perry; 66
R2 Mickelson; 134
R3 Cochran; 205

Lowest Scores
R2 Leonard; 66
R3 Cochran; 65
R4 Sindelar, Stricker, Tolles, Weibring; 67

THE MASTERS 1997

Augusta National Golf Club, Augusta, Georgia
(10–13 April)

6925 yards: Par 72 (288)

Records galore fell to the new *enfant terrible* of golf. Eldrick 'Tiger' Woods, after many years of hype and a sparkling amateur record, had announced himself to the world of professional golf. At 21 he became the youngest winner of the Masters, cancelling out the successive records of Jack Nicklaus, then Seve Ballesteros, and in doing, so changed the public perception of this middle-class, middle-brow, middle-aged, white man's sport so dramatically it may be now be irrevocable. Tiger so destroyed the Augusta course (a record low for the Masters) and the field (a record winning margin for the Masters), and created so many records on the way (first rookie to win a Major since Jerry Pate in 1976; shot the last 54 holes in 200; the first black golfer to win a Major, etc) he almost disguised the most amazing facet of his emergence. Here was a role model for all youth, black and white alike. His maturity off course was commented upon as much as his golfing genius – and left all in awe and wonder of what this new comet was about to inflict on the world of golf over the next couple of decades.

1	**TIGER WOODS** ($486000)	70	66	65	69	270
2	Tom Kite	77	69	66	70	282
3	Tommy Tolles	72	72	72	67	283
4	Tom Watson	75	68	69	72	284
5=	Costantino Rocca	71	69	70	75	285
	Paul Stankowski	68	74	79	74	285
7=	Fred Couples	72	69	73	72	286
	Bernhard Langer	72	72	74	68	286
	Justin Leonard	76	69	71	70	286
	Davis Love III	72	71	72	71	286
	Jeff Sluman	74	67	72	73	286
12=	Steve Elkington	76	72	72	67	287
	Per-Ulrik Johansson	72	73	73	69	287
	Tom Lehman	73	76	69	69	287
	Jose Maria Olazabal	71	70	74	72	287
	Willie Wood	72	76	71	68	287
17=	Mark Calcavecchia	74	73	72	69	288
	Ernie Els	73	70	71	74	288
	Fred Funk	74	73	69	72	288
	Vijay Singh	75	74	69	70	288
21=	Stuart Appleby	72	76	70	71	289
	John Huston	67	77	75	70	289
	Jesper Parnevik	73	72	71	73	289
24=	Nick Price	71	71	75	74	291
	Lee Westwood	77	71	73	70	291
26=	Lee Janzen	72	73	74	73	292
	Craig Stadler	77	72	71	72	292
28=	Paul Azinger	69	73	77	74	293
	Jim Furyk	74	75	72	72	293
30=	Scott McCarron	77	71	72	74	294
	Larry Mize	79	69	74	72	294
	Colin Montgomerie	72	67	74	81	294
	Mark O'Meara	75	74	70	75	294

Round Leader(s)
R1   Huston; 67
R2   Woods; 136
R3   Woods; 201

Lowest Scores
R2   Woods; 66
R3   Woods; 65
R4   Elkington, Tolles; 67

US OPEN 1997

Congressional Golf Club, Bethesda, Maryland
(12–15 June)

7213 yards: Par 70 (280)

The Woods bandwagon could not get up the expected head of steam, and despite a Round Two 67 which put him briefly in contention, Tiger rarely threatened in what was to become a three-horse race amongst those consistent performers, Lehman, Montgomerie and Els. Once again, though, Montgomerie was to be found wanting at the very end, as Lehman faded and the Scotsman, coming into the 17th, was tying with Els. True, the juxtaposition of the 18th green where Lehman and Maggert were putting out created a diversion, but Monty's temperament failed him as he delayed, and perhaps threatened in what – over a fatal five-footer. Els was made of sterner stuff and the South African collected his second US Open, at the age of 27.

1	**ERNIE ELS** ($465000)	71	67	69	69	276
2	Colin Montgomerie	65	76	67	69	277
3	Tom Lehman	67	70	68	73	278
4	Jeff Maggert	73	66	68	74	281
5=	Olin Browne	71	71	69	71	282
	Jim Furyk	74	68	69	71	282
	Jay Haas	73	69	68	72	282
	Tommy Tolles	74	67	69	72	282
	Bob Tway	71	71	70	70	282
10=	Scott Hoch	71	68	72	72	283
	Scott McCarron	73	71	69	70	283
	David Ogrin	70	69	71	73	283
13=	Billy Andrade	75	67	69	73	284
	Stewart Cink	71	67	74	72	284
	Loren Roberts	72	69	72	71	284
16=	Bradley Hughes	75	70	71	69	285
	Davis Love III	75	70	69	71	285
	Jose Maria Olazabal	71	71	71	71	285
19=	Nick Price	71	74	71	70	286
	Paul Stankowski	75	70	68	73	286
	Hal Sutton	66	73	73	74	286
	Lee Westwood	71	71	73	71	286
	Tiger Woods	74	67	73	72	286
24=	Scott Dunlap	75	66	75	71	287
	Steve Elkington	75	68	72	72	287
	Edward Fryatt	72	73	73	69	287
	Len Mattiace	71	75	73	68	287
28=	Paul Azinger	72	72	74	70	288
	Kelly Gibson	72	69	72	75	288
	Paul Goydos	73	72	74	69	288
	Hideki Kase	68	73	73	74	288
	Mark McNulty	67	73	75	73	288
	Jeff Sluman	69	72	72	75	288
	Payne Stewart	71	73	73	71	288
	Fuzzy Zoeller	72	73	69	74	288

Round Leader(s)
R1   Montgomerie; 65
R2   Lehman; 137
R3   Lehman; 205

Lowest Scores
R2   Dunlap, Maggert; 66
R3   Montgomerie; 67
R4   Mattiace; 68

BRITISH OPEN 1997

Royal Troon GC, Ayrshire, Scotland
(17–20 July)
7079 yards: Par 71 (284)

After Woods and Els, Justin Leonard became the third twentysomething in a row to a win a Major. He shot a brilliant last round to destroy Parnevik, who had been in a similar position three years earlier at Turnberry, that time succumbing to Nick Price. With all the early attention in Round Four on the scrap between Ulsterman Clarke and the quirky Swede, Leonard proceeded to compile the lowest score of the day up ahead: he was almost unnoticed until he birdied 17, and set a meaningful target for those behind. Playing in-and-out golf, Parnevik still had the Championship in his grasp when he approached the 13th. Four bogeys home, including 16, 17 and 18, sealed his fate and put a question-mark over his big-time nerve. Leonard continued the good form of the Americans in recent years, making it three Opens in a row.

1	**JUSTIN LEONARD**	69	66	72	65	272
	(£250000)					
2=	Darren Clarke	67	66	71	71	275
	Jesper Parnevik	70	66	66	73	275
4	Jim Furyk	67	72	70	70	279
5=	Stephen Ames	74	69	66	71	280
	Padraig Harrington	75	69	69	67	280
7=	Fred Couples	69	68	70	74	281
	Peter O'Malley	73	70	70	68	281
	Eduardo Romero	74	68	67	72	281
10=	Robert Allenby	76	68	66	72	282
	Mark Calcavecchia	74	67	72	69	282
	Ernie Els	75	69	69	69	282
	Retief Goosen	75	69	70	68	282
	Tom Kite	72	67	74	69	282
	Davis Love III	70	71	74	67	282
	Shigeki Maruyama	74	69	70	69	282
	Frank Nobilo	74	72	68	68	282
	Tom Watson	71	70	70	71	282
	Lee Westwood	73	70	67	72	282
20=	Stuart Appleby	72	72	68	71	283
	Brad Faxon	77	67	72	67	283
	Mark James	76	67	70	70	283
	Jose Maria Olazabal	75	68	73	67	283
24=	Jay Haas	71	70	73	70	284
	Tom Lehman	74	72	72	66	284
	Peter Lonard	72	70	69	73	284
	Phil Mickelson	76	68	69	71	284
	Colin Montgomerie	76	69	69	70	284
	David A Russell	75	72	68	69	284
	Tiger Woods	72	74	64	74	284
	Ian Woosnam	71	73	69	71	284

Round Leader(s)
R1 Clarke, Furyk; 67
R2 Clarke; 133
R3 Parnevik; 202

Lowest Scores
R2 Clarke, Leonard, Parnevik, David Tapping (44); 66
R3 Woods; 64
R4 Leonard; 65

US PGA 1997

Winged Foot Golf Club, Mamaroneck, New York
(14–17 August)
6987 yards: Par 70 (280)

An emotional Davis Love finally made the Majors breakthrough he had been seeking for so long, by first seeing off in-form Leonard and then pulling away from the field to win in the end by some margin – and with some panache (he birdied the last). The win was much more than just quenching an overlong thirst: it was the manifestation of a family dream after his father, Davis Love Jr, had contested several Majors without success (he finishes sixth in the 1969 British Open). The win was even more poignant as his father was killed in an air crash in 1988. Love's win continued the uncanny sequence of a new champion every year since the advent of strokeplay. The last back-to-back winner of the Wanamaker Trophy was Denny Shute, way back in 1937. Love's pair of 66s to round off, equalled Steve Elkington's record of 1995 for the lowest second 36 holes, and despite being beaten later, it is still the joint-lowest in any Major win.

1	**DAVIS LOVE III**	66	71	66	66	269
	($470000)					
2	Justin Leonard	68	70	65	71	274
3	Jeff Maggert	69	69	73	65	276
4	Lee Janzen	69	67	74	69	279
5	Tom Kite	68	71	71	70	280
6=	Phil Blackmar	70	68	74	69	281
	Jim Furyk	69	72	72	68	281
	Scott Hoch	71	72	68	70	281
9	Tom Byrum	69	73	70	70	282
10=	Tom Lehman	69	72	72	70	283
	Scott McCarron	74	71	67	71	283
	Joey Sindelar	72	71	71	69	283
13=	David Duval	70	70	71	73	284
	Tim Herron	72	73	68	71	284
	Colin Montgomerie	74	71	67	72	284
	Greg Norman	68	71	74	71	284
	Mark O'Meara	69	73	75	67	284
	Nick Price	72	70	72	70	284
	Vijay Singh	73	66	76	69	284
	Tommy Tolles	75	70	73	66	284
	Kirk Triplett	73	70	71	70	284
	Bob Tway	68	75	72	69	284
23=	Mark Calcavecchia	71	74	73	76	285
	John Cook	71	71	74	69	285
	Bernhard Langer	73	71	72	69	285
	Doug Martin	69	75	74	67	285
	Shigeki Maruyama	68	70	74	73	285
	Kenny Perry	73	68	73	71	285
29=	Ronnie Black	76	69	71	70	286
	Fred Couples	71	67	73	75	286
	John Daly	66	73	77	70	286
	Paul Goydos	70	72	71	73	286
	Hale Irwin	73	70	71	72	286
	Phil Mickelson	69	69	73	75	286
	Frank Nobilo	72	73	67	74	286
	Don Pooley	72	74	70	70	286
	Payne Stewart	70	70	72	74	286
	Lee Westwood	74	68	71	73	286
	Tiger Woods	70	70	71	75	286

Round Leader(s)
R1 Daly, Love III; 66
R2 Janzen; 136
R3 Leonard, Love III; 203

Lowest Scores
R2 Singh; 66
R3 Leonard; 65
R4 Maggert; 65

THE MASTERS 1998

Augusta National Golf Club, Augusta, Georgia
(9–12 April)

6925 yards: Par 72 (288)

In a memorable Masters for golden oldies, Mark O'Meara, at 41, won his first Major at the 57th time of asking. He birdied the final two holes – something which hadn't been achieved since Palmer in his landmark win in 1960 – to overcome the stuttering Duval and long-time leader Couples at the death. Nicklaus rolled back the years (he would break his run of 154 consecutive Majors after the upcoming US Open due to a hip operation) by becoming the oldest Top Ten finisher in the Masters. His venerable partner-in-crime, Gary Player, at 62, became the oldest to beat the cut at Augusta; whilst Gay Brewer became the oldest to shoot a par-or-better round, aged 66.

1	**MARK O'MEARA** ($576000)	74	70	68	67	279
2=	Fred Couples	69	70	71	70	280
	David Duval	71	68	74	67	280
4	Jim Furyk	76	70	67	68	281
5	Paul Azinger	71	72	69	70	283
6=	Jack Nicklaus	73	72	70	68	285
	David Toms	75	72	72	64	285
8=	Darren Clarke	76	73	67	69	286
	Justin Leonard	74	73	69	69	286
	Colin Montgomerie	71	75	69	70	286
	Tiger Woods	71	72	72	70	285
12=	Jay Haas	72	71	71	72	286
	Per-Ulrik Johannson	74	75	67	70	286
	Phil Mickelson	74	69	69	74	286
	Jose Maria Olazabal	70	73	71	72	286
16=	Mark Calcavecchia	74	74	69	70	287
	Ernie Els	75	70	70	72	287
	Scott Hoch	70	71	73	73	287
	Scott McCarron	73	71	72	71	287
	Ian Woosnam	74	71	72	70	287
21=	Matt Kuchar (a)	72	76	68	72	288
	Willie Wood	74	74	70	70	288
23=	Stewart Cink	74	76	69	70	289
	John Huston	77	71	70	71	289
	Jeff Maggert	72	73	72	72	289
26=	Brad Faxon	73	74	71	72	290
	David Frost	72	73	74	71	290
	Steve Jones	75	70	75	70	290
29	Michael Bradley	73	74	72	72	291
30	Steve Elkington	75	75	71	71	292

Round Leader(s)
R1   Couples; 69
R2   Couples, Duval; 139
R3   Couples; 210

Lowest Scores
R2   Duval; 68
R3   Clarke, Furyk, Johansson, Love III; 67
R4   Toms; 64

US OPEN 1998

Olympic Club, San Francisco, California
(18–21 June)

6979 yards: Par 70 (280)

Two major pieces of good fortune on the Olympic Club's testing course – at the 5th and the 11th – on the last day, helped Lee Janzen turn around a five-shot disadvantage to overcome a faltering Payne Stewart, and win his second US Open. Janzen, in all fairness, had played the most solid golf of all the leading protagonists over the last 18, repeating his triumph over the luckless Stewart in 1993. Stewart, ahead of the field by four starting the day, had enough in hand to win over the rest of the pack, and indeed finished three clear of Tway in third place. But Janzen's second-best-of-the-day 68 was enough to make him a multiple Major champion, and elevate him from the hardly extraordinary list of one-win wonders who had begun to typify the Majors during the 90s.

1	**LEE JANZEN** ($535000)	73	66	73	68	280
2	Payne Stewart	66	71	70	74	281
3	Bob Tway	68	70	73	73	284
4	Nick Price	73	68	71	73	285
5=	Tom Lehman	68	75	68	75	286
	Steve Stricker	73	71	69	73	286
7=	David Duval	75	68	75	69	287
	Jeff Maggert	69	69	75	74	287
	Lee Westwood	72	74	70	71	287
10=	Stuart Appleby	73	74	70	71	288
	Stewart Cink	73	68	73	74	288
	Phil Mickelson	71	73	74	70	288
	Jeff Sluman	72	74	74	68	288
14=	Paul Azinger	75	72	77	65	289
	Jim Furyk	74	73	68	74	289
	Matt Kuchar (a)	70	69	76	74	289
	Jesper Parnevik	69	74	76	70	289
18=	Frank Lickliter	73	71	72	74	290
	Colin Montgomerie	70	74	77	69	290
	Jose Maria Olazabal	68	77	72	74	290
	Loren Roberts	71	76	71	72	290
	Tiger Woods	74	72	71	73	290
23=	Glen Day	73	72	71	75	291
	Casey Martin	74	71	74	72	291
25=	Thomas Bjorn	72	75	70	75	292
	Mark Carnevale	67	73	74	78	292
	Per-Ulrik Johansson	71	75	73	73	292
	Chris Perry	74	71	72	75	292
	Eduardo Romero	72	70	76	74	292
	Vijay Singh	73	72	73	74	292
	DA Weibring	72	72	75	73	292

Round Leader(s)
R1   Stewart; 66
R2   Stewart; 137
R3   Stewart; 207

Lowest Scores
R2   Janzen; 66
R3   Furyk, Lehman; 68
R4   Azinger; 65

BRITISH OPEN 1998

Royal Birkdale Golf Club, Southport, Lancashire, England
(16–19 July)
7018 yards: Par 70 (280)

In a magical last day, which capped the best Major since the Faldo-Norman Masters of 1996, Mark O'Meara's sheer 1998 impetus saw him squeak home for his second Major of the year, after play-off with US exile Brian Watts. The severity of the weather on the Saturday sorted out the field – much like the mayhem caused at a fence in a steeplechase race – leaving just a handful of serious contenders left to fight for the spoils. The consistency of Woods, Furyk and Parnevik was again in evidence, but a new British sporting hero appeared to be born in a mercurial performance from the teenage amateur Justin Rose. He finished at the 72nd hole with an outrageous chip in, and fourth place. The birth was to prove somewhat premature, however, as almost every cut in tournaments he played over the next 12 months was missed. The trauma would take fully two seasons to get out of his sytem after that.

1	**MARK O'MEARA***	72	68	72	68	280
	(£300000)				
2	Brain Watts	68	69	73	70	280
3	Tiger Woods	65	73	77	66	281
4=	Jim Furyk	70	70	72	70	282
	Jesper Parnevik	68	72	72	70	282
	Justin Rose (a)	72	66	75	69	282
	Raymond Russell	68	73	75	66	282
8	Davis Love III	67	73	77	68	283
9=	Thomas Bjorn	68	71	76	71	286
	Costantino Rocca	72	74	70	70	286
11=	David Duval	70	71	75	71	287
	Brad Faxon	67	74	74	72	287
	John Huston	65	77	73	72	287
14	Gordon Brand, Jr	71	70	76	71	288
15=	Peter Baker	69	72	77	71	289
	Jose Maria Olazabal	73	72	75	69	289
	Des Smyth	74	69	75	71	289
	Greg Turner	68	75	75	71	289
19=	Robert Allenby	67	76	78	69	290
	Mark James	71	74	74	71	290
	Sandy Lyle	70	73	75	72	290
	Vijay Singh	67	74	78	71	290
	Curtis Strange	73	73	74	70	290
24=	Stephen Ames	68	72	79	72	291
	Bob Estes	72	70	76	73	291
	Lee Janzen	72	69	80	70	291
	Peter O'Malley	71	71	78	71	291
	Sam Torrance	69	77	75	70	291
29=	Scott Dunlap	72	79	80	71	292
	Ernie Els	73	72	75	72	292
	Sergio Garcia (a)	69	75	76	72	292
	Shigeki Maruyama	70	73	75	74	292
	Nick Price	66	72	82	72	292
	Loren Roberts	66	76	76	74	292

* Mark O'Meara beat Brian Watts in a four-hole Play-off

Round Leader(s)
R1 Huston, Woods; 65
R2 Watts; 137
R3 Watts; 210

Lowest Scores
R2 Rose; 66
R3 Katsuyoshi Tomori (44), Rocca; 70
R4 Russell, Woods; 66

US PGA 1998

Sahalee Country Club, Redmond, Washington
(13–16 August)
6906 yards: Par 70 (280)

Popular Fijian, Vijay Sigh, deservedly collected his first Major at the typically tight Salahee course in the pretty Pacific North West. Overcoming many hassles during his globe-trotting career, his solid game seems ideally suited to the strictures of the PGA Championship – proved here when pulling away from Steve Stricker over the last round. Once again the winner came from the Southern Hemisphere, and once again there was an almost non-existent challenge from a disappointing group of Europeans. O'Meara tinkered with the immortality that sharing Ben Hogan's 1953 three-Majors record would surely bring – picking up three shots over the final day's first five holes – but staggered back into the pack, to finish five adrift of the winner, no doubt contemplating on what a wonderful game golf is.

1	**VIJAY SINGH**	70	66	67	68	271
	($540000)				
2	Steve Stricker	69	68	66	70	273
3	Steve Elkington	69	69	69	67	274
4=	Frank Lickliter	68	71	69	68	276
	Mark O'Meara	69	70	69	68	276
	Nick Price	70	73	68	65	276
7=	Davis Love III	70	68	69	70	277
	Billy Mayfair	73	67	67	70	277
9	John Cook	71	68	70	69	278
10=	Skip Kendall	72	68	68	71	279
	Kenny Perry	69	72	70	68	279
	Tiger Woods	66	72	70	71	279
13=	Robert Allenby	72	68	69	71	280
	Paul Azinger	68	73	70	69	280
	Fred Couples	74	71	67	68	280
	Brad Faxon	70	68	74	68	280
	Steve Flesch	75	69	67	69	280
	Bill Glasson	68	74	69	69	280
	John Huston	70	71	68	71	280
	Bob Tway	69	76	67	68	280
21=	Ernie Els	72	72	71	66	281
	Andrew Magee	70	68	72	71	281
23=	Fred Funk	70	71	71	70	282
	Scott Gump	68	69	72	73	282
	Per-Ulrik Johansson	69	74	71	68	282
	Greg Kraft	71	73	65	73	282
27=	Jeff Sluman	71	73	70	69	283
	Hal Sutton	72	68	72	71	283
29=	Glen Day	68	71	75	70	284
	Scott Hoch	72	69	70	73	284
	Tom Lehman	71	71	70	72	284
	Lee Rinker	70	70	71	73	284
	Ian Woosnam	70	75	67	72	284

Round Leader(s)
R1 Woods; 66
R2 Singh; 136
R3 Singh, Stricker; 203

Lowest Scores
R2 Singh; 66
R3 Kraft; 65
R4 Price; 65

THE MASTERS 1999

Augusta National Golf Club, Augusta, Georgia
(8–11 April)
6985 yards: Par 72 (288)

In a Masters tournament that weather-wise resembled a windswept British Open, two Augusta favourites reprised the good old days when Olazabal and Norman dominated the fourth round. A third, and the man to whom the appeal of the Masters owes so much, Gene Sarazen, was, sadly for all concerned, to tee-off ceremonially for the last time, aged 97. That the two latter-day heroes should even be playing at the top level again was remarkable, as Norman missed most of 1998, and all the Majors, and of course Olazabal's gloomy prognosis during 1995 and 1996 that he may never walk again is well-known. Olazabal returned to golf in 1997 and played solidly, if not spectacularly: the Masters win hopefully means a return to a hugely successful career. Greg just seemed genuinely happy to be in contention again. He eventually gave way to Olazabal at the 16th, after the latter had birdied the hole to go clear by two, and having made his first killer blow at 13. Previously, Davis Love had chipped in at 16 to move into second place on his own, being at five under par with Norman since Greg had dropped a shot at the 12th. He could do nothing more then par out, however, leaving the respected Spaniard Champion by two. For the first time since 1959 there was no Jack Nicklaus – out after a hip operation.

1	**JOSE MARIA OLAZABAL** ($720000)	70	66	73	71	280
2	Davis Love III	69	72	71	73	282
3	Greg Norman	71	68	71	73	283
4=	Bob Estes	71	72	69	72	284
	Steve Pate	71	75	65	73	284
6=	David Duval	71	74	70	70	285
	Carlos Franco	72	72	68	73	285
	Phil Mickelson	74	69	71	71	285
	Nick Price	69	72	72	72	285
	Lee Westwood	75	71	68	71	285
11=	Steve Elkington	72	70	71	74	287
	Bernhard Langer	76	66	72	73	287
	Colin Montgomerie	70	72	71	74	287
14=	Jim Furyk	72	73	70	73	288
	Lee Janzen	70	69	73	76	288
	Brandt Jobe	72	71	74	71	288
	Ian Woosnam	71	74	71	72	288
18=	Brandel Chamblee	69	73	75	72	289
	Bill Glasson	72	70	73	74	289
	Justin Leonard	70	72	73	74	289
	Scott McCarron	69	68	76	76	289
	Tiger Woods	72	72	70	75	289
23	Larry Mize	76	70	72	72	290
24=	Brad Faxon	74	73	68	76	291
	Per-Ulrik Johansson	75	72	71	73	291
	Vijay Singh	72	76	71	72	291
27=	Stewart Cink	74	70	71	77	292
	Fred Couples	74	71	76	71	292
	Ernie Els	71	72	69	80	292
	Rocco Mediate	73	74	69	76	292

Round Leader(s)
R1   Chamblee, Love III, McCarron; 69
R2   Olazabal; 136
R3   Olazabal; 209

Lowest Scores
R2   Langer, Olazabal; 66
R3   Pate; 65
R$ Duval; 70

US OPEN 1999

Pinehurst Resort and Country Club, Pinehurst, North Carolina
(17–20 June)
7175 yards: Par 70 (280)

Pinehurst, arguably the spiritual home of US golf, finally played host to American golf's premier event. 42 year-old Payne Stewart added a second US Open title and third Major (with his PGA win in 1989) when he fought back into contention over the last few holes at Pinehurst No 2 course. Five months later he was to be forever taken from the world of golf in a tragic, bizarre flying accident. Two long saving putts from Stewart on 16 and 18 sandwiched a meticulously set-up birdie on the 17th – clawing back shots on leaders Phil Mickelson and Tiger Woods, and eventually finishing ahead of them at one under par. Payne had wiped out the memories of 1993 and 1998 and the spectre of Lee Janzen. Mickelson was consigned to the next Major still as a Majors nearly-man along with Duval, Montgomerie, Furyk and one or two others; whilst John Daly, after an opening round 68, finished 77, 81 and 83, cursed the USGA and threatened to boycott Pebble Beach in 2000. Masters Champion Jose Maria Olazabal broke his hand in an unusual fit of temper after his opening 75, and withdrew, as did three-time US Open Champion, Hale Irwin.

1	**PAYNE STEWART** ($625000)	68	69	72	70	279
2	Phil Mickelson	67	70	73	70	280
3=	Vijay Singh	69	70	73	69	281
	Tiger Woods	68	71	72	70	281
5	Steve Stricker	70	73	69	73	285
6	Tim Herron	69	72	70	75	286
7=	David Duval	67	70	75	75	287
	Jeff Maggert	71	69	74	73	287
	Hal Sutton	69	70	76	72	287
10=	Darren Clarke	73	70	74	71	288
	Billy Mayfair	67	72	74	75	288
12=	Paul Azinger	72	72	75	70	289
	Paul Goydos	67	74	74	74	289
	Davis Love III	70	73	74	72	289
15=	Justin Leonard	69	75	73	73	290
	Colin Montgomerie	72	72	74	72	290
17=	Jim Furyk	69	73	77	72	291
	Jay Haas	74	72	73	72	291
	Dudley Hart	73	73	76	69	291
	John Huston	71	69	75	76	291
	Jesper Parnevik	71	71	76	73	291
	Scott Verplank	72	73	72	74	291
23=	Miguel Angel Jimenez	73	70	72	77	292
	Nick Price	71	74	74	73	292
	Tim Scherrer	72	72	74	74	292
	Brian Watts	69	73	77	73	292
	DA Weibring	69	74	74	75	292
28=	David Berganio, Jr	68	77	76	72	293
	Tom Lehman	73	74	73	73	293
30=	Bob Estes	70	71	77	76	294
	Geoffrey Sisk	71	72	76	75	294

Round Leader(s)
R1   Duval, Goydos, Mayfair, Mickelson; 67
R2   Duval, Mickelson, Stewart; 137
R3   Stewart; 209

Lowest Scores
R2   Huston, Maggert, Stewart; 69
R3   Stricker; 69
R4   Hart, Singh; 69

BRITISH OPEN 1999

Carnoustie Golf Club, Angus, Scotland
(15–18 July)
7361 yards: Par 71 (284)

After the outstanding Open of Royal Birkdale the previous year, no one had the right to expect anything approaching the same in 1999. A golfing classic it may not have been, but few sporting events could match the 1999 Open Championship for the dramatic, suspenseful, heart-wrenching, heroic, and sporting (in the Corinthian sense) scenes witnessed at Carnoustie on the Sunday evening. Aberdeen-born Paul Lawrie won the Open after beating Justin Leonard and Jean Van de Velde in the four-hole play-off – those are the facts of the matter. Those facts don't tell the story, though, of the golf course's record length and its over-punishing rough; of Rodney Pampling's first-round lead and cut demise – unique in Majors history; of 19-year-old Sergio Garcia finishing in tears, last of all players to complete two rounds; of Lawrie's win being the first by a qualifier (Van de Velde also qualified), and a Scotsman on his own soil since James Braid won over the Old Course in 1910 (if Messrs Hutchison and Armour do not count). Nor does it, or can it begin to tell the tragic tale of Frenchman Van de Velde's farce at the 72nd hole, already a piece of classic golfing folklore; his self-destruction in the Barry Burn – with and without shoes – after charging the green unnecessarily and surrendering a three-shot lead at the tee. In a piece of pure theatre spectators looked on aghast as the plot of the 18th hole unfolded, and the leader moved from one disaster to another – at every move twisting a self-inserted knife even deeper whilst seeming to get more and more sympathy from the disbelieving galleries. Who said this is only a game?

1	**PAUL LAWRIE***	73	74	76	67	290
	(£350000)					
2=	Justin Leonard	73	74	71	72	290
	Jean Van de Velde	75	68	70	77	290
4=	Angel Cabrera	75	69	77	70	291
	Craig Parry	76	75	67	73	291
6	Greg Norman	76	70	75	72	293
7=	David Frost	80	69	71	74	294
	Davis Love III	74	74	77	69	294
	Tiger Woods	74	72	74	74	294
10=	Scott Dunlap	72	77	76	70	295
	Jim Furyk	78	71	76	70	295
	Retief Goosen	76	75	73	71	295
	Jesper Parnevik	74	71	78	72	295
	Hal Sutton	73	78	72	72	295
15=	Colin Montgomerie	74	76	72	74	296
	Scott Verplank	80	74	73	69	296
	Tsuyoshi Yoneyama	77	74	73	72	296
18=	Andrew Coltart	74	74	72	77	297
	Bernhard Langer	72	77	73	75	297
	Frank Nobilo	76	76	70	75	297
	Costantino Rocca	81	69	74	73	297
	Patrik Sjoland	74	72	77	74	297
	Lee Westwood	76	75	74	72	297
24=	Ernie Els	74	76	76	72	298
	Miguel Angel Martin	74	76	72	76	298
	Peter O'Malley	76	75	74	73	298
	Brian Watts	74	73	77	74	298
	Ian Woosnam	76	74	74	74	298
29	Padraig Harrington	77	74	74	74	299
30=	Thomas Bjorn	79	73	75	73	300
	Darren Clarke	76	75	76	73	300
	Pierre Fulke	75	75	77	73	300
	Tim Herron	81	70	74	75	300
	Jeff Maggert	75	77	73	75	300
	Len Mattiace	73	74	75	78	300
	Payne Stewart	79	73	74	74	300

* Paul Lawrie (5-4-3-3) beat Justin Leonard (5-4-4-5) and Jean Van de Velde (6-4-3-5) in the Four-hole Play-off

Round Leader(s)
R1 Rodney Pampling (cut); 71
R2 Van de Velde; 143
R3 Van de Velde; 213

Lowest Scores
R2 Van de Velde; 68
R3 Parry; 67
R4 Lawrie; 67

US PGA 1999

Medinah Country Club, Medinah, Illinois
(12–15 August)
7398 yards: Par 72 (288)

When Tiger Woods won the Masters in 1997, many predicted that his 12-shot demolition of Augusta, and the competition, would hasten in an era of unchallenged golfing supremacy for the brilliant youngster. Between the first Major of 1997 and the last of 1999, despite being the only golfer to have made the Top 30 in every one of the ten intervening Majors, he has disappointed by his own high standards. It was only a matter of time, however, before he would win again. He did so at Medinah No 3, (at almost 7400 yards the longest course in Majors history after the columbine giant of 1968), but he was not have it all his own way. Enter Sergio Garcia, the 19 year-old Spaniard, into the PGA and Majors limelight, who seemed to flatter to deceive earlier in the year. He won for the first time as a pro in Ireland; he came second at Loch Lomond; then he shot a humiliating 172 for two rounds at the Open hell of Carnoustie – all in consecutive weeks. Garcia stunned everyone in leading the field at Medinah by two at the end of Round One; and was just two behind the Tiger after a third-round 68. Mike Weir's challenge evaporated (he beacme the only player in the history of the Majors to have carded, over four rounds, scores in the 60s and 80s, but none in the 70s!), but Garcia made birdie at the 13th, and saw Woods follow with a double-bogey, cutting his lead to one. Sergio bogeyed 15 but then came possibly the best moment of the Championship – and of many others. Stuck 170 yards from the pin on the 16th, the ball trapped amongst some tree roots, he blasted the ball to within 40 feet, chasing and leaping after his ball like some demented animal. Woods dropped a shot but just about held everything together thereafter for his second Major. But what of El Niño?

1	**TIGER WOODS**	70	67	68	72	277
	($650000)					
2	Sergio Garcia	66	73	68	71	278
3=	Stewart Cink	69	70	68	73	280
	Jay Haas	68	67	75	70	280
5	Nick Price	70	71	69	71	281
6=	Bob Estes	71	70	72	69	282
	Colin Montgomerie	72	70	70	70	282
8=	Jim Furyk	71	70	69	74	284
	Steve Pate	72	70	73	69	284
10=	David Duval	70	71	72	72	285
	Miguel Jimenez	70	70	73	70	285
	Jesper Parnevik	72	70	73	70	285
	Corey Pavin	69	74	71	71	285
	Chris Perry	70	73	71	71	285
	Mike Weir	68	68	69	80	285
16=	Mark Brooks	70	73	70	74	287
	Gabriel Hjertstedt	72	70	73	72	287
	Brandt Jobe	69	74	69	75	287
	Greg Turner	73	69	70	75	287
	Lee Westwood	70	68	74	75	287
21=	David Frost	75	68	74	71	288
	Scott Hoch	71	71	75	71	288
	Skip Kendall	74	65	71	78	288
	JL Lewis	73	70	74	71	288
	Kevin Wentworth	72	70	72	74	288
26=	Fred Couples	73	69	75	72	289
	Carlos Franco	72	71	71	75	289
	Jerry Kelly	69	74	71	75	289
	Hal Sutton	72	73	73	71	289
	Jean Van de Velde	73	70	71	76	290

Round Leader(s)
R1 Garcia; 66
R2 Haas; 135
R3 Weir, Woods; 205

Lowest Scores
R2 Kendall; 65
R3 Cink, Garcia, Woods; 68
R4 Mark James (31); 67

THE MASTERS 2000

Augusta National Golf Club, Augusta, Georgia
(6–9 April)
6985 yards: Par 72 (288)

If competitors at the 64th Masters thought the infamously quick greens were even more slippery in Rounds One and Two, those who missed the cut were perhaps the lucky ones. The hot temperatures of Friday dipped with alarming alacrity overnight, the winds got up and the threat of storms persisted all day – resulting in play being suspended for two hours. 37-year old Fijian Singh showed that class, married to stacks of hard work, will always win through as he pocketed his second Major trophy in three years, seemingly undeterred by the atmospherics, both natural and man-made, all around him. He maintained his three-shot overnight advantage over the final 18 holes, and although at one time this was cut to one, the progressive challenges of Duval, Loren Roberts, then Els all dissipated. Tiger Woods' round stuttered between the brilliance of his Saturday performance, the misfortune of lipping-out on three birdie chances around Amen Corner, and, frankly, uncommon mediocrity. After Tommy Jacobs in 1952, the Masters welcomed its younger competitor, Korean amateur, Sung Yoon Kim, who at two months short of his 18th birthday failed to make the cut – as did another amateur, Aaron Baddeley, winner of the Australian Open. To celebrate the millennium, the galleries witnessed The Big Three of Palmer, Player and Nicklaus going out together on Thursday and Friday.

1	**VIJAY SINGH**	72	67	70	69	278
	($828000)					
2	Ernie Els	72	67	74	68	281
3=	David Duval	73	65	74	70	282
	Loren Roberts	73	69	71	69	282
5	Tiger Woods	75	72	68	69	284
6	Tom Lehman	69	72	75	69	285
7=	Carlos Franco	79	68	70	69	286
	Davis Love III	75	72	68	71	286
	Phil Mickelson	71	68	76	71	286
10	Hal Sutton	72	75	71	69	287
11=	Fred Couples	76	72	70	70	288
	Greg Norman	80	68	70	70	288
	Nick Price	74	69	73	72	288
14=	Jim Furyk	73	74	71	71	289
	John Huston	77	69	72	71	289
	Dennis Paulson	68	76	73	72	289
	Chris Perry	73	75	72	69	289
18	Jeff Sluman	73	69	77	71	290
19=	Glen Day	79	67	74	71	291
	Bob Estes	72	71	77	71	291
	Padraig Harrington	76	69	75	71	291
	Colin Montgomerie	76	69	77	69	291
	Steve Stricker	70	73	75	73	291
	Jean Van de Velde	76	70	75	70	291
25=	Steve Jones	71	70	76	75	292
	Larry Mize	78	67	73	74	292
	Craig Parry	75	71	72	74	292
28=	Paul Azinger	72	72	77	72	293
	Thomas Bjorn	71	77	73	72	293
	Stewart Cink	75	72	72	74	293
	Dudley Hart	75	71	72	75	293
	Nick Faldo	72	72	74	75	293
	Bernhard Langer	71	71	75	76	293
	Justin Leonard	72	71	77	73	293
	Jumbo Ozaki	72	72	74	75	293
	Mike Weir	75	70	70	78	293

Round Leader(s)
R1 Paulson; 68
R2 Duval; 138
R3 Singh; 209

Lowest Scores
R2 Duval; 65
R3 Love III, Woods; 68
R4 Els; 68

US OPEN 2000

Pebble Beach Golf Links, Pebble Beach, California
(15–18 June)
6828 yards: Par 71 (284)

During a year that was to be submerged in a welter of records unprecedented in the 140 year history of Major Championships, Tiger Woods re-established the (slightly wavering) belief that he could the best-ever player in the history of the sport when he took the US Open by the scruff of the neck. So arduous do the USGA set US Open courses that a cursory glance at the Records part of this book indicates that low scores in this particular Major are the most difficult to come by. The litany of Tiger's achievements must begin with the largest winning margin – 15 strokes – of any Major, taking away Old Tom Morris' record 12 shots victory in the third-ever Open Championship in 1862: the margin also shattered Willie Smith's achievement in the US Open of 11 strokes in 1899. The only player under par throughout (no one else achieved the 72-hole par of 284), Woods led after successive rounds by one stroke, then six (a record at the US Open in itself), and ten (again a record) at the end of Round Three. In doing so he made a mockery, both of some of the best players in the world, and the much-vaunted Pebble Beach ocean-side trial. His 272 equalled the US Open record of Jack Nicklaus and Lee Janzen, and also tied the 36-hole record along the way. Spaniard Miguel Angel Jimenez tied with Ernie Els to lead an international supporting cast home, among whom Nick Faldo made his first return to a Majors final leaderboard since the 1996 British Open. Very few others managed to steal any limelight, however, in this, the most complete victory in the entire Majors catalogue.

1	**TIGER WOODS**	65	69	71	67	272
	($800000)					
2=	Ernie Els	74	73	68	72	287
	Miguel Angel Jimenez	66	74	76	71	287
4	John Huston	67	75	76	70	288
5=	Padraig Harrington	73	71	72	73	289
	Lee Westwood	71	71	76	71	289
7	Nick Faldo	69	74	76	71	290
8=	Stewart Cink	77	72	72	70	291
	David Duval	75	71	74	71	291
	Loren Roberts	68	78	73	72	291
	Vijay Singh	70	73	80	68	291
12=	Paul Azinger	71	73	79	69	292
	Michael Campbell	71	77	71	73	292
	Retief Goosen	77	72	72	71	292
	Jose Maria Olazabal	70	71	76	75	292
16=	Fred Couples	70	75	75	73	293
	Scott Hoch	73	76	75	69	293
	Justin Leonard	73	73	75	72	293
	Phil Mickelson	71	73	73	76	293
	David Toms	73	76	72	72	293
	Mike Weir	76	72	76	69	293
22	Notah Begay III	74	75	72	73	294
23=	Mike Brisky	71	73	79	72	295
	Tom Lehman	71	73	78	73	295
	Bob May	72	76	75	72	295
	Hal Sutton	69	73	83	70	295
27=	Hale Irwin	68	78	81	69	296
	Steve Jones	75	73	75	73	296
	Nick Price	77	70	78	71	296
	Steve Stricker	75	74	75	72	296
	Tom Watson	71	74	78	73	296

Round Leader(s)
R1 Woods; 65
R2 Woods; 134
R3 Woods; 205

Lowest Scores
R2 John Daly (cut & w/d), Dave Eichelberger (57), Woods; 69
R3 Els; 68
R4 Woods; 67

BRITISH OPEN 2000

Royal & Ancient Golf Club, St Andrews, Fife, Scotland
(20–23 July)
7115 yards: Par 72 (288)

The king is dead: long live the king. As Jack Nicklaus was caught for posterity waving to the crowd from the Swilcan Bridge for the last time in an Open Championship, the young pretender to the Golden Bear's mantle of golfing supremacy, Tiger Woods, was putting the final touches to the second lowest 36 holes in an Open shot at the Home of Golf. Just one behind Faldo's record at St Andrews at half-way and again after 54 holes, Woods followed up his record-breaking success at Pebble Beach a month earlier by stretching out to an eight-shot win in the Open, his final 69 eventually pipping Nick's Championship total over the Old Course by one. In doing so Woods equalled some truly great Champions' margins from the previous century – those of JH Taylor (twice) and James Braid; and they are only headed in the lists by the Morrises, Old and Young, from the dim and distant 19th century. Tiger, as if this was not enough, became only the fifth player in history to achieve a career slam of all four Majors after Sarazen, Hogan, Nicklaus and Player. At 24, he was easily the youngest of the group, and the feat had been accumulated over just four years – against Jack's first 'slam' over five seasons, Hogan's over six, Player's seven and Sarazen's 14 years. Woods also did the Open double in the same year for the first time since Tom Watson in 1982, and before that only Jones (twice), Sarazen and Hogan had accomplished the feat. His 19 under par total was the lowest against the card in any Major, beating his own record at Augusta in 1997. Playing conditions on the fairways were the hardest and fastest in memory for the showcase millennium event: Ernie Els was runner up to Tiger again (and for the third time in succsession), and really, it would not have mattered if the course was like a swamp – Ernie, nor anyone else, would have caught the Tiger. There was more to come...

1	**TIGER WOODS**	67	66	67	69	269
	(£500000)					
2=	Thomas Bjorn	69	69	68	71	277
	Ernie Els	66	72	70	69	277
4=	Tom Lehman	68	70	70	70	288
	David Toms	69	67	71	71	288
6	Fred Couples	70	68	72	69	279
7=	Paul Azinger	69	72	72	67	280
	Darren Clarke	70	69	68	73	280
	Pierre Fulke	69	72	70	69	280
	Loren Roberts	69	68	70	73	280
11=	Stuart Appleby	73	70	68	70	281
	David Duval	70	70	66	75	281
	Bernhard Langer	74	70	66	71	281
	Davis Love III	74	66	74	67	281
	Mark McNulty	69	72	70	70	281
	Bob May	72	72	66	71	281
	Phil Mickelson	72	66	71	72	281
	Dennis Paulson	68	71	69	73	281
	Vijay Singh	70	70	73	68	281
20=	Notah Begay III	69	73	69	71	282
	Bob Estes	72	69	70	71	282
	Steve Flesch	67	70	71	74	282
	Padraig Harrington	68	72	70	72	282
	Paul McGinley	69	72	71	70	282
	Steve Pate	73	70	71	68	282
26=	Mark Calcavecchia	73	70	71	69	283
	Miguel Angel Jimenez	73	71	71	68	283
	Colin Montgomerie	71	70	72	70	283
	Mark O'Meara	70	73	69	71	283
	Dean Robertson	73	70	68	72	283

Round Leader(s)
R1   Els; 66
R2   Woods; 133
R3   Woods; 200

Lowest Scores
R2   Jose Coceres (36),
     Love III, Mickelson,
     Woods; 66
R3   Duval, Langer, May; 66
R4   Azinger, Love III; 67

US PGA 2000

Valhalla Golf Club, Louisville, Kentucky
(17–20 August)
7167 yards: Par 72 (288)

Perhaps the most telling comment came from Jack Nicklaus who famously re-quoted what the immortal Bobby Jones said about him when Jack arrived on the scene in the early 1960s, 'Tiger is playing a game I am not familiar with'. Indeed, in this year of all years, and very possibly in Jack's last PGA Championship, the greatest player of the second half of the 20th century was grouped in the early rounds of the Championship with perhaps the greatest to be produced in the first half of the 21st. Jones, Nicklaus and Woods – three pillars of progress in golf – one acknowledging the seachange created by another. At Valhalla, Woods became the first player since Denny Shute in 1937 to defend the PGA Championship successfully, and the first of the strokeplay era. Tiger also emulated Hogan's great 1953 feat of three successive Major victories, something denied to even Nicklaus in his great pomp. Unlike the earlier Opens of 2000, the PGA was not the expected walk, or prowl, in the park for Tiger. Despite shooting 18 under – a figure only he himself had previously beaten or equalled in Majors – stalwart of the European Tour and an American vitually unknown in his own country, Bob May, took Woods to his first ever play-off in a Major after catching him over the last round. May equalled the record low for the last 36 holes in a Major to catch Woods, as did Olazabal, who, in a group of reasonably placed overseas players, also became the latest player to equal the Majors low score of 63.

1	**TIGER WOODS***	66	67	70	67	270
	($900000)					
2	Bob May	72	66	66	66	270
3	Thomas Bjorn	72	68	67	68	275
4=	Stuart Appleby	70	69	68	69	276
	Greg Chalmers	71	69	66	70	276
	Jose Maria Olazabal	76	68	63	69	276
7	Franklin Langham	72	71	65	69	277
8	Notah Begay III	72	66	70	70	278
9=	Darren Clarke	68	72	72	67	279
	Scott Dunlap	66	68	70	75	279
	Fred Funk	69	68	74	68	279
	Davis Love III	68	69	72	70	279
	Phil Mickelson	70	70	69	70	279
	Tom Watson	76	70	65	68	279
15=	Stewart Cink	72	71	70	67	280
	Mike Clark II	73	70	67	70	280
	Chris DiMarco	73	70	69	68	280
	Lee Westwood	72	72	69	67	280
19=	Robert Allenby	73	71	68	69	281
	Angel Cabrera	72	71	71	67	281
	JP Hayes	69	68	68	76	281
	Lee Janzen	76	70	70	65	281
	Tom Kite	70	72	69	70	281
24=	Paul Azinger	72	71	66	73	282
	Steve Jones	72	71	70	69	282
	Jarmo Sandelin	74	72	68	68	282
27=	Brad Faxon	71	74	70	68	283
	Skip Kendall	72	72	69	70	283
	Tom Pernice, Jr	74	69	70	70	283
30=	Stephen Ames	69	71	71	73	284
	Kenny Perry	78	68	70	68	284
	Jean Van de Velde	70	74	69	71	284
	Mike Weir	76	69	68	71	284

* Tiger Woods beat Bob May at the third hole of the Sudden Death Play-off

Round Leader(s)
R1   Dunlap, Woods; 66
R2   Woods; 133
R3   Woods; 203

Lowest Scores
R2   Begay III, May; 66
R3   Olazabal; 63
R4   Janzen; 65

The 65th Masters Tournament

AUGUSTA NATIONAL GOLF CLUB
Augusta, Georgia
5–8 April 2001
6985 yards PAR 72 (288)

WOODS SHOUTS 'FOUR!'
Tiger makes first 4-timer in Majors history

Tiger Woods, as if he hadn't already done so, wrote his name into the history books of golf and all sports when he duly collected his fourth consecutive Major Championship at Augusta – a feat never previously achieved. Tom Morris, Jr did win four Opens in a row, between 1868 and 1872, when the only Major was an Open Championship, but as there was no competition in 1871, Tommy's achievement straddled five years. Tiger's 'slam' took just eight months, including the off-season. Very few people in the annals of sport have achieved anything similar: Sir Donald Bradman in cricket and Muhammad Ali in boxing come to mind. In modern times one can only consider the unquestioned supremacy of Michael Schumacher in Formula 1 motor sport – possibly – in the same light.

Throughout 2000, players, sportswriters and fans alike ran out of superlatives to describe what Woods had done. To add the seemingly elusive fourth Major to the sequence sent them into orbit. For weeks after the event the great debate was whether this, like in 1930 when Bob Jones had won double-double of Opens and Amateur Championships, could be classed as the 'Grand Slam'. If, because the feat traversed two seasons it cannot qualify, then there is only one person playing golf today who might someday achieve it. Certainly I don't think Tiger Woods minds what it is called, and because of its uniqueness it may always be remembered as a Tiger Slam. Some tribute, but somehow I believe Woods has a burning ambition to surpass even this and go on and settle the Grand Slam argument once and for all one day.

Tiger's fourth successive Majors win didn't come easy, and the young Champion admitted feeling the strain of the final back nine, when both Duval and Mickleson were breathing down his neck. His first Masters, in 1997, was a joyful, youthful, naïve romp: an almost expected conversion of exuberant promise into a masterful victory over course and opposition. In 2001, Woods conveyed a somewhat haunted look of a man both in pursuit of greatness, and being pursued by those wishing to deny him such deification: the strain of maintaining such a high level of consistency and brilliance beginning to age that smiling visage of adolescence.

Augusta in 2001, after a blustery beginning to the week, looked its usual charming self, the pretty façade masking a few sharper teeth for those straying off the fairways. Woods' prize money was the first million dollar cheque for any Major, a far cry from the $1500 won by Byron Nelson in both his Masters victories. After appearing in all but the first tournament in 1934, the grand old man of golf (now that his two erstwhile cohorts, Ben Hogan and Gene Sarazen had passed away in the previous four years) ceremonially teed-off on Thursday for the last time. He was 89, and his drive, if slightly down the right hand side, was – as ever – in shape.

FINAL LEADERBOARD

I	**TIGER WOODS (USA)** ($1008000)	70	66	68	68	272
2	David Duval (USA)	71	66	70	67	274
3	Phil Mickelson (USA)	67	69	69	70	275
4=	Mark Calcavecchia (USA)	72	66	68	72	278
	Toshi Izawa (JAP)	71	66	74	67	278
6=	Ernie Els (RSA)	71	68	68	72	279
	Jim Furyk (USA)	69	71	70	69	279
	Bernhard Langer (GER)	73	69	68	69	279
	Kirk Triplett (USA)	68	70	70	71	279
10=	Angel Cabrera (ARG)	66	71	70	73	280
	Chris DiMarco (USA)	65	69	72	74	280
	Brad Faxon (USA)	73	68	68	71	280
	Miguel Angel Jimenez (ESP)	68	72	71	69	280
	Steve Stricker (USA)	66	71	72	71	280
15=	Paul Azinger (USA)	70	71	71	69	281
	Rocco Mediate (USA)	72	70	66	73	281
	Jose Maria Olazabal (ESP)	70	68	71	72	281
18=	Tom Lehman (USA)	75	68	71	68	282
	Vijay Singh (FIJ)	69	71	73	69	282
20=	John Huston (USA)	67	75	72	69	283
	Jeff Maggert (USA)	72	70	70	71	283
	Mark O'Meara (USA)	69	74	72	68	283
	Jesper Parnevik (SWE)	71	71	72	69	283
24	Darren Clarke (IRL)	72	67	72	73	284
25	Tim Scherrer (USA)	71	71	70	73	285
26	Fred Couples (USA)	74	71	73	68	286
27=	Padraig Harrington (IRL)	75	69	72	71	287
	Steve Jones (USA)	74	70	72	71	287
	Justin Leonard (USA)	73	71	72	71	287
31=	Stuart Appleby (AUS)	72	70	70	76	288
	Mark Brooks (USA)	70	71	77	70	288
	Lee Janzen (USA)	67	70	72	79	288
	David Toms (USA)	72	72	71	73	288
	Duffy Waldorf (USA)	72	70	71	75	288
36	Hal Sutton (USA)	74	69	71	75	289
37=	Scott Hoch (USA)	74	70	72	74	290
	Chris Perry (USA)	68	74	74	74	290
	Loren Roberts (USA)	71	74	73	72	290
40=	Shingo Katayama (JAP)	75	70	73	74	292
	Franklin Langham (USA)	72	73	75	72	292
	Steve Lowery (USA)	72	72	78	70	292
43=	Dudley Hart (USA)	74	70	78	71	293
	Jonathan Kaye (USA)	74	71	74	74	293
	Bob May (USA)	71	74	73	75	293
46	Carlos Franco (PAR)	71	71	77	75	294
47	Robert Allenby (AUS)	71	74	75	75	295

Leaders (Round-by-round)

R1	65	C DiMarco
	66	A Cabrera, S Stricker
	67	J Huston, L Janzen, P Mickelson
R2	134	C DiMarco; 65,69
	136	P Mickelson; 67,69, T Woods; 70,66
	137	A Cabrera; 66,71, D Duval; 71,66, T Izawa; 71,66, L Janzen; 67,70; S Stricker; 66,71
R3	204	T Woods; 70,66,68
	205	P Mickelson; 67,69,69
	206	M Calcavecchia; 72,66,68, C DiMarco; 65,69,72

Lowest Scores

R2	66	M Calcavecchia, D Duval, T Izawa, T Woods
	67	D Clarke
	68	E Els, B Faxon, T Lehman, J M Olazabal
R3	66	R Mediate
	68	M Calcavecchia, E Els, B Faxon, B Langer, T Woods
	69	P Mickelson
R4	67	D Duval, T Izawa
	68	Couples, T Lehman, M O'Meara, T Woods
	69	P Azinger, J Furyk, J Huston, M A Jimenez, B Langer, J Parnevik, V Singh

The 101st US Open Championship

SOUTHERN HILLS CC
Tulsa, Oklahoma
14–18 June 2001
6973 yards PAR 70 (280)

RETIEF RELIEF!
Woods Spell is broken at last

The Woods bubble finally burst at Southern Hills. Retief Goosen became the fourth South African after Locke, Player and Els to win a Major Championship, and only the third (as Locke's successes were all in the British Open) to lift the US Open trophy. In doing so he denied Tiger the immortality of five back-to-back Major wins. To be truthful the young legend had somewhat gone off the boil, almost like a road-racing cyclist dropping back into the peleton for a breather having just won a sprint or mountain stage, and was to remain relatively anonymous for the rest of the year's Majors. That this period has been a time for recharging batteries I have no doubt. Even when just ticking over, everyone knows that a 65 could be imminent from a dozing Tiger and suddenly he's back in contention again. It must not be forgotten, too, that even if 2001 was not to match the dizzy heights of success he experienced the year before, since his first Masters win in 1997 (and extending through to the end of the 2001 season), he will have finished in the Top 30 of all 20 Majors played. No one in the history of Major Championships since the Masters made it four events in a year has matched such consistency. And 2002 is another year...

While all the talk on Thursday at Southern Hills may have been about Woods, come Sunday the galleries drifted away in stunned amazement, not knowing the winner or really what had gone on during a crazy last hour of play. The leaderboard announced that there would be an 18-hole play-off on the following day (isn't it time the PGA came up with something less anti-cli-

mactic in the case of ties?) between 1996 PGA Champion Mark Brooks and Goosen, the South African with several years European Tour experience. But this didn't begin to tell the story.

There was a four-horse race coming into the final stretch, with Goosen and Brooks being pushed all the way by Majors hopefuls Stewart Cink and Rocco Mediate. Sergio Garcia, well placed at the start of the day, fell well away, still seeming to be a year or two away from a Major win at this stage. Mediate gave it his best but the pressure finally told on him, leaving just three coming to the last hole. Firstly Brooks took three from just 40 feet, and he, along with everyone else now felt that Goosens was home and dry – having two shots for the Championship from about 12 feet. Indeed Cink was so certain Goosen had already won, he tried to be the gentleman and putt in his 18-incher to leave the arena for the imminent crowning of the champion. Of course he embarrassingly missed, and was mortified when Goosens too turned to jelly and fluffed his second putt from two feet, Cink knowing his carelessness had cost him a place in a play-off. This left Goosens tied with a bemused Brooks, who had found all these shenanigans quite inexplicable.

In the protracted shoot-out, Brooks' waywardness off the tee presented the Championship to an untroubled Goosens. If Brooks had won, he would have been the first Majors winner at Southern Hills over three US Opens and three PGA Championships to have made par on the 72nd hole! The record persists.

FINAL LEADERBOARD

1	**RETIEF GOOSEN* (RSA)** ($900000)	66	70	69	71	276
2	Mark Brooks (USA)	72	64	70	70	276
3	Stewart Cink (USA)	69	69	67	72	277
4	Rocco Mediate (USA)	71	68	67	72	278
5=	Paul Azinger (USA)	74	67	69	71	281
	Tom Kite (USA)	73	72	72	64	281
7=	Angel Cabrera (ARG)	70	71	72	69	282
	Davis Love III (USA)	72	69	71	70	282
	Phil Mickelson (USA)	70	69	68	75	282
	Vijay Singh (FIJ)	74	70	74	64	282
	Kirk Triplett (USA)	72	69	71	70	282
12=	Michael Allen (USA)	77	68	67	71	283
	Matt Gogel (USA)	70	69	74	70	283
	Sergio Garcia (ESP)	70	68	68	77	283
	Tiger Woods (USA)	74	71	69	69	283
16=	Chris DiMarco (USA)	69	73	70	72	284
	David Duval (USA)	70	69	71	74	284
	Scott Hoch (USA)	73	73	69	69	284
19=	Corey Pavin (USA)	70	75	68	72	285
	Chris Perry (USA)	72	71	73	69	285
	Mike Weir (CAN)	67	76	68	74	285
22=	Thomas Bjorn (DEN)	72	69	73	72	286
	Scott Verplank (USA)	71	71	73	71	286
24=	Olin Browne (USA)	71	74	71	71	287
	Mark Calcavecchia (USA)	70	74	73	70	287
	Joe Durant (USA)	71	74	70	72	287
	Tom Lehman (USA)	76	68	59	74	287
	Steve Lowery (USA)	71	73	72	71	287
	Hal Sutton (USA)	70	75	71	71	287
30=	Darren Clarke (IRL)	74	71	71	72	288
	Bob Estes (USA)	70	72	75	71	288
	Padraig Harrington (IRL)	73	70	71	74	288
	Gabriel Hjertstedt (SWE)	72	74	70	72	288
	Steve Jones (USA)	73	73	72	70	288
	JL Lewis (USA)	69	68	77	75	288
	Bob May (USA)	72	72	69	75	288
	Bryce Molder [a] (USA)	75	71	68	74	288
	Jesper Parnevik (SWE)	73	73	74	68	288
	Dean Wilson (USA)	71	74	72	71	288
40=	Briny Baird (USA)	71	72	70	76	289
	Tim Herron (USA)	71	74	73	71	289
	Bernhard Langer (USA)	71	73	71	74	289
	Shaun Micheel (USA)	73	70	75	71	289
44=	Tom Byrum (USA)	74	72	72	72	290
	Brandel Chamblee (USA)	72	71	71	76	290
	Fred Funk (USA)	78	68	71	73	290
	Toshi Izawa (JAP)	69	74	74	73	290
	Jeff Maggert (USA)	69	73	72	76	290
	Kevin Sutherland (USA)	73	72	73	72	290
	Duffy Waldorf (USA)	75	68	69	78	290
51	Eduardo Romero (ARG)	74	72	72	73	291
52=	Jose Coceres (ARG)	70	73	75	74	292
	Scott Dunlap (USA)	74	70	73	75	292
	Hale Irwin (USA)	67	75	74	76	292
	Brandt Jobe (USA)	77	68	71	76	292
	Frank Lickliter (USA)	75	71	70	76	292
	Colin Montgomerie (SCO)	71	70	77	74	292
	Loren Roberts (USA)	69	76	69	78	292
	Bob Tway (USA)	75	71	72	74	292
	Jimmy Walker (USA)	79	66	74	73	292
	Mark Wiebe (USA)	73	72	74	73	292
62=	Jim Furyk (USA)	70	70	71	82	293
	Dudley Hart (USA)	71	73	74	75	293
	Tim Petrovic (USA)	74	71	75	73	293
	Richard Zokol (CAN)	72	71	74	76	293

66=	Ernie Els (RSA)	71	74	77	72	294
	Dan Forsman (USA)	75	71	77	71	294
	Harrison Frazar (USA)	73	73	76	72	294
	Peter Lonard (AUS)	76	69	70	79	294
	David Peoples (USA)	73	73	72	76	294
	David Toms (USA)	71	71	77	75	294
72=	Nick Faldo (ENG)	76	70	74	75	295
	Franklin Langham (USA)	75	71	75	74	295
74=	Mathias Gronberg (SWE)	74	69	74	79	296
	Thongchai Jaidee (THA)	73	73	72	78	296
	Anthony Kang (USA)	74	72	77	73	296
	Gary Orr (SCO)	74	72	74	76	296
78	Jim McGovern (USA)	71	73	77	76	297
79	Stephen Gangluff (USA)	74	72	78	77	301

* Retief Goosen (70) beat Mark Brooks (72) in the 18-Hole Play-off

Leaders (Round-by-round)

R1	66	R Goosen
	67	H Irwin, M Weir
	68	JL Lewis
R2	136	M Brooks; 72,64, R Goosen; 66,70, JL Lewis; 68,68
	138	S Cink; 69,69, S Garcia; 70,68
	139	D Duval; 70,69, P Mickelson; 70,69, R Mediate; 71,68
R3	205	S Cink; 69,69,67, R Goosen; 66,70,69
	206	M Brooks; 72,64,70, S Garcia; 70,68,68, R Mediate; 71,68,67
	207	P Mickelson; 70,69,68

Lowest Scores

R2	64	M Brooks
	66	J Walker
	67	P Azinger
R3	67	M Allen, S Cink, R Mediate
	68	S Garcia, P Mickelson, B Molder (a), C Pavin, M Weir
	69	P Azinger, R Goosen, S Hoch, T Lehman, B May, L Roberts, D Waldorf, T Woods
R4	64	T Kite, V Singh
	68	J Parnevik
	69	A Cabrera, S Hoch, C Perry, T Woods

The 130th (British) Open Championship

ROYAL LYTHAM & ST ANNE'S GC
Lancashire, England
19–22 July 2001
6905 yards PAR 71 (284)

DUVAL'S BREAKTHROUGH
Woosie woe as one of bridesmaids gets hitched

David Duval finally escaped the mantle he disputed with several others as being the best player never to have won a Major when the gods finally smiled on him at Lytham. After a frenetic bunch of around 20 real hopefuls set off on Sunday morning, the sombre-faced American eventually sauntered to the Open Championship, his first Major, doffed a cap that erstwhile seemed to be permanently attached to his skull, and removed his shades to reveal a sun mark reminiscent of an emerging coal miner. David even smiled, and his victor's address to the great and the good on the 18th green was full of bonhomie, so out of character from the carefully stage-managed frosty façade the golfing public was used to getting. An early birdie took him away from the pack, and with all around dropping shots or not making forward progress, Duval's length allowed him to birdie all the par 5s and cruise home by three. Young Swede Niclas Fasth suggested he could be one for the future in matching the winner's final round 67 to bypass the pack into second place.

Duval's win came after six years of contending and one or two before that getting the feel of Major Championships. For the only other man to have topped the World Ranking during the Woods dynasty, this success must have seemed a long time coming. His win, once it came though, was impressive, as just a glance at the final leaderboard shows. The chasing pack is studded with Major Champions or those riding high in the Ranking. After Fasth, there was was a six-way tie for third, featuring amongst them some old Majors warhorses in Els, Langer and Woosnam. In fact Woos-

nam made a Majors Top Five for the first time since the Muirfield Open of 1992, and he could have gone much better.

The big background drama running alongside Duval's victory was the Welshman's penalty of two strokes for carrying a 15th club in his bag. Sharing the lead at the start of play, Woosie promptly birdied the par-3 1st after a signature iron off the tee made for a virtual tap-in. On the 2nd tee, now level with the already-finished Fasth and one better than the pack, Woosnam's caddie Miles Byrne, with some trepidation, told his boss the gut-wrenching news. Woosnam somehow parred 2, but obviously not focused, dropped shots at 3 and 4, and his chance, with Duval, Clarke, Els and others on the hunt, to add to his 1991 Masters triumph had gone. It is to his credit that he held things altogether from there in, and even threatened briefly once more. It is also to his credit that he publicly supported his caddie (once the early expletives died away) despite quite a brouhaha in the press for a few days to come. Woosnam's magnanimity ran out a few weeks later, however, when the unhappy Irish bagman failed to turn up at a Tour event.

A magical Major in many ways, but not if you were one of the eight former Open Champions who failed to make the cut. Gary Player, Bob Charles and Tom Watson might be excused on the grounds of venerability, but sadly, champions of more recent vintage, Messrs Ballesteros, Faldo (for only the second time in 25 years), Daly, Lehman and Leonard all packed their bags early.

FINAL LEADERBOARD

1	**DAVID DUVAL (USA)**	69	73	65	67	274
	£600,000					
2	Niclas Fasth (SWE)	69	69	72	67	277
3=	Darren Clarke (IRL)	70	69	69	70	278
	Ernie Els (RSA)	71	71	67	69	278
	Miguel Angel Jimenez (ESP)	69	72	67	70	278
	Billy Mayfair (USA)	69	72	67	70	278
	Bernhard Langer (GER)	71	69	67	71	278
	Ian Woosnam (WAL)	72	68	67	71	278
9=	Sergio Garcia (ESP)	70	72	67	70	279
	Mikko Ilonen (FIN)	68	75	70	66	279
	Jesper Parnevik (SWE)	69	68	71	71	279
	Kevin Sutherland (USA)	75	69	68	67	279
13=	Billy Andrade (USA)	69	70	70	71	280
	Alex Cejka (GER)	69	69	69	73	280
	Retief Goosen (RSA)	74	68	67	71	280
	Raphael Jacquelin (FRA)	71	68	69	72	280
	Colin Montgomerie (SCO)	65	70	73	72	280
	Loren Roberts (USA)	70	70	70	70	280
	Vijay Singh (FIJ)	70	70	71	69	280
	Des Smyth (IRL)	74	65	70	71	280
21=	Davis Love III (USA)	73	67	74	67	281
	Nick Price (ZIM)	73	67	68	73	281
23=	Michael Campbell (NZL)	71	72	71	68	282
	Greg Owen (ENG)	69	68	72	73	282
25=	Bob Estes (USA)	74	70	73	66	283
	Joe Ogilvie (USA)	69	68	71	75	283
	Eduardo Romero (ARG)	70	68	72	73	283
	Tiger Woods (USA)	71	68	73	71	283
29	Barry Lane (ENG)	70	72	72	70	284
30=	Stewart Cink (USA)	71	72	72	70	285
	David Dixon [a] (ENG)	70	71	70	74	285
	Phil Mickelson (USA)	70	72	72	71	285
	Phillip Price (WAL)	74	69	71	71	285
	Justin Rose (ENG)	69	72	74	70	285
	Nicolas Vanhootegem (BEL)	72	68	70	75	285
	Scott Verplank (USA)	71	72	70	72	285
37=	Andrew Coltart (SCO)	75	68	70	73	286
	Padraig Harrington (IRL)	75	68	70	73	286
	Dudley Hart (USA)	74	69	69	74	286
	Frank Lickliter (USA)	71	71	73	71	286
	Toru Taniguchi (JAP)	72	69	72	73	286
42=	Richard Green (AUS)	71	70	72	74	287
	JP Hayes (USA)	69	71	74	73	287
	Paul Lawrie (SCO)	72	70	69	76	287
	Mark O'Meara (USA)	70	69	72	76	287
	Steve Stricker (USA)	71	69	72	75	287
47=	Robert Allenby (AUS)	73	71	71	73	288
	Chris DiMarco (USA)	68	74	72	74	288
	Brad Faxon (USA)	68	71	74	75	288
	Matt Gogel (USA)	73	70	71	74	288
	Peter Lonard (AUS)	72	70	74	72	288
	Adam Scott (AUS)	73	71	70	74	288
	Lee Westwood (ENG)	73	70	71	74	288
54=	Mark Calcavecchia (USA)	72	70	72	75	289
	Paul Curry (ENG)	72	71	71	75	289
	Carlos Franco (PAR)	71	71	73	74	289
	Paul McGinley (IRL)	69	72	72	76	289
	Jose Maria Olazabal (ESP)	69	74	73	73	289
	Rory Sabbatini (RSA)	70	69	76	74	289
	Duffy Waldorf (USA)	70	73	69	77	289
61	Stuart Appleby (AUS)	69	75	72	74	290
62=	Gordon Brand Jr (SCO)	70	72	75	74	291
	Brandel Chamblee (USA)	72	69	74	76	291
	Pierre Fulke (SWE)	69	67	72	83	291
65	Neil Cheetham (ENG)	72	72	73	78	295
66=	Alexandre Balicki (FRA)	69	75	75	77	296
	Thomas Levet (FRA)	72	72	77	75	296

68	David Smail (NZL)	71	72	76	79	298
69=	Scott Henderson (SCO)	75	69	81	76	301
	Sandy Lyle (SCO)	72	71	77	81	301

Leaders (Round-by-round)

R1	65	C Montgomerie
	68	DiMarco, B Faxon, M Ilonen
	69	B Andrade, S Appleby, A Balicki, A Cejka, D Duval, N Fasth, P Fulke, JP Hayes, MA Jimenez, P McGinley, B Mayfair, G Owen, J Ogilvie, JM Olazabal, J Parnevik, J Rose
R2	135	C Montgomerie; 65,70
	136	P Fulke; 69,67
	137	J Ogilvie; 69,68. G Owen; 69,68, J Parnevik; 69,68
R3	207	A Cejka; 69,69,69, D Duval; 69,73,65, B Langer; 71,69,68, I Woosnam; 72,68,67
	208	D Clarke; 70,69,69, P Fulke; 69,67,72, R Jacquelin; 71,68,69; MA Jimenez; 69,72,67, B Mayfair; 69,72,67, C Montgomerie; 65,70,73, J Ogilvie; 69,68,71, J Parnevik; 69,68,71
	209	B Andrade; 69,70,70, E Els; 71,71,67, S Garcia; 70,72,67, G Owen; 69,68,72, R Goosen; 74,68,67, D Smyth; 74, 65,70,71

Lowest Scores

R2	65	D Smyth
	66	P Harrington
	67	D Love III, N Price
R3	65	D Duval
	67	E Els, S Garcia, R Goosen, MA Jimenez, B Mayfair, I Woosnam
	68	N Price, K Sutherland
R4	66	B Estes, M Ilonen
	67	D Duval, N Fasth, D Love III, K Sutherland
	68	M Campbell

The 83rd US PGA Championship

ATLANTA ATHLETIC CLUB
Duluth, Georgia
16–19 August 2001
7213 yards PAR 70 (280)

RECORD HAUL FOR TOMS
Unprecedented low-scoring as Atlanta burns again

P GA Championship and Majors records went straight out of the window *en masse* at the Atlanta Athletic Club, as David Toms fulfilled a season and more of promise to capture his first Major title. A 5-wood hole-in-one on the par-3 15th on Saturday suggested the portents were good for the 34 year-old from Louisiana. A safety-first lay-up out of a poor lie approaching the 72nd green suggested that under pressure there was still a cool tactical brain to match the crusading flair. Once more, Phil Mickelson was to flatter to deceive, gaining his second runner-up spot and 14th Top Ten place in a Major where he seemed to be in the driving seat throughout. After a blistering 64 in Round Two, Japan's Shingo Katayama became a firm favourite with a crowd spoilt with a surfeit of Americans in the top dozen home.

Toms' victory with a 15 under par 265 was the lowest total to win any Major competed for over 72 holes. So complete was destruction of the Atlanta course, which had held its dignity in its two previous Majors (US Open 1976 and the PGA in 1981), that Mickleson's 266 became the second-lowest total, and of course, now the lowest total *not* to win, in a Major. In third place, Steve Lowery's 268 was not only his best ever finish in a Major Championship, his total, before Atlanta 2001, had only been bettered three times in history. Along the way, Toms and Katayama equalled the 36-hole PGA record of 131 held by Mark O'Meara in 1995, just one

off Nick Faldo's all-time Majors best at Muirfield three years before that. After 54 holes, Toms created a new record low of 196, while, two behind, Mickelson shot the joint-third lowest total in Majors history. Jetting into fourth place, 1989 Open Champion Mark Calcavecchia, having a better year in 2001 than any since the time of his Troon triumph, set an all-time low for Majors over the final 36 holes of 131.

Tiger Woods' gentle summer perambulated on, finishing as low in a Major as he had done since the PGA at Winged Foot during his rookie professional year (1997), but still maintaining a record of a Top 30 finish in every Major since that famous first Masters. That he was more interested in telling the press some shaggy-bear(!) story about him and his mate O'Meara while fishing in Alaska perhaps summed up his state of mind. Perhaps, deliberately, he was taking the heat off his golf and all the hype that was surrounding it.

Despite playing for the minor places, this for many Europeans was one of the last opportunities of the season to obtain meaningful points for the upcoming Ryder Cup. Sweating in 10th place in the standings, Phillip Price of Wales, thought his Third Round 76 and resultant share of 59th place had scuppered his chances, but no other European could finish high enough at Atlanta, nor in the remaining Tour events following, to stop him. The urgency of it all after 11 September now seems totally futile.

FINAL LEADERBOARD

1	**DAVID TOMS (USA)**	66	65	65	69	265
	($936000)					
2	Phil Mickelson (USA)	66	66	66	68	266
3	Steve Lowery (USA)	67	67	66	68	268
4=	Mark Calcavecchia (USA)	71	68	66	65	270
	Shingo Katayama (JAP)	67	64	69	70	270
6	Billy Andrade (USA)	68	70	68	66	272
7=	Jim Furyk (USA)	70	64	71	69	274
	Scott Hoch (USA)	68	70	69	67	274
	Scott Verplank (USA)	69	68	70	67	274
10=	David Duval (USA)	66	68	67	74	275
	Justin Leonard (USA)	70	79	67	69	275
	Kirk Triplett (USA)	68	70	71	66	275
13=	Ernie Els (RSA)	67	67	70	72	276
	Steve Flesch (USA)	73	67	70	66	276
	Jesper Parnevik (SWE)	70	68	70	68	276
16=	Robert Allenby (AUS)	68	67	73	68	277
	Stuart Appleby (AUS)	66	70	68	73	277
	Jose Coceres (ARG)	69	68	73	67	277
	Chris DiMarco (USA)	68	67	71	71	277
	Dudley Hart (USA)	66	68	73	70	277
	Mike Weir (CAN)	69	72	66	70	277
22=	Paul Azinger (USA)	68	67	69	74	278
	Briny Baird (USA)	70	69	72	67	278
	Brian Gay (USA)	70	68	69	71	278
	Charles Howell III (USA)	71	67	69	71	278
	Paul McGinley (IRL)	68	72	71	67	278
	Shigeki Maruyama (JAP)	68	72	71	67	278
	Mark O'Meara (USA)	72	63	70	73	278
29=	KJ Choi (KOR)	66	68	72	73	279
	Niclas Fasth (SWE)	66	69	72	72	279
	Carlos Franco (PAR)	67	72	71	69	279
	Greg Norman (AUS)	70	68	71	70	279
	Nick Price (ZIM)	71	67	71	70	279
	Chris Smith (USA)	68	71	68	71	279
	Bob Tway (USA)	69	69	71	70	279
	Tiger Woods (USA)	73	67	69	70	279
37=	Angel Cabrera (ARG)	69	69	70	72	280
	Andrew Coltart (SCO)	67	72	71	70	280
	Fred Couples (USA)	70	69	70	71	280
	Bob Estes (USA)	67	65	75	73	280
	Retief Goosen (RSA)	69	70	66	75	280
	Davis Love III (USA)	71	67	65	77	280
	Jose Maria Olazabal (ESP)	71	70	68	71	280
44=	Greg Chalmers (AUS)	68	70	69	74	281
	Jerry Kelly (USA)	69	67	72	73	281
	Andrew Oldcorn (SCO)	73	67	74	67	281
	Kenny Perry (USA)	68	70	71	72	281
	Rick Schuller (USA)	68	70	72	71	281
	Hal Sutton (USA)	67	71	73	70	281
	Lee Westwood (ENG)	71	68	68	74	281
51=	Scott Dunlap (USA)	69	72	70	71	282
	Joe Durant (USA)	68	71	72	71	282
	Nick Faldo (ENG)	67	74	71	70	282
	Frank Lickliter (USA)	71	69	71	71	282
	Tom Pernice Jr (USA)	69	69	74	70	282
	Chris Riley (USA)	68	71	73	70	282
	Vijay Singh (FIJ)	73	68	70	71	282
	Ian Woosnam (WAL)	71	70	73	68	282
59=	Stewart Cink (USA)	68	72	71	72	283
	Brad Faxon (USA)	66	70	74	73	283
	Phillip Price (WAL)	68	69	76	70	283
	Grant Waite (NZL)	64	74	73	72	283
63=	Thomas Bjorn (DEN)	67	71	73	73	284
	Jonathan Kaye (USA)	67	68	78	71	284
	Skip Kendall (USA)	72	67	73	72	284
66=	Robert Damron (USA)	68	73	71	73	285
	Rocco Mediate (USA)	71	65	73	76	285
	Steve Stricker (USA)	75	65	75	70	285

	Tom Watson (USA)	69	70	76	70	285
70=	Fred Funk (USA)	69	67	73	77	286
	Scott McCarron (USA)	69	67	73	77	286
72	John Huston (USA)	67	68	75	77	287
73	Bob May (USA)	71	70	76	74	291
74	Paul Stankowski (USA)	67	71	76	79	293
75	Steve Pate (USA)	71	69	71	83	294
Also	Colin Montgomerie (SCO)	71	69	74	d/q	

Leaders (Round-by-round)

R1 64 G Waite
66 S Appleby, KJ Choi, D Duval, N Fasth,
B Faxon, F Funk, D Hart, P Mickelson,
D Toms
67 A Coltart, T Bjorn, E Els, B Estes, N Faldo,
C Franco, J Huston, S Katayama, J Kaye,
S Lowery, P Stankowski, H Sutton
R2 131 S Katayama; 67,64, D Toms; 66,65
132 B Estes; 67,65, P Mickelson; 66,66
134 KJ Choi; 66,68, D Duval; 66,68, E Els; 67,67,
J Furyk; 70,64, D Hart; 66,68, S Lowery; 67,67
R3 196 D Toms; 66,65,65
198 P Mickelson; 66,66,66
200 S Katayama; 67,64,69, S Lowery; 67,67,66

Lowest Scores

R2 63 M O'Meara
64 J Furyk, S Katayama
65 B Estes, R Mediate, S Stricker, D Toms
R3 65 D Toms, D Love III
66 M Calcavecchia, R Goosen, S Lowery,
P Mickelson, M Weir
67 D Duval, J Leonard
R4 65 M Calcavecchia
66 B Andrade, S Flesch, K Triplett
67 B Baird, J Coceres, S Hoch, P McGinley,
S Maruyama, A Oldcorn, S Verplank

THE MAJOR CHAMPIONSHIPS: THE FUTURE

THE MASTERS

As usual, the Masters will take place each April at the home of its organizers, Augusta National Golf Club. It is expected that the year 2002 will see the greatest alterations to the course since the days of Bob Jones and Alister MacKenzie, with the intention of offering a tougher test to the longer hitter. Overall, nine holes are being changed, including seven par 4s and two par 5s. The yardage on the course will increase to approximately 7270 yards from 6985. In more detail (yardages are approximate):

Hole 1 Tees moving back 20–25 yards. Reshaping fairway bunker, extending it 10–15 yards towards the green and making the carry 300 yards. (Total) 435 yards

Hole 7 Tees moving back 40–45 yards. 410 yards

Hole 8 Tees moving back 15–20 yards and 10 yards to the right. Reshaping and nearly doubling the size of the fairway bunker, making the carry 305 yards. 570 yards

Hole 9 Tees moving back 25–30 yards. 460 yards

Hole 10 Tees moving back 5–10 yards and 5 yards to the left. 495 yards

Hole 11 Tees moving back 30–35 yards and moving 5 yards to the right. 490 yards

Hole 13 Tees moving back 20–25 yards. 510 yards

Hole 14 Tees moving back 30-35 yards. 440 yards

Hole 18 Tees moving back 55-60 yards and 5 yards to the right. Adjusting bunker complex by making bunkers 10% larger and making the carry 320 yards. 465 yards

Dates:

2002 11–14 April

2003 10–13 April

2004 8–11 April

THE (BRITISH) OPEN

The Open roster's page falls open on the **Muirfield** home of the Hon Co of Edinburgh Golfers for 2002. They will play hosts at the lovely links to the east of Scotland's capital for the 15th time, and, if the old Musselburgh venue is taken into account, the 21st. In a return to the English Channel the following year, **Royal St George's** at Sandwich makes it Open No 13 for this famous club, while in 2004 it heads for Scotland's west coast and **Royal Troon's** seventh Championship. Although not confirmed, the R&A have plans to bring back Royal Liverpool at Hoylake to the Open list, perhaps as early as 2006. Roberto de Vicenzo was the last winner there in 1967.

Dates:

2002 **Muirfield**, 18–21 July

2003 **Royal St George's**, 17–20 July

2004 **Royal Troon**, 15–18 July

US OPEN

The USGA visits **Bethpage State Park** at Farmingdale, Long Island, New York in 2002, the first new location since Pinehurst, and before that, Pebble Beach in 1972. The Black Course will be the first public golf course to host the US Open. 2003 sees an unexpected return to historic **Olympia Fields**, 75 years since Johnny Farrell won the US Open when it was played there for the only time. It was last used for a Major in 1962, when the PGA Championship visited. More nostalgia as **Shinnecock Hills** is the site of the 2004 US Open: although it has been utilized more by the USGA over the last few years as much as it did in the first 100 of the event.

Dates:

2002 **Bethpage State Park**, 13–16 June

2003 **Olympia Fields**, 12–15 June

2004 **Shinnecock Hills**, 17–20 June

USPGA CHAMPIONSHIP

Hazeltine National at Ceska, Minnesota will host the PGA Championship for the first time in 2002. Famous for Tony Jacklin's win at the US Open in 1970, it also staged the 1991 US Open, when Payne Stewart triumphed. Tree-lined **Oak Hill** was originally planned tree-less by Donald Ross, but over 30000 were subsequently planted by a botanist member whose campaign brought in varieties from all over the world. It holds the PGA Championship for the second time in 2003, having already played host for three US Opens. The PGA of America, in typical pioneering vein, have awarded the 2004 event to the **Whistling Straits** Club at Kohler, Wisconsin – a first for the Club and state. Almost a British links in character, bounded by high dunes, Lake Michigan's offshore influences are expected to be as testing as anything on course.

Dates:

2002 **Hazeltine National**, 15–18 August

2003 **Oak Hill**, 14–17 August

2004 **Whistling Straits**, 12–15 August

Part

	Yr	M	AS	USO	BOP	PGA
AARON, Tommy (USA)						
	1960	25				
	1964					21
	1965	11				8
	1966	13		30		22
	1967	8				20
	1968	7				26
	1969	8				
	1970	5				
	1971	22				
	1972					2
	1973	W				
	1975			29		
	1979	28				
ABBOTT, Patrick (USA)						
	1952			28		
ADAM, Robert [a] (SCO)						
	1890				25	
ADAMS, GC (USA)						
	1916					Last 32
ADAMS, Jimmy (SCO)						
	1934				26	
	1936				2	
	1937				17	
	1938				2	
	1939				13	
	1947				12	
	1949				8	
	1950				12	
	1951				4	
	1954				5	
	1956				25	
	1959				29	
ADAMS, John (USA)						
	1993			11		
ADAMS, Sam (USA)						
	1977			23		
ADWICK, James (ENG)						
	1925				28	
ADWICK, KWC (ENG)						
	1956				28	
ALBUS, Jim (USA)						
	1984			30		
ALCROFT, Albert (USA)						
	1927					Last 32
	1928					Last 32
	1929					Last 32

	Yr	M	AS	USO	BOP	PGA
ALERIDGE, Clayton (USA)						
	1944					Last 32
ALEXANDER, Andrew (SCO)						
	1882				13	
ALEXANDER, Skip (USA)						
	1948			11		Last 16
	1949		30	27		Last 32
	1950		14	18		Last 32
	1952		27			
	1953		29			
ALLAN, Jamie (SCO)						
	1878				8	
	1879				2	
	1885				29	
	1888				18	
ALLAN, John (SCO)						
	1866				8	
	1868				5	
	1870				8	
	1878				9	
	1890				15	
	1893				23	
ALLAN, Matthew (SCO)						
	1875				13	
	1884				11	
ALLEN, Brian (ENG)						
	1963				14	
ALLEN, Michael (USA)						
	2001			12		
ALLEN, TW (ENG)						
	1950				24	
ALLENBY, Robert (AUS)						
	1995				15	
	1997				10	
	1998				19	13
	2000					18
	2001					16
ALLIN, Buddy (Brian) (USA)						
	1974	15		10		
	1975	20		25		10
	1976	19				
ALLISS, Percy (ENG)						
	1922				10	
	1925				6	
	1927				9	
	1928				4	

ALLISS, Percy (cont)

Yr	M AS	USO	BOP	PGA
1929			4	
1930			17	
1931			3	
1932			4	
1934			9	
1935			15	
1936			5	
1937			15	
1939			9	
1946			17	

ALLISS, Peter (ENG)

Yr	M AS	USO	BOP	PGA
1953			9	
1954			8	
1957			12	
1958			11	
1959			16	
1961			8	
1962			8	
1963			18	
1966			20	
1968			13	
1969			8	

ALLOTT, Fred (ENG)

Yr	M AS	USO	BOP	PGA
1950			29	
1952			21	

ALVES, Grange (USA)

Yr	M AS	USO	BOP	PGA
1911		20		

AMBO, Walter (USA)

Yr	M AS	USO	BOP	PGA
1947				Last 32

AMES, Stephen (TRI)

Yr	M AS	USO	BOP	PGA
1997		5		
1998		24		
2000				29

ANDERSON, Bill (SCO)

Yr	M AS	USO	BOP	PGA
1939			17	
1946			14	

ANDERSON, Brad (USA)

Yr	M AS	USO	BOP	PGA
1971				22

ANDERSON, Carl (USA)

Yr	M AS	USO	BOP	PGA
1919				Last 32
1923				Last 32

ANDERSON, D [a] (SCO)

Yr	M AS	USO	BOP	PGA
1890			17	

ANDERSON Sr, David (SCO)

Yr	M AS	USO	BOP	PGA
1876			14	
1879			7	
1882			21	
1885			21	

ANDERSON Jr, David (SCO)

Yr	M AS	USO	BOP	PGA
1888			2	
1890			14	
1891			22	
1892			16	
1893			22	
1895			6	
1896			24	
1900			14	

ANDERSON, Iain (SCO)

Yr	M AS	USO	BOP	PGA
1955			15	

ANDERSON, Jamie (SCO)

Yr	M AS	USO	BOP	PGA
1869			6	
1870			7	
1873			2	
1874			5	
1876			12	
1877			W	
1878			W	
1879			W	
1881			2	
1882			3	
1884			15	

ANDERSON, John G (USA)

Yr	M AS	USO	BOP	PGA
1912		16		

ANDERSON, LS [a] (SCO)

Yr	M AS	USO	BOP	PGA
1893			19	

ANDERSON, PC [a] (SCO)

Yr	M AS	USO	BOP	PGA
1893			19	

ANDERSON, R (USA)

Yr	M AS	USO	BOP	PGA
1896		27		

ANDERSON, Stuart [a] (SCO)

Yr	M AS	USO	BOP	PGA
1894			25	

ANDERSON Jr, Tom (USA)

Yr	M AS	USO	BOP	PGA
1909		7		
1910		8		
1912		10		

ANDERSON (Sr), Willie (SCO)

Yr	M AS	USO	BOP	PGA
1885			24	
1888			27	

ANDERSON (Jr), Willie (SCO/USA)

Yr	M AS	USO	BOP	PGA
1897		2		
1898		3		
1899		5		
1900		11		
1901		W		
1902		5		

ANDERSON (Jr), Willie (cont)

Yr	MAS	USO	BOP	PGA
1903		W		
1904		W		
1905		W		
1906		5		
1907		15		
1908		4		
1909		4		
1910		11		

ANDRADE, Billy (USA)

Yr	MAS	USO	BOP	PGA
1990				14
1992			25	12
1995		21		
1996		23		
1997		13		
2001			13	6

ANDREW, R [a] (SCO)

Yr	MAS	USO	BOP	PGA
1908			27	

ANDREW, Robert (SCO)

Yr	MAS	USO	BOP	PGA
1860			4	
1861			5	
1863			6	
1864			3	
1865			7	
1866			3	
1867			7	
1868			2	

ANDREWS, Robert [a] (USA)

Yr	MAS	USO	BOP	PGA
1913		21		

ANGELINI, Alfonso (ITA)

Yr	MAS	USO	BOP	PGA
1954			12	

ANNON, Fred (USA)

Yr	MAS	USO	BOP	PGA
1944				Last 16

AOKI, Isao (JAP)

Yr	MAS	USO	BOP	PGA
1977	28			
1978			7	
1979			7	
1980		2	12	
1981		11	11	4
1982		30	20	
1983	19			
1984	25	16		
1985	16			
1987		14		
1988	25		7	
1989				17

APPLEBY, Stuart (AUS)

Yr	MAS	USO	BOP	PGA
1997	21		20	
1998		10		
2000			11	4
2001				16

ARCHER, George (USA)

Yr	MAS	USO	BOP	PGA
1966		17		
1967	16			
1968	22	16		4
1969	W	10		
1970		30		
1971		5		
1972	12			
1977	19	27		19
1980				17
1981	11			
1982	30			
1983	12			
1984	25			

ARMITAGE, R [a] (SCO)

Yr	MAS	USO	BOP	PGA
1873			12	
1879			29	

ARMOUR, Tommy (SCO/USA)

Yr	MAS	USO	BOP	PGA
1924		13		
1925				QF
1926		9	12	
1927		W		QF
1928		16		Last 32
1929		5	10	
1930				W
1931			W	QF
1932		21	17	
1933		4		
1934				Last 16
1935				RU
1936	20	22		
1937	8			
1938		23		
1939	10	22		
1940		12		
1942	28			

ARMOUR III, Tommy (USA)

Yr	MAS	USO	BOP	PGA
1988			28	
1989				24

ARMSTRONG, Wally (USA)

Yr	MAS	USO	BOP	PGA
1977		16		
1978	5	20		19
1979			13	

ARUNDEL, Thomas (SCO)

Yr	MAS	USO	BOP	PGA
1879			15	
1880			10	
1882			27	
1883			21	

AUBREY, Emlyn (ENG)

Yr	MAS	USO	BOP	PGA
1989		29		
1996				24

Yr	M AS	USO	BOP	PGA

AUCHTERLONIE, Laurie
(SCO/USA)

Yr	M AS	USO	BOP	PGA
1888		14		
1891		18		
1895		13		
1899	9			
1900	4			
1901	5			
1902	W			
1903	7			
1904	4			
1905	24			
1906	3			
1907	11			
1908	21			
1909	23			

AUCHTERLONIE, Willie (SCO)

Yr	M AS	USO	BOP	PGA
1888		18		
1891		8		
1893		W		
1894		23		
1896		12		
1897		18		
1900		5		
1901		29		
1910		28		

AULBACH, George (USA)

Yr	M AS	USO	BOP	PGA
1924				Last 32
1926				Last 32

AUSTIN, Woody (USA)

Yr	M AS	USO	BOP	PGA
1995				23
1996	23			

AVESTON, Willie (WAL)

Yr	M AS	USO	BOP	PGA
1895		27		
1899		15		
1908		28		

AYCOCK, Tommy (USA)

Yr	M AS	USO	BOP	PGA
1974				11

AYTON, David (SCO)

Yr	M AS	USO	BOP	PGA
1873		18		
1879		15		
1882		7		
1885		3		
1887		12		
1888		9		
1890		17		
1891		22		

AYTON Sr, Laurie (SCO/USA)

Yr	M AS	USO	BOP	PGA
1910		4		
1911		9		
1912		5		

AYTON Sr, Laurie (cont)

Yr	M AS	USO	BOP	PGA
1913		30		
1920		17		Last 16
1921		18		Last 16
1922		11		
1924		25		
1925		9		Last 32
1926		16		Last 32
1930				Last 16
1931		23		
1933			21	
1935			9	
1939			30	

AYTON Jr, Laurie (SCO)

Yr	M AS	USO	BOP	PGA
1956			25	
1957			30	
1960			28	

AZINGER, Paul (USA)

Yr	M AS	USO	BOP	PGA
1987	17		2	
1988		6		2
1989	14	9	8	
1990		24		
1993				W
1995	17			
1996	18			
1997	28	28		
1998	5	14		13
1999		12		
2000	28	12	6	23
2001	15	5		22

BAIOCCHI, Hugh (RSA)

Yr	M AS	USO	BOP	PGA
1973			18	
1974	22			
1975			23	
1980			29	
1984			9	

BAIRD, Briny (USA)

Yr	M AS	USO	BOP	PGA
2001				22

BAIRD, Butch (USA)

Yr	M AS	USO	BOP	PGA
1966				28
1976		4		

BAKER, Peter (ENG)

Yr	M AS	USO	BOP	PGA
1993			21	
1998			15	

BAKER-FINCH, Ian (AUS)

Yr	M AS	USO	BOP	PGA
1984			9	
1985			20	
1989			30	
1990			6	
1991	7		W	
1992	6		19	

BAKER-FINCH, Ian (cont)

Yr	M	AS	USO	BOP	PGA
1993			19		
1994	10				

BALDIE, D [a] (SCO)

Yr	M	AS	USO	BOP	PGA
1883				30	

BALDING, Al (CAN)

Yr	M	AS	USO	BOP	PGA
1956	29		17		
1957	16				
1958	26				
1961	27				
1962	24				
1967			12	8	
1968				9	
1970	18				

BALFOUR, Leslie [a] (SCO)

Yr	M	AS	USO	BOP	PGA
1885				16	
1888				5	
1892				28	

BALL, Donald (USA)

Yr	M	AS	USO	BOP	PGA
1908			12		

BALL, Errie (USA)

Yr	M	AS	USO	BOP	PGA
1934					Last 32
1936			23		Last 32
1948					Last 32
1956		22			

BALL, Frank (USA)

Yr	M	AS	USO	BOP	PGA
1921				19	
1923				16	
1924				3	
1925				24	
1928		22			
1935				26	

BALL Jr, John [a] (ENG)

Yr	M	AS	USO	BOP	PGA
1878				4	
1890				W	
1891				11	
1892				2	
1893				8	
1894				13	
1895				18	
1897				17	
1899				25	
1902				15	
1904				17	
1907				15	
1908				13	
1910				19	

BALL, Tom (ENG)

Yr	M	AS	USO	BOP	PGA
1906				24	
1907				10	

BALL, Tom (cont)

Yr	M	AS	USO	BOP	PGA
1908				2	
1909				2	
1910				12	
1911				15	
1912				26	
1913				30	

BALLESTEROS, Severiano (Seve) (ESP)

Yr	M	AS	USO	BOP	PGA
1976				2	
1977				15	
1978	18	16		17	
1979	12			W	
1980	W			19	
1982	3			13	13
1983	W		4	6	27
1984			30	W	5
1985	2	5			
1986	4	24		6	
1987	2	3			10
1988	11			W	
1989	5				12
1990	7				
1991	22			9	23
1992		23			
1993	11				
1994	18	18			

BALLINGALL, JH (ENG)

Yr	M	AS	USO	BOP	PGA
1938				15	

BAMFORD, Brian (ENG)

Yr	M	AS	USO	BOP	PGA
1962				24	
1965				21	

BANNERMAN, Harry (SCO)

Yr	M	AS	USO	BOP	PGA
1971				11	
1972				19	

BANNISTER, Eric (ENG)

Yr	M	AS	USO	BOP	PGA
1920				14	

BARBARO, Louis (USA)

Yr	M	AS	USO	BOP	PGA
1953			30		

BARBER, JM (ENG)

Yr	M	AS	USO	BOP	PGA
1924				9	

BARBER, Jerry (USA)

Yr	M	AS	USO	BOP	PGA
1953	21	30			
1954	6				QF
1956	6				Last 32
1957	26	9			
1958		19			
1959					2
1960		9			
1961					W
1962	5				

BARBER, Miller (USA)

Yr	M AS	USO	BOP	PGA
1962		22		
1966		26		
1967		18		
1968	12	24		8
1969	7	6	10	5
1970	21	6		
1971				4
1972		29		16
1973		25		24
1974	15			
1975	26	24		
1977				25
1978	24			
1979	12			28

BARBER, Tom (ENG)

Yr	M AS	USO	BOP	PGA
1923			16	
1926			5	
1930			9	

BARBIERI, Romualdo (ARG)

Yr	M AS	USO	BOP	PGA
1955			10	

BARKER, HH (ENG/USA)

Yr	M AS	USO	BOP	PGA
1908		17		
1909		7		
1910		8		
1911		7		
1915		24		

BARNES, Brian (SCO)

Yr	M AS	USO	BOP	PGA
1967			25	
1968			6	
1972			5	
1973			10	
1975			23	
1976			14	
1981			14	

BARNES, Jim (ENG/USA)

Yr	M AS	USO	BOP	PGA
1912		18		
1913		4		
1914		13		
1915		4		
1916		3		W
1919		11		W
1920		6	6	Last 16
1921		W	6	RU
1922		24	2	Last 32
1923		12		QF
1924				RU
1925		29	W	
1926			17	Last 32
1927		24	16	
1928			6	Last 16
1929			7	
1930			6	

BARNETT, Robert (USA)

Yr	M AS	USO	BOP	PGA
1921				Last 32
1923				Last 32

BARNUM, John (USA)

Yr	M AS	USO	BOP	PGA
1958				16

BARONI, Fred (USA)

Yr	M AS	USO	BOP	PGA
1922				Last 32
1924				Last 32
1927		15		Last 32

BARR, Dave (CAN)

Yr	M AS	USO	BOP	PGA
1985		2		
1986	16			
1988		25		

BARRETT, Percy (ENG/CAN)

Yr	M AS	USO	BOP	PGA
1904		6		
1905		3		
1908		8		
1912		15		

BARRON, Herman (USA)

Yr	M AS	USO	BOP	PGA
1929				Last 16
1930		28		
1931		15		
1933		13		QF
1934		23		Last 32
1935		14		
1936		11		
1939				Last 32
1941		5		
1945				Last 16
1946	25	4		Last 16
1947	17	27		Last 32
1948	25	7		
1949	13	27		Last 16

BASS, Vic (USA)

Yr	M AS	USO	BOP	PGA
1942				Last 32

BASSLER, Charles (USA)

Yr	M AS	USO	BOP	PGA
1951		21		SF
1953				Last 32
1954				Last 16
1957				Last 32
1961				29

BASSLER, Harry (USA)

Yr	M AS	USO	BOP	PGA
1938				Last 16
1941				Last 32
1944				Last 16
1946				Last 16
1947				Last 32

BASSLER, Newton (USA)

Yr	M AS	USO	BOP	PGA
1946				Last 32

	Yr	M AS	USO	BOP	PGA
BATLEY, Jas (ENG)					
	1912			27	
	1914			21	
BATTELL, Bert (USA)					
	1916		24		
BAXTER, Alex (SCO/USA)					
	1906		17		
BAYER, George (USA)					
	1957		22		
	1958	29			
	1960	29	12		
	1961				22
	1962				3
	1963	28			
	1964		11		
	1965	15			
BEACH, Ralph (USA)					
	1927				Last 16
BEAN, Andy (USA)					
	1977	19	23		
	1978	24	6		7
	1979	28	25		12
	1980	12		6	2
	1982	10			
	1983			2	30
	1984	18	11	14	16
	1985	25	15		3
	1986		24	14	
	1988		12	16	
	1989				2
BEARD, Frank (USA)					
	1965	8	3		
	1966	22	17		11
	1967	26			7
	1968	5			6
	1969	19			10
	1970	9			
	1971	9			13
	1972			19	
	1973	24	25		
	1974	22	12		11
	1975		3		
BECK, Alf (ENG)					
	1932			25	
	1934			21	
	1935			26	
BECK, Chip (USA)					
	1982		12		
	1983		10		23

	Yr	M AS	USO	BOP	PGA
BECK, Chip (cont)	1984		21		25
	1986		2		16
	1987	12			
	1988	21	21	28	
	1989	8	2	26	
	1990		29		5
	1991			17	23
	1992			12	
	1993	2	25		
	1994	15	25		
BEGAY III, Notah (USA)					
	2000		22	20	8
BELFORE, Joe (USA)					
	1938		27		
BELL, Art (USA)					
	1935				Last 32
	1944				QF
	1946				Last 16
	1947				SF
	1948	23	25		
	1955		28		
BELL, David (USA)					
	1900		2		
BELL, RK [a] (ENG)					
	1946			23	
BELLWOOD, Frank (USA)					
	1913		30		
BELLWORTHY, AE (ENG)					
	1904			29	
	1909			26	
BEMAN, Deane (USA)					
	1960	29a			
	1961		12a		
	1962		14a		
	1964	25a			
	1965		11a		
	1966		30a		
	1967		6	13	
	1969	19	2		
	1970	23			
BEMBRIDGE, Maurice (ENG)					
	1968			5	
	1970			13	
	1972			19	
	1974	9			
	1975	26		16	
BEMISH, Walter (USA)					
	1931				Last 32

Yr	M AS	USO	BOP	PGA
BENEPE, Jim (USA)				
1988			28	
1990		14		
BENNETT, Stephen (ENG)				
1989			26	
BERGANIO Jr, David (USA)				
1996		16		
1999		28		
BERGIN, Bill (USA)				
1984			14	
BERNARDI, Sam (USA)				
1937				Last 32
1949		27		
1952				Last 32
BERNARDINI, Roberto (ITA)				
1969	29			
1970			17	
1972			13	
BERTOLINO, Enrique (ARG)				
1939			13	
1956			6	
BESSELINK, Al (USA)				
1950		12		
1951	20	6		
1952	3			
1953	9			
1954	9			
BEVERIDGE, James (SCO)				
1880			23	
BIAGETTI, Leo (USA)				
1957		30		
BIES, Don (USA)				
1967				7
1968		5		26
1969				11
1973		29		30
1974				9
1982		30		
BINNIE, William (SCO)				
1910			24	
BISDORF, Bill (USA)				
1964				28
1967				30
BISHOP, Simon (ENG)				
1985			16	

Yr	M AS	USO	BOP	PGA
BJORN, Thomas (DEN)				
1998		25	9	
1999			30	
2000	28		2	3
2001		22		
BLACK, David (SCO/USA)				
1912		30		
BLACK, Jimmy (ENG)				
1938			20	
BLACK, John (USA)				
1922		2		
1923		26		
BLACK, Ronnie (USA)				
1984	6			
1986				21
1987				28
1988				25
1997				29
BLACKMAR, Phil (US)				
1997				6
BLACKWELL, Edward BH (Ted) [a] (SCO)				
1892			13	
1900			30	
1904			26	
1911			21	
BLACKWELL, Ernley RH [a] (SCO)				
1891			22	
1892			27	
BLAIR, David [a] (SCO)				
1950			30	
1960			9	
BLAKE, Jay Don (USA)				
1987		24		
1988				25
1989		18		
1991	27			13
1992		6		
BLAKESLEE, Jack (USA)				
1925				Last 32
BLANCAS, Homero (USA)				
1971		19		
1972	5	4		
BLAND, John (RSA)				
1980			16	
BLANTON, Julian (USA)				
1928				Last 16

BLISS Jr, Rodney [a] (USA)

Yr	M AS	USO	BOP	PGA
1934		28		

BLUM, Arnold (USA)

Yr	M AS	USO	BOP	PGA
1952	24			
1958	29			

BLYTH, AD [a] (ENG)

Yr	M AS	USO	BOP	PGA
1894			10	

BOLETSA, George (USA)

Yr	M AS	USO	BOP	PGA
1951				Last 16

BOLSTAD, Lester [a] (USA)

Yr	M AS	USO	BOP	PGA
1933		19		

BOLT, Tommy (USA)

Yr	M AS	USO	BOP	PGA
1951		29		
1952	3	7		
1953	5			Last 32
1954	12	6		SF
1955	22	3		SF
1956	8	22		
1957				Last 16
1958		W		5
1959	30			17
1960	20			
1961	4	22		
1962				30
1965	8			
1966	17			
1967	26			
1971				3

BONALLACK, Michael [a] (ENG)

Yr	M AS	USO	BOP	PGA
1959			11	
1966			27	
1968			21	
1971			22	

BONNAR, Tom (USA)

Yr	M AS	USO	BOP	PGA
1910		14		

BONTEMPO, Henry (USA)

Yr	M AS	USO	BOP	PGA
1935				Last 21

BOOBYER, Fred (ENG)

Yr	M AS	USO	BOP	PGA
1960			28	
1965			25	
1966			30	
1967			29	
1969			25	

BOOMER, Aubrey (ENG)

Yr	M AS	USO	BOP	PGA
1921			26	
1922			17	
1924			6	

BOOMER, Aubrey (cont)

Yr	M AS	USO	BOP	PGA
1925			26	
1927			2	
1928			6	
1929			15	
1931			20	
1933			18	
1935			11	
1936			15	

BOON, Neil (SCO)

Yr	M AS	USO	BOP	PGA
1875			11	
1878			19	

BOOTHBY, Fitz [a] (SCO)

Yr	M AS	USO	BOP	PGA
1882			3	

BOOTHBY, RT [a] (SCO)

Yr	M AS	USO	BOP	PGA
1892			16	

BOREK, Gene (USA)

Yr	M AS	USO	BOP	PGA
1971				30

BOROS, Julius (USA)

Yr	M AS	USO	BOP	PGA
1950		9		
1951	17	4		
1952	7	W		
1953	10	17		
1954	16	23		
1955	4	5		
1956	24	2		
1957		4		
1958		3		5
1959	8	28		
1960	5	3		24
1962	11			11
1963	3	W		13
1964				21
1965		4		17
1966	28	17	15	5
1967	5			5
1968	16	16		W
1969		13		25
1970	23	12		26
1972		29		
1973		7		
1974	26			

BOTTOMLEY, Steven (ENG)

Yr	M AS	USO	BOP	PGA
1995			3	

BOURNE, Walter (USA)

Yr	M AS	USO	BOP	PGA
1921			26	
1924		17		

BOUSE, GJ (USA)

Yr	M AS	USO	BOP	PGA
1907		20		

Yr	M	AS	USO	BOP	PGA

BOUSFIELD, Ken (ENG)

Yr	M	AS	USO	BOP	PGA
1947				27	
1948				21	
1949				11	
1952				21	
1955				5	
1956				22	
1959				11	
1960				21	
1961				8	
1963				30	

BOWDEN, George (USA)

Yr	M	AS	USO	BOP	PGA
1919		8			
1920		30			Last 32

BOYD, Bob (USA)

Yr	M	AS	USO	BOP	PGA
1983					30
1990					19
1994					30

BOYD, James (SCO)

Yr	M	AS	USO	BOP	PGA
1875				14	
1887				20	

BOYD, Tom (USA)

Yr	M	AS	USO	BOP	PGA
1919					Last 32
1920					Last 32
1921			26		Last 16
1922					Last 32
1925			20		
1929			30		

BOYD, W (SCO)

Yr	M	AS	USO	BOP	PGA
1870				15	

BOYER, Auguste (FRA)

Yr	M	AS	USO	BOP	PGA
1930				9	
1931		29			
1933				14	
1934				29	
1935				10	

BOYLE, Hugh (IRL)

Yr	M	AS	USO	BOP	PGA
1962				27	
1965				12	
1967				8	
1973				18	

BOYNTON, Frank (USA)

Yr	M	AS	USO	BOP	PGA
1962			27		
1966					22
1968					8

BRADBEER, Bob (ENG)

Yr	M	AS	USO	BOP	PGA
1928				23	

BRADBEER, James (ENG)

Yr	M	AS	USO	BOP	PGA
1907				19	
1913				7	
1914				14	

BRADLEY, Jackson (USA)

Yr	M	AS	USO	BOP	PGA
1948					Last 32
1950					Last 16
1951					Last 16
1953					Last 16
1960			19		

BRADLEY, Michael (USA)

Yr	M	AS	USO	BOP	PGA
1998		29			

BRADSHAW, Harry (IRL)

Yr	M	AS	USO	BOP	PGA
1946				11	
1949				2	
1950				16	
1951				15	
1952				9	
1954				12	
1956				23	
1957				19	
1958				24	
1959				16	
1961				20	
1962				30	

BRADY, Mike (USA)

Yr	M	AS	USO	BOP	PGA
1907			16		
1908			17		
1909			12		
1911			2		
1912			3		
1913			14		
1914			5		
1915			6		
1916			9		Last 16
1919			2		Last 16
1920			14		
1921			14		
1922			8		Last 32
1923			20		
1924			9		Last 32
1925			7		Last 16
1926			16		Last 16

BRAID, George (SCO/USA)

Yr	M	AS	USO	BOP	PGA
1902			26		
1904			15		

BRAID, James (SCO)

Yr	M	AS	USO	BOP	PGA
1894				10a	
1896				6	
1897				2	
1898				10	

	Yr	M	AS	USO	BOP	PGA
BRAID, James (cont)	1899				5	
	1900				3	
	1901				W	
	1902				2	
	1903				5	
	1904				2	
	1905				W	
	1906				W	
	1907				5	
	1908				W	
	1909				2	
	1910				W	
	1911				5	
	1912				3	
	1913				18	
	1914				10	
	1920				21	
	1921				16	
	1924				18	
	1926				26	
	1927				29	
BRAID, Robert (SCO/USA)						
	1899			27		
BRANCH, William J (Bill) (ENG)						
	1935				8	
	1937				13	
	1949				14	
	1950				24	
	1955				23	
BRAND, D (SCO)						
	1973				22	
BRAND, Fred (USA)						
	1906			18		
	1907			11		
	1914			28		
	1922					Last 32
BRAND, Gordon J (ENG)						
	1981				19	
	1985				25	
	1986				2	
BRAND Jr, Gordon (SCO)						
	1987				26	
	1988				20	
	1992				5	
	1998				14	
BRANNAN, Mike (USA)						
	1982			22		
BRANTLY, Edward [a] (USA)						
	1961			29		

	Yr	M	AS	USO	BOP	PGA
BREDEMUS, John (USA)						
	1919					Last 32
BREWER, Gay (USA)						
	1962		11	5		
	1964		25	5		8
	1965			16		28
	1966		2			27
	1967		W			28
	1968			9	6	20
	1969				15	25
	1970			7		
	1971			9		
	1972			25		7
	1973		10		10	
	1974					17
	1976		23			
	1977			26		
	1978		29			
	1981		15			
BREWS, Sid (ENG/RSA)						
	1923				22	
	1929				18	
	1934				2	
	1935			21	30	
	1938				13	
BRIGGS, Eldon (USA)						
	1955					Last 32
	1957					Last 32
BRION, Stan (USA)						
	1974					22
BRISKY, Mike (USA)						
	1996					14
	2000			23		
BRITTON, Bill (USA)						
	1990		7			4
	1992					21
BRITZ, Tienie (RSA)						
	1978				29	
	1983				19	
BROADHURST, Paul (ENG)						
	1990				12	
	1991				17	
	1996				27	
BROKAW, George T [a] (USA)						
	1903			26		
BROOKS, Mark (USA)						
	1990			5		26

BROOKS, Mark (cont)

Yr	MAS	USO	BOP	PGA
1991		19		
1992				15
1994		20		
1995		3		
1996		16	5	W
1999				16
2001		2		

BROSCH, Al (USA)

Yr	MAS	USO	BOP	PGA
1936		28		
1937		6		
1939				Last 32
1940				Last 16
1948				Last 32
1949		13		Last 16
1950				Last 32
1951		10		QF
1952		15		

BROWN, A (SCO)

Yr	MAS	USO	BOP	PGA
1874			30	
1880			16	

BROWN, Billy Ray (USA)

Yr	MAS	USO	BOP	PGA
1990		3		
1991		19		
1992	19			

BROWN, David (SCO/USA)

Yr	MAS	USO	BOP	PGA
1880			4	
1883			24	
1886			W	
1887			9	
1889			4	
1890			10	
1891			7	
1892			24	
1894			13	
1895			6	
1896			7	
1897			7	
1901		7		
1902		12		
1903		2		
1907		8		
1908		27		

BROWN, Eric (SCO)

Yr	MAS	USO	BOP	PGA
1950			23	
1952			9	
1953			9	
1955			12	
1957			3	
1958			3	
1960			9	
1961			5	
1965			17	

BROWN, Eric (cont)

Yr	MAS	USO	BOP	PGA
1966			23	
1968			18	
1969			16	

BROWN, George (SCO)

Yr	MAS	USO	BOP	PGA
1860			5	
1861			9	
1863			5	

BROWN, Hugh (SCO)

Yr	MAS	USO	BOP	PGA
1872			7	

BROWN, J (SCO)

Yr	MAS	USO	BOP	PGA
1870			11	

BROWN, Ken (SCO)

Yr	MAS	USO	BOP	PGA
1979			19	
1980			6	
1982			19	
1984			14	
1987			17	24

BROWN, Stuart (ENG)

Yr	MAS	USO	BOP	PGA
1970			28	

BROWN, T (SCO)

Yr	MAS	USO	BOP	PGA
1874			17	
1880			10	

BROWN, W (USA)

Yr	MAS	USO	BOP	PGA
1916				Last 16

BROWN, Willie (SCO)

Yr	MAS	USO	BOP	PGA
1874			25	
1877			5	
1880			8	
1883			3	
1885			23	
1889			7	

BROWNE, Olin (USA)

Yr	MAS	USO	BOP	PGA
1997		5		
2001		24		

BROWNING, Jim (USA)

Yr	MAS	USO	BOP	PGA
1953				Last 16
1954				Last 16
1955				Last 32

BRUE, Bob (USA)

Yr	MAS	USO	BOP	PGA
1961		22		
1973				12

BRUEN, James (Jimmy) [a] (IRL)

Yr	MAS	USO	BOP	PGA
1939			13	

	Yr	M	AS	USO	BOP	PGA
BRYANT, Brad (USA)						
	1992			23		
	1995			13		
	1996			23		
BUCKLE, GR (ENG)						
	1913				30	
	1920				9	
	1927				16	
BULLA, Johnny (USA)						
	1939			6	2	
	1940	21				
	1941			3		
	1946	16		22	2	
	1947	13			6	Last 32
	1948	13	8		7	QF
	1949	2	14		27	Last 32
	1950			12	14	
	1951	8				QF
	1952			4		
	1956			24		
BULLOCK, Fred (ENG)						
	1938				8	
	1947				15	
	1950				7	
	1952				8	
	1959				2	
BUNN, Oscar (USA)						
	1896			21		
BURGESS, Jack (USA)						
	1922					Last 16
BURGESS, Michael [a] (ENG)						
	1965				29	
BURKE, Billy (USA)						
	1928			18		Last 32
	1929			15		
	1930			28		Last 32
	1931			W		SF
	1932			7		
	1934	3		6		
	1936	28		18		Last 16
	1937	29		16		Last 32
	1938	13				Last 16
	1939	3				Last 16
	1940					Last 32
	1942	22				
	1947			27		
	1950	29				
BURKE, Eddie (USA)						
	1934					Last 32

	Yr	M	AS	USO	BOP	PGA
BURKE, Eddie (cont)	1942					Last 32
	1948					Last 32
	1949					Last 32
	1950					Last 16
BURKE Sr, Jack (USA)						
	1909			30		
	1910			27		
	1911			18		
	1914			28		
	1920			2		
	1922			28		
	1925					Last 16
	1928					Last 32
	1929			26		
BURKE Jr, Jack (USA)						
	1949			27		
	1951	11				QF
	1952	2				Last 32
	1953	8		14		
	1954	6		15		
	1955	13		10		QF
	1956	W				W
	1957	7				
	1958					4
	1959					17
	1960	11				29
	1961	7				
	1962					17
	1963			21		
	1965					8
	1969	24				
BURKEMO, Walter (USA)						
	1951					RU
	1952					Last 16
	1953					W
	1954	22				RU
	1955	15				
	1956	17		29		Last 16
	1957			4		SF
	1958			5		16
	1959	22				17
	1960	6				22
	1961	11				14
	1963			8		
	1964					17
	1966			22		
BURNS, George (USA)						
	1975	30			10	
	1976				10	
	1977				5	19
	1978					19
	1979					28
	1980			28		
	1981			2		
	1982			30		

BURNS, Jack (SCO)

Yr	M	AS	USO	BOP	PGA
1882				23	
1885				7	
1888				W	
1889				14	

BURNS, Stewart (SCO)

Yr	M	AS	USO	BOP	PGA
1928				16	
1930				24	

BURROWS, Gaylord (USA)

Yr	M	AS	USO	BOP	PGA
1977				26	

BURTON, Richard (Dick) (ENG)

Yr	M	AS	USO	BOP	PGA
1936				12	
1938				4	
1939				W	
1946				12	
1947				5	
1948				18	
1949				14	
1951				12	

BURTON, John (ENG)

Yr	M	AS	USO	BOP	PGA
1934				12	
1937				29	

BUSSON, JH (Harry) (ENG)

Yr	M	AS	USO	BOP	PGA
1939				25	
1947				25	

BUSSON, JJ (Jack) (ENG)

Yr	M	AS	USO	BOP	PGA
1935				11	
1937				23	
1938				4	

BUTCHART, Arthur (SCO)

Yr	M	AS	USO	BOP	PGA
1909				26	
1921				26	
1924				23	

BUTEL, Fred (ENG)

Yr	M	AS	USO	BOP	PGA
1898				29	

BUTLER, Peter (ENG)

Yr	M	AS	USO	BOP	PGA
1957				30	
1961				20	
1964	13			30	
1966	13			16	
1967	24				
1971				25	
1972				15	
1973				6	
1976				10	
1977				15	

BUTLER, Tony (USA)

Yr	M	AS	USO	BOP	PGA
1931					Last 32

BYMAN, Bob (USA)

Yr	M	AS	USO	BOP	PGA
1978				17	
1979				7	21

BYRD, Sam (USA)

Yr	M	AS	USO	BOP	PGA
1939			16		
1940	14				
1941	3		26		
1942	4				Last 32
1944					Last 16
1945					RU
1947			23		

BYRUM, Curt (USA)

Yr	M	AS	USO	BOP	PGA
1987					14

BYRUM, Tom (USA)

Yr	M	AS	USO	BOP	PGA
1997					9

CABRERA, Angel (ARG)

Yr	M	AS	USO	BOP	PGA
1999			4		
2000					18
2001	10		7		

CADLE, George (USA)

Yr	M	AS	USO	BOP	PGA
1977					15
1978					26

CAHILL, Michael (AUS)

Yr	M	AS	USO	BOP	PGA
1978			11		
1985			25		

CAIRNCROSS, Douglas (SCO)

Yr	M	AS	USO	BOP	PGA
1937				25	

CALCAVECCHIA, Mark (USA)

Yr	M	AS	USO	BOP	PGA
1986			14		
1987	17		17	11	
1988	2				17
1989				W	
1990	20				
1991	12				
1992				28	
1993	17		25	14	
1994				11	
1995				24	
1996	15				
1997	17			10	23
1998	16				
2000				26	
2001	4		24		4

CALDWELL, Rex (USA)

Yr	M	AS	USO	BOP	PGA
1978					3
1980					20
1984	11				25

CAMPBELL, Albert [a] (CAN)

Yr	M	AS	USO	BOP	PGA
1936	26				

	Yr	M	AS	USO	BOP	PGA
CAMPBELL, Alec (USA)						
	1923					Last 16
CAMPBELL, Alex (SCO/USA)						
	1899			12		
	1900			11		
	1901			8		
	1902			20		
	1903			15		
	1904			13		
	1905			6		
	1906			18		
	1907			3		
	1908			12		
	1909			13		
	1910			16		
	1911			12		
	1912			5		
	1913			13		
	1915			10		
	1916			28		
CAMPBELL, Andrew (USA)						
	1909			7		
CAMPBELL, Ben (SCO)						
	1883				10	
	1885				22	
	1886				3	
	1887				10	
	1890				15	
	1892				16	
CAMPBELL, Jack (SCO/USA)						
	1902			14		
	1903			6		
	1904			20		
	1907			19		
	1909			22		
	1910			18		
	1912			23		
CAMPBELL, James (SCO/USA)						
	1902			26		
	1903			26		
	1907			22		
CAMPBELL, Joe (USA)						
	1957			22a		
	1958	29a				
	1959			25		
	1962			28		27
	1969			25		
CAMPBELL, John (SCO)						
	1875				10	
CAMPBELL, Matt (USA)						
	1913			15		

	Yr	M	AS	USO	BOP	PGA
CAMPBELL, Michael (NZL)						
	1995				3	17
	2000			12		
	2001				23	
CAMPBELL, WW (SCO/USA)						
	1896			25		
CAMPBELL, William [a] (USA)						
	1954			23		
CAMPBELL, Willie (SCO/USA)						
	1880				10	
	1881				5	
	1883				5	
	1884				4	
	1885				9	
	1886				2	
	1887				3	
	1888				4	
	1889				7	
	1891				22	
	1895			6		
	1896			14		
	1898			26		
CANAUSA, Fred (USA)						
	1921					Last 32
CANIZARES, Jose Maria (ESP)						
	1982				22	
	1985				11	
	1986				11	
CARMICHAEL, Sam (USA)						
	1967					14
CARMICHAEL, T [a] (SCO)						
	1893				23	
CARNEVALE, Mark (USA)						
	1998			25		
CARPENTER, Mel (USA)						
	1952					Last 32
CARR, Joe [a] (IRL)						
	1951				24	
	1960				8	
CARRICK, John [a] (SCO)						
	1887				25	
CARTER, G (ENG)						
	1907				19	

	Yr	M AS	USO	BOP	PGA
CASPER, Billy (USA)					
	1956		14		
	1957	16			
	1958	20	13		2
	1959		W		17
	1960	4	12		24
	1961	7	17		15
	1962	15			
	1963	11			
	1964	5	4		9
	1965		17		2
	1966	10	W		3
	1967	24	4		19
	1968	16	9	4	6
	1969	2		25	
	1970	W	8	17	18
	1971	13		7	2
	1972	17	11		4
	1973	17			
	1975	6			5
	1976	8			
	1977	14			
	1978		30		
CASTANON, Aurelio (ARG)					
	1939			29	
CATLIN, Arthur (ENG)					
	1913			27	
CAWKWELL, George (ENG)					
	1904			26	
CAWSEY, George (ENG)					
	1903			9	
	1904			18	
	1906			15	
	1909			16	
CAYGILL, Alex (ENG)					
	1964			17	
	1966			16	
	1968			24	
	1969			25	
CEJKA, Alexander (GER)					
	1996			11	
	2001			13	
CERDA, Antonio (ARG)					
	1951			2	
	1952			5	
	1953			2	
	1954			5	
	1955			5	
	1956			8	
	1957			9	

	Yr	M AS	USO	BOP	PGA
CERDA, Antonio (cont)	1958			26	
	1959			16	
	1961	24			
CERRUDO, Ron (USA)					
	1969				21
	1974		30		
CHALMERS, Greg (AUS)					
	2000			4	
CHAMBERS, Peter [a] (SCO)					
	1863			11	
CHAMBERS Jr, Robert [a] (SCO)					
	1861			10	
CHAMBLEE, Brandel (USA)					
	1999	18			
CHAMP, Frank (USA)					
	1939				Last 32
	1952				QF
CHAPMAN, Dick [a] (USA)					
	1941	19			
	1947	14			
	1951	20			
	1954	11	21		
CHAPMAN, Roger (ENG)					
	1989			13	
	1991			12	
CHARLES, Bob (NZL)					
	1962	25		5	
	1963	15	19	W	13
	1964		3	17	19
	1968	19	7	2	2
	1969	29		2	
	1970	17	3	13	26
	1971		13	18	13
	1972	22		15	
	1973	29	11	7	
	1975			12	
	1979			10	
	1986			19	
	1988			20	
CHARTER, Brien (USA)					
	1955				Last 16
	1957				Last 32
CHEN, Ching-Po (TPE)					
	1963	15			
	1966	22			

	Yr	M	AS	USO	BOP	PGA
CHEN, Tze-Chung (TPE)						
	1985			2		23
	1986	23				
	1987	12				
	1988	19				
CHEN, Tze-Ming (TPE)						
	1985					3
CHERRY, Don [a] (USA)						
	1955	30				
	1959	25				
	1960			9		
CHIAPETTA, Louis (USA) 1929				16		
CHIN, Chick (JAP)						
	1936	20				
CHISHOLM, John (SCO)						
	1873				20	
CHOI, KJ (Kyoung-Ju) (KOR)						
	2001					29
CHRIST, George (USA)						
	1926					QF
	1928					Last 16
	1934					Last 32
CHRISTIAN, Neil (USA)						
	1924					Last 32
	1928		18			
	1929					Last 16
	1944					Last 32
CHURIO, Marcos (ARG)						
	1931				7	
CINK, Stewart (USA)						
	1996			16		
	1997			13		
	1998	23		10		
	1999	27				3
	2000	28		8		14
	2001			3	30	
CIRCELLI, Pat (USA)						
	1931					Last 32
	1935					Last 16
CIUCI, Al (USA)						
	1922					Last 16
CIUCI, Henry (USA)						
	1924					QF

	Yr	M	AS	USO	BOP	PGA
CIUCI, Henry (cont)						
	1928			6		
	1929			7		Last 16
	1930					Last 32
	1931			29		Last 32
	1932			14		
	1933			15		
	1934	25		17		
CLAAR, Brian (USA)						
	1989			5		
	1990			29		
	1992					9
CLAMPETT, Bobby (USA)						
	1978			30a		
	1979	23				
	1981					27
	1982			3	10	
	1987					28
CLARK, Arthur (USA)						
	1940					Last 16
	1948			30		
CLARK, Barney (USA)						
	1945					Last 32
CLARK, Clarence (USA)						
	1929					Last 32
	1932			11		
	1933			9		Last 16
	1935	19				
	1936			3		
	1937	13		7		
CLARK, Clive (ENG)						
	1967				3	
	1970				17	
	1972				11	
CLARK, Howard (ENG)						
	1977				13	
	1981				8	
	1983				26	
	1988				28	
	1989				13	
	1993				21	
CLARK, Jimmy (USA)						
	1953					QF
CLARK II, Mike (USA)						
	2000					14
CLARK, Walter (USA)						
	1901			22		
	1905			18		
	1907			22		

	Yr	M	AS	USO	BOP	PGA
CLARKE, Charles (USA)						
	1921					Last 16
CLARKE, Darren (IRL)						
	1996				11	
	1997				2	
	1998	8				
	1999			10	30	
	2000				6	
	2001	24		30	3	
CLARKSON, F (USA)						
	1916					Last 32
CLAYDON, Russell (ENG)						
	1994				11	
CLAYTON, D (SCO)						
	1874				29	
CLEMENTS, Lennie (USA)						
	1983			13		
	1984			16		
	1986			24		
	1987			9		
	1994			28		30
COBURN, George (SCO)						
	1900				26	
	1903				29	
	1904				16	
	1908				24	
COCERES, Angel (ARG)						
	2001					16
COCHRAN, Russ (USA)						
	1984					10
	1987					28
	1992				28	7
	1993	21				
	1996					17
COE, Charles R [a] (USA)						
	1949	16				
	1951	12				
	1953	16				
	1954	20				
	1958	23		13		
	1959	6				
	1961	2				
	1962	9				
	1970	23				
COLBERT, Jim (USA)						
	1971			3		
	1973			10		12

	Yr	M	AS	USO	BOP	PGA
COLBERT, Jim (cont)	1974	4		5		28
	1976	12				
	1977	14				
	1980	14				30
	1981	25		26		
	1982					16
	1984					25
COLE, Bobby (RSA)						
	1966				30a	
	1968				13	
	1969					21
	1970			12	28	
	1971			13		
	1974				7	3
	1975	15			3	
	1977				15	
	1978	28				
COLEMAN, Fay (USA)						
	1934					Last 16
	1936					Last 32
	1941					Last 32
	1946					Last 32
COLES, Neil (ENG)						
	1959				21	
	1961				3	
	1963				20	
	1965				12	
	1968				6	
	1969				11	
	1970				6	
	1971				22	
	1973				2	
	1974				13	
	1975				7	
	1976				28	
	1980				29	
COLLINGE, T (ENG)						
	1937				24	
COLLINS, Al (USA)						
	1932					QF
COLLINS, Bill (USA)						
	1960					12
	1961	7				
	1962	29				
	1964			7		
COLLINS, Fred (ENG)						
	1901				15	
	1904				18	
	1905				22	
	1907				15	

Yr	M AS	USO	BOP	PGA
COLLINS, Fred (cont)				
1908			13	
1909			21	
1911			12	
1912			7	
1913			11	
1923			16	
COLLINS, JB (USA)				
1935				Last 32
COLLINS, Jock (USA)				
1925				Last 32
1930				Last 16
1931				Last 32
COLLINS, WS (ENG)				
1939			26	
COLTART, Andrew (SCO)				
1994			24	
1995			20	
1999			18	
COLTART, Bruce (USA)				
1939				Last 16
1940		29		
1941				Last 16
1942				Last 32
1944				Last 32
COLTART, Frank (USA)				
1923				Last 32
COMPSTON, Archie (ENG)				
1920			9	
1922			26	
1924			21	
1925			2	
1927		7	22	
1928		22	3	
1929			12	
1930			6	
1931			28	
1932			10	
1933			12	
1946			18	
CONGDON, Chuck (USA)				
1944				SF
1946				QF
1948		12		
CONNER, Frank (USA)				
1979				23
1981		6		
CONRAD, Joe [a] (USA)				
1955		18	23	

Yr	M AS	USO	BOP	PGA
COODY, Charles (USA)				
1967		28		
1968	30	16		8
1969	5	13		7
1970	12			
1971	W		5	
1972	12			15
1973	29	29		
1974	29			
1976	5			8
1977				4
1978		30		
COOK, John (USA)				
1980				19
1981	21	4		
1983				20
1987	24			28
1991		19		
1992		13	2	2
1993		25		6
1994		5		4
1996		16		
1997				23
1998				9
COOP, AB (ENG)				
1958			20	
1961			13	
1962			22	
1964			24	
COOPER, Derrick (ENG)				
1986			21	
1989			19	
COOPER, Harry (ENG/USA)				
1923				Last 32
1925				SF
1926				Last 32
1927		2		Last 16
1930		4		Last 16
1931		15		
1932		7		
1933		29		Last 16
1934		3		Last 16
1935	25	28		
1936	2	2		Last 16
1937	4	4		QF
1938	2	3		
1939		12		
1940	4			
1941	14			
1942	18			QF
COOPER, Pete (USA)				
1948		25		Last 32

	Yr	M AS	USO	BOP	PGA
COOPER, Pete (cont)	1949	21	8		
	1950	29	29		
	1953		4		Last 16
	1954	22			
	1955	24			
	1956	12	14		
	1958				25
	1959				17
	1960				15
	1962				30
CORLETT, Charles (ENG)					
	1926			28	
CORSTORPHINE, D (SCO)					
	1879			23	
	1880			16	
	1883			26	
COSGROVE, Ned (SCO)					
	1880			3	
	1881			3	
COSGROVE, R (SCO)					
	1874			22	
COSGROVE, William (SCO)					
	1874			20	
	1877			3	
	1878			6	
	1883			16	
	1884			16	
	1885			29	
	1886			20	
COTTON, Henry (ENG)					
	1927			8	
	1928			18	
	1930			8	
	1931			9	
	1932			10	
	1933			7	
	1934			W	
	1935			7	
	1936			3	
	1937			W	
	1938			3	
	1939			13	
	1946			4	
	1947			6	
	1948	25		W	
	1952			4	
	1956			6	
	1957	13		9	
	1958			8	
COTTON, LT (ENG)					
	1934			29	

	Yr	M AS	USO	BOP	PGA
COUPLES, Fred (USA)					
	1982				3
	1983				23
	1984	10	9	4	20
	1985	10			6
	1988	5	10	4	
	1989	11	21	6	
	1990	5		25	2
	1991		3	3	27
	1992	W	17		21
	1993	21	16	9	
	1994		16		
	1995	10			
	1996	15		7	
	1997	7		7	29
	1998	2			13
	1999	27			26
	2000	11	16	6	
	2001	26			
COURTNEY, Chuck (USA)					
	1971				22
COWAN, Gary [a] (CAN)					
	1964	25			
COWAN, John (USA)					
	1919		7		
	1923				Last 32
COX, Bill (ENG)					
	1935			11	
	1936			12	
	1937			21	
	1938			8	
COX, Reg (ENG)					
	1935			22	
COX, Wiffy (USA)					
	1924		29		
	1928				Last 32
	1929		11		Last 32
	1930				Last 32
	1931		4		
	1932		5		
	1934		3		
	1936	13	5		
	1937	12			
	1938	25			
COXON, Barry (AUS)					
	1967			18	
CRAMPTON, Bruce (AUS)					
	1956			13	
	1957	21			

CRAMPTON, Bruce (cont)

Yr	M AS	USO	BOP	PGA
1958	26	19		
1960	16			
1961		22		
1962	29			17
1963	11	5		3
1964	21	14		
1965	11			20
1966	17			
1967				26
1968				23
1969	13	6		15
1970		30		6
1971	18			
1972	2	2		24
1973			18	2
1974	11	23		
1975				2
1976	27			

CRAPPER, H (ENG)

Yr	M AS	USO	BOP	PGA
1930			21	

CRAWFORD, Charlie (SCO)

Yr	M AS	USO	BOP	PGA
1886			29	
1892			30	

CRAWFORD, Dick (USA)

Yr	M AS	USO	BOP	PGA
1960	29			
1967				20
1968				26
1969		25		
1970		22		

CRAWLEY, Leonard [a] (ENG)

Yr	M AS	USO	BOP	PGA
1939			23	

CREAVY, Tom (USA)

Yr	M AS	USO	BOP	PGA
1931				W
1932				SF
1933				QF
1934	25	8		

CREAVY, William (USA)

Yr	M AS	USO	BOP	PGA
1923		26		
1925				Last 32

CREMIN, Eric (AUS)

Yr	M AS	USO	BOP	PGA
1951			16	

CRENSHAW, Ben (USA)

Yr	M AS	USO	BOP	PGA
1971		27a		
1972	19a			
1973	24a			
1974	22		28	
1975	30	3		10
1976	2	8		8
1977	8		5	
1978			2	16
1979		11	2	2

CRENSHAW, Ben (cont)

Yr	M AS	USO	BOP	PGA
1980	6		3	
1981	8	11	8	
1982	24	19	15	
1983	2			9
1984	W		22	
1986	16	6	21	11
1987	4	4	4	7
1988	4	12	16	17
1989	3			17
1990	14			
1991	3			
1994	18			9
1995	W		15	
1996			27	

CRICHTON, Marshall (USA)

Yr	M AS	USO	BOP	PGA
1926				Last 16

CROKE, Jack (USA)

Yr	M AS	USO	BOP	PGA
1912		21		
1913		21		

CROWDER, Waldo (USA)

Yr	M AS	USO	BOP	PGA
1928		6		

CROWLEY, Bob (USA)

Yr	M AS	USO	BOP	PGA
1930				Last 16
1931				Last 16
1933		26		
1934				QF

CRUICKSHANK, Bobby (SCO/USA)

Yr	M AS	USO	BOP	PGA
1921		26		Last 16
1922		28		SF
1923		2		SF
1924		4		Last 16
1925				Last 16
1926				Last 32
1927		11		Last 32
1929			6	
1932		2		QF
1933				Last 16
1934	28	3		
1935	9	14		
1936	4			Last 16
1937	17	3		
1938	18			
1939		25		
1942	15			

CRUICKSHANK, JI [a] (SCO/ARG)

Yr	M AS	USO	BOP	PGA
1925			17	

CULLEN, Gary (ENG)

Yr	M AS	USO	BOP	PGA
1980			23	

	Yr	M AS	USO	BOP	PGA
CUMMINGS, George (USA)					
	1903		22		
	1904		28		
	1905		9		
	1906		18		
	1910		14		
	1911		20		
	1912		23		
CUNNINGHAM, Alex (SCO/USA)					
	1916		29		
	1919		21		
	1920				Last 16
CUNNINGHAM, James (SCO)					
	1890			27	
CUPIT, Buster (USA)					
	1958			8	
	1959			17	
	1962			30	
CUPIT, Jacky (USA)					
	1961		9		
	1962	20	17		
	1963		2		
	1964		28		17
	1965				8
	1966				6
	1967	15			
CURL, Rod (USA)					
	1975	15			
	1978		30		26
	1980				20
CURLEY, Jack (USA)					
	1927				Last 32
	1933				Last 32
CURTIS, Donald (ENG)					
	1927			19	
CURTIS, JF (USA)					
	1898		16		
CUTHBERT, John (SCO)					
	1897			30	
DAILEY, Allan (SCO)					
	1933			27	
	1934			16	
	1938			4	
DALLEMAGNE, Marcel (FRA)					
	1931			16	
	1934			4	

	Yr	M AS	USO	BOP	PGA
DALLEMAGNE, Marcel (cont)	1936			3	
	1937			26	
	1938			23	
DALY, Fred (IRL)					
	1946			8	
	1947			W	
	1948			2	
	1950			3	
	1951			4	
	1952			3	
	1953			11	
	1955			12	
	1958			20	
DALY, John (USA)					
	1991				W
	1992	19			
	1993	3		14	
	1995			W	
	1996	29	27		
	1997				29
DALZIEL, C [a] (SCO)					
	1901			24	
D'ANGELO, Jimmy (US)					
	1944				Last 32
DARCY, Eamonn (IRL)					
	1976			15	
	1981			14	
	1983			26	
	1985			11	
	1987			17	
	1990			22	
	1991			5	
DAVENPORT, RRW (Robin) (ENG)	1967			25	
DAVIES, Bill (ENG)					
	1925			6	
	1928			10	
	1929			18	
	1930			24	
	1931		29	7	
	1932			7	
	1934			13	
	1936			14	
	1939			20	
DAVIS, Mark (ENG)					
	1989			30	
DAVIS, Rodger (AUS)					
	1979			5	

DAVIS, Rodger (cont)

Yr	M AS	USO	BOP	PGA
1983			26	
1987			2	
1988	29		20	
1991			12	
1993			24	

DAVIS, WF (Willie) (ENG/USA)

Yr	M AS	USO	BOP	PGA
1895		5		
1896		13		
1897		15		
1898		18		
1901		27		

DAWSON, George [a] (USA)

Yr	M AS	USO	BOP	PGA
1933		17		

DAWSON, John [a] (USA)

Yr	M AS	USO	BOP	PGA
1934	23			
1935	17			
1936	9			
1949	16			

DAWSON, Peter (ENG)

Yr	M AS	USO	BOP	PGA
1974			18	
1977			22	

DAY, Arthur (ENG)

Yr	M AS	USO	BOP	PGA
1920			29	

DAY, Glen (USA)

Yr	M AS	USO	BOP	PGA
1994				15
1998		23		29
2000	19			

DEBOYS, Alec [a] (SCO)

Yr	M AS	USO	BOP	PGA
1960			21	

DeFOY, Craig (WAL)

Yr	M AS	USO	BOP	PGA
1971			4	
1972			23	

de la TORRE, Angel (ESP)

Yr	M AS	USO	BOP	PGA
1920			16	
1923			19	

de la TORRE, Manuel (ESP)

Yr	M AS	USO	BOP	PGA
1963				17

de LUCA, Fidel (ARG)

Yr	M AS	USO	BOP	PGA
1960			16	

del VECCHIO, Perry (USA)

Yr	M AS	USO	BOP	PGA
1927		15		
1928				QF

de MANE, Arthur (USA)

Yr	M AS	USO	BOP	PGA
1926		23		

DEMARET, Jimmy (USA)

Yr	M AS	USO	BOP	PGA
1937		16		
1938				Last 16
1939		22		
1940	W			Last 32
1941	12			
1942	6			SF
1946	4	6		SF
1947	W			
1948	18	2		SF
1949	8			QF
1950	W	20		SF
1951	30	14		
1952		15		
1953		4		
1954	29	29	10	
1957	3	3		
1958	14			
1962	5			

DEMASSEY, Mike (USA)

Yr	M AS	USO	BOP	PGA
1944				Last 32
1949				Last 32

DENNIS, Clark (USA)

Yr	M AS	USO	BOP	PGA
1994		6		

DENNY, CS (ENG)

Yr	M AS	USO	BOP	PGA
1931			15	

DERR, Ray (USA)

Yr	M AS	USO	BOP	PGA
1923				Last 16
1924				SF
1925				Last 16

de VICENZO, Roberto (ARG)

Yr	M AS	USO	BOP	PGA
1948			3	
1949			3	
1950	12		2	
1951	20	29		
1952				Last 16
1953			6	
1954				QF
1956	17	27		
1957		8		
1960			3	
1961	22			
1964			3	
1965			4	
1966	22		20	
1967	10		W	
1968	2	24	10	
1969			3	
1970			17	
1971	9		11	
1972	22			
1973			28	
1975			28	

	Yr	M AS	USO	BOP	PGA
DEVLIN, Bruce (AUS)					
	1964	4		5	
	1965	15	6	8	6
	1966	28	26	4	28
	1967	10	23	8	
	1968	4	9	10	
	1969	19	10	16	
	1970		8	25	18
	1971	13	27		13
	1972	5		26	
	1973	8		18	24
	1974				22
	1975	15			
	1976	19			
	1980				30
	1981		26		
	1982		10		
de WIT, Gerard (NED)					
	1956			22	
	1958			24	
DICK, CE [a] (ENG)					
	1894			20	
DICKINSON, Gardner (USA)					
	1953		21		
	1959		17		
	1961		9		
	1962	15	23		
	1963		21		8
	1964				23
	1965		21		5
	1966	28			18
	1967		6		28
	1968	22			30
	1969	29			
	1972	22			
	1973	10			
DICKSON, Bob (USA)					
	1969				25
	1973	17			
DIEGEL, Leo (USA)					
	1920		2		Last 32
	1921		26		
	1922		7		
	1923		8	25	
	1924		25		Last 32
	1925		8		QF
	1926		3		RU
	1927		11		
	1928		18		W
	1929		8	3	W
	1930		11	2	Last 16
	1931		3		Last 32

	Yr	M AS	USO	BOP	PGA
DIEGEL, Leo (cont)	1932		4		
	1933		17	3	Last 32
	1934	16	17		Last 32
	1935	19			
	1938				Last 32
	1939				
DIEHL, Terry (USA)					
	1977		7		
	1980				10
DIETZ, Mike (USA)					
	1956		29		
DILL, Terry (USA)					
	1964		14		
	1965	24			
	1966	17			
	1970				26
	1971				30
	1975		18		
DILLARD, Andy (USA)					
	1992		17		
DiMARCO, Chris (USA)					
	2000				14
	2001	10	16		16
DINGWALL, John (SCO/USA)					
	1901		28		
	1909		27		
	1912		18		
DIXON, David [a] (ENG)					
	2001			30	
DODSON, Leonard (USA)					
	1937		10		
	1952				Last 32
DOERING, Arthur (USA)					
	1954				Last 32
DOLEMAN, A [a] (SCO)					
	1870			9	
DOLEMAN, F (SCO)					
	1870			14	
DOLEMAN, William [a] (SCO)					
	1865			6	
	1866			6	
	1867			6	
	1868			8	
	1869			7	
	1870			5	

	Yr	M AS	USO	BOP	PGA
DOLEMAN, William (cont)	1872			3	
	1874			20	
	1875			8	
	1879			18	
	1884			16	
DONALD, Mike (USA)	1990		2		
DONALDSON, James (SCO/USA)	1910		28		
	1911		15		
	1913		30		
	1914		5		
	1915		19		
	1916		21		Last 32
	1923				Last 32
DONOVAN, William (USA)	1899			30	
DORRESTEIN, Jan (NED)	1972			15	
DOSER, Clarence (USA)	1929				Last 32
	1935				Last 32
	1936				Last 32
	1939				Last 16
	1945				SF
	1947				Last 32
	1950				Last 32
	1952		13		QF
	1953		17		
DOUGHERTY, Ed (USA)	1975				22
DOUGLAS, Dave (USA)	1949		6		Last 16
	1950				QF
	1951	5	6		
	1952	30			Last 32
	1953				QF
	1955				Last 32
	1961		14		
	1962		28		
DOUGLAS, Edward (ENG)	1926			22	
DOUGLAS, Findlay [a] (SCO/USA)	1897		19		
	1903		8		
	1909		23		
DOUGLAS, George (SCO/USA)	1892			25	
	1896		4		

	Yr	M AS	USO	BOP	PGA
DOUGLASS, Dale (USA)	1969	19	13		
	1971	27			
	1974		18		
	1975		24		27
	1978		24		
DOW, George (USA)	1924				Last 32
DOW, J (SCO)	1874			24	
DOW, Robert (SCO)	1879			23	
DOW, William (SCO)	1861			3	
	1862			4	
	1864			5	
	1865			3	
	1867			8	
	1868			7	
	1870			17	
DOWIE, A [a] (SCO)	1946			27	
DOWLING, Jack (USA)	1912		7		
	1913		26		
	1915		22		
	1916		12		QF
DOYLE, Pat (USA)	1913		10		
	1919		18		Last 32
	1920				Last 32
	1926				QF
	1928				Last 16
DREW, Norman (IRL)	1954			20	
	1957			15	
	1958			20	
DRUMMOND, R (SCO)	1880			21	
DUDAS, Stan (USA)	1958		27		
DUDLEY, Ed (USA)	1925				Last 16
	1927				Last 16
	1928		6		QF
	1929			18	

	Yr	MAS	USO	BOP	PGA
DUDLEY, Ed (cont)	1930		17		
	1931		15		Last 32
	1932		14		SF
	1933			7	QF
	1934	5			
	1935	19	21		QF
	1936	6			Last 16
	1937	3	5	6	Last 16
	1938	6			Last 32
	1939	10	12		
	1940	4	10		Last 16
	1941	5	10		Last 32
	1942				QF
	1944				QF
	1945				Last 32
	1947				Last 32
	1948	18			
DUFFY, Matt (USA)					
	1922				Last 32
DUNCAN, George (SCO)					
	1906			8	
	1907			7	
	1908			18	
	1909			21	
	1910			3	
	1911			8	
	1912			4	
	1914			10	
	1920			W	
	1921		8	5	
	1922		6	2	
	1923			6	
	1924			6	
	1925			28	
	1926			20	
	1928			18	
	1929			22	
DUNLAP, Scott (USA)					
	1997	24			
	1998			29	
	1999			10	
	2000				9
DUNN, Jamie (SCO)					
	1861			11	
DUNN, John (SCO/USA)					
	1898		25		
DUNN, Tom (SCO)					
	1878			9	
	1879			8	
	1882			18	
	1883			17	

	Yr	MAS	USO	BOP	PGA
DUNN, Tom (cont)	1884			7	
	1886			16	
DUNN Sr, Willie (SCO)					
	1861			7	
	1866			10	
	1867			10	
	1868			10	
	1874			22	
DUNN Jr, Willie (SCO/USA)					
	1883			9	
	1884			11	
	1886			27	
	1895		2		
	1896		12		
	1897		3		
	1898		7		
DUPREE, Charles (USA)					
	1956				Last 32
DURANT, Joe (USA)					
	2001		24		
DURNIAN, Denis (ENG)					
	1983			8	
DUTRA, Mortie (USA)					
	1924				Last 16
	1925				SF
	1927				QF
	1928				Last 32
	1929				Last 32
	1930		17		
	1931		7		
	1932		23		
	1933		6		Last 32
	1934	11	28		
	1935		14		Last 32
	1936				Last 32
DUTRA, Olin (USA)					
	1928				Last 32
	1930		25		
	1931		21		
	1932		7		W
	1933		7	6	Last 16
	1934		W		
	1935	3	12		
	1937				Last 32
	1938		16		
	1939		16		
DUVAL, David (USA)					
	1995		28	20	
	1996	18		14	

	Yr	M AS	USO	BOP	PGA
DUVAL, David (cont)	1997				13
	1998	2	7	11	
	1999	6	7		
	2000	3	8	11	
	2001	2	16	W	10
EASTERBROOK, Syd (ENG)	1932			13	
	1933			3	
	1935			7	
EASTWOOD, Bob (USA)	1980				30
	1987		14		
	1988		21		
EATON, Zell (USA)	1934		28a		
	1936		28		
	1948				Last 32
	1952		28		Last 32
EDGAR, JD (Douglas) (ENG/USA)	1909			26	
	1912			20	
	1914			14	
	1919			21	QF
	1920			20	RU
	1921			26	
EDMUNDSON, James (IRL)	1908			11	
EDWARDS, Danny (USA)	1974			5	
	1975			23	
	1976		19		
	1977	19			
	1982	24	12		22
	1983				20
	1984	18			
	1986	28		21	
	1987		24	29	
EDWARDS, David (USA)	1980		28		30
	1981				16
	1984	3			
	1987				14
	1988				25
	1993		11		
	1994	18	13		
	1995	24			
	1996				17
EDWARDS, Kenneth (USA)	1904		26		

	Yr	M AS	USO	BOP	PGA
EDWARDS, Thurman (USA)	1944				Last 32
EGAN, H Chandler [a] (USA)	1904		20		
	1906		8		
	1911		23		
EHRESMAN, Clarence (USA)	1932				Last 32
EICHELBERGER, Dave (USA)	1971	20	19		
	1972		29		
	1976		21		
	1986		24		
ELDER, Lee (USA)	1972		29		24
	1973				24
	1974				11
	1976				15
	1977	19			
	1978		30		
	1979	17	11		
	1980				26
ELDRED, Vincent (USA)	1931				Last 32
	1932		12		Last 16
	1933				Last 32
	1935		12		
ELKINGTON, Steve (AUS)	1989		21		
	1990		21		
	1991	22			
	1992				18
	1993	3			14
	1994				7
	1995	5		6	W
	1996				3
	1997	12	24		
	1998	30			3
	1999	11			
ELLIS Jr, Wes (USA)	1956		9		
	1960				6
	1961				5
	1962				30
	1963	24			17
	1965	15	24		13
	1966		8		
	1967	16	12		25
ELPHICK, Jack (USA)	1923				Last 32

Yr	M AS	USO	BOP	PGA
ELS, Ernie (RSA)				
1992			5	
1993		7	6	
1994	8	W	24	25
1995			11	3
1996	12	5	2	
1997	17	W	10	
1998	16		29	21
1999	27		24	
2000	2	2	2	
2001	6		3	13
ELSWORTHY, Sherman (USA)				
1948				Last 32
EMERY, Clare (USA)				
1959				28
EMMETT, Devereux (USA)				
1897		28		
ENDERBY, Kep [a] (AUS)				
1951			17	
ERICKSON, Bob (USA)				
1968		24		
ESPINOSA, Abe (USA)				
1924		7		
1925				Last 32
1926				QF
1931				QF
1932				Last 16
1933		24		
1939				Last 32
ESPINOSA, Al (USA)				
1924				QF
1925		9		Last 16
1926		13		Last 32
1927		18		SF
1928		14		RU
1929		2		QF
1930				QF
1931		10		Last 32
1933				Last 16
1934	7	21		
1935	17	28		
1936	15			
1937	29			Last 32
ESTES, Bob (USA)				
1993				6
1994			24	
1995	29			6
1996	27			
1998			24	

Yr	M AS	USO	BOP	PGA
ESTES, Bob (cont)	1999	4	30		6
2000	19		20	
2001		30	25	
EVANS Jr, Charles (Chick) [a] (USA)				
1914		2		
1915		18		
1916		W		
1919		10		
1920		6		
1921		4		
1922		16		
1923		14		
1924		10		
1926		13		
EVANS, Max (USA)				
1954		23		Last 32
1955	27	28		
EVERARD, HSC [a] (SCO)				
1885			18	
1888			11	
1891			28	
FABEL, Brad (USA)				
1987				28
FAIRBAIRN, THT (ENG)				
1953			14	
FAIRFIELD, Don (USA)				
1955				QF
1957		17		
1958		27		
1961				22
1964		28		
FAIRLIE, FA [a] (SCO)				
1892			19	
1893			28	
FAIRLIE, JO (Col James Ogilvy) [a] (SCO)				
1861			8	
FALDO, Nick (ENG)				
1976			28	
1978			7	
1979			19	
1980			12	
1981			11	
1982			4	14
1983	20		8	
1984	15		6	20
1985	25			
1986			5	
1987			W	28

	Yr	M AS	USO	BOP	PGA
FALDO, Nick (cont)	1988	30	2	3	4
	1989	W	18	11	9
	1990	W	3	W	19
	1991	12	16	17	16
	1992	13	4	W	2
	1993			2	3
	1994			8	4
	1995	24			
	1996	W	16	4	
	2000	28	7		
FALLON, Johnny (SCO)					
	1936			23	
	1938			26	
	1939			3	
	1948			21	
	1949			8	
	1955			2	
	1957			19	
FARINA, Armand (USA)					
	1948				Last 32
FARLOW, Charles (USA)					
	1949		27		
	1957				Last 32
FARQUHAR, John [a] (USA)					
	1964		28		
FARRELL, Billy (USA)					
	1962				17
	1966				22
	1967		23		11
FARRELL, Jack (USA)					
	1927				Last 32
FARRELL, Johnny (USA)					
	1919				Last 32
	1921				Last 32
	1922		11		Last 16
	1923		5	19	Last 16
	1924		19		QF
	1925		3		QF
	1926		3		SF
	1927		7		Last 32
	1928		W		
	1929			2	RU
	1930		8		QF
	1931		10	5	Last 32
	1933		9		SF
	1934				Last 32
	1936	29	22		
	1937				Last 16
	1939				Last 32
	1940	14	28		

	Yr	M AS	USO	BOP	PGA
FASTH, Niclas (SWE)					
	2001			2	29
FAULKNER, Gus (ENG)					
	1922			27	
	1931			12	
FAULKNER, Max (ENG)					
	1936			21	
	1939			23	
	1948			15	
	1949			6	
	1950			5	
	1951			W	
	1952			17	
	1953			12	
	1954			20	
	1957			9	
	1958			16	
	1963			20	
	1965			10	
	1969			30	
FAXON, Brad (USA)					
	1988			11	
	1992				15
	1993	9			14
	1994	15		7	30
	1995	17		15	5
	1996	25			17
	1997			20	
	1998	26		11	13
	1999	24			
	2000				26
	2001	10			
FAZIO, George (USA)					
	1941				Last 32
	1946				Last 32
	1948	30	25		QF
	1949				Last 32
	1950	21	3		Last 32
	1951	18			
	1952	14	5		
	1953		4		
	1954		27		
	1958				25
FEHERTY, David (IRL)					
	1987			26	
	1989			6	
	1991				7
	1994			4	
FEHR, Rick (USA)					
	1984	25			
	1985		9		

Yr	M AS	USO	BOP	PGA
FEHR, Rick (cont)				
1991		26		27
1992				18
FEMINELLI, Al (USA)				
1960		23		
FENN, AH (USA)				
1901		17		
1903		30		
FENTON, Jas (SCO)				
1873			12	
1874			24	
FERGUS, Keith (USA)				
1979		9		
1980	26	3		
1981				4
1983	16			14
1984				29
FERGUSON, Bob (SCO)				
1874			8	
1875			4	
1877			3	
1879			6	
1880			W	
1881			W	
1882			W	
1883			2	
1886			4	
FERGUSON, Jacky (SCO)				
1886			24	
FERGUSON, James (SCO/USA)				
1916		29		Last 32
FERGUSON, R (SCO)				
1953			29	
FERGUSSON, J (SCO)				
1874			10	
FERNANDEZ, Vicente (ARG)				
1971			25	
1976			10	
1986			21	
FERNIE, George (SCO)				
1884			7	
1885			18	
1887			17	
1890			21	
FERNIE, Peter (SCO)				
1882			21	

Yr	M AS	USO	BOP	PGA
FERNIE, Peter (cont)				
1884			9	
1886			22	
1887			24	
FERNIE, Tom (SCO)				
1911			29	
1923			5	
1925			14	
FERNIE, Willie (SCO)				
1873			10	
1879			12	
1881			8	
1882			2	
1883			W	
1884			2	
1885			4	
1886			8	
1887			7	
1888			14	
1889			6	
1890			2	
1891			2	
1892			8	
1893			23	
1894			5	
1895			6	
1896			3	
1897			22	
1898			7	
1899			5	
1902			12	
1903			24	
FERREE, Jim (USA)				
1957		17		
1958		19		
1964				28
FERREE, Purvis (USA)				
1944				Last 32
FERRIER, Jim (AUS/USA)				
1940	26a	29a		
1941	29	30		
1942	15			
1946	4			Last 16
1947	6	6		W
1948	4			Last 32
1949	16	23		SF
1950	2			Last 32
1951	7			Last 16
1952	3			Last 32
1953	16			
1960				2
1961		22		
1963				7
1964	5			

Yr	MAS	USO	BOP	PGA
FETCHICK, Mike (USA)				
1956				Last 32
1957	16	13		
1958		27		
1963		14		
1964				23
1967		28		
FEZLER, Forrest (USA)				
1974		2		
1975	30	24		
FIELD, Stewart (ENG)				
1950			24	
FINDLAY, AH (Alex) (SCO/USA)				
1898		13		
1899		11		
1902		30		
FINSTERWALD, Dow (USA)				
1955		28		
1956	24			
1957	7	13		RU
1958	17			W
1959	18	11		4
1960	3	3		15
1961		6		
1962	3			11
1963	5	12		3
1964	9	8		
1965	21			
1966				12
FIORI, Ed (USA)				
1980	6			
FISCHER, Johnny [a] (USA)				
1932		27		
FITZJOHN, Ed (USA)				
1901		28		
FITZJOHN, Val (USA)				
1899		2		
1900		10		
1901		12		
FITZSIMMONS, Pat (USA)				
1975	22	9		
FLECK, Jack (USA)				
1955		W		Last 16
1956				Last 32
1957	26	26		
1959	18	19		
1960		3		

Yr	MAS	USO	BOP	PGA
FLECK, Jack (cont)				
1961		27		19
1962	11			7
1965				20
FLECKMAN, Marty (USA)				
1967		18a		
1968				4
FLEISHER, Bruce (USA)				
1992	25			
1993				14
FLESCH, Steve (USA)				
1998				13
2000		20		
2001				13
FLOYD, Ray(mond) (USA)				
1964		14		
1965		6		17
1966	8			18
1967				20
1968	7			
1969		13		W
1970		22		8
1971	13	8		
1972				4
1973		16		
1974	22	15		11
1975	30	12	23	10
1976	W	13	4	2
1977	8		8	
1978	16	12	2	
1979	17			
1980	17			17
1981	8		3	19
1982	7		15	W
1983	4	13	14	20
1984	15			13
1985	2	23		
1986		W	16	
1987			17	14
1988	11	17		9
1989		26		
1990	2			
1991	17	8		7
1992	2		12	
1993	11	7		
1994	10			
1995	17			
1996	25			
FOORD, Ernest (ENG)				
1905			24	
1906			30	
1909			21	
1910			28	
1914			19	

FORD, Bob (USA)

Yr	M	AS	USO	BOP	PGA
1983			26		

FORD, Doug (USA)

Yr	M	AS	USO	BOP	PGA
1952	21		19		
1953	21		21		
1955			7		W
1956	6		9		Last 32
1957	W		17		Last 16
1958	2				11
1959	25		5		11
1960	25				7
1961			6		5
1962			8		5
1963	11				27
1964			24		
1965					20
1966	17				

FOREMAN, J (SCO)

Yr	M	AS	USO	BOP	PGA
1880			10		

FOREMAN, Roger (ENG)

Yr	M	AS	USO	BOP	PGA
1962			16		

FORRESTER, George (SCO)

Yr	M	AS	USO	BOP	PGA
1882			23		

FORRESTER, Jack (USA)

Yr	M	AS	USO	BOP	PGA
1921					Last 32
1923			4		Last 32
1924					Last 32
1925			20		
1926			13		
1928			17		
1929			23		
1930			28		

FORSBRAND, Anders (SWE)

Yr	M	AS	USO	BOP	PGA
1985				8	
1986				16	
1987				29	
1992					9
1993	11				
1994				4	

FORSMAN, Dan (USA)

Yr	M	AS	USO	BOP	PGA
1992					7
1993	7		19		
1994	14				
1996			13		

FORTINO, Tony (USA)

Yr	M	AS	USO	BOP	PGA
1956					Last 32

FOSTER, Martin (ENG)

Yr	M	AS	USO	BOP	PGA
1975				23	
1977				26	

FOTHERINGHAM, Arthur (USA)

Yr	M	AS	USO	BOP	PGA
1916			24		

FOTHERINGHAM, George (USA)

Yr	M	AS	USO	BOP	PGA
1912			13		
1916					Last 32
1919			29		Last 16

FOUGHT, John (USA)

Yr	M	AS	USO	BOP	PGA
1983					5

FOULIS, David (SCO/USA)

Yr	M	AS	USO	BOP	PGA
1897			8		
1899			18		

FOULIS, James (SCO/USA)

Yr	M	AS	USO	BOP	PGA
1895			3		
1896			W		
1897			3		
1899			20		
1900			14		
1901			11		
1902			20		
1904			9		
1906			22		

FOULIS, Jim (USA)

Yr	M	AS	USO	BOP	PGA
1928					Last 32
1931					Last 16
1934	28				Last 32
1937					Last 16
1938			19		QF
1939			25		
1940	29		16		Last 16
1941	29				Last 32
1942	26				
1946	11				

FOULIS, Robert (SCO/USA)

Yr	M	AS	USO	BOP	PGA
1897			15		
1900			29		

FOULIS, TJ (SCO/USA)

Yr	M	AS	USO	BOP	PGA
1911			29		

FOURIE, John (RSA)

Yr	M	AS	USO	BOP	PGA
1976				15	
1977				22	

FOVARGUE, Walter (USA)

Yr	M	AS	USO	BOP	PGA
1906			14		
1909			18		
1911			28		
1914			24		
1916			13		Last 32

FOWLER, WH [a] (SCO)

Yr	M	AS	USO	BOP	PGA
1900				26	

	Yr	M	AS	USO	BOP	PGA
FOWNES Jr, WC [a] (USA)						
	1913			11		
FRANCIS, Francis [a] (ENG)						
	1936				23	
	1937		28			
FRANCIS, Red (USA)						
	1940					Last 32
FRANCIS, William (USA)						
	1939					Last 32
FRANCO, Carlos (PAR)						
	1999		6			26
	2000		7			
	2001					29
FRANK, Joe (USA)						
	1930					Last 32
FRANKLIN, Barry (RSA)						
	1967				25	
FRASER, Leo (USA)						
	1934					Last 32
FRENCH, Emmett (USA)						
	1915			10		
	1916					Last 16
	1919					QF
	1921			5	26	SF
	1922			19		RU
	1923			22		
	1924			22		QF
	1925			20		Last 32
	1926			27	8	
	1927			4		
FROST, David (RSA)						
	1985			23	25	
	1986			15		21
	1987			17	6	10
	1988		8		7	
	1989		18	18		27
	1993				24	
	1994					25
	1995		5			
	1996		10			
	1998		26			
	1999				7	21
FROSTICK, FH (ENG)						
	1912				24	
FRY, Earl (USA)						
	1930					Last 32

	Yr	M	AS	USO	BOP	PGA
FRY, Mark (USA)						
	1930					Last 32
	1934			16		
	1941					Last 16
	1944					Last 16
FRY, SH [a] (ENG)						
	1902				14	
FRYATT, Ed(ward) (ENG)						
	1997			24		
FULKE, Pierre (SWE)						
	1999				30	
	2000				6	
FUNK, Fred (USA)						
	1985			23		
	1993			7		
	1996					26
	1997		17			
	1998					23
	2000					9
FUNSETH, Rod (USA)						
	1965					8
	1966			13		
	1968			16		
	1971					30
	1972			25		
	1973			20		
	1976			11		
	1977		14	10		
	1978		2			
	1979					23
FURGOL, Ed (USA)						
	1946			12		
	1947			13		
	1948		6			
	1951		15			
	1953					Last 16
	1954			W		Last 32
	1955		24		20	Last 16
	1956		24	4		SF
	1957		6			
	1963		5			
	1964			14		13
FURGOL, Marty (USA)						
	1948			28		
	1949					Last 16
	1950			20		
	1951			23		Last 32
	1952					Last 32
	1953			9		Last 32
	1954		22	18		

	Yr	M	AS	USO	BOP	PGA
FURGOL, Marty (cont)	1955			25		Last 16
	1957	11				
	1958			13		
FURYK, Jim (USA)						
	1994			28		
	1995					13
	1996	29		5		17
	1997	28		5	4	6
	1998	4		14	4	
	1999	14		17	10	8
	2000	14				
	2001	6				7
GADD, Bert (ENG)						
	1933			22		
	1934			21		
	1935			4		
	1936			21		
	1938			10		
GADD, Chas (ENG)						
	1927			27		
GADD, George (ENG)						
	1922			12		
	1923			29		
	1924			9		
	1926			22		
	1928			23		
GADDIE, Clay (USA)						
	1949					Last 32
GAFFORD, Ray (USA)						
	1950					QF
	1951			19		Last 32
	1952			28		
GAIRDNER, JR [a] (ENG)						
	1898			21		
GAJDA, Bob (USA)						
	1952					Last 32
	1957					Last 32
	1958					25
GALE, Terry (AUS)						
	1979			13		
	1983			29		
	1984			28		
GALLACHER, Bernard (SCO)						
	1973			18		
	1974			24		
	1975			19		
	1978			22		

	Yr	M	AS	USO	BOP	PGA
GALLACHER, Bernard (cont)	1982			25		
	1983			19		
GALLAGHER Jr, Jim (USA)						
	1989					12
	1991	17		11		3
	1992	25				2
	1993	29				
GALLARDO, Angel (ESP)						
	1974			24		
	1977			26		
GALLETT, Francis (USA)						
	1922					Last 16
	1923			5		
	1924					Last 16
	1925			20		
	1926					Last 32
	1927					QF
	1930			25		
GAMEZ, Robert (USA)						
	1990					12
GARAIALDE, Jean (FRA)						
	1958				14	
	1959				21	
	1961				26	
	1962				12	
	1963				9	
	1964				13	
	1969				30	
GARCIA, Sergio (ESP)						
	1998				29a	
	1999					2
	2001			12	9	
GARDNER, Buddy (USA)						
	1985	6				
	1989	17				
GARDNER, Robert (USA)						
	1911			23		
GARDNER, Robert W (USA)						
	1961	11				
GARDNER, Stewart (USA)						
	1900			9		
	1901			4		
	1902			2		
	1903			3		
	1904			6		
	1905			5		
	1906			7		
	1907			21		

GARNER, John (ENG)

Yr	M AS	USO	BOP	PGA
1972			28	
1974			11	

GARRIDO, Antonio (ESP)

Yr	M AS	USO	BOP	PGA
1978			24	

GASSIAT, Jean (FRA)

Yr	M AS	USO	BOP	PGA
1912			7	
1913			22	
1914			14	
1920			29	
1922			7	
1926			28	
1927			19	
1928			23	

GAUDIN, A (ENG)

Yr	M AS	USO	BOP	PGA
1920			16	

GAUDIN, EP (ENG)

Yr	M AS	USO	BOP	PGA
1909			14	
1910			8	

GAUDIN, HA (Herbert) (ENG)

Yr	M AS	USO	BOP	PGA
1925			13	
1926			10	

GAUDIN, JW (ENG)

Yr	M AS	USO	BOP	PGA
1921			15	
1923			29	
1924			16	
1925			6	

GAUDIN, PJ (Philip) (ENG/USA)

Yr	M AS	USO	BOP	PGA
1900			22	
1901			9	
1904			23	
1906			19	
1907			11	
1908			9	
1910			12	
1912			23	
1914			8	
1922				Last 32

GAUDIN, WC (ENG/USA)

Yr	M AS	USO	BOP	PGA
1907		30		

GAUNTT, Jimmy (USA)

Yr	M AS	USO	BOP	PGA
1942				Last 32

GAY, Brian (USA)

Yr	M AS	USO	BOP	PGA
2001				22

GEIBERGER, Al (USA)

Yr	M AS	USO	BOP	PGA
1961	12			
1963				5

GEIBERGER, Al (cont)

Yr	M AS	USO	BOP	PGA
1964	13	14		19
1965	24	4		19
1966		30		W
1967		28		5
1968	30	9		8
1969	13	2		
1970				16
1971	24			30
1972	12	21		
1973		13		18
1974		18	13	8
1976	15	2		
1977		10		6
1979		19		

GENTA, Tomas (ARG)

Yr	M AS	USO	BOP	PGA
1931			11	

GERLAK, Alex (USA)

Yr	M AS	USO	BOP	PGA
1933				Last 32
1940				Last 32

GETCHELL, George (USA)

Yr	M AS	USO	BOP	PGA
1948				Last 32

GHEZZI, Vic (USA)

Yr	M AS	USO	BOP	PGA
1932				Last 32
1933				Last 32
1934	25			Last 16
1935	8	20		Last 32
1936	15	18		Last 16
1937	8	20		Last 16
1938	10	11		
1939	12	29		Last 32
1940		15		Last 32
1941	6	19		W
1942				Last 32
1945				QF
1946	13	2		Last 32
1947	21	6	18	SF
1948	18	14		
1950	14			
1951				Last 16
1952	30			Last 16
1954	29			
1955				Last 32
1956	29			

GIANFERANTE, Jerry (USA)

Yr	M AS	USO	BOP	PGA
1936		22		
1941		30		

GIBSON, Andrew (USA)

Yr	M AS	USO	BOP	PGA
1940		20		

GIBSON, Charles (ENG)

Yr	M AS	USO	BOP	PGA
1894			28	
1897			30	

GIBSON, John (USA)

Yr	M AS	USO	BOP	PGA
1940				Last 32
1945				Last 32

GIBSON, Kelly (USA)

Yr	M AS	USO	BOP	PGA
1997		28		

GIBSON, Leland (USA)

Yr	M AS	USO	BOP	PGA
1942				Last 16
1946		26		
1947		6		QF
1948		14		Last 16
1949	13			
1950	14			
1952		22		
1953	13			
1954		18		
1955		25		

GILBERT, Gibby (USA)

Yr	M AS	USO	BOP	PGA
1971				6
1973				18
1975				17
1979				5
1980	2			
1981	28			

GILDER, Bob (USA)

Yr	M AS	USO	BOP	PGA
1978				19
1979		16		16
1981	15			4
1982	14			8
1985				18
1988		8		6
1991				5
1992		6		

GILES III, Marvin [a] (USA)

Yr	M AS	USO	BOP	PGA
1968	22			
1973		17		

GILFORD, David (ENG)

Yr	M AS	USO	BOP	PGA
1995	24			

GILLAN, DH [a] (SCO)

Yr	M AS	USO	BOP	PGA
1890			30	

GINN, Stewart (AUS)

Yr	M AS	USO	BOP	PGA
1976			21	

GLASSON, Bill (USA)

Yr	M AS	USO	BOP	PGA
1984		25		
1986	25			
1989		21		
1994	19			19
1995		4	24	
1998				13
1999	18			

GLENZ, David (USA)

Yr	M AS	USO	BOP	PGA
1974		30		

GLOVER, Randy (USA)

Yr	M AS	USO	BOP	PGA
1976		19		

GOALBY, Bob (USA)

Yr	M AS	USO	BOP	PGA
1959				5
1960		19		
1961		2		15
1962	25	14		2
1963				17
1966		22		
1967		6		7
1968	W			8
1971		19		
1972	17			
1973	6			18
1974	22			

GODFREY, Walter (NZL)

Yr	M AS	USO	BOP	PGA
1970			22	

GOETZ, Bob (USA)

Yr	M AS	USO	BOP	PGA
1958		16		
1963		30		

GOFF, Bruce [a] (SCO)

Yr	M AS	USO	BOP	PGA
1885			29	

GOFF, WH [a] (SCO)

Yr	M AS	USO	BOP	PGA
1885			26	

GOGEL, Matt (USA)

Yr	M AS	USO	BOP	PGA
2001		12		

GOGGIN, Willie (USA)

Yr	M AS	USO	BOP	PGA
1933		9		RU
1934				Last 32
1936		18	23	Last 16
1937				Last 32
1940	4			
1941	9			
1942	14			Last 16
1944				QF
1952			9	

GOLDEN, John (USA)

Yr	M AS	USO	BOP	PGA
1920		17		
1921		22		QF
1922		8		SF
1923				Last 16
1924		25		
1925		18		Last 16
1926				SF
1927		7		SF
1928				Last 32

	Yr	M AS	USO	BOP	PGA
GOLDEN, John (cont)	1929			13	Last 32
	1930		5		Last 32
	1931		27		Last 16
	1932				Last 16
	1933		21		QF
	1934	21	17		
GOLDSTRAND, Joel (USA)					
	1970		12		
GONZALES, Mario (BRA)					
	1948			11	
GONZALEZ, Jaime (BRA)					
	1984			28	
	1985			20	
GOOD, DJ (ENG)					
	1973			18	
GOOD, G (ENG)					
	1936			19	
GOODLOE Jr, William [a] (USA)					
	1955	28			
GOODMAN, Johnny [a] (USA)					
	1930		11		
	1932		14		
	1933		W		
	1936		22		
	1937		8		
GOOSEN, Retief (RSA)					
	1997			10	
	1999			10	
	2000		12		
	2001		W	13	
GOOSIE, JC (USA)					
	1963				27
GOSS, Dan (USA)					
	1922				Last 32
GOSSETT, Thomas (SCO)					
	1886			4	
GORDON, George (USA)					
	1919				Last 16
GORDON, Jack (USA)					
	1920				Last 32
	1921				Last 16
GOULD, Harold (WAL)					
	1948			30	

	Yr	M AS	USO	BOP	PGA
GOURLAY, Tom (SCO/USA)					
	1896		19		
GOURLAY, Walter (SCO)					
	1873			6	
	1876			8	
	1879			8	
GOYDOS, Paul (USA)					
	1997		28		29
	1999		12		
GRADY, Wayne (AUS)					
	1986				21
	1987			17	
	1989			2	
	1990	27			W
	1991			26	
	1992	13	17		
	1993			9	
	1994				30
GRAHAM, David (AUS)					
	1973	29			
	1974		18	11	
	1975		29	28	10
	1976			21	4
	1977	6			
	1978	9			
	1979		7		W
	1980	5		29	26
	1981	7	W	14	
	1982	19	6	27	
	1983		8	14	14
	1984	6	21		
	1985	10	23	3	
	1986	28	15	11	7
	1987	27			
	1988				17
	1990			8	
GRAHAM, Jack [a] (ENG)					
	1897			18	
	1901			9	
	1904			7	
	1906			4	
	1907			13	
	1908			18	
	1913			11	
GRAHAM, Lou (USA)					
	1965		23		
	1967		28		
	1968				8
	1970				22
	1972		19		
	1973	17			30

Yr	M AS	USO	BOP	PGA
GRAHAM, Lou (cont)				
1974		3		
1975		W		
1976	12	28		22
1977	6	2		6
1979	23	25		10
1980	26			
GRANT, D [a] (ENG)				
1920			29	
GRANT, David (SCO)				
1879			23	
1880			8	
1883			24	
1884			20	
1886			8	
1887			7	
1888			6	
1889			7	
1890			7	
1891			14	
1893			17	
1894			20	
GRANT, James A [a] (US)				
1966	28			
GRAPPASONI, Ugo (ITA)				
1949			28	
1951			19	
1953			27	
1954			17	
GRAVATT, Morrie (USA)				
1944				Last 32
GRAY, Claude (ENG)				
1913			18	
GRAY, Ernest (ENG)				
1903			15	
1904			18	
1905			5	
1906			24	
1908			13	
GRAY, Reg (ENG)				
1907			18	
GREEN, Hubert (USA)				
1972	22			16
1973	14			
1974	9	26	4	3
1975	8	18		
1976	19	6	5	30
1977	8	W	3	
1978	2		29	26

Yr	M AS	USO	BOP	PGA
GREEN, Hubert (cont)				
1979	10	24		16
1980	4	6		
1981	11		23	27
1983			19	
1984		30		14
1985				W
1988	19			
1989	9			
GREEN, Ken (USA)				
1983		26		
1986				26
1987		29		
1989	11			
1991				16
1996		7		
GREEN, Tom (ENG)				
1930			29	
1934			26	
1936			5	
GREEN, WH (ENG)				
1939			19	
GREENE, Bert (USA)				
1969				3
1970	12			
1971	12			
GREENE, Christy (IRL)				
1958			20	
1964			13	
1965			21	
1966			30	
GREENWALDT, Phil (USA)				
1941				Last 32
GREGSON, Malcom (ENG)				
1964			19	
1968			27	
1971			25	
GREIG, William [a] (SCO)				
1885			16	
1888			23	
1891			28	
1900			16	
GREINER, Otto (USA)				
1948		14		
1963		27		
GRIFFIN, George (USA)				
1925				Last 32

	Yr	M AS	USO	BOP	PGA
GRIFFITHS, AS (USA)					
	1902		16		
GROH, Gary (USA)					
	1975		18		
GROSSART, T (SCO)					
	1883			14	
GROUT, Dick (USA)					
	1926				Last 16
GROUT, Jack (USA)					
	1941				Last 16
	1945				Last 16
	1953				Last 32
GUEST, Charles (USA)					
	1927				Last 16
	1929				Last 16
	1930		17		Last 32
	1931		19		
GUILFORD, Jesse [a] (USA)					
	1919		24		
	1921		26		
	1922		19		
	1924		29		
GULDAHL, Ralph (USA)					
	1933		2		
	1934		8		
	1936		8		
	1937	2	W	11	Last 32
	1938	2	W		Last 32
	1939	W	7		Last 32
	1940	14	5		SF
	1941	14	21		Last 16
	1942	21			
	1949		22		
GULLANE, Henry (SCO/USA)					
	1899		8		
	1900		25		
GULLICKSON, Lloyd (USA)					
	1920				Last 32
	1922		28		
GUMP, Scott (USA)					
	1998				23
GUSA, Arthur (USA)					
	1931				Last 32
GUSTIN, John (USA)					
	1964				9

	Yr	M AS	USO	BOP	PGA
GUTHRIE, James (SCO)					
	1875			12	
HAAS, Fred (USA)					
	1946	15			
	1947	17			
	1948	18			
	1949	29	19		
	1950	10	18		
	1951		29		
	1952				QF
	1953	26	12		Last 32
	1954		6		Last 32
	1955				Last 32
	1956	29	14		Last 32
	1962				23
	1963				27
HAAS, Jay (USA)					
	1975		18a		
	1977	5			
	1979				7
	1980	17			
	1981				19
	1982		6	27	5
	1983	27		19	9
	1984	21	11		
	1985	5	15		
	1986	6			
	1987	7			28
	1988		25		
	1992		23		
	1993				20
	1994	5			14
	1995	3	4		8
	1996			22	
	1997		5	24	
	1998	12			
	1999		17		3
HACKBARTH, Alfred (USA)					
	1921		11		
HACKBARTH, Otto (USA)					
	1906		22		
	1910		23		
	1911		29		
	1912		7		
	1914		27		
	1915		29		
	1916		19		
	1919		26		Last 16
	1920				Last 32
	1921		22		
HACKNEY, Clarence (USA)					
	1919		13		Last 32

	Yr	MAS	USO	BOP	PGA
HACKNEY, Clarence (cont)	1920		12		QF
	1921		8	23	Last 32
	1923				Last 16
	1924		13		
	1925		17		
	1926		22		
	1930				Last 32
	1935				Last 32
HACKNEY, Dave (USA)					
	1929				Last 32
	1931				Last 32
	1933				Last 32
HACKNEY, George (USA)					
	1922		17		
HAGAWA, Yakata (JAP)					
	1982	15			
HAGEN, Walter (USA)					
	1913		4		
	1914		W		
	1915		10		
	1916		7		SF
	1919		W		
	1920		11		
	1921		2	6	W
	1922		5	W	
	1923		18	2	RU
	1924		4	W	W
	1925		5		W
	1926		7	3	W
	1927		6		W
	1928		4	W	QF
	1929		19	W	SF
	1930		17		
	1931		7	22	Last 32
	1932		10		Last 32
	1933		4		
	1934	13			Last 32
	1935	15	3		
	1936	11			
	1937			26	
	1940				Last 16
HAGER, Joe (USA)					
	1980		12		
	1982		22		
	1984		25		
HALIBURTON, Tom (SCO)					
	1946			30	
	1948			23	
	1953			29	
	1959			29	
	1963			30	

	Yr	MAS	USO	BOP	PGA
HALL, Charles (USA)					
	1920		30		
HALLBERG, Gary (USA)					
	1980		22a		
	1984				6
	1985	6			
	1993				14
	1995		28		
HALLDORSAN, Dan (USA)					
	1982				16
HALLETT, Jim (USA)					
	1987				21
	1991				27
HALSALL, Bobby (ENG)					
	1954			15	
	1955			23	
HAM, Arthur (USA)					
	1924				Last 32
HAMBLETON, Walter (ENG)					
	1914			25	
HAMBRICK, Archie (USA)					
	1933		21		
HAMBRO, CE [a] (ENG)					
	1894			25	
	1899			21	
HAMILL, Harry (IRL)					
	1906			19	
HAMILTON, Bob (USA)					
	1944				W
	1945				Last 32
	1946	3			Last 32
	1947		29		
	1948	18			
	1949	23			Last 32
	1951				Last 32
	1952				SF
	1953	4			
HAMMOND, Donnie (USA)					
	1984				16
	1986	11			11
	1987	27			
	1990	24		8	
	1992		23	5	
HAMPTON, Harry (USA)					
	1919		11		Last 16

	Yr	M AS	USO	BOP	PGA
HAMPTON, Harry (cont)	1920		22		SF
	1921		22		Last 32
	1922		19		Last 16
	1924				Last 32
	1925		20		
	1926		27		QF
	1927		7		
	1928		25		
HANCOCK, Phil (USA)	1978		20	16	
HANCOCK, Roland (USA)	1927				Last 32
	1928		3		
HARBERT, MR (Chick) (USA)	1939	18			
	1942	10			
	1946	7	8		
	1947		12		RU
	1948	3	28		QF
	1949		23		
	1950	24			Last 16
	1951				Last 32
	1952		24		RU
	1953	5			
	1954	12			W
	1955				Last 32
	1957		8		
	1958	17			
	1959	14	26		28
	1961		29		
	1962				11
HARCKE, Byron (USA)	1945				Last 32
HARDEN, Jack (USA)	1949				Last 32
	1951				Last 16
HARGREAVES, Jack (ENG)	1948			3	
	1951			19	
	1952			27	
	1954			20	
	1956			17	
HARLAND, John (USA)	1895		7		
	1898		17		
	1901		28		
	1902		20		
HARMON, Claude (USA)	1945				SF

	Yr	M AS	USO	BOP	PGA
HARMON, Claude (cont)	1946	18	15		
	1947	26	19		Last 16
	1948	W		27	SF
	1949	11	8		Last 32
	1950				Last 16
	1952	14			
	1953				SF
	1954		15		Last 32
	1955	28			Last 16
	1956				Last 32
	1957				QF
	1958	9			
	1959		3		
	1960	16	27		
HARMON Jr, Tom (USA)	1924				Last 32
	1926		27		Last 16
	1927		29		Last 16
HARNEY, Paul (USA)	1959	25			14
	1960		12		18
	1961	6			11
	1962	15	28		7
	1963		4		23
	1964	5			
	1965	11			
	1966	8			15
	1967	6	18		
	1970		18		
	1972	22			
	1973	24			
HARPER, Chandler (USA)	1942	13			
	1946	19	15		Last 16
	1947	8			Last 32
	1948				Last 32
	1950				W
	1952				Last 32
	1953	10			
	1959	14			
HARPER Jr, Charles (USA)	1956				Last 16
	1957				Last 32
HARRIMAN, Herbert M [a] (USA)	1899		13		
HARRINGTON, Padraig (IRL)	1996			18	
	1997			5	
	1999			24	
	2000	19	5	20	
	2001	27	30		

	Yr	M AS	USO	BOP	PGA
HARRIS, Bob (USA)					
	1955		21		
	1960		15		
HARRIS Sr, Labron (USA)					
	1952				Last 32
	1953				Last 16
	1958		27		
HARRIS Jr, Labron (USA)					
	1964		28		
	1965		24		
	1967		28		
HARRIS, Robert [a] (SCO)					
	1911			27	
	1925			11	
HARRISON, EJ (Dutch) (USA)					
	1939		25		SF
	1941		7		
	1942	7			Last 32
	1945				Last 32
	1946		10		Last 16
	1947	29	13		
	1948	13			
	1949	23			
	1950		4		
	1951	15			
	1953		14		Last 32
	1954	4			Last 16
	1956		17		
	1958		23		
	1960		3		
	1961		17		
	1965		28		
	1967		16		
HARRISON, John (USA)					
	1896		24		
	1897		24		
HARRISON, Robert (USA)					
	1961		29		
HART, Dick (USA)					
	1962				30
	1963				17
	1964				28
HART, Dudley (USA)					
	1992		23		
	1993				6
	1999		17		
	2000	28			
	2001				16

	Yr	M AS	USO	BOP	PGA
HART, PO (USA)					
	1921		30		
	1923		24		
	1926		23		
	1927		24		
	1929		13		Last 32
HARTER, Charles (USA)					
	1952				Last 32
HARTLEY, Lister [a] (ENG)					
	1926			13	
	1932			25	
HARWOOD, Mike (AUS)					
	1991			2	
HASSANEIN, H (EGY)					
	1950			30	
	1953			17	
	1955			28	
HASTINGS, Willie (SCO)					
	1938			23	
HATALSKY, Morris (USA)					
	1982	24			
	1990				14
	1991	29			
HAVERS, Arthur (ENG)					
	1920			7	
	1921			4	
	1922			12	
	1923			W	
	1924			29	
	1925			20	
	1926			26	
	1927		15	7	
	1929			11	
	1931			9	
	1932			3	
	1933			14	
	1937			17	
	1947			27	
HAWKES, Jeff (RSA)					
	1989			30	
HAWKINS, Fred (USA)					
	1951		6		
	1952	7			
	1953	10			
	1955		19		QF
	1956	29			QF
	1957	16	6		
	1958	2			14

HAWKINS, Fred (cont)

Yr	M AS	USO	BOP	PGA
1959	7	11		28
1960	16			10
1961	24			22

HAYES, Dale (RSA)

Yr	M AS	USO	BOP	PGA
1971			17	
1978			11	
1976	19			

HAYES, JP (John Patrick) (USA)

Yr	M AS	USO	BOP	PGA
2000				18

HAYES, Mark (USA)

Yr	M AS	USO	BOP	PGA
1975				22
1976		14		15
1977			9	19
1978			14	
1979			30	
1980		6		
1981		14		
1982	10			
1983	20	26		

HAYES, Otway (RSA)

Yr	M AS	USO	BOP	PGA
1948			28	

HAYES Jr, Ted (USA)

Yr	M AS	USO	BOP	PGA
1970		22		

HEAFNER, Clayton (USA)

Yr	M AS	USO	BOP	PGA
1939		16		
1941	12	21		
1946	7	12		
1947	29			Last 32
1949	8	2		QF
1950	7			
1951	20	2		
1952	24			
1953		26		

HEAFNER, Vance (USA)

Yr	M AS	USO	BOP	PGA
1981				11

HEARD, Jerry (USA)

Yr	M AS	USO	BOP	PGA
1971		13		9
1972	5	29	28	7
1973		7		
1974	11			
1975	26	29		25
1976				22

HEBERT, Jay (USA)

Yr	M AS	USO	BOP	PGA
1953		9		
1954	16	17		
1955	15			Last 32
1956		17		
1957	10			QF

HEBERT, Jay (cont)

Yr	M AS	USO	BOP	PGA
1958	9	7		5
1959	8	17		25
1960				W
1961	30			13
1962		17		10
1963	27			
1964	30			
1966	10			12
1967	21			
1968	28			

HEBERT, Lionel (USA)

Yr	M AS	USO	BOP	PGA
1955				Last 32
1956				Last 16
1957				W
1958				16
1959		28		
1960	9	27		18
1961	30			
1962	20	23		
1963		14		
1964		21		
1967	8			14
1968	7			30
1969	8			

HEDBLOM, Peter (SWE)

Yr	M AS	USO	BOP	PGA
1996			7	

HEINLEIN, William (USA)

Yr	M AS	USO	BOP	PGA
1941				Last 32
1946				Last 32

HEINTZELMAN, Webb (USA)

Yr	M AS	USO	BOP	PGA
1990		24		

HELD, Eddie [a] (USA)

Yr	M AS	USO	BOP	PGA
1923		26		

HENDERSON, Willie John (SCO)

Yr	M AS	USO	BOP	PGA
1951			19	
1955			15	

HENDRY, Jock (SCO/USA)

Yr	M AS	USO	BOP	PGA
1926				Last 32
1929				Last 32

HENDRY, TS [a] (SCO)

Yr	M AS	USO	BOP	PGA
1885			27	

HENKE, Nolan (USA)

Yr	M AS	USO	BOP	PGA
1989		21		
1991		7		
1992	6			
1993	27	7		6
1995				23

Yr	MAS	USO	BOP	PGA
HENNING, Alan (RSA)				
1966			30	
HENNING, Harold (RSA)				
1957			29	
1958			13	
1959			23	
1960			3	
1961			10	
1962	11		30	
1963			20	
1964			8	
1966	22		13	
1967			6	
1968	22			
1969	13		16	
1970			3	
1973			10	
1983			6	
HENNINGER, Brian (USA)				
1995	10			
HENRY, Bunky (USA)				
1969		9	11	
1970		30		
HEPBURN, James (SCO)				
1903			24	
1904			29	
1905			24	
1906			30	
1908			24	
1909			8	
1910			19	
1911			10	
HERD, Alex (Sandy) (SCO)				
1888			8	
1891			13	
1892			2	
1893			3	
1894			8	
1895			2	
1896			5	
1897			5	
1898			17	
1899			16	
1900			10	
1901			5	
1902			W	
1903			4	
1904			9	
1905			15	
1906			19	
1907			12	
1908			4	

Yr	MAS	USO	BOP	PGA
HERD, Alex (Sandy) (cont)				
1909			8	
1910			2	
1911			3	
1912			5	
1913			11	
1914			29	
1920			2	
1921			6	
1923			22	
1924			13	
1925			14	
1926			20	
1927			9	
HERD, David (SCO)				
1894			20	
1895			20	
1896			27	
1898			21	
1899			28	
1901			25	
1902			28	
HERD, Fred (SCO/USA)				
1898		W		
1899		25		
1900		16		
1902		24		
HERON, Al [a] (USA)				
1930		11		
HERON, George (USA)				
1925		29		
HERRESHOFF, Fred [a] (USA)				
1910		20		
1913		16		
HERRON, Tim (USA)				
1997				13
1999		6	30	
HESLER, Phil (USA)				
1920				Last 32
HEZLET, Charles [a] (IRL)				
1928			17	
HIGGINS, Doug (USA)				
1956		27		
HILGENDORF, Charles (USA)				
1922				Last 32
1928		18		
1929		13		
1930		28		

Yr	M	AS	USO	BOP	PGA

HILL, Dave (USA)

Yr	M	AS	USO	BOP	PGA
1963					17
1966		22			
1967		18			11
1968		16			17
1969		24	13		15
1970		5	2		
1971		27			6
1972		29			
1973				18	
1974	11				3
1975	7				7
1976	15				22

HILL, Mike (USA)

Yr	M	AS	USO	BOP	PGA
1970					16
1973					24
1974					11
1975					17
1976					15

HILL, Ray (USA)

Yr	M	AS	USO	BOP	PGA
1940					Last 32
1949					QF
1955					Last 32

HILLS, Percy (ENG)

Yr	M	AS	USO	BOP	PGA
1904				29	
1905				22	

HILTON, Harold [a] (ENG)

Yr	M	AS	USO	BOP	PGA
1892				W	
1893				8	
1896				23	
1897				W	
1898				3	
1899				12	
1900				16	
1901				4	
1902				6	
1903				24	

HILTON, Horace [a] (ENG)

Yr	M	AS	USO	BOP	PGA
1911				3	

HINCKLE, Lon (USA)

Yr	M	AS	USO	BOP	PGA
1975			19		
1980			3		3
1981	28		6		
1982					9

HINES, Jimmy (USA)

Yr	M	AS	USO	BOP	PGA
1932					Last 32
1933					SF
1934		7	8		
1935		9			Last 32
1936					QF

HINES, Jimmy (cont)

Yr	M	AS	USO	BOP	PGA
1937		10	20		QF
1938		10	11		SF
1939		22	20		
1940		27	20		Last 16
1941		19	24		QF
1942					Last 32
1944					Last 16
1948					Last 32
1950					Last 32
1952				21	

HINSON, Larry (USA)

Yr	M	AS	USO	BOP	PGA
1970					4
1971		30	9		13
1973					12
1974			23		26
1975					28

HIRIGOYEN, Pierre (FRA)

Yr	M	AS	USO	BOP	PGA
1930				21	
1932				29	

HISKIE, Babe (USA)

Yr	M	AS	USO	BOP	PGA
1973					17

HITCHCOCK, Jimmy (ENG)

Yr	M	AS	USO	BOP	PGA
1954				29	
1957				23	
1959				11	
1962				30	
1963				26	
1966				16	

HJERTSTEDT, Gabriel (SWE)

Yr	M	AS	USO	BOP	PGA
1999					16
2001		30			

HOARE, WT (USA)

Yr	M	AS	USO	BOP	PGA
1896			15		
1897			5		

HOARE, WV (USA)

Yr	M	AS	USO	BOP	PGA
1898			6		
1900			27		

HOBDAY, Simon (ZIM)

Yr	M	AS	USO	BOP	PGA
1975				28	
1976				21	
1979				30	
1983				19	

HOBENS, Jack (USA)

Yr	M	AS	USO	BOP	PGA
1902			14		
1903			9		
1904			11		
1905			7		
1906			10		

Yr	M	AS	USO	BOP	PGA
HOBENS, Jack (cont)					
1907			4		
1908			6		
1909			4		
1910			7		
1916					Last 16
1919					Last 32
HOCH, Scott (USA)					
1983	27				
1985					12
1987					3
1988			21		25
1989	2		13		7
1990	14		8		
1991			6		
1993			5		6
1994			13		
1995	7				
1996	5		7		
1997			10		6
1998	16				29
1999					21
2000			16		
2001			16		7
HODSON, Bert (WAL)					
1927				7	
1930				12	
1931				25	
1932				17	
1934				7	
HOFFNER, Charles (USA)					
1914			13		
1915			24		
1919			13		
1920					Last 32
1922			19		Last 32
1924					Last 32
1925					Last 32
HOGAN, Ben (USA)					
1938	25				
1939	9				Last 16
1940	10		5		QF
1941	4		3		QF
1942	2				QF
1946	2		4		W
1947	4		6		
1948	6		W		W
1950	4		W		
1951	W		W		
1952	7		3		
1953	W		W	W	
1954	2		6		
1955	2		2		
1956	8		2		

Yr	M	AS	USO	BOP	PGA
HOGAN, Ben (cont)					
1958	14		10		
1959	30		8		
1960	6		9		
1961			14		
1964	9				9
1965	21				15
1966	13		12		
1967	10				
HOLGUIN, Tony (USA)					
1949	19				
1955					Last 32
1957					Last 32
HOLLAND, Len (ENG)					
1920				5	
1921				16	
1922				12	
1923				25	
1924				6	
1927				22	
1931				22	
1935				26	
HOLLAND, Mike (USA)					
1982					29
HOLSCHER, Bud (USA)					
1955			7		
HONEYMAN, David (USA)					
1910			28		
1912			30		
HONEYMAN, W (SCO)					
1882				16	
HONSBERGER, Ray (USA)					
1952					Last 16
HOOD, Tom [a] (SCO)					
1865				10	
1866				11	
1874				14	
HOOPER, Herb (USA)					
1971					18
HOPE, WL [a] (ENG)					
1928				23	
1932				15	
HORNE, Reg (ENG)					
1947				2	
1948				28	
1949				20	
1950				17	

HORNE, Reg (cont)

Yr	M AS	USO	BOP	PGA
1953			20	
1955			23	
1957			24	

HORNE, Stanley (CAN)

Yr	M AS	USO	BOP	PGA
1938	15			

HORNE, William (ENG)

Yr	M AS	USO	BOP	PGA
1907			25	
1909			7	
1912			20	
1920			9	

HORTON, Tommy (ENG)

Yr	M AS	USO	BOP	PGA
1965			17	
1967			8	
1968			13	
1969			11	
1970			9	
1975			19	
1976			5	
1977			9	

HORVATH, Rudy (CAN)

Yr	M AS	USO	BOP	PGA
1954		13		

HOUGHTON, Al (USA)

Yr	M AS	USO	BOP	PGA
1933				Last 32
1934				QF

HOWARD, George (USA)

Yr	M AS	USO	BOP	PGA
1925				Last 32

HOWELL III, Charles (USA)

Yr	M AS	USO	BOP	PGA
2001				22

HOWELL, Ron (USA)

Yr	M AS	USO	BOP	PGA
1966				28

HOYLE, M (ENG)

Yr	M AS	USO	BOP	PGA
1967			13	

HSU, Chi-San (TPE)

Yr	M AS	USO	BOP	PGA
1976			21	

HUCKABY, Charles (USA)

Yr	M AS	USO	BOP	PGA
1965		17		

HUGE, Ted (USA)

Yr	M AS	USO	BOP	PGA
1945				Last 32

HUGGETT, Brian (WAL)

Yr	M AS	USO	BOP	PGA
1961			26	
1962			3	
1963			14	
1965			2	
1967			25	

HUGGETT, Brian (cont)

Yr	M AS	USO	BOP	PGA
1968			13	
1969			16	
1970			28	
1971			25	
1972			26	

HUGHES, Bradley (AUS)

Yr	M AS	USO	BOP	PGA
1997		16		

HUGHES, Cyril (ENG/USA)

Yr	M AS	USO	BOP	PGA
1913			22	
1914			19	
1920			25	
1922		24		
1923		11		

HUISH, David (SCO)

Yr	M AS	USO	BOP	PGA
1976			21	

HULBERT, Mike (USA)

Yr	M AS	USO	BOP	PGA
1986				7
1989				27
1990		29		
1991				23
1992	19	6		28
1995		28		

HUME, Jimmy (ENG)

Yr	M AS	USO	BOP	PGA
1967			29	

HUNT, Bernard (ENG)

Yr	M AS	USO	BOP	PGA
1955			5	
1957			24	
1958			30	
1959			11	
1960			3	
1962			16	
1963			11	
1964			4	
1965	26		5	
1969			23	
1971			20	

HUNT, Geoff (ENG)

Yr	M AS	USO	BOP	PGA
1960			28	
1964			30	

HUNT, Guy (ENG)

Yr	M AS	USO	BOP	PGA
1972			7	
1975			28	
1977			15	
1978			17	

HUNTER, Charlie (SCO)

Yr	M AS	USO	BOP	PGA
1860			6	
1861			12	
1862			3	

Yr	MAS	USO	BOP	PGA
HUNTER, Charlie (cont)				
1863			7	
1868			9	
1870			9	
1872			6	
1874			27	
HUNTER, David (SCO/USA)				
1899		30		
1901		25		
1902		30		
1907		16		
1908		16		
1909		30		
HUNTER, J (SCO)				
1870			15	
HUNTER, James [a] (SCO)				
1882			29	
1884			18	
HUNTER, John (SCO)				
1893			15	
1896			18	
1898			8	
1903			21	
HUNTER, Mac (USA)				
1959		19		
HUNTER, P [a] (SCO)				
1921			19	
HUNTER, Robert [a] (SCO/USA)				
1904		23		
HUNTER, T [a] (SCO)				
1867			8	
1870			13	
1874			16	
HUNTER, William [a] (SCO)				
1872			8	
1878			20	
HUNTER Sr, Willie (SCO/USA)				
1901		28		
1902		20		
1903			13	
1905			24	
1906			12	
1914			17	
HUNTER Jr, William I (SCO/USA)				
1920			26a	
1922		24a	22a	
1923				Last 32

Yr	MAS	USO	BOP	PGA
HUNTER Jr, William I (cont)				
1925		13		
1926		8		
1928		28		
1929		26		
1930		17		
1931			16	
1934		14		
1935		28		
1938		15		
HUSKE, Al (USA)				
1938		24		
1940		29		
HUSTON, John (USA)				
1990	3	14		
1991	29			7
1992	25			18
1994	10			
1995	17			
1996	17			
1997	21			
1998	23		11	13
1999		17		
2000	14	4		
2001	20			
HUTCHINGS, Charles [a] (ENG)				
1891			18	
1893			13	
1894		.	25	
HUTCHINSON, Dennis (RSA)				
1961			18	
1962			16	
1965			21	
1966			27	
1967			22	
HUTCHINSON, Horace [a] (ENG)				
1885			11	
1886			16	
1887			10	
1890			6	
1891			22	
1892			10	
HUTCHINSON, James (SCO)				
1898			21	
1901			25	
HUTCHINSON Tom (SCO/USA)				
1900		7		
HUTCHISON, CK [a] (SCO)				
1909			19	
1910			24	
1914			29	

Yr	M AS	USO	BOP	PGA
HUTCHISON, James (SCO)				
1866			12	
HUTCHISON, Jock (SCO/USA)				
1908		8		
1909		23		
1910		8		
1911		5		
1912		23		
1913		16		
1915		8		
1916		2		RU
1919		3		QF
1920		2		W
1921		18	W	Last 16
1922		8	4	QF
1923		3		
1924				Last 32
1925		27		
1927		23		
1928				QF
HUTCHISON Jr, Jock (USA)				
1940		23		
HUTCHISON, Ralph (USA)				
1945				QF
HUTCHISON, W (SCO)				
1874			26	
HYNDMAN III, William [a] (USA)				
1957		13		
1958	26			
1959	18			
ILONEN, Mikko (FIN)				
2001			9	
INGHAM, Mike (ENG)				
1969			30	
INGRAM, David (SCO)				
1977			26	
INMAN Jr, Joe (USA)				
1975		14		
1976		23		22
1977		16		11
1978	9	12		11
1979	23			
1980		16		17
1981				19
INMAN, John (USA)				
1990		14		

Yr	M AS	USO	BOP	PGA
INMAN Jr, Walker (USA)				
1955		14		
1956	29			
IRWIN, Hale (USA)				
1971	13	19		22
1972				11
1973				9
1974	4	W	24	
1975	4	3	9	5
1976	5	26		
1977	5			
1978	8	4	24	12
1979	23	W	6	
1980	25	8		30
1981				16
1983	6		2	14
1984	21	6	14	25
1985		14		
1986				26
1988		17		
1990		W		12
1991	10	11		
1992			19	
1993	27			6
1994	18	18		
1995	14			
1996	29			
1997				29
2000		27		
ISAACS, Jack (USA)				
1949		23		Last 32
1952				Last 16
1953				SF
1954				Last 32
ISHII, Tomoo (JAP)				
1964	26			
IVERSON, Don (USA)				
1973				6
1974	29			
IZAWA, Toshi(mitsu) (JAP)				
2001	4			
JACK, Reid [a] (SCO)				
1959			5	
1960			16	
JACKLIN, Tony (ENG)				
1963			30	
1965			25	
1966			30	
1967	16		5	
1968	22		18	

	Yr	M	AS	USO	BOP	PGA
JACKLIN, Tony (cont)	1969			25	W	25
	1970	12		W	5	
	1971				3	
	1972	27			3	
	1973				14	
	1974				18	
	1979				24	
	1981				23	
JACKSON, D [a] (IRL)						
	1896				24	
JACKSON, F (ENG)						
	1902				23	
JACKSON, Gardner (USA)						
	1961					19
JACKSON, Hugh (IRL)						
	1970				8	
	1971				22	
JACKSON, James [a] (USA)						
	1959			19		
JACOBS, JA (ENG)						
	1935				15	
	1946				23	
	1948				25	
	1952				25	
JACOBS, John (ENG)						
	1952				27	
	1953				14	
	1954				20	
	1955				12	
	1956				16	
	1961				20	
JACOBS, Tommy (USA)						
	1958			10		
	1959					14
	1962			6		23
	1963	28				8
	1964			2		
	1965	15		28		
	1966	2				
JACOBSEN, Gary (USA)						
	1977			5		
JACOBSEN, Peter (USA)						
	1979					23
	1980			22		10
	1981	11				27
	1982	20				
	1983	20			12	3

	Yr	M	AS	USO	BOP	PGA
JACOBSEN, Peter (cont)	1984	25		7	22	18
	1985				11	10
	1986	25				3
	1987			24		20
	1988			21		
	1989			8	30	27
	1990	30			16	26
	1991	17				
	1992					28
	1993					28
	1994				24	
	1995					23
	1996			23		
JACQUELIN, Raphael (FRA)						
	2001				13	
JAECKEL, Barry (USA)						
	1976			28		
JAGGER, David (ENG)						
	1974				28	
JAMES, Mark (ENG)						
	1976				5	
	1979				4	
	1981				3	
	1983				29	
	1985				20	
	1989				13	
	1991				26	
	1993				27	
	1994				4	
	1995				8	
	1996				22	
	1997				20	
	1998				19	
JAMIESON, Jim (USA)						
	1971					6
	1972	5				2
	1973	3				18
	1974			26		
JANUARY, Don (USA)						
	1958			7		
	1959			19		
	1960	20				5
	1961	4				2
	1962	20				27
	1963	9		11		
	1964	18		11		
	1966	6		17		12
	1967	16		3		W
	1968	14		24		
	1969	5				15
	1970	12				12

	Yr	M AS	USO	BOP	PGA
JANUARY, Don (cont)	1971	4	27		
	1972		11		
	1973	10			
	1975		29		10
	1976		14		2
	1977	8			6
	1978	11			19
	1979				7
	1981				19
JANZEN, Lee (USA)					
	1992				21
	1993		W		22
	1994	30			
	1995	12	13	24	23
	1996	12	10		8
	1997	26			4
	1998		W	24	
	1999	14			
	2000				18
JARMAN, Edward (ENG)					
	1934			13	
JENKINS, JLC [a] (SCO)					
	1914			8	
JENKINS, Tom (USA)					
	1974				17
	1976		26		
JEWELL, FC (ENG)					
	1922			12	
	1923			25	
JIMENEZ, Miguel Angel (ESP)					
	1995		28		13
	1996				24
	1999		23		10
	2000		2	26	
	2001	10		3	
JOB, Nick (ENG)					
	1978			22	
	1981			14	
JOBE, Brandt (USA)					
	1999	14			10
JOHANSSON, Per-Ulrik (SWE)					
	1995			15	
	1996				8
	1997	12			
	1998	12	25		23
	1999	24			

	Yr	M AS	USO	BOP	PGA
JOHNS, Charlie (ENG)					
	1909			4	
	1920			16	
	1922			11	
	1924			16	
	1927			16	
JOHNSON, Gunnar (USA)					
	1930				Last 32
	1933				Last 32
JOHNSON, Howie (USA)					
	1967		23		
	1969		13		19
	1970	18			
	1971			20	
JOHNSON, Jimmy (USA)					
	1949				Last 32
JOHNSON, Norman (ENG)					
	1961			14	
JOHNSON, Terl (USA)					
	1938				Last 32
	1945				Last 16
	1956				QF
JOHNSTON, Bill (USA)					
	1956				SF
	1957	28			
	1960			26	
	1963				8
JOHNSTON, Harrison [a] (USA)					
	1926		23		
	1927		18		
	1928		22		
JOHNSTON, JF [a] (SCO)					
	1862			6	
	1863			11	
JOHNSTON, Ralph (USA)					
	1971		27		
	1973		13		
	1974	15			
	1975	20			
JOHNSTON, RH [a] (SCO)					
	1891			28	
JOHNSTONE, JC (SCO)					
	1905			18	
	1911			29	

Yr	M AS	USO	BOP	PGA

JOLLY, Herbert (ENG)

Yr	M AS	USO	BOP	PGA
1923			8	
1926			21	
1929			15	

JOLLY, Jack (USA)

1905		26		
1906		14		
1907		25		

JONES, Brian (AUS)

1981			8	

JONES, DC (WAL)

1933			22	

JONES, Ernest (ENG)

1911			24	
1913			18	
1914			21	

JONES, Gordon (USA)

1965				20

JONES, Grier (USA)

1975		18		
1976		28		30
1977				25
1978				16

JONES, JW [a] (ENG)

1952			27	

JONES, Jack (USA)

1952				Last 32

JONES, John (USA)

1898		8		
1901		12		
1908		5		

JONES, Robert Tyre (Bobby) [a] (USA)

1920		8		
1921		5		
1922		2		
1923		W		
1924		2		
1925		2		
1926		W	W	
1927		11	W	
1928		2		
1929		W		
1930			W	W
1934	13			
1935	25			
1937	29			
1938	16			
1942	28			

JONES, Rowland (ENG)

Yr	M AS	USO	BOP	PGA
1894			29	
1901			11	
1902			12	
1903			24	
1904			26	
1905			2	
1906			5	
1908			24	
1909			26	
1911			16	
1912			27	
1924			23	

JONES, Steve (US)

1988	30			9
1990	20	8	16	
1996		W		
1998	26			
2000	25	27		23
2001	27	30		

JORDAN, Pete (USA)

1995		21		
1996		27		

JOSEPH, Eddie (USA)

1947				Last 16

JOWLE, Frank (ENG)

1946			18	
1948			18	
1955			3	

JURADO, Jose (ARG)

1926			8	
1928			6	
1929			25	
1931			2	
1932		6		

KAISER, Bill (USA)

1935		21		

KANE, C (IRL)

1954			17	

KANE, Jim (USA)

1992		23		

KARLSSON, Robert (SWE)

1992			5	

KASE, Hideki (JAP)

1997		28		

KATAYAMA, Shingo (JAP)

Yr	MAS	USO	BOP	PGA
2001				4

KAY, James (SCO)

Yr	MAS	USO	BOP	PGA
1887			12	
1890			11	
1891			14	
1892			5	
1893			6	
1895			25	
1896			14	
1897			25	
1898			12	
1900			22	
1905			30	
1906			30	

KAY, Robert (USA)

Yr	MAS	USO	BOP	PGA
1956		24		Last 16

KEDDIE, James (USA)

Yr	MAS	USO	BOP	PGA
1886			29	

KEISER, Herman (USA)

Yr	MAS	USO	BOP	PGA
1940				Last 32
1941		26		
1942	22			
1946	W			
1947	24			
1948	10	14		
1949	11			
1950	14			
1957				Last 32

KELLER, Bob (USA)

Yr	MAS	USO	BOP	PGA
1961				29

KELLY, Jerry (USA)

Yr	MAS	USO	BOP	PGA
1999				26

KELLY, Paul (USA)

Yr	MAS	USO	BOP	PGA
1965				28

KENDALL, Skip (USA)

Yr	MAS	USO	BOP	PGA
1998				10
1999				21
2000				26

KENNEDY, Les (USA)

Yr	MAS	USO	BOP	PGA
1949		19		

KENNETT, Tom (USA)

Yr	MAS	USO	BOP	PGA
1920				Last 16

KENNETT, William (USA)

Yr	MAS	USO	BOP	PGA
1927			29	

KENNEY, Dan (USA)

Yr	MAS	USO	BOP	PGA
1914		20		
1922				Last 32

KENNY, Donald (SCO)

Yr	MAS	USO	BOP	PGA
1906			24	

KENNY, Joseph (USA)

Yr	MAS	USO	BOP	PGA
1930				Last 32

KENYON, Ernest WH (ENG)

Yr	MAS	USO	BOP	PGA
1931			28	
1932			22	
1935			11	
1938			28	
1939			9	
1949			29	

KEPLER, Bob (USA)

Yr	MAS	USO	BOP	PGA
1945				Last 16

KERRIGAN, Tom (USA)

Yr	MAS	USO	BOP	PGA
1914		20		
1915		10		
1916		29		QF
1919		26		Last 16
1920		23		
1921			3	Last 32
1922				QF
1924		19		
1925		18		QF
1936		11		

KERTES, Stanley (USA)

Yr	MAS	USO	BOP	PGA
1938		27		

KESSELRING, Gerald (CAN)

Yr	MAS	USO	BOP	PGA
1957		26		

KETTLEY, AF (ENG)

Yr	MAS	USO	BOP	PGA
1911			29	

KIDD, Harry (SCO)

Yr	MAS	USO	BOP	PGA
1907			25	

KIDD, Tom (SCO)

Yr	MAS	USO	BOP	PGA
1873			W	
1874			8	
1879			5	
1882			11	

KIDD, Willie (SCO/USA)

Yr	MAS	USO	BOP	PGA
1919				Last 32
1920		30		
1927				Last 32
1928				Last 32

Yr	M	AS	USO	BOP	PGA
KIMBALL, Richard (USA)					
1908		10			
KINCH, Henry (USA)					
1921				23	
1927				22	
KINDER, Joe (USA)					
1932					Last 16
KINDER, John (USA)					
1931		21			
1940					Last 32
KING, Alex (ENG)					
1963				11	
KING, Sam (ENG)					
1935				22	
1936				28	
1937				29	
1938				23	
1939				3	
1947				6	
1948				7	
1949				4	
1950				9	
1952				5	
1953				7	
1954				8	
1957				24	
1958				30	
1959				5	
KING Sr, Tom (ENG)					
1922				22	
KING Jr, Tom (ENG)					
1927				27	
KINGSLEY, EC [a] (USA)					
1948			11		
KINNELL, David (SCO)					
1898				6	
1903				18	
1906				11	
1908				5	
KINNELL, James (SCO)					
1895				23	
1897				20	
1898				15	
1899				7	
1901				7	
1902				6	
1903				15	

Yr	M	AS	USO	BOP	PGA
KINNELL, James (cont)					
1905				4	
1906				28	
1907				30	
1910				8	
KINSMAN, George (USA)					
1951			29		
KINSMAN, Robert (SCO)					
1876				11	
1879				18	
1882				29	
1885				27	
KIRK, Bob (SCO)					
1865				4	
1866				5	
1867				5	
1868				4	
1869				4	
1870				2	
1873				3	
1876				8	
1878				2	
KIRK, Eddie (USA)					
1940			23		QF
KIRK, James (SCO)					
1882				28	
KIRK, Walter (ENG)					
1896				24	
KIRKALDY, Andrew (SCO)					
1879				2	
1880				7	
1888				6	
1889				2	
1890				4	
1891				2	
1892				13	
1893				4	
1894				3	
1895				3	
1896				14	
1897				10	
1898				21	
1899				3	
1900				10	
1901				18	
1902				10	
1903				11	
1904				7	
1905				24	

Yr	M AS	USO	BOP	PGA
KIRKALDY, Hugh (SCO)				
1887			19	
1888			11	
1889			10	
1890			7	
1891			W	
1892			2	
1893			4	
1894			13	
1895			15	
KIRKALDY, John (SCO)				
1879			12	
1882			3	
1884			9	
1885			11	
1887			12	
1888			18	
1891			14	
1900			19	
KIRKWOOD Sr, Joe (AUS/USA)				
1921			6	
1922		13	19	
1923		12	4	QF
1924		22		
1925			14	
1926			22	
1927			4	
1929		19		Last 32
1930				SF
1931			25	Last 32
1932		23		Last 32
1933		9	14	
1934		12	4	
1936	29			
1942				Last 16
1946			8	
1947		23		
1948		28		
KIRKWOOD Jr, Joe (USA)				
1948		21		
1949	7			
1950	14	5		
1951	20	21		
1952	19			
1957				Last 32
KITE, Tom (USA)				
1972	27a	19a		
1974		8		
1975	10			
1976	5		5	13
1977	13			13
1978	18	20	2	
1979	5		30	

Yr	M AS	USO	BOP	PGA
KITE, Tom (cont)				
1980	6		27	20
1981	5	20		4
1982	5	29		9
1983	2	20	29	
1984	6		22	
1985		13	8	12
1986	2			26
1987	24			10
1988			20	4
1989	18	9	19	
1990	14			
1992		W	19	21
1993		14		
1994	4		8	9
1996			27	
1997	2		10	5
2000				18
2001		5		
KLEIN, Willie (USA)				
1923				Last 32
1926		9		
1927				Last 16
1928				Last 32
1931		23		
1933				Last 32
1936				Last 32
KNIGHT, Dick (USA)				
1959		10		
KNIGHT, G (ENG)				
1946			21	
KNIGHT, James (a) (SCO)				
1862			5	
1863			8	
KNIGHT, Reg (ENG)				
1953			24	
1957			30	
1959			23	
1961			14	
KNIPE, J (ENG)				
1949			14	
KNOX, Kenny (USA)				
1987		17		
1988				9
1991				4
KNUDSON, George (CAN)				
1964				28
1965	10	17		20
1966	6			
1968	28			
1969	2			25

KOCH, Gary (USA)

Yr	M AS	USO	BOP	PGA
1979				10
1982		6		
1983		24	14	
1985	16		11	
1986	16	15	6	
1987	22			
1988	25		4	
1989			30	

KOCSIS, Charles [a] (USA)

Yr	M AS	USO	BOP	PGA
1936		14		
1937		10		
1938	22			
1951		16		
1952	14			
1959	22			

KOCSIS, Emerick (USA)

Yr	M AS	USO	BOP	PGA
1929		30		
1939				QF

KONO, Takaaki (JAP) 1969 13

Yr	M AS	USO	BOP	PGA
1970	12			
1972	19			

KOONTZ, Charles (USA)

Yr	M AS	USO	BOP	PGA
1927				Last 32

KOVACH, Steve (USA)

Yr	M AS	USO	BOP	PGA
1946		15		

KOWAL, Matt (USA)

Yr	M AS	USO	BOP	PGA
1939		25		

KOZAK, Walter (USA)

Yr	M AS	USO	BOP	PGA
1930		28		

KRAFT, Greg (USA)

Yr	M AS	USO	BOP	PGA
1998				23

KRAK, Mike (USA)

Yr	M AS	USO	BOP	PGA
1956				Last 32
1957				Last 32

KRATZERT, Bill (USA)

Yr	M AS	USO	BOP	PGA
1977	24	19		25
1978	5	6		12
1979	17			
1980	19			
1985	14			

KRINGLE, Frank (USA)

Yr	M AS	USO	BOP	PGA
1945				Last 32

KROLL, Ed (USA)

Yr	M AS	USO	BOP	PGA
1964				23

KROLL, Ted (USA)

Yr	M AS	USO	BOP	PGA
1950		25		Last 16
1951	25			
1952	14	7		SF
1953	7	7		
1954		27		Last 16
1955				Last 32
1956		4		RU
1957				Last 16
1958	23			20
1959	14	11		25
1960	13	3		12
1961	24	27		4
1962	25			30
1964				23
1965		24		

KRUEGER, Alvin (USA)

Yr	M AS	USO	BOP	PGA
1934		14		
1935		6		Last 16
1936				Last 32
1937				Last 32
1938		27		Last 32

KUCHAR, Matt [a] (USA)

Yr	M AS	USO	BOP	PGA
1998	21	14		

KUNES, Gene (USA)

Yr	M AS	USO	BOP	PGA
1932				Last 16
1934				SF
1935	28	21		
1940		16		
1941	19	20		Last 32
1942	10			
1944				Last 32
1946	29	19		
1947		19		
1951				Last 16

KURAMOTO, Masahiro (JAP)

Yr	M AS	USO	BOP	PGA
1982			4	
1986			30	

KYLE, Alex [a] (SCO)

Yr	M AS	USO	BOP	PGA
1939			20	

KYLE, DH [a] (SCO)

Yr	M AS	USO	BOP	PGA
1921			26	

LACEY, Arthur (ENG)

Yr	M AS	USO	BOP	PGA
1930			24	
1931			8	
1932			7	
1935			22	
1936			8	
1937			7	
1938			17	
1949			20	

LACEY, Charles (USA)

Yr	M AS	USO	BOP	PGA
1930		7		SF
1932		23		Last 32
1938		22		

LAFFOON, Ky (USA)

Yr	M AS	USO	BOP	PGA
1933		26		
1934	18	23		Last 16
1935	28	28		Last 16
1936	6	5		Last 32
1937	5	20		SF
1938	27			Last 32
1939	22	9		Last 32
1940				Last 32
1942				Last 16
1945				QF
1946	4			
1947				QF
1948				Last 16

LAFITTE, L (FRA)

Yr	M AS	USO	BOP	PGA
1920			13	

LAGERBLADE, Herbert (USA)

Yr	M AS	USO	BOP	PGA
1916		15		
1919		26		

LAIDLAW, W (SCO)

Yr	M AS	USO	BOP	PGA
		17		
1935			7	
	1937			

LAIDLAY, Johnny [a] (SCO)

Yr	M AS	USO	BOP	PGA
1885			13	
1886			8	
1887			4	
1888			10	
1889			4	
1890			11	
1891			18	
1893			2	
1895			17	
1896			18	
1897			29	
1900			26	
1901			7	

LAMB, David [a] (ENG)

Yr	M AS	USO	BOP	PGA
1876			12	

LAMB, Henry [a] (ENG)

Yr	M AS	USO	BOP	PGA
1873			9	
1876			7	
1879			15	
1882			11	

LAMBERGER, Larry (USA)

Yr	M AS	USO	BOP	PGA
1946				Last 32

LAMBERT, John (SCO)

Yr	M AS	USO	BOP	PGA
1886			12	

LANCASTER, Neal (USA)

Yr	M AS	USO	BOP	PGA
1995		4		

LANDRUM, Ralph (USA)

Yr	M AS	USO	BOP	PGA
1983		8		

LANE, Barry (ENG)

Yr	M AS	USO	BOP	PGA
1991			17	
1993	16		13	
1994				25
1995			20	
2001			29	

LANGER, Bernhard (GER)

Yr	M AS	USO	BOP	PGA
1981			2	
1982			13	
1984			2	
1985	W		3	
1986	16	8	3	
1987	7	4	17	21
1988	9			
1989	26			
1990	7			
1991			9	
1992		23		
1993	W		3	
1994	25	23		25
1995			24	
1997	7			23
1999	11		18	
2000	28	11		
2001	6		3	

LANGHAM, Frank(lin) (USA)

Yr	M AS	USO	BOP	PGA
2000				7

LANNER, Mats (SWE)

Yr	M AS	USO	BOP	PGA
1992			28	

l'ANSON, John (ENG/USA)

Yr	M AS	USO	BOP	PGA
1896		22		

LARGE, Bill (ENG)

Yr	M AS	USO	BOP	PGA
1971			25	

LARGE, Harry (ENG)

Yr	M AS	USO	BOP	PGA
1930			21	

LARGE, William (ENG)

Yr	M AS	USO	BOP	PGA
1930			17	

LASSEN, EA (Bertie) [a] (ENG)

Yr	M AS	USO	BOP	PGA
1909			10	
1913			14	
1914			17	

Yr	M AS	USO	BOP	PGA
LAWRIE, Paul (SCO)				
1992			22	
1993			6	
1994			24	
1999			W	
LEACH, Bill (USA)				
1921				Last 32
1925				Last 32
1926				Last 16
1928	6			
LEACH, Fred (ENG)				
1911			27	
1912			17	
1914			21	
1920			29	
1921			6	
1924			23	
LEAVER, William (ENG)				
1903			8	
1906			12	
1908			13	
LEE, Robert (ENG)				
1985			25	
1986			21	
LEEDER, Malcolm (ENG)				
1963			20	
LEEDS, HC [a] (USA)				
1898		8		
LEES, Arthur (ENG)				
1946			18	
1947			6	
1948			11	
1949			6	
1950			7	
1952			9	
1953			13	
LEES, Walter (ENG)				
1949			17	
LeGRANGE, Cobie (RSA)				
1965			17	
1969			11	
LEHMAN, Tom (USA)				
1993	3	19		
1994	2		24	
1995		3		
1996	18	2	W	14
1997	12	3	24	10
1998		5		29

Yr	M AS	USO	BOP	PGA
LEHMAN, Tom (cont)				
1999		28		
2000	6	23	4	
2001	18	24		
LEITCH, D [a] (SCO)				
1883			20	
1888			26	
1890			13	
LEITCH, Dan (USA)				
1899		22		
LEMA, Tony (USA)				
1963	2	5		13
1964	9	20	W	9
1965	21	8	5	
1966	22	4	30	
LEONARD, Justin (USA)				
1995				8
1996	27			5
1997	7		W	2
1998	8			
1999	18	15	2	
2000	28	16		
2001	27			10
LEONARD, Paul (IRL)				
1975			12	
LEONARD, Stan (CAN)				
1955	8			
1956	24			
1957	11			
1958	4			
1959	4			
1960	9			
1961	15			
1962		25		
1963	21			
LEPRE, Charles (USA)				
1956				Last 32
LESLIE, R (USA)				
1897		21		
LESTER, Eric (ENG)				
1953			17	
1954			20	
1956			22	
1957			15	
1958			8	
1961			26	
LEVI, Wayne (USA)				
1976		28		

LEVI, Wayne (cont)

Yr	MAS	USO	BOP	PGA
1979		25		
1981	25			
1982	24			
1983	12			
1984	11			
1985	18			18
1986				30
1991				16
1993		25		

LEWIS, Alf (ENG)

Yr	MAS	USO	BOP	PGA
1901			18	

LEWIS, Hugh (ENG)

Yr	MAS	USO	BOP	PGA
1963			14	

LEWIS, JL (John) (USA)

Yr	MAS	USO	BOP	PGA
1999				21
2001		30		

LICHARDUS, Milton (Babe) (USA)

Yr	MAS	USO	BOP	PGA
1956				Last 32
1959				17

LICKLITER, Frank (USA)

Yr	MAS	USO	BOP	PGA
1998		18		4

LIETZKE, Bruce (USA)

Yr	MAS	USO	BOP	PGA
1977	28	19		15
1978		20		
1979	6			16
1980			19	30
1981	11	17	6	4
1982	20			16
1983				6
1985	6			18
1986				5
1987				28
1991				2
1992	13			
1995				23

LINNARS, Dick (USA)

Yr	MAS	USO	BOP	PGA
1926				Last 16

LISTER, John (USA)

Yr	MAS	USO	BOP	PGA
1898		14		

LISTER, John (NZL)

Yr	MAS	USO	BOP	PGA
1971			25	
1977		27		

LITTLE, Lawson (USA)

Yr	MAS	USO	BOP	PGA
1934		25a		
1935	6a		4a	
1936	20			
1937	19			

LITTLE, Lawson (cont)

Yr	MAS	USO	BOP	PGA
1938	10			
1939	3			
1940	19	W		
1941	8	17		
1942	7			
1946	21	10	10	Last 32
1947	14			
1949	23			
1950	9			
1951	6			Last 32
1956	28			

LITTLER, Gene (USA)

Yr	MAS	USO	BOP	PGA
1954	22	2		
1955	22	15		
1956	12			
1958		4		
1959	8	11		10
1960				18
1961	15	W		5
1962	4	8		23
1963	24	21		
1964	13	11		
1965	6	8		28
1966				3
1967	26			7
1968				30
1969	8			
1970	2	12		4
1971	4			
1973	17			
1974			18	28
1975	22			7
1976	12			22
1977	8			2
1978	24			
1979	10			16
1982		22		

LIVIE, David (USA)

Yr	MAS	USO	BOP	PGA
1912		30		

LLOYD, Joe (ENG/USA)

Yr	MAS	USO	BOP	PGA
1893			17	
1894			17	
1896		3		
1897		W	20	
1898		4		
1901		20		
1903		24		
1905		16		

LOCKE, AD (Arthur D'Arcy - Bobby) (RSA)

Yr	MAS	USO	BOP	PGA
1936			8a	
1937			17a	
1938			10	
1939			9	

LOCKE, AD (cont)

Yr	M AS	USO	BOP	PGA
1946			2	
1947	14	3		
1948	10	4		
1949	13	4	W	
1950			W	
1951		3	6	
1952	21		W	
1953		14	8	
1954		5	2	
1955		4		
1957			W	
1958			16	
1959			29	

LOCKHART, Gordon (SCO)

Yr	M AS	USO	BOP	PGA
1923			12	

LOCKWOOD, AG [a] (USA)

Yr	M AS	USO	BOP	PGA
1901		17		
1905		11		

LOEFFLER, Emil (NED/USA)

Yr	M AS	USO	BOP	PGA
1921		10		Last 32
1922				QF

LOMAS, Jonathan (ENG)

Yr	M AS	USO	BOP	PGA
1994			11	

LONARD, Peter (AUS)

Yr	M AS	USO	BOP	PGA
1997			24	

LONG, Harold (USA)

Yr	M AS	USO	BOP	PGA
1927				Last 32

LONGMUIR, Bill (SCO)

Yr	M AS	USO	BOP	PGA
1979			30	

LONGWORTH, Ted (USA)

Yr	M AS	USO	BOP	PGA
1929		23		
1932				Last 32
1944				Last 32

LONIE, JC (SCO)

Yr	M AS	USO	BOP	PGA
1914			29	

LoPRESTI, Tom (USA)

Yr	M AS	USO	BOP	PGA
1936				Last 32

LOOS, Eddie (USA)

Yr	M AS	USO	BOP	PGA
1919				Last 32
1920		17		Last 32
1921		12		
1922		15		
1924		10		
1927		11		
1934		25		Last 32
1935				Last 32

LOTT, Lyn (USA)

Yr	M AS	USO	BOP	PGA
1976		8		
1977		7		25
1982		12		

LOTZ, Dick (USA)

Yr	M AS	USO	BOP	PGA
1970	18			8
1971	24	24		

LOVE Jr, Davis (USA)

Yr	M AS	USO	BOP	PGA
1963		14		
1969			6	

LOVE III, Davis (USA)

Yr	M AS	USO	BOP	PGA
1989			23	17
1991		11		
1992	25			
1994		28		
1995	2	4		
1996	7	2		
1997	7	16	10	W
1998		8		7
1999	2	12	7	
2000	7		11	9
2001		7	21	

LOVEKIN, WR (USA)

Yr	M AS	USO	BOP	PGA
1906		22		

LOVING, Ben (USA)

Yr	M AS	USO	BOP	PGA
1942				Last 32

LOVING, Elmer (USA)

Yr	M AS	USO	BOP	PGA
1913		11		

LOW Sr, George (SCO)

Yr	M AS	USO	BOP	PGA
1878			18	
1882			13	

LOW Jr, George (SCO/USA)

Yr	M AS	USO	BOP	PGA
1899		2		
1900		6		
1901		9		
1902		12		
1904		23		
1905		15		
1906		11		
1907		5		
1908		12		
1909		27		
1910		12		
1911		15		
1915		7		

LOW, GW (George) (SCO)

Yr	M AS	USO	BOP	PGA
1962			29	

Yr	M AS	USO	BOP	PGA
LOWERY, Steve (USA)				
1994		16		
1995				8
2001		24		3
LU, CS (TPE)				
1983			29	
LU, Liang-Huan (TPE)				
1964			24	
1971			2	
1974			5	
LUCAS, PB (Laddie) [a] (ENG)				
1935			22	
LUMSDEN, A (ENG)				
1894			30	
LUNN, Bob (USA)				
1968		24		30
1969				21
1970	10	3		
1971		27		9
LUTHER, Ted (USA)				
1934		12		
1935		26		
LYE, Mark (USA)				
1980		26		
1984	6			
1989		13		
LYLE, Alexander (Sandy) (SCO)				
1979			19	
1980			12	
1981	28		14	
1982			8	
1984			14	
1985	25		W	
1986	11		30	
1987	17		17	
1988	W	25	7	
1990			16	
1991		16		16
1992			12	
1993	21			
1998			19	
LYNCH, Levi (USA)				
1935				Last 16
LYONS, Denny (USA)				
1973		20		12

Yr	M AS	USO	BOP	PGA
LYONS, Toby (USA)				
1953		30		
1954				Last 32
1956				Last 16
McANDREWS, RG (SCO/USA)				
1897		21		
1898		8		
1900		23		
M'CACHNIE, G (SCO)				
1874			10	
McBEE, Rives (USA)				
1966		13		
McCALLISTER, Blaine (USA)				
1988				25
1989				17
1990				19
1993		19		
McCALLISTER, Bob (USA)				
1962				11
1963		21		
1965				8
McCARRON, Scott (USA)				
1996	10			
1997	30	10		10
1998	16			
1999	18			
McCOLL, Bill (SCO)				
1980			23	
McCULLOCH, Duncan (SCO)				
1925			20	
1927			26	
1928			18	
1930			30	
1931			28	
McCULLOUGH, Mike (USA)				
1977		10		
1978		12		
1983			29	
McCUMBER, Mark (USA)				
1979				28
1984		16	8	
1985	18			
1986	11	8		
1987	12			5
1988	24			
1989		2		
1991	17			

	Yr	M	AS	USO	BOP	PGA
McCUMBER, Mark (cont)	1992			13		
	1994					19
	1995			13		
	1996				2	
McDEEVER, Tom (SCO/USA)						
	1904			29		
McDERMOTT, Fred (USA)						
	1928					Last 32
McDERMOTT, John (USA)						
	1910			2		
	1911			W		
	1912			W		
	1913			8	5	
	1914			9		
MacDONALD, Bob (USA)						
	1913			28		
	1915			3		
	1916			8		Last 16
	1919			29		SF
	1920			10		QF
	1922			13		
	1925			15		
	1926			27		
	1927			29		
	1928					Last 16
	1932			27		
MacDONALD, Charles [a] (SCO/USA)	1897			11		
	1900			30		
MacDONALD, Ian (ENG)						
	1963				14	
MacDONALD, John (ENG)						
	1960				21	
	1963				20	
	1964				19	
MacDONALD, Keith (ENG)						
	1962				27	
	1966				26	
	1968				24	
McDONALD, Robert (USA)						
	1911			29		
MacDOWALL, James (SCO)						
	1926				28	
	1934				16	
McELLIGOTT, Ed (USA)						
	1928					Last 32

	Yr	M	AS	USO	BOP	PGA
McEVOY, Peter [a] (ENG)						
	1979				17	
McEWAN, David (SCO)						
	1887				27	
	1895				25	
	1896				18	
	1901				29	
	1906				19	
	1907				25	
McEWAN, Douglas (SCO)						
	1892				25	
	1895				27	
McEWAN Sr, Peter (SCO)						
	1862				6	
McEWAN Jr, Peter (SCO)						
	1896				11	
	1897				14	
	1898				17	
	1900				21	
McEWAN, William (SCO)						
	1890				9	
	1892				19	
	1893				28	
	1899				24	
	1902				25	
MacFARLANE, Willie (SCO/USA)	1912			18		
	1916					SF
	1920			8		Last 32
	1923					QF
	1924					Last 16
	1925			W		
	1926			20		
	1927			18		
	1928			14		Last 16
	1929			26		
	1931					Last 16
	1934	6				
	1937			19		Last 32
MacFIE, Allan [a] (SCO)						
	1887				22	
	1888				18	
McGEE, Jerry (USA)						
	1971			13		22
	1972	5				29
	1974			30		
	1976	15				8
	1977	28		19		6
	1978	11		27		
	1979					12

	Yr	M AS	USO	BOP	PGA
McGINLEY, Paul (IRL)					
	1996			14	
	2000			20	
	2001				22
McGOVERN, Jim (USA)					
	1993				22
	1994	5	13		
McGOWAN, Pat (USA)					
	1978		27		
	1980		16		
	1983		13		4
McHALE Jr, James [a] (USA)					
	1947		23		
	1949		27		
	1950			17	
	1953		26		
McINTOSH, D (SCO/USA)					
	1906		22		
McINTOSH, Gregor (SCO)					
	1949			20	
McINTYRE, Neal (USA)					
	1926				Last 16
	1929				Last 32
	1932				Last 32
McKAY, James (SCO)					
	1890			29	
McKENNA, Charles (USA)					
	1927				Last 32
McKENNA, John (IRL)					
	1951			28	
MacKENZIE, Fred (SCO/USA)					
	1904		3		
	1905		16		
	1910			16	
MacKENZIE, JH (SCO)					
	1923			8	
MacKENZIE, Malcolm (ENG)					
	1992			5	
	1993			27	
MacKENZIE, W Willis [a] (SCO)					
	1929			25	
MACKEY Jr, Lee (USA)					
	1950		25		

	Yr	M AS	USO	BOP	PGA
MACKIE, Isaac (USA)					
	1901		16		
	1903		13		
	1905		29		
	1907		22		
	1908		23		
	1909		4		
	1919		13		
	1920				Last 32
MACKIE, John (USA)					
	1902		29		
McCLELLAND, Doug (ENG)					
	1972			23	
	1973			14	
	1974			28	
MACKRELL, JN (USA)					
	1896		16		
M'LEAN, Jack [a] (SCO)					
	1933			18	
	1934			16	
	1937			26	
	1938			22	
McLEAN, George (SCO/USA)					
	1916		19		Last 16
	1919		5		SF
	1920		30		SF
	1921			26	QF
	1923				SF
	1926		16		
McLENDON, Mac (USA)					
	1968		22		
	1975				25
	1978	29			
McLEOD, Fred (SCO/USA)					
	1903		26		
	1904		29		
	1905		19		
	1907		5		
	1908		W		
	1909		13		
	1910		4		
	1911		4		
	1912		13		
	1914		3		
	1915		8		
	1916		24		
	1919		8		RU
	1920		13		
	1921		2		QF
	1923				QF

Yr	M AS	USO	BOP	PGA
McLEOD, Fred (cont)				
1924				Last 32
1926			7	Last 32
McMINN, William (SCO)				
1931			28	
1949			20	
MACNAMARA, TL (IRL)				
1913			25	
McNAMARA, Frank (USA)				
1920		14		
McNAMARA, Tom (USA)				
1905		20		
1907		14		
1908		10		
1909		2		
1910		5		
1911		29		
1912		2		
1913		16		
1914		13		
1915		2		
1916		15		Last 32
1919		3		Last 16
McNEILL, Hughie (IRL)				
1912			15	
1913			18	
McNICKLE, Artie (USA)				
1978		16		
1979	17			28
1980				30
McNULTY, Mark (ZIM)				
1980			23	
1981			23	
1987			11	
1988	16	17	28	17
1989			11	
1990			2	8
1991				27
1992			28	
1993			14	
1994			11	15
1996			14	
1997		28		
2000			11	
McNULTY, Robert (USA)				
1916				Last 32
McSPADEN, Harold (USA)				
1934	7			
1935	19			

Yr	M AS	USO	BOP	PGA
McSPADEN, Harold (cont)				
1936	15	18		QF
1937		20		RU
1938	16	16		Last 32
1939	12	9		
1940	17	12		SF
1941	9	7		Last 16
1942	18			Last 16
1944				QF
1945				Last 32
1946	29			SF
1947	4			
1948		12		
McWATT, Thomas (SCO)				
1886			12	
MADISON, Les (USA)				
1936				Last 32
MAGEE, Andrew (USA)				
1991	7			13
1992	19	17	5	
1998				21
MAGEE, Jerry (USA)				
1958		19		
MAGGERT, Jeff (USA)				
1992				6
1993	21			
1994		9	24	
1995		4		3
1996	7		5	
1997		4		3
1998	23	7		
1999		7	30	
2001	20			
MAGUIRE, Willie (USA)				
1926				Last 32
MAHAFFEY, John (USA)				
1973		29		30
1974		12		9
1975		2	10	28
1976		4		
1978				W
1980		28		15
1981	8			
1982		22		
1984		30		20
1985	14			23
1986			30	
1987		24		
1988				15
MAHON, PJ (IRL)				
1938			20	

Yr	M AS	USO	BOP	PGA
MAIR, James [a] (SCO)				
1890			26	
MAIDEN, James (USA)				
1905		26		
1906		3		
1909		27		
MAKALENA, Ted (USA)				
1963		27		
1964		23		
MALLORY, Leo (USA)				
1937		28		
MALTBIE, Roger (USA)				
1976	9			
1977			26	
1983				14
1985				28
1986	23			
1987	4			28
MANERO, Tony (USA)				
1927				Last 16
1928				Last 32
1929				QF
1931		19		
1933		29		
1935				Last 16
1936		W		QF
1937	13			SF
1938	27			Last 32
1939	26			Last 32
1940	29			
1944				Last 16
MANGRUM, Lloyd (USA)				
1940	2	5		
1941	9	10		SF
1942				Last 16
1946	16	W		
1947	8	23		QF
1948	4	21		Last 32
1949	2	14		SF
1950	6	2		QF
1951	3	4		Last 16
1952	6	10		Last 32
1953	2	3	24	
1954	4	3		
1955	7			
1956	4			
1957	28			
1960		23		
MANGRUM, Ray (USA)				
1935	13	4		Last 32

Yr	M AS	USO	BOP	PGA
MANGRUM, Ray (cont)	1936	6	11		Last 32

Yr	M AS	USO	BOP	PGA
MANGRUM, Ray (cont)				
1936	6	11		Last 32
1937	24	14		
1938		27		Last 16
1939				Last 32
1940		27		Last 32
1941	28			
MANSFIELD, James [a] (SCO)				
1882			7	
MANTON, HR (ENG)				
1936			28	
MANZIE, R (SCO)				
1873			16	
MARCHBANK, Brian (SCO)				
1986			8	
1989			30	
MARR, Dave (USA)				
1959		15		
1960		17		10
1961				22
1962	2			
1963		21		
1965				W
1966		4	8	18
1967	16	9		
1968	20			
1969		10		
1970		30		
1972			11	
MARSH, Graham (AUS)				
1970			25	
1975	22		6	
1976	9		17	
1977			15	
1978				7
1979	28	16	7	16
1981			19	
1982			25	
1983			4	
1984			9	
1985			20	
1987			11	
MARSHALL, William (USA)				
1897		11		
1906		22		
MARSTON, Max [a] (USA)				
1915		19		
MARTI, Elroy (USA)				
1954				Last 16

MARTI, Fred (USA)	Yr	MAS	USO	BOP	PGA
	1969				25
	1971				9

MARTIN, Bob (SCO)

Yr	MAS	USO	BOP	PGA
1873			10	
1874			4	
1875			2	
1876			W	
1878			4	
1879			21	
1881			4	
1882			3	
1885			W	
1887			2	
1888			16	

MARTIN, Casey (USA)

Yr	MAS	USO	BOP	PGA
1998				23

MARTIN, Doug (USA)

Yr	MAS	USO	BOP	PGA
1997				23

MARTIN, Earl (USA)

Yr	MAS	USO	BOP	PGA
1947				Last 32

MARTIN, Hutt (USA)

Yr	MAS	USO	BOP	PGA
1923		29		

MARTIN, Iverson (USA)

Yr	MAS	USO	BOP	PGA
1953				Last 32

MARTIN, Jimmy (IRL)

Yr	MAS	USO	BOP	PGA
1960			28	
1962			16	
1964			24	

MARTIN, Miguel Angel (ESP)

Yr	MAS	USO	BOP	PGA
1989			30	
1999			24	

MARTINDALE, Bill (USA)

Yr	MAS	USO	BOP	PGA
1966				15

MARTUCCI, Louis (USA)

Yr	MAS	USO	BOP	PGA
1919				Last 32

MARUSIC, Milon (USA)

Yr	MAS	USO	BOP	PGA
1951				Last 32
1952		15		Last 16
1957				Last 16
1961		29		

MARUYAMA, Shigeki (JAP)

Yr	MAS	USO	BOP	PGA
1996			14	
1997			10	23
1998			29	
2001				22

MASON, Carl (ENG)

Yr	MAS	USO	BOP	PGA
1978			24	
1980			4	
1996			22	

MASON, George (SCO)

Yr	MAS	USO	BOP	PGA
1891			22	

MASSENGALE, Don (USA)

Yr	MAS	USO	BOP	PGA
1966				28
1967				2
1972		15		
1974				24
1976				22

MASSENGALE, Rik (USA)

Yr	MAS	USO	BOP	PGA
1974		30		
1975		14		
1976	23			30
1977	3		26	
1981		26		

MASSY, Arnaud (FRA)

Yr	MAS	USO	BOP	PGA
1902			10	
1905			5	
1906			6	
1907			W	
1908			9	
1910			22	
1911			2	
1912			10	
1913			7	
1914			10	
1920			29	
1921			6	

MATTHEWS, Alf (ENG)

Yr	MAS	USO	BOP	PGA
1904			23	
1906			28	
1907			17	

MATTIACE, Len (USA)

Yr	MAS	USO	BOP	PGA
1997		24		
1999			30	

MAXWELL, Billy (USA)

Yr	MAS	USO	BOP	PGA
1955	18	27		
1956		12		
1957		8		
1958	9	27		25
1959	8	26		11
1960	25			24
1961		22		27
1962	5	8		
1963	15	5		5
1964	18			13
1965	26	14		
1970				10

MAXWELL, Robert [a] (SCO)

Yr	M	AS	USO	BOP	PGA
1900				7	
1902			4		
1903				13	
1904				10	
1906				7	
1909				13	

MAY, Bob (USA)

Yr	M	AS	USO	BOP	PGA
2000			23	11	2
2001			30		

MAY, Dick (ENG)

Yr	M	AS	USO	BOP	PGA
1925				24	

MAYER, Dick (USA)

Yr	M	AS	USO	BOP	PGA
1950			12		
1951	25				
1952			28		
1953	16				
1954	29		3		
1955	10				
1957			W		QF
1958			23		14
1959	4				
1961	19				
1963	15				

MAYFAIR, Billy (USA)

Yr	M	AS	USO	BOP	PGA
1988			25a		
1990					5
1991	12				
1992			23		
1993					28
1995					23
1998					7
1999			10		
2001				3	

MAYFIELD, Shelley (USA)

Yr	M	AS	USO	BOP	PGA
1954			6		QF
1955			12		SF
1956	8		29		Last 32
1961					22
1962					30

MAYO, Charles (ENG/USA)

Yr	M	AS	USO	BOP	PGA
1907				17	
1908				30	
1911				16	
1912				11	
1913				27	
1920					Last 16
1925			26		

MEARNS, Bob (SCO)

Yr	M	AS	USO	BOP	PGA
1890				23	

MEARNS, Bob (cont)

Yr	M	AS	USO	BOP	PGA
1891				14	
1893				23	

MEDIATE, Rocco (USA)

Yr	M	AS	USO	BOP	PGA
1991	22				16
1993			25		
1996			18		
1999	27				
2001	15				

MEEHAN, James (USA)

Yr	M	AS	USO	BOP	PGA
1923					Last 32

MEHLHORN, Bill (USA)

Yr	M	AS	USO	BOP	PGA
1919					Last 32
1920			27		Last 16
1922			4	16	
1923			8		
1924			3		Last 32
1925			15		RU
1926			3	8	
1927			5		Last 32
1928				9	Last 32
1929					Last 16
1930			9		Last 32
1931			4		Last 16
1934					Last 32
1936					SF

MEISTER Jr, Edward [a] (USA)

Yr	M	AS	USO	BOP	PGA
1962			25		

MELNYK, Steve (USA)

Yr	M	AS	USO	BOP	PGA
1971	24				
1973	12				
1975			29		17
1977			16		

MENGERT, Al (USA)

Yr	M	AS	USO	BOP	PGA
1953	23		21		
1954			13		
1955			16		
1956	24				
1957	21				
1958	9				
1961					29
1966			26		
1968					20
1970					18

MERCER, JH (USA)

Yr	M	AS	USO	BOP	PGA
1898			23		

METZ, Dick (USA)

Yr	M	AS	USO	BOP	PGA
1933					Last 32
1934					QF
1935			10		Last 32

Yr	MAS	USO	BOP	PGA
METZ, Dick (cont)				
1936	27	28		Last 32
1938	8	2		Last 16
1939		7		SF
1940	21	9		Last 16
1941	19	10		
1942				Last 32
1946		8		Last 32
1947	8	13		Last 16
1948	10			
1949	30			
1950		20		Last 32
1952		6		
1953	23	7		
1954		29		
1958		7		
MICKELSON, Phil (USA)				
1990		29a		
1993				6
1994				3
1995	7	4		
1996	3			8
1997			24	29
1998	12	10		
1999	6	2		
2000	7	16	11	9
2001	3	7	30	2
MIDDLECOFF, Cary (USA)				
1946	12a			
1947	29			
1948	2	21		
1949	23	W		
1950	7	10		
1951	12	24		
1952	11	24		QF
1953	27			Last 32
1954	9	11		SF
1955	W	21		RU
1956	3	W		
1957		2	14	
1958	6	27		20
1959	2	19		8
1960				29
1961				11
1962	29			15
MIGUEL, Angel (ESP)				
1956			13	
1957			4	
1958			29	
1959	25			
1960			16	
1961			14	
1964			8	

Yr	MAS	USO	BOP	PGA
MIGUEL, Sebastian (ESP)				
1957			15	
1958			26	
1960			26	
1961			14	
1962			12	
1963			9	
1965			8	
1966			8	
1967			6	
1968			21	
MILLAR, J (SCO)				
1870			12	
MILLER, Allen (USA)				
1975	15			
MILLER, David (ENG)				
1961			30	
MILLER, G [a] (SCO)				
1883			19	
MILLER, James [a] (SCO)				
1863			9	
MILLER, Johnny (USA)				
1966		8a		
1970		18		12
1971	2	5		20
1972		7	15	20
1973	6	W	2	18
1974	15		10	
1975	2		3	
1976	23	10	W	
1977		27	9	11
1978		6		
1981	2	23		
1982			22	
1983	12			30
1984		4		
1985	25	8		
1986	28			
MILLER, Lindy [a] (USA)				
1978	16			
MILLER, Massie (USA)				
1929		21		
MILLER, William (SCO)				
1865			9	
MILLS, Peter (ENG)				
1959			23	
1960			20	
1967			22	

Yr	M AS	USO	BOP	PGA
MILNE, John (SCO)				
1903			24	
MINER, RS (USA)				
1922				Last 16
1923				Last 32
MITCHELL, Abe (ENG)				
1914			4	
1920			4	
1921			13	
1922		17	18	
1923			8	
1925			5	
1926			5	
1928			21	
1929			4	
1930			13	
1931			11	
1932			10	
1933			7	
MITCHELL, Bobby (USA)				
1969		25		
1970		12		
1971	22	27		
1972	2	21		
1974		23		
MITCHELL-INNES, G [a] (SCO)				
1869			8	
MITCHELL, Joe (USA)				
1900		23		
1914		13		
1915		26		
1916		21		Last 16
MITCHELL, Peter (ENG)				
1992			22	
1995			20	
1996			27	
MITCHELL, William [a] (SCO)				
1862			6	
1863			13	
MIZE, Larry (USA)				
1984	11			6
1985				23
1986	16	24		
1987	W	4	26	
1988		12		
1989	26		19	17
1990	14	14		12
1991	17			
1992	6			

Yr	M AS	USO	BOP	PGA
MIZE, Larry (cont)				
1993	21		27	
1994	3		11	15
1996	23			8
1997	30			
1999	23			
2000	25			
MIZUMAKI, Yoshinori (JAP)				
1993			27	
MOE, Donald [a] (USA)				
1930			15	
MOE, Kristen (USA)				
1985			25	
MOFFAT, William [a] (SCO)				
1863			14	
MOFFITT, Ralph (ENG)				
1960			21	
1961			26	
1962			11	
1964			13	
MOLDER, Bryce [a] (USA)				
2001		30		
MONAGHAN, A (SCO)				
1887			17	
MONK, Arthur (ENG)				
1922			27	
MONTGOMERIE, Colin (SCO)				
1991			26	
1992		3		
1994		2	8	
1995	17	28		2
1996		10		
1997	30	2	24	13
1998	8	18		
1999	11	15	15	6
2000	19		26	
2001			13	
MONTI, Eric (USA)				
1949		11		
1950	30			
1955		28		
1958				20
1961		6		
1965		21		
MOODY, Orville (USA)				
1969		W	16	8
1970	18			

Yr	M	AS	USO	BOP	PGA
MOODY, Orville (cont)					
1971	20		27		
1972			15		
1973					30
1978				11	
1979				19	
MOORE, Eric (RSA)					
1950				5	
1956				25	
1958				16	
MOORE, Frank (USA)					
1936			14		
1938			7		Last 32
1939	22				
1946					QF
1948			28		Last 32
1949					Last 32
MOORE, James (SCO)					
1878				21	
MORAN, Michael (IRL)					
1909				21	
1910				14	
1911				21	
1912				15	
1913				3	
1914				25	
MORE, WD (ENG)					
1891				5	
1892				21	
MORELAND, Gus [a] (USA)					
1933			7		
MORGAN, Gil (USA)					
1975					17
1976					8
1977					15
1978	18				4
1979					28
1980	19		16	10	3
1981	21				19
1982			22		22
1983	8		3		
1984	3		21	22	
1985			23		28
1987					21
1990					3
1991					16
1992			13		21
1993				14	
MORGAN, John (ENG)					
1974				13	
1978				29	

Yr	M	AS	USO	BOP	PGA
MORLEY, Mike (USA)					
1976			14		15
1977			27		
1980			8		
MORRIS, JOF (James Ogilvy Fairlie) (SCO)					
1873				12	
1874				10	
1878				3	
1879				8	
1884				13	
1885				9	
1886				11	
1888				23	
MORRIS, Jack (SCO)					
1873				17	
1878				16	
1887				25	
MORRIS, Johnny (USA)					
1941			26		
MORRIS Sr, Tom (SCO)					
1860				2	
1861				W	
1862				W	
1863				2	
1864				W	
1865				5	
1866				4	
1867				W	
1868				6	
1869				2	
1870				4	
1872				4	
1873				7	
1874				18	
1876				4	
1878				11	
1879				18	
1881				5	
1883				10	
1884				13	
1885				29	
1886				27	
1888				27	
MORRIS Jr, Tom (SCO)					
1866				4	
1867				4	
1868				W	
1869				W	
1870				W	
1872				W	
1873				3	
1874				2	

MORRISON, Fred (USA)

Yr	MAS	USO	BOP	PGA
1929				Last 16
1932		14		

MORRISON, Hugh (SCO)

Yr	MAS	USO	BOP	PGA
1875			8	

MORSE, John (USA)

Yr	MAS	USO	BOP	PGA
1996		4		

MOSEL, Stan [a] (USA)

Yr	MAS	USO	BOP	PGA
1952		28		

MOSES, JR (ENG)

Yr	MAS	USO	BOP	PGA
1959			23	

MOTHERSOLE, Charles (USA)

Yr	MAS	USO	BOP	PGA
1921		22		Last 16
1923		16		

MOULAND, Mark (WAL)

Yr	MAS	USO	BOP	PGA
1991			17	

MOWRY, Larry (USA)

Yr	MAS	USO	BOP	PGA
1969				11

MOZEL, Joe (USA)

Yr	MAS	USO	BOP	PGA
1944				Last 32

MUDD, Jodie (USA)

Yr	MAS	USO	BOP	PGA
1982	20a			
1986		15		
1987	4	17		
1989	7		5	
1990	30		4	
1991	7	26	5	
1992			28	

MUNDAY, Rod (USA)

Yr	MAS	USO	BOP	PGA
1939				QF
1942				Last 32
1950				Last 32
1951				Last 32

MUNGER, Jack [a] (USA)

Yr	MAS	USO	BOP	PGA
1936		28		

MUNN, LO [a] (ENG)

Yr	MAS	USO	BOP	PGA
1932			29	

MUNRO, Jack (USA)

Yr	MAS	USO	BOP	PGA
1914		25		

MURE FERGUSSON, R [a] (SCO)

Yr	MAS	USO	BOP	PGA
1891			4	

MURE FERGUSSON, S [a] (SCO)

Yr	MAS	USO	BOP	PGA
1869			3	
1873			15	
1885			24	
1892			15	
1893			15	
1894			18	
1897			12	
1901			15	

MURPHY, Bob (USA)

Yr	MAS	USO	BOP	PGA
1966		15a		
1967		23a		
1969		5		
1970	23			2
1971	13			
1973		20		
1975		3		25
1976	28			
1977				25
1979		25		
1980	20			
1981	18			

MURPHY, Eddie (USA)

Yr	MAS	USO	BOP	PGA
1926		27		
1927				Last 32

MURRAY, A (RSA)

Yr	MAS	USO	BOP	PGA
1964			19	

MURRAY, AH (USA)

Yr	MAS	USO	BOP	PGA
1912		26		

MURRAY, Charles (SCO/CAN)

Yr	MAS	USO	BOP	PGA
1904		11		
1905		29		
1909		30		
1912		9		
1913		21		
1921		21		

MURRAY, D (IRL)

Yr	MAS	USO	BOP	PGA
1927			29	

MURRAY, Walter (USA)

Yr	MAS	USO	BOP	PGA
1931				Last 16

MUSCROFT, Hedley (ENG)

Yr	MAS	USO	BOP	PGA
1967			18	
1969			28	

MYLES, Reggie (USA)

Yr	MAS	USO	BOP	PGA
1932				Last 16
1933				Last 32
1947				Last 16
1951				QF

	Yr	M AS	USO	BOP	PGA
NABHOLTZ, Larry (USA)					
	1924				SF
	1926				Last 32
	1927		24		
	1929				Last 16
NAGLE, Kel (AUS)					
	1951			19	
	1955			20	
	1960			W	
	1961		17	5	
	1962			2	
	1963			4	
	1964	21			
	1965	15	2	5	20
	1966			4	
	1967		9	22	
	1968	30		13	
	1969			9	
	1970		30		
	1971			11	
NAKAJIMA, Tommy (JAP)					
	1978			17	
	1983	16	26		
	1984				10
	1986	8		8	
	1987		9		
	1988				3
	1991	10			
	1992				21
NAKAMURA, Tohru (JAP)					
	1979			24	
	1982			20	
	1983			29	
NARY, Bill (USA)					
	1947		13		
	1950		8		
	1951	25			
	1953		17		QF
	1954				Last 32
	1955				Last 32
NEAVES, Charles (SCO)					
	1901			22	
NELSON, Al (USA)					
	1946				Last 32
NELSON, Byron (USA)					
	1932				Last 32
	1935	9			
	1936	13			
	1937	W	20	5	QF
	1938	5	5		QF

	Yr	M AS	USO	BOP	PGA
NELSON, Byron (USA) (cont)	1939	7	W		RU
	1940	3	5		W
	1941	2	17		RU
	1942	W			SF
	1944				RU
	1945				W
	1946	7	2		QF
	1947	2			
	1948	8			
	1949	8			
	1950	4			
	1951	8			
	1952	24			
	1953	29			
	1954	12			
	1955	10	28		
	1957	16			
	1958	20			
	1965	15			
NELSON, CP (USA)					
	1911		14		
	1914		28		
NELSON, Gunnar (USA)					
	1926				Last 32
	1932				Last 32
NELSON, Larry (USA)					
	1976		21		
	1978				12
	1979		4		28
	1980	6		12	
	1981		20		W
	1982	7	19		
	1983		W		
	1984	5			
	1985				23
	1987				W
	1988			13	
	1989		13		
	1990		14		
	1991		3		
	1992				28
NELSON, Wallie (USA)					
	1920				Last 32
NETTLEBLADT, Harry (USA)					
	1938				Last 32
	1940				Last 32
	1942				Last 32
	1944				Last 32
	1945				Last 32
NEWTON, Jack (AUS)					
	1975			2	

NEWTON, Jack (cont)

Yr	M AS	USO	BOP	PGA
1976			17	
1978			24	
1979	12			
1980	2		10	20

NICHOLLS, Bernard (ENG/USA)

Yr	M AS	USO	BOP	PGA
1897		6		
1898		8		
1899		17		
1901		5		
1902		28		
1903		19		
1904		4		
1905		20		
1906		10		
1907		8		
1909			10	

NICHOLLS, Gilbert (USA)

Yr	M AS	USO	BOP	PGA
1898		23		
1899		20		
1901		14		
1902		18		
1903		15		
1904		2		
1905		7		
1906		8		
1907		2		
1909		17		
1910		5		
1911		5		
1915		10		
1916		4		
1919		16		
1920		23		
1924			13	

NICHOLS, Bobby (USA)

Yr	M AS	USO	BOP	PGA
1962		3		6
1963	24	14		23
1964	25	14		W
1966	22	7		
1967	2	23		14
1968	30	4		
1969	29			
1970				26
1971		9		
1972		11		
1973	24	20		
1974	7			
1975	4			
1978				19
1979		25		

NICKLAUS, Jack (USA)

Yr	M AS	USO	BOP	PGA
1960	13a	2a		
1961	7a	4a		

NICKLAUS, Jack (cont)

Yr	M AS	USO	BOP	PGA
1962	15	W		3
1963	W		3	W
1964	2	23	2	2
1965	W		12	2
1966	W	3	W	22
1967		W	2	3
1968	5	2	2	
1969	24	25	6	11
1970	8		W	6
1971	2	2	5	W
1972	W	W	2	13
1973	3	4	4	W
1974	4	10	3	2
1975	W	7	3	W
1976	3	11	2	4
1977	2	10	2	3
1978	7	6	W	
1979	4	9	2	
1980		W	4	W
1981	2	6	23	4
1982	15	2	10	16
1983			29	2
1984	18	21		25
1985	6			
1986	W	8		16
1987	7			24
1988	21		25	
1989	18		30	27
1990	6			
1991				23
1993	27			
1994		28		
1996		27		
1998	6			

NICOLETTE, Mike (USA)

Yr	M AS	USO	BOP	PGA
1983		13		

NIELSON, Lonnie (USA)

Yr	M AS	USO	BOP	PGA
1986				11

NIEPORTE, Tom (USA)

Yr	M AS	USO	BOP	PGA
1958		17		
1960				18
1962				30
1964	5			26

NOBILO, Frank (NZL)

Yr	M AS	USO	BOP	PGA
1990			16	
1993				22
1994		9	11	
1995		10		
1996	4	13	27	8
1997			10	29
1999			18	

NOKE, Eddie (ENG)

Yr	M AS	USO	BOP	PGA
1952			21	

NOLAN, William (IRL)

Yr	M AS	USO	BOP	PGA
1929			23	
1934			21	

NORDONE, Augie (USA)

Yr	M AS	USO	BOP	PGA
1941				Last 32
1945				Last 32

NORMAN, Greg (AUS)

Yr	M AS	USO	BOP	PGA
1978			29	
1979			10	
1981	4			4
1982			27	5
1983	30		19	
1984	25	2	6	
1985		15	16	
1986	2	12	W	2
1987	2			
1988	5			9
1989	3		2	12
1990		5	6	19
1991			9	
1992	6		18	15
1993			W	2
1994	18	6	11	4
1995	3	2	15	20
1996	2	10	7	17
1997				13
1999	3		6	
2000	11			
2001				29

NORTH, Andy (USA)

Yr	M AS	USO	BOP	PGA
1975		12		4
1976		14		
1977	24			
1978		W		
1979	12	11		
1980	24	8		15
1981				11
1982		22		
1983	30	10		
1985		W		
1990	27			

NORTON, Willie (ENG/USA)

Yr	M AS	USO	BOP	PGA
1896		26		
1900		19		
1902		11		
1903		20		

OAKLEY, Bud (USA)

Yr	M AS	USO	BOP	PGA
1941				Last 32

OBENDORF, Herbert (USA)

Yr	M AS	USO	BOP	PGA
1923				Last 32

O'BRIEN, JJ (USA)

Yr	M AS	USO	BOP	PGA
1914		13		
1916		9		QF
1920		23		

OCKENDEN, James (ENG)

Yr	M AS	USO	BOP	PGA
1911			29	
1914			7	
1923			25	
1925			20	
1928			23	

O'CONNOR Sr, Christy (IRL)

Yr	M AS	USO	BOP	PGA
1953			24	
1954			20	
1955			10	
1956			10	
1957			19	
1958			3	
1959			5	
1961			3	
1962			16	
1963			6	
1964			6	
1965			2	
1966			13	
1967			21	
1969			5	
1970			17	
1972			23	
1973			7	
1974			24	
1976			5	

O'CONNOR Jr, Christy (IRL)

Yr	M AS	USO	BOP	PGA
1983			8	
1985			3	
1986			11	
1990			25	

O'CONNOR, Tom (USA)

Yr	M AS	USO	BOP	PGA
1939				Last 16

O'DONNELL, John (USA)

Yr	M AS	USO	BOP	PGA
1954				Last 32

OGDEN, Bill (USA)

Yr	M AS	USO	BOP	PGA
1953		12		
1956		17		
1963		30		
1965		21		

OGG, Willie (USA)

Yr	M AS	USO	BOP	PGA
1922		19		Last 32

	Yr	M AS	USO	BOP	PGA
OGG, Willie (cont)	1923		18		Last 16
	1924		15		Last 32
	1925				Last 32
	1928				Last 32
OGILVIE, David (SCO/USA)					
	1903		20		
	1907		26		
	1908		27		
	1909		18		
	1912		16		
	1915		29		
OGILVIE, Joe (USA)2001			25		
OGILVIE, W (SCO/USA)					
	1907		30		
OGLE, Brett (AUS)					
	1995		21	11	
O'GRADY, Mac (USA)					
	1987		9		
	1988	30			
OGRIN, David (USA)					
	1983		13		
	1997		10		
O'HARA, Pat (USA)					
	1920				Last 32
	1921		30		Last 32
O'HARA, Peter (USA)					
	1920		27		QF
	1921		18		Last 32
	1924		7		
	1929		8		
	1930		11		
	1931				Last 16
OKE, JH (ENG)					
	1901			15	
	1903			29	
	1907			30	
OKE, William (ENG)					
	1931			16	
OLAZABAL, Jose Maria (ESP)					
	1985			25a	
	1986			16	
	1987			11	
	1989	8	9	23	
	1990	13	8	16	14
	1991	2	8		
	1992			3	

	Yr	M AS	USO	BOP	PGA
OLAZABAL, Jose Maria (cont)	1993	7			
	1994	W			7
	1995	14	28		
	1997	12	16	20	
	1998	12	16	15	
	1999	W			
	2000		12		4
	2001	15			
O'LEARY, John (IRL)					
	1977			26	
	1979			13	
OLIVER, Ed (USA)					
	1939		29		
	1940	19			
	1946		6		RU
	1947	8	3		Last 16
	1948				Last 16
	1951		24		Last 32
	1952	30	2		
	1953	2			
	1954	22			Last 16
	1957		22		
	1958				8
	1959	14			11
	1960	20			
O'LOUGHLIN, Martin (IRL/USA)	1907		16		
	1910		23		
O'MALLEY, Peter (AUS)					
	1997			7	
	1998			24	
	1999			24	
O'MEARA, Mark (USA)					
	1984		7		25
	1985	24	15	3	28
	1987	24			
	1988		3	27	9
	1989	11			
	1990				19
	1991	27		3	
	1992	4		12	
	1993	21			
	1994	15			
	1995				6
	1996	18	16		26
	1997	30			13
	1998	W		W	4
	2000			26	
	2001	20			22
O'NEILL, George (USA)					
	1906		29		

OOSTERHUIS, Peter (ENG)

Yr	M AS	USO	BOP	PGA
1970			6	
1971			18	
1972			28	
1973	3		18	
1974			2	
1975		7	7	
1976	23			
1977		10		
1978	14	27	6	26
1980			23	
1982	24	30	2	22
1983	20			
1984		25		

OOSTHUIZEN, Andries (RSA)

Yr	M AS	USO	BOP	PGA
1975			12	

OPPERMAN, Steve (USA)

Yr	M AS	USO	BOP	PGA
1965		15		

OSBORNE, HE (ENG)

Yr	M AS	USO	BOP	PGA
1949			26	

OSBORNE, HJ (Herbert) (ENG)

Yr	M AS	USO	BOP	PGA
1922			19	

OTT, Leonard (USA)

Yr	M AS	USO	BOP	PGA
1941				Last 16

OUIMET, Francis [a] (USA)

Yr	M AS	USO	BOP	PGA
1913		W		
1914		5		
1919		18		
1923		29		
1925		3		

OVERTON, Jay (USA)

Yr	M AS	USO	BOP	PGA
1988				17

OWEN, Greg (ENG)

Yr	M AS	USO	BOP	PGA
2001			23	

OWEN, Simon (NZL)

Yr	M AS	USO	BOP	PGA
1978			2	
1979			13	
1981			23	

OZAKI, Masashi (Jumbo) (JAP)

Yr	M AS	USO	BOP	PGA
1973	8			
1978			14	
1979			10	
1987		17	11	
1989	18	6	30	
1990	23	24		
1992		23		
1994		28		
1995	29	28		
2000	28			

OZAKI, Naomichi (Joe) (JAP)

Yr	M AS	USO	BOP	PGA
1992				28
1993		25		

PADGETT, Don (ENG)

Yr	M AS	USO	BOP	PGA
1977		27		

PADGHAM, Alf (ENG)

Yr	M AS	USO	BOP	PGA
1932			4	
1933			7	
1934			3	
1935			2	
1936			W	
1937			7	
1938			4	
1946			30	
1947			13	
1948			7	
1950			20	

PALETTI, Joe (USA)

Yr	M AS	USO	BOP	PGA
1934				Last 32

PALMER, Arnold (USA)

Yr	M AS	USO	BOP	PGA
1955	10	21		
1956	21	7		
1957	7			
1958	W	23		
1959	3	5		14
1960	W	W	2	7
1961	2	14	W	5
1962	W	2	W	17
1963	9	3	26	
1964	W	5		2
1965	2		16	
1966	4	2	8	6
1967	4	2		14
1968			10	2
1969	27	6		2
1970			12	
1971	18	24		18
1972		3	7	16
1973	24	4	14	
1974	11	5		28
1975	13	9	16	
1976				15
1977		19	7	19
1980	24			
1981			23	
1982			27	

PALMER, Johnny (USA)

Yr	M AS	USO	BOP	PGA
1941		21		
1942	26			
1947	17	6		
1948	28			Last 32
1949	4	8		RU

PALMER, Johnny (cont)

Yr	M AS	USO	BOP	PGA
1950	24	10		QF
1951	30	24		
1952	12			
1953	13			
1955	18			Last 16
1956	11			
1957	24			

PANTON, John (SCO)

Yr	M AS	USO	BOP	PGA
1950			20	
1951			11	
1952			15	
1953			27	
1956			5	
1957			15	
1959			5	
1962			16	
1965			10	
1970			9	

PARK, David (SCO)

Yr	M AS	USO	BOP	PGA
1861			4	
1863			3	
1866			2	
1872			4	
1874			6	

PARK, Jack (SCO/USA)

Yr	M AS	USO	BOP	PGA
1899		6		
1901		9		
1902		25		
1915		10		

PARK, Mungo (SCO)

Yr	M AS	USO	BOP	PGA
1874			W	
1875			3	
1876			4	
1877			7	
1878			17	
1880			20	
1883			27	

PARK Sr, Willie (SCO)

Yr	M AS	USO	BOP	PGA
1860			W	
1861			2	
1862			2	
1863			W	
1864			4	
1865			2	
1866			W	
1867			2	
1868			3	
1870			6	
1874			13	
1875			W	
1876			3	
1878			6	

PARK Sr, Willie (cont)

Yr	M AS	USO	BOP	PGA
1880			14	
1882			7	
1883			22	

PARK Jr, Willie (SCO)

Yr	M AS	USO	BOP	PGA
1880			15	
1881			5	
1882			18	
1883			8	
1884			4	
1885			4	
1886			4	
1887			W	
1888			11	
1889			W	
1890			4	
1891			6	
1892			7	
1893			19	
1894			12	
1896			14	
1897			22	
1898			2	
1899			14	
1900			6	
1901			18	
1902			23	
1903			15	
1904			12	
1905			13	

PARKIN, Philip (WAL)

Yr	M AS	USO	BOP	PGA
1985			25	
1986			21	

PARKS Jr, Sam (USA)

Yr	M AS	USO	BOP	PGA
1935	15	W		Last 16
1936	20			
1937		16		Last 32
1938	24			
1940		29		
1941	19			
1942				Last 32

PARNEVIK, Jesper (SWE)

Yr	M AS	USO	BOP	PGA
1993			21	
1994			2	
1995			24	20
1996				5
1997	21		2	
1998		14	4	
1999		17	10	10
2001	20	30	9	13

PARRY, Craig (AUS)

Yr	M AS	USO	BOP	PGA
1990			22	
1991		11	8	

PARRY, Craig (cont)

Yr	MAS	USO	BOP	PGA
1992	13		28	
1993		3		
1994	30	25		19
1999			4	
2000	25			

PATE, Jerry (USA)

Yr	MAS	USO	BOP	PGA
1975		18a		
1976		W		4
1977	14	15		5
1978	18	16		2
1979		2	26	5
1980	6		16	10
1981	5	26	19	11
1982	3			9
1983				23

PATE, Steve (USA)

Yr	MAS	USO	BOP	PGA
1987		24		
1988		3		
1989	26		13	
1990			8	
1991	3			7
1992	6		4	
1993		19		
1994		21		
1999	4			8
2000			20	

PATRICK, Alexander (SCO)

Yr	MAS	USO	BOP	PGA
1878			15	

PATRICK, AH (SCO/USA)

Yr	MAS	USO	BOP	PGA
1896		16		
1899		13		

PATRICK, John (SCO/USA)

Yr	MAS	USO	BOP	PGA
1895		7		
1896		19		

PATRICK, N (SCO)

Yr	MAS	USO	BOP	PGA
1874			28	

PATRICK, P (USA)

Yr	MAS	USO	BOP	PGA
1952		28		

PATRICK, RS (SCO/USA)

Yr	MAS	USO	BOP	PGA
1899		27		
1901		25		
1902		30		

PATRONI, Jack (USA)

Yr	MAS	USO	BOP	PGA
1932		23		
1936				Last 32
1949				Last 16

PATTON, Billy Joe [a] (USA)

Yr	MAS	USO	BOP	PGA
1954	3	6		
1956	12	13		
1957		8		
1958	8			
1959	8			
1960	13			

PATTON, Mike (USA)

Yr	MAS	USO	BOP	PGA
1925				Last 32
1926				Last 32

PAULSEN, Guy (USA)

Yr	MAS	USO	BOP	PGA
1929				Last 32
1931		13		

PAULSON, Dennis (USA)

Yr	MAS	USO	BOP	PGA
1999	14			
2000			11	

PAUTKE, Ben (USA)

Yr	MAS	USO	BOP	PGA
1933				Last 32

PAVELLA, Mike (USA)

Yr	MAS	USO	BOP	PGA
1951				Last 32
1955				Last 32

PAVIN, Corey (USA)

Yr	MAS	USO	BOP	PGA
1984			22	20
1985	25	9		6
1986	11			21
1987	27			
1988				17
1990		24	8	14
1991	22	8		
1992	3			12
1993	11	19	4	
1994	8			2
1995	17	W	8	
1996	7		27	26
1999				10
2001		19		

PAXTON, Edwin (SCO)

Yr	MAS	USO	BOP	PGA
1878			13	
1879			23	

PAXTON, George (SCO)

Yr	MAS	USO	BOP	PGA
1874			3	
1876			8	
1879			4	
1880			4	
1883			5	

PAXTON, James (SCO)

Yr	MAS	USO	BOP	PGA
1863			10	

PAXTON, Peter (SCO)

Yr	M	AS	USO	BOP	PGA
1880				2	
1883				10	
1885				8	
1886				23	
1896				30	
1898				21	
1900				19	

PAYTON, George (USA)

Yr	M	AS	USO	BOP	PGA
1947			19		

PEACH, Stanley (AUS)

Yr	M	AS	USO	BOP	PGA
1967				13	

PEARCE, Eddie (USA)

Yr	M	AS	USO	BOP	PGA
1975			14		
1976					28

PEARSON, George (USA)

Yr	M	AS	USO	BOP	PGA
1897			21		

PEEBLES, Frank (SCO/USA)

Yr	M	AS	USO	BOP	PGA
1912			10		

PEEBLES, Robert (SCO/USA)

Yr	M	AS	USO	BOP	PGA
1905			28		
1908			12		
1914			13		
1916			15		

PEEBLES, Tom (SCO/USA)

Yr	M	AS	USO	BOP	PGA
1909			7		

PEETE, Calvin (USA)

Yr	M	AS	USO	BOP	PGA
1976			23		
1979			11		
1980	19		28		
1981	21		14		
1982	30		10		3
1983			4		
1984	15				4
1985					18
1986	11		24		30

PEMBERTON, RH (Bob) (ENG)

Yr	M	AS	USO	BOP	PGA
1938				28	

PENECALE, Sam (USA)

Yr	M	AS	USO	BOP	PGA
1957			26		

PENNA, Toney (USA)

Yr	M	AS	USO	BOP	PGA
1937			28		
1938			3		
1939	10				
1940	10				
1941	19				Last 32

PENNA, Toney (cont)

Yr	M	AS	USO	BOP	PGA
1942	22				Last 16
1944					Last 16
1945					Last 16
1946	21		15		Last 32
1947	8				Last 32
1948			8		
1949	23				
1959	21				
1951					Last 32

PERELLI, Johnny (USA)

Yr	M	AS	USO	BOP	PGA
1927					Last 32
1932					Last 16

PERKINS, Phil (ENG/USA)

Yr	M	AS	USO	BOP	PGA
1927			9a		
1928			14a		
1929			23a		
1931		7a			
1932		2			
1934		21			
1935	28				

PERNICE Jr, Tom (USA)

Yr	M	AS	USO	BOP	PGA
1989			13		
2000					26

PERRY, Alf (ENG)

Yr	M	AS	USO	BOP	PGA
1930				30	
1932				17	
1933				26	
1934				26	
1935				W	
1938				15	
1939				3	
1946				25	
1947				18	
1948				23	

PERRY, Chris (USA)

Yr	M	AS	USO	BOP	PGA
1987					28
1989					17
1990					26
1998			25		
1999					10
2000	14				
2001			19		

PERRY, Kenny (USA)

Yr	M	AS	USO	BOP	PGA
1993			25		
1995	12				
1996				2	
1997					23
1998					10
2000					29

Yr	MAS	USO	BOP	PGA
PERSONS, Peter (USA)				
1991		19		
PFEIL, Mark (USA)				
1982				22
1983				30
PHELPS, Mason (USA)				
1911		20		
PHILLIPS, Frank (AUS)				
1963			18	
1964			12	
PICARD, Henry (USA)				
1932				Last 16
1933				Last 16
1934	23			
1935	4	6	6	
1936	9	5		Last 16
1937		10	15	QF
1938	W	7		SF
1939	8	12		W
1940	7	12		Last 16
1941		26		
1942	15			
1946	25	12		
1947	6			
1948	25			
1949	21			
1950	14	12		SF
1951		24		Last 32
PINERO, Manuel (ESP)				
1981			6	
1985			25	
1986			19	
PIPER, J (ENG)				
1911			13	
PIRIE, Jack (USA)				
1921				Last 32
PITTMAN, Jerry (US)				
1958		17		
1967		16		
1968	7	7		
PLATTS, Lionel (ENG)				
1961			20	
1962			24	
1967			13	
PLAYER, Gary (RSA)				
1956			4	
1957	24		24	

Yr	MAS	USO	BOP	PGA
PLAYER, Gary (cont)				
1958		2	7	
1959	8	15	W	
1960	6	19	7	
1961	W	9		29
1962	2	6		W
1963	5	8	7	8
1964	5	23	8	13
1965	2	W		
1966	28	15	4	3
1967	6	12	3	
1968	7	16	W	
1969			23	2
1970	3			12
1971	6	27	7	4
1972	10	15	6	W
1973		12	14	
1974	W	8	W	7
1975	30			
1976	28	23	28	13
1977	19	10	22	
1978	W	6		26
1979	17	2	19	23
1980	6			26
1981	15	26		
1982	15			
1983		20		
1984	21			2
1990	24			
PLAYFAIR, N [a] (SCO)				
1888			25	
PLEMMONS, Broyles (USA)				
1953				Last 32
POHL, Dan (USA)				
1981				3
1982	2	3		
1983	8			8
1985				12
1986				26
1987		9		14
1988	16	12		8
1989		29		24
POLLAND, Eddie (IRL)				
1973			18	
POLLOCK, R [a] (SCO)				
1862			6	
POMEROY, Ewing (USA)				
1957				Last 32
POOLEY, Don (USA)				
1981	19			19
1983				23

	Yr	M AS	USO	BOP	PGA
POOLEY, Don (cont)	1985		15		
	1986		24		16
	1987		24		5
	1988	5		16	
	1989	14	26	19	
	1990				8
	1997				29
POPE, Charles (ENG)	1912			27	
PORTER, Joe (USA)	1976				29
POSE, Martin (ARG)	1939			8	
	1941	29			
POTT, Johnny (USA)	1959		19		
	1960		15		15
	1961	19			5
	1962	20			27
	1963	21			
	1964	13	9		
	1965				28
	1969	28			19
POULTON, A (ENG)	1951			28	
	1952			25	
	1953			29	
POWERS, Greg (USA)	1978				26
	1982		30		
PRICE, Nick (ZIM)	1980			27	
	1981			23	
	1982			2	
	1985				5
	1986	5			
	1987	22	17	8	10
	1988	14		2	17
	1990			25	
	1991		19		
	1992	6	4		W
	1993		11	6	
	1994			W	W
	1995		13		
	1996	18			8
	1997	24	19		13
	1998		4	29	4
	1999	6	23		5
	2000	11	27		
	2001			21	29

	Yr	M AS	USO	BOP	PGA
PRICE, Phil(lip) (WAL)	2001			30	
PRICE, Terry (AUS)	1994			24	
PRINGLE, Bob (SCO)	1873			21	
	1874			14	
	1875			7	
	1877			2	
	1878			22	
	1880			4	
	1882			23	
	1883			4	
	1886			16	
PROWSE, H (ENG)	1932			13	
PRUITT, Dillard (USA)	1992	13			
PULFORD, George (ENG)	1895			4	
	1897			3	
	1898			13	
	1902			22	
	1903			18	
	1906			30	
	1907			3	
	1908			18	
	1909			10	
PURSE, W (USA)	1932			29	
PURSEY, W (ENG)	1921			13	
	1922			22	
PURTZER, Tom (USA)	1977		4		
	1978		24		
	1979		8		
	1981				19
	1982			4	16
	1984	25	16		
	1989	24			
	1992			22	21
PYMAN, Iain [a] (ENG)	1993			27	
QUICK, Lyman (Smiley) (USA)	1946		26a		
	1948		8		

	Yr	M AS	USO	BOP	PGA
QUICK, Lyman (Smiley) (cont)	1951		10		
	1952	27			
	1955		16		
QUIGLEY, N (ENG)					
	1947			27	
RACHELS, Sammy (USA)					
	1981		6		
RAFFERTY, Ronan (IRL)					
	1984			9	
	1986			21	
	1990	14			
	1994			11	
RAGAN, Dave (USA)					
	1960	25			22
	1962	25			7
	1963		12		2
RAINFORD, Peter (ENG)					
	1899			16	
	1902			28	
	1909			14	
RAJOPPI, TJ (USA)					
	1921				Last 32
RANDOLPH, Sam [a] (USA)					
	1985	18			
RANSOM, Henry (USA)					
	1940		29		
	1941		13		
	1946		22		Last 32
	1947		29		Last 32
	1948				Last 16
	1949				Last 32
	1950		5		
	1951	25	16		
	1953				QF
	1954				Last 32
	1956				QF
	1957	21			Last 16
	1959		28		
RASSETT, Joey (USA)					
	1983		26		
RAUTENBUSCH, WM [a] (USA)					
	1914		11		
RAWLINS, Harry (ENG/USA)					
	1900		19		
	1908		21		

	Yr	M AS	USO	BOP	PGA
RAWLINS, Horace (ENG/USA)					
	1895		W		
	1896		2		
	1897		8		
	1898		19		
	1899		13		
	1901		17		
	1902		16		
	1903		12		
	1904		14		
	1907		26		
RAY, Edward (Ted) (ENG)					
	1899			16	
	1900			13	
	1901			12	
	1902			9	
	1903			23	
	1904			12	
	1905			11	
	1906			8	
	1907			5	
	1908			3	
	1909			6	
	1910			5	
	1911			5	
	1912			W	
	1913	3		2	
	1914			10	
	1920	W		3	
	1921			19	
	1923			12	
	1925			2	
	1926			28	
	1927	27		29	
	1930			24	
REASOR, Mike (USA)					
	1974		15		
REED, Elmer (USA)					
	1950				Last 16
REEKIE, WM [a] (USA)					
	1923		5		
REES, Dai (WAL)					
	1935			30	
	1936			11	
	1937			21	
	1938			13	
	1939			12	
	1946			4	
	1947			21	
	1948			15	
	1950			3	
	1951			12	

Yr	M AS	USO	BOP	PGA
REES, Dai (cont)				
1952			27	
1953			2	
1954			2	
1955			28	
1956			13	
1957			30	
1958			14	
1959			9	
1960			9	
1961			2	
REFRAM, Dean (USA)				
1962		28		
1963		14		
1964	30			
1965		28		
1969		13		
REGALADO, Victor (MEX)				
1974				28
1975	30			
1978		24		
1984				10
REID, John (USA)				
1895		10		
1896		16		
1903		24		
REID, Mike (USA)				
1979		25		
1980		6		
1981		20		
1983				9
1984				14
1985		23		
1986		24		
1988				2
1989	6			
1991		26	26	
REID, Steve (USA)				
1968				26
REID, Wilfred (ENG/USA)				
1909			21	
1910			24	
1911			16	
1912			20	
1913		16	26	
1915		10		
1916		4		Last 32
1919		21		Last 16
1923				Last 32
1925		27		

Yr	M AS	USO	BOP	PGA
REINHART, FO (USA)				
1903		13		
RENNER, Jack (USA)				
1979				12
1980	14			
1981		17		
1982	20	30		
1983	16			
1984	11			
1985		9		
RENNIE, James (SCO)				
1875		5		
1879		12		
1881		7		
1885		18		
RENOUF, TG (ENG)				
1897		14		
1898		9		
1899		12		
1901		12		
1902		20		
1904		22		
1905		16		
1906		8		
1907		17		
1908		28		
1909		5		
1910		8		
1911		13		
1912		19		
1913		5		
REVOLTA, Johnny (USA)				
1933		15		Last 16
1934	18	8		Last 16
1935	13			W
1936	25	14		Last 32
1937	13	28		Last 32
1938	18	16		Last 32
1939		22		Last 16
1940	27	16		
1945				Last 16
1951		19		
1952	13			
1954		29		Last 16
1957		30		
RHYAN, Dick (USA)				
1964				23
1968				20
RICHARDSON, JC (SCO)				
1970			13	

	Yr	MAS	USO	BOP	PGA
RICHARDSON, Steven (ENG)					
	1991				5
RICKETTS, Alfred (ENG/USA)					
	1896		10		
	1897		6		
	1899		16		
RIEGEL, Robert (Skee) (USA)					
	1948	13a			
	1949	30a	14a		
	1950	21	12		
	1951	2	10		
	1952	14			
	1953	29			
	1955	13			
	1956				Last 32
	1957				Last 32
RINKER, Larry (USA)					
	1982		15		
	1986		24		
	1992			12	
RINKER, Lee (USA)					
	1998				29
RISDON, PWL [a] (ENG)					
	1935			26	
RISEBOROUGH, Ernest (ENG)					
	1906			24	
RISEBOROUGH, Herbert (ENG)					
	1910			28	
RITCHIE, William (SCO)					
	1910			16	
	1920			29	
RIVERO, Jose (ESP)					
	1985			3	
	1988			16	
	1990			25	
	1993			14	
ROBB, J (SCO)					
	1895			13	
ROBBINS Jr, Hillman [a] (USA)					
	1955	24			
	1956	17			
ROBERTS, Charles (ENG)					
	1907			25	
	1910			24	
	1912			27	
	1913			14	

	Yr	MAS	USO	BOP	PGA
ROBERTS, Hugh (WAL)					
	1921			26	
ROBERTS, Loren (USA)					
	1990				5
	1991				27
	1993		11		28
	1994	5	2	24	9
	1995	25			
	1996	23		18	
	1997		13		
	1998		18	29	
	2000	3	8	6	
	2001			13	
ROBERTSON, AM (SCO)					
	1946			27	
ROBERTSON, Argyll, [a] (SCO)					
	1879			28	
ROBERTSON, DD [a] (SCO)					
	1890			23	
ROBERTSON, Dave (USA)					
	1904		19		
	1906		29		
	1907		13		
	1908		20		
	1912		28		
	1922				Last 32
	1924		10		
ROBERTSON, Dean (SCO)					
	2000			26	
ROBERTSON, Fred (SCO)					
	1933			22	
	1937			17	
ROBERTSON, Jock (SCO/USA)					
	1924				Last 32
ROBERTSON, Peter (US)					
	1904		29		
	1905		3		
	1906		14		
	1907		5		
	1908		6		
	1909		20		
	1911		9		
	1912		28		
	1913		21		
ROBERTSON, William (SCO)					
	1924			23	

	Yr	M	AS	USO	BOP	PGA
ROBINSON, WD (USA)						
	1907			26		
	1910			26		
ROBSON, Fred (ENG)						
	1908				18	
	1910				5	
	1911				10	
	1923				29	
	1924				23	
	1925				11	
	1926				17	
	1927				2	
	1928				4	
	1930				4	
	1931				20	
	1932				9	
ROCCA, Costantino (ITA)						
	1995				2	17
	1997		5			
	1998				9	
	1999				18	
RODGERS, Phil (USA)						
	1958	22				
	1962			3	3	
	1963				2	
	1964	25			19	
	1966	17		6	4	
	1967					28
	1969			13		
	1972					7
	1973	23				
	1974	7				
RODGERS, Phillip H (ENG)						
	1927				9	
	1930				15	
	1931				28	
	1932				25	
	1935				17	
RODRIGUEZ, Chi Chi (PUR)						
	1964	21				
	1967	26				
	1969					15
	1970	10		27		
	1971	30		13		
	1972			9		24
	1973	10		29	28	24
	1974	20		26		
	1975					22
	1981			6		
ROE, Mark (ENG)						
	1987				17	

	Yr	M	AS	USO	BOP	PGA
ROE, Mark (cont)	1990				16	
	1993				24	
	1995			13		
ROGERS, Bill (USA)						
	1978	29				
	1979			4		
	1980			16	19	8
	1981			2	W	27
	1982			3	22	29
	1983				8	
ROGERS, Jock (SCO/USA)						
	1924			19		
	1926			20		
	1929			11		
ROGERS, Johnny (USA)						
	1938			24		
	1939			20		
ROLLAND, Douglas (SCO)						
	1882				13a	
	1883				10	
	1884				2	
	1894				2	
ROMANS, Walter (USA)						
	1949					Last 16
ROMERO, Eduardo (ARG)						
	1988				13	
	1989				8	
	1991				26	
	1993					20
	1997				7	
	1998			25		
	2001				25	
ROONEY, Michael (USA)						
	1956					Last 32
ROSBURG, Bob (USA)						
	1953			21		
	1954	6		29		
	1955	4		5		
	1956	16				
	1958			5		11
	1959	30		2		W
	1960	20		23		
	1961	15		21		19
	1962			13		
	1964			9		
	1966	10				
	1967	21				
	1968	30				
	1969			2		
	1971			3		9

Yr	M AS	USO	BOP	PGA
ROSE, DG [a] (SCO)				
1888			27	
ROSE, James (USA)				
1919				Last 32
ROSE, Justin (ENG)				
1998			4a	
2001			30	
ROSMAN, Joe (USA)				
1919				Last 32
1920				Last 32
ROSS, AM [a] (SCO)				
1889			13	
1895			27	
ROSS, Alex (SCO/USA)				
1902		10		
1903		9		
1904		15		
1905		13		
1906		6		
1907		W		
1908		23		
1910		22		
1911		9		
1914		22		
1919		16		
1920		27		
ROSS, Donald (SCO/USA)				
1901		21		
1902		9		
1903		5		
1904		10		
1905		25		
1907		10		
1910			8	
ROSS, Jack (SCO)				
1895			24	
1896			18	
1901			25	
ROSS, Jack B (SCO)				
1913			30	
ROSSI, Ricardo (ARG)				
1956			17	
ROTAR, Charles (USA)				
1955		28		
ROWE, Charles (USA)				
1909		20		

Yr	M AS	USO	BOP	PGA
ROWE, Charles (USA) (cont)	1912		27	
1920		14		
1922				QF
ROWE, John (ENG)				
1894			23	
1897			28	
1902			15	
1904			16	
1905			11	
1907			23	
1910			22	
ROYER Jr, Hugh (USA)				
1968		22		
RUDOLPH, Mason (USA)				
1960				22
1961	28			
1962		28		
1963	15	27		23
1964	18			4
1965	4	11		20
1966		8		22
1967	10			28
1968	14			17
1969	11			
1970		27		10
1973	14			3
RUIZ, Leopoldo (ARG)				
1958			5	
1959			9	
RUMMELLS, Dave (USA)				
1988				6
1989				5
RUNYAN, Paul (USA)				
1931				Last 16
1932		12		Last 32
1933				QF
1934	3	28		W
1935	7	10		QF
1936	4	8		
1937	19	14		Last 16
1938	4	7		W
1939	16	9		QF
1940	12			QF
1941		5		
1942	3			
1946		21		
1947		6		
1950		25		
1951		6		
1952		22		
1961			18	

Yr	M AS	USO	BOP	PGA
RUSSELL, David A (ENG)				
1997			24	
RUSSELL, David J (ENG)				
1988			11	
RUSSELL, Raymond (SCO)				
1998			4	
RUTHERFORD, W [a] (USA)				
1898		28		
RYAN, Jack (US)				
1939				Last 32
1940		29		
1941	17			Last 32
SAAVEDRA, Armando (ARG)				
1979			30	
SALERNO, Gus (USA)				
1955				Last 32
SAMPSON, Harold (USA)				
1930				QF
1935				Last 32
SANDELIN, Jarmo (SWE)				
2000			23	
SANDERS, Doug (USA)				
1958				2
1960	29			3
1961	11	2		3
1962		11		15
1963	28	21		17
1964			11	28
1965	11	11		20
1966	4	8	2	6
1967	16		18	28
1968	12			8
1970			2	
1971			9	
1972			4	7
1973			28	
1976			28	
SANDERSON, AJ (USA)				
1915		21		
SANDERSON, J (USA)				
1919		24		
SANUDO, Cesar (USA)				
1972		9		

Yr	M AS	USO	BOP	PGA
SARAZEN, Gene (USA)				
1920		30		
1921		17		QF
1922		W		W
1923		16		W
1924		17		Last 16
1925		5		Last 32
1926		3		Last 16
1927		3		QF
1928		6	2	SF
1929		3	8	QF
1930		28		RU
1931		4	3	SF
1932		W	W	
1933		26	3	W
1934		2	21	Last 16
1935	W	6		Last 32
1936	3	28	5	
1937	19	10		Last 32
1938	13	10		QF
1939	5			
1940	21	2		QF
1941	19	7		SF
1942	28			
1945				Last 32
1947	26			Last 16
1948	23			Last 16
1950	10			
1951	12			Last 32
1955				Last 32
1956				Last 16
SARGENT, Alfred (USA)				
1931				Last 32
SARGENT, George (ENG/USA)				
1909		W		
1910		16		
1911		7		
1912		6		
1913		21		
1914		3		
1915		10		
1916		4		
1919		29		
1923		29		
SAUBABER, Jean (FRA)				
1936			28	
SAUERS, Gene (USA)				
1986				30
1987				24
1992				2
1993				22
SAVEL, Steve (USA)				
1944				Last 32

	Yr	M AS	USO	BOP	PGA
SAWYER, DE [a] (USA)					
	1911		18		
SAWYER, Pat (USA)					
	1937		16		
SAYERS, Bernard (Ben) (SCO)					
	1878			12	
	1879			22	
	1880			19	
	1882			18	
	1883			7	
	1884			6	
	1885			15	
	1886			16	
	1887			5	
	1888			2	
	1889			3	
	1890			19	
	1891			9	
	1892			5	
	1893			12	
	1894			5	
	1895			9	
	1896			7	
	1897			12	
	1898			19	
	1899			11	
	1900			9	
	1902			19	
	1903			21	
	1905			10	
	1908			30	
	1909			17	
	1915		29		
SAYERS, George (ENG/USA)					
	1915		28		
SAYNER, Cedric (ENG)					
	1925			28	
	1929			25	
	1932			29	
SCHEIDER, F (USA)					
	1935				Last 32
SCHERRER, Tom (USA)					
	1999		23		
	2001	25			
SCHLEE, John (USA)					
	1973		2		
	1974	26			17
	1975				10
	1976				4
	1977	8			

	Yr	M AS	USO	BOP	PGA
SCHLOTMAN, JB (USA)					
	1900		22		
SCHMUTTE, Leonard (USA)					
	1928		25		
	1929		26		
	1950				Last 32
	1952				Last 32
SCHNEIDER, Charles (USA)					
	1930				Last 32
	1933				Last 32
	1935				Last 32
	1937				Last 32
SCHNEITER, George (USA)					
	1934		28		
	1941				Last 32
	1944				SF
	1945				Last 32
	1946	13			Last 16
	1947	26			Last 32
	1948		14		
	1949				Last 32
	1955		19		
SCHROEDER, John (USA)					
	1971		27		22
	1977			9	19
	1978			7	12
	1979				21
	1981		4		
	1982	24			
SCHULTZ, Eddie (USA)					
	1929				Last 16
	1931				Last 32
	1932				Last 32
	1935				QF
SCHULZ, Ted (USA)					
	1992	6			
SCHWAB, Pat (USA)					
	1968		24		
SCHWARTZ, Bill (USA)					
	1933		29		
	1934	18	28		
SCOTT, Andrew (SCO)					
	1896			7	
	1897			16	
	1898			29	
	1899			25	
	1900			22	
	1901			18	
	1903			6	

	Yr	M AS	USO	BOP	PGA
SCOTT, Michael [a] (ENG)					
	1922			19	
SCOTT Jr, R [a] (SCO)					
	1923			22	
SCOTT, Syd (ENG)					
	1952			9	
	1953			22	
	1954			2	
	1955			20	
	1956			28	
	1959			4	
	1960			9	
	1961			10	
	1962			10	
	1964			19	
SEAVALL, Eric (USA)					
	1930				Last 32
SECKEL, Albert [a] (USA)					
	1911		11		
SELLMAN, Jack (USA)					
	1963				13
SENIOR, Peter (AUS)					
	1991			17	
	1992			25	
	1993			4	
	1994			20	
SERAFIN, Felix (USA)					
	1928		28		
	1936		22		
	1937	19			
	1938	6			Last 16
	1939	16	29		
	1940		20		
	1941	19			
	1942	18			
	1945				Last 32
	1946	21			
SERRA, Enrique (URU)					
	1939			17	
SERVAS, LC (USA)					
	1901		28		
SEWELL, Doug (ENG)					
	1963			26	
	1965			25	
	1966			20	
	1971			25	

	Yr	M AS	USO	BOP	PGA
SEWGOLUM, Sewsunker (RSA)					
	1963			13	
SEYMOUR, Mark (ENG)					
	1924			29	
	1929			18	
	1931			22	
	1932			22	
	1935			17	
SHADE, Ronnie (SCO)					
	1966			16a	
	1970			25	
	1974			22	
SHAFER, George (USA)					
	1950				Last 32
SHANKLAND, Bill (ENG)					
	1938			18	
	1939			3	
	1946			13	
	1947			4	
	1949			11	
	1951			6	
SHANKS, PJ (ENG)					
	1959			29	
SHAVE Sr, Bob (USA)					
	1925		20		
	1927				Last 32
	1929				Last 32
	1930		17		Last 16
	1938				Last 32
SHAVE Jr, Bob (USA)					
	1960		27		
	1966		26		
SHAW, Bob (USA)					
	1968			27	
	1972				20
SHAW, QA [a] (USA)					
	1898		21		
SHAW, Tom (USA)					
	1969				21
	1970			28	
	1973		25		
SHEA, Leo (USA)					
	1926				Last 32
SHEARER, Bob (AUS)					
	1976			21	

Yr	MAS	USO	BOP	PGA
SHEARER, Bob (cont)				
1977			15	
1978		16	7	26
SHELTON, Ben (ENG)				
1954			29	
SHEPARD, B (ENG)				
1947			27	
SHEPPARD, Charles (USA)				
1938		26		
1940				Last 32
1941				Last 32
1957				QF
SHERBORNE, Andrew (ENG)				
1991			17	
SHERLOCK, James (ENG)				
1897			27	
1902			17	
1904			6	
1905			8	
1910			28	
1911			16	
1913			7	
1920			16	
1924			9	
SHERMAN, Mike (USA)				
1916				Last 32
SHIPPEN, John (USA)				
1896		6		
1899		25		
1900		27		
1902		5		
SHOEMAKER, Dick (USA)				
1946				Last 16
1951				Last 16
1958				29
SHUTE, Densmore (Denny) (USA)				
1928		6		
1929		3		Last 32
1930		25		Last 16
1931		25		RU
1932		14		Last 32
1933		21	W	
1934	13		20	SF
1935	5	4		Last 16
1936	11	10		W
1937	13	10	14	W
1938		11		Last 16
1939	15	3		Last 16
1941	18	2		QF

Yr	MAS	USO	BOP	PGA
SHUTE, Densmore (cont)				
1942				Last 32
1945				QF
1946	25			
1947	20			
1950				Last 16
1951				Last 32
SIECKMANN, Tom (USA)				
1985		23		
1990		8		
1991		19		
SIFFORD, Charles (USA)				
1964		27		
1972		21		
SIGEL, Jay [a] (USA)				
1980	26			
SIKES, Dan (USA)				
1963	15	10		
1964	13			
1965	5			
1966				28
1967				3
1968		15		8
1969	12			25
1970		27		18
1972				13
1973				6
1974	15			17
SIKES, RH (Richard) (USA)				
1965				13
1966			12	28
1967				14
SILLS, Tony (USA)				
1985		15		
1986				16
SIMONS, Jim (USA)				
1971		5a		
1972		15a		
1977				25
1979	23	16		
1980	19	22		
1981	15			
1982	15			5
1983				30
SIMPSON, Archie (SCO)				
1885			2	
1886			4	
1887			5	
1888			16	
1889			12	

Yr	M	AS	USO	BOP	PGA
SIMPSON, Archie (cont)					
1890				2	
1891				11	
1892				9	
1893				14	
1894				13	
1895				5	
1896				12	
1897				7	
1898				16	
1899				16	
1900				7	
1902				30	
1903				29	
SIMPSON, Bob (SCO)					
1885				4	
1886				15	
1887				16	
1888				30	
1893				6	
1898				29	
SIMPSON, David (SCO)					
1882				23	
1886				26	
1891				18	
SIMPSON, George (SCO/USA)					
1911			2		
1912			13		
1914			13		
1916			24	Last 16	
SIMPSON, Harry (ENG)					
1914				3	
SIMPSON, Jack (SCO)					
1883				17	
1884				W	
1885				13	
1886				12	
1887				12	
1892				28	
SIMPSON, James (SCO/USA)					
1914			11		
SIMPSON, JB (SCO/USA)					
1911			23		
1916			15		
SIMPSON, RL (SCO/USA)					
1911			17		
SIMPSON, Robert (SCO/USA)					
1900			14		
1901			14		
1904			6		

Yr	M	AS	USO	BOP	PGA
SIMPSON, Scott (USA)					
1980					30
1981			23		
1982			15		
1983		11	13		9
1984			25		6
1985			15		12
1986		25			
1987		27	W		
1988		6			
1989		6	6	26	
1990		7	14		
1991		22	2		
1992		13			
1993		11		9	6
1994		27			
1995			28		
1996		29			
SIMPSON, Tim (USA)					
1984			11		25
1985		18			
1987			14		
1989					27
1990			5	12	8
1991			26		
SIMPSON, Tom (ENG)					
1900				14	
1905				9	
1906				15	
1908				7	
1913				27	
SINDELAR, Joey (USA)					
1985			15		28
1986			15		
1988			17		
1992			6		
1993		27			
1996					14
1997					10
SINGH, Vijay (FIJ)					
1989			23		
1990			12		
1991			12		
1993					4
1994		27	20		
1995			10	6	
1996			7	11	5
1997		17			13
1998			25	19	W
1999		24	3		
2000		W	8	11	
2001		18	7	13	

Yr	M	AS	USO	BOP	PGA
SISK, Geoffrey (USA)					
1999			30		
SJOLAND, Patrik (SWE)					
1999				18	
SKERRITT, Paddy (IRL)					
1968				18	
SLINGERLAND, G (USA)					
1935					Last 32
SLUMAN, Jeff (USA)					
1986					30
1987					14
1988					W
1989	8				24
1990	27		14	25	
1991	29				
1992	4		2		12
1993	17		11		
1994	25		9		25
1995			13		8
1997	7		28		
1998			10		27
2000	18				
SMALLDON, DF (WAL)					
1955				17	
1956				28	
SMITH (of Cambridge) (ENG)					
1879				23	
SMITH, AW [a] (SCO/USA)					
1879				11	
1895			3		
1896			4		
SMITH, Al (USA)					
1948	16				Last 16
1952					Last 16
1953					Last 16
1957					Last 32
SMITH, Alexander (SCO)					
1860				7 or 8	
SMITH, Alex (SCO/USA)					
1898			2		
1899			7		
1900			13		
1901			2		
1902			18		
1903			4		
1904			18		
1905			2	16	

Yr	M	AS	USO	BOP	PGA
SMITH, Alex (cont)					
1906			W		
1907				25	
1908			3		
1909			3		
1910			W		
1911			23		
1912			3		
1913			16		
1915			22		
1916					Last 16
1921			5		
SMITH, Alfred (USA)					
1947			19		
1948			21		
SMITH, Arthur (SCO/USA)					
1900			16		
1903			26		
1905			10		
1908			29		
1914			9		
SMITH, Bob E (USA)					
1971			24		20
1972					24
1976			28		
1979			25		
SMITH, C Ralph (SCO)					
1897				30	
1898				27	
1900				30	
1902				27	
1914				21	
1920				28	
SMITH, Chris (USA)					
2001					29
SMITH, G (SCO)					
1884				20	
SMITH, GG (Garden) [a] (SCO)					
1892				21	
SMITH, George (SCO/USA)					
1906			18		
1910			21		
SMITH, George B (USA)					
1925					Last 32
1929			16		
1932			21		Last 32
1934					Last 32

	Yr	M AS	USO	BOP	PGA
SMITH, George M (USA)					
	1930		11		
SMITH, Horton (USA)					
	1928		28		SF
	1929		10	25	Last 32
	1930		3	4	QF
	1931		27	11	QF
	1932				Last 32
	1933		24	14	Last 32
	1934	W	17		
	1935	19	6		QF
	1936	W	22		QF
	1937	19		10	Last 16
	1938	22	19		QF
	1939	26	15		QF
	1940		3		
	1941	19	13		Last 16
	1942	5			
	1946	21			
	1947	22			
	1949	23	23		Last 32
	1950	12			
	1952	30	15		
	1954				Last 16
SMITH, Ian (ENG)					
	1960			16	
SMITH, Jack (USA)					
	1925			17	
	1927			22	
	1928			13	
	1947				Last 32
SMITH, Mac(donald) (SCO/USA)					
	1910		2		
	1913		4		
	1923		20	3	
	1924		4		
	1925		11	4	
	1926		9		
	1927		18		
	1928		6		
	1929		23	15	
	1930		2	2	
	1931		10	5	
	1932		14	2	
	1933		19		
	1934	7	6	4	
	1935		14	17	
	1936		4		
SMITH, Mel (USA)					
	1927				Last 32
SMITH, Norman (USA)					
	1930				Last 32

	Yr	M AS	USO	BOP	PGA
SMITH, WB [a] (USA)					
	1897		29		
SMITH, WD (Dick) [a] (SCO)					
	1957			5	
SMITH, Warren (USA)					
	1957				Last 16
SMITH, William B (ENG)					
	1920			21	
	1922			22	
SMITH, Willie (SCO/USA)					
	1898		5		
	1899		W		
	1900		4		
	1901		3		
	1902		4		
	1903		9		
	1905		13		
	1906		2		
	1907		2		
	1908		2		
	1910			5	
SMITHERS, Wally (ENG)					
	1936			15	
	1949			8	
	1950			12	
	1951			28	
	1952			17	
SMYTH, Des (IRL)					
	1982			4	
	1993			27	
	1998			15	
	2001			13	
SNEAD, JC (USA)					
	1972	30			20
	1973	2			3
	1974	26	21		24
	1975	10			28
	1976		14		15
	1977		27		19
	1978		2		
	1979	22			
	1980	14	22		
	1981				15
	1982		15		
	1983	12			
SNEAD, Sam (USA)					
	1937	18	2	11	Last 16
	1938				RU
	1939	2	5		

SNEAD, Sam (cont)

Yr	M AS	USO	BOP	PGA
1940	7	16		RU
1941	6	13		QF
1942	7			W
1946	7	19	W	Last 32
1947	22	2		Last 32
1948	16	5		QF
1949	W	2		W
1950	3	12		Last 32
1951	8	10		W
1952	W	10		
1953	16	2		Last 32
1954	W	11		QF
1955	3	3		Last 32
1956	4	24		QF
1957	2	8		Last 16
1958	13			3
1959	22	8		8
1960	11	19		3
1961	15	17		27
1962	15		6	17
1963	3			27
1965		24		6
1966				6
1967	10			
1968		9		
1970	23			12
1972	27			4
1973	29	29		9
1974	20			3

SNEED, Ed (USA)

Yr	M AS	USO	BOP	PGA
1975		29		
1978	18			
1979	2	11	26	28
1980		8		

SNELL, David (ENG)

Yr	M AS	USO	BOP	PGA
1958			30	

SOMERS, Vaughan (AUS)

Yr	M AS	USO	BOP	PGA
1986			21	

SOMERVILLE, Ross [a] (CAN)

Yr	M AS	USO	BOP	PGA
1933			28	

SOTA, Ramon (ESP)

Yr	M AS	USO	BOP	PGA
1960			15	
1961			12	
1963			7	
1964			30	
1965	6		25	
1971			11	

SOTO, Arturo (ARG)

Yr	M AS	USO	BOP	PGA
1955			17	

SOUCHAK, Frank [a] (USA)

Yr	M AS	USO	BOP	PGA
1953		9		

SOUCHAK, Mike (USA)

Yr	M AS	USO	BOP	PGA
1955	4	10		
1956	17	29	8	
1957				Last 16
1958	14			8
1959	25	3		5
1960	16	3		12
1961	28	4		
1962	5	14		
1963	11			23
1964	9			12
1965				15
1967				20
1972				29

SOUTHERDEN, EA (ENG)

Yr	M AS	USO	BOP	PGA
1949			20	

SPARK, W (SCO)

Yr	M AS	USO	BOP	PGA
1933			28	

SPEARS, Herschel (USA)

Yr	M AS	USO	BOP	PGA
1948		14		
1949		11		
1950	27			

SPENCE, Jamie (ENG)

Yr	M AS	USO	BOP	PGA
1990			22	
1992			12	

SPENCE, TW (Bill) (ENG)

Yr	M AS	USO	BOP	PGA
1954			12	

SPENCER, Glen (USA)

Yr	M AS	USO	BOP	PGA
1928				Last 16

SPRAY, Steve (USA)

Yr	M AS	USO	BOP	PGA
1968		5		

SPRINGER, Mike (USA)

Yr	M AS	USO	BOP	PGA
1994		25	24	

SPROGELL, Frank (USA)

Yr	M AS	USO	BOP	PGA
1922				Last 16

STACKHOUSE, WA (USA)

Yr	M AS	USO	BOP	PGA
1944				Last 32

STADLER, Craig (USA)

Yr	M AS	USO	BOP	PGA
1978				6
1979	7			
1980	26	16	6	
1981		26		
1982	W	22		16

Yr	M AS	USO	BOP	PGA
STADLER, Craig (cont)				
1983	6	10	12	
1984		28	18	
1985	6		18	
1986		15	30	
1987	17	24	8	28
1988	3	25		15
1989			13	7
1990	14	8		
1991	12	19		7
1992	25			
1994			24	19
1995				8
1996	29			
1997	26			
STAHL, Marvin (USA)				
1938				Last 16
STAIT, Jack (USA)				
1923				Last 16
1924		25		
STANDLY, Mike (USA)				
1993		16		
STANKOWSKI, Paul (USA)				
1997	5	19		
STANLEY, Ian (AUS)				
1986			30	
STANTON, Bob (USA)				
1966			27	
1969		22		
1970				22
STARK, George (USA)				
1922				Last 32
STARKS, Nate (USA)				
1975		29		
STEEL, William (SCO)				
1860			7 or 8	
STEELSMITH, Jerry (USA)				
1961		29		
STEPHENSON, David (SCO)				
1905			28	
STEVENS, LB [a] (ENG)				
1911			24	
STEVENS, Tom (USA)				
1926		23		
1927			19	

Yr	M AS	USO	BOP	PGA
STEWART, Earl (USA)				
1951		24		
1952		10		
1953	16			
1954	22			
1958		23		
1962		17		
1963				27
1967				26
STEWART, Payne (USA)				
1984	21			
1985	25	5	2	12
1986	8	6		5
1987			4	24
1988	25	10	7	9
1989	24	13	8	W
1990			2	8
1991		W		13
1993	9	2	12	
1995		21	11	13
1996		27		
1997		28		29
1998		2		
1999		W	30	
STEWART, WG [a] (USA)				
1897		20		
STICKLEY, Arnold (ENG)				
1959			11	
STILL, Ken (USA)				
1963		19		
1970		5		
1971	6	19		
STINCHCOMB, Verl (USA)				
1945				Last 32
STOCKTON, Dave (USA)				
1968		9		17
1969	18	25		
1970	5			W
1971	9		11	
1972	10			
1973	14			12
1974	2			26
1975	26			
1976				W
1978		2		19
1980	26			
STODDART, WE (USA)				
1898		29		

	Yr	M AS	USO	BOP	PGA
STONEHOUSE, Ralph (USA)					
	1932				QF
	1934	16			
	1941				Last 32
STOREY, Eustace [a] (ENG)					
	1938			26	
STRAFACI, Frank [a] (USA)					
	1937		9		
STRANAHAN, Frank (USA)					
	1946	20a			
	1947	2a	13a	2a	
	1948			23a	
	1949	19a		13a	
	1950	14a		9a	
	1951			12a	
	1952	19a			
	1953	14a	21a	2a	
	1954			29a	
	1955	15	12		
	1956	22		12	
	1957		13	19	
	1958		10		
	1962				17
STRANAHAN, Richard (USA)					
	1960		27		
STRANGE, Curtis (USA)					
	1976	15a			
	1980		16		5
	1981	19	17		27
	1982	7		15	14
	1983		26	29	
	1984		3		
	1985	2			
	1986	21		14	
	1987	12	4		9
	1988	21	W	13	
	1989	18	W		2
	1990	7	21		
	1992		23		
	1993		25		
	1994	27	4		19
	1995	9			17
	1996		27		26
	1998			19	
STRATH, Andrew (SCO)					
	1860			3	
	1863			4	
	1864			2	
	1865			W	
	1866			6	
	1867			3	

	Yr	M AS	USO	BOP	PGA
STRATH, Davie (SCO)					
	1869			5	
	1870			2	
	1872			2	
	1873			5	
	1874			18	
	1875			6	
	1876			2	
	1877			5	
STRATH, George (SCO/USA)					
	1878			14	
	1879			29	
	1880			16	
	1883			29	
	1886			24	
	1896		22		
STRATH, William (SCO)					
	1864			6	
	1865			8	
STRECK, Ron (USA)					
	1977		23		
	1979				4
	1982				22
STRICKER, Steve (USA)					
	1995		13		23
	1996			22	26
	1998		5		2
	1999		5		
	2000	19	27		
	2001	10			
STRINGER, Irving (USA)					
	1910		28		
STRONG, Herbert (USA)					
	1908		29		
	1913		9		
	1915		26		
STUART, A [a] (SCO)					
	1887			22	
STUPPLE, Bob (USA)					
	1937		20		
SULLIVAN, Mike (USA)					
	1980				30
	1983			14	
	1984		25		
	1989				12
SULLIVAN, Vince (USA)					
	1966		30		

SUNESSON, Magnus (SWE)

Yr	M AS	USO	BOP	PGA
1991			12	

SUTHERLAND, Kevin (USA)

Yr	M AS	USO	BOP	PGA
2001			9	

SUTTON, Hal (USA)

Yr	M AS	USO	BOP	PGA
1982		19		29
1983	27	6	29	W
1984		16		6
1985		23		
1986		4		21
1987			11	28
1989		29		
1991				7
1997		19		
1998				27
1999		7	10	26
2000	10	23		
2001		24		

SUTTON, Norman (ENG)

Yr	M AS	USO	BOP	PGA
1930			24	
1936			23	
1947			17	
1949			19	
1951			6	
1952			20	
1953			29	
1954			27	
1955			28	
1957			30	

SUZUKI, Norio (JAP)

Yr	M AS	USO	BOP	PGA
1976			10	
1977			26	
1980			19	

SWAELENS, Don (BEL)

Yr	M AS	USO	BOP	PGA
1958			11	
1962			23	
1969			30	
1974			7	

SWEETSER, Jess [a] (USA)

Yr	M AS	USO	BOP	PGA
1921		14		
1939	29			

SWEENY, HR [a] (USA)

Yr	M AS	USO	BOP	PGA
1898		27		

SYLVESTER, Joe (USA)

Yr	M AS	USO	BOP	PGA
1919				Last 32
1920				Last 16
1921				Last 32
1923		24		

SZWEDKO, Andrew [a] (USA)

Yr	M AS	USO	BOP	PGA
1940		29		

TAGGART, Fred (SCO)

Yr	M AS	USO	BOP	PGA
1928			11	
1939			26	

TAILER, Tommy (USA)

Yr	M AS	USO	BOP	PGA
1938	18			
1939	21			

TAIT, Bob (SCO)

Yr	M AS	USO	BOP	PGA
1883			28	
1886			20	
1888			18	

TAIT, Freddie [a] (SCO)

Yr	M AS	USO	BOP	PGA
1891			28	
1892			21	
1894			9	
1895			15	
1896			3	
1897			3	
1898			5	
1899			7	

TAPIE, Alan (USA)

Yr	M AS	USO	BOP	PGA
1974			13	
1975			16	
1976			21	
1979				23
1980				20

TAYLOR, Alex (USA)

Yr	M AS	USO	BOP	PGA
1901		22		
1904		23		

TAYLOR Jr, Frank [a] (USA)

Yr	M AS	USO	BOP	PGA
1956		29		
1957	13			
1960	20			

TAYLOR, Gerard (AUS)

Yr	M AS	USO	BOP	PGA
1987			25	

TAYLOR, HE [a] (ENG)

Yr	M AS	USO	BOP	PGA
1911			16	

TAYLOR, JH (John Henry) (ENG)

Yr	M AS	USO	BOP	PGA
1893			10	
1894			W	
1895			W	
1896			2	
1897			10	
1898			4	
1899			4	
1900		2	W	

	Yr	M	AS	USO	BOP	PGA
TAYLOR, JH (cont)	1901				3	
	1902				6	
	1903				9	
	1904				2	
	1905				2	
	1906				2	
	1907				2	
	1908				7	
	1909				W	
	1910				14	
	1911				5	
	1912				11	
	1913			30	W	
	1914				2	
	1920				12	
	1921				26	
	1922				6	
	1924				5	
	1925				6	
	1926				10	
TAYLOR, Josh (ENG)						
	1911				24	
	1913				14	
	1914				25	
TAYLOR, JW (ENG)						
	1896				29	
	1897				30	
	1898				27	
	1899				25	
	1900				18	
TAYLOR, Philip (ENG)						
	1912				24	
	1913				17	
	1920				16	
TAYLOR, Scott (USA)						
	1989			29		
TELLIER, Louis (FRA/USA)						
	1913			4	22	
	1914			8		
	1915			4		
	1916			13		Last 32
	1919			5		Last 32
	1921			14		
TENNYSON, Brian (USA)						
	1989					27
	1990					26
TERRY, Orrin (USA)						
	1908			17		
	1909			15		

	Yr	M	AS	USO	BOP	PGA
TEWELL, Doug (USA)						
	1980					30
	1982					22
	1983					9
	1984					25
	1985					12
	1986					10
	1988		14			
THOM, Charles (USA)						
	1902			7		
	1910			12		
	1913			26		
	1921					Last 32
THOMAS, Dave (WAL)						
	1956				17	
	1957				5	
	1958				2	
	1959	30				
	1962				8	
	1963				26	
	1964				13	
	1966				2	
	1968				27	
THOMAS, Emery (USA)						
	1950					Last 32
THOMPSON, Alec (SCO)						
	1904				25	
THOMPSON, Alvie (CAN)						
	1963		28			
THOMPSON, George (USA)						
	1920					Last 16
THOMPSON, John (SCO)						
	1876				14	
THOMPSON, Leonard (USA)						
	1974			21		17
	1975					10
	1976					22
	1977					15
	1978		24			
	1979		7			
	1980					26
	1981					22
THOMPSON, RM (USA)						
	1914			25		
THOMPSON, Rocky (USA)						
	1973			18		

THOMPSON, W (USA)

Yr	M	AS	USO	BOP	PGA
1899			24		

THOMSON, Cyril (ENG)

Yr	M	AS	USO	BOP	PGA
1935				30	

THOMSON, George (USA)

Yr	M	AS	USO	BOP	PGA
1904			15		

THOMSON, Hector (SCO)

Yr	M	AS	USO	BOP	PGA
1936				15a	
1950				14	
1953				22	

THOMSON, James (SCO/USA)

Yr	M	AS	USO	BOP	PGA
1910			18		
1916					Last 32

THOMSON, Jimmy (SCO/USA)

Yr	M	AS	USO	BOP	PGA
1926			16		
1929				13	
1935			2		Last 32
1936	15		14		RU
1937	6		28		Last 16
1938	8				Last 32
1939	18				
1942	12				Last 32
1946	25				Last 32
1949					Last 32

THOMSON, Peter (AUS)

Yr	M	AS	USO	BOP	PGA
1951				6	
1952				2	
1953			26	2	
1954	16			W	
1955	18			W	
1956			4	W	
1957	5		22	2	
1958	23			W	
1959				23	
1960				9	
1961	19			7	
1962				6	
1963				5	
1964				24	
1965				W	
1966				8	
1967				8	
1968				24	
1969				3	
1970				9	
1971				9	
1977				13	
1978				24	
1979				26	

THOMSON, R (SCO)

Yr	M	AS	USO	BOP	PGA
1873				18	

THOMSON, Robert (SCO)

Yr	M	AS	USO	BOP	PGA
1903				6	
1904				12	
1905				7	
1906				30	
1909				17	
1911				29	
1912				13	

THOMSON, William (SCO)

Yr	M	AS	USO	BOP	PGA
1874				6	
1876				4	
1880				21	
1882				16	
1883				23	
1889				10	

THOREN, John (USA)

Yr	M	AS	USO	BOP	PGA
1938					Last 32
1957					Last 32

THORPE, Jim (USA)

Yr	M	AS	USO	BOP	PGA
1981			11		
1982			30		
1983			13		14
1984			4		
1985	18				
1986					7
1987			9		

TILLINGHAST, AW (Albert Warren) [a] (USA)

Yr	M	AS	USO	BOP	PGA
1910			25		

TIMBERMAN, Wayne (USA)

Yr	M	AS	USO	BOP	PGA
1945					Last 32

TINGEY Sr, Albert (ENG)

Yr	M	AS	USO	BOP	PGA
1895				21	
1896				28	
1897				30	
1899				9	
1908				30	

TINGEY Jr, Albert (ENG)

Yr	M	AS	USO	BOP	PGA
1924				18	

TINSLEY, Dave (USA)

Yr	M	AS	USO	BOP	PGA
1946					Last 32

TODA, Torchy (JAP)

Yr	M	AS	USO	BOP	PGA
1936	29				

TODD, Harry (USA)

Yr	M	AS	USO	BOP	PGA
1941			13a		
1946			22		
1947	29		13		
1948	8				

	Yr	M AS	USO	BOP	PGA
TODD, Harry (cont)	1949		14		
	1952		13		
TOLIFSON, AC (USA)					
	1897		30		
	1900		25		
TOLLES, Tommy (USA)					
	1996				3
	1997	3	5		13
TOLLEY, Cyril [a] (ENG)					
	1924			18	
	1925			28	
	1929			25	
	1933			18	
	1938			28	
TOMORI, Katsuyoshi (JAP)					
	1995			24	
TOMS, David (USA)					
	1998	6			
	2000		16	4	
	2001				W
TOOGOOD, AH (ENG)					
	1894			4	
	1895			9	
	1896			17	
	1897			22	
	1899			23	
	1903			18	
	1904			12	
	1907			24	
	1908			18	
TOOGOOD, Peter [a] (AUS)					
	1954			15	
TOOGOOD, Walter (ENG)					
	1895			27	
	1896			22	
	1897			26	
	1898			19	
	1899			20	
	1901			28	
	1902			20	
	1905			28	
	1906			15	
	1907			13	
	1908			18	
TOPPING, Lambert (ENG)					
	1954			20	

	Yr	M AS	USO	BOP	PGA
TORPEY, Bunny (USA)					
	1933				Last 32
	1937				Last 32
TORRANCE, Sam (SCO)					
	1975			19	
	1981			5	
	1982			12	
	1984			9	
	1985			16	
	1986			21	
	1994		21		30
	1995			11	23
	1996		16		
	1998			24	
TORRANCE, Thomas [a] (SCO)					
	1932			22	
TORRANCE, WB [a] (SCO)					
	1927			9	
TORZA, Felice (ITA/USA)					
	1952		24		
	1953	29			RU
TOSKI, Bob (USA)					
	1950		20		Last 16
	1951	18			
	1953				Last 32
	1954	22	18		Last 32
	1956		17		Last 32
	1958				20
TOWNS, Eddie (USA)					
	1916				Last 32
	1921				Last 32
	1922				Last 16
	1924				Last 16
TOWNSEND, Peter (ENG)					
	1966			23a	
	1969			16	
	1972			13	
	1974			13	
	1981			19	
TRAVERS, Jerome [a] (USA)					
	1907		26		
	1913		28		
	1915		W		
TRAVIANI, P (ITA)					
	1951			24	
TRAVIS, Walter [a] (AUS/USA)					
	1902		2		

	Yr	M	AS	USO	BOP	PGA
TRAVIS, Walter (cont)	1903		15			
	1905		11			
	1908		23			
	1909		7			
	1912		10			
TREVINO, Lee (USA)						
	1967		5			
	1968		W			23
	1969	19				
	1970		8	3		26
	1971		W	W		13
	1972		4	W		11
	1973		4	10		18
	1974					W
	1975	10	29			
	1976	28				
	1977		27	4		13
	1978	14	12	29		7
	1979	12	19	17		
	1980	26	12	2		7
	1981			11		
	1983	20		5		14
	1984		9	14		W
	1985	10		20		2
	1986		4			11
	1987			17		
	1989	18				
	1990	24		25		
	1991			17		
TRIPLETT, Kirk (USA)						
	1994		23			15
	1995					13
	1997					13
	2001	6	7			10
TRISH, John (USA)						
	1952					Last 32
TROMBLEY, Bill (USA)						
	1952		19			
	1954					Last 32
TUCKER, Ken (USA)						
	1939					Last 32
TUCKER, Samuel (ENG/USA)						
	1895		9			
	1897		25			
TUCKER, Willie (ENG/USA)						
	1896		8			
	1897		15			
	1898		14			
	1899		27			

	Yr	M	AS	USO	BOP	PGA
TUPLING, Peter [a] (ENG)						
	1969				28	
TURNBULL, George (USA)						
	1905			20		
	1916			21		
TURNER, Greg (NZL)						
	1994				20	
	1996				7	
	1998				15	
	1999					16
TURNER, Ted (USA)						
	1934					Last 16
	1935			14		
	1936				15	
TURNESA, Jim (USA)						
	1942					RU
	1945					Last 16
	1946					QF
	1947					Last 16
	1948			3		
	1949		4	4		Last 16
	1951					Last 32
	1952					W
	1953	27		17		Last 32
	1954				5	
	1956	22				Last 16
TURNESA, Joe (USA)						
	1923			14		
	1924			15		
	1925			11		
	1926			2		Last 32
	1927			27		RU
	1928			6		
	1929				25	
	1930			17		
	1932					Last 32
	1935	9				
TURNESA, Mike (USA)						
	1934	28				
	1935	25				
	1939					Last 32
	1941					Last 16
	1942					Last 32
	1945					Last 16
	1946			26		
	1947					Last 16
	1948					RU
	1953					Last 32
TURNESA, Willie [a] (USA)						
	1939	26				

TURPIE, Harry (SCO/USA)

Yr	MAS	USO	BOP	PGA
1897		14		
1898		12		
1899		18		
1900		8		
1901		22		
1902		8		
1903		23		
1904		20		
1906		13		
1911		12		

TUTEN, Billy (USA)

Yr	MAS	USO	BOP	PGA
1990		24		

TWAY, Bob (USA)

Yr	MAS	USO	BOP	PGA
1986	8	8		W
1988		25	20	
1991		26	5	
1995		10		
1996	12			
1997		5		13
1998		3		13
2001				29

TWEDDELL, W [a] (ENG)

Yr	MAS	USO	BOP	PGA
1927			29	

TWIGGS, Greg (USA)

Yr	MAS	USO	BOP	PGA
1993				22

TWINE, William (ENG)

Yr	MAS	USO	BOP	PGA
1927			29	
1928			14	
1931			25	
1932			25	
1934			11	

TWITTY, Howard (USA)

Yr	MAS	USO	BOP	PGA
1979				7
1980				5
1989				27
1991				16
1993	17			

TYNER, Tray (USA)

Yr	MAS	USO	BOP	PGA
1992		17		

TYNG, JA [a] (USA)

Yr	MAS	USO	BOP	PGA
1897		15		
1898		19		

ULRICH, Wally (USA)

Yr	MAS	USO	BOP	PGA
1953				Last 16
1954				Last 32
1955				Last 16

UPTON Jr, FR [a] (USA)

Yr	MAS	USO	BOP	PGA
1909		15		

URZETTA, Sam (USA)

Yr	MAS	USO	BOP	PGA
1951	25a	29a		
1956	12			

VALENTINE, Tommy (USA)

Yr	MAS	USO	BOP	PGA
1981		26		11

VAN de VELDE, Jean (FRA)

Yr	MAS	USO	BOP	PGA
1999			2	26
2000	19			29

van DONCK, Flory (BEL)

Yr	MAS	USO	BOP	PGA
1946			27	
1947			21	
1948			7	
1950			9	
1951			24	
1952			7	
1953			20	
1954			10	
1955			5	
1956			2	
1957			5	
1958			5	
1959			2	

VANHOOTEGEM, Nicolas (BEL)

Yr	MAS	USO	BOP	PGA
2001			30	

VARDON, Harry (ENG)

Yr	MAS	USO	BOP	PGA
1893			23	
1894			5	
1895			9	
1896			W	
1897			6	
1898			W	
1899			W	
1900		W	2	
1901			2	
1902			2	
1903			W	
1904			5	
1905			9	
1906			3	
1907			7	
1908			5	
1909			26	
1910			16	
1911			W	
1912			2	
1913		2	3	
1914			W	
1920		2	14	
1921			23	

VARDON, Harry (cont)

Yr	M AS	USO	BOP	PGA
1922			8	
1925			17	

VARDON, Tom (ENG)

Yr	M AS	USO	BOP	PGA
1891			9	
1892			12	
1893			28	
1894			19	
1895			9	
1896			10	
1897			7	
1900			10	
1902			5	
1903			2	
1904			4	
1906			12	
1907			3	
1908			13	
1909		23	19	
1912		21		
1916		9		

VAUGHAN, David (WAL)

Yr	M AS	USO	BOP	PGA
1972			7	

VENTURI, Ken (USA)

Yr	M AS	USO	BOP	PGA
1954	16a			
1956	2a	8a		
1957	13	6		
1958	4		20	
1959			5	
1960	2	23	9	
1961	11			
1962	9			
1964		W	5	
1966	16	17	15	
1967	21	28	11	

VERPLANK, Scott (USA)

Yr	M AS	USO	BOP	PGA
1986		15		
1994		18		
1995		21		
1999		17	15	
2001		22	30	7

VERWEY, Bob (RSA)

Yr	M AS	USO	BOP	PGA
1965		17		
1966		22		
1967		18		
1979			30	

VICKERS, RD (ENG)

Yr	M AS	USO	BOP	PGA
1927			9	

VINES, Ellsworth (USA)

Yr	M AS	USO	BOP	PGA
1946		26		
1947	24			

VINES, Ellsworth (cont)

Yr	M AS	USO	BOP	PGA
1948	28	14		
1949		14		
1950				Last 32
1951				SF
1957				Last 32

VINES, Randall (AUS)

Yr	M AS	USO	BOP	PGA
1971			25	

von ELM, George [a] (USA)

Yr	M AS	USO	BOP	PGA
1926		3		
1928	4			
1929	5			
1930	11			
1931	2			
1932	27			
1934	28			
1938	11			

von NIDA, Norman (AUS)

Yr	M AS	USO	BOP	PGA
1946			4	
1947			6	
1948			3	
1950	27			
1952	27		9	

VOSSLER, Ernie (USA)

Yr	M AS	USO	BOP	PGA
1955		21		
1959		5		17
1960				24
1961				15
1966				18

WADE, Jim (ENG)

Yr	M AS	USO	BOP	PGA
1949			25	

WADKINS, Bobby (USA)

Yr	M AS	USO	BOP	PGA
1980		12		
1983				27
1986		15		
1987	21	4		7

WADKINS, Lanny (USA)

Yr	M AS	USO	BOP	PGA
1971		13a		
1972	19	25		16
1973	29	7	7	3
1974		26		
1975			22	
1977				W
1978	18			
1979	7	19		
1980				30
1981	21	14		
1982		6		2
1983	8	7	29	
1984		11	4	3
1985	18	5		10

WADKINS, Lanny (cont)

Yr	MAS	USO	BOP	PGA
1986		2		11
1987	12		29	2
1988	11	12		25
1989	26		26	
1990	3			
1991	3			
1993	3			14
1994	18			

WADKINS, Lloyd (USA)

Yr	MAS	USO	BOP	PGA
1947				Last 32

WAGNER, Leonard (USA)

Yr	MAS	USO	BOP	PGA
1955				Last 32

WAITES, Brian (ENG)

Yr	MAS	USO	BOP	PGA
1983			19	

WALDORF, Duffy (USA)

Yr	MAS	USO	BOP	PGA
1992			25	9
1994		9		
1995	24	13		20
1996	5			

WALKER, Cyril (ENG/USA)

Yr	MAS	USO	BOP	PGA
1916				QF
1921		13		SF
1923		23		Last 16
1924		W		
1926			17	
1931				QF

WALKER, Harry (ENG)

Yr	MAS	USO	BOP	PGA
1926			13	

WALKER, Peter (SCO/USA)

Yr	MAS	USO	BOP	PGA
1899		9		

WALL, Art (USA)

Yr	MAS	USO	BOP	PGA
1953		26		
1955		16		
1956				Last 32
1958	6			11
1959	W			25
1961				5
1962		11		23
1963	21			8
1967		9		
1968	22			
1971	27			
1972				24
1975	15			
1976	28			

WALPER, Leo (USA)

Yr	MAS	USO	BOP	PGA
1936				Last 16

WALSH, Frank (USA)

Yr	MAS	USO	BOP	PGA
1928		27		
1929				Last 32
1930		28		
1931		13		
1932				RU
1933		29		Last 16
1935		26		
1936				Last 32
1937		20		
1938	27			Last 32
1939	29			
1940	12	10		Last 32

WALSH, Peter (USA)

Yr	MAS	USO	BOP	PGA
1922				Last 32

WALTON, Philip (IRL)

Yr	MAS	USO	BOP	PGA
1989			13	

WALTON, Thomas (ENG)

Yr	MAS	USO	BOP	PGA
1922			8	
1923			19	

WALZEL, Bobby (USA)

Yr	MAS	USO	BOP	PGA
1979		19		
1980				8

WAMPLER, Fred (USA)

Yr	MAS	USO	BOP	PGA
1959		28		

WARD, Charlie (ENG)

Yr	MAS	USO	BOP	PGA
1932			17	
1933			28	
1934			13	
1939			30	
1946			4	
1947			6	
1948			3	
1949			4	
1951			3	
1953			17	
1956			17	

WARD Jr, E Harvie [a] (USA)

Yr	MAS	USO	BOP	PGA
1952	21			
1953	14			
1954	20			
1955	8	7		
1957	4	26		

WARD, Marvin (Bud) (USA)

Yr	MAS	USO	BOP	PGA
1939		4a		
1940	21a			
1941		30a		
1942	14a			
1946		26a		

	Yr	M	AS	USO	BOP	PGA
WARD, Marvin (Bud) (cont)	1947			5a		
	1948	30a				
	1955	30				
	1957			17		
WARGO, Tom (USA)						
	1992					28
WARRENDER, T (USA)						
	1896			28		
WATERS, Alan (ENG)						
	1947				23	
	1948				11	
	1949				18	
	1951				17	
WATERS, L (SCO/RSA)						
	1895				18	
	1901				22	
WATROUS, Al (USA)						
	1922					Last 32
	1923		8			
	1924					Last 16
	1925		13			Last 32
	1926				2	Last 32
	1927		18			
	1928				8	Last 16
	1929					SF
	1930		17			Last 16
	1931		15			
	1932					Last 32
	1933		13			
	1934	11				QF
	1935		14			SF
	1936	29				
	1937	7				Last 32
	1938	27				
	1939	25				Last 16
	1940	21				Last 32
	1950					Last 32
WATSON, Denis (ZIM)						
	1982				15	
	1985		2			
	1986		12			
	1987	27				
WATSON, James (SCO/USA)						
	1904			29		
	1906			27		
WATSON, RC (USA)						
	1911			23		

	Yr	M	AS	USO	BOP	PGA
WATSON, Tom (USA)						
	1972			29		
	1973					12
	1974			5		11
	1975	8		9	W	9
	1976			7		15
	1977	W		7	W	6
	1978	2		6	14	2
	1979	2			26	12
	1980	12		3	W	10
	1981	W		23	23	
	1982	5		W	W	9
	1983	4		2	W	
	1984	2		11	2	
	1985	10				6
	1986	6		24		16
	1987	7		2	7	14
	1988	9			28	
	1989	14			4	9
	1990	7				19
	1991	3		16	26	
	1993			5		5
	1994	13		6	11	9
	1995	14				
	1996			13		17
	1997	4			10	
	2000			27		9
WATT, David (SCO)						
	1914				25	
WATT, Tom (SCO)						
	1905				18	
	1908				11	
WATT, William (SCO)						
	1911				21	
	1921				19	
	1922				27	
	1923				8	
WATTS, Brian (USA)						
	1998				2	
	1999			23	24	
WAY, Ernest (USA)						
	1899			23		
	1900			21		
	1906			27		
WAY, Paul (ENG)						
	1984				22	
WAY, WH (USA)						
	1896			11		
	1897			25		
	1899			2		

Yr	M AS	USO	BOP	PGA
WAY, WH (cont)				
1900		16		
1903		15		
1904		26		
1905		20		
1908		29		
WEASTALL, BS (ENG)				
1924			21	
WEAVER, Bert (USA)				
1963				27
WEAVER, Dewitt (USA)				
1974		18		
WEBB, Gene (USA)				
1949		19		
WEBSTER, DL (SCO)				
1968			21	
WEBSTER, Steven [a] (ENG)				
1995			24	
WEETMAN, Harry (ENG)				
1951			6	
1952			15	
1953			14	
1955			5	
1956			10	
1957			12	
1958			8	
1959			16	
1960			9	
1962			12	
1964			6	
1965			29	
WEHRLE, Wilfred [a] (USA)				
1939		16		
1940		23		
WEIBRING, DA (Donald Albert) (USA)				
1979		19		
1983		20		
1985			8	
1986			30	4
1987	7			3
1988		3		
1989		21		
1991		11		
1992	25			
1996				17
1998		25		
1999		23		

Yr	M AS	USO	BOP	PGA
WEIR, Mike (CAN)				
1999				10
2000	28	16		29
2001		19		16
WEISKOPF, Tom (USA)				
1967		15		
1968	16	24		
1969	2	22		
1970	23	30	22	
1971	6			22
1972	2	8	7	
1973		3	W	6
1974	2	15	7	3
1975	2	29	15	
1976	9	2	17	8
1977	14	3	22	
1978	11	4	17	4
1979		4		
1980			16	10
1981				27
1982	10			
1983	20	24		30
WEITZEL, Johnny (USA)				
1954		21		
WELCH, Michael (ENG)				
1996			18	
WENTWORTH, Kevin (USA)				
1999				21
WEST, James (Jimmy) (USA)				
1916				Last 32
1919		18		QF
1920		20		
1921				Last 16
1923				Last 32
1924		22		
WESTON, Percy (ENG)				
1924			9	
1932			29	
1934			21	
WESTWOOD, Lee (ENG)				
1997	24	19	10	29
1998		7		
1999	6		18	16
2000		5		14
WETHERED, Roger [a] (ENG)				
1921			2	
WHEILDON, Dick (ENG)				
1920			21	
1922			17	

Yr	M	AS	USO	BOP	PGA
WHIGHAM, Charles [a] (SCO)					
1890				27	
WHIGHAM, HJ [a] (SCO/USA)					
1896		6			
1897		8			
WHITCOMBE, Charles (ENG)					
1922				5	
1923				6	
1926				22	
1927				6	
1930				9	
1931				28	
1932				4	
1934				7	
1935				3	
1936				19	
1937				4	
1938				10	
WHITCOMBE, Ernest E (ENG)					
1937				29	
1946				21	
1947				18	
1948				15	
1950				17	
1951				24	
1959				29	
WHITCOMBE, Ernest R (ENG)					
1914				29	
1922				12	
1924				2	
1925				26	
1927				4	
1930				17	
1931				22	
1933				12	
1934				9	
1935				17	
1938				19	
WHITCOMBE, Reg (ENG)					
1925				20	
1926				13	
1928				23	
1930				13	
1931				16	
1932				17	
1933				7	
1934				16	
1936				8	
1937				2	
1938				W	
1939				3	
1946				14	

Yr	M	AS	USO	BOP	PGA
WHITCOMBE, Reg (cont)	1947			13	
	1948			18	
WHITE, Buck (USA)					
1949			6		
1951			16		Last 32
1953					Last 32
1957					Last 32
WHITE, DK (USA)					
1920			23		
1923					Last 32
WHITE, GM (ENG)					
1949				30	
WHITE, Jack (SCO)					
1893				10	
1895				21	
1898				13	
1899				2	
1900				4	
1901				6	
1902				18	
1903				3	
1904				W	
1905				18	
WHITE, Orville (USA)					
1934					Last 32
1935			25		Last 32
1936	15				
WHITE, R (USA)					
1897			27		
WHITE, Ronnie [a] (ENG)					
1946				30	
WHITECROSS, Robert [a] (SCO)					
1906				15	
WHITEHEAD, George (USA)					
1938					Last 32
WHITEHEAD, Ross (ENG)					
1962				12	
WHITING, Albert (ENG)					
1928				11	
WHITT, Don (USA)					
1957					SF
1958					29
1960			17		
1961					15
1962			17		30

WHITTEN, Buddy (USA)

Yr	M AS	USO	BOP	PGA
1983				27

WIEBE, Mark (USA)

Yr	M AS	USO	BOP	PGA
1988		25		
1989				12
1990				19

WIECHERS, Jim (USA)

Yr	M AS	USO	BOP	PGA
1972		25		29
1975		14		

WILCOCK, Peter (ENG)

Yr	M AS	USO	BOP	PGA
1973			18	

WILCOX, Leland (USA)

Yr	M AS	USO	BOP	PGA
1940		23		

WILCOX, Pat (USA)

Yr	M AS	USO	BOP	PGA
1937				Last 32

WILCOX, Terry (USA)

Yr	M AS	USO	BOP	PGA
1965		28		
1969				7
1970	21			

WILKES, Brian (RSA)

Yr	M AS	USO	BOP	PGA
1963			20	

WILKES, Trevor (RSA)

Yr	M AS	USO	BOP	PGA
1957			24	
1958			26	

WILL, George (SCO)

Yr	M AS	USO	BOP	PGA
1961			30	
1964			29	
1965			21	
1966			23	

WILLIAMS, Dan (USA)

Yr	M AS	USO	BOP	PGA
1924				Last 16
1925				Last 16
1926		9		

WILLIAMS, David (ENG)

Yr	M AS	USO	BOP	PGA
1991			12	

WILLIAMS, Eddie (USA)

Yr	M AS	USO	BOP	PGA
1931		25		

WILLIAMS, Harold (USA)

Yr	M AS	USO	BOP	PGA
1950		20		Last 32

WILLIAMS Jr, Henry (USA)

Yr	M AS	USO	BOP	PGA
1944				Last 32
1948				Last 32
1949				QF
1950		29		RU

WILLIAMS Jr, Henry (cont)

Yr	M AS	USO	BOP	PGA
1952				Last 16
1953				Last 16
1954				Last 32

WILLIAMSON, EB (ENG)

Yr	M AS	USO	BOP	PGA
1954			27	

WILLIAMSON, JM (SCO)

Yr	M AS	USO	BOP	PGA
1900			29	

WILLIAMSON, Tom (ENG)

Yr	M AS	USO	BOP	PGA
1898			21	
1899			9	
1902			30	
1903			11	
1905			13	
1906			19	
1907			7	
1910			19	
1912			17	
1913			7	
1914			4	
1920			26	
1921			6	
1922			27	
1923			12	
1924			13	
1926			13	
1927			9	
1928			21	
1929			25	
1931			11	

WILSON, Dave (USA)

Yr	M AS	USO	BOP	PGA
1919				Last 32

WILSON, Dean (USA)

Yr	M AS	USO	BOP	PGA
2001		30		

WILSON, James [a] (SCO)

Yr	M AS	USO	BOP	PGA
1946			25	

WILSON, P [a] (SCO)

Yr	M AS	USO	BOP	PGA
1887			20	

WILSON, Robert (ENG)

Yr	M AS	USO	BOP	PGA
1890			22	
1896		9		
1897		11		

WILSON, Reg (ENG)

Yr	M AS	USO	BOP	PGA
1912			7	
1914			6	
1920			21	
1923			29	
1928			23	

WILSON, Sandy (ENG)

Yr	M AS	USO	BOP	PGA
1968			27	

WINGATE, Sydney (ENG)

Yr	M AS	USO	BOP	PGA
1920			7	
1923			12	
1924			23	
1925			6	
1928			23	

WINNINGER, Bo (USA)

Yr	M AS	USO	BOP	PGA
1951		29a		
1952		24		
1953	29			
1957		21		
1958	17	27		16
1959	18	19		
1960				29
1962		17		
1963	8			27
1964	21			7
1965	26			4

WISE, Larry (USA)

Yr	M AS	USO	BOP	PGA
1972				20

WOLFF, Randy (USA)

Yr	M AS	USO	BOP	PGA
1970		18		

WOLSTENHOLME, Guy (ENG/AUS)

Yr	M AS	USO	BOP	PGA
1959			16a	
1960			6	
1962			24	
1965			17	
1967			13	
1969			11	
1970			22	
1976			17	

WOOD, Craig (USA)

Yr	M AS	USO	BOP	PGA
1929		16		QF
1930		9		
1932		14		Last 32
1933		3	2	
1934	2			RU
1935	2	21		
1936	20			SF
1937	26			Last 32
1939	6	2		
1940	7	4		Last 32
1941	W	W		Last 32
1942	22			QF
1944				Last 16
1949		27		

WOOD, Larry (USA)

Yr	M AS	USO	BOP	PGA
1971				22

WOOD, Warren [a] (USA)

Yr	M AS	USO	BOP	PGA
1914		22		

WOOD, Willie (USA)

Yr	M AS	USO	BOP	PGA
1985				23
1992		17		
1997	12			
1998	21			

WOODS, Eldrick (Tiger) (USA)

Yr	M AS	USO	BOP	PGA
1996			22a	
1997	W	19	24	29
1998	8	18	3	10
1999	18	3	7	W
2000	5	W	W	W
2001	W	12	25	29

WOODWARD, Jim (USA)

Yr	M AS	USO	BOP	PGA
1987		17		

WOOSNAM, Ian (WAL)

Yr	M AS	USO	BOP	PGA
1985			16	
1986			3	30
1987			8	
1988			25	
1989	14	2		6
1990	30	21	4	
1991	W		17	
1992	19	6	5	
1993	17			22
1994				9
1995	17	21		
1996	29			
1997			24	
1998	16			29
1999	14		24	
2001			3	

WORSHAM, Lew (USA)

Yr	M AS	USO	BOP	PGA
1946		22		Last 32
1947		W		QF
1948	30	6		Last 16
1949	6	27		Last 16
1950				Last 32
1951	3	14		Last 32
1952	7	7		Last 32
1954	12	23		
1955				QF
1956				Last 16
1961	22			
1962	29			

WORTHINGTON, JS [a] (ENG)

Yr	M AS	USO	BOP	PGA
1904			21	

WRENN, Robert (USA)

Yr	M AS	USO	BOP	PGA
1988	25			
1989		26		

WRIGHT, A (SCO)

Yr	M AS	USO	BOP	PGA
1890			20	

	Yr	M AS	USO	BOP	PGA
WRIGHT Jr, Fred [a] (USA)					
	1922		24		
WRIGHT, Jimmy (USA)					
	1969				4
	1970	29			
WYNN, Bob (USA)					
	1975				28
	1977	24			
WYNNE, Philip (SCO)					
	1898			10	
WYSONG, Dudley (USA)					
	1964		23		
	1965		8		
	1966				2
YANCEY, Bert (USA)					
	1966				23
	1967	3			
	1968	3	3		
	1969	13	22	16	
	1970	4	22	13	22
	1971		9	11	22
	1972	12	11	19	29
	1973		25	5	24
	1974		3		
	1975	30			
YATES, Charlie [a] (USA)					
	1934	21			
	1935	19			
	1937	26			
	1939	18			
	1940	17			
	1942	28			
YEOMAN, Tom (ENG)					
	1901			12	
	1902			25	
YONEYAMA, Tsuyosho (JAP)					
	1999			15	
YOUDS, Jack (ENG/USA)					
	1898		21		
YOUNG, Arthur (ENG)					
	1930			17	
YUNG-YO, Hsieh (TPE)					
	1970	29			
ZARHARDT, Joe (USA)					
	1939				Last 32
	1941		25		
	1944				Last 32

	Yr	M AS	USO	BOP	PGA
ZARLEY, Kermit (USA)					
	1968	20			8
	1969		13		
	1970				22
	1969		13		
	1971		27		
	1972		6		
	1973	17			9
	1975		24		
	1978				19
ZENDER, Bob (USA)					
	1976				30
	1978				26
ZIEGLER, Larry (USA)					
	1968		24		
	1969				5
	1970		8		
	1971	30			
	1973		13		
	1974		12		
	1975	13			
	1976	3			
ZIMMERMAN, Al (USA)					
	1932		27		
	1935				SF
	1936				Last 32
	1938		19		
	1946	29			
ZIMMERMAN, Emery (USA)					
	1938		5		
ZOELLER, Fuzzy (USA)					
	1978				10
	1979	W			
	1980	19			
	1981				2
	1982	10	15	8	
	1983	20		14	6
	1984		W	14	
	1985		9	11	
	1986	21	15	8	
	1987	27		29	
	1988	16	8		
	1989	26			
	1990	20	8		14
	1991	12	5		
	1992	19			
	1993	11		14	
	1994			3	19
	1995		21		
	1997		28		
ZOKOL, Richard (CAN)					
	1988				17
	1993				14

Part

THE MAJOR CHAMPIONSHIPS RECORDS

Most Wins in Major Championships

1	JACK NICKLAUS	18
2	Walter Hagen	11
3=	Ben Hogan	9
	Gary Player	9
5	Tom Watson	8
6=	Bobby Jones	7
	Arnold Palmer	7
	Gene Sarazen	7
	Sam Snead	7
	Harry Vardon	7
11=	Nick Faldo	6
	Lee Trevino	6
	Tiger Woods	6
14=	Seve Ballesteros	5
	James Braid	5
	Byron Nelson	5
	JH Taylor	5
	Peter Thomson	5
19=	Willie Anderson Jr	4
	Jim Barnes	4
	Ray Floyd	4
	Bobby Locke	4
	Tom Morris Jr	4
	Tom Morris Sr	4
	Willie Park Sr	4
26=	Jamie Anderson	3
	Tommy Armour	3
	Julius Boros	3
	Billy Casper	3
	Henry Cotton	3
	Jimmy Demaret	3
	Bob Ferguson	3
	Ralph Guldahl	3
	Hale Irwin	3
	Cary Middlecoff	3
	Larry Nelson	3
	Nick Price	3
	Denny Shute	3
	Payne Stewart	3

Most Wins in Individual Majors

British Open

1	HARRY VARDON	6
2=	James Braid	5
	JH Taylor	5
	Peter Thomson	5
	Tom Watson	5
6=	Walter Hagen	4
	Tom Morris Jr	4
	Tom Morris Sr	4
	Willie Park Sr	4
11=	Jamie Anderson	3
	Seve Ballesteros	3
	Henry Cotton	3
	Nick Faldo	3
	Bob Ferguson	3
	Bobby Jones	3
	Jack Nicklaus	3
	Gary Player	3

US Open

1=	WILLIE ANDERSON	4
	BEN HOGAN	4
	BOBBY JONES	4
	JACK NICKLAUS	4
5	Hale Irwin	3
6=	Julius Boros	2
	Billy Casper	2
	Ernie Els	2
	Ralph Guldahl	2
	Walter Hagen	2
	Lee Janzen	2
	John McDermott	2
	Cary Middlecoff	2
	Andy North	2
	Gene Sarazen	2
	Alex Smith	2
	Payne Stewart	2
	Curtis Strange	2
	Lee Trevino	2

US PGA

1=	WALTER HAGEN (All Matchplay – MP)	5
	JACK NICKLAUS (All Strokeplay – SP)	5
3=	Gene Sarazen (All MP)	3
	Sam Snead (All MP)	3
5=	Jim Barnes (All MP)	2
	Leo Diegel (All MP)	2
	Ray Floyd (All SP)	2
	Ben Hogan (All MP)	2
	Byron Nelson (All MP)	2
	Larry Nelson (All SP)	2
	Gary Player (All SP)	2
	Nick Price (All SP)	2
	Paul Runyan (All MP)	2
	Denny Shute (All MP)	2
	Dave Stockton (All SP)	2
	Lee Trevino (All SP)	2
	Tiger Woods (All SP)	2

The Masters

1	JACK NICKLAUS	6
2	Arnold Palmer	4
3=	Jimmy Demaret	3
	Nick Faldo	3
	Gary Player	3
	Sam Snead	3
7=	Seve Ballesteros	2
	Ben Crenshaw	2
	Ben Hogan	2
	Bernhard Langer	2
	Byron Nelson	2
	Jose Maria Olazabal	2
	Horton Smith	2
	Tom Watson	2
	Tiger Woods	2

Winners of All Four Majors

JACK NICKLAUS (3+ times)	USO:	1962, 1967, 1972, 1980
	MAS:	1963, 1965, 1966, 1973, 1975, 1986
	PGA:	1963, 1971, 1973, 1975, 1980
	BOP:	1966, 1970, 1978
Ben Hogan (1+)	PGA:	1946, 1948
	USO:	1948, 1950, 1951, 1953
	MAS:	1951, 1953
Gary Player (1+)	BOP:	1959, 1968, 1974
	MAS:	1961, 1974, 1978
	PGA:	1962, 1972
	USO:	1965
Gene Sarazen (1+)	USO:	1922, 1932
	PGA:	1922, 1923, 1933
	BOP:	1932
	MAS:	1935
Tiger Woods (1+)	MAS:	1997, 2001
	PGA:	1999, 2000
	USO:	2000
	BOP:	2000

In the days before the Masters Tournament, the three Majors on offer had only been won by Walter Hagen and Jim Barnes, apart, of course, from Sarazen.

Multiple Wins in the Same Year

JACK NICKLAUS (5 times)	MAS, PGA (1963)
	MAS, BOP (1966)
	MAS, USO (1972)
	MAS, PGA (1975)
	USO, PGA (1980)
Ben Hogan (3)	MAS, USO, BOP (1953)
	USO, PGA (1948)
	MAS, USO (1951)
Bobby Jones (2)	USO, BOP (1926)
	USO, BOP (1930)
Arnold Palmer (2)	MAS, USO (1960)
	MAS, BOP (1962)
Gene Sarazen (2)	USO, PGA (1922)
	USO, BOP (1932)
Tom Watson (2)	MAS, BOP (1977)
	USO, BOP (1982)
Jack Burke, Jr (1)	MAS, PGA (1956)
Nick Faldo (1)	MAS, BOP (1990)
Walter Hagen (1)	BOP, PGA (1924)
Mark O'Meara (1)	MAS, BOP (1998)
Gary Player (1)	MAS, BOP (1974)
Nick Price (1)	BOP, PGA (1994)
Sam Snead (1)	MAS, PGA (1949)
Craig Wood (1)	MAS, USO (1941)
Tiger Woods (1)	USO, BOP, PGA (2000)

Winners of Consecutive Majors

TOM MORRIS, Jr (4 in a row)*	BOP 1868, 1869, 1870, 1872
TIGER WOODS (4)	USO 2000, BOP 2000, PGA 2000, MAS 2001
Jamie Anderson (3)	BOP 1877, 1878, 1879
Bob Ferguson (3)	BOP 1880, 1881, 1882
Ben Hogan (3)**	MAS 1953, USO 1953, BOP 1953
Tommy Armour (2)	PGA 1930, BOP 1931
Walter Hagen (2)	PGA 1921, BOP 1922
	and BOP 1924, PGA 1924
	and PGA 1927, BOP 1928
Ben Hogan (2)	PGA 1948, USO 1948
	and MAS 1951, USO 1951
Bobby Jones (2)	BOP 1926, USO 1926
	and BOP 1930, USO 1930
Tom Morris, Sr (2)	BOP 1861, 1862
Jack Nicklaus (2)	MAS 1972, USO 1972
Arnold Palmer (2)	MAS 1960, USO 1960
Nick Price (2)	BOP 1994, PGA 1994
Gene Sarazen (2)	USO 1922, PGA 1922
	and BOP 1932, USO 1932
Sam Snead (2)	MAS 1949, PGA 1949
JH Taylor (2)	BOP 1894, 1895
Lee Trevino (2)	USO 1971, BOP 1971
Tom Watson (2)	USO 1982, BOP 1982
Craig Wood (2)	MAS 1941, USO 1941

*There was no championship in 1871
**For all practical purposes the PGA and BOP overlapped

Back-to-Back Winners of the Same Major

WALTER HAGEN (4 in a row)	PGA 1924, 1925, 1926, 1927
TOM MORRIS, Jr (4)*	BOP 1868, 1869, 1870, 1872
Jamie Anderson (3)	BOP 1877, 1878, 1879
Willie Anderson (3)	USO 1903, 1904, 1905
Bob Ferguson (3)	BOP 1880, 1881, 1882
Peter Thomson (3)	BOP 1954, 1955, 1956
Jim Barnes (2)**	PGA 1916, 1919
James Braid (2)	BOP 1905, 1906
Leo Diegel (2)	PGA 1928, 1929
Nick Faldo (2)	MAS 1989, 1990
Ralph Guldahl (2)	USO 1937, 1938
Walter Hagen (2)	BOP 1928, 1929
Ben Hogan (2)	USO 1950, 1951
Bobby Jones (2)	USO 1926, 1927
	and USO 1929, 1930
Bobby Locke (2)	BOP 1949, 1950
John McDermott (2)	USO 1911,1912
Tom Morris, Sr (2)	BOP 1861, 1862
Jack Nicklaus (2)	MAS 1965, 1966
Arnold Palmer (2)	BOP 1961, 1962
Gene Sarazen (2)	PGA 1922, 1923
Denny Shute (2)	PGA 1936,1937
Curtis Strange (2)	USO 1988, 1989
JH Taylor (2)	BOP 1894, 1895
Lee Trevino (2)	BOP 1971, 1972
Harry Vardon (2)	BOP 1898, 1899
Tom Watson (2)	BOP 1982, 1983
Tiger Woods (2)	PGA 1999, 2000

*There was no championship in 1871
**There were no championships in 1917 and 1918

Longest Spans between First & Last Wins (Years)

1	JACK NICKLAUS	24 (1962 USO to 1986 MAS)
2=	Gary Player	19 (1959 BOP to 1978 MAS)
	JH Taylor	19 (1894 BOP to 1913 BOP)
4	Harry Vardon	18 (1896 BOP to 1914 BOP)
5	Ray Floyd	17 (1969 PGA to 1986 USO)
6=	Julius Boros	16 (1952 USO to 1968 PGA)
	Hale Irwin	16 (1974 USO to 1990 USO)
	Lee Trevino	16 (1968 USO to 1984 PGA)
9=	Walter Hagen	15 (1914 USO to 1929 BOP)
	Willie Park, Sr	15 (1860 BOP to 1875 BOP)
11	Henry Cotton	14 (1934 BOP to 1948 BOP)
12	Gene Sarazen	13 (1922 USO to 1935 MAS)
13	Sam Snead	12 (1942 PGA to 1954 MAS)
14=	Billy Casper	11 (1959 USO to 1970 MAS)
	Ben Crenshaw	11 (1984 MAS to 1995 MAS)
	Peter Thomson	11 (1954 BOP to 1965 BOP)

Longest Gaps between Wins

11 years	Julius Boros (USO 1952 to USO 1963)
	Henry Cotton (BOP 1937 to BOP 1948)
	Ben Crenshaw (MAS 1984 to MAS 1995)
	Hale Irwin (USO 1979 to USO 1990)

It is pure coincidence that these time spans happen to be between the same Major Championships. The longest span between victories in two different Majors is nine years for Gene Sarazen (PGA 1923 to BOP 1932). The longest gap between two wins in the same Major (although they both achieved success elsewhere between-times) was 13 years for Gary Player (MAS 1961 to 1974) and Ray Floyd (PGA 1969 to PGA 1982).

Youngest Winners

TOM MORRIS, Jr (BOP, 1868)	17 years	5 months 8 days
Tom Morris Jr (BOP, 1869)	18 years	5 months 1 day
Tom Morris Jr (BOP, 1870)	19 years	5 months
John McDermott (USO, 1911)	19 years	10 months 12 days
Francis Ouimet (USO, 1913)	20 years	4 months 11 days
Gene Sarazen (USO, 1922)	20 years	4 months 16 days
Gene Sarazen (PGA, 1922)	20 years	5 months 20 days
Tom Creavy (PGA, 1931)	20 years	7 months 17 days
John McDermott (USO, 1912)	20 years	11 m则ths 21 days
Willie Auchterlonie (BOP, 1893)	21 years	24 days
Tiger Woods (MAS, 1997)	21 years	3 months 15 days

Oldest Winners

JULIUS BOROS (PGA, 1968)	48 years	4 months 18 days
Tom Morris, Sr (BOP, 1867)	46 years	3 months 9 days
Jack Nicklaus (MAS, 1986)	46 years	2 months 23 days
Jerry Barber (PGA, 1961)	45 years	3 months 6 days
Hale Irwin (USO, 1990)	45 years	15 days
Lee Trevino (PGA, 1984)	44 years	8 months 18 days
Roberto de Vicenzo (BOP, 1967)	44 years	4 months 3 days
Ray Floyd (USO, 1986)	43 years	9 months 11 days
Ted Ray (USO, 1920)	43 years	4 months 16 days
Julius Boros (USO, 1963)	43 years	3 months 20 days
Ben Crenshaw (MAS, 1995)	43 years	2 months 29 days

Largest Winning Margins

15	TIGER WOODS	USO, 2000
13	Tom Morris Sr	BOP, 1862
12	Tom Morris Jr	BOP, 1870
	Tiger Woods	MAS, 1997
11	Willie Smith	USO, 1899
9	Jim Barnes	USO, 1921
	Jack Nicklaus	MAS, 1965
8	James Braid	BOP, 1908
	Ray Floyd	MAS, 1976
	JH Taylor	BOP, 1900
	JH Taylor	BOP, 1913
	Tiger Woods	BOP, 2000
7	Fred Herd	USO, 1898
	Tony Jacklin	USO, 1970
	Cary Middlecoff	MAS, 1955
	Jack Nicklaus	PGA, 1980

Play-Offs (Extra holes in Matchplay PGA)

Out of 379 Major Championship events, 74 have resulted in ties at the end of the regulation rounds. Of these, five occurred in the 39 matchplay PGA Championships (1916–1957) which went to extra holes in the Final. The Open Championship has provided 16 play-offs in the 130 events to date (a ratio of one play-off every eight years or so); the Masters, 11 out of 65 (one every six years); and the PGA an additional 10 in the 44 occasions (every four to five years) since strokeplay was introduced in 1958. The most play-offs by some margin, however, seem to be in the US Open, where overtime has been needed in no fewer than 32 of the 101 Championships – almost one year in three.

1876 BOP:	Bob Martin bt Davie Strath (36 holes)*
1883 BOP:	Willie Fernie bt Bob Ferguson (36 holes)
1889 BOP:	Willie Park, Jr bt Andrew Kirkaldy (36 holes)
1895 BOP:	Harry Vardon bt JH Taylor (36 holes)
1901 USO:	Willie Anderson bt Alex Smith (18 holes)
1903 USO:	Willie Anderson bt David Brown (18 holes)
1907 USO:	Fred McLeod bt Willie Smith (18 holes)
1910 USO:	Alex Smith bt John McDermott (18 holes)
1911 USO:	John McDermott bt Mike Brady & George Simpson (18 holes)
1912 BOP:	Harry Vardon bt Arnaud Massy (after 35)
1913 USO:	Francis Ouimet bt Harry Vardon & Ted Ray (18 holes)
1919 USO:	Walter Hagen bt Mike Brady (18 holes)
1921 BOP:	Jock Hutchison bt Roger Wethered (36 holes)
1923 USO:	Bobby Jones bt Bobby Cruickshank (18 holes)
1923 PGA:	Gene Sarazen bt Walter Hagen (after 38)
1925 USO:	Willie McFarlane bt Bobby Jones (2x18 holes)
1927 USO:	Tommy Armour bt Harry Cooper (18 holes)
1928 USO:	Johnny Farrell bt Bobby Jones (36 holes)
1929 USO:	Bobby Jones bt Al Espinosa (36 holes)
1931 USO:	Billy Burke bt George Von Elm (2x36 holes)
1933 BOP:	Denny Shute bt Craig Wood (36 holes)
1934 PGA:	Paul Runyan bt Craig Wood (after 38)
1935 MAS:	Gene Sarazen bt Craig Wood (36 holes)
1937 PGA:	Denny Shute bt Harold McSpaden (after 37)
1939 USO:	Byron Nelson bt Craig Wood & Denny Shute (2x18 holes)
1939 PGA:	Henry Picard bt Byron Nelson (after 37)
1940 USO:	Lawson Little bt Gene Sarazen (18 holes)
1941 PGA:	Vic Ghezzi bt Byron Nelson (after 38)
1942 MAS:	Byron Nelson bt Ben Hogan (18 holes)

1946 USO: Lloyd Mangrum bt Byron Nelson & Vic Ghezzi (2x18 holes)
1947 USO: Lew Worsham bt Sam Snead (18 holes)
1949 BOP: Bobby Locke bt Harry Bradshaw (36 holes)
1950 USO: Ben Hogan bt Lloyd Mangrum & George Fazio (18 holes)
1954 MAS: Sam Snead bt Ben Hogan (18 holes)
1955 USO: Jack Fleck bt Ben Hogan (18 holes)
1956 USO: Dick Mayer bt Cary Middlecoff (18 holes)
1957 BOP: Peter Thomson bt Dave Thomas (36 holes)
1961 PGA: Jerry Barber bt Don January (18 holes)
1962 MAS: Arnold Palmer bt Gary Player & Dow Finsterwald (18 holes)
1962 USO: Jack Nicklaus bt Arnold Palmer (18 holes)
1963 USO: Julius Boros bt Jacky Cupit & Arnold Palmer (18 holes)
1963 BOP: Bob Charles bt Phil Rodgers (36 holes)
1965 USO: Gary Player bt Kel Nagle (18 holes)
1966 MAS: Jack Nicklaus bt Tommy Jacobs & Gay Brewer (18 holes)
1966 USO: Billy Casper bt Arnold Palmer (18 holes)
1967 PGA: Don January bt Don Massingale (18 holes)
1970 MAS: Billy Casper bt Gene Littler (18 holes)
1970 BOP: Jack Nicklaus bt Doug Sanders (18 holes)
1971 USO: Lee Trevino bt Jack Nicklaus (18 holes)
1975 USO: Lou Graham bt John Mahaffey (18 holes)
1975 BOP: Tom Watson bt Jack Newton (18 holes)
1977 PGA: Lanny Wadkins bt Gene Littler (s/d)
1978 PGA: John Mahaffey bt Jerry Pate & Tom Watson (s/d)
1979 MAS: Fuzzy Zoeller bt Ed Sneed & Tom Watson (s/d)
1979 PGA: David Graham bt Ben Crenshaw (s/d)
1982 MAS: Craig Stadler bt Dan Pohl (s/d)
1982 USO: Fuzzy Zoeller bt Greg Norman (18 holes)
1987 MAS: Larry Mize bt Greg Norman & Seve Ballesteros (s/d)
1987 PGA: Larry Nelson bt Lanny Wadkins (s/d)
1988 USO: Curtis Strange bt Nick Faldo (18 holes)
1989 MAS: Nick Faldo bt Scott Hoch (s/d)
1989 BOP: Calcavecchia bt Wayne Grady & Greg Norman (4 holes)
1990 MAS: Nick Faldo bt Ray Floyd (s/d)
1990 USO: Hale Irwin bt Mike Donald (18 holes, s/d)
1991 USO: Payne Stewart bt Scott Simpson (18 holes)
1993 PGA: Paul Azinger bt Greg Norman (s/d)
1994 USO: Ernie Els bt Loren Roberts & Colin Montgomerie (18 holes, s/d)
1995 BOP: John Daly bt Costantino Rocca (4 holes)
1995 PGA: Steve Elkington bt Colin Montgomerie (s/d)
1996 PGA: Mark Brooks bt Kenny Perry (s/d)
1998 BOP: Mark O'Meara bt Brian Watts (4 hole)
1999 BOP: Paul Lawrie bt Jean Van de Velde & Justin Leonard (4 holes)
2000 PGA: Tiger Woods bt Bob May (s/d)
2001 USO: Retief Goosen bt Mark Brooks (18 holes)

Never took place when Strath refused to play off

Most (and Least) Successful Players in Play-Offs (Min 2)

WILLIE ANDERSON	2-0
BILLY CASPER	2-0
NICK FALDO	2-0
FUZZY ZOELLER	2-0
Jack Nicklaus	3-1
Gene Sarazen	2-1
Denny Shute	2-1
Harry Vardon	2-1
Bobby Jones	2-2
Mark Brooks	1-1
Walter Hagen	1-1
Don January	1-1
John McDermott	1-1
Gary Player	1-1
Alex Smith	1-1
Sam Snead	1-1
Byron Nelson	2-3
Tom Watson	1-2
Ben Hogan	1-3
Arnold Palmer	1-3
Mike Brady	0-2
Colin Montgomerie	0-2
Greg Norman	0-4
Craig Wood	0-4

Most Runners-up (against No of Wins)

1	JACK NICKLAUS (BOP 7; USO 4; PGA 4; MAS 4)	19 (18)
2	Arnold Palmer (BOP 1; USO 4; PGA 3; MAS 2)	10 (6)
3=	Greg Norman (BOP 1; USO 2; PGA 2; MAS 3)	8 (2)
	Sam Snead (USO 4; PGA 2; MAS 2)	8 (6)
4=	JH Taylor (BOP 6; USO 1)	7 (5)
	Tom Watson (BOP 1; USO 2; PGA 1; MAS 3)	7 (8)
6=	Ben Hogan (USO 2; MAS 4)	6 (9)
	Byron Nelson (USO 1; PGA 3; MAS 2)	6 (5)
	Gary Player (USO 2; PGA 2; MAS 2)	6 (9)
	Harry Vardon (BOP 4; USO 2)	6 (7)
10=	Ben Crenshaw (BOP 2; PGA 1; MAS 2)	5 (2)
	Ray Floyd (BOP 1; PGA 1; MAS 3)	5 (4)
	Tom Weiskopf (USO 1; MAS 4)	5 (1)
	Craig Wood (BOP 1; USOP 1; PGA 1; MAS 2)	5 (2)

The following players have recorded the most Runner-Up positions without ever winning a Major title:

Harry Cooper (USO 2; MAS 2)	4
Bruce Crampton* (USO 1; PGA 2; MAS 1)	4
Doug Sanders (BOP 2; USO 1; PGA 1)	4
Macdonald Smith (BOP 2; USO 2)	4
Andy Bean (BOP 1; PGA 2)	3
Chip Beck (USO 2; MAS 1)	3
Johnny Bulla (BOP 2; MAS 1)	3
Andrew Kirkaldy (BOP 3)	3
Tom McNamara (USOP 3)	3
Colin Montgomerie (USOP 2; PGA 1)	3
Ed Oliver (USOP 1; PGA 1; MAS 1)	3
Dai Rees (BOP 3)	3
Frank Stranahan (BOP 2; MAS 1)	3
Davie Strath (BOP 3)	3

On every occasion he was runner-up, Bruce Crampton was beaten by Jack Nicklaus!

Most Top 5 Finishes

1	JACK NICKLAUS	56
2=	Arnold Palmer	26
	Sam Snead	26
4=	Gene Sarazen	24
	Tom Watson	24
6=	Walter Hagen	22
	Ben Hogan	22
8=	Gary Player	19
	Greg Norman	19
10=	Nick Faldo	18
	Byron Nelson	18
	JH Taylor	18
	Harry Vardon	18

The players with most Top 5 finishes who have never recorded a win are:

Harry Cooper	11
Macdonald Smith	10
Bobby Cruickshank	8
Andrew Kirkaldy	8
Doug Sanders	8

The players with most Top 5 finishes who have never recorded a win or a second place are:

Jay Haas	8
Ed Dudley	6
Bruce Devlin	6
Phil Mickelson	6

Most Top 10 Finishes

1	JACK NICKLAUS	73
2	Sam Snead	46
3	Tom Watson	45
4	Gary Player	40
5	Ben Hogan	39
6	Arnold Palmer	38
7	Gene Sarazen	35
8=	Ray Floyd	28
	Walter Hagen	28
	Byron Nelson	28

The players with most Top 10 finishes who have never recorded a win are:

Ed Dudley	19
Bruce Devlin	16
Macdonald Smith	15
Phil Mickelson	14

Most Top 20 Finishes

1	JACK NICKLAUS	84
2	Sam Snead	65
3	Tom Watson	62
4	Ray Floyd	60
5	Gary Player	56
6	Arnold Palmer	54
7	Gene Sarazen	52
8	Ben Hogan	45
8=	Billy Casper	44
	Tom Kite	44

The players with most Top 20 finishes who have never recorded a win are:

Ed Dudley	31
Bruce Devlin	25
Doug Sanders	24

Most Top 30 Finishes

1	JACK NICKLAUS	101
2	Sam Snead	81
3	Gary Player	75
4	Tom Watson	70
5=	Ray Floyd	67
	Gene Sarazen	67
7	Arnold Palmer	65
8	Lee Trevino	52
9	Tom Kite	51
10	Ben Crenshaw	51

The players with most Top 30 finishes who have never recorded a win are:

Ed Dudley	37
Bruce Devlin	34
Bruce Crampton	33

Lowest Totals and Scores

Totals

265	DAVID TOMS	Atlanta AC, PGA 2001
266	Phil Mickelson*	Atlanta AC, PGA 2001
267	Steve Elkington	Riviera CC, PGA 1995
	Colin Montgomerie*	Riviera CC, PGA 1995
	Greg Norman	Royal St George's, BOP 1993
268	Steve Lowery*	Atalanta AC, PGA 2001
	Nick Price	Turnberry, BOP 1994
	Tom Watson	Turnberry, BOP 1977
269	Ernie Els*	Riviera CC, PGA 1995
	Nick Faldo*	Royal St George's, BOP 1993
	Davis Love III	Winged Foot, PGA 1999
	Jeff Maggert*	Riviera CC, PGA 1995
	Jack Nicklaus*	Turnberry, BOP 1977
	Jesper Parnevik*	Turnberry, BOP 1994
	Nick Price	Southern Hills, PGA 1994
	Tiger Woods	St Andrews, BOP 2000
270	Mark Calcavecchia*	Atlanta AC, PGA 2001
	Nick Faldo	St Andrews, BOP 1990
	Shingo Katayama*	Atlanta AC, PGA 2001
	Bernhard Langer*	Royal St George's, BOP 1993
	Tiger Woods	Augusta National, MAS 1997
	Bob May*	Valhalla GC, PGA 2000
	Tiger Woods	Valhalla GC, PGA 2000
271	Brad Faxon*	Riviera CC, PGA 1995
	Ray Floyd	Augusta National, MAS 1976
	Tom Lehman	Royal Lytham, BOP 1996
	Bobby Nichols	Columbus CC, PGA 1964
	Jack Nicklaus	Augusta National, MAS 1965
	Tom Watson	Muirfield, BOP 1980
	Fuzzy Zoeller*	Turnberry, BOP 1994
272	Billy Andrade*	Atlanta AC, PGA 2001
	Paul Azinger	Inverness, PGA 1993
	Ian Baker-Finch	Royal Birkdale, BOP 1991
	Ben Crenshaw*	Oakland Hills, PGA 1979
	Nick Faldo	Muirfield, BOP 1992
	Ray Floyd	Southern Hills, PGA 1982
	David Graham	Oakland Hills, PGA 1979
	Lee Janzen	Baltusrol, USO 1993
	Jack Nicklaus	Baltusrol, USO 1980
	Greg Norman*	Inverness, PGA 1993
	Corey Pavin*	Royal St George's, BOP 1993
	Peter Senior*	Royal St George's, BOP 1993
	Jeff Sluman	Oak Tree GC, PGA 1988
	Tiger Woods	Pebble Beach, USO 2000
	Tiger Woods	Augusta National, MAS 2001

* Not winning totals

18 Holes

63	MICHAEL BRADLEY	Riviera CC, PGA 1995
	RAY FLOYD	Southern Hills, PGA 1982
	JACK NICKLAUS	Baltusrol, USO 1980
	GREG NORMAN	Augusta National, MAS 1996
	TOM WEISKOPFf	Baltusrol, USO 1980
64	Rodger Davis	Muirfield, BOP 1987
	Mike Donald	Augusta National, MAS 1990
	Ray Floyd	Muirfield, BOP 1992
	Jim Gallagher, Jr	Riviera CC, PGA 1995
	Lee Mackey, Jr	Merion, USO 1950
	Lloyd Mangrum	Augusta National, MAS 1940
	Bobby Nichols	Columbus CC, PGA 1964
	Christy O'Connor, Jr	Royal St George's, BOP 1985
	Mark O'Meara	Riviera CC, PGA 1995
	Steve Pate	Muirfield, BOP 1982
	Scott Simpson	Inverness, PGA 1993
	Craig Stadler	Royal Birkdale, BOP 1983
	Doug Tewell	Cherry Hills, PGA 1985
	David Toms	Augusta National, MAS 1998

36 Holes

130	NICK FALDO (66,64)	Muirfield, BOP 1992
131	Ernie Els (66,65)	Riviera CC, PGA 1995
	Shingo Katayama (67,64)	Atlanta AC, PGA 2001
	Ray Floyd (65,66)	Augusta National, MAS 1976
	Mark O'Meara (64,67)	Riviera CC, PGA 1995
	Vijay Singh (68,63)	Inverness, PGA 1993
	Hal Sutton (65,66)	Riviera CC, PGA 1983
	David Toms (66,65)	Atlanta AC, PGA 2001
132	Nick Faldo (67,65)	St Andrews, BOP 1990
	Nick Faldo (69,63)	Royal St George's, BOP 1993
	Bob Estes (67,65)	Atlanta AC, PGA 2001
	Ray Floyd (63,69)	Southern Hills, PGA 1982
	Phil Mickelson (66,66)	Atlanta AC, PGA 2001
	Nick Price (67,65)	Southern Hills, PGA 1994

The lowest 36-hole total in the US Open is 134, shared by the following players:

Tze-Chung Chen (65,69)	Oakland Hills, 1985
Lee Janzen (67,67)	Baltusrol, 1993
Jack Nicklaus (63,71)	Baltusrol, 1980
Tiger Woods (65,69)	Pebble Beach, 2000

54 Holes

196	DAVID TOMS (66,65,65)	Atlanta AC, PGA 2001
197	Ernie Els (66,65,66)	Riviera CC, PGA 1995
198	Tom Lehman (67,67,64)	Royal Lytham, BOP 1996
	Phil Mickelson (66,66,66)	Atlanta AC, PGA 2001
199	Nick Faldo (67,65,67)	St Andrews, BOP 1990
200	Ray Floyd (63,69,68)	Southern Hills, PGA 1982
	Shingo Katayama (67,64,69)	Atlanta AC, PGA 2001
	Steve Lowery (67,67,66)	Atalanta AC, PGA 2001
	Jeff Maggert (66,69,65)	Riviera CC, PGA 1995
	Mark O'Meara (64,67,69)	Riviera CC, PGA 1995
	Tiger Woods (67,66,67)	St Andrews, BOP 2000
201	Ray Floyd (65,66,70)	Augusta National, MAS 1976
	Tiger Woods (70,66,65)	Augusta National, MAS 1997

The lowest 54-hole total in the US Open is 203, shared by the following players:

George Burns (69,66,68)	Merion CC, 1981
Tze-Chung Chen (65,69,69)	Oakland Hills, 1995
Lee Janzen (67,67,69)	Baltusrol, 1993

Lowest Rounds

2nd Round

63	BRUCE CRAMPTON	Firestone CC, PGA 1975
	NICK FALDO	Royal St George's, BOP 1993
	MARK HAYES	Turnberry, BOP 1977
	GREG NORMAN	Turnberry, BOP 1993
	MARK O'MEARA	Atlanta AC, PGA 2001
	GARY PLAYER	Shoal Creek, PGA 1984
	VIJAY SINGH	Inverness, PGA 1993
64	Miller Barber	Augusta National, MAS 1979
	Don Bies	NCR CC, PGA 1969
	Mark Brooks	Turnberry, BOP 1994
	Mark Brooks	Southern Hills, USO 2001
	Horacio Carbonetti	Muirfield, BOP 1980
	Nick Faldo	Muirfield, BOP 1992
	Jim Furyk	Atanta AC, PGA 2001
	Jay Haas	Augusta National, MAS 1995
	Shingo Katayama	Atlanta AC, PGA 2001
	Tommy Jacobs	Congressional, USO 1964
	Rives McBee	Olympic Club, USO 1966
	Blaine McCallister	Southern Hills, PGA 1994
	Gary Player	Augusta National, MAS 1974
	Dave Rummells	Oak Tree GC, PGA 1988
	Craig Stadler	Kemper Lakes, PGA 1989
	Curtis Strange	Oak Hill, USO 1989
	Steve Stricker	Riviera CC, PGA 1995

3rd Round

63	ISAO AOKI	Muirfield, BOP 1980
	PAUL BROADHURST	ST Andrews, BOP 1990
	JOSE MARIA OLAZABAL	Valhalla, PGA 2000
	NICK PRICE	Augusta National, MAS 1986
64	Ian Baker-Finch	St Andrews, BOP 1990
	Ian Baker-Finch	Royal Birkdale, BOP 1991
	Miller Barber	NCR CC, PGA 1969
	Keith Clearwater	Olympic Club, USO 1987
	Ben Crenshaw	Merion, USO 1981
	Wayne Grady	Royal St George's, BOP 1993
	Hubert Green	Muirfield, BOP 1980
	Jay Haas	Riviera CC, PGA 1995
	Larry Mize	Turnberry, BOP 1994
	Jack Nicklaus	Augusta National, MAS 1965
	Loren Roberts	Oakmont, USO 1994
	Hal Sutton	Shoal Creek, PGA 1984
	Bob Tway	Inverness, PGA 1986
	Tom Watson	Muirfield, BOP 1980
	Fuzzy Zoeller	Turnberry, BOP 1994

4th Round

63	BRAD FAXON	Riviera CC, PGA 1995
	JOHNNY MILLER	Oakmont, USO 1973
	JODIE MUDD	Royal Birkdale, BOP 1991
	PAYNE STEWART	Royal St George's, BOP 1993
64	Seve Ballesteros	Turnberry, BOP 1986
	Maurice Bembridge	Augusta National, MAS 1974
	Fred Couples	Royal Birkdale, BOP 1991
	Steve Elkington	Riviera CC, PGA 1995
	Nick Faldo	Turnberry, BOP 1994
	Anders Forsbrand	Turnberry, BOP 1994
	Hale Irwin	Augusta National, MAS 1975
	Peter Jacobsen	Brookline, USO 1988
	Tom Kite	Southern Hills, USO 2001
	Graham Marsh	Royal Birkdale, BOP 1983
	Jack Nicklaus	Columbus CC, PGA 1964
	Greg Norman	Augusta National, MAS 1988
	Greg Norman	Royal Troon, BOP 1989
	Greg Norman	Royal St George's, BOP 1993
	Gary Player	Augusta National, MAS 1978
	Vijay Singh	Southern Hills, USO 2001
	David Toms	Augusta National, MAS 1998

Most-used Venues (Min 2 Majors)

Naturally having hosted every Masters Tournament since its inception in 1934, Augusta National GC would head any list with 65. It is perhaps unfair on the other host venues to include it in this list.

1	Old Course, St Andrews (1873–2000)	26 (BOP)
2	Prestwick (1860–1925)	24 (BOP)
3	Muirfield (1892–1992)	14 (BOP)
4	(Royal) St George's (1894–1993)	12 (BOP)
5=	Oakmont (1922–1994)	10 (7 USO; 3 PGA)
	Royal Liverpool, Hoylake (1897–1967)	10 (BOP)
	Royal Lytham & St Annes (1926–2001)	10 (BOP)
8=	Oakland Hills (1924–1996)	8 (6 USO; 2 PGA)
	(Royal) Birkdale (1954–1998)	8 (BOP)
10	Baltusrol (1903–1993)	7 (USO)
11=	Carnoustie (1931–1999)	6 (BOP)
	Inverness (1920–1993)	6 (4 USO; 2 PGA)
	Musselburgh (1874–1889)	6 (BOP)
	(Royal) Troon (1923–1997)	6 (BOP)
	Southern Hills (1958–2001)	6 (3 USO; 3 PGA)
16=	Cherry Hills (1938–1985)	5 (3 USO; 2 PGA)
	Pebble Beach (1972–2000)	5 (4 USO; 1 PGA)
	Winged Foot (1929–1997)	5 (4 USO; 1 PGA)
19=	Medinah (1949–1999)	4 (3 USO; 1 PGA)
	Merion (1934–1981)	4 (USO)
	Myopia Hunt (1898–1908)	4 (USO)
	Oak Hill (1956–1989)	4 (3 USO; 1 PGA)
	Olympic (1955–1998)	4 (USO)
24=	Atlanta Athletic Club (1976–2001)	3 (1 USO; 2 PGA)
	Brookline (1913–1988)	3 (USO)
	Canterbury (1940–1973)	3 (2 USO; 1 PGA)
	Congressional (1964–1997)	3 (2 USO; 1 PGA)
	Firestone (1960–75)	3 (PGA)
	Olympia Fields (1925–1961)	3 (1 USO; 2 PGA)
	Riviera (1948–1995)	3 (1 USO; 2 PGA)
	Shinnecock Hills (1896–1996)	3 (USO)
	Turnberry (1977–1994)	3 (BOP)
33=	Bellerive (1965–1992)	2 (1 USO; 1 PGA)
	Chicago (1897–1900)	2 (USO)
	Fresh Meadow (1930–1932)	2 (1 USO; 1 PGA)
	Hazeltine International (1970–1991)	2 (USO)
	Inwood (1921–1923)	2 (1 USO; 1 PGA)
	PGA National (1971–1987)	2 (PGA)
	Pinehurst (1936–1999)	2 (1 USO; 1 PGA)
	Scioto (1926–1950)	2 (1 USO; 1 PGA)
	Shoal Creek (1984–1990)	2 (PGA)
	Valhalla (1996–2000)	2 (PGA)

THE PLAYERS' PERFORMANCE CHARTS

The following pages take the statistics of the previous sections in an effort to quantify the performances (by way of allocating points for positions attained) of the leading golfers in Major Championships. It is divided into three main areas, and taking the same premise of the 'Top 30' as used in the main 'Year-by-Year' section earlier, the top players in each era using this system are listed in charts.

Leading Players of Different Generations

This section identifies five naturally-defined eras in the history of golf covering the first century of Major Championships – 1860–1960 – and the ensuing completed decades (1961–70; 1971–80; 1981–90; 1991–2000), making nine charts in all.

The first chart covers the period 1860-1894, when there was only the British Open to play for (and the points allocation here is adjusted to accommodate that); then 1895–1916 – the years of the 'Great Triumvirate' and the rapid progress of golf in America; the third, 1919–30 – the days of Hagen, Jones and Sarazen; fourth, 1931–1942, from the beginnings of the Masters to the start of World War II; and 1944–60 – Nelson, Hogan and Snead and the polarization of the British Open. The remaining four look at succeeding decades in more detail.

Last 5 Years

Here the most recent history is analyzed with rolling charts which, updated every year, depict the most current trends and performances. This chart shows the positions of players over the same period up to the previous year, in much the same way as a music, film or book chart does, so that comparative performances this year against last can be identified.

The Hall of Fame Top 100 All-Time List

Taking the statistics in the same way as the above, but over the spread of some 140 years, this section collates all the points accruing for each golfer and calculates from their totals which golfers make up the Top 100 of all time – a statistical Hall of Fame. Like the 5-year chart, these will be updated annually, so that there will be positional movement, and, from time to time, the loss of some older 'great' to accommodate a younger one. C'est la vie.

It is appreciated that with quantity, the very best should also have quality, and that the Bobby Jones's and Ben Hogans of this world should be higher in such a listing than their points accumulation over a relatively short, or interrupted career, can permit. However, the points tallies are remarkably close to what most people would surmise – and how else is one ever going to settle the 19th-hole argument as to who actually was, or is, the best player never to win a Major?

LEADING PLAYERS OF DIFFERENT GENERATIONS

The following tables take the performances of the leading players of different eras and apply points to the positions they achieved in Major Championships during that time. With the exception of the period 1860–1894 (see below for details), which pertains to the period when only the British Open was contested and fields were often limited in size and standard, uniform points-to-positions values apply throughout. They are: 20 points for 1st place; 8 for 2nd; 5 for 3rd to 5th (SF in PGA when matchplay); 3 for 6th to 10th (QF); 2 for 11th to 20th (Last 16); and 1 for 21st to 30th (Last 32).

Pos.	Player	Win (12pts)	R/UP (5pts)	3–5 (3pts)	6–10 (2pts)	11–20 (1pts)	TOTAL POINTS
1	Tom Morris, Sr	4 (48)	3 (15)	6 (18)	3 (6)	4 (4)	91
2	Willie Park, Sr	4 (48)	4 (20)	3 (9)	3 (6)	2 (2)	85
3	Tom Morris, Jr	4 (48)	1 (5)	3 (9)			62
4	Jamie Anderson	3 (36)	2 (10)	2 (6)	2 (4)	2 (2)	58
5	Bob Ferguson	3 (36)	1 (5)	3 (9)	2 (4)		54
6	Willie Fernie	1 (12)	4 (20)	2 (6)	6 (12)	2 (2)	52
7	Willie Park, Jr	2 (24)		5 (15)	3 (6)	5 (5)	50
8	Bob Martin	2 (24)	2 (10)	4 (12)	1 (2)	1 (1)	49
9=	Bob Kirk		2 (10)	6 (18)	1 (2)		30
	Ben Sayers		1 (5)	4 (12)	3 (6)	7 (7)	30
11	Andrew Kirkaldy		3 (15)	3 (9)	2 (4)	1(1)	29
12	Andrew Strath	1 (12)	1 (5)	3 (9)	1 (2)		28
13=	Hugh Kirkaldy	1 (12)	1 (5)	1 (3)	2 (4)	3 (3)	27
	Davie Strath		3 (15)	3 (9)	1 (2)	1 (1)	27
15	Willie Campbell		1 (5)	5 (15)	3 (6)		26
16	David Brown	1 (12)		2 (6)	3 (6)	1 (1)	25
17	John Ball, Jr (a)	1 (12)	1 (5)	1 (3)	1 (2)	2 (2)	24
18=	Robert Andrew		1 (5)	4 (12)	3 (6)		23
	Mungo Park	1(12)		2 (6)	1 (2)	3 (3)	23
	Archie Simpson		2 (10)	2 (6)	1 (2)	5 (5)	23
21	William Doleman (a)			2 (6)	6 (12)	3 (3)	21
22=	Tom Kidd	1 (12)		1 (3)	1 (2)	1 (1)	18
	Johnny Laidlay (a)		1 (5)	2 (6)	2 (4)	3 (3)	18
24	William Dow			4 (12)	2 (4)	1 (1)	17
25=	David Grant				6 (12)	4 (4)	16
	David Park		1 (5)	3 (9)	1 (2)		16
	Jack Simpson	1 (12)				4 (4)	16
28=	Willie Auchterlonie	1 (12)			1 (2)	1 (1)	15
	Jack Burns	1 (12)			1 (2)	1 (1)	15
	Bob Pringle		1 (5)	2 (6)	1 (2)	2 (2)	15

The 1892 Open Champion, amateur Horace Hilton, was 31st, tied with the emerging genius, JH Taylor. Sandy Herd, only just beginning his 54-year span of Opens, was 33rd.

1895–1916

Pos.	Player	Win (20pts)	R/UP (8pts)	3–5 (5pts)	6–10 (3pts)	11–20 (2pts)	21–30 (1pt)	TOTAL POINTS
1	Harry Vardon	7 (140)	5 (40)	4 (20)	4 (12)	1 (2)	1 (1)	215
2=	James Braid	5 (100)	4 (32)	6 (30)	3 (9)	1 (2)		173
	JH Taylor	4 (80)	7 (56)	4 (20)	4 (12)	2 (4)	1 (1)	173
4	Willie Anderson, Jr	4 (80)	1 (8)	6 (18)		3 (6)		112
5	Alex Smith	2 (40)	3 (24)	4 (20)	1 (3)	6 (12)	3 (3)	102
6	Sandy Herd	1 (20)	2 (16)	7 (35)	3 (9)	6 (12)	1 (1)	93
7	Ted Ray	1 (20)	1 (8)	5 (25)	4 (12)	5 (10)	1 (1)	76
8	Willie Smith	1 (20)	3 (24)	5 (25)	1 (3)	1 (2)		74
9	John McDermott	2 (40)	1 (8)	1 (5)	2 (6)			59
10	Gilbert Nicholls		2 (16)	3 (15)	3 (12)	5 (10)	1 (1)	54
11=	Fred McLeod	1 (20)	2 (20)		1 (3)	3 (6)	3 (3)	52
	Arnaud Massy	1 (20)	1 (8)	1 (5)	6 (18)		1 (1)	52
13	Laurie Auchterlonie	1 (20)		4 (20)	2 (6)	1 (2)	3 (3)	51
14	Jack White	1 (20)	1 (8)	2 (10)	1 (3)	3 (6)	1 (1)	48
15	Tom Vardon		1 (8)	3 (15)	5 (15)	3 (6)	2 (2)	46
16	Horace Rawlins	1 (20)	1 (8)		1 (3)	6 (12)	1 (1)	44
17	Tom McNamara		3 (24)	1 (5)	1 (3)	5 (10)	1 (1)	43
18=	Alex Campbell			2 (10)	3 (9)	11 (22)	1 (1)	42
	James Foulis	1 (20)		2 (10)	1 (3)	4 (8)	1 (1)	42
	George Sargent	1 (20)		2 (10)	3 (9)	1 (2)	1 (1)	42
21=	Jim Barnes	1 (20)		3 (15)		2 (4)		39
	Harold Hilton (a)	1 (20)		2 (10)	1 (3)	2 (4)	2 (2)	39
	Alex Ross	1 (20)			4 (12)	2 (4)	3 (3)	39
24=	Joe Lloyd	1 (20)		2 (10)		3 (6)	1 (1)	37
	TG Renouf			2 (10)	3 (9)	8 (16)	2 (2)	37
26=	Walter Hagen	1 (20)		2 (10)	2 (6)			36
	George Low, Jr		1 (8)	1 (5)	3 (9)	6 (12)	2 (2)	36
28	Jock Hutchison		2 (16)	1 (5)	3 (9)	1 (2)	2 (2)	34
29	Stewart Gardner		1 (8)	3 (15)	3 (9)		1 (1)	33
30=	Charles Evans, Jr (a)	1 (20)	1 (8)			1 (2)		30
	Andrew Kirkaldy			2 (10)	4 (12)	3 (6)	2 (2)	30

Mike Brady tied for 33rd, while the 1913 US Open conquerer of Vardon and Ray, Francis Ouimet who struck a blow for the amateur and the native-born American golfer tied 36th.

1919–1930

Pos.	Player	Win (20pts)	R/UP (8pts)	3–5 (5pts)	6–10 (3pts)	11–20 (2pts)	21–30 (1pt)	TOTAL POINTS
1	Walter Hagen	10 (200)	3 (24)	6 (30)	4 (12)	4 (8)		274
2	Bobby Jones (a)	7 (140)	4 (32)	1 (5)	1 (3)	1 (2)		182
3	Gene Sarazen	3 (60)	2 (16)	5 (25)	5 (15)	5 (10)	3 (3)	129
4	Jim Barnes	3 (60)	3 (24)		7 (21)	6 (12)	5 (5)	122
5	Leo Diegel	2 (40)	3 (24)	2 (10)	5 (15)	4 (8)	5 (5)	102
6=	Johnny Farrell	1 (20)	2 (16)	4 (20)	5 (15)	5 (10)	3 (3)	84
	Jock Hutchison	2 (40)	1 (8)	3 (15)	4 (12)	2 (4)	3 (3)	82
8	Tommy Armour	2 (40)		1 (5)	4 (12)	3 (6)	1 (1)	64
9	Bill Mehlhorn		1 (8)	4 (20)	4 (12)	4 (8)	6 (6)	54
10	George Duncan	1 (20)	1 (8)	1 (5)	4 (12)	2 (4)	2 (2)	51
11	John Golden			4 (20)	3 (9)	5 (10)	5 (5)	44
12	Al Espinosa		2 (16)	1 (5)	4 (12)	4 (8)	1 (1)	42
13=	Emmett French		1 (8)	3 (15)	3 (9)	2 (4)	5 (5)	41
	Arthur Havers	1 (20)		1 (5)	2 (6)	4 (8)	2 (2)	41
	Ted Ray	1 (20)	1 (8)	1 (5)		2 (4)	4 (4)	41
	Macdonald Smith		2 (16)	2 (10)	2 (6)	4 (8)	1 (1)	41
	Bobby Cruickshank		1 (8)	3 (15)	1 (3)	4 (8)	4 (4)	38
17=	Willie MacFarlane	1 (20)			2 (6)	5 (10)	2 (2)	38
	Joe Kirkwood, Sr			3 (15)	2 (6)	5 (10)	3 (3)	34
19=	Al Watrous		1 (8)	1 (5)	2 (6)	6 (12)	3 (3)	34
	Mike Brady		1 (8)		3 (9)	7 (14)	2 (2)	33
21	Fred McLeod		2 (16)		4 (12)	1 (2)	2 (2)	32
22=	Abe Mitchell			4 (20)	1 (3)	4 (8)	1 (1)	32
	Cyril Walker	1 (20)		1 (5)		3 (6)	1 (1)	32
	Joe Turnesa		2 (16)		1 (3)	4 (8)	3 (3)	30
25	Archie Compston		1 (8)	1 (5)	3 (9)	1 (2)	4 (4)	28
26	Harry Hampton			1 (5)	2 (6)	5 (10)	6 (6)	27
27	Fred Robson		1 (8)	2 (10)	1 (3)	1 (2)	2 (2)	25
28	Harry Cooper		1 (8)	2 (10)		2 (4)	2 (2)	24
29=	George MacLean			4 (20)		1 (2)	2 (2)	24
	Horton Smith			3 (15)		2 (6)	3 (3)	24

American dominance, and the opportunity to play in more Majors (the PGA started in 1916), paints a totally different picture to the previous era, so much the preserve of the 'Great Triumvirate'. It was the end of Majors success for JH Taylor (38th) and Sandy Herd (33rd) both of whom had featured in the 1860–1894 and 1894–1916 league tables. Percy Alliss was 32nd and 1916 US Open winner, the amateur Chick Evans, was tied for 34th.

1931–1942

Pos.	Player	Win (20pts)	R/UP (8pts)	3–5 (5pts)	6–10 (3pts)	11–20 (2pts)	21–30 (1pt)	TOTAL POINTS
1	Gene Sarazen	4 (80)	2 (16)	8 (40)	6 (18)	4 (8)	7 (7)	169
2	Byron Nelson	4 (80)	3 (24)	6 (30)	4 (12)	3 (6)		152
3	Denny Shute	3 (60)	2 (16)	4 (20)	3 (9)	11 (22)	4 (4)	131
4	Craig Wood	2 (40)	5 (40)	3 (15)	4 (12)	2 (4)	7 (7)	118
5	Ralph Guldahl	3 (60)	3 (24)	2 (10)	3 (9)	4 (8)	5 (5)	116
6	Paul Runyan	2 (40)		5 (25)	9 (27)	7 (14)	2 (2)	108
7	Horton Smith	2 (40)		2 (10)	7 (21)	11 (22)	7 (7)	100
8	Henry Picard	2 (40)		3 (15)	8 (24)	8 (16)	2 (2)	97
9	Sam Snead	1 (20)	4 (32)	1 (5)	4 (12)	5 (10)		79
10	Ed Dudley			6 (30)	10 (30)	7 (14)	3 (3)	77
11	Harry Cooper		3 (24)	5 (25)	2 (6)	7 (14)	3 (3)	72
12=	Henry Cotton	2 (40)		2 (10)	4 (12)	1 (2)		64
	Olin Dutra	2 (40)		1 (5)	3 (9)	4 (8)	2 (2)	64
14	Vic Ghezzi	1 (20)			4 (12)	11 (22)	8 (8)	62
15	Billy Burke	1 (20)		3 (15)	2 (6)	6 (12)	5 (5)	58
16	Tommy Armour	1 (20)	1 (8)	1 (5)	3 (9)	4 (8)	5 (5)	55
17	Harold McSpaden		1 (8)	1 (5)	5 (15)	12 (24)	1 (1)	53
18=	Jimmy Hines		8 (24)	2 (10)		6 (12)	6 (6)	52
	Johnny Revolta	1 (20)			1 (3)	11 (22)	7 (7)	52
20	Lawson Little	1 (20)		2 (10)	4 (12)	4 (8)	1 (1)	51
21	Alf Padgham	1 (20)	1 (8)	3 (15)	2 (6)			49
22	Reg Whitcombe	1 (20)	1 (8)	1 (5)	2 (6)	3 (6)		45
23	Dick Metz		1 (8)	1 (5)	6 (18)	3 (6)	7 (7)	44
24	Bobby Cruickshank		1 (8)	3 (15)	2 (6)	6 (12)	2 (2)	43
25=	Ky Laffoon			3 (15)	2 (6)	5 (10)	11 (11)	42
	Tony Manero	1 (20)		1 (5)	1 (3)	4 (8)	6 (6)	42
27	Ben Hogan		1 (8)	3 (15)	5 (15)	1 (2)	1 (1)	41
28	Macdonald Smith		1 (8)	3 (15)	3 (9)	4 (8)		40
29=	Jimmy Demaret	1 (20)		1 (5)	1 (3)	3 (6)	2 (2)	36
	Jimmy Thomson		2 (16)		2 (6)	5 (10)	4 (4)	36

The post Jones-Hagen era brought a more even spread of victories, and with the advent of the Masters in 1934, an even greater imbalance between the US and Britain. Some Brits, such as Cotton, Padgham and Reg Whitcombe, may have featured even more strongly in this table if they had competed in the American Majors and had performed as well as they had done in the British Open. Other British Open winners included Alf Perry (32nd) and Dick Burton (37th): the last amateur winner of the US Open, Johnny Goodman, tied 38th, and 1931 PGA Champion, Tom Creavy, was 31st.

1944–1960

Pos.	Player	Win (20pts)	R/UP (8pts)	3–5 (5pts)	6–10 (3pts)	11–20 (2pts)	21–30 (1pt)	TOTAL POINTS
1	Ben Hogan	9 (180)	5 (40)	4 (20)	9 (27)	1 (2)	1 (1)	270
2	Sam Snead	6 (120)	4 (32)	7 (35)	10 (30)	9 (18)	8 (8)	243
3	Bobby Locke	4 (80)	2 (16)	6 (30)	3 (9)	4 (8)	2 (2)	145
4	Cary Middlecoff	3 (60)	4 (32)	2 (10)	6 (18)	7 (14)	10 (10)	144
5	Peter Thomson	4 (80)	3 (24)	2 (10)	2 (6)	2 (4)	4 (4)	128
6	Lloyd Mangrum	1 (20)	3 (24)	8 (40)	7 (21)	3 (6)	7 (7)	118
7	Jimmy Demaret	2 (40)	1 (8)	7 (35)	4 (12)	5 (10)	2 (3)	108
8	Arnold Palmer	3 (60)	1 (8)	2 (10)	4 (12)	1 (2)	3 (3)	95
9	Julius Boros	1 (20)	1 (8)	8 (40)	4 (12)	3 (6)	4 (4)	90
10	Jack Burke, Jr	2 (40)	1 (8)	1 (5)	6 (18)	6 (12)	3 (3)	86
11	Doug Ford	2 (40)	1 (8)	1 (5)	4 (12)	5 (10)	6 (6)	81
12	Jim Ferrier	1 (20)	2 (16)	4 (20)	3 (9)	4 (8)	4 (4)	77
13=	Chick Harbert	1 (20)	2 (16)	2 (10)	4 (12)	5 (10)	8 (8)	76
	Claude Harmon	1 (20)		4 (20)	3 (9)	10 (20)	7 (7)	76
	Byron Nelson	1 (20)	3 (24)	1 (5)	6 (18)	3 (6)	3 (3)	76
16	Tommy Bolt	1 (20)		6 (30)	3 (9)	4 (8)	5 (5)	72
17	Walter Burkemo	1 (20)	2 (16)	3 (15)	1 (3)	6 (12)	4 (4)	70
18	Frank Stranahan		3 (24)		2 (6)	13 (26)	4 (4)	60
19	Lew Worsham	1 (20)		1 (5)	6 (18)	5 (10)	6 (6)	59
20	Jim Turnesa	1 (20)		4 (20)	1 (3)	5 (10)	4 (4)	57
21=	Johnny Bulla		2 (16)	1 (5)	6 (18)	6 (12)	5 (5)	56
	Ted Kroll		1 (8)	3 (15)	3 (9)	9 (18)	6 (6)	56
	Bob Rosburg	1 (20)	1 (8)	3 (15)	1 (3)	3 (6)	4 (4)	56
24	Ed Oliver		3 (24)	1 (5)	3 (9)	6 (12)	5 (5)	55
25=	Fred Daly	1 (20)	1 (8)	3 (15)	1 (3)	3 (3)	3 (3)	52
	Jay Hebert	1 (20)		1 (5)	5 (15)	5 (10)	2 (2)	52
27=	Ed Furgol	1 (20)		2 (10)	2 (6)	6 (12)	3 (3)	51
	Gary Player	1 (20)	1 (8)	1 (5)	4 (12)	2 (4)	2 (2)	51
29	Flory van Donck		2 (16)	3 (15)	4 (12)	1 (2)	3 (3)	48
30=	Billy Casper	1 (20)	1 (8)	1 (5)		6 (12)	1 (1)	46
	Dick Mayer	1 (20)		2 (10)	2 (6)	3 (6)	4 (4)	46

The British Open became increasingly marginalized as the Americans stayed away in droves. The Ryder Cup, which had been in existence since 1927 had, up to 1955, gone 9–2 in favour of the Americans over the British and Irish, a clear indication of the gulf in standards. The momentum swung back momentarily in 1957 with a famous victory for the home team at Lindrick in Yorkshire. Its captain, Dai Rees, was 32nd in this table. Henry Cotton was 31st, Bob Hamilton, winner of the 1944 PGA was 33rd, Ken Venturi 34th, tied with Roberto de Vicenzo, and 1951 British Open Champion, Max Faulkner, 36th.

1961–1970

Pos.	Player	Win (20pts)	R/UP (8pts)	3–5 (5pts)	6–10 (3pts)	11–20 (2pts)	21–30 (1pt)	TOTAL POINTS
1	Jack Nicklaus	8 (160)	7 (56)	6 (30)	4 (12)	3 (6)	4 (4)	268
2	Sam Snead	6 (120)	4 (32)	7 (35)	10 (30)	9 (18)	8 (8)	243
3	Arnold Palmer	4 (80)	8 (64)	5 (25)	5 (15)	5 (10)	2 (2)	196
4	Gary Player	4 (80)	3 (24)	6 (30)	8 (24)	5 (10)	4 (4)	172
5	Billy Casper	2 (40)	2 (16)	5 (25)	6 (18)	9 (18)	2 (2)	119
6	Julius Boros	2 (40)		5 (25)		10 (20)	5 (5)	90
7	Bob Charles	1 (20)	3 (24)	3 (15)	1 (3)	8 (16)	3 (3)	81
8	Gene Littler	1 (20)	1 (8)	4 (20)	5 (15)	4 (8)	6 (6)	77
9	Don January	1 (20)	1 (8)	3 (15)	2 (6)	11 (22)	2 (2)	73
10	Doug Sanders		3 (24)	2 (10)	3 (9)	11 (22)	4 (4)	69
11	Al Geiberger	1 (20)	1 (8)	3 (15)	2 (6)	7 (14)	4 (4)	67
12	Gay Brewer	1 (20)	1 (8)	2 (10)	4 (12)	4 (8)	5 (5)	63
13	Tony Jacklin	2 (40)		2 (10)		3 (6)	6 (6)	62
14	Bruce Devlin			4 (20)	9 (27)	4 (8)	5 (5)	601
15	Tony Lema	1 (20)	1 (8)	3 (15)	3 (9)	2 (4)	3 (3)	59
16	Bobby Nichols	1 (20)	1 (8)	2 (10)	2 (6)	3 (6)	8 (8)	58
17	Roberto de Vicenzo	1 (20)	1 (8)	3 (15)	2 (6)	2 (4)	3 (3)	56
18	Kel Nagle		2 (16)	4 (20)	2 (6)	4 (8)	4 (4)	54
19	Bob Goalby	1 (20)	2 (16)		3 (9)	3 (6)	2 (2)	53
20	Dave Marr	1 (20)	1 (8)	1 (5)	3 (9)	3 (6)	3 (3)	51
21=	Peter Thomson	1 (20)		2 (10)	5 (15)	1 (2)	2 (2)	49
	Ray Floyd	1 (20)			4 (12)	5 (10)	1 (1)	43
	Mason Rudolph			2 (10)	3 (12)	7 (14)	7 (7)	43
23	Ken Venturi	1 (20)		1 (5)	1 (3)	5 (10)	2 (2)	40
24	Bruce Crampton			2 (10)	2 (6)	8 (16)	6 (6)	38
25	Lee Trevino	1 (20)		2 (10)	1 (3)	1 (2)	2 (2)	37
26=	George Archer	1 (20)		1 (5)	1 (3)	3 (6)	2 (2)	36
	Paul Harney			2 (10)	4 (12)	6 (12)	2 (2)	36
28=	Phil Rodgers		1 (8)	3 (15)	1 (3)	3 (6)	2 (2)	34
	Sam Snead			1 (5)	5 (15)	5 (10)	4 (4)	34
30=	Frank Beard			2 (10)	5 (15)	3 (6)	2 (2)	33
	Dave Stockton	1 (20)		1 (5)	1 (3)	2 (4)	1 (1)	33

Thanks to Jack Nicklaus, Gary Player and most significantly Arnold Palmer, the British Open regained its former perceived status among the Major Championships. More transatlantic journeys were made from west to east, and from this decade, the tables can be said to be representative of the world's best players competing in the world's best tournaments. Failing to make this Top 30 were Christy O'Connor Sr, Dow Finsterwald and Bob Rosburg (all tied 32nd).

1971–1980

Pos.	Player	Win (20pts)	R/UP (8pts)	3–5 (5pts)	6–10 (3pts)	11–20 (2pts)	21–30 (1pt)	TOTAL POINTS
1	Jack Nicklaus	9 (180)	8 (64)	12 (60)	6 (18)	2 (4)		326
2	Tom Watson	4 (80)	3 (24)	2 (10)	8 (24)	6 (12)	2 (2)	152
3	Gary Player	4 (80)	1 (8)	1 (5)	9 (27)	7 (14)	9 (9)	143
4	Lee Trevino	4 (80)	1 (8)	3 (15)	4 (12)	10 (20)	5 (5)	140
5	Tom Weiskopf	1 (20)	4 (32)	6 (30)	8 (24)	7 (14)	3 (3)	123
6	Johnny Miller	2 (40)	3 (24)	2 (10)	6 (18)	6 (12)	2 (2)	106
7	Hale Irwin	2 (40)		7 (35)	5 (15)	4 (8)	7 (7)	105
8	Hubert Green	1 (20)	1 (8)	5 (25)	6 (18)	5 (10)	6 (6)	87
9	Ray Floyd	1 (20)	2 (16)	2 (10)	4 (12)	11 (22)	3 (3)	83
10	Ben Crenshaw		4 (32)	3 (15)	5 (15)	3 (6)	5 (5)	73
11	Jerry Pate	1 (20)	2 (16)	3 (15)	2 (6)	6 (12)	1 (1)	70
12	Seve Ballesteros	2 (40)	1 (8)			6 (12)		60
13	Lou Graham	1 (20)	1 (8)	1 (5)	3 (9)	3 (6)	6 (6)	54
14	Dave Stockton	1 (20)	2 (16)		2 (6)	4 (8)	3 (3)	53
15	David Graham	1 (20)		2 (10)	4 (12)	2 (4)	6 (6)	52
16=	Tom Kite		1 (8)	3 (15)	3 (9)	7 (14)	3 (3)	49
	Lanny Wadkins	1 (20)		1 (5)	3 (9)	5 (10)	5 (5)	49
18	Arnold Palmer			3 (15)	3 (9)	10 (20)	4 (4)	48
19	Charles Coody	1 (20)		1 (15)	1 (3)	2 (4)	4 (4)	46
20	John Mahaffey	1 (20)	1 (8)	1 (5)	1 (3)	2 (4)	4 (4)	44
21	Bruce Crampton		4 (32)			3 (6)	3 (3)	41
22	Andy North	1 (20)		1 (5)	1 (3)	5 (10)	2 (2)	40
23	JC Snead		2 (16)	1 (5)	1 (3)	4 (8)	7 (7)	39
24=	Billy Casper		1 (8)	2 (10)	3 (9)	5 (10)	1 (1)	38
	Don January		1 (8)	1 (5)	5 (15)	4 (8)	2 (2)	38
26	Peter Oosterhuis		1 (8)	1 (5)	4 (12)	3 (6)	5 (5)	36
27=	Al Geiberger		1 (8)		3 (9)	7 (14)	3 (3)	34
	Gene Littler		1 (8)	1 (5)	3 (9)	4 (8)	4 (4)	34
29	Tommy Aaron	1 (20)	1 (8)				3 (3)	31
30=	Jim Colbert			3 (15)	1 (3)	4 (8)	1 (1)	27
	Gil Morgan			2 (10)	2 (6)	5 (10)	1 (1)	27

A second decade of Nicklaus domination, with Jack's two Majors in 1980, suggesting he was finishing as strongly as he started it. Bert Yancey, Jerry Magee and the unfortunate Jack Newton shared 31st place, while 1979 Masters Champion, Fuzzy Zoeller, was just emerging on the scene and claimed 33rd spot.

1981–1990

Pos.	Player	Win (20pts)	R/UP (10pts)	3–5 (6pts)	6–10 (4pts)	11–20 (2pts)	21–30 (1pt)	TOTAL POINTS
1	Tom Watson	4 (80)	4 (32)	3 (15)	9 (27)	5 (10)	4 (4)	168
2	Nick Faldo	4 (80)	1 (8)	5 (25)	3 (9)	8 (16)	3 (3)	141
3	Seve Ballesteros	3 (60)	2 (16)	7 (35)	4 (12)	4 (8)	3 (3)	134
4	Greg Norman	1 (20)	4 (32)	6 (30)	3 (9)	6 (12)	3 (3)	106
5	Ray Floyd	2 (40)	2 (16)	2 (10)	3 (9)	12 (24)	2 (2)	101
6	Curtis Strange	2 (40)	2 (16)	2 (10)	3 (9)	8 (16)	6 (6)	97
7	Ben Crenshaw	1 (20)	1 (8)	5 (25)	5 (15)	10 (20)	3 (3)	91
8	Jack Nicklaus	1 (20)	3 (24)	1 (5)	6 (18)	5 (10)	9 (9)	86
9	Payne Stewart	1 (20)	2 (16)	3 (15)	7 (21)	2 (4)	5 (5)	81
10	Larry Nelson	3 (60)		1 (5)	1 (3)	5 (10)	1 (1)	79
11	Lanny Wadkins		3 (24)	4 (20)	4 (12)	7 (14)	6 (6)	76
12	Tom Kite		2 (16)	4 (20)	5 (15)	8 (16)	5 (5)	72
13=	Bernhard Langer	1 (20)	2 (16)	3 (15)	4 (12)	3 (6)	2 (2)	71
	Fuzzy Zoeller	1 (20)	1 (8)		7 (21)	9 (18)	4 (4)	71
15	Craig Stadler	1 (20)		1 (5)	6 (18)	9 (18)	7 (7)	68
16	David Graham	1 (20)		1 (5)	7 (21)	7 (14)	5 (5)	65
17	Sandy Lyle	2 (40)			2 (6)	6 (12)	4 (4)	62
18	Lee Trevino	1 (20)	1 (8)	2 (10)	2 (6)	7 (14)	2 (2)	60
19	Fred Couples		1 (8)	5 (25)	6 (18)	2 (4)	3 (3)	58
20	Scott Simpson	1 (20)			5 (15)	6 (12)	5 (5)	52
21	Hale Irwin	1 (20)	1 (8)		2 (6)	6 (12)	3 (3)	49
22	Larry Mize	1 (20)		1 (5)	1 (3)	8 (16)	4 (4)	48
23	Peter Jacobsen			2 (10)	3 (9)	8 (16)	10 (10)	45
24	Hal Sutton	1 (20)		1 (5)	2 (6)	3 (6)	7 (7)	44
25	Andy Bean		2 (16)	1 (5)	1 (3)	8 (16)	3 (3)	43
26=	Chip Beck		2 (16)	1 (5)	2 (6)	3 (6)	8 (8)	41
	Nick Price		2 (16)	2 (10)	2 (6)	3 (6)	3 (3)	41
28	Mark Calcavecchia	1 (20)	1 (8)			6 (12)		40
29	Bill Rogers	1 (20)	1 (8)	1 (5)	1 (3)		3 (3)	39
30	Jay Haas			2 (10)	4 (12)	4 (8)	5 (5)	35

The 80s proved to be much more open, with no real outstanding or obvious successors to the 'Big Three'. It also saw the re-emergence of Europe as a power in golf, with Ballesteros and Faldo in the vanguard. PGA Champions Andy North (for the second time in 1985), Bob Tway (1986), Jeff Sluman (1988) and Wayne Grady (1990) were out of the Top 30 at, respectively, 37th (tied with Gil Morgan), 36th, 34th (tied with Paul Azinger) and 31st (tied with Ian Woosnam).

1991–2000

Pos	Player	Win (20pts)	R/UP (8pts)	3–5 (5pts)	6–10 (3pts)	11–20 (2pts)	21–30 (1pt)	TOTAL POINTS
1	Tiger Woods	5	0	3	3	3	3	133
2	Ernie Els	2	4	3	5	4	6	116
3	Nick Price	3	0	4	4	5	4	110
4	Nick Faldo	2	2	4	2	6	2	96
5	Greg Norman	1	2	3	6	9	0	87
6=	Jose Maria Olazabal	2	1	2	3	8	1	84
	Vijay Singh	2	0	3	4	7	3	84
8	Davis Love III	1	3	1	8	3	4	83
9	Tom Lehman	1	2	5	2	4	5	80
10	Fred Couples	1	1	2	6	7	6	74
11	Mark O'Meara	2	0	3	1	5	5	73
12	Lee Janzen	2	0	1	2	5	7	68
13	Corey Pavin	1	1	2	5	4	3	64
14	Colin Montgomerie	0	3	1	4	7	5	60
15	Justin Leonard	1	2	1	3	3	2	58
16	Steve Elkington	1	0	4	2	4	3	57
17	Tom Kite	1	1	2	3	3	2	55
18	Ian Woosnam	1	0	1	3	5	6	53
19=	John Daly	2	0	1	0	2	3	52
	Phil Mickelson	0	1	3	7	3	2	52
21	Payne Stewart	1	2	0	1	3	5	50
22=	Paul Azinger	1	0	1	1	6	4	46
	Tom Watson	0	0	4	4	6	2	46
24=	Bernhard Langer	1	0	1	2	3	7	44
	Jeff Maggert	0	0	5	5	0	4	44
26	Loren Roberts	0	1	2	3	4	6	41
27=	Mark Brooks	1	0	2	0	5	0	40
	John Cook	0	2	2	2	3	2	40
	Jeff Sluman	0	1	1	4	5	5	40
30	Jay Haas	0	1	5	1	4	3	39

Wood's five wins didn't come until the last four years of the decade, but he still had enough in hand to be the leading player over the whole ten years. Of course, some players' careers span from the middle of one decade to another, so that Nick Faldo and Greg Norman, for instance, may not have topped any list which for the sake of neatness covers an easily identifiable period of time, but they were still good enough to feature in the Top Five for both decades. By the same token Tom Watson was still good enough to hang around the Top 30 during the 90s, after being No 2 in the 70s and topping the lot for the ten years in between!

Last 5 Years

Pos	Player	Win (20pts)	R/UP (8pts)	3–5 (5pts)	6–10 (3pts)	11–20 (2pts)	21–30 (1pt)	TOTAL POINTS
1	Tiger Woods	6	0	3	3	4	4	156
2	David Duval	1	2	1	6	4	0	67
3=	Ernie Els	1	3	1	2	3	4	65
	Vijay Singh	2	0	1	2	6	2	65
5	Davis Love III	1	1	0	8	3	1	59
6	Justin Leonard	1	2	0	3	3	2	53
7	Mark O'Meara	2	0	1	0	2	3	52
8	Phil Mickelson	0	2	1	5	3	3	45
9	Jim Furyk	0	0	4	5	4	1	44
10	Jose Maria Olazabal	1	0	1	0	8	0	41
11	Jesper Parnevik	0	1	1	3	4	2	32
12=	Lee Janzen	1	0	1	0	2	2	31
	Colin Montgomerie	0	1	0	2	7	3	31
	Payne Stewart	1	1	0	0	0	3	31
15=	Retief Goosen	1	0	0	2	2	0	30
	Tom Lehman	0	0	3	2	2	5	30
	Nick Price	0	0	3	1	3	6	30
	David Toms	1	0	1	1	1	0	30
19	Paul Azinger	0	0	2	1	5	5	28
20	Fred Couples	0	1	0	3	3	4	27
21	Darren Clarke	0	1	1	3	0	3	25
22=	Stewart Cink	0	0	2	2	2	4	24
	Steve Stricker	0	1	2	1	1	1	24
	Lee Westwood	0	0	1	3	4	2	24
25	Tom Kite	0	1	2	1	1	0	22
26	Miguel Angel Jimenez	0	1	1	2	0	2	21
27=	Thomas Bjorn	0	1	1	1	0	4	20
	Mark Calcavecchia	0	0	2	1	2	3	20
	Paul Lawrie	1	0	0	0	0	0	20
	Jeff Maggert	0	0	2	2	1	2	20

Perhaps the biggest shake out of players since the last edition of *The Golf Majors* occurs in this section. Gone are the old guard like Norman, Faldo, Langer and Woosnam, although all have suggested in recent Majors that they are still well capable of accumulating 'Hall of Fame' points. This is the dawn of the Woods era, and the evidence for this is starkly apparent in the statistics. Tiger's harvest of a quarter of all the Majors contested during this period leaves the chart peppered with wannabees, several of whom have held the press mantle of 'best player never to have won a Major' at some time or another.

The Hall of Fame Top 100 of All Time

Pos. in 2001	Pos. in 2000	Player (No of Years Featured: Span of Entries)	Win 20*	R/UP 8*	3–5 5*	6–10 3*	11–20 2*	21–30 1*	TOTAL POINTS*
1	1	**Jack Nicklaus (36/39: 1960–98)**	18	19	19	17	11	17	697
2	2	Gary Player (29/34: 1956–90)	9	6	8	21	17	18	383
3	3	Sam Snead (33/38: 1937–74)	7	8	11	20	20	15	374
4	4	Tom Watson (26/29: 1972–2000)	8	7	9	21	17	8	366
5	5	Arnold Palmer (26/28: 1955–82)	7	9	10	12	16	11	341
6	6	Walter Hagen (23/28: 1913–40)	11	3	10	8	8	5	339
7	7	Ben Hogan (23/30: 1938–67)	9	6	7	17	6	3	329
8	8	Gene Sarazen (31/37: 1920–56)	7	4	13	12	13	15	314
9	9	Ray Floyd (33/33: 1964–96)	4	5	4	15	32	7	256
10	10	Nick Faldo (21/25: 1976–2000)	6	3	9	6	16	6	245
11	11	Lee Trevino (23/25: 1967–91)	6	2	7	7	20	9	241
12	12	Harry Vardon (25/33: 1893–1925)**	7	6	5	5	3	3	234
13	13	Byron Nelson (22/33: 1932–65)	5	6	7	10	7	4	231
14=	16	Greg Norman (22/24: 1978–2001)	2	8	9	10	15	5	214
	14	JH Taylor (28/34: 1893–1926)**	5	7	5	8	3	2	214
16	15	Seve Ballesteros (18/19: 1976–94)	5	3	7	5	13	6	206
17	17	Billy Casper (22/23: 1956–78)	3	4	8	9	20	4	203
18	18	Ben Crenshaw (23/26: 1971–96)	2	5	9	11	15	9	197
19	19	Bobby Jones (16/23: 1920–42)	7	4	1	1	3	3	189
20	20	Julius Boros (23/25: 1950–74)	3	1	13	5	13	11	185
21	21	Peter Thomson (24/29: 1951–79)	5	3	4	8	4	8	184
22	22	James Braid (27/34: 1894–1927)**	5	4	6	4	3	3	182
23	23	Tom Kite (26/309: 1972–2001)	1	4	10	11	18	10	181
24	24	Hale Irwin (24/30: 1971–2000)	3	1	7	9	15	14	174
25	25	Jim Barnes (17/19: 1912–30)	4	3	3	7	8	5	161
26	38	Tiger Woods (6/6: 1996–2001)	6	0	3	3	4	5	157
27	26	Bobby Locke (18/24: 1936–59)	4	2	6	6	5	2	156
28=	29	Nick Price (20/22: 1980–2001)	3	2	6	6	10	10	154
	27	Denny Shute (17/24: 1928–51)	3	2	5	5	15	8	154
30	28	Payne Stewart (14/16: 1984–99)	3	4	3	8	6	10	153
31=	29	Jimmy Demaret (19/26: 1937–62)	3	1	9	5	8	5	149
	29	Cary Middlecoff (17/17: 1946–62)	3	4	2	6	9	11	149
33	31	Tom Weiskopf (17/17: 1967–83)	1	5	6	9	10	11	148
34	32	Lloyd Mangrum (16/21: 1940–60)	1	4	10	9	4	7	144
35	33	Gene Littler (26/29: 1954–82)	1	3	6	10	12	13	141
36	34	Lanny Wadkins (22/24: 1971–84)	1	3	7	7	14	11	139
37=	35	Johnny Miller (16/21: 1966–86)	2	4	3	8	9	7	136
	35	Horton Smith (21/27: 1928–54)	2	0	5	9	14	16	136
39	38	Fred Couples (18/20: 1982–2001)	1	2	8	13	7	10	135
40	40	Leo Diegel (18/20: 1920–39)	2	3	5	5	8	10	130
41	41	Sandy Herd (32/40: 1888–1927)**	1	4	8	7	10	2	127
42=	56	Ernie Els (10/10: 1992–2001)	2	4	4	6	5	6	126
	42	Craig Wood (14/21: 1929–49)	2	5	3	5	4	8	126
44=	43	Don January (21/24: 1958–81)	1	2	5	8	18	4	125
	43	Curtis Strange (18/23: 1976–98)	2	2	4	4	13	11	125
46	45	Willie Anderson (14/14: 1897–1910)	4	1	6	0	3	0	124
47	55	Bernhard Langer (19/21: 1981–2001)	2	2	5	7	6	9	123
48	46	Hubert Green (16/18: 1972–89)	2	1	5	7	9	9	121
49=	47	Tommy Armour (18/19: 1924–42)	3	1	2	7	7	6	119
	47	Paul Runyan (17/31: 1931–61)	2	0	5	11	8	5	119
51	49	Fuzzy Zoeller (19/20: 1978–97)	2	1	2	8	15	6	118
52=	50	Henry Cotton (19/32: 1927–1958)	3	0	4	10	3	1	117
	50	David Graham (17/18: 1973–90)	2	0	3	11	9	11	117

	50	Ralph Guldahl (10/17: 1933–49)	3	3	2	3	4	6	117
	50	Ted Ray (23/32: 1899–1930)	2	2	6	4	7	5	117
56=	54	Jock Hutchison (17/21: 1908–28)	2	3	4	7	3	5	116
	54	Henry Picard (18/20: 1932–51)	2	0	4	9	11	7	116
58	58	Johnny Farrell (19/22: 1919–40)	1	2	6	7	7	9	110
59=	61	Jose Maria Olazabal (15/17: 1985–2001)	2	1	2	6	14	3	107
	59	Alex Smith (19/24: 1898–1921)	2	3	5	1	6	3	107
61	60	Roberto de Vicenzo (22/28: 1948–75)	1	2	6	6	7	8	106
62=	61	Bob Charles (13/27: 1962–88)	1	3	3	3	16	5	105
	61	Doug Ford (14/15: 1952–66)	2	1	1	8	8	8	105
64	65	Mark O'Meara (16/18: 1984–2001)	2	0	5	3	9	11	103
65=	64	Al Geiberger (16/19: 1961–79)	1	2	3	5	14	7	101
	64	Vic Ghezzi (18/23: 1932–56)	1	1	1	6	18	14	101
67=	67	Harry Cooper (17/20: 1923–42)	0	4	7	3	9	5	99
	67	Ed Dudley (22/24: 1925–48)	0	0	6	13	12	6	99
	67	Larry Nelson (15/17: 1976–92)	3	0	3	2	7	4	99
	67	Macdonald Smith (22/27: 1910–36)	0	4	7	5	8	1	99
71=	71	Jack Burke Jr (16/21: 1949–69)	2	1	1	8	7	5	96
	71	Doug Sanders (13/17: 1958–76)	0	4	4	5	11	7	96
	71	Craig Stadler (19/20: 1978–97)	1	0	1	11	13	12	96
74	79	Vijay Singh (12/13: 1989–2001)	2	0	3	5	18	4	94
75	74	Jim Ferrier (14/25: 1940–64)	1	2	5	4	5	9	92
76	75	Tom Morris Sr (23/29: 1860–88)*	4	3	6	3	4	3	91
77=	76	Tommy Bolt (16/21: 1951–71)	1		8	4	5	8	90
	83	Davis Love III (11/13: 1989–2001)	1	3	1	9	5	4	90
79=	77	Dow Finsterwald (12/12: 1955–66)	1	1	6	4	8	3	89
	77	Jerry Pate (9/9: 1975–83)	1	2	5	3	8	3	89
81	83	Corey Pavin (14/17: 1984–2001)	1	1	2	8	9	8	88
82=	79	Bruce Crampton (20/21: 1956–76)	0	4	2	2	14	11	87
	79	Bruce Devlin (16/19: 1964–82)	0	0	5	11	9	11	87
	79	Bob Rosburg (15/19: 1953–71)	1	2	4	4	6	7	87
85=	83	Jay Haas (20/25: 1975–99)	0	0	7	6	10	8	86
	83	Dave Stockton (11/13: 1968–80)	2	2	1	3	6	4	86
	92	Ian Woosnam (16/17: 1985–2001)	1	1	4	4	8	10	86
88	86	Willie Park Sr (18/24:1860–83)*	4	4	3	3	2	1	85
89=	87	Chick Harbert (17/24: 1939–62)	1	2	2	5	7	9	84
	87	Fred McLeod (18/24: 1903–26)	1	2	4	5	4	5	84
91=	90	Gay Brewer (16/20: 1962–81)	1	1	2	8	6	9	83
	94	Tom Lehman (9/9: 1993–2001)	1	2	5	2	5	6	83
93=	–	Paul Azinger (12/15: 1987–2001)	1	2	2	4	9	6	82
	91	Ken Venturi (11/14: 1954–67)	1	2	3	4	8	3	82
95	92	Bobby Cruickshank (17/22: 1921–42)	0	2	6	3	10	6	81
96=	94	Walter Burkemo (14/16: 1951–66)	1	2	3	2	9	5	80
	94	Kel Nagle (14/21: 1951–71)	1	2	4	2	7	4	80
98	97	Tony Jacklin (13/19: 1963–81)	2	0	4	0	5	9	79
99	98	Bobby Nichols (15/18: 1962–79)	1	1	3	4	6	10	77
100=	99	George Duncan (17/24: 1906–29)	1	2	3	8	3	3	76
	99	Claude Harmon (15/16: 1945–60)	1	0	4	3	10	7	76

* Pre 1985 Points System.

** Combinations of both Points Systems.

Woods has made inexorable progress up the Hall of Fame Chart since he burst in at position 38 in 2000, and the performances in recent years of Els, Singh and Love are reflected here too. We must say farewell finally to Mexico City's Willie Smith, and probably finally with the new competition bursting through, to former champions Scott Simpson and Sandy Lyle. David Duval, leads the charge of a handful of modern players who just need a couple of Top Ten finishes in Majors to enter the chart.

BIBLIOGRAPHY & PERIODICALS

The Open Championship Annuals, 1894–1994/5 (R&A)
History of the Open Golf Championship, (The Guardian)
The British Professional Golfers, 1887–1930 – A Register, Alan F Jackson
USGA Record Books, 1895–1959; 1960–1980; 1981–90, (USGA)
The Official US Open Almanac, Salvatore Johnson
PGA of America Media Guides
Records of the Masters Tournament, 1934–81, (Augusta National GC)
The Who's Who of Golf, Peter Alliss
Golf and All its Glory, Bruce Critchley with Bob Ferrier
Encyclopedia of Golf, Webster Evans
Golf Monthly
Golf World
Golf Weekly
Golf Digest
The (London) Times
The Sunday Times
The Guardian
The Observer
The Daily Telegraph
The Sunday Telegraph
The Independent
The Independent on Sunday
The American Sports Weekly
Sports Illustrated